DAVID BUSCH'S NIKON® D810

GUIDE TO DIGITAL SLR PHOTOGRAPHY

David D. Busch

Cengage Learning PTR

CENGAGE Learning®

Professional • Technical • Reference

Australia, Brazil, Japan, Korea, Mexico, Singapore, Spain, United Kingdom, United States

CENGAGE Learning®

Professional • Technical • Reference

David Busch's Nikon® D810 Guide to Digital SLR Photography
David D. Busch

Publisher and General Manager, Cengage Learning PTR:
Stacy L. Hiquet

Manager of Editorial Services:
Heather Talbot

Product Team Manager:
Kevin Harreld

Project Editor:
Jenny Davidson

Series Technical Editor:
Michael D. Sullivan

Interior Layout Tech:
Bill Hartman

Cover Designer:
Mike Tanamachi

Indexer:
Valerie Haynes Perry

Proofreader:
Sara Gullion

WCN: 01-100

Library of Congress Control Number: 2014949526

ISBN-13: 978-1-305-57727-5

ISBN-10: 1-305-57727-2

Cengage Learning PTR
20 Channel Center Street
Boston, MA 02210
USA

Cengage Learning is a leading provider of customized learning solutions with office locations around the globe, including Singapore, the United Kingdom, Australia, Mexico, Brazil, and Japan. Locate your local office at: **international.cengage.com/region**

Cengage Learning products are represented in Canada by Nelson Education, Ltd.

For your lifelong learning solutions, visit **cengageptr.com**

Visit our corporate website at **cengage.com**

Printed in Canada
1 2 3 4 5 6 7 16 15 14

For Cathy

Acknowledgments

Once again thanks to the folks at Cengage Learning PTR, who recognized that a professional-level camera like Nikon D810 deserves in-depth full-color coverage at a price anyone can afford. Special thanks to product team manager Kevin Harreld, who always gives me the freedom to let my imagination run free with a topic, as well as my veteran production team including project editor Jenny Davidson and series technical editor Mike Sullivan. Also thanks to Bill Hartman, layout; Valerie Haynes Perry, indexing; Sara Gullion, proofreading; Mike Tanamachi, cover design; and my agent, Carole Jelen, who has the amazing ability to keep both publishers and authors happy.

Also, big thanks to the folks at Campus Camera (www.campuscamera.net), who sold me my Nikon D810 when it arrived from Nikon Professional Services on the first day they were available. Their help made it possible for me to be using this great camera and putting together this book while most Nikonphiles were still waiting for delivery.

Thanks again to master photographer Nancy Balluck (www.nancyballuckphotography.com) for the front and back cover photos of yours truly.

About the Author

With more than two million books in print, **David D. Busch** is the world's #1 selling digital camera guide author, and the originator of popular digital photography series like *David Busch's Pro Secrets* and *David Busch's Quick Snap Guides.* He has written more than four dozen hugely successful guidebooks and compact guides for Nikon digital SLR models, several dozen additional user guides for other camera models, as well as many popular books devoted to dSLRs, including *Mastering Digital SLR Photography, Fourth Edition* and *Digital SLR Pro Secrets.* As a roving photojournalist for more than 20 years, he illustrated his books, magazine articles, and newspaper reports with award-winning images. He's operated his own commercial studio, suffocated in formal dress while shooting weddings-for-hire, and shot sports for a daily newspaper and upstate New York college. His photos and articles have been published in magazines as diverse as *Popular Photography, Rangefinder, Professional Photographer*, and hundreds of other publications. He's also reviewed dozens of digital cameras for CNet Networks and other CBS publications. His advice has been featured on National Public Radio's *All Tech Considered.*

When About.com named its top five books on Beginning Digital Photography, debuting at the #1 and #2 slots were Busch's *Digital Photography All-In-One Desk Reference for Dummies* and *Mastering Digital Photography.* During the past year, he's had as many as five of his books listed in the Top 20 of Amazon.com's Digital Photography Bestseller list—simultaneously! Busch's 200 other books published since 1983 include bestsellers like *David Busch's Quick Snap Guide to Using Digital SLR Lenses.*

Busch is a member of the Cleveland Photographic Society (www.clevelandphoto.org), which has operated continuously since 1887. Visit his website at http://www.dslrguides.com/blog.

Contents

Chapter 6
Advanced Techniques 175

Chapter 7
Working with Lenses 201

PART III: WORKING WITH LIGHT

Chapter 8 Making Light Work for You 237

Chapter 9 Electronic Flash with the Nikon D810 255

Chapter 10
Wireless and Multiple Flash 287

PART IV: CONFIGURING YOUR NIKON D810

Chapter 11
Playback and Shooting Menus 303

Chapter 13 The Setup Menu, Retouch Menu, and My Menu 413

PART V: INTRODUCTION TO MOVIE MAKING

Chapter 14 Basics of Live View 447

Chapter 15 Shooting Movies with the D810 461

Chapter 16 Advanced Movie-Making Techniques 471

PART VI: BONUS MATERIAL

Appendix A
Nikon D810: Pre-Flight Checklist 491

Appendix B
What Lenses Can Do for You 507

Appendix C
Software Tools 525

Appendix D
Nikon D810: Troubleshooting and Prevention 533

Index 559

Preface

You don't want good pictures from your new Nikon D810—you demand *outstanding photos.* After all, the revamped D810 is the most advanced camera in the $3,300 price range that Nikon has ever introduced. It boasts 36 megapixels of resolution, blazing-fast automatic focus, and professional-level video capabilities. But your gateway to pixel proficiency is dragged down by the fat but confusing book included in the box as a manual.

You know everything you need to know is in there, somewhere, but you don't know where to start. In addition, the camera manual doesn't offer much information on photography or digital photography. Nor are you interested in spending hours or days studying a comprehensive book on digital SLR photography that doesn't necessarily apply directly to your D810.

What you need is a guide that explains the purpose and function of the D810's basic controls, how you should use them, and *why.* Ideally, there should be information about file formats, resolution, aperture/priority exposure, and special autofocus modes, but you'd prefer to read about those topics only after you've had the chance to go out and take a few hundred great pictures with your new camera. Why isn't there a book that summarizes the most important information in its first two or three chapters, with lots of illustrations showing what your results will look like when you use this setting or that? This is that book.

If you can't decide on what basic settings to use with your camera because you can't figure out how changing ISO or white balance or focus defaults will affect your pictures, you need this guide. I won't talk down to you, either; this book isn't padded with dozens of pages of checklists telling you how to take a travel picture, a sports photo, or how to take a snapshot of your kids in overly simplistic terms. There are no special sections devoted to "real world" recipes here. All of us do 100 percent of our shooting in the real world! So, I give you all the information you need to cook up great photos on your own!

Introduction

I've owned every Nikon digital SLR offered since the Nikon D70 (nearly two dozen different models in all), and few of them made the first impression that the D810 and its predecessors the D800 and D800E did. The first time I picked up a 36 megapixel camera, the absolutely stunning image quality threw me for a loop, but I wondered if I was holding a highly specialized camera that sacrificed shooting speed and ISO performance for resolution.

That didn't prove to be the case. Unlike my first "high definition" camera, a Nikon D3x (which boasted a paltry 24MP), Nikon's 36 megapixels of resolution didn't come with the expected heavy penalties. Two days after I unpacked my D810, I was using it at ISO 6400 to grab shots of a model at a seminar at 5 frames per second. Yes, there was some noise, but a lot less than I expected from a camera with 4.8-micron pixels. (Nikon's current speed champ, the D4s, sucks in photons with pixels that are 1.5X larger at 7.3 microns.) And 5 fps is respectable for just about any application; even fast-moving sports. Indeed, switch to DX mode and add the optional MB-D12 battery pack/grip and you've got a mini-D4s that can shoot at up to 7 frames per second. The D810 is truly a versatile, multi-purpose camera for anyone with $3,300 to spend.

While the improvements of the D810 over the D800/D800E aren't enough to convince owners of the older camera to convert en masse, this new edition is a worthy upgrade. Despite its bulging feature list, the D810 retains the ease of use that smoothes the transition for those new to digital photography. For those just dipping their toes into the digital pond, the experience is warm and inviting. The Nikon D810 isn't just a full-featured full-frame camera—it's a tool for the most serious thinking photographer.

Once you've confirmed that you made a wise purchase decision, the question comes up, *how do I use this thing?* All those cool features can be mind-numbing to learn, if all you have as a guide is the manual furnished with the camera. Help is on the way. I sincerely believe that this book is your best bet for learning how to use your new camera, and for learning how to use it well.

If you're a Nikon D810 owner who's looking to learn more about how to use this great camera, you've probably already explored your options. There are DVDs and online tutorials—but who can learn how to use a camera by sitting in front of a television or computer screen? Do you want to watch a movie or click on HTML links, or do you want to go out and take photos with your camera? Videos are fun, but not the best answer.

There's always the manual furnished with the D810. It's thick and filled with information, but there's really very little about *why* you should use particular settings or features. Its organization makes it difficult to find what you need. Multiple cross-references send you searching back and forth between two or three sections of the book to find what you want to know. The basic manual is also hobbled by black-and-white line drawings and tiny monochrome pictures that aren't very good examples of what you can do.

I've tried to make *David Busch's Nikon D810 Guide to Digital SLR Photography* different from your other D810 learn-up options. The roadmap sections use larger, color pictures to show you where all the buttons and dials are, and the explanations of what they do are longer and more comprehensive. I've tried to avoid overly general advice, including the two-page checklists on how to take a "sports picture" or a "portrait picture" or a "travel picture." You won't find half the content of this book taken up by generic chapters that tell you how to shoot Landscapes, Portraits, or Product photographs. Instead, you'll find tips and techniques for using all the features of your Nikon D810 to take *any kind of picture* you want. If you want to know where you should stand to take a picture of a quarterback dropping back to unleash a pass, there are plenty of books that will tell you that. This one concentrates on teaching you how to select the best autofocus mode, shutter speed, f/stop, or flash capability to take, say, a great sports picture under any conditions.

This book is not a lame rewriting of the manual that came with the camera. Some folks spend five minutes with a book like this one, spot some information that also appears in the original manual, and decide "Rehash!" without really understanding the differences. Yes, you'll find information here that is also in the owner's manual, such as the parameters you can enter when changing your D810's operation in the various menus. Basic descriptions—before I dig in and start providing in-depth tips and information—may also be vaguely similar. There are only so many ways you can say, for example, "Hold the shutter release down halfway to lock in exposure." But not *everything* in the manual is included in this book. If you need advice on when and how to use the most important functions, you'll find the information here.

David Busch's Nikon D810 Guide to Digital SLR Photography is aimed at both Nikon and dSLR veterans as well as newcomers to digital photography and digital SLRs. Both groups can be overwhelmed by the options the D810 offers, while underwhelmed by the explanations they receive in their user's manual. The manuals are great if you already know what you don't know, and you can find an answer somewhere in a booklet arranged by menu listings and written by a camera vendor employee who last threw together instructions on how to operate a camcorder.

Once you've read this book and are ready to learn more, I hope you pick up one of my other guides to digital SLR photography, including my nuts-and-bolts exploration of digital SLR technology and techniques, *David Busch's Mastering Digital SLR Photography, Fourth Edition,* and *David Busch's Compact Field Guide for the Nikon D810,* which condenses the most essential information about settings, menus, and options into a pocket-sized format you can tuck in a camera bag. It's a spiral-bound, lay-flat book with advice on using every setting and control your D810 offers. While my "big books" contain everything you need to know, the compact versions make sure you'll have the must-have information, when you need it.

Family Resemblance

If you've owned previous models in the Nikon digital camera line, and copies of my books for those cameras, you're bound to notice a certain family resemblance. Nikon has been very crafty in introducing upgraded cameras that share the best features of the models they replace, while adding new capabilities and options. You benefit in two ways. If you used a Nikon D700 or even a D800/D800E prior to switching to this latest D810 model, you'll find that the parts that haven't changed have a certain familiarity for you, making it easy to make the transition to the newest model. There are lots of features and menu choices of the D810 that are exactly the same as those in the most recent models. This family resemblance will help level the learning curve for you.

Similarly, when writing books for each new model, I try to retain the easy-to-understand explanations that worked for previous books dedicated to earlier camera models, and concentrate on expanded descriptions of things readers have told me they want to know more about, a solid helping of fresh sample photos, and lots of details about the latest and greatest new features. Rest assured, this book was written expressly for you, and tailored especially for the D810. Indeed, I completely reorganized the content of this book, relegating some of the introductory stuff to the appendixes. If you need to learn the basics of lenses, or how to unbox and set up your D810, you can find what you need to know in those "bonus" sections. The rest of this book is all meat.

Who Am I?

After spending many years as the world's most successful unknown author, I've become slightly less obscure in the past few years, thanks to a horde of camera guidebooks and other photographically oriented tomes. You may have seen my photography articles in *Popular Photography* magazine. I've also written about 2,000 articles for magazines like *Rangefinder*, *Professional Photographer*, and dozens of other photographic publications. But, first, and foremost, I'm a photojournalist and made my living in the field until I began devoting most of my time to writing books. Although I love writing, I'm happiest when I'm out taking pictures, which is why I spend four to six weeks in the Florida Keys each winter as a base of operations for photographing the wildlife, wild natural settings, and wild people in the Sunshine State. In recent years, I've spent a lot of time overseas, too, photographing people and monuments. You'll find photos of some of these visual treasures within the pages of this book.

Like all my digital photography books, this one was written by a Nikon devotee with an incurable photography bug who has used Nikon cameras professionally for longer than I care to admit. Over the years, I've worked as a sports photographer for an Ohio newspaper and for an upstate New York college. I've operated my own commercial studio and photo lab, cranking out product shots on demand and then printing a few hundred glossy 8 × 10s on a tight deadline for a press kit. I've served as a photo-posing instructor for a modeling agency. People have actually paid me to shoot their weddings and immortalize them with portraits. I even prepared press kits and articles on photography as a PR consultant for a large Rochester, N.Y., company, which older readers may recall as an industry giant. My trials and travails with imaging and computer technology have made their way into print in book form an alarming number of times, including a few dozen on scanners and photography.

Like you, I love photography for its own merits, and I view technology as just another tool to help me get the images I see in my mind's eye. But, also like you, I had to master this technology before I could apply it to my work. This book is the result of what I've learned, and I hope it will help you master your Nikon D810 digital SLR, too.

Guide to the Guide

Whether you subscribe to the "my camera is just a tool" theory, or belong to the "an exquisite camera adds new capabilities to my shooting arsenal" camp, picking up a new Nikon D810 is a special experience. Those who simply wield tools will find this camera as comforting as an old friend, a solid piece of fine machinery ready and able to do their bidding as part of any creative process that calls for high resolution and reliability.

Other photographers see the ultra-high res 36-megapixel sensor, advanced movie-making capabilities, unexpectedly good (for its resolution) higher ISO performance, and sophisticated tools like built-in high dynamic range (HDR) capabilities, and gain a sense of empowerment. *Here* is a camera with fewer limitations and more capabilities for exercising renewed creative vision. In either case, using less mawkish terms, the D810 is one of the coolest cameras Nikon has ever offered. Whether you're upgrading from another brand, from another Nikon model, or (O brave one!) your D810 is your first digital camera and/or SLR, welcome to the club.

But, now that you've unwrapped and recharged the beast, mounted a lens, and fueled it with a memory card, what do you *do* with it? That's where this book should come in handy. Like many of you, I am a Nikon user of long standing. And, like other members of our club, I had to learn at least some aspects of my newest camera for the very first time at some point. Experienced pro, or Nikon newbie, you bought this book because you wanted to get the most from a very powerful tool, and I'm here to help.

Depending on your path to the camera, the Nikon D810 is either the company's most ambitious camera for the avid amateur, or most affordable entry-level "pro" camera (if you discount the similarly-priced Nikon Df, which I also love dearly, but is something of a niche camera). "Amateur" and "Pro" are both distinctions that I find almost meaningless in the greater scheme of things. I know consummate professionals who produce amazing images with a D90 even today and experienced wedding photographers who can evoke the most romantic photos from an old Nikon D200.

The Nikon D810 is a professional camera in most of the traditional senses: built like a tank with a magnesium body, reliable for hundreds of thousands of exposures, capable of lightning-fast autofocusing and superb image quality, whether you're shooting in a studio or drenched in driving rain. But whether your *images* are of professional quality, both technically and inspirationally, depends on what's between your ears, and how you apply it. The goal of this book is to provide you with the information you need to put your brain cells together with your Nikon's electro-mechanical components to work productively.

There's a lot to learn, but you don't have to master every detail all at once. Some of the other camera guides I've seen winnow this information down to about one-third as many pages. Indeed, I find it odd that those guidebooks use the same basic template for the advanced D810 cameras as for a resolutely amateur-level model like the Nikon D3300. A camera like the D810 has a lot more depth than that, and deserves the in-depth coverage you'll find here.

Some readers who visit my blog have told me that the Nikon D810 is such an advanced camera that few people really need the kind of basics that so many camera guides concentrate on. "Leave out all the basic photography information!" On the other hand, I've had many pleas from those who are trying to master digital photography as they learn to use their D810, and they've asked me to help them climb the steep learning curve.

Rather than write a book for just one of those two audiences, I've tried to meet the needs of both. You veterans will find plenty of information on getting the most from the D810's features, and may even learn something from an old hand's photo secrets. I'll bet there was a time when you needed a helping hand with some confusing photographic topic. I've tucked most of the really basic material away in the bonus appendixes. And those who are looking to learn about photography and their camera will find just what you need in this book, too.

Here's a quick guide to my Guide:

- **Part I: Introducing the Nikon D810.** I won't insult you by giving you the newbie tour outlining the procedure for unboxing your camera and charging the battery. At least, not here. If you really do want the 50-cent introduction to your camera, you'll find it in the "bonus" material in Appendix A. Part I is devoted to letting you hit the ground running, with a quickie guide to exposure, autofocus, and other controls, a Streetsmart Roadmap that shows you what every component is, and how/when to use it, and a full chapter of recommended settings. Nikon's default settings for your D810 are nice, but mine are better.
- **Part II: Mastering Your Tools.** The four thick chapters in this Part tell you everything you need to know about exposure (including my dismantling of the myth of the 18-percent gray card), autofocus, HDR, and other tools. There's a chapter where I evaluate most of the current Nikon lens line-up (and a few old favorites). Beginners who need to know basics of using lenses can jump to Appendix B in the bonus section at the end of the book.
- **Part III: Working with Light.** Three chapters here explain the nature of light, and how to use it, with a full chapter on electronic flash (even the basics), and another on using the Nikon Creative Lighting System's wireless/multiple flash modes.

- **Part IV: Configuring Your Nikon D810.** Most guidebooks have a chapter near the front of the book that lists all the menu options available, and what they do. Just like Nikon's own manual, only with more words. Part IV, more than 100 pages long, not only tells you when and why to use each of the dozens of shooting, custom, and setup options of your Nikon D810—but when *not* to use them.
- **Part V: Introduction to Movie Making.** How far we've come! When the Nikon D90 was introduced, I explained movie making in part of a chapter that also discussed live view and other techniques. Now, with the Nikon D810's full HD video mode, I needed three full chapters to explain just what you need to know to get started. If you're serious about movie making, this Part will ready you for more in-depth study. Entire books have been written about dSLR movie making (I've written one myself with video guru Rob Sheppard), but these chapters offer a good summary of the tools and techniques at your disposal.
- **Part VI: Bonus Material.** You'll find four appendixes here, each with kernels of essential information that was better put at the end, keeping the main body of this humongous guidebook more streamlined. You'll learn about the D810 and its accessories; basics of wide-angle, telephoto, zoom, prime, and specialized lens technology; how to choose your software tools, from Lightroom 4 to Photoshop CS 6 to Nikon Capture NX 2 and Camera Control 2. There's also an appendix on troubleshooting your camera, upgrading firmware, and cleaning your sensor.

In closing, I'd like to ask a special favor: let me know what you think of this book. If you have any recommendations about how I can make it better, visit my website at www.dslrguides.com/blog, click on the E-Mail Me tab, and send your comments, suggestions on topics that should be explained in more detail, or, especially, any typos. (The latter will be compiled on the Errata page you'll also find on my website.) I really value your ideas, and appreciate it when you take the time to tell me what you think! Some of the content of the book you hold in your hands came from suggestions I received from readers like yourself. If you found this book especially useful, tell others about it. Visit http://www.amazon.com and leave a positive review. Your feedback is what spurs me to make each one of these books better than the last. Thanks!

Part I

Introducing the Nikon D810

This first part of the book, consisting of just three short chapters, is designed to familiarize you with the basics of your Nikon D810 as quickly as possible, even though I have no doubt that you've already been out shooting a few hundred (or thousand) photographs with your pride and joy. After all, inserting a memory card, mounting a lens, stuffing a charged battery into the base, and removing the lens cap to fire off a shot or two isn't rocket science. Even the rawest neophyte can rotate the mode dial (located at top left on the camera body) to the P (Programmed auto) indicator, point the D810 at something interesting, and press the shutter release. Presto! A pretty good picture will pop up on the color LCD on the back of the camera. It's easy!

But in digital photography, there is such a thing as *too* easy. If you bought a D810, you certainly had no intention of using the camera as a point-and-shoot snapshooter. After all, the D810 is a tool suitable for the most advanced photographic pursuits, with an extensive array of customization possibilities. As such, you don't want the camera's operation to be brainless; you want *access* to the advanced features to be easy.

You get that easy access with the Nikon D810. However, you'll still need to take the time to learn how to use these features, and I'm going to provide everything those who are new to this type of camera need to know to begin shooting in these first three chapters. To help you decide which sections are important to you, I'm including green-accented "executive summaries" and chapter descriptions like the following:

This part of the book is intended for anyone who needs basic information on getting started with the Nikon D810. You can learn the basic functions needed to begin shooting immediately, discover the function of every control, and review my recommended changes from Nikon's default settings.

- **Chapter 1:** *This chapter is optional for many of those who have extensive experience with a Nikon mid- or pro-level dSLR.* The information is fairly basic, but contains the kind of Quick Start descriptions that many readers have told me is essential for those who may not be old hands with Nikon cameras at this level of sophistication. I promise you we didn't charge anything extra for this chapter, so skim over it if you don't need it.

  But the D810 does have some interesting new features, including the most advanced autofocus systems ever seen in a Nikon camera body (and which deserves an entire chapter of its own later in this book). But even with all the goodies to play with and learning curve still to climb, you'll find that Chapter 1 will get you shooting quickly with a minimum of fuss. If you're a newbie who wants the most basic fundamentals of the camera and its accessories, that material has been tucked away in Appendix A.

- **Chapter 2:** This is a Streetsmart Roadmap to the Nikon D810. Confused by the tiny little diagrams and multiple cross-references for each and every control that send you scurrying around looking for information you know is buried somewhere in the inadequate manual stuffed in the box? This chapter uses multiple large full-color pictures that show every dial, knob, and button, and explain the basics of using each in clear, easy-to-understand language. I'll give you the basics up front, and, even if I have to send you deeper into the book for a full discussion of a complex topic, you'll have what you need to use a control right away.
- **Chapter 3:** This is a "Recommended Settings" introduction that consists of several parts. At the beginning of the chapter I'll provide recommendations about default settings of the Nikon D810 as it comes from the factory that you probably should change right away. I'll tell you why to make these changes, and list some exceptions for sticking with Nikon's defaults. Later in the chapter I'll list some recommended settings for various types of shooting situations, based on my experience with this camera. If you're just starting out with the Nikon D810, you might want to try out my recommendations, and alter them to fit your own needs as you gain experience.

Once you've finished (or skimmed through) these three chapters, you'll be ready for Part II, which explains how to use the most important basic features, such as the D810's exposure controls, nifty improved autofocus system, and the related tools that put techniques like high dynamic range (HDR) photography and movie-making tools at your fingertips. Then, you can visit Part III, which shows you how to work with light, Part IV, which explains all the dozens of setup options that can be used to modify the capabilities you've learned to use so far, and Part V, which provides an introduction to movie shooting with the D810 and related accessories.

1

Nikon D810 Quick Start

Now it's time to fire up your Nikon D810 and take some photos. The easy part is turning on the power—the Off-On switch is on the right side, concentric with the shutter release button. Turn on the camera, and, if you mounted a lens and inserted a fresh battery and memory card, you're ready to begin. You'll need to select a release mode, exposure mode, metering mode, focus mode, and, if need be, elevate the D810's built in flash.

Choosing a Release Mode

This section shows you how to choose from Single frame, Continuous mode, Self-timer mode, Remote control mode, two "quiet" modes, and a special vibration-damping Mirror Up (Mup) mode. Unless you have need of burst shooting or the self-timer, you can set your camera to Single frame mode and skip ahead to "Selecting an Exposure Mode" (next). Just press the release mode dial lock release button at the 11 o'clock position on the release mode dial (at the top-left edge of the camera) and rotate to the first, or S position, if it's been changed to something else. (See Figure 1.1, left.)

The shooting mode determines when (and how often) the D810 makes an exposure. If you're coming to the dSLR world from a point-and-shoot camera, you might have used a model that labels these options as drive modes, dating back to the film era when cameras could be set for single shot or "motor drive" (continuous) shooting modes. Your D810 has seven release (shooting) modes: Single frame, Continuous low speed, Continuous high speed, Quiet shutter release, Quiet Continuous shutter release, Self-timer, and Mirror Up. I'll explain all these modes in more detail and provide tips for using them in particular situations in Chapter 2.

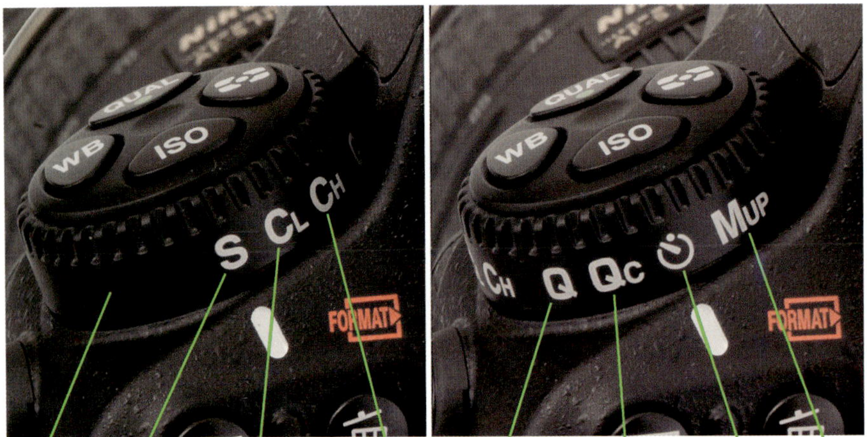

Release mode dial *Single shooting* *Continuous low* *Continuous high* *Quiet shutter release* *Quiet continuous shutter release* *Self-timer* *Mirror up*

Figure 1.1
Hold down the lock release and rotate the dial to choose a release mode.

The shooting modes are as follows:

- **Single frame.** In single shot mode, the D810 takes one picture each time you press the shutter release button down all the way. If you press the shutter and nothing happens (which is very frustrating!), you may be using a focus mode that requires sharp focus to be achieved before a picture can be taken. This is called focus priority, and is discussed in more detail under "Choosing a Focus Mode," later in this chapter.
- **Continuous low speed (C_L).** This "low speed" shooting mode can be set to produce bursts of 1 to 6 frames per second. The 6 fps option hardly qualifies as *low* speed. You can set the frame rate in Custom Setting d2. I use this setting when slicing a scene into tiny fragments of time isn't necessary or desirable (say, I'm bracketing in three shot bursts, or don't want a zillion versions of a scene that really isn't changing that fast). This setting also determines the frame advance rate when using Interval Timer Shooting (described in Chapter 11).
- **Continuous high speed (C_H).** This mode fires off shots at up to 5 or 6 fps (or a maximum of 7 fps when using DX Image Area and the MB-D12 vertical grip), depending on the image size you select. (I'll explain the various image size/frame rate combinations in Chapter 12.) The frame rate can slow down as your D810's memory buffer fills, which forces the camera to wait until some of the pictures you have already taken are written to the memory card, freeing up more space in the buffer. The frame rate may also decrease at shutter speeds slower than 1/250th second, or when operations like Continuous-servo autofocus (described later in this chapter) force the D810 to work at a slightly slower interval. **Note:** Continuous shooting is not available if the built-in flash is elevated; the D810's flash cannot recycle quickly enough to allow shooting in bursts.

SHOOTING MOVIES

You'll learn more about shooting HDTV movie clips with your D810 in Chapters 14 to 16. But if you want to get started right away, it's easy. Just select live view mode by rotating the Live View (Lv) switch located just south of the multi selector to the position with the movie camera icon. When you want to start shooting, press the button in the center of the Lv switch, followed by the movie button on top of the camera (it has a red dot in the middle). Press the movie button again to stop shooting. That's it!

- **Quiet shutter release.** This setting, marked with a Q symbol, activates the D810's "quiet mode," which silences the camera's beep noise, reduces the sound the mirror makes when it flips back down, and delays that "noise" until you release the shutter button or return it to the half-pressed position.
- **Quiet continuous shutter release.** Marked with a QC symbol, takes images at a frame rate of about 3 fps in a quieter shooting mode. I use this at concerts and other venues where quiet moments may occur unexpectedly and I don't want to attract attention to the camera.
- **Self-timer.** You can use the self-timer as a replacement for a remote release, to reduce the effects of camera/user shake when the D810 is mounted on a tripod or, say, set on a firm surface, or when you want to get in the picture yourself. Use Custom Setting c3 to specify delays of 2, 5, 10, or 20 seconds. You can also specify the number of shots taken at the end of the elapsed period, and the interval between those shots (see Chapter 11 for detailed instructions). Any time you use the camera on a tripod (with the self-timer or otherwise) make sure there is no bright light shining on the viewfinder window; if so, use the D810's built-in eyepiece shutter (the lever is located to the left of the eyepiece window).
- **Mirror Up (Mup).** This mode delays the taking of the picture until after the mirror is flipped up out of the way (blanking the viewfinder), producing a short delay that also minimizes the effect of the mirror's movement on a picture taken using a long shutter speed. When shooting with telephoto lenses or during close-up photography, a "long" shutter speed can be anything from 1/125th seconds to several seconds. (Mirror movement has only an imperceptible effect on exposures longer than a second or two.) When Mup is activated, pressing the shutter release down all the way once lifts the mirror; pressing it a second time takes the picture and returns the mirror to its down position. To use Mup to take a picture after a delay, press the shutter just once. About 30 seconds after the mirror is raised, the camera will take the picture automatically, with no further action required on your part. When working with Mup mode, you can optionally activate the D810's electronic front-curtain shutter (use Custom Setting d5), which opens the physical shutter prior to the actual exposure, but doesn't begin capturing an image until vibration from the "real" shutter has subsided.

Note

The Mup facility is an offbeat way of producing a self-timer delay of 30 seconds, rather than the maximum 20 seconds that the D810's self-timer feature provides.

Selecting an Exposure Mode

This section shows you how to choose an exposure mode. If you'd rather have the D810 make most of the decisions for you, just press the MODE button, located just in front of the top-panel monochrome control panel LCD, and rotate the main control dial until P (Program auto) appears on the status LCD. You can read about the P options available in this mode later in this section, or jump to the section titled "Reviewing the Pictures You've Taken." If you'd rather choose one of the camera's semi-automatic modes, you should definitely continue reading this section.

While P mode is a good all-around option, and a must for "grab" shots when you don't have time to make other settings, those who have more photographic experience might want to opt for one of the semi-automatic modes. These, too, are described in more detail in Chapter 4. These modes all let you apply a little more creativity to your camera's settings. Any of these can be dialed in by pressing the MODE button and rotating the main command dial.

- **P (Program).** This mode allows the D810 to select the basic exposure settings, but you can still override the camera's choices to fine-tune your image, while maintaining metered exposure, as I'll explain in Chapter 4.
- **S (Shutter-priority).** This mode is useful when you want to use a particular shutter speed to stop action or produce creative blur effects. Choose your preferred shutter speed by rotating the main command dial when the meter is active, and the D810 will select the appropriate f/stop for you.
- **A (Aperture-priority).** Choose when you want to use a particular lens opening, especially to control sharpness or how much of your image is in focus. Specify the f/stop you want using the sub-command dial when the meter is "awake" (tap the shutter release to activate the meter, if necessary), and the D810 will select the appropriate shutter speed for you.
- **M (Manual).** Select when you want full control over the shutter speed and lens opening, either for creative effects or because you are using a studio flash or other flash unit not compatible with the D810's automatic flash metering. Use the main command dial and sub-command dial when the exposure meter is active to specify the shutter speed and f/stop (respectively).

Choosing a Metering Mode

This section shows you how to choose the area the D810 will use to measure exposure, giving emphasis to the center of the frame; evaluating many different areas of the frame; or measuring light from a small spot in the center of the frame.

The metering mode you select determines how the D810 calculates exposure. You might want to select a particular metering mode for your first shots, although the default Matrix metering is probably the best choice as you get to know your camera. I'll explain when and how to use each of the three metering modes later. To change metering modes, press the metering mode button, located on the left shoulder of the camera on top of the release mode dial, and rotate the main dial, which is positioned on the back right corner, just to the right of the button labeled AF-ON. The choices that are displayed in the viewfinder and on the top-mounted control panel are as follows: (See Figure 1.2.)

- **Matrix metering.** The standard metering mode; the D810 attempts to intelligently classify your image and choose the best exposure based on readings from a 91,000-point RGB color CCD sensor that interprets light reaching the viewfinder using a database of hundreds of thousands of patterns.
- **Center-weighted metering.** The D810 meters the entire scene, but gives the most emphasis to the central area of the frame, measuring about 12mm. (You can change the size of this area to 8, 15, or 20mm, as described in Chapter 12.)
- **Spot metering.** Exposure is calculated from a smaller 4mm spot, about 1.5 percent of the image area, centered on whichever of the 51 focus points is currently the active point.
- **Highlight-weighted.** The D810 measures highlights and assigns the emphasis to them, preventing overexposure when, say, an important subject is surrounded by very dark areas.

You'll find a detailed description of each of these modes in Chapter 4.

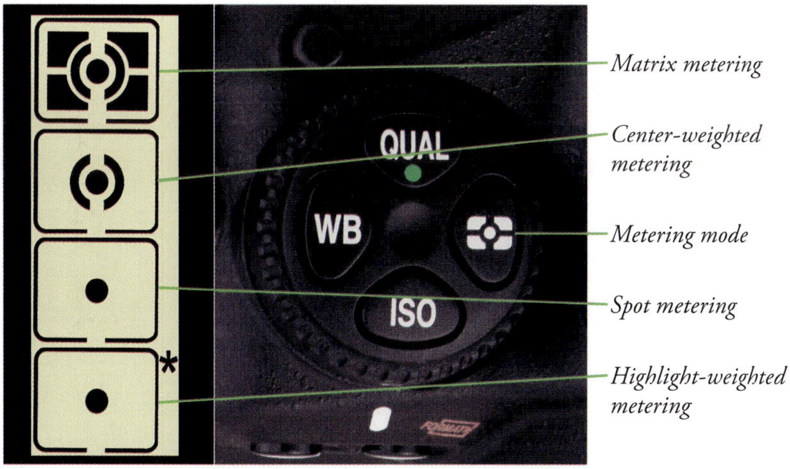

Figure 1.2
Metering modes are selected using the metering mode selector (right). The individual icons for the modes are shown at left.

Choosing a Focus Mode

This section shows how to select *when* the D810 calculates focus: all the time (continuously), only once when you press a control like the shutter release button (single autofocus), or manually when you rotate a focus ring on the lens.

You can easily switch between automatic and manual focus by moving the AF/MF or M-AF/MF switch on the lens mounted on your camera (if present; some older lenses lack the switch). There is also an AF/MF lever on the camera body. (See Figure 1.3.) When using autofocus, you have additional choices. You can select the autofocus mode (*when* the D810 measures and locks in focus) and autofocus pattern (*which* of the 51 available autofocus points or zones are used to interpret correct focus). To specify when the D810 locks in focus, follow these steps:

1. **Activate autofocus.** Make sure the camera is set for autofocus mode by sliding any MA/M or AF/M switch on the lens to the MA or AF position. The camera body AF/M switch (see Figure 1.3) must also be set in the AF position. Note that the autofocus/manual focus switches on the lens and camera body must agree; if either is set to manual focus, then the D810 defaults to manual focus regardless of how the other switch is set. Nikon, in fact, specifically warns using autofocus lenses with the lens switch set to M and the camera body switch to AF, saying that doing so could damage the camera.
2. **Enter setting mode.** Press and hold the autofocus mode button in the center of the AF/M switch.
3. **Choose AF mode.** While holding down the AF-mode button, rotate the main dial until AF-S or AF-C is shown on the top-panel monochrome LCD, as well as on the back-panel color LCD when the information display screen is visible (press the Info button, located to the immediate right of the LCD, at the bottom, to produce it). (See Figure 1.4.) While the button is held down, you'll also see AFS or AFC in green at the bottom of the optical viewfinder and on the control panel. If you haven't activated autofocus mode, as described in Step 1, nothing will happen while the button is pressed and the main command dial is rotated. The two focus modes are described in more detail next.

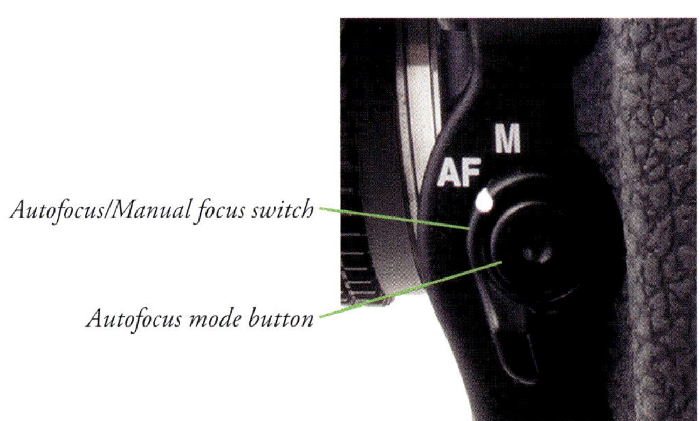

Figure 1.3
Activate autofocus mode on the camera body.

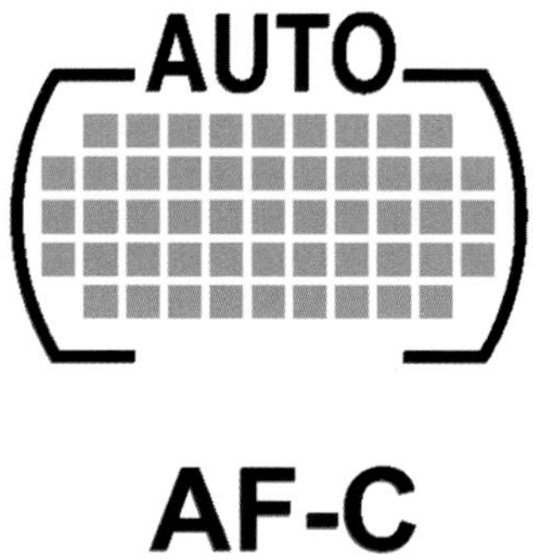

Figure 1.4
The autofocus mode you select is displayed on the back-panel LCD when the Info button is pressed (pictured) in the viewfinder, and on the top control panel LCD (not shown).

The two autofocus modes are as follows:

- **(AF-C) Continuous-servo autofocus.** This mode, sometimes called *continuous autofocus*, or AF-C, sets focus when you partially depress the shutter button (or other autofocus activation button), but continues to monitor the frame and refocuses if the camera or subject is moved. This is a useful mode for photographing sports and moving subjects. Focus or release-priority can be specified for AF-C mode using Custom Setting a1.
- **(AF-S) Single-servo autofocus.** This mode, sometimes called *single autofocus*, or AF-S, locks in a focus point when the shutter button is pressed down halfway (there are other autofocus activation button options, described in Chapter 5), and the focus confirmation light glows at bottom left in the viewfinder. The focus will remain locked until you release the button or take the picture. This mode is best when your subject is relatively motionless. As you'll learn in Chapter 12, you can set your Nikon D810 using Custom Setting a2 so that the camera will not take a photo unless sharp focus is achieved (*focus-priority*), or so that it will go ahead and snap a photo while still adjusting focus (*release-priority*).

Choosing the Focus Area Mode

The Nikon D810 uses up to 51 different focus points to calculate correct focus, using one or more points you can select yourself, or which the camera can choose. To choose a focus area mode, follow these steps:

1. **Enter setting mode.** Press and hold the autofocus mode button in the center of the AF/M switch.
2. **Rotate sub-command dial.** The dial, on the front of the camera, can be used to select one of the modes. The current AF area mode chosen will be displayed on the back-panel color LCD (see Figure 1.5, left) and an equivalent indicator in the viewfinder (see Figure 1.5, right).
3. **Choose AF-area mode.** For now, you should set to Auto-area AF and allow the D810 to choose the focus zone for you.

The AF area modes are as follows.

- **Single-point.** The camera focuses on a point you select, using the multi selector directional buttons, when the AF point lock lever (located just below the multi selector) is not set to the L (lock) position.
- **9-point dynamic-area AF.** You select the focus point, and the camera also uses information from surrounding AF points (nine points, total) to calculate focus.
- **21-point dynamic-area AF.** You select the focus point, and the camera also uses information from surrounding AF points (21 points, total) to calculate focus.
- **51-point dynamic-area AF.** You select the focus point, and the camera also uses information from all 51 focus points to calculate focus.
- **3D-tracking.** You select the focus point, and the camera will track your subject, using any of the other focus points, as needed, when using AF-A and AF-C modes. (In AF-S mode, focus tracking is not used, as focus is locked in when you press the shutter release halfway.)
- **Group-Area AF.** The D810 uses a group of focus points that you select, thereby enlarging the focus area compared to single-point focus. Faces that are detected when using AF-S focus mode will be given priority.
- **Auto-area AF.** The D810 chooses a focus point.

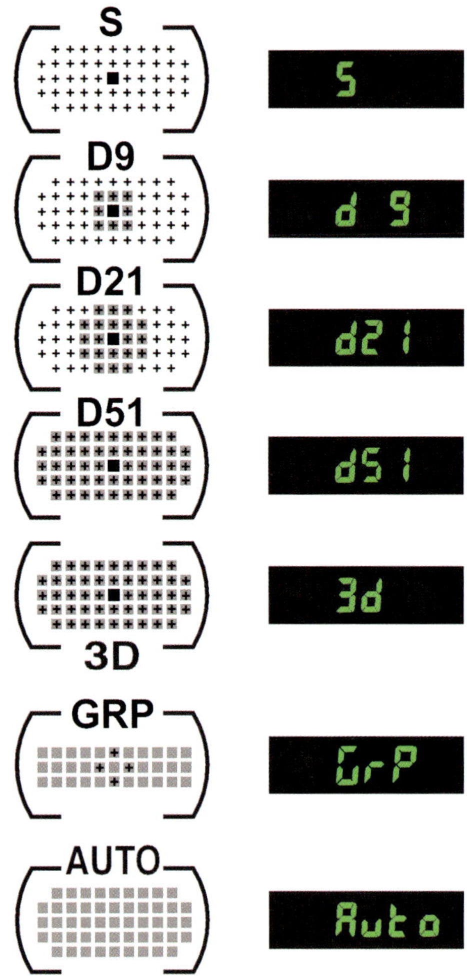

Figure 1.5 Focus area modes shown on the top control panel LCD (left) and in the viewfinder (right) are, top to bottom, Single-point, 9-point dynamic-area AF, 21-point dynamic-area AF, 51-point dynamic-area AF, 3D-tracking, Group-Area AF, and Auto-area AF. While the illustration shows the focus points centered, the active points can be moved by the user in single-, 9-, and 21-point modes.

Other Settings

This section describes some optional features you can select if you feel you need to choose the white balance, change the camera's sensitivity setting, or delay taking a picture with the self-timer.

There are a few other settings you can make if you're feeling ambitious, but don't feel ashamed if you postpone using these features until you've racked up a little more experience with your D810.

Adjusting White Balance and ISO

If you like, you can custom-tailor your white balance (color balance) and ISO sensitivity settings. To start out, it's best to set white balance (WB) to Auto, and ISO to ISO 200 for daylight photos, and ISO 400 for pictures in dimmer light. (Don't be afraid of ISO 1600 or even higher, however; the D810 does a *much* better job of producing low-noise photos at higher ISOs than earlier generations.) You can adjust either one now by pressing the WB (for white balance) or ISO buttons on top of the release mode dial on the left side of the camera, and rotating the main command dial until the setting you want appears on the control panel LCD on top of the camera.

MAKING SETTINGS UNDER LOW LIGHT

When working under low light levels, you might experience some difficulty seeing the white balance, ISO, or other settings on the top monochrome control panel LCD as you make them. You can always rotate the ON-OFF switch an additional push in the clockwise direction to illuminate the LCD backlight, but there is a better way. Instead, press the Info button (at the bottom of the right side of the camera to the right of the LCD) to show the much larger and easier-to-read shooting information display on the color LCD. Then press the WB or ISO button (or the button for whatever setting you're changing) and rotate the appropriate dial until the value you want appears on the shooting information display. Indeed, you can press the Info button at any time to pop up this information screen, which is especially helpful when working with the camera on a tripod, or under dim illumination.

Using the Self-Timer

If you want to set a short delay before your picture is taken, you can use the self-timer. Press the lock release button to free the release mode dial, and rotate it five clicks clockwise until the self-timer icon appears next to the indicator line. Press the shutter release to lock focus and start the timer. The self-timer lamp on the front of the camera will blink and the beeper will sound (unless you've silenced it in the menus) until the final two seconds, when the lamp remains on and the beeper beeps more rapidly. The default delay is 10 seconds, but you can set it to 2, 5, 10, or 20 seconds using Custom Setting c3, and choose the number of shots snapped after the delay has elapsed (1 to 9 images), and the interval between those shots (0.5-3 seconds) as described in Chapter 12. As I mentioned earlier, you can also use the Mup release mode to get a 30-second delay.

Reviewing the Images You've Taken

Read this section when you're ready to take a closer look at the images you've taken, and want to know how to review pictures and zoom in.

The Nikon D810 has a broad range of playback and image review options, and I'll cover them in more detail in Chapter 11. For now, you'll want to learn just the basics. Here is all you really need to know at this time, as shown in Figure 1.6:

- **View image.** Press the Playback button (marked with a white right-pointing triangle) at the upper-left corner of the back of the camera to display the most recent image on the LCD.
- **View additional images.** Press the multi selector left or right buttons.
- **Change information display.** Press the multi selector button up or down to change among overlays of basic image information or detailed shooting information.

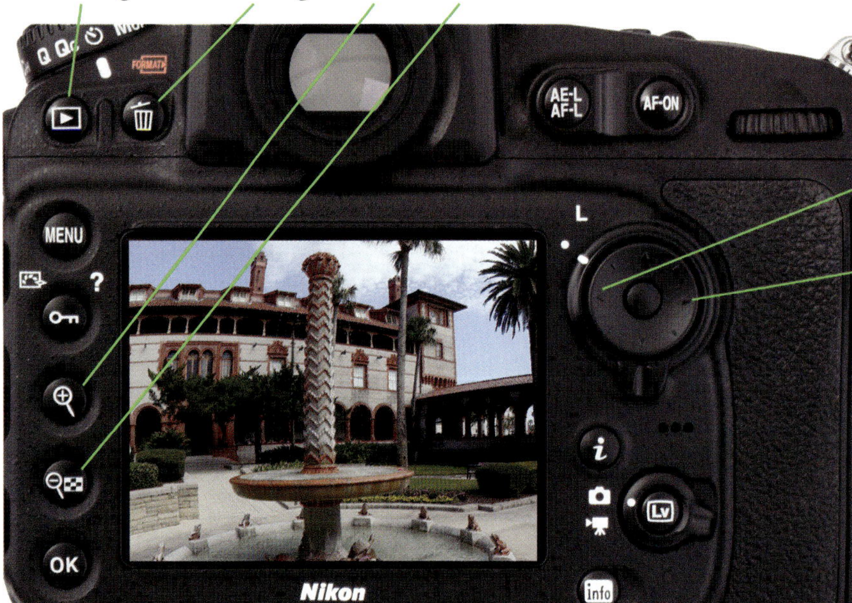

Figure 1.6
Review your images.

- **Change magnification.** Press the Zoom In button repeatedly to zoom in on the image displayed; the Zoom Out button reduces the image. (Both buttons are located to the left of the color LCD.) A thumbnail representation of the whole image appears in the lower-right corner with a yellow rectangle showing the relative level of zoom. At intermediate zoom positions, the yellow rectangle can be moved around within the frame using the multi selector.
- **Exit image review.** Press the Playback button again, or just tap the shutter release button to exit playback view.

You'll find information on viewing thumbnail indexes of images, automated playback, and other options in Chapter 11.

Using the Built-in Flash

Working with the D810's built-in flash (as well as external flash units like the Nikon SB-910) deserves detailed coverage, and I'm providing the information you need (see Chapters 8–10). But the built-in flash is easy enough to work with that you can begin using it right away, either to provide the main lighting of a scene or as supplementary illumination to fill in the shadows. For example, if you choose Matrix or Center-weighted metering (as described earlier), you can even use the flash in full daylight, as the D810 will even automatically balance the amount of light emitted from the flash so that it illuminates the shadows nicely, without overwhelming the highlights and producing a glaring "flash" look. (Think *Baywatch* when they're using too many reflectors on the lifeguards!)

The D810's flash has a power rating of 12/39 (meters/feet) at ISO 100, using the GN (guide number) system that dates back to the film era and before electronic flash units had any sort of automatic features. I'll explain guide numbers (which can be a little confusing) in more detail in Chapter 9, but in plain terms, the flash's rating means that the unit is powerful enough to allow proper illumination of a subject that's 10 feet away at f/4 at the ISO 100 (sensitivity) setting of your camera. Boost the ISO (or use a wider f/stop) and you can shoot subjects that are located at a great distance. For example, at ISO 800, the D810's flash is good enough for a subject at 20 feet using f/5.6 or, alternatively, you can expose that scene at the original 10 feet distance at f/11. Ordinarily, the D810 takes care of all these calculations for you. If you need a bigger blast of light, you can add an external flash, like the Nikon SB-910, which lets you reach out to 32 to 45 feet at ISO 200 and f/5.6 (or even farther at larger f/stops).

To use the built-in flash, for Program, Shutter-priority, Aperture-priority, or Manual modes, just press the flash pop-up button (shown in Figure 1.7). When you're finished using it, you need to push it back down. When the flash is fully charged, a lightning bolt symbol will flash at the right side of the viewfinder display. When using P (Program) or A (Aperture-priority) exposure modes,

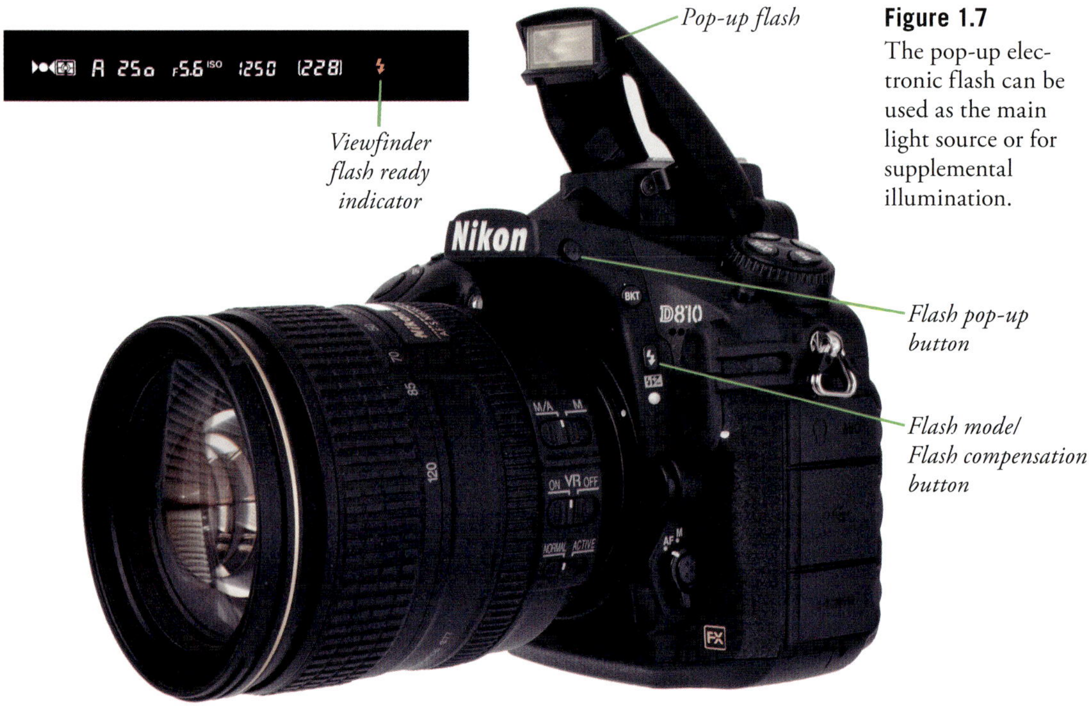

Figure 1.7
The pop-up electronic flash can be used as the main light source or for supplemental illumination.

the D810 will select a shutter speed for you automatically from the range 1/250th to 1/60th seconds (with a couple exceptions described in Chapter 9). In S (Shutter-priority) and M (Manual) modes, you select the shutter speed from 1/250th to 30 seconds (again, with a couple exceptions that I won't get into here). When using the built-in flash, if you select a shutter speed higher than 1/250th second (which prevents the camera from synchronizing with the shutter; see Chapter 9), the D810 will set 1/250th second for you automatically.

When using PSAM modes, you can preview the effect of your flash visually by pressing the depth-of-field button, which activates a brief, continuous series of bursts (which look to the eye like a single, long flash of light)—unless you've disabled this "modeling flash" using Custom Setting e5.

You'll also learn in Chapter 9 how to change the flash syncing mode (and why you might want to do so), as well as how to increase/reduce the effects of the flash on your scene using *flash compensation* adjustments.

Transferring Photos to Your Computer

The final step in your picture-taking session will be to transfer the photos you've taken to your computer for printing, further review, or image editing. Your D810 allows you to print directly to PictBridge-compatible printers and to create print orders right in the camera, plus you can select which images to transfer to your computer. I'll outline those options in Chapter 11.

I always recommend using a card reader attached to your computer to transfer files, because that process is generally a lot faster and doesn't drain the D810's battery. However, you can also use a cable for direct transfer, which may be your only option when you have the cable and a computer, but no card reader (perhaps you're using the computer of a friend or colleague, or at an Internet café).

To transfer images from the camera to a Mac or PC computer using the USB cable:

1. Turn off the camera.
2. Pry back the rubber cover that protects the D810's USB port, and plug the USB cable furnished with the camera into the USB port. (See Figure 1.8.)
3. Connect the other end of the USB cable to a USB port on your computer.
4. Turn on the camera. The operating system itself, or installed software such as Nikon Transfer or Adobe Photoshop Elements Transfer, usually detects the camera and offers to copy or move the pictures. Or, the camera appears on your desktop as a mass storage device, enabling you to drag and drop the files to your computer.

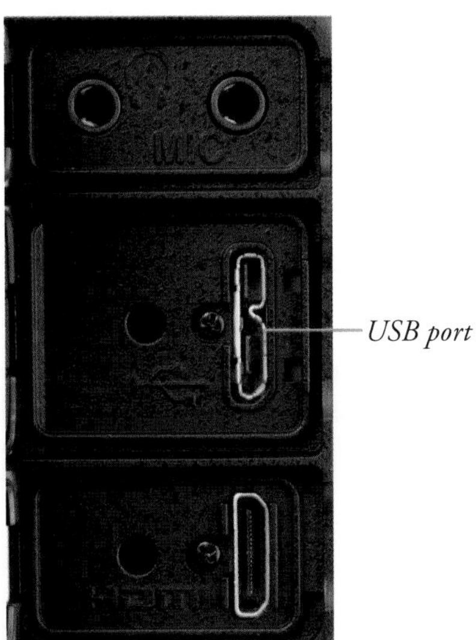

Figure 1.8
Images can be transferred to your computer using a USB cable connected to this port.

To transfer images from a memory card to the computer using a card reader, as shown in Figure 1.9:

1. Turn off the camera.
2. Open the memory card door and extract the Secure Digital card.
3. Insert the memory card into your memory card reader. Your installed software detects the files on the card and offers to transfer them. The card can also appear as a mass storage device on your desktop, which you can open and then drag and drop the files to your computer.

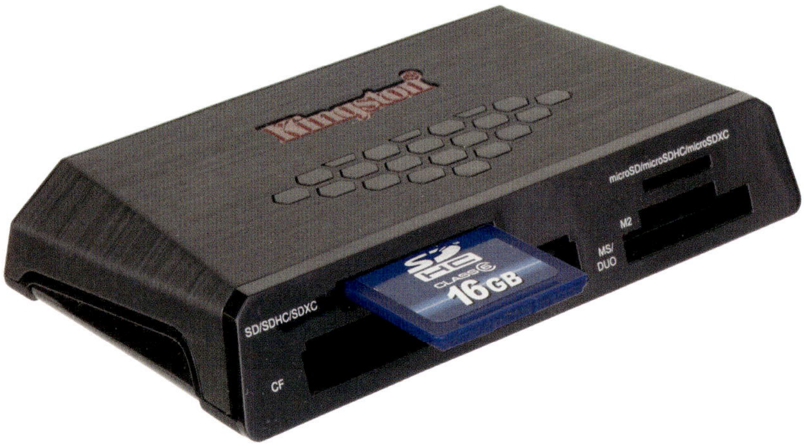

Figure 1.9
A card reader is the fastest way to transfer photos.

2

Nikon D810 Roadmap

Most of the Nikon D810's key functions and settings that are changed frequently can be accessed directly using the array of dials, buttons, and knobs that populate the camera's surface. With so many dedicated controls available, you'll find that the bulk of your shooting won't be slowed down by a visit to the vast thicket of text options called Menu-land. That's a distinct paradigm shift from early point-and-shoot cameras, which had only four or five buttons, and relied on menus to control virtually every setting you might want to make. With the D810, you can press specific buttons dedicated to image quality, white balance, ISO sensitivity, shooting mode, exposure compensation, and playback options, and then spin a command dial or make adjustments using the multi selector.

While it might take some time to learn the position and function of each of these controls, once you've mastered them, the D810 camera is remarkably easy to use. That's because dedicated buttons with only one or two functions each are much faster to access than the alternative—a maze of menus that must be navigated every time you want to use a feature. The advantage of menu systems—dating back to early computer user interfaces of the 1980s—is that they are easy to *learn.* The ironic disadvantage of menus is that they are clumsy to *use.*

Imagine that you are familiar with digital SLRs in general, but know virtually nothing about the Nikon D810. Perhaps you've upgraded from a Canon EOS model, which uses a control and menu layout that's much different from most Nikon cameras. You've decided that you want to format the memory card. A-ha! There's a big ol' MENU button on the left side of the camera. Press it, and you'll see a series of different menu icons, which, when you scroll through them, have titles like Playback menu, Shooting menu, Custom Settings menu, and Setup menu. You might guess that the Setup menu is the likely repository for a Format command, but even if you guess wrong, it takes only a minute or two to check out the other menus and discover the Format command tucked away within the Setup menu. A couple more button presses (you'll need to choose between which of the two memory card slots you want to format—if both contain cards) and you've successfully formatted your memory card.

You didn't really need instructions—the menu system itself led you to the right command. If you don't format another card for weeks and weeks, you can come back to the menus and discover how to perform the task all over again. The main cost to you was the time required to negotiate through all the menus to carry out the function; while menus are easy to learn, the multiple steps they call for (10 or more button presses may be required) can be cumbersome to use. Direct access buttons are the exact opposite: you have to teach yourself how to use them, and then remember what you've learned over time, but once learned, buttons are much faster to use.

For example, simple direct button presses can also format your memory card. It's easy to just hold down the metering mode button and the trash can button simultaneously for about two seconds. When the characters For and the exposures remaining displays blink in the viewfinder and top control panel LCD, select the slot containing the memory card you want to format (rotate the main command dial), press the pair of buttons again, and the D810 formats your card. To cancel the format, press any other button. The sequence may be tricky to learn or remember (although red Format labels appear next to the pair of buttons), but it's much faster to use than threading through a series of menu options.

If you want to operate your D810 efficiently, you'll need to learn the location, function, and application of all these controls. What you really need is a street-level roadmap that shows where everything is, and how it's used. But what Nikon gives you in the user's manual is akin to a world globe with an overall view and many cross-references to the pages that will tell you what you really need to know. Check out the "Getting to Know the Camera" section starting on Page 1 of Nikon's manual, which offers four tiny black-and-white line drawings of the camera body that show front, back, two sides, and the top and bottom of the D810, plus several insets. There are about six dozen callouts pointing to various buttons and dials. If you can find the control you want in this cramped layout, you'll still need to flip back and forth among multiple pages (individual buttons can have several different cross-references!) to locate the information.

Most other third-party books follow this format, featuring black-and-white photos or line drawings of front, back, and top views, and many labels. I originated the up-close-and-personal, full-color, street-level roadmap (rather than a satellite view) that I use in this book and my previous camera guidebooks. I provide you with many different views and lots of explanation accompanying each zone of the camera, so that by the time you finish this chapter, you'll have a basic understanding of every control and what it does. I'm not going to delve into menu functions here—you'll find a discussion of your Playback, Shooting, Custom Settings, and Setup options in Chapters 11, 12, and 13. Everything here is devoted to the button pusher and dial twirler in you.

You'll also find this "roadmap" chapter a good guide to the rest of the book, as well. I'll try to provide as much detail here about the use of the main controls as I can, but some topics (such as autofocus and exposure) are too complex to address in depth right away. As much as I'd like to explain *everything* in just one place, 200-page chapters can be tiresome. So, I'll point you to the relevant chapters that discuss things like setup options, exposure, use of electronic flash, and working with lenses with the occasional cross-reference.

Nikon D810: Full Frontal

This is the side seen by your subjects as you snap away (Figure 2.1). For the photographer, though, the front is the surface your fingers curl around as you hold the camera, and there are really only a few buttons to press, all within easy reach of the fingers of your left and right hands. There are additional controls on the lens itself. You'll need to look at several different views to see everything.

Figure 2.1 shows the front of the D810 with the lens removed. The components shown in this view include:

- **Aperture lever.** This mechanical lever pivots to physically move the diaphragm inside the lens to the f/stop that will be used to take the picture. The actual size of the aperture is determined by the setting calculated by the D810's exposure system, or specified by you in Manual exposure mode, and conveyed to the camera through the electrical contacts located at the top edge of the lens mount.
- **Electronic contacts.** These eight contact points mate with matching points on the bayonet mount of the lens itself, and allow two-way communication between the camera and lens for functions like aperture size and autofocus information.
- **Lens indexing ring.** This sliding lever mates with a notch on the edge of the lens barrel. Its position tells the camera the maximum aperture of the lens as well as the currently selected f/stop of lenses that have their own built-in aperture ring. Lens indexing allows the D810 to use older lenses (such as non-autofocus AI or AI-S lenses) for automatic exposure using Aperture-priority.

  You'll need to enter the maximum aperture and focal length of such lenses one time in the Non-CPU Lens Data entry of the Setup menu, and then tell the D810 when you have mounted this lens. (I'll show you how to do this in Chapter 13.)

  The presence of the lens indexing ring is the reason why you need to lock the aperture of your autofocus D-type lenses at the minimum setting (usually f/16 or f/22) using a lock switch on the lens itself, so that the lens can communicate aperture information electronically. The indexing makes no difference when using G-type lenses that lack an aperture ring.

Figure 2.1

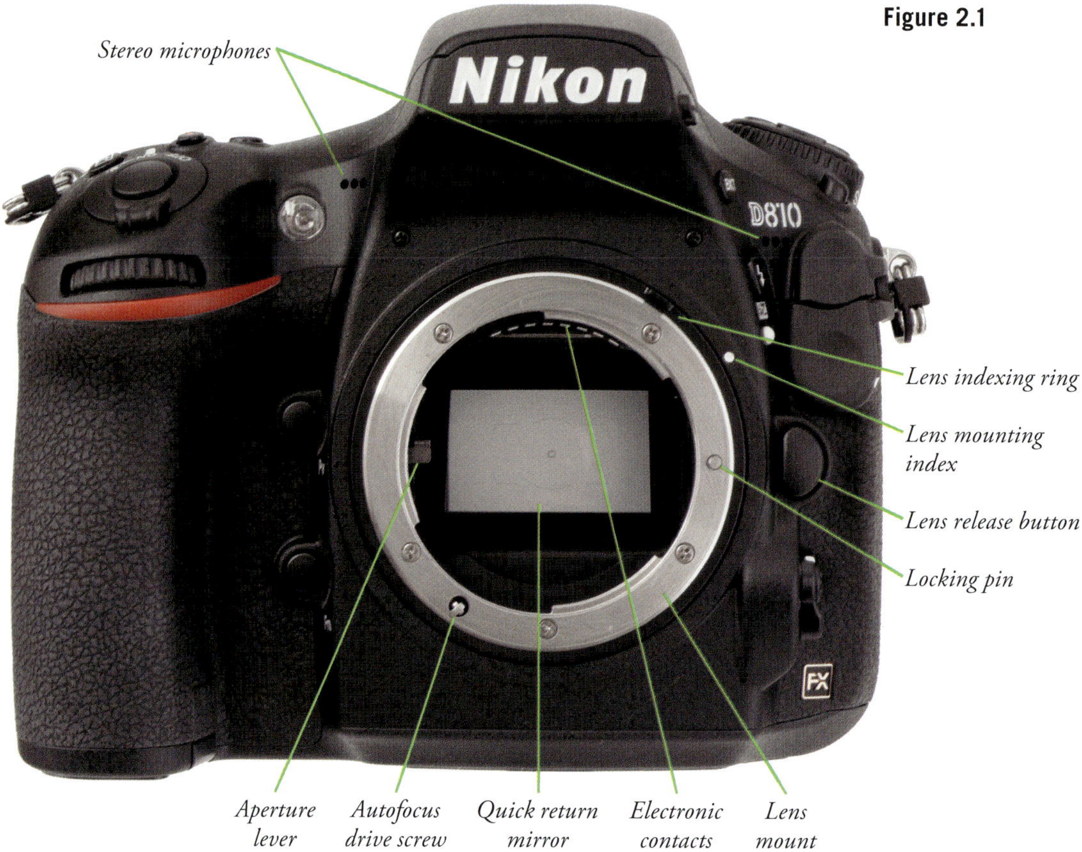

- **Autofocus drive screw.** This feature, along with the lens indexing ring, are two components lacking in Nikon's most recent entry-level cameras, but present in more advanced models like the D810. The drive screw is connected to a motor in the camera body to allow the camera to adjust focus of lenses that lack an AF motor within the lens itself. These lenses are marked with an AF designation instead of AF-S (the S stands for Silent Wave motor). The D810 can autofocus any AF or AF-S lens, whereas entry-level models like the Nikon D3xxx and D5xxx series (which don't have the camera-body motor and this drive screw) autofocus only the AF-S lenses. I'll explain autofocus and lens features in more detail in Chapters 5 and 7.
- **Lens mounting index.** Line up this dot with the matching dot on the lens barrel to mount your lens on the D810.
- **Lens mount.** This precision bayonet mount mates with the matching mount on the back of each compatible lens. The mount configuration is basically unchanged since the original Nikon F was introduced in 1959, with only a few changes, such as the lens indexing ring introduced in 1977, and autofocus motor/pin in 1986.

- **Lens release button.** Press this button to retract the locking pin on the lens mount so a lens can be rotated to remove it from the camera.
- **Locking pin.** This pin slides inside a matching hole in the lens to keep it from rotating until the lens release button is pressed.
- **Quick return mirror.** This flip-up mirror directs the image seen by the lens upward to the viewing screen and exposure metering system, and thence onward to the eyepiece of the optical viewfinder. Semi-silvered locations on the mirror allow some illumination to be directed downward to the autofocus mechanism located on the floor of the compartment.
- **Stereo microphones.** The D810 has a pair of microphones built into the front of the camera, each seen as a trio of holes set in a horizontal line. This is an upgrade from the previous D800/D800E models, which included only a single monaural microphone on the front of the camera.

Figure 2.2 shows a view of the left side Nikon D810, as seen from the front. The main components you need to know about are as follows:

- **Shutter release.** Angled on top of the hand grip is the shutter release button, which has multiple functions. Press this button down halfway to lock exposure and focus. Press it down all the way to actually take a photo or sequence of photos if you've changed the mode dial to either of the continuous shooting modes, C_L or C_H (Continuous shooting low speed and Continuous shooting high speed), or if you've redefined the behavior of the self-timer to take 1 to 9 exposures when its delay has expired. (I'll show you how to take multiple shots with the self-timer in Chapter 11.) Tapping the shutter button when the D810's exposure meters have turned themselves off reactivates them, and a tap can be used to remove the display of a menu or image from the rear color LCD monitor.
- **On/Off switch.** Rotating this switch to the detent turns the camera on. Continuing to rotate past the detent to the farthest position illuminates the top control panel LCD lamp, so you can read settings in dim lighting.
- **Sub-command dial.** This dial is used to change shooting settings. When settings are available in pairs (such as shutter speed/aperture), this dial will be used to make one type of setting, such as aperture, while the main command dial (on the back of the camera) will be used to make the other, such as shutter speed. Using the Custom Settings menu adjustments in Custom Setting f9, you can reverse the default rotational direction, swap the functions of the sub-command and main command dials, control how the sub-command dial is used to set aperture, and tell the D810 that you want to use the main command dial to scroll through menus and images. All these options are discussed in more detail in Chapter 12.
- **AF-assist illuminator/Red-eye reduction/Self-timer lamp.** This LED provides a blip of light shortly before a flash exposure to cause the subjects' pupils to close down, reducing the effect of red-eye reflections off their retinas. When using the self-timer, this lamp also flashes to mark the countdown until the photo is taken. It can also illuminate to provide assistance for the D810's autofocus mechanism at fairly close distances.

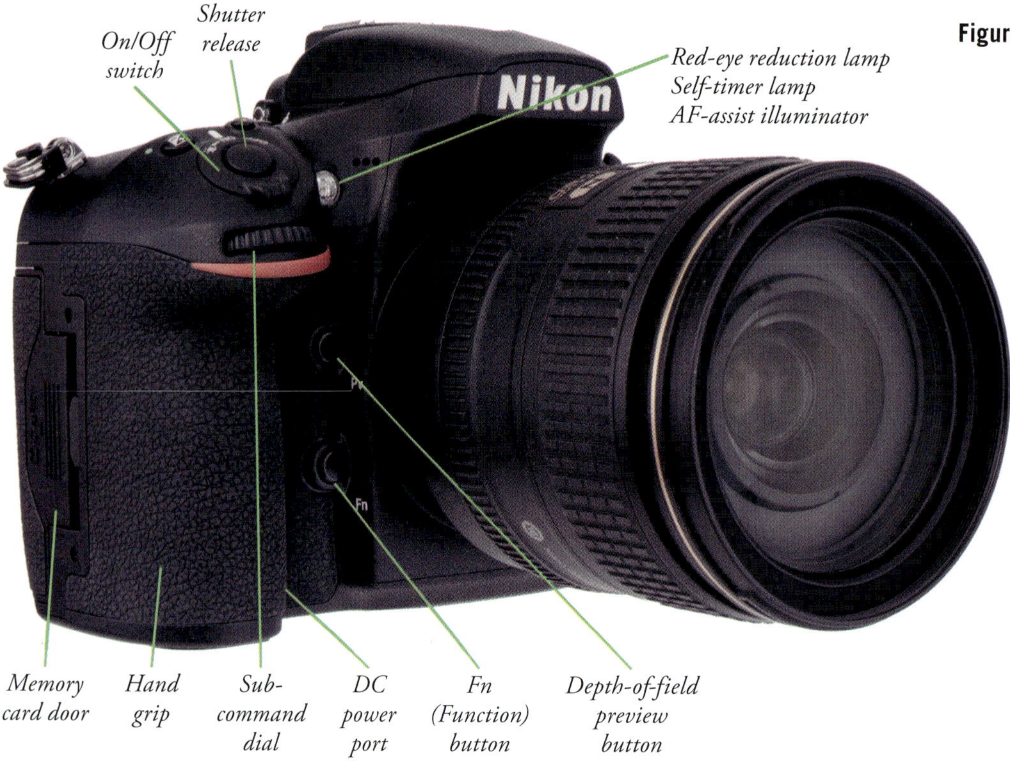

Figure 2.2

- **Hand grip.** This provides a comfortable hand-hold, and also contains the D810's battery. Unlike some earlier Nikon models which had their electrical contacts inside the battery compartment, it's not necessary to remove the battery of the D810 to mount the MB-D12 accessory battery/vertical grip. Its contacts are located on the bottom of the camera, protected by a rubber cover.
- **Fn (Function button).** This conveniently located button has no function by default, but can be programmed to perform any one of 12 different actions, ranging from metering modes (Matrix, Center-weighted, Spot) to flash off or bracketing bursts. You can choose separate actions for both a standard Fn button press (17 options, plus Off), or the Fn button and command dial spin (5 options, plus Off).

TIP

Note that on some earlier Nikon cameras that have both a Fn button and depth-of-field preview (described next), the position of these two is swapped. If you'd rather have this button (the upper one) act as a DOF button, as on those earlier cameras, you can define it for that function. I'll explain how to define a function using Custom Setting f4 in Chapter 12.

- **Depth-of-field (preview) button.** By default, this button closes down the lens aperture to the opening that will be used to take the picture, as set by the D810's light meters or by you (when in Manual or Aperture-priority modes). The DOF button can be redefined using the same functions offered for the Fn button. I'll explain how to define a function using Custom Setting f5 in Chapter 12.
- **Memory card door.** Your Secure Digital and/or Compact Flash memory cards can be inserted here when you slide the door toward the rear of the camera to open it.
- **DC power port.** This opening on the inside edge of the hand grip (not really visible in the figure) provides a place for the optional AC adapter connector to exit.

You'll find more controls on the other side of the D810, shown in Figure 2.3. In the illustration, you can see the mode dial on top, and the rubber covers on the side that protects the camera's USB, HDMI, microphone ports, and headphone jack. The main points of interest shown include:

- **Neck strap eyelet.** It comes with a split-ring attached that can be used to fasten a neck strap to the D810.
- **Port covers.** These two rubber covers protect the USB, HDMI, microphone ports, and headphone connectors when not in use.

Figure 2.3

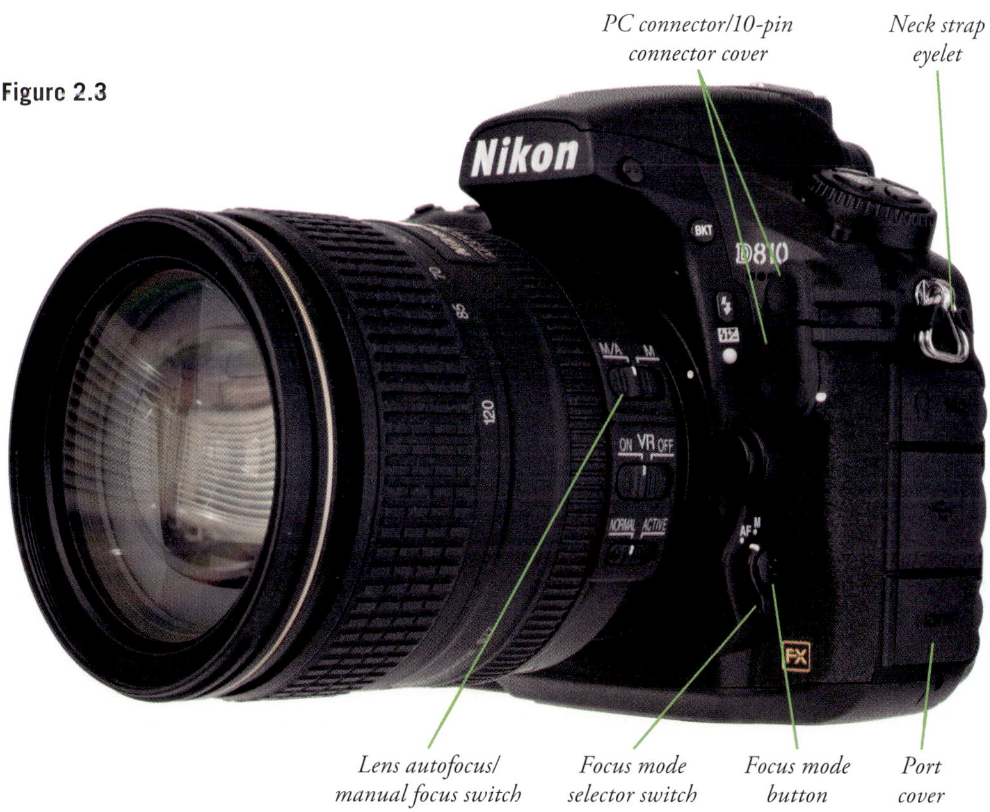

- **Focus mode selector switch.** Rotate to change from autofocus to manual focus. You should remember that the modes selected with this switch and the autofocus/manual focus switch on the lens must agree. If you've chosen A (or M/A, which allows for manual fine-tuning of autofocus) on the lens, then the camera body switch must be set to AF. If either the lens or body switch (or both) are set to M, then the lens must be focused manually.
- **Focus mode button.** Press this button and rotate the main command dial to change from Continuous-servo autofocus (AF-C) to Single-servo autofocus (AF-S) or Manual focus (M). Rotate the sub-command dial to change autofocus area selection modes. Both options were described in Chapter 1, and will be explained in more detail in Chapter 5.
- **Flash sync connector.** This connector hides beneath a PC connector/10-pin connector cover, along with the 10-pin remote terminal. You can see the two connectors uncovered in Figure 2.4. Connect a standard PC/X-contact cable or other accessory to this connector. If you are connecting a non-dedicated flash unit to your Nikon D810 (say, a studio strobe or some other non-automatic non-Nikon flash), it would plug in here.
- **10-pin remote terminal.** This connector is used for a variety of accessories, including cable release cords, remote releases of other types (including radio/IR receivers), GPS links (to the Nikon GP-1), and so forth.

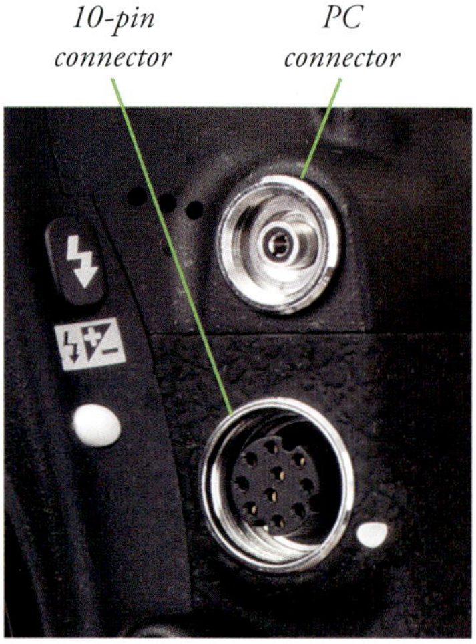

Figure 2.4

LOSE THE RUBBER COVER

I don't like the rubber cover over the flash sync and 10-pin remote connectors. I use studio flash and remote devices so often that the cover ends up dangling at the side of the camera 90 percent of the time. If you're in the same boat, help is on the way. The rubber cover fastens to the D810 around the neck strap lug, so you can carefully remove it (it's easier to do this when no neck strap is attached, obviously) and store the cover away for re-installation when you sell your D810. If you'd rather not leave your connectors "naked" (or just want to protect them when shooting in rain and other harsh conditions), the plastic PC connector and 10-pin terminal covers provided for earlier Nikon pro cameras screw into the connectors just fine. They can be purchased for a few dollars each from www.bocaphoto.com, which offers many other inexpensive Nikon replacement parts. I buy a bunch of them at a time, because the tiny connectors are easy to lose, but I find the inconvenience of screwing one of these connectors on and off from time to time (say, when I'm shooting in rain or snow), or replacing a lost one is much less of a hassle than dealing with that floppy rubber cover installed at the factory.

Controls for using the D810's built-in electronic flash (also called a strobe or Speedlight) are shown in Figure 2.5. These components include:

- **Pop-up flash.** The flash elevates from the top of the camera, theoretically reducing the chances of red-eye reflections, because the higher light source is less likely to reflect back from your subjects' eyes into the camera lens. In practice, the red-eye effect is still possible (and likely), and can be further minimized with the D810's red-eye reduction lamp (which flashes before the exposure, causing the subjects' pupils to contract), and the after-shot red-eye elimination offered in the Retouch menu. (Your image editor may also have anti-red-eye tools.) Of course, the best strategy is to use an external Speedlight that mounts on the accessory shoe on top of the camera (and thus is even higher) or a flash that is bounced (rather than aimed directly at the subject's eyes), or located off-camera entirely.
- **Flash pop-up button.** This button releases the built-in flash so it can flip up and start the charging process. If you decide you do not want to use the flash, you can turn it off by pressing the flash head back down.
- **Flash mode/Flash compensation button.** This button is held down while spinning the main command dial (to choose flash mode) or sub-command dial (to add or subtract exposure using flash compensation). I'll explain how to use the various flash modes (red-eye reduction, front/rear curtain sync, and slow sync) in Chapter 9, along with some tips for adjusting flash exposure.

Figure 2.5

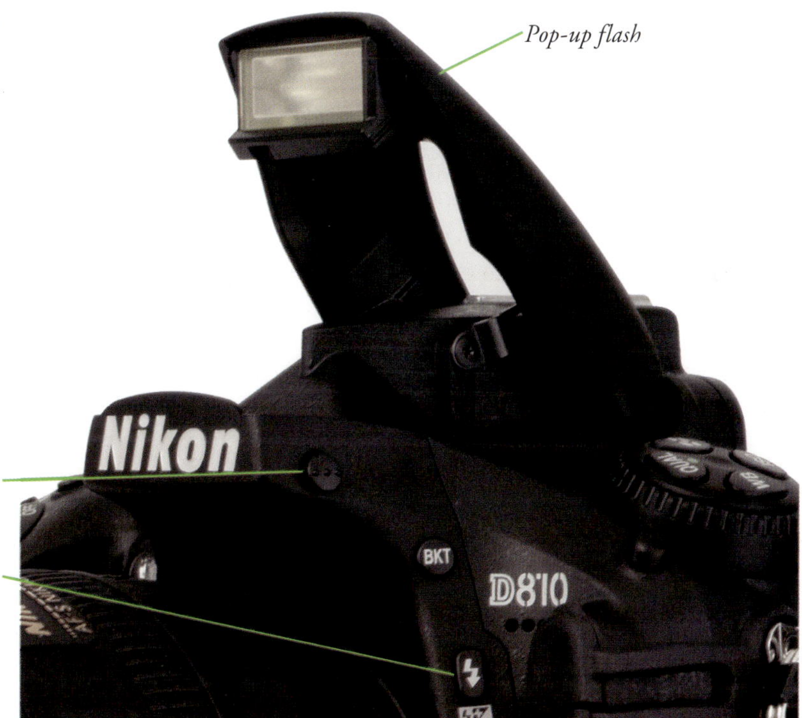

The main features on the side of the Nikon D810 are three rubber covers that protect the connector ports underneath from dust and moisture. The connectors, shown in Figure 2.6, with the rubber covers removed, are as follows:

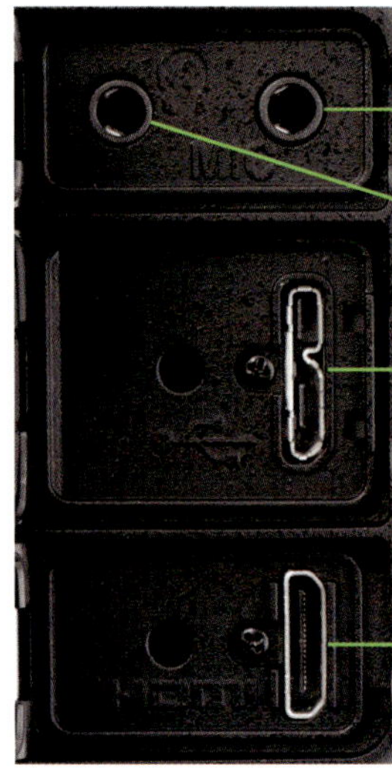

Figure 2.6

- **Headphone port.** Serious movie shooters will want to connect an earphone or headphone to this port so they can monitor exactly what sound is being recorded by the camera during video capture. I'll have more audio recommendations in Chapter 15.
- **Microphone port.** Although the D810 has a built-in microphone on the front, if you want better quality (and want to shield your video clip soundtracks from noises emanating from the camera and/or your handling of it), you can plug in an accessory mic here.
- **USB port.** Plug in the USB 3.0 cable furnished with your Nikon D810 and connect the other end to a USB port in your computer to transfer photos, to upload Picture Control settings, or to upload/download other settings between your camera and computer. If you attach a supplied USB port clip to your cable, the hole to the immediate left of the USB port accepts a pin on the clip to keep the cable securely plugged into the camera.
- **HDMI port.** You need to buy an accessory cable to connect your D810 to an HDTV, as one to fit this port is not provided with the camera. If you have a high-resolution television, it's worth the expenditure to be able to view your camera's output in all its glory. An HDMI cable clip is also provided in the box with your camera, and can be used to secure the HDMI cable to the port.

The Nikon D810's Business End

The back panel of the Nikon D810 (see Figure 2.7) bristles with more than a dozen different controls, buttons, and knobs. That might seem like a lot of controls to learn, but you'll find, as I noted earlier, that it's a lot easier to press a dedicated button and spin a dial than to jump to a menu every time you want to change a setting.

Figure 2.7

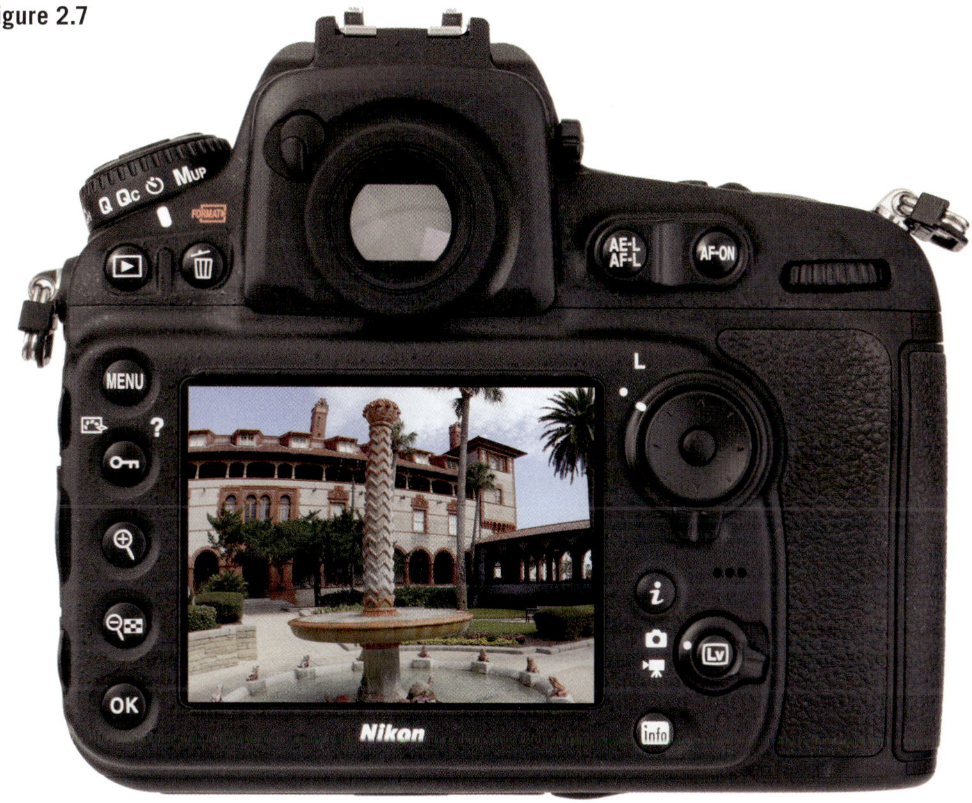

You can see the controls clustered along the top edge of the back panel in Figure 2.8. The key buttons and components and their functions are as follows:

- **Playback button.** Press this button to review images you've taken, using the controls and options I'll explain in the next section. To remove the displayed image, press the Playback button again, or simply tap the shutter release button.
- **Trash/Format #1.** Press to erase the image shown on the LCD monitor. A display will pop up on the LCD asking you to press the Trash button once more to delete the photo, or press the Playback button to cancel. Hold down this button and the metering mode button on the top-right surface of the camera (both are marked with red Format labels). "For" will appear in the monochrome control panel LCD. Choose which memory card you want to erase (rotate the main command dial). Press the buttons again to begin formatting your memory card.
- **Viewfinder eyepiece.** You can frame your composition by peering into the viewfinder. It's surrounded by a soft rubber frame that seals out extraneous light when pressing your eye tightly up to the viewfinder, and it also protects your eyeglass lenses (if worn) from scratching.

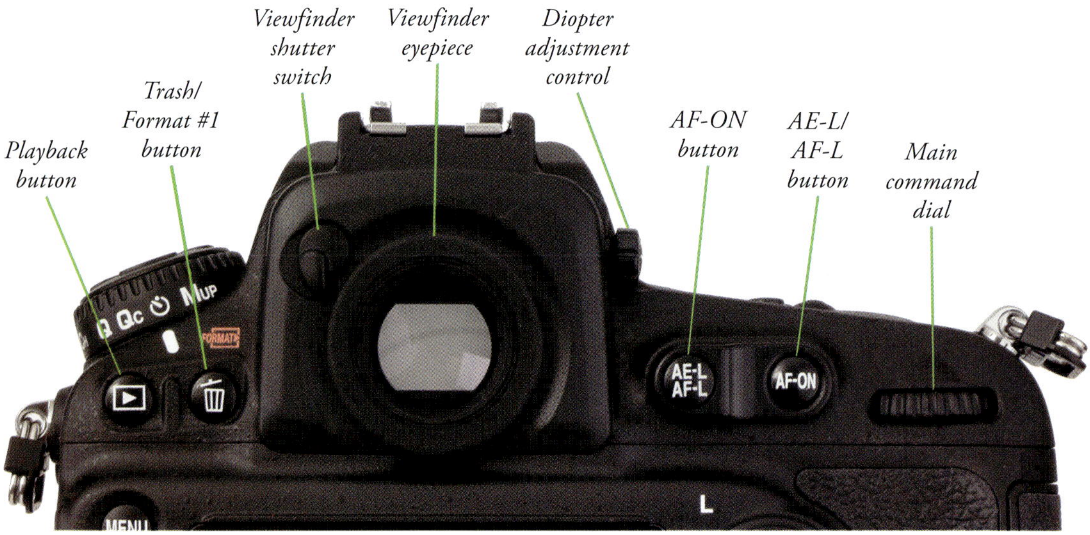

Figure 2.8

- **Viewfinder shutter switch.** You should ensure that light coming from the back of the camera doesn't venture inside and possibly affect the exposure reading when taking pictures while not looking through the viewfinder (say, the camera is mounted on a tripod). Flip this switch to block off illumination coming from the rear. Shielding the viewfinder with your hand may be more convenient (unless you're using the self-timer to get in the photo yourself).
- **Diopter adjustment control.** Pull it out, and then rotate this to adjust the diopter correction for your eyesight, as described in Chapter 1. Push it back in to lock your setting.
- **AE-L/AF-L (autoexposure/autofocus) lock.** This button can be programmed by you to provide a variety of autoexposure/autofocus locking functions, which I'll explain in Chapter 12. By default, it locks the exposure or focus that the camera sets when you partially depress the shutter button. The exposure lock indication (AE-L icon) appears in the viewfinder. If you want to recalculate exposure or autofocus with the shutter button still partially depressed, press the button again. The exposure/autofocus will be unlocked when you release the shutter button or take the picture. To retain the exposure/autofocus lock for subsequent photos, keep the button pressed while shooting.
- **AF-ON.** Press this button to activate the autofocus system without needing to partially depress the shutter release. This control, used with other buttons, allows you to lock exposure and focus separately: Lock exposure by pressing the shutter release halfway, or by pressing the AE lock (AE-L) button; autofocus by pressing the shutter release halfway, or by pressing the AF-ON button. There are lots of cool ways you can use the AF-ON button, and I'll explain them in detail in Chapter 12.

- **Main command dial.** This is the main control dial of the D810, used to set or adjust most functions, such as shutter speed, bracketing sequence, white balance, ISO, and so forth, either alone or when another button is depressed simultaneously. It is often used in conjunction with the sub-command dial on the front of the camera when pairs of settings can be made, such as image formats (main command dial: image format; sub-command dial: resolution); exposure (main: shutter speed; sub: aperture); flash (main: flash mode; sub: flash compensation); or white balance (main: WB preset; sub: fine-tune WB). You can swap functions of the main and sub-command dials, reverse the rotation direction, choose whether the aperture ring on the lens or the sub-command dial will be used to set the f/stop, and activate the main command dials to navigate menus and images. You'll learn about these Custom Settings menu options in Chapter 12.

You'll be using the five buttons to the left of the LCD monitor (shown in Figure 2.9) quite frequently, so learn their functions now.

- **MENU button.** Summons/exits the menu displayed on the rear LCD monitor of the D810. When you're working with submenus, this button also serves to exit a submenu and return to the main menu.
- **Help/Protect/Picture Controls button.** When viewing most menu items on the monitor, pressing this button produces a concise Help screen with tips on how to make the relevant setting. This triple-duty button also can be used to protect an image from accidental erasure when

Figure 2.9

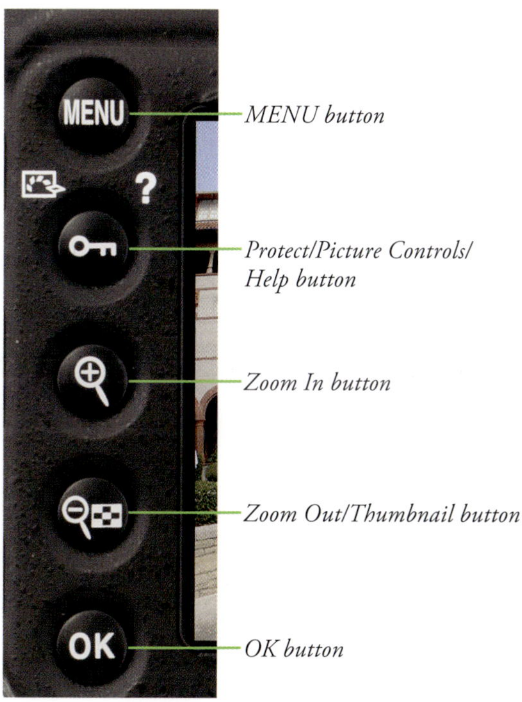

reviewing a picture on the LCD monitor. Press once to protect the image, a second time to unprotect it. A key symbol appears when the image is displayed to show that it is protected. (This feature safeguards an image from erasure when deleting or transferring pictures only; when you format a card, protected images are removed along with all the others.) The button also summons the setting screen for Picture Controls (explained in Chapter 11).

- **Zoom Out/Thumbnail button.** Use this button to change from full-screen view to four, nine, or 72 thumbnails, or to zoom out. I'll explain zooming and other playback options in the next section. The button also accesses ISO sensitivity settings.
- **Zoom In button.** Press to zoom in on an image.
- **OK button.** Press to confirm your choices.

More buttons reside on the right side of the back panel, as shown in Figure 2.10. The key controls and their functions are as follows:

- **Live view selector switch.** Rotate this switch clockwise to select either Live View (for still images) or Live View (for movie shooting).
- **Lv button.** Press the Live View button to activate live view, again to stop live view.
- **Multi selector.** This joypad-like button can be shifted up, down, side to side, and diagonally for a total of eight directions, or pressed. It can be used for several functions, including AF point selection, scrolling around a magnified image, trimming a photo, or setting white balance

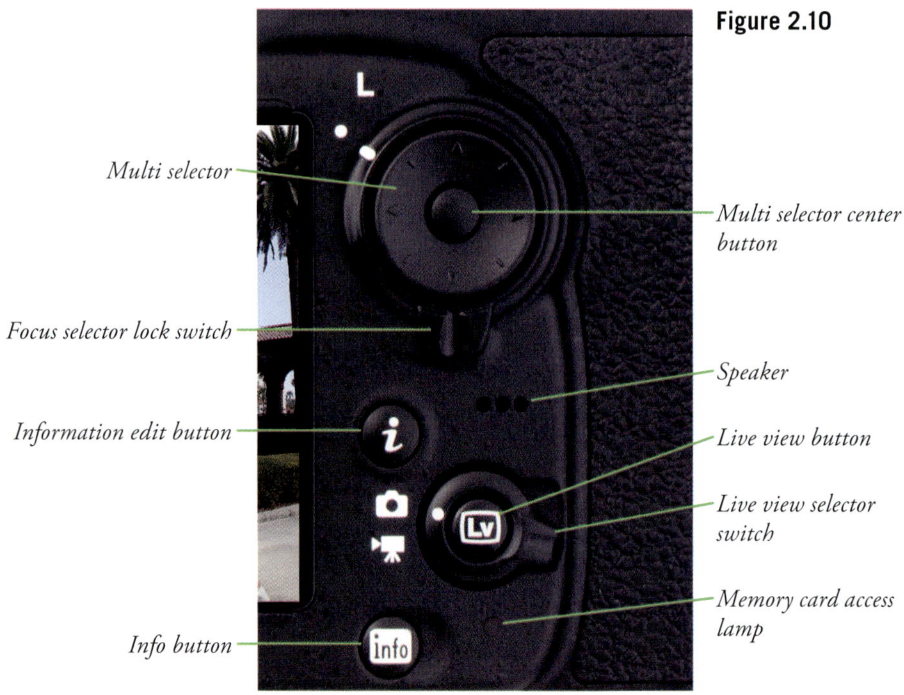

Figure 2.10

correction. Within menus, pressing the up/down arrows moves the on-screen cursor up or down; pressing toward the right selects the highlighted item and displays its options; pressing left cancels and returns to the previous menu.

- **Multi selector center button.** The button in the center of the multi selector can be pressed to choose a highlighted selection in a menu and to confirm choices.
- **Focus selector lock switch.** Rotate this switch to the L position to disable changing the focus point with the multi selector.
- **Speaker.** Sound emitted by your D810 emerges here.
- **Memory card access lamp.** When lit or blinking, this lamp indicates that a memory card is being accessed.
- **Info button.** Press this button to activate the shooting information display. Press again to turn the display off. That is the primary function of this button, which is easily confused with the *other* "information" button (the *i* button) described next.
- **Information edit (*i*) button.** Press this button once to produce the information edit screen shown in Figure 2.11. You can change any of the parameters in the bottom two rows of the display: just use the multi selector to highlight the option and press the OK button to produce a screen with options for the highlighted selection.

  That's simple enough, but Nikon couldn't leave well enough alone. When the information edit screen is displayed, pressing the *i* button additional times toggles back and forth between the edit screen and the shooting information display. That overlap of functions with the Info button can be confusing; it would have been smarter to dedicate the *i* button to do nothing but provide access to the information edit screen, and allow the Info button to produce the shooting information screen as needed. In this book I will use the term *i* button or, information edit (*i*) button (to remind you of its function), and the Info button to refer to the shooting information display on/off button.

Figure 2.11

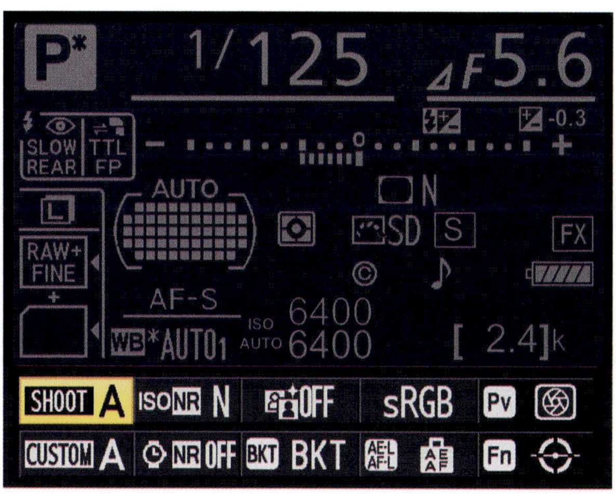

Playing Back Images

Reviewing images is a joy on the Nikon D810's big 3.2-inch monitor. The display is big and bright, and there is abundant detail on that 1,228,800-dot, VGA-resolution screen.

Here are the basics involved in reviewing images on the monitor screen (or on a television/HDTV screen you have connected with a cable). You'll find more details about some of these functions later in this chapter, or, for more complex capabilities, in the chapters that I point you to. This section just lists the must-know information.

- **Start review.** To begin review, press the Playback button at the upper-left corner of the back of the D810. The most recently viewed image will appear on the LCD monitor.
- **Playback card.** If you have two memory cards installed in your D810, you can change which card is used for playback by pressing the Zoom Out/Thumbnail button until the 72 thumbnails view (described later) is shown. Press the button one more time, and the Playback Slot and Folder screen will appear. If images are on both cards, you can highlight either SD Card Slot or CF Card Slot. Press the right button to see a list of available playback folders. Choose the folder/card you want to use. You can also select the folder using the Playback Folder option (choose a named folder, All, or Current folder) in the Playback menu. See Chapter 11 for more information.
- **View thumbnail images.** To change the view from a single image to four, nine, or 72 thumbnails, follow the instructions in the "Viewing Thumbnails" section that follows.
- **Zoom in and out.** To zoom in or out, press the Zoom Out/Thumbnail key, following the instructions in the "Zooming the Nikon D810 Playback Display" in the next section. (It also shows you how to move the zoomed area around using the multi selector keypad.)
- **Move back and forth.** To advance to the next image, press the right edge of the multi selector pad; to go back to a previous shot, press the left edge. When you reach the beginning/end of the photos in your folder, the display "wraps around" to the end/beginning of the available shots. **Note:** You can assign a special behavior to the sub-command dial such that rotating it skips ahead either 10 or 50 images, or allows you to change folders. See the discussion of Custom Setting f9 in Chapter 12 for more information.
- **See different types of data.** To change the type of information about the displayed image that is shown, press the up and down portions of the multi selector pad. To learn what data is available, read the "Using Shooting Data" section later in this chapter.
- **Remove images.** To delete an image that's currently on the screen, press the Trash button once, then press it again to confirm the deletion. To select and delete a group of images, use the Delete option in the Playback menu to specify particular photos to remove, as described in more detail in Chapter 11.
- **Cancel playback.** To cancel image review, press the Playback button again, or simply tap the shutter release button.

Zooming the Nikon D810 Playback Display

The Nikon D810 zooms in and out of preview images using the procedure that follows:

1. When an image is displayed (use the Playback button to start), press the Zoom In button to fill the screen with a slightly magnified version of the image.
2. A navigation window appears in the lower-right corner of the monitor showing the entire image. Keep pressing to continue zooming in to the maximum of 46X enlargement (with a full resolution large image). Medium images can be zoomed in by a factor of 34X; small images by 22X.
3. A yellow box in the navigation window shows the zoomed area within the full image. The entire navigation window vanishes from the screen after a few seconds, leaving you with a full-screen view of the zoomed portion of the image. (See Figure 2.12.)
4. To detect faces, rotate the sub-command dial while an image is zoomed. Up to 35 faces will be detected by the D810, indicated by white borders in the navigation window. Rotate the sub-command dial to move highlighting to the individual faces.
5. Use the main command dial to move to the same zoomed area of the next/previous image.
6. Use the Zoom Out/Thumbnail button to zoom back out of the image.
7. Use the multi selector buttons to move the zoomed area around within the image. The navigation window will reappear for reference when zooming or scrolling around within the display.
8. To exit zoom in/zoom out display, keep pressing the Zoom Out button until the full screen/full image/information display appears again.

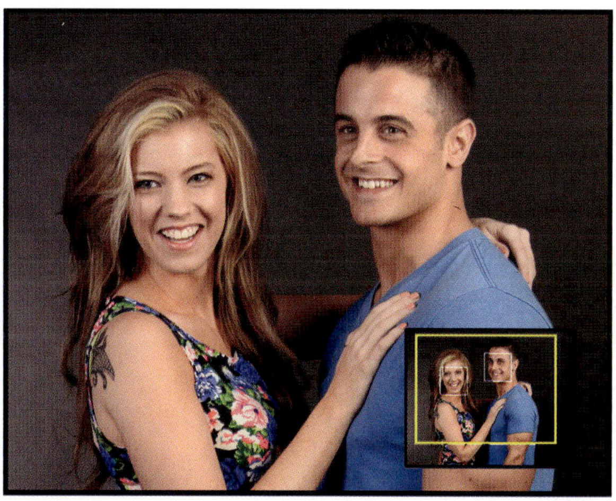

Figure 2.12
The Nikon D810 incorporates a small thumbnail image with a yellow box showing the current zoom area.

Viewing Thumbnails

The Nikon D810 provides other options for reviewing images in addition to zooming in and out a single monitor, switching among single image view and either four, nine, or 72 reduced-size thumbnail images on screen. (Note: The D810 lacks the "calendar view" found in Nikon mid- and entry-level models, which shows images grouped by the date they were shot.)

Pages of thumbnail images offer a quick way to scroll through a large number of pictures quickly to find the one you want to examine in more detail. As I said, the D810 lets you switch quickly from single- to four- to nine- to 72-image views, with a scroll bar displayed at the right side of the screen to show you the relative position of the displayed thumbnails within the full collection of images in the active folder on your memory card. Figure 2.13 offers a comparison between the three levels of thumbnail views. The Zoom In and Zoom Out/Thumbnail buttons are used.

- **Add thumbnails.** To increase the number of thumbnails on the screen, press the Zoom Out button. The D810 will switch from single image to four thumbnails to nine thumbnails to 72 thumbnails. (The display doesn't cycle back to single image again.)
- **Reduce number of thumbnails.** To decrease the number of thumbnails on the screen, press the Zoom In button to change from 72 to nine thumbnails to four thumbnails, or from four to single-image display. Continuing to press the Zoom In button once you've returned to single-image display starts the zoom process described in the previous section.

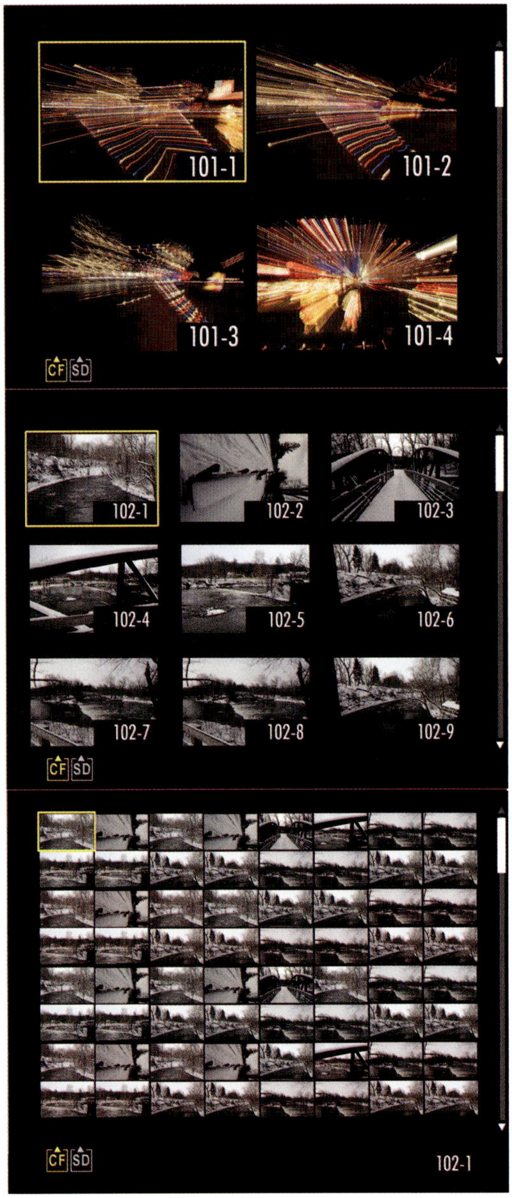

Figure 2.13 Switch between four thumbnails (top), nine thumbnails (center), or 72 thumbnails (bottom), by pressing the Zoom Out and Zoom In buttons.

- **Change slot and folder.** When viewing 72 thumbnails, if two memory cards are installed in the D810, then pressing the Zoom Out button one additional time produces a screen that allows you to choose the memory card slot and folder that contains the images you want to view. Press the Playback button to back out of this option and return to the 72-thumbnail view.
- **Switch between thumbnails and full image.** When viewing thumbnails, you can quickly switch between thumbnail view and full image display by pressing the button in the center of the multi selector.
- **Switching to Retouch menu.** When viewing thumbnails or a full screen image, press the OK button located to the left of the monitor until the Retouch menu, described in Chapter 13, appears. If you want to return to thumbnail views instead, press the Zoom In button.
- **Change highlighted thumbnail area.** Use the multi selector to move the yellow highlight box around among the thumbnails.
- **Protect and delete images.** When viewing thumbnails or a single page image, press the Protect button to preserve the image against accidental deletion (a key icon is overlaid over the full-page image and thumbnails; press Protect again to remove protection).
- **Exit image review.** Tap the shutter release button or press the Playback button to exit image review. You don't have to worry about missing a shot because you were reviewing images; a half-press of shutter release automatically brings back the D810's exposure meters, the autofocus system, and cancels image review.

Working with the Shooting Information/ Photo Data Displays

Your Nikon D810 can display two types of information on the color monitor as you are reviewing or taking pictures:

- **Shooting information display.** This is the screen of information that appears when you press the Info button on the back of the camera (located just to the right of the bottom edge of the color monitor). The shooting information display partially duplicates some of the data shown on the top control panel LCD, but has an additional feature as noted earlier: you can change any of the parameters listed in the bottom two rows of the display, by pressing the *i* button. I'll describe exactly how to do this next.
- **Photo Data.** These are a series of up to eight screens (including GPS data, which appears only if you used a GPS device to take the picture) that provide various types of shooting and other information *about a particular image* that you are reviewing. The data shown applies only to that image, and does not reflect your D810's current shooting settings (unless you're viewing an image you've just taken). I'll show you each of these screens, too, and explain how you can use them.

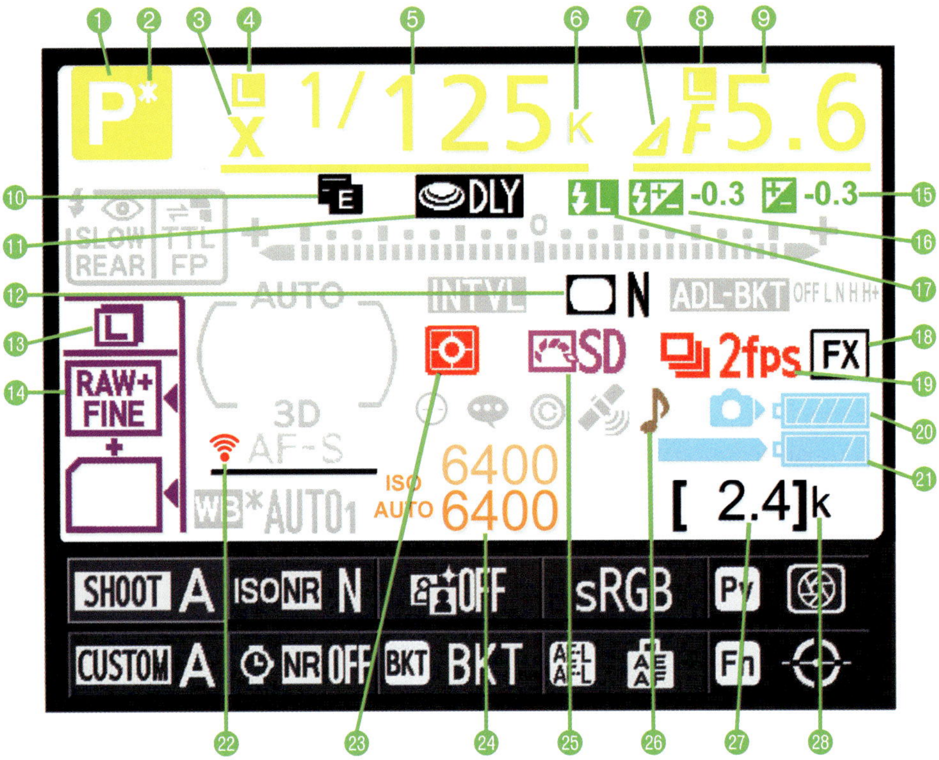

❶ *Exposure mode*

❷ *Flexible program indicator*

❸ *Flash sync indicator*

❹ *Flash lock*

❺ *Shutter speed/White balance fine-tuning/Color temperature/ Number of shots in bracketing/ Number of shots in multiple exposure/Focal length of non-CPU lens*

❻ *Color temperature*

❼ *Aperture stop indicator*

❽ *Aperture lock*

❾ *Aperture/Bracketing increment/ Number of shots in ADL bracketing/Maximum aperture of non-CPU lens*

❿ *Electronic first-curtain shutter*

⓫ *Delay mode*

⓬ *Vignette control*

⓭ *Image size*

⓮ *Image quality*

⓯ *Exposure compensation*

⓰ *Flash exposure compensation*

⓱ *Flash value lock*

⓲ *Image area*

⓳ *Release mode/Continuous shooting*

⓴ *Camera battery status*

㉑ *MB-D12 battery type*

㉒ *Eye-Fi connection*

㉓ *Metering mode*

㉔ *ISO sensitivity/Auto ISO indicator*

㉕ *Picture Control*

㉖ *Beep*

㉗ *Exposures remaining/Manual lens number/Time-lapse recording*

㉘ *Thousands of exposures*

Figure 2.14 The shooting information display has this kind of information, color-coded here for simplicity.

Using the Shooting Information Display

The shooting information display is toggled on or off when you press the Info button to the lower right of the color monitor. This display shows for about 10 seconds by default, but you can change this to a period of up to 10 minutes using Custom Setting c4, as described in Chapter 12. Hide this display by pressing the Info button a second time, or by tapping the shutter release button. (The D810 will always clear the monitor screen when you depress the shutter release button, and activate the exposure meter at the same time, so you'll be ready to take a shot if you want.)

The shooting information display provides a lot of basic shooting data. Figures 2.14 and 2.15 show a color-coded version. It does *not* appear colored like this on your LCD monitor, and, for clarity, I'm showing some options that don't appear on the screen at the same time; for example, your display will have only some of the flash information that I've coded in pink in my illustration.

I've applied some labels highlighting the basic kinds of settings you'll find on this screen. I've simplified the labels here; you'll find similar callouts of the individual icons later in this chapter in the section on the top-panel monochrome display, which largely duplicates the information you see

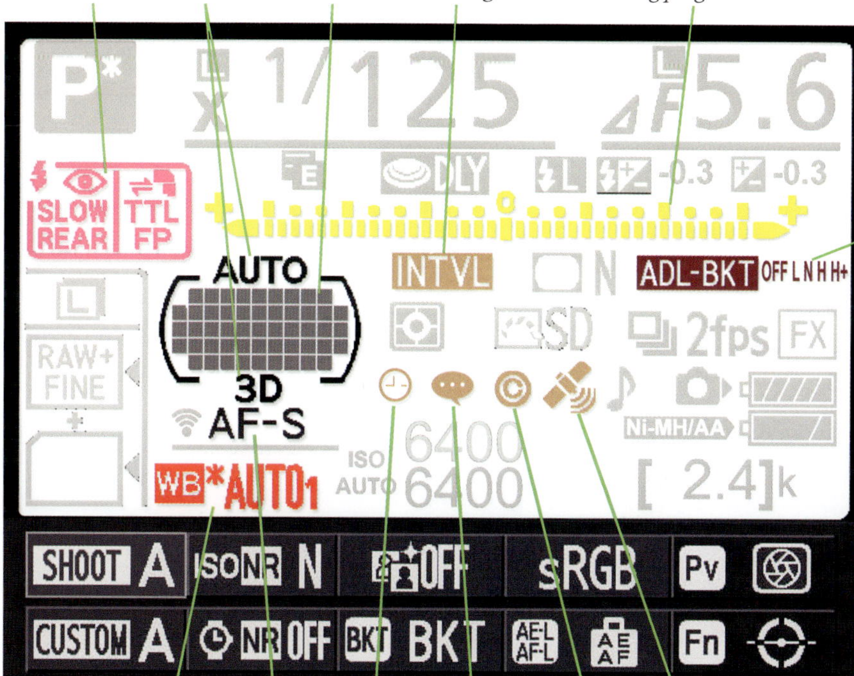

Figure 2.15
Shooting information display continued.

here. As I noted, this rendition just provides an overview of the kind of data you'll find on the color monitor; not every readout will appear on your screen, and certainly not all at once.

To change the parameters in the bottom two rows (shown in Figure 2.16), press the *i* button. Use the multi selector buttons to move the yellow highlighting to the parameter you want to adjust and press the OK button *or* the multi selector center button to produce a menu with your options. If you decide you don't want to make a change, press the OK button or multi selector center button again to back out of the options menu.

If you've set Custom Setting d9 (Screen Tips) to On (the default), a handy tool tip appears near a highlighted entry, so you can easily tell what each of the parameters does. Once you've learned the functions, you can turn the tool tips off in the Custom Settings menu. The specs you can change include the following. (I'll describe the options for each of them in Chapters 11, 12, and 13.)

- **Shooting menu bank.** Choose from Banks A, B, C, or D.
- **Custom Settings bank.** Choose from Banks A, B, C, or D.
- **ISO Noise Reduction/Long Exposure Noise Reduction.** You can turn each of these two types of noise reduction off, or to high, normal, or low settings.
- **Active D-Lighting.** Choose to extend the dynamic range of your image to one of four levels (Low, Normal, High, Extra High), plus Auto or Off. I'll explain the pitfalls/advantages of Active D-Lighting in Chapter 4.
- **Picture Control.** Choose a Picture Control style, or make adjustments to an existing style.
- **Color Space.** Switch between Adobe RGB and sRGB color spaces.
- **AE-L/AF-L button, Function button, Depth-of-field preview button, Bracket button assignment.** Change the function of each of these four buttons, so that pressing them performs a function of your choice (such as locking the flash off, changing metering mode, or triggering a burst of bracketed shots). You'll find out how to use these (seemingly) infinite combinations of useful shortcuts in Chapter 12.

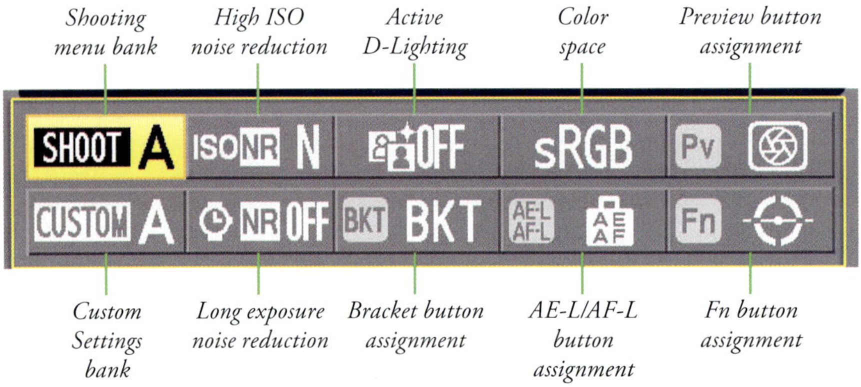

Figure 2.16
The information edit display allows changing many settings quickly.

Using the Photo Data Displays

When reviewing an image on the screen, your D810 can supplement the image itself with a variety of shooting data, ranging from basic information presented at the bottom of the LCD monitor, to three text overlays that detail virtually every shooting option you've selected. There is also a display for GPS data if you're using a GPS device, and two views of histograms. There's actually a third histogram view that can be summoned when you reprogram the center button of the multi selector. I'll explain how to do that and how to work with histograms in the discussion on achieving optimum exposure in Chapter 4. However, this is a good place to provide an overview of the kind of information you can view when playing back your photos.

You can change the *types* of information displayed using the Display Mode entry in the Playback menu. There you will find checkboxes you can mark for both basic photo information (overexposed highlights and the focus point used when the image was captured) and detailed photo information (which includes an RGB histogram and various data screens). I'll show you how to activate these info options in Chapter 11, and provide more detailed reasons why you might want to see this data when you review your pictures. This section will simply show you the type of information available. Most of the data is self-explanatory, so the labels in the accompanying figures should tell you most of what you need to know. To change to any of these views while an image is on the screen in Playback mode, press the multi selector up/down buttons.

- **Information display.** The basic full image review display looks like Figure 2.17. Press the multi selector down button to advance to the next information screen.
- **Highlights.** When highlights display is active (after being chosen in the Display Mode entry of the Playback menu, as described in Chapter 11), any overexposed areas will be indicated by a flashing black border. As I am unable to make the printed page flash, you'll have to check out this effect for yourself. You can visualize what these "blinkies" look like in Figure 2.18.
- **RGB histogram.** Another optional screen is the RGB histogram, which you can see in Figure 2.19. I'm going to leave the discussion of histograms for Chapter 4. Note that while using this view you can press the Zoom In and Zoom Out buttons to get a closer look at the large thumbnail of the image in the upper-left corner. A small navigation window with a yellow position box appears to the lower right of the large thumbnail to show you what portion of the image is being zoomed.
- **Shooting Data 1.** This is the first in a series of four screens that collectively provide everything else you might want to know about a picture you've taken. I'm not providing any labels in Figure 2.20, because the information in the first seven lines in the screen should be obvious.
- **Shooting Data 2.** This screen shows white balance data and adjustments, the color space you've selected, and lists any Picture Control tweaks you've entered. (See Figure 2.21.)
- **Shooting Data 3.** The next screen shows any noise reduction you've specified, Active D-Lighting status, and any Retouch menu changes you may have made. Although none of

them apply to the background image shown in Figure 2.22, I've added a few entries to show the kind of changes that can be made. You'll learn more about the Retouch menu in Chapter 13, which also will tell you how to create an image comment, like the one shown in the figure.

- **Shooting Data 4.** This screen appears *only* if you've entered artist and/or copyright information in the Copyright Information setting of the Setup menu, as described in Chapter 13. I'm not providing an illustration for this screen, because it shows nothing except the name of the photographer (artist) and the copyright.
- **GPS data.** This screen appears *only* if the image was taken using the GPS device, such as the Nikon GP-1a. It includes latitude, longitude, altitude, and time information, as shown in Figure 2.23.
- **Overview data.** This screen, shown in Figure 2.24, provides a smaller image of your photo, but more information, including a luminance (brightness) histogram, metering mode used, lens focal length, exposure compensation, flash compensation, and lots of other data that's self-explanatory.

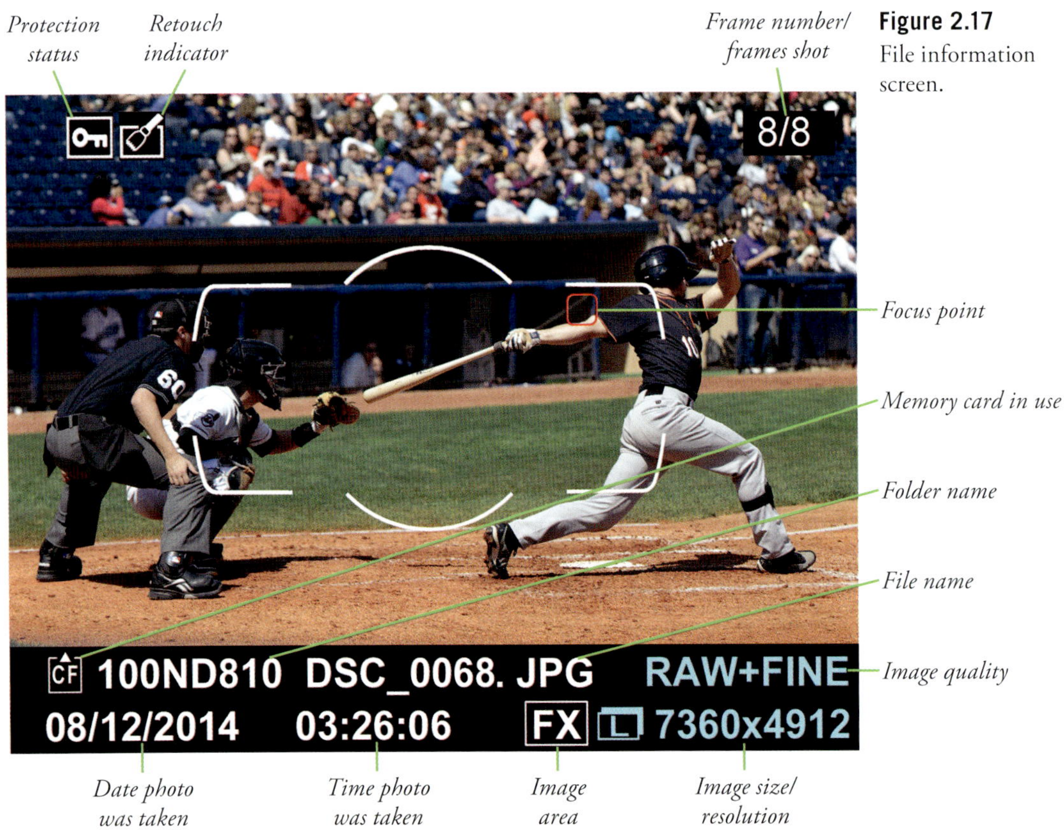

Figure 2.17
File information screen.

Figure 2.18
Highlights screen.

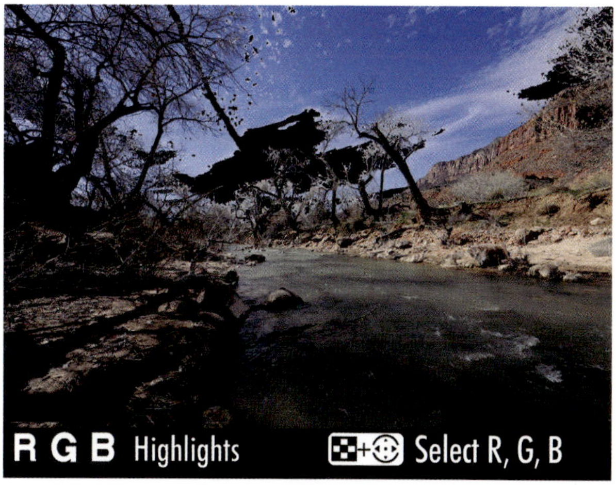

Figure 2.19
RGB histogram screen.

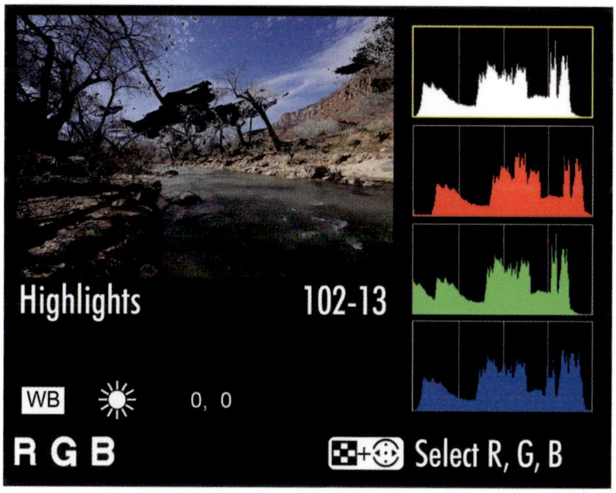

Figure 2.20
Shooting Data 1 screen.

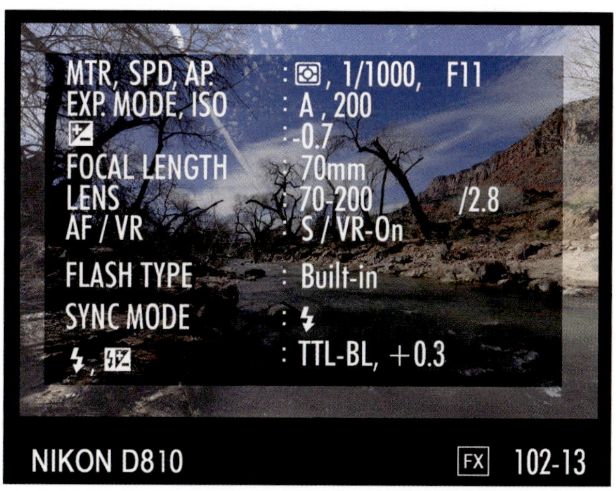

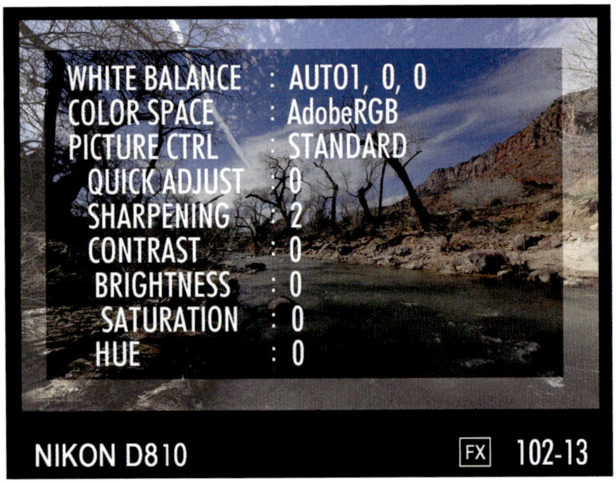

Figure 2.21
Shooting Data 2 screen.

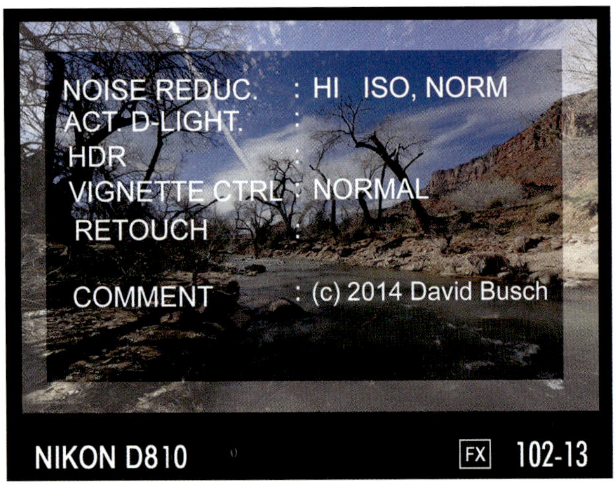

Figure 2.22
Shooting Data 3 screen.

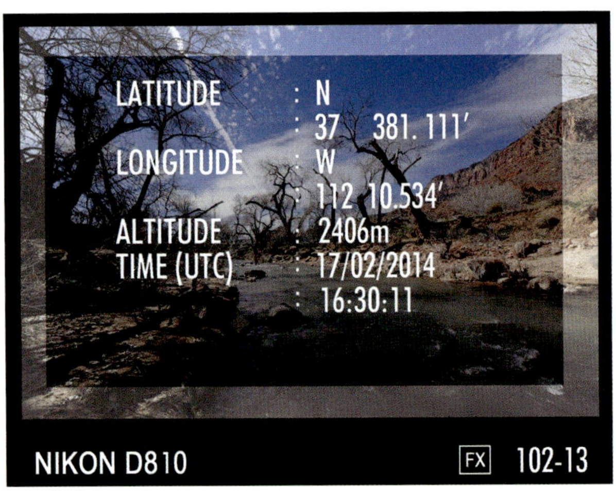

Figure 2.23
GPS data screen.

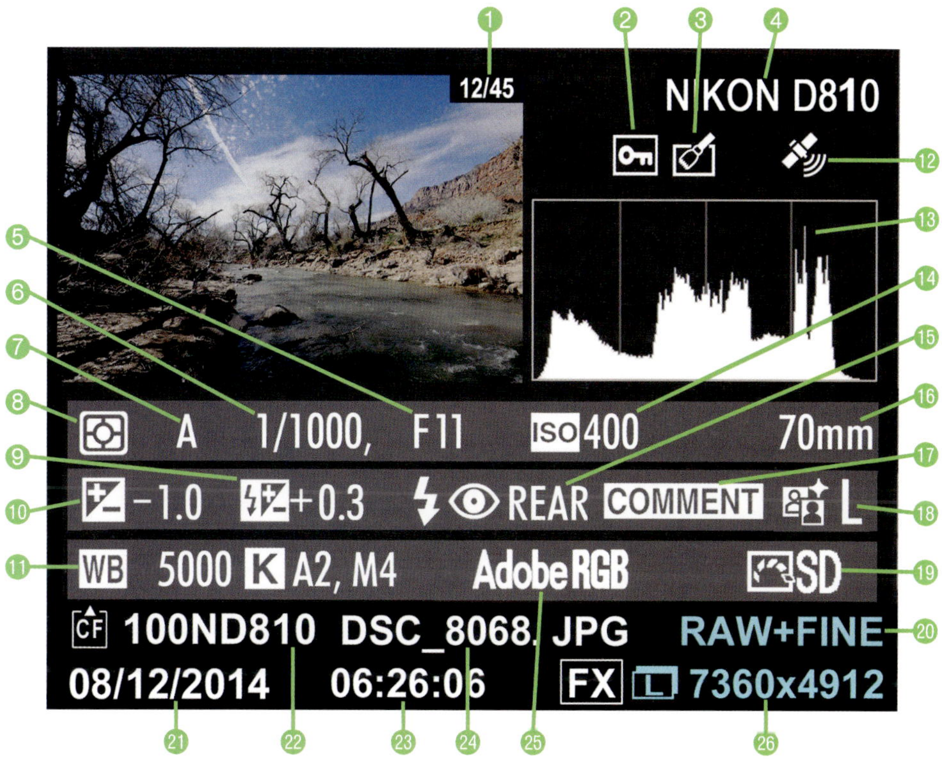

1 *Frame number/frames shot*
2 *Protection status*
3 *Retouch indicator*
4 *Camera name*
5 *Aperture*
6 *Shutter speed*
7 *Exposure mode*
8 *Metering method*
9 *Flash compensation*
10 *Exposure compensation*
11 *White balance settings and adjustments*
12 *GPS active*
13 *Luminance (brightness) histogram*
14 *ISO setting*
15 *Flash mode*
16 *Lens focal length*
17 *Image comment active*
18 *Active D-Lighting status*
19 *Picture Control*
20 *JPEG image quality*
21 *Date photo taken*
22 *Folder name*
23 *Time photo taken*
24 *File name*
25 *Color space*
26 *Size (resolution)*

Figure 2.24 Overview data screen.

Going Topside

The top surface of the Nikon D810 (see Figure 2.25) has its own set of frequently accessed controls. I'm going to divide them into two parts: those to the left side of the camera, and those on the right side. The left side controls offer some settings that you may change frequently, perhaps even during a shooting session (metering mode, white balance and ISO sensitivity), and one that you'll probably change once at the beginning: image quality (when you choose whether to shoot RAW, JPEG [and which compression level you want], or a combination of the two). Also on the left side of the camera is the release mode dial itself, which you'll use to flip among Single frame, Continuous shooting L, Continuous shooting H, Self-timer, Quiet shutter, Quiet Shutter continuous, and Mup modes. Figure 2.26 shows the left top side of the D810 up close.

- **Release mode dial lock release.** Before you can choose any of the release mode dial's settings, you must hold down this button to free the dial so it can rotate.
- **Direct Access buttons.** These are available for Image Quality/Size, White Balance, Metering Mode, and ISO. Hold each button and rotate the main or sub-command dials to make your adjustment. The Qual button also serves as the second reset button (used with the exposure compensation button on top of the camera, and described next).
- **Release mode dial.** Your choices include S (Single frame), C_L (Continuous low speed), C_H (Continuous high speed), Quiet shutter release, Quiet shutter continuous, Self-timer, and Mup (Mirror Up).

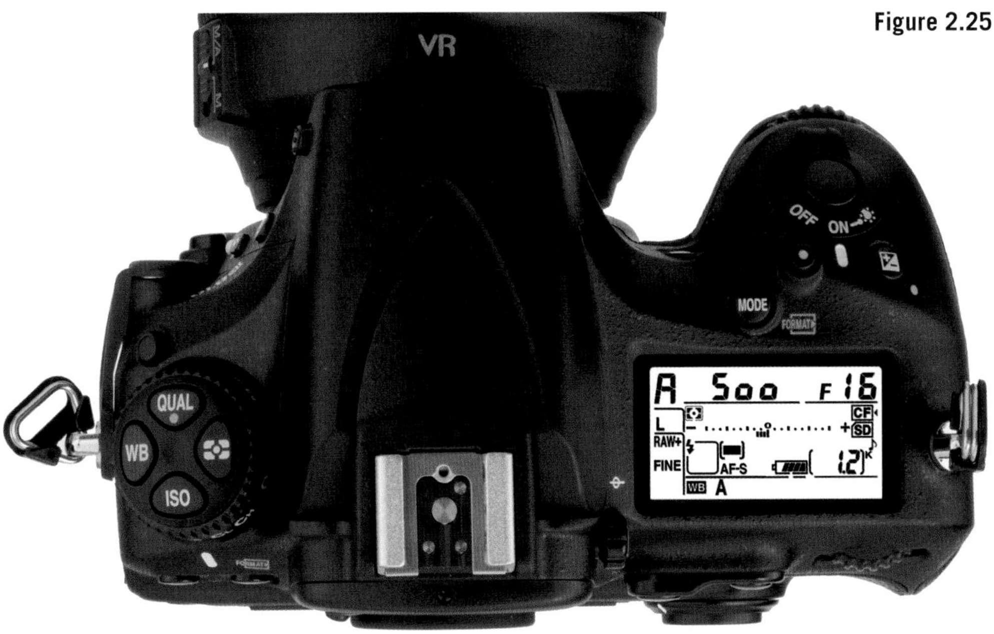

Figure 2.25

Figure 2.26

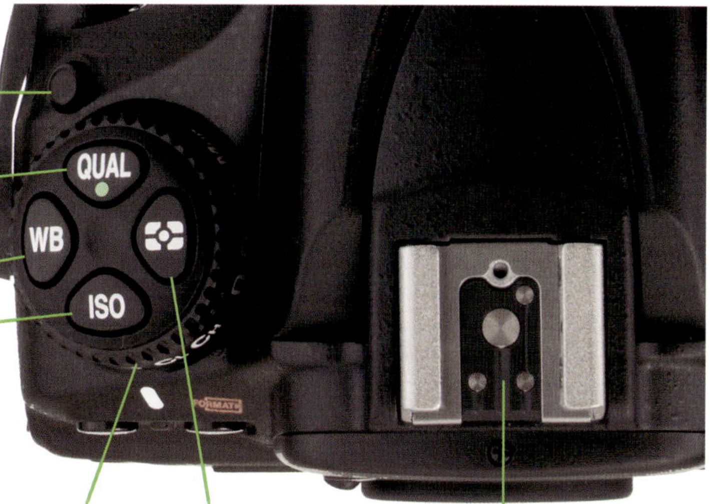

- **Accessory shoe.** Slide an electronic flash into this mount when you need a more powerful Speedlight. A dedicated flash unit, like the Nikon SB-910, can use the multiple contact points shown to communicate exposure, zoom setting, white balance information, and other data between the flash and the camera. There's more on using electronic flash in Chapter 9. You can also mount other accessories on this shoe, such as the Nikon GP-1 GPS adapter or Nikon ME-1 microphone.

On the right side of the camera is another batch of controls and a display panel, as shown in Figure 2.27:

- **Power switch.** Rotate this switch clockwise to turn on the Nikon D810 (and virtually all other Nikon dSLRs). Continue past the ON position to illuminate the monochrome control panel's backlight for a few seconds. If you'd rather have the backlight remain on for the length of time the exposure meters are active, you can specify this using Custom Setting d11 (LCD Illumination: set to On). For this setting to be useful, you'll need to set the automatic meter-off delay to something other than the default six seconds. If you're carefree about battery usage, you can specify meter-off delays of four seconds to 10 minutes using Custom Setting c2 (Standby Timer), as described in Chapter 12.
- **Shutter release button.** Partially depress this button to activate the exposure meter (and the main and sub-command dials that adjust metering settings), lock in exposure, and focus (unless you've redefined the focus activation button, as outlined in Chapter 12). Press all the way to take the picture. Tapping the shutter release when the camera has turned off the autoexposure and autofocus mechanisms reactivates both. When a review image is displayed on the back-panel color monitor, tapping this button removes the image from the display and reactivates the autoexposure and autofocus mechanisms.

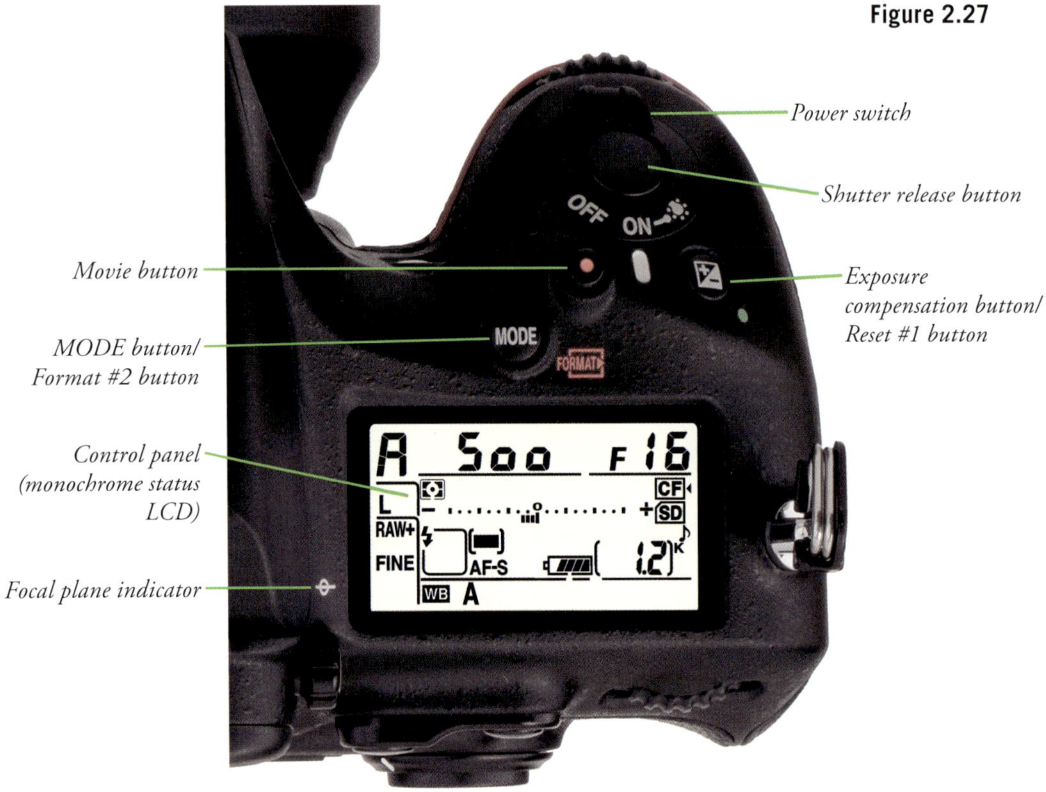

Figure 2.27

- **MODE button/Format #2.** Press this button and rotate the main command dial while watching the top control panel LCD to change to Aperture-priority, Shutter-priority, Program Auto, or Manual exposure modes. You can hold this button down at the same time as the Trash button on the back of the camera (which I call Format #1) to reformat a memory card.
- **Exposure compensation button/Reset #1.** Hold down this button and spin the main command dial to add or subtract exposure when using Program, Aperture-priority, or Shutter-priority modes. (In Manual mode, the exposure remains the same, but the "ideal" exposure shown in the electronic analog display [more on that in the next section] is modified to reflect the extra/reduced exposure you're calling for.) The exposure compensation amount is shown on the monochrome status panel as plus or minus values. This button is also used in conjunction with the QUAL button described earlier to provide a quick two-button reset of the camera to many of the factory default settings, as described in Chapter 3. (Any reassignment of the AE-L/AF-L button you made using Custom Setting f6 is unaffected.) Hold down the two buttons, each marked with a green dot, for about two seconds to effect the reset.

- **Focal plane indicator.** This indicator shows the *plane* of the sensor, for use in applications where exact measurement of the distance from the focal plane to the subject is necessary. (These are mostly scientific/close-up applications.)
- **Movie button.** Press to begin video capture; press a second time to stop.
- **Control panel.** This useful indicator shows the status of many settings. Unfortunately, because it's on top of the camera, you may not be able to *see* those settings when the camera is elevated (especially on a tripod). In that case, use the shooting information display, described earlier in this chapter, which can show much of the same information on the back-panel color LCD monitor when you press the Info button.

Control Panel Readouts

The top panel of the Nikon D810 (see Figure 2.28) contains a monochrome LCD readout (the "control panel") that displays status information about most of the shooting settings. All of the information segments available are shown in Figures 2.29 and 2.30. I've color-coded the display and divided the figure into two parts to avoid drowning you in labels for this intensely dense readout. The information does *not* appear in color on the actual D810, and all of these indicators will not appear at once. Many of the information items are mutually exclusive (that is, in the white balance area at bottom, only one of the possible settings illustrated will appear).

Figure 2.28

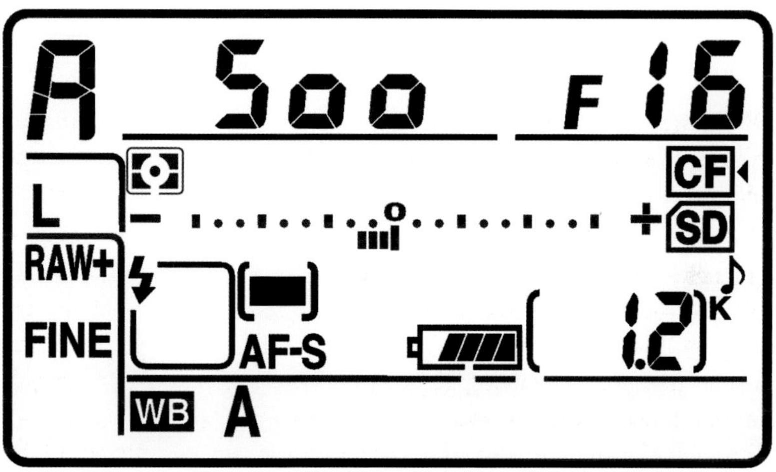

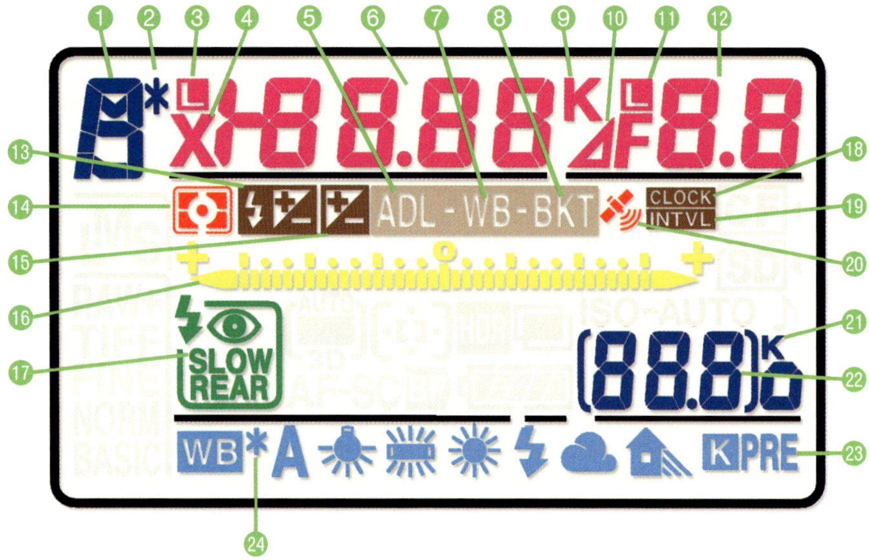

1 *Exposure mode*

2 *Flexible program indicator*

3 *Shutter speed lock indicator*

4 *Flash sync indicator*

5 *Active D-Lighting indicator*

6 *Shutter speed/Exposure compensation value/Flash compensation value/White balance fine-tuning/Color temperature/White balance preset number/Number of shots in bracketed sequence/Number of intervals with interval timer/ Focal length of non-CPU lens*

7 *WB bracketing indicator*

8 *Exposure and flash bracketing indicator*

9 *Color temperature indicator*

10 *Aperture stop indicator*

11 *Aperture lock indicator*

12 *F/stop/Number of stops/ Bracketing increment/Number of shots per interval/Maximum aperture of non-CPU lens/PC mode indicator*

13 *Flash compensation indicator*

14 *Metering mode*

15 *Exposure compensation indicator*

16 *Analog scale*

17 *Flash mode*

18 *Interval timer*

19 *GPS indicator*

20 *Clock not set indicator*

21 *Thousands of exposures*

22 *Number of exposures remaining/ Number of shots remaining until buffer fills/Capture mode indicator/ISO sensitivity/Preset white balance recording indicator/Active D-Lighting amount/Manual lens number/ HDMI-CEC connection indicator*

23 *White balance setting*

24 *White balance fine-tuning indicator*

Figure 2.29

Figure 2.30

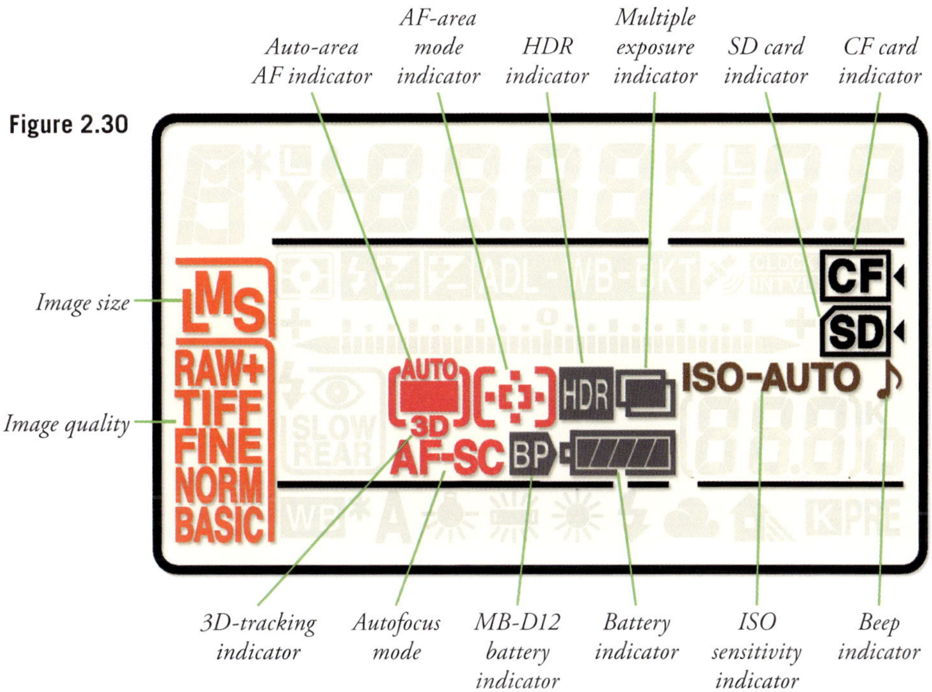

Lens Components

The lens shown at left in Figure 2.31 is a typical lens that might be mounted on a Nikon dSLR. Components found on this lens include:

- **Filter thread.** Most lenses have a thread on the front for attaching filters and other add-ons. Some also use this thread for attaching a lens hood (you screw on the filter first, and then attach the hood to the screw thread on the front of the filter). Some lenses, such as the AF-S Nikkor 14-24mm f/2.8G ED lens, have no front filter thread, either because their front elements are too curved to allow mounting a filter and/or because the front element is so large that huge filters would be prohibitively expensive. Some of these front-filter-hostile lenses allow using smaller filters that drop into a slot at the back of the lens.
- **Lens hood bayonet.** Lenses like the 17-35mm zoom shown in the figure use this bayonet to mount the lens hood. Such lenses generally will have a dot on the edge showing how to align the lens hood with the bayonet mount.
- **Focus ring.** This is the ring you turn when you manually focus the lens, or fine-tune autofocus adjustment.

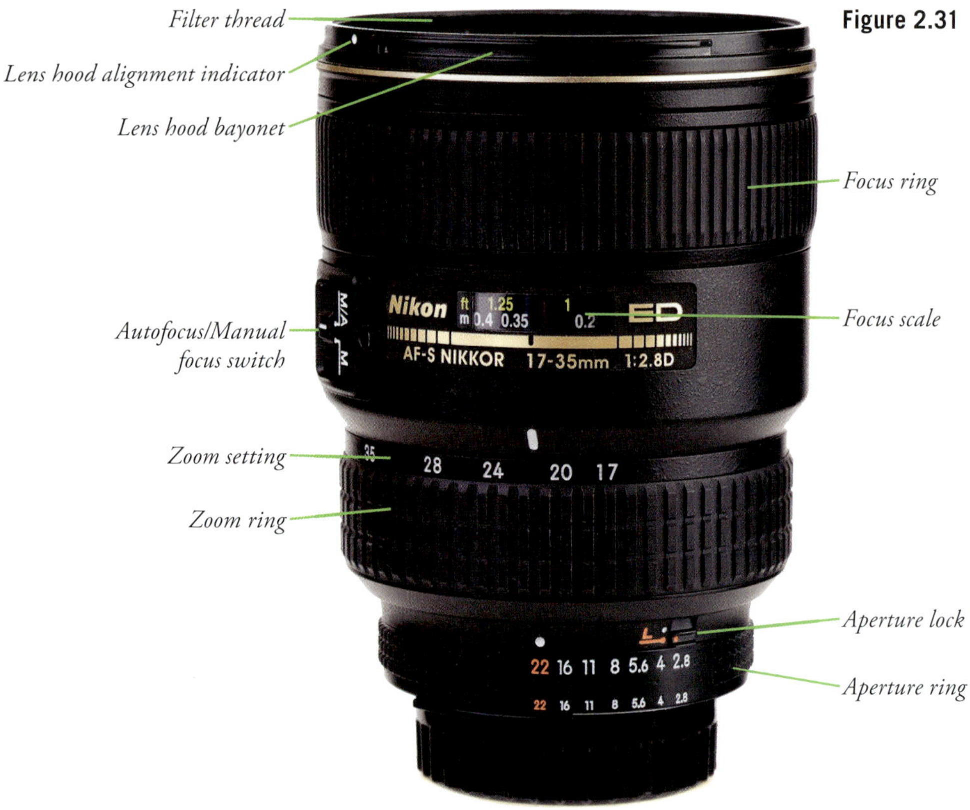

Figure 2.31

- **Focus scale.** This is a readout found on many lenses that rotates in unison with the lens's focus mechanism to show the distance at which the lens has been focused. It's a useful indicator for double-checking autofocus, roughly evaluating depth-of-field, and for setting manual focus guesstimates. Chapter 7 deals with the mysteries of lenses and their controls in more detail.
- **Zoom setting.** These markings on the lens show the current focal length selected.
- **Zoom ring.** Turn this ring to change the zoom setting.
- **Autofocus/Manual switch.** Allows you to change from automatic focus to manual focus.
- **Aperture ring.** Some lenses have a ring that allows you to set a specific f/stop manually, rather than use the camera's internal electronic aperture control. An aperture ring is useful when a lens is mounted on a non-automatic extension ring, bellows, or other accessory that doesn't couple electronically with the camera. Aperture rings also allow using a lens on an older camera that lacks electronic control. In recent years, Nikon has been replacing lenses that have aperture rings with versions that only allow setting the aperture with camera controls.
- **Aperture lock.** If you want your D810 (or other Nikon dSLR) to control the aperture electronically, you must set the lens to its smallest aperture (usually f/22 or f/32) and lock it with this control.

- **Focus limit switch.** Some lenses have this switch (shown in Figure 2.32), which limits the focus range of the lens, thus potentially reducing focus seeking when shooting distant subjects. The limiter stops the lens from trying to focus at closer distances (in this case, closer than 2.5 meters).
- **Vibration reduction switch.** Lenses with Nikon's Vibration Reduction (VR) feature include a switch for turning the stabilization feature on and off, and, in some cases, for changing from normal vibration reduction to a more aggressive "active" VR mode useful for, say, shooting from moving vehicles. More on VR and other lens topics in Chapter 7.

Figure 2.32
Some lenses have focus limit switches and controls for vibration reduction (VR) features.

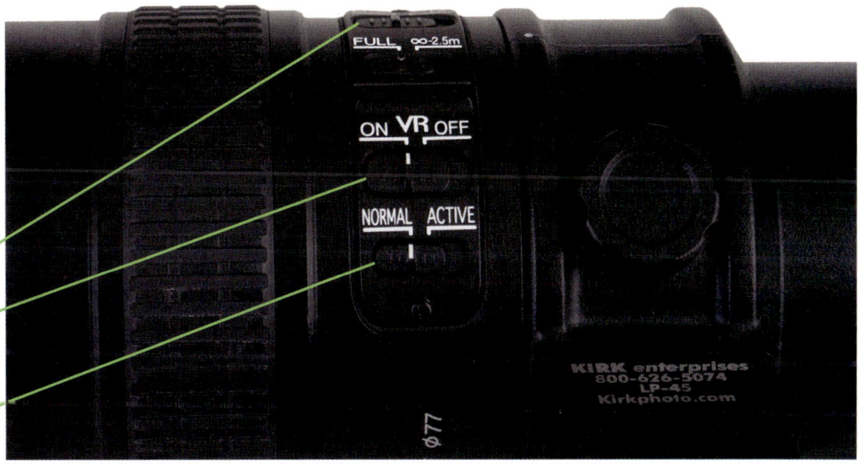

Focus limit switch

Vibration reduction On/Off switch

Normal/Active VR mode switch

The back end of a lens intended for use on a Nikon camera has other components that you seldom see (except when you swap lenses), shown in Figure 2.33, but still should know about:

- **Lens bayonet mount.** This is the mounting mechanism that attaches to a matching mount on the camera. Although the lens bayonet is usually metal, some lower-priced lenses use a rugged plastic for this key component.
- **Automatic diaphragm lever.** This lever is moved by a matching lever in the camera to adjust the f/stop from wide open (which makes for the brightest view) to the *taking aperture*, which is the f/stop that will be used to take the picture. The actual taking aperture is determined by the camera's metering system (or by you when the D810 is in Manual mode), and is communicated to the lens through the electronic contacts described next. (An exception is when the aperture ring on the lens itself is unlocked and used to specify the f/stop.) However, the spring-loaded physical levers are what actually push the aperture to the selected f/stop—even with advanced cameras like the D810 or D3. The aperture lever is also activated when you press the DOF (depth-of-field) button.
- **Electronic contacts.** These metal contacts pass information to matching contacts located in the camera body allowing a firm electrical connection so that exposure, distance, and other information can be exchanged between the camera and lens.

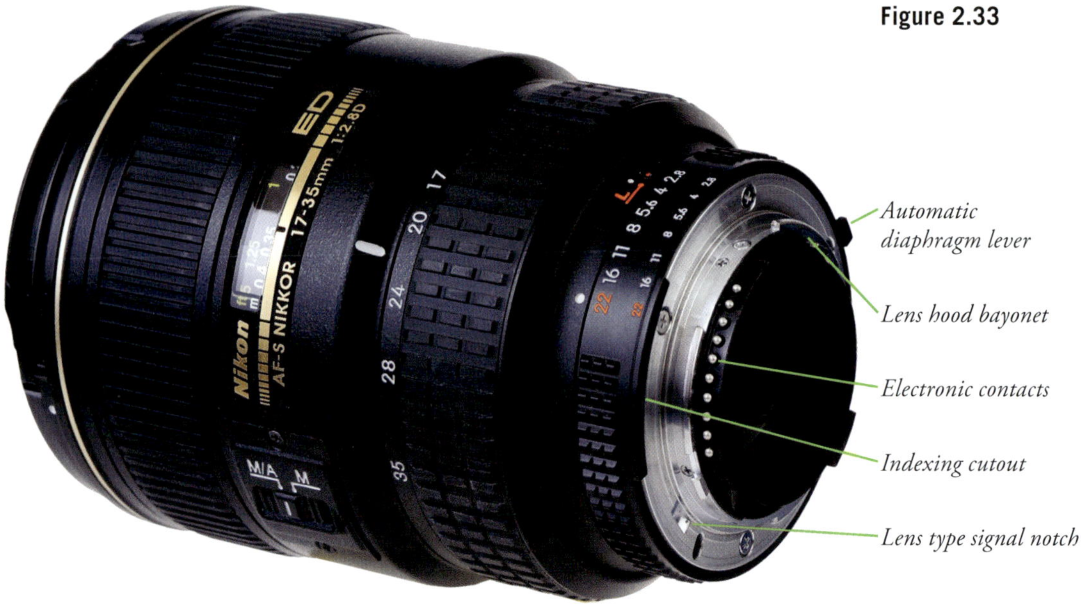

Figure 2.33

- **Lens type signal notch.** This is a machined groove in the lens mount, designed to tell older (non-dSLR) cameras that the aperture stops were linear. Today, this information would be conveyed electronically, except that all current lenses already have linear f/stops.
- **Indexing cutout.** The base of any Nikon lens made after 1977 that has an aperture ring includes a cutout notch that mates with a ring around the lens mount of Nikon's advanced cameras. It tells the camera what the maximum aperture is and what f/stop has been set. For a D810 owner, this means that older manual focus lenses (including pre-1977 lenses that have been converted to this system) can be used for automatic metering with the Aperture-priority exposure mode, and for manual metering in Manual exposure mode.
- **Autofocus drive screw slot.** (Not shown in the figure.) As you'll learn in Chapter 7, older autofocus lenses (given the AF designation in Nikon nomenclature) lack an internal autofocus motor. Focus is set using a screw drive built into the camera body of every Nikon autofocus camera (film or digital) except (at the time I write this) the entry-level models including the Nikon D40/D40x, D60, D3xxx-series, and D5xxx-series. Lenses given the AF-S designation lack this connection, because autofocus is achieved internally using a tiny motor.

Looking Inside the Viewfinder

Much of the important shooting status information is shown inside the viewfinder of the Nikon D810. As with the control panel LCD up on top, not all of this information will be shown at any one time. Figure 2.34 shows what you can expect to see.

These readouts include:

- **Focus points.** Can display the 51 areas used by the D810 to focus. The camera can select the appropriate focus zone for you, or you can manually select one or all of the zones.
- **Active focus point.** The currently selected focus point can be highlighted with red illumination, depending on focus mode.
- **AF area bracket.** Shows the area covered by the autofocus sensors.
- **Focus indicator.** This green dot stops blinking when the subject covered by the active autofocus zone is in sharp focus, whether focus was achieved by the AF system, or by you using manual focusing. Left and right arrows show whether focus is set ahead of or behind the subject.
- **Autoexposure (AE) lock/Flash value lock indicator.** Shows that exposure or flash exposure has been locked.
- **Flash sync.** Shows that the shutter speed has been locked in S or M modes at the x250 (1/250th second) setting (located, not between 1/125th and 1/500th second, but as the speed *past* bulb and 30 seconds).
- **Shutter speed.** Displays the current shutter speed selected by the camera, or by you in Manual exposure mode.
- **Aperture.** Shows the current aperture chosen by the D810's autoexposure system, or specified by you when using Manual exposure mode.
- **Automatic ISO indicator.** Is shown as a reminder that the D810 has been set to adjust ISO sensitivity automatically.
- **Flash compensation indicator.** Appears when flash EV changes have been made.
- **Exposure compensation indicator.** This is shown when exposure compensation (EV) changes have been made. It's easy to forget you've dialed in a little more or less exposure, and then shoot a whole series of pictures of a different scene that doesn't require such compensation. Beware!
- **Electronic analog exposure display.** This scale shows the current exposure level, with the bottom indicator centered when the exposure is correct as metered. The indicator may also move to the left or right to indicate over- or underexposure (respectively). The scale is also used to show the amount of exposure compensation dialed in and the exposure compensation and degree of horizontal tilt.
- **Exposures remaining/maximum burst available/other data.** Normally displays the number of exposures remaining on your memory card, but while shooting it changes to show a number that indicates the number of frames that can be taken in continuous shooting mode using the current settings. This indicator also shows other information, such as ISO sensitivity, exposure compensation value, and Active D-Lighting amount.

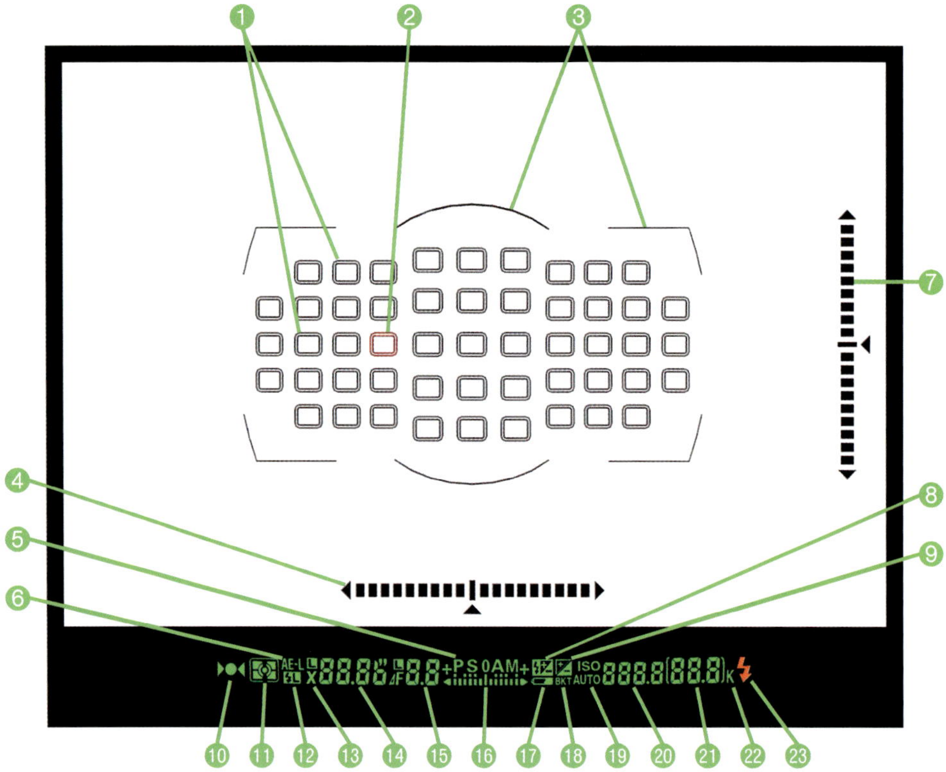

1 *Focus points*

2 *Active focus point*

3 *AF-area bracket*

4 *Side-to-side tilt indicator*

5 *Exposure mode*

6 *Autoexposure (AE) lock*

7 *Front/back tilt indicator*

8 *Flash compensation indicator*

9 *Exposure compensation indicator*

10 *Focus indicator*

11 *Metering mode*

12 *Flash exposure lock*

13 *Flash sync*

14 *Shutter speed/AF mode*

15 *Aperture*

16 *Electronic analog exposure display/Exposure compensation display*

17 *Battery status*

18 *Bracketing indicator*

19 *Automatic ISO indicator*

20 *ISO sensitivity*

21 *Exposures remaining/Shots remaining until buffer fills/ISO sensitivity/Preset white balance recording indicator/Exposure compensation value/Flash compensation value/Active D-Lighting amount/AF-area mode indicator*

22 *Thousands of exposures*

23 *Flash ready indicator*

Figure 2.34

- **Thousands of exposures.** Displayed when more than 999 exposures remaining; the readout to the left will then show number of shots remaining in thousands.
- **Flash ready indicator.** This icon appears when the flash is fully charged.
- **Battery status.** Shows amount of remaining power.
- **Bracketing indicator.** Shows when Active D-Lighting, exposure, flash, or white balance bracketing is underway.
- **ISO sensitivity.** This useful indicator shows the current ISO setting value. Those who have accidentally taken dozens of shots under bright sunlight at ISO 1600 because they forgot to change the setting back after some indoor shooting will treasure this addition.

Underneath Your Nikon D810

There's not a lot going on with the bottom panel of your Nikon D810. You'll find the battery compartment access door, and a tripod socket, which secures the camera to a tripod. The socket accepts other accessories, such as quick release plates that allow rapid attaching and detaching the D810 from a matching platform affixed to your tripod. The socket is also used to secure the optional MB-D12 battery grip, which provides more juice to run your camera to take more exposures with a single charge. Figure 2.35 shows the underside view of the camera.

Figure 2.35

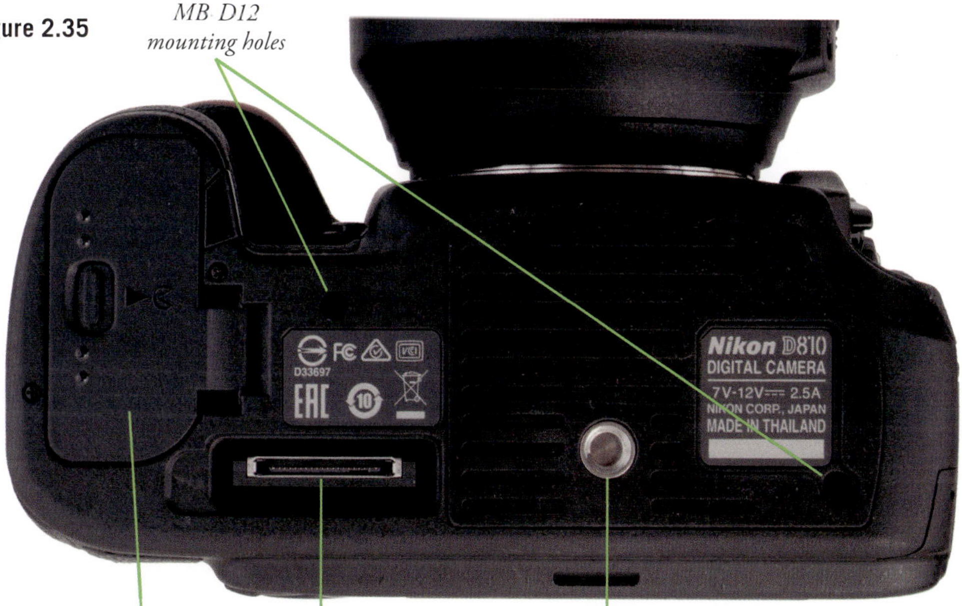

Using the MB-D12 Multi-Power Battery Pack/Vertical Grip

One optional accessory that you might want to consider is the Nikon MB-D12 battery pack/vertical grip, which attaches to the underside of the D810 and provides extra power for those long shooting sessions. It also adds a vertically oriented shutter release, main command dial, sub-command dial, an AE-L/AF-L button, and a miniature joystick-like version of the multi selector, all arranged for easier shooting when the camera is rotated to a vertical position. There's a terminal connector under a rubber cover to provide a connection between the D810 and accessories that fasten to the underside. This accessory (see Figure 2.36 for front and back views) is available for about $616.

FALSE ECONOMY

Yes, the MB-D12 costs $600 or more, and you can expect serviceable knock-offs to be available soon from several Asian sources for a lot less. I've checked out previous models carefully. They're made of lightweight plastic, don't look especially durable, and are probably not a serious option for anything other than light-duty use. If you plan on giving your battery/grip a real workout, I'd recommend springing for the real thing. I don't know what would happen to a D810 if one of these units shorted out, and don't plan to find out. Keep in mind that the MB-D12 may work with future cameras as well, now that Nikon has stopped giving its grips nomenclature linked to the camera model. But, even if it does not, you'll have a grip that can be resold to owners of compatible models, so the resale value is likely to be higher. A battery pack/grip is one place that I recommend not cutting corners.

To use the MB-D12, just follow these steps:

1. **Expose contacts.** Remove the rubber protective cover over the contacts on the bottom of the D810 body. (See Figure 2.35, earlier.) Don't worry about losing the cover: it fits in a matching well inside the MB-D12. Retrieve the cover from that safe location when you remove the grip. Next, remove the white plastic protective cover from the terminal contacts on the MB-D12.
2. **Line up the camera and grip.** There are two holes on the underside surface of the D810 that mate with matching pins on the MB-D12. Line up those components, the tripod socket and tripod screw, and the contacts, and slide the MB-D12 onto the underside of the camera.

TIP

Unlike some earlier battery grips, you don't need to remove the battery in the camera; the D810 can use both, in the order you specify (use Custom Setting d13, described in Chapter 12). I recommend using the battery in the MB-D12 grip first; as it poops out, you can replace it with a fresh EN-EL15 or set of AA batteries without the need to remove the grip. (You do own several back-up batteries, don't you?) Use the D810's internal battery only when you have no other replacements available.

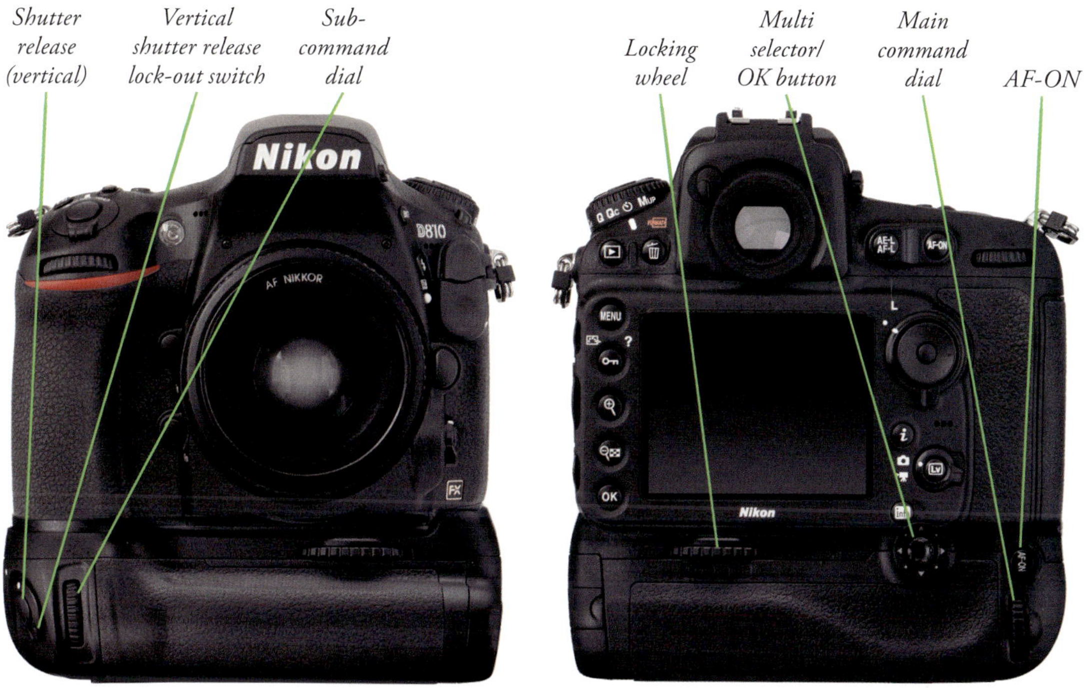

Figure 2.36 The Nikon MB-D12 Multi-Power Grip can double the length of your battery-powered shooting session, while adding convenient vertically oriented controls.

3. **Tighten the connection.** When the grip and D810 are fit snugly together, rotate the large wheel under the base of the MB-D12 to lock the device onto the D810.
4. **Add batteries.** The MB-D12 is furnished with two trays to hold batteries. You can add a second EN-EL15 battery to one tray to double your available power. Or you can use eight AA alkaline, nickel-metal hydride, nickel-manganese, or lithium batteries with the supplied holder. Slide the battery tray inside the base of the grip, and rotate the locking knob. Use Custom Setting d11 to tell the D810 which type of AA batteries you are using.
5. **Fire away.** To use the shutter release on the vertical grip, you must turn the rotating switch so the dot aligns with the line on the grip, indicating that the shutter release is unlocked. If you're holding the camera in horizontal orientation and using the regular shutter release, it's easy to accidentally trip the vertical release with the palm of your right hand. (This accounts for the "phantom" shutter releases that mystify new users of this grip.)
6. **Remove the grip.** To remove the grip, reverse these steps.

3

Recommended Settings

This chapter is purely optional, especially for those who are new to an advanced Nikon at the D810's level, who should skip it entirely for now, and return when they've gained some experience with this full-featured camera. This section is for the benefit of those who want to know *now* some of the most common changes I recommend to the default settings of your D810. Nikon has excellent reasons for using these settings as a default; I have better reasons for changing them.

Changing Default Settings

Even if this is your first experience with a Nikon digital SLR, you can easily make a few changes to the default settings that I'm going to recommend, and then take your time learning *why* I suggest these changes when they're explained in the more detailed chapters of this book. I'm not going to provide step-by-step instructions for changing settings here; I'll give you an overview of how to make any setting adjustment, and leave you to navigate through the fairly intuitive D810 menu system to make the changes yourself. Or, you can jump ahead to Chapters 11-13 for more detailed instructions on a particular setting.

Resetting the Nikon D810

If you want to change from the factory default values, you might think that it would be a good idea to make sure that the Nikon D810 is set to the factory defaults in the first place. After all, even a brand-new camera might have had its settings changed at the retailer, or during a demo. Unfortunately, Nikon doesn't make it easy to reset *all* settings in the camera to their factory defaults. In fact, there are no fewer than *four* different ways to "reset" the D810, each of which does slightly different things.

Those ways include:

- **Two-button reset.** This type of "rebooting" changes the most basic settings in your camera listed in Table 3.1, and is useful when you want to cancel the most common changes you make when adjusting your camera. It does not affect all Shooting menu settings, or any of the Custom Settings memory banks, described next. I'll show you how to perform the two-button reset shortly.
- **Shooting menu bank reset.** The Shooting menu has a separate Reset Shooting menu option that zeroes out the changes you've made to the default options. In the screen shown in Figure 3.1, you can switch from one shooting menu bank to another, replace the generic A, B, C, and D labels for the individual shooting menu banks with a name of your choice, or perform an individual reset for each menu bank separately.
- **Custom Settings menu bank reset.** The Custom Settings menu also has a screen (shown in Figure 3.2), that allows selecting the active Custom Settings bank, and which includes a separate Reset Custom Settings option that zeroes out most of the changes you've made to the default options. A two-button reset does not affect any of the settings in the Custom Settings menu banks. As with the shooting menu banks, you can rename them or reset the banks individually; changing or resetting one bank does not affect the settings in the others.
- **Cold reset.** The only way to reset *all* of the D810's internal settings is to remove the battery and allow the internal backup battery to run down until the settings are lost, which can take as long as several weeks. You can remove the battery and then turn on the camera briefly to reset *most* settings, but this won't zero out all settings to the factory defaults as long as some juice remains in the backup battery (which is tucked deep inside the camera and not user-accessible). You might want to try a cold reset if your camera is hopelessly locked up, and you'd like to make one last attempt at restoring it to factory operation before sending it in for service.

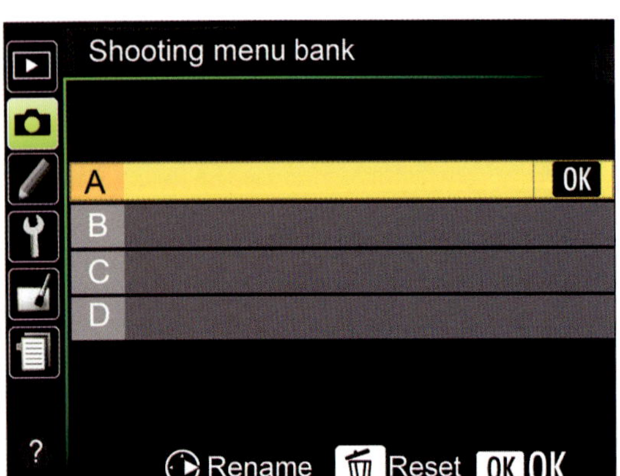

Figure 3.1 Switch shooting menu banks, rename a bank, or reset a bank from this screen.

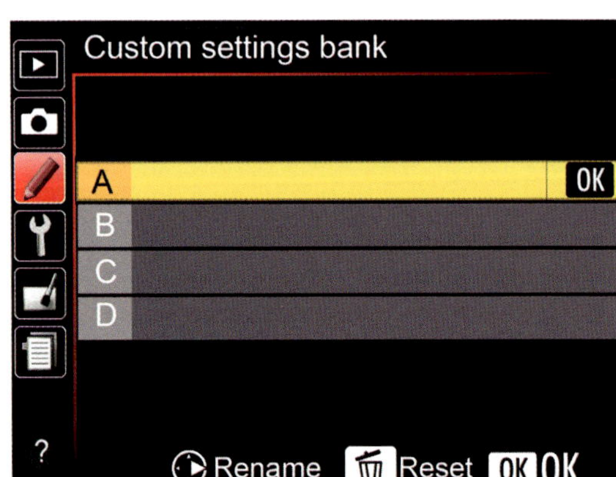

Figure 3.2 Switch from one Custom Settings bank, apply a new name, or reset a bank here.

Two-Button Reset

Just follow these steps to perform a two-button reset of the camera:

1. **Find reset buttons.** Locate the QUAL button on the back left side of the camera, and the EV button on the top panel of the D810, just southeast of the shutter release button. Each is marked with a green dot. Figure 3.3 shows the two buttons highlighted in yellow.
2. **Start reset.** Press and hold the two buttons for more than two seconds. The monochrome LCD control panel switches off momentarily while the settings are reset.
3. **Release the two buttons.** Your camera's settings have been returned to the factory default, as described below.

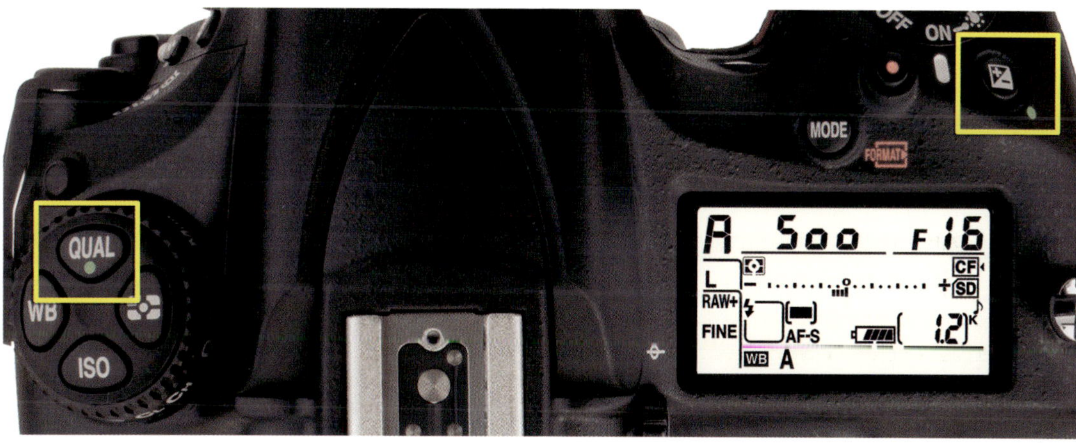

Figure 3.3 Perform a two-button reset by holding down the QUAL and EV buttons for more than two seconds.

Once a two-button reset has been performed, the following settings shown in Table 3.1 will be restored to their defaults (all these options are described in Chapters 11, 12, and 13).

Shooting Menu/Custom Settings Menu Reset

Resetting banks individually affects more settings than the two-button reset, as shown in Tables 11.1 (Shooting Menu Defaults) and 12.1 to 12.7 (Custom Settings Defaults) in Chapters 11 and 12. I won't duplicate them here. If you'd like to reset all the options in the Shooting menu and Custom Settings menu for each bank (that is, A, B, C, or D individually), follow these steps:

1. **Access menus.** Press the MENU button at the top of the array of five buttons located to the immediate left of the back-panel LCD.
2. **Choose Shooting menu or Custom Settings menu.** Press the multi selector down button to scroll down to either the Shooting menu (represented by a camera icon; the second icon from the top in the left-column of the menus) or the Custom Settings menu (represented by a pencil icon; the third icon from the top). Press the right multi selector button to reveal the Shooting or Custom Settings menus.

3. **Access banks.** Use the directional buttons to select Shooting Menu Bank or Custom Settings Bank down button to scroll to the Reset Shooting Menu or Reset Custom Settings choices, then press the right button to reveal the screens shown earlier in Figures 3.1 and 3.2.
4. **Choose bank to reset.** Scroll down to highlight the bank you'd like to reset, then press OK to activate that bank.
5. **Reset bank.** Press the Trash button, located just to the left of the viewfinder window, to reset that bank. A message will appear asking you to confirm. Highlight Yes and press OK to reset. You can repeat steps 2 to 4 to reset other banks, if desired.
6. **Exit.** Press MENU or tap the shutter release to exit.

Table 3.1 Two-Button Reset Defaults

Shooting Menu		Other Settings	
Option	**Default Value**	**Option**	**Default Value**
Image quality	JPEG Normal	Focus point	Center
JPEG/TIFF recording		Preset focus point	Center
Image Size	Large	Exposure mode	Programmed auto
NEF (RAW Recording		Flexible program	Off
Image Size	Large	Exposure compensation	Off
White balance	Auto>Normal	AE lock hold	Off
Fine-tuning	A-B:0 G-M:0	Aperture lock	Off
Picture Control	Unmodified	Autofocus mode	AF-S
HDR (High dynamic range)	Off	AF-area mode	
		Viewfinder	Single-point AF
ISO sensitivity settings		Live view/movie live view	Normal-area AF
ISO sensitivity	100	Photo live view display white balance	None
Auto ISO sensitivity control	Off	Highlight display	Off
Multiple exposure	Off	Headphone volume	15
Interval timer shooting	Off	Metering	Matrix
		Bracketing	Off
		Flash mode	Front-curtain sync
		Flash compensation	Off
		FV lock	Off
		Exposure delay mode	Off
		+NEF (RAW)	Off

Recommended Default Changes

Although I won't be explaining how to use the Nikon D810's menu system in detail until Chapters 11, 12, and 13, you can make some simple changes now. These general instructions will serve you to make any of the setting changes I recommend next. To change any menu setting, follow these steps:

1. **Access menus.** Press the MENU button at the top of the array of five buttons located to the immediate left of the back-panel LCD monitor.
2. **Choose the main menu you need to access.** Press the multi selector down button to scroll down to the menu containing the entry you want to change. The available menus include (from top to bottom in the left column of the Menu screen: Playback menu (right-pointing triangle icon); Shooting menu (camera icon); Custom Settings menu (pencil icon); Setup menu (wrench icon); Retouch menu (paintbrush icon); and My Menu (text page/text page with checkmark icon).
3. **Select main menu.** Press the right multi selector button to choose the menu heading containing the submenu entry you want to change.
4. **Choose menu entry.** Press the down multi selector button to move within the main menu to the entry you want to change. A scroll bar at the right side shows your progress through the menu, as all the main menus except for the Custom Settings menu and My Menu (if it contains fewer than five custom entries) have more items than can fit on a single screen.
5. **Choose options.** Press the right multi selector button to choose the highlighted menu entry, and view a screen with options. Select the options you want, and press OK to confirm. Some menus allow you to confirm by pressing the right button again, or require you to move to a Done selection and choose that before exiting.
6. **Exit menus.** Usually you can exit the menu system by pressing the MENU button. If an option has variations, I'll explain them when I discuss each of the menu choices in Chapters 11, 12, and 13.

Here are some of the changes I recommend you make to the defaults that Nikon sets up for you. (I have no changes to recommend for the Playback, Setup, and My Menu settings, which are fine the way they are for most people, nor for the Retouch menu, which doesn't have parameters that can be stored.)

Shooting Menu

Make these changes to the Shooting menu entries listed. Some of the changes I suggest may or may not apply to you, depending on the kind of shooting you do. I'll point out when you should, and when you should not make these changes. Jump to Chapter 11 for more information about each particular setting.

- **File Naming.** The D810 applies a generic DSC filename prefix to all your image files. That makes it easy to confuse your D810 images with those taken with other cameras that use the same DSC nomenclature. Unless you import images using an application that changes the filenames during import, it's a good idea to change from the DSC prefix to something more distinctive. I use 810.
- **Primary slot selection.** The D810 automatically assumes that the SD card slot is your preferred memory card slot. If you've been using CF cards with your previous camera, you'll probably want to change the primary slot to CF, *unless* your SD cards are larger, faster, and more numerous than the CF cards in your collection.
- **Secondary slot function.** The D810 sets this to Overflow. That's actually fine for most users. But pros and others who absolutely can't afford to lose a shot may want to change the default to Backup (images copied to both cards), or RAW Primary, JPEG secondary.
- **Image Quality.** Change from JPEG Normal to JPEG Fine, to produce better image quality. Please!
- **High ISO NR.** Change from default Normal to Off, until you've had a chance to evaluate whether the D810 performs to your liking at high sensitivity settings. Off produces the least amount of noise reduction (Nikon doesn't allow you to disable NR completely), but also doesn't degrade the amount of detail as much as any of the On settings.

Custom Settings Menu

Make these changes to the Custom Settings menu entries listed:

- **Custom Setting a10: Built-in AF-assist illuminator.** Change from the default Auto to Off, unless you frequently take photos in low light situations from relatively close distances, and the lamp's illumination won't prove annoying. This feature doesn't work well, except very close and when the lamp isn't blocked by your fingers, and is annoying at other times. At concerts, religious ceremonies, and other situations the lamp can be distracting.
- **Custom Setting c2: Standby timer.** If you shoot sports or other events where you don't want the camera going to sleep and delaying your ability to snap off a shot *now*, change from the default 6 seconds to 30 seconds, 1 minute, 5 minutes, or 10 minutes. You'll use more power, but won't lose a shot from a split-second delay while the camera wakes up.
- **Custom Setting d1: Beep.** Choose the Volume setting and turn to OFF to quiet the camera during self-timer countdowns and single-servo autofocus confirmation. If you decide you need this reminder, you can always turn it back on, but most of the time it's annoying and calls attention to your shooting.
- **Custom Setting e8: Bracketing Order.** The default is to shoot the metered exposure first, followed by the under- and overexposures. Changing to Under > Metered > Over provides a more convenient progression, especially when shooting HDR.

- **Custom Setting f11: Slot empty release lock.** This controls what happens when you press the shutter release while no memory card is loaded in the camera. Change from the default Enable Release to Release Locked. Why would you want to be able to take pictures with no memory card in the camera, other than to demonstrate the camera or a few other reasons? Even though a DEMO label appears on the LCD when you "take" pictures with no memory card inserted, it's easy to overlook. Turn this capability to LOCK.

Recommended Customized Settings

I'm going to finish off this chapter with some tables listing recommended settings for your Shooting and Custom Settings banks. I will outline how to set the four Shooting menu banks, A, B, C, and D in Chapter 11, and show you how to assign each of them a suitable name so you could more easily remember the shooting situations the customized settings were tailored for. In Chapter 12, I'll explain the four Custom Settings banks (also named A, B, C, and D by default), and some of the ways you could set up groups of settings for different kinds of picture-taking opportunities.

I've divided the recommended settings into a group of tables, rather than one or two huge tables that would be more difficult to read. The tables show the "default" settings for the Shooting menu banks and Custom Settings banks, as they come from the factory, plus eight groups intended for Basic, Studio flash, Portrait, Long exposure, Sports—Indoors, Sports—Outdoors, Landscapes, and Portraits. For the Custom Settings menu, I add one more group of settings, for exposure bracketing.

Each setting includes options that I consider best suited for their particular shooting situations. For example, when I am bracketing exposures, I like to shoot off a single bracket burst fairly quickly, so I choose C_L release mode, with the shooting speed set to 5 frames per second. When I press the shutter release, all the exposures are taken consecutively in a brief period of time. Similarly, when I am shooting indoor sports, I like to use ISO 3200 and set my autofocus priority to Release + Focus. That lets me shoot bursts of pictures with minimal shutter lag when I press the shutter release button, but still gives the camera a little extra time to get that first picture in sharp focus. I understand that the continuous shooting speed may be a little slower in that mode, but it works for me.

Now, obviously, your D810 has only four Shooting banks and four Custom Settings banks, plus the Extended banks to add additional parameters, so you'll have to choose which of my recommendations to "install" in the four available banks that reside in your camera. I also suggest further customizing these settings to best suit your own habits and needs. In addition, there are some settings that I do not suggest changes for, but which can easily be modified by you, if you like.

For example, you may not have known that you can select both a folder name and file naming scheme for *each* Shooting menu bank. So, you can deposit your image files in a different folder, if you like, based on which Shooting menu bank you've selected. Similarly, you could conceivably use different filename prefixes for each bank (say, to separate SPT_ [sports] shots from LND_ [landscape] pictures). That seems like a lot of trouble to me, but you can do it.

Shooting Menu Recommendations

I'll list my Shooting menu bank suggestions first. The Custom Settings menu bank recommendations are divided into the exact same categories but, of course, deal with different options. In Table 3.2, the second column shows the default settings, as the D810 comes from the factory. Note that when a setting is entirely up to your personal preference or a given shooting situation (for example, Primary Slot choice or White Balance Fine-Tuning), I may not list that setting or provide a recommendation.

Custom Settings Menu Bank Recommendations

Next come the Custom Settings menu bank recommendations. They are divided into the exact same categories, but with the addition of a new category for bracketed shots. And, of course, they all deal with different options. Note that I have no special recommendations for settings related to your personal preference for limiting AF-area mode selections (a11), anything relating to the MB-D12 or movie making (g1 to g4).

Table 3.2 Shooting Menu Recommendations #1

Option	Camera Default	Basic Setting	Studio Flash	Portrait
Extended menu banks	Off	Off	Off	Off
File naming	DSC/_DSC	Your choice	Your choice	Your choice
Secondary slot function	Overflow	Overflow	Backup	Backup
Image quality	JPEG Normal	NEF(RAW)+ JPEG Fine	NEF	NEF+JPEG Fine
JPEG/TIFF recording				
Image size	Large	Large	Large	Large
JPEG compression	Size Priority	Optimal quality	Optimal quality	Optimal quality
NEF (RAW) recording				
Image size	FX	FX	FX	FX
NEF (RAW) compression	Lossless compressed	Lossless compressed	Lossless compressed	Lossless compressed
NEF (RAW) bit depth	14-bit	14-bit	14-bit	14-bit
Image area				
Choose image area	FX	FX	FX	FX
Auto DX crop	On	On	On	On

Table 3.2 Shooting Menu Recommendations #1 (continued)

Option	Camera Default	Basic Setting	Studio Flash	Portrait
White balance	Auto1	Auto1	Flash	Auto2
Set Picture Control	Standard	C-1 (Standard+ Sharp 7)	Standard	C-3 (Neutral + Sharp -2)
Color space	sRGB	Adobe RGB	Adobe RGB	Adobe RGB
Active D-Lighting	Off	Off	Off	Off
Vignette control	Normal	Off	Off	Normal
Long exp. NR	Off	Off	Off	Off
High ISO NR	Normal	Low	Low	Low
ISO sensitivity settings				
ISO sensitivity	100	200	100	100
ISO sensitivity auto control:	Off	On	Off	Off
>*Maximum sensitivity*	3200	800	1600	1600
>*Minimum shutter speed*	1/30 s	1/60 s	1/60 s	1/60 s
Movie settings				
Frame Size/rate	1920 × 1080; 60 fps	1920 × 1080; 30 fps	1920 × 1080; 30 fps	1920 × 1080; 30 fps
Movie Quality	High Quality	High Quality	High Quality	High Quality
Microphone sensitivity	Auto sensitivity	Auto sensitivity	Auto sensitivity	Auto sensitivity
Frequency response	Wide range	Wide range	N/A	Wide range
Wind noise reduction	Off	Off	N/A	Off
Destination	SD Card Slot	Slot with fastest card	N/A	Slot with fastest card
Movie ISO sensitivity				
>*ISO sensitivity (Mode M)*	100	100	N/A	100
>*Auto ISO control (Mode M)*	Off	Off	N/A	Off
>*Maximum sensitivity*	12800	12800	N/A	3200

Table 3.3 Shooting Menu Recommendations #2

Option	Long Exposure	Sports Indoors	Sports Outdoors	Landscape
Extended menu banks	Off	On	On	Off
File naming	DSC/_DSC	Your choice	Your choice	Your choice
Secondary slot function	Overflow	Overflow	Overflow	Backup
Image quality	JPEG Normal	JPEG Fine	JPEG Fine	NEF+JPEG Fine
JPEG/TIFF recording				
Image size	Large	Large	Large	Large
JPEG compression	Size Priority	Optimal quality	Optimal quality	Optimal quality
NEF (RAW) recording				
Image size	FX	FX	FX	FX
NEF (RAW) compression	Lossless compressed	Lossless compressed	Lossless compressed	Lossless compressed
NEF (RAW) bit depth	14-bit	14-bit	14-bit	14-bit
Image area				
Choose image area	FX	FX	FX/DX	FX
Auto DX crop	On	On	On	On
White balance	Auto1	Auto1	Auto1	Auto1
Set Picture Control	Standard	Standard	Standard	C-2 (Vivid + Sharp 5)
Color space	Adobe RGB	Adobe RGB	Adobe RGB	Adobe RGB
Active D-Lighting	Off	Off	Off	Normal
Vignette control	Off	Off	Off	Normal
Long exp. NR	On	Off	Off	Off
High ISO NR	Low	Normal	Low	Low
ISO sensitivity settings				
ISO sensitivity	400	3200	800	200
ISO sensitivity auto control:	Off	On	Off	Off
>*Maximum sensitivity*	3200	3200	1600	800
>*Minimum shutter speed*	1/30 s	1/60 s	1/60 s	1/60 s

Table 3.3 Shooting Menu Recommendations #2 (continued)

Option	Long Exposure	Sports Indoors	Sports Outdoors	Landscape
Movie settings				
Frame Size/rate	1920 × 1080; 60 fps	1920 × 1080; 30 fps	1920 × 1080; 30 fps	1920 × 1080; 30 fps
Movie Quality	High Quality	High Quality	High Quality	High Quality
Microphone sensitivity	Auto sensitivity	Auto sensitivity	Auto sensitivity	Auto sensitivity
Frequency response	Wide range	Wide range	Wide range	Wide Range
Wind noise reduction	Off	Off	On	On
Destination	SD Card Slot	Slot with fastest card	Slot with fastest card	Slot with fastest card
Movie ISO sensitivity				
>*ISO sensitivity (Mode M)*	100	400	200	200
>*Auto ISO control (Mode M)*	Off	On	On	Off
>*Maximum sensitivity*	12800	12800	12800	3200

Table 3.4 Shooting Menu Recommendations #3

Option	HDR	Candids/People	Concerts	Vacation
Extended menu banks	Off	Off	Off	Off
File naming	DSC/_DSC	Your choice	Your choice	Your choice
Secondary slot function	Overflow	Overflow	Backup	Backup
Image quality	NEF	JPEG Fine	NEF	NEF+JPEG Fine
JPEG/TIFF recording				
Image size	Large	Large	Large	Large
JPEG compression	Size Priority	Optimal quality	Optimal quality	Optimal quality
NEF (RAW) recording				
Image size	FX	FX	DX or 1.2X crop	FX
NEF (RAW) compression	Lossless compressed	Lossless compressed	Lossless compressed	Lossless compressed
NEF (RAW) bit depth	14-bit	12-bit	14-bit	14-bit

Table 3.4 Shooting Menu Recommendations #3 (continued)

Option	HDR	Candids/People	Concerts	Vacation
Image area				
Choose image area	FX	FX	FX	FX
Auto DX crop	On	On	On	On
White balance	Auto1	Auto1	Auto or Tungsten	Auto1
Set Picture Control	Standard	Standard	Standard	Vivid
Color space	Adobe RGB	Adobe RGB	Adobe RGB	Adobe RGB
Active D-Lighting	Off	Off	Off	Normal
Vignette control	Off	Off	Off	Normal
Long exp. NR	Off	Off	Off	Off
High ISO NR	Low	Normal	Low	Low
ISO sensitivity settings				
ISO sensitivity	100	200	200	200
ISO sensitivity auto control:	Off	On	Off	Off
>*Maximum sensitivity*	100	3200	800	200
>*Minimum shutter speed*	1/30 s	1/60 s	1/60 s	1/60 s
Movie settings				
Frame Size/rate	1920 × 1080; 60 fps	1920 × 1080; 30 fps	1920 × 1080; 30 fps	1920 × 1080; 30 fps
Movie Quality	High Quality	High Quality	High Quality	High Quality
Microphone sensitivity	Auto sensitivity	Auto sensitivity	Auto sensitivity	Auto sensitivity
Frequency response	Wide range	Wide range	Wide Range	Wide Range
Wind noise reduction	Off	On	Off	On
Destination	SD Card Slot	Slot with fastest card	NA	Slot with fastest card
Movie ISO sensitivity				
>*ISO sensitivity (Mode M)*	100	100	3200	100
>*Auto ISO control (Mode M)*	Off	Off	On	Off
>*Maximum sensitivity*	12800	12800	12800	12800

Table 3.5 Custom Settings Menu Bank Recommendations #1

Item	Option	Camera Default	Basic Setting	Studio Flash	Portrait	Long Exposure
Autofocus						
a1	AF-C priority selection	Release	Release	Release	Release	Release
a2	AF-S priority selection	Focus	Focus	Focus	Focus	Focus
a3	Focus tracking with lock-on	Normal	Normal	Normal	Normal	Normal
a4	AF activation	Shutter/ AF-ON (ON)	Shutter/ AF-ON (ON)	Shutter/ AF-ON (ON)	Shutter/ AF-ON (ON)	Shutter/ AF-ON (ON)
a5	Focus point illumination					
	Manual focus mode	On	On	On	On	On
	Dynamic-area AF display	Off	On	On	On	On
	Group-area AF illumination	Squares	Squares	Squares	Squares	Squares
a6	AF point illumination	Auto	Auto	Auto	Auto	Auto
a7	Focus point wrap-around	No wrap (OFF)	No wrap (OFF)	No wrap (OFF)	No wrap (OFF)	No wrap (OFF)
a8	Number of focus points	51 points	51 points	11 points	51 points	51 points
a9	Store by orientation	Off	Off	Off	On	Off
a10	Built-in AF illuminator	On	Off	Off	Off	Off
a12	Autofocus mode restrictions	No restrictions	No restrictions	No restrictions	No restrictions	No restrictions
Metering/exposure						
b1	ISO sensitivity step value	1/3 step	1/3 step	1/3 step	1/3 step	1/3 step
b2	EV steps for exposure control	1/3 step	1/3 step	1/3 step	1/3 step	1/3 step

Table 3.5 Custom Settings Menu Bank Recommendations #1 (continued)

Item	Option	Camera Default	Basic Setting	Studio Flash	Portrait	Long Exposure
Metering/exposure						
b3	Exp./Flash comp. step value	1/3 step	1/3 step	1/3 step	1/3 step	1/3 step
b4	Easy exposure compensation	Off	Off	Off	Off	Off
b5	Matrix metering	Face detection on	Face detection on	Face Detection on	Face detection on	Off
b6	Center-weighted area	12mm	12mm	12mm	8mm	8mm
b7	Fine-tune optimal exposure:					
	Matrix metering	0	0	0	0	0
	Center-weighted	0	0	0	0	0
	Spot metering	0	0	0	0	0
	Highlight-weighted metering	0	0	0	0	0
Timers/AE Lock						
c1	Shutter-release button AE-L	Off	Off	Off	Off	Off
c2	Standby timer	6 sec	6 sec	6 sec	6 sec	6 sec
c3	Self-timer delay	10 sec	20 sec	10 sec	10 sec	2 sec
c4	Monitor off delay					
	Playback	10 sec	10 sec	10 sec	10 sec	20 sec
	Menus	20 sec	20 sec	20 sec	20 sec	20 sec
	Information display	10 sec	10 sec	20 sec	20 sec	20 sec
	Image review	4 sec	10 sec	4 sec	4 sec	4 sec
	Live view	10 min.	10 min.	10 min	10 min.	10 min.
Shooting/display						
d1	Beep	Volume: Off; Pitch: High	Volume: Off; Pitch: High	Volume: Off; Pitch: High	Volume: Off; Pitch: High	Volume: Off; Pitch: High
d2	CL Mode Shooting speed	2 fps	2 fps	1 fps	2 fps	1 fps

Table 3.5 Custom Settings Menu Bank Recommendations #1 (continued)

Item	Option	Camera Default	Basic Setting	Studio Flash	Portrait	Long Exposure
Shooting/display						
d3	Max. continuous release	100	20	20	20	20
d4	Exposure delay mode	Off	Off	Off	Off	On
d5	Electronic front-curtain shutter	Off	Off	Off	On	On
d6	File no. Sequence	On	On	On	On	On
d7	Viewfinder grid display	Off	Off	On	On	Off
d8	ISO display and adjustment	Frame Count	Frame Count	ISO	ISO	ISO
d9	Screen tips	On	On	On	On	On
d10	Information Display	Auto	Auto	Auto	Auto	Dark on Light
d11	LCD illumination	Off	Off	Off	Off	On
Bracketing/Flash						
e1	Flash sync speed	1/250	1/250	1/250	1/250	1/250
e2	Flash shutter speed	1/60	1/60	1/15	1/15	1/60
e3	Flash cntrl for built-in flash	TTL	TTL	TTL	TTL	TTL
e4	Exposure comp. for flash	Entire frame	Entire frame	Entire frame	Entire frame	Entire frame
e5	Modeling flash	ON	ON	ON	ON	ON
e6	Auto bracketing set	AE & Flash	AE & Flash	AE & Flash	AE & Flash	AE & Flash
e7	Auto bracketing (mode M)	Flash/ Speed	Flash/ Speed	Flash/ Speed	Flash/ Speed	Flash/ Speed
e8	Bracketing order	Meter> Under> Over	Meter> Under> Over	Meter> Under> Over	Meter> Under> Over	Meter> Under> Over

Table 3.5 Custom Settings Menu Bank Recommendations #1 (continued)

Item	Option	Camera Default	Basic Setting	Studio Flash	Portrait	Long Exposure
Controls						
f1	Illuminator switch	LCD backlight	LCD backlight	LCD backlight	LCD backlight	Information and LCD display
f2	Multi selector center button					
	Shooting mode	Select center focus point	Select center focus point	Select center focus point	Select center focus point	Select center focus point
	Playback mode	Thumbnail On/Off	View histograms	View histograms	View histograms	View histograms
	Live view	Select center focus point	Select center focus point	Select center focus point	Select center focus point	Select center focus point
f3	Multi selector	Do nothing (OFF)	Do nothing (OFF)	Do nothing (OFF)	Do nothing (OFF)	Do nothing (OFF)
f4	Assign Fn button					
	Fn button press	Viewfinder virtual horizon	Viewfinder virtual horizon	FV Lock	FV Lock	None
	Fn button + dials	None	None	Bracketing Burst	Bracketing Burst	Bracketing Burst
f5	Assign preview button					
	Preview button press	Preview	Preview	Preview	Preview	Preview
	Preview button + dials	None	None	None	None	None
f6	Assign AE-L/AF-L button					
	AE-L/AF-L button press	AE-AF lock	AE-AF lock	AE-AF lock	AE-AF lock	AE-AF lock
	AE-L/AF-L button + dials	None	None	None	None	None
f7	Shutter spd & aperture lock	Off/Off	Off/Off	On/Off	Off/Off	Off/Off

Table 3.5 Custom Settings Menu Bank Recommendations #1 (continued)

Item	Option	Camera Default	Basic Setting	Studio Flash	Portrait	Long Exposure
Controls						
f8	Assign BKT button	Auto bracketing	Auto bracketing	Auto bracketing	Auto bracketing	Auto bracketing
f9	Customize command dials					
	Reverse rotation	No (OFF)	No (OFF)	No (OFF)	No (OFF)	No (OFF)
	Change main/sub	No (OFF)	No (OFF)	No (OFF)	No (OFF)	No (OFF)
	Aperture setting	ON (Sub-command dial)	ON (Sub-command dial)	ON (Sub-command dial)	ON (Sub-command Dial)	ON (Sub-command dial)
	Menus and playback	Off	Off	Off	Off	Off
	Sub-dial frame advance	10 frames	10 frames	10 frames	10 frames	10 frames
f10	Release button to use dial	No (OFF)	No (OFF)	No (OFF)	No (OFF)	No (OFF)
f11	Slot Empty Release Lock	Enable release (OK)	Release locked (LOCK)	Release locked (LOCK)	Release locked (LOCK)	Release locked (LOCK)
f12	Reverse indicators	+ 0 -	+ 0 -	+ 0 -	+ 0 -	+ 0 -
f13	Assign movie record button	None	None	None	None	None
f14	Live view button options	Enable	Enable	Enable	Enable	Enable
f15	Assign MB-D12 AF-ON	AF-ON	AF-ON	AF-ON	AF-ON	AF-ON
f16	Assign remote (WR) Fn button	None	None	None	None	None
f17	Lens focus function button	AF Lock Only	AF Lock Only	AF Lock Only	AF Lock Only	AF Lock Only

Table 3.6 Custom Settings Menu Bank Recommendations #2

Item	Option	Sports Indoors	Sports Outdoors	Landscape	Bracketing
Autofocus					
a1	AF-C priority selection	Release	Release	Focus	Release
a2	AF-S priority selection	Focus	Focus	Focus	Focus
a3	Focus tracking with lock-on	5 (long)	Normal	5 (long)	5 (long)
a4	AF activation	AF-ON only	AF-ON only	Shutter/ AF-ON (ON)	Shutter/ AF-ON (ON)
a5	Focus point illumination				
	Manual focus mode	On	On	On	On
	Dynamic-area AF display	Off	On	On	On
	Group-area AF illumination	Squares	Squares	Squares	Squares
a6	AF point illumination	Auto	Auto	Auto	Auto
a7	Focus point wrap-around	No wrap (OFF)	No wrap (OFF)	No wrap (OFF)	No wrap (OFF)
a8	Number of focus points	11 points	11 points	11 points	51 points
a9	Store by orientation	Off	On	On	Off
a10	Built-in AF illuminator	On	Off	Off	Off
a12	Autofocus mode restrictions	No restrictions	AF-C	AF-C	No restrictions
Metering/exposure					
b1	ISO sensitivity step value	1/3 step	1/3 step	1/3 step	1/3 step
b2	EV steps for exposure control	1/3 step	1/3 step	1/3 step	1/3 step
b3	Exp./Flash comp. step value	1/3 step	1/3 step	1/3 step	1/3 step
b4	Easy exposure compensation	Off	Off	Off	Off
b5	Matrix metering	Face detection On	Face detection On	Face detection Off	Face detection Off

Table 3.6 Custom Settings Menu Bank Recommendations #2 (continued)

Item	Option	Sports Indoors	Sports Outdoors	Landscape	Bracketing
Metering/exposure					
b6	Center-weighted area	12mm	12mm	12mm	8mm
b7	Fine-tune optimal exposure:				
	Matrix metering	0	0	0	0
	Center-weighted	0	0	0	0
	Spot metering	0	0	0	0
	Highlight-weighted metering	0	0	0	0
Timers/AE Lock					
c1	Shutter-release button AE-L	Off	Off	Off	Off
c2	Standby timer	1 min	1 min	6 sec	6 sec
c3	Self-timer delay	10 sec	20 sec	10 sec	10 sec
c4	Monitor off delay				
	Playback	2 sec	2 sec	10 sec	10 sec
	Menus	10 sec	20 sec	20 sec	20 sec
	Information display	10 sec	10 sec	20 sec	20 sec
	Image review	2 sec	2 sec	4 sec	4 sec
	Live view	10 min.	10 min.	10 min	10 min.
Shooting/display					
d1	Beep	Volume: Off; Pitch: High	Volume: Off; Pitch: High	Volume: Off; Pitch: High	Volume: Off; Pitch: High
d2	CL Mode Shooting speed	2 fps	2 fps	1 fps	2 fps
d3	Max. continuous release	100	20	20	20
d4	Exposure delay mode	Off	Off	Off	Off
d5	Electronic front-curtain shutter	Off	Off	Off	On
d6	File no. Sequence	On	On	On	On
d7	Viewfinder grid display	Off	Off	On	On
d8	ISO display and adjustment	Frame Count	Frame Count	ISO	ISO

Table 3.6 Custom Settings Menu Bank Recommendations #2 (continued)

Item	Option	Sports Indoors	Sports Outdoors	Landscape	Bracketing
Shooting/display					
d9	Screen tips	Off	Off	Off	Off
d10	Information Display	Auto	Auto	Auto	Auto
d11	LCD illumination	Off	Off	Off	Off
Bracketing/Flash					
e1	Flash sync speed	1/250	1/250	1/250	1/250
e2	Flash shutter speed	1/60	1/60	1/15	1/15
e3	Flash cntrl for built-in flash	TTL	TTL	TTL	TTL
e4	Exposure comp. for flash	Entire frame	Entire frame	Entire frame	Entire frame
e5	Modeling flash	ON	ON	ON	ON
e6	Auto bracketing set	AE & Flash	AE & Flash	AE & Flash	AE & Flash
e7	Auto bracketing (mode M)	Flash/Speed	Flash/Speed	Flash/Speed	Flash/Speed
e8	Bracketing order	Meter> Under>Over	Meter> Under>Over	Meter> Under>Over	Meter> Under>Over
Controls					
f1	Illuminator switch	LCD backlight	LCD backlight	LCD backlight	LCD backlight
f2	Multi selector center button				
	Shooting mode	Select center focus point	Select center focus point	Select center focus point	Select center focus point
	Playback mode	Thumbnail On/Off	View histograms	View histograms	View histograms
	Live view	Select center focus point	Select center focus point	Select center focus point	Select center focus point
f3	Multi selector	Do nothing (OFF)	Do nothing (OFF)	Do nothing (OFF)	Do nothing (OFF)
f4	Assign Fn button				
	Fn button press	Viewfinder virtual horizon	Viewfinder virtual horizon	Viewfinder virtual horizon	FV Lock
	Fn button + dials	None	None	Bracketing Burst	Bracketing Burst

Table 3.6 Custom Settings Menu Bank Recommendations #2 (continued)					
Item	**Option**	**Sports Indoors**	**Sports Outdoors**	**Landscape**	**Bracketing**
Controls					
f5	Assign preview button				
	Preview button press	Preview	Preview	Preview	Preview
	Preview button + dials	None	None	None	None
f6	Assign AE-L/AF-L button				
	AE-L/AF-L button press	AE-AF lock	AE-AF lock	AE-AF lock	AE-AF lock
	AE-L/AF-L button + dials	None	None	None	None
f7	Shutter spd & aperture lock	Off/Off	Off/Off	On/Off	Off/Off
f8	Assign BKT button	Auto bracketing	Auto bracketing	Auto bracketing	Auto bracketing
f9	Customize command dials				
	Reverse rotation	No (OFF)	No (OFF)	No (OFF)	No (OFF)
	Change main/sub	No (OFF)	No (OFF)	No (OFF)	No (OFF)
	Aperture setting	ON (Sub-command dial)	ON (Sub-command dial)	ON (Sub-command dial)	ON (Sub-command Dial)
	Menus and playback	Off	Off	Off	Off
	Sub-dial frame advance	10 frames	10 frames	10 frames	10 frames
f10	Release button to use dial	No (OFF)	No (OFF)	No (OFF)	No (OFF)
f11	Slot Empty Release Lock	Enable release (OK)	Release locked (LOCK)	Release locked (LOCK)	Release locked (LOCK)
f12	Reverse indicators	+ 0 -	+ 0 -	+ 0 -	+ 0 -
f13	Assign movie record button	None	None	None	None
f14	Live view button options	Enable	Enable	Enable	Enable
f15	Assign MB-D12 AF-ON	AF-ON	AF-ON	AF-ON	AF-ON
f16	Assign remote (WR) Fn button	None	None	None	None
f17	Lens focus function button	AF Lock Only	AF Lock Only	AF Lock Only	AF Lock Only

Table 3.7 Custom Settings Menu Bank Recommendations #3

Item	Option	HDR	Candid/ People	Indoor Concerts	Vacation
Autofocus					
a1	AF-C priority selection	Release	Release	Release	Release+ Focus
a2	AF-S priority selection	Focus	Focus	Focus	Focus
a3	Focus tracking with lock-on	5 (long)	Normal	Normal	Normal
a4	AF activation	Shutter/ AF-ON (ON)	Shutter/ AF-ON (ON)	Shutter/ AF-ON (ON)	Shutter/ AF-ON (ON)
a5	Focus point illumination				
	Manual focus mode	On	On	On	On
	Dynamic-area AF display	On	On	On	On
	Group-area AF illumination	Squares	Squares	Squares	Squares
a6	AF point illumination	Auto	Auto	Auto	Auto
a7	Focus point wrap-around	No wrap (OFF)	No wrap (OFF)	No wrap (OFF)	No wrap (OFF)
a8	Number of focus points	51 points	51	11 points	51 points
a9	Store by orientation	Off	Off	Off	On
a10	Built-in AF illuminator	Off	Off	Off	Off
a12	Autofocus mode restrictions	No restrictions	No restrictions	No restrictions	No restrictions
Metering/exposure					
b1	ISO sensitivity step value	1/3 step	1/3 step	1/3 step	1/3 step
b2	EV steps for exposure control	1/3 step	1/3 step	1/3 step	1/3 step
b3	Exp./Flash comp. step value	1/3 step	1/3 step	1/3 step	1/3 step
b4	Easy exposure compensation	Off	Off	Off	Off
b5	Matrix metering	Face detection Off	Face detection On	Face detection On	Face detection On

Table 3.7 Custom Settings Menu Bank Recommendations #3 (continued)

Item	Option	HDR	Candid/ People	Indoor Concerts	Vacation
Metering/exposure					
b6	Center-weighted area	12mm	12mm	8mm	12mm
b7	Fine-tune optimal exposure:				
	Matrix metering	0	0	0	0
	Center-weighted	0	0	0	0
	Spot metering	0	0	0	0
	Highlight-weighted metering	0	0	0	0
Timers/AE Lock					
c1	Shutter-release button AE-L	Off	Off	Off	Off
c2	Standby timer	6 sec	6 sec	6 sec	6 sec
c3	Self-timer delay	10 sec	20 sec	10 sec	10 sec
c4	Monitor off delay				
	Playback	10 sec	10 sec	10 sec	20 sec
	Menus	20 sec	20 sec	20 sec	20 sec
	Information display	10 sec	20 sec	20 sec	20 sec
	Image review	10 sec	4 sec	4 sec	4 sec
	Live view	10 min	10 min	10 min	10 min
Shooting/display					
d1	Beep	Volume: Off; Pitch: High	Volume: Off; Pitch: High	Volume: Off; Pitch: High	Volume: Off; Pitch: High
d2	CL Mode Shooting speed	2 fps	2 fps	3 fps	2 fps
d3	Max. continuous release	20	20	20	20
d4	Exposure delay mode	Off	Off	Off	On
d5	Electronic front-curtain shutter	Off	Off	On	On
d6	File no. Sequence	On	On	On	On
d7	Viewfinder grid display	Off	On	On	Off
d8	ISO display and adjustment	Frame Count	ISO	ISO	ISO

Table 3.7 Custom Settings Menu Bank Recommendations #3 (continued)

Item	Option	HDR	Candid/ People	Indoor Concerts	Vacation
Shooting/display					
d9	Screen tips	On	On	On	On
d10	Information Display	Auto	Auto	Auto	Dark on Light
d11	LCD illumination	Off	Off	Off	On
Bracketing/Flash					
e1	Flash sync speed	1/250	1/250	1/250	1/250
e2	Flash shutter speed	1/60	1/15	1/15	1/60
e3	Flash cntrl for built-in flash	TTL	TTL	TTL	TTL
e4	Exposure comp. for flash	Entire frame	Entire frame	Entire frame	Entire frame
e5	Modeling flash	ON	ON	ON	ON
e6	Auto bracketing set	AE & Flash	AE & Flash	AE & Flash	AE & Flash
e7	Auto bracketing (mode M)	Flash/Speed	Flash/Speed	Flash/Speed	Flash/Speed
e8	Bracketing order	Meter> Under>Over	Meter> Under>Over	Meter> Under>Over	Meter> Under>Over
Controls					
f1	Illuminator switch	LCD backlight	LCD backlight	LCD backlight	Information and LCD display
f2	Multi selector center button				
	Shooting mode	Select center focus point	Select center focus point	Select center focus point	Select center focus point
	Playback mode	View histograms	View histograms	View histograms	View histograms
	Live view	Select center focus point	Select center focus point	Select center focus point	Select center focus point
f3	Multi selector	Do nothing (OFF)	Do nothing (OFF)	Do nothing (OFF)	Do nothing (OFF)

Table 3.7 Custom Settings Menu Bank Recommendations #3 (continued)

Item	Option	HDR	Candid/ People	Indoor Concerts	Vacation
Controls					
f4	Assign Fn button				
	Fn button press	Viewfinder virtual horizon	FV Lock	FV Lock	None
	Fn button + dials	None	Bracketing Burst	Bracketing Burst	Bracketing Burst
f5	Assign preview button				
	Preview button press	Preview	Preview	Preview	Preview
	Preview button + dials	None	None	None	None
f6	Assign AE-L/AF-L button				
	AE-L/AF-L button press	AE-AF lock	AE-AF lock	AE-AF lock	AE-AF lock
	AE-L/AF-L button + dials	None	None	None	None
f7	Shutter spd & aperture lock	Off/Off	On/Off	Off/Off	Off/Off
f8	Assign BKT button	Auto bracketing	Auto bracketing	Auto bracketing	Auto bracketing
f9	Customize command dials				
	Reverse rotation	No (OFF)	No (OFF)	No (OFF)	No (OFF)
	Change main/sub	No (OFF)	No (OFF)	No (OFF)	No (OFF)
	Aperture setting	ON (Sub-command dial)	ON (Sub-command dial)	ON (Sub-command Dial)	ON (Sub-command dial)
	Menus and playback	Off	Off	Off	Off
	Sub-dial frame advance	10 frames	10 frames	10 frames	10 frames
f10	Release button to use dial	No (OFF)	No (OFF)	No (OFF)	No (OFF)
f11	Slot Empty Release Lock	Release locked (LOCK)	Release locked (LOCK)	Release locked (LOCK)	Release locked (LOCK)
f12	Reverse indicators	+ 0 -	+ 0 -	+ 0 -	+ 0 -
f13	Assign movie record button	None	None	None	None

Table 3.7 Custom Settings Menu Bank Recommendations #3 (continued)					
Item	**Option**	**HDR**	**Candid/ People**	**Indoor Concerts**	**Vacation**
Controls					
f14	Live view button options	Enable	Enable	Enable	Enable
f15	Assign MB-D12 AF-ON	AF-ON	AF-ON	AF-ON	AF-ON
f16	Assign remote (WR) Fn button	None	None	None	None
f17	Lens focus function button	AF Lock Only	AF Lock Only	AF Lock Only	AF Lock Only

Part II

Mastering Your Tools

Even if you've learned the fundamentals and controls of the D810, there is lots of room to learn more and master the features of the camera so you can use them to their fullest. Even if you're getting great exposures a high percentage of the time, you can fine-tune tonal values and use your shutter speed, aperture, and ISO controls creatively. Your camera's high performance autofocus system may zero in on your subject in most situations—but you still need to be able to tell the D810 *what* to focus on, and *when*. Other tools at your disposal let you freeze an instant of time, create multiple exposures on a single frame, and improve your images in other imaginative ways. The chapters in this part will help you move your photography to the next level by understanding exposure, mastering the mysteries of autofocus, and using the Nikon D810's advanced features.

This part of the book contains the core chapters that will help you improve your images by nailing the best exposure, every time; by using the (often confusing, sometimes conflicting) features of the camera's advanced autofocus system and exploring some advanced techniques like trap focus, stacked focus, and in-camera HDR. I'll also clear up any questions you might have about which lenses are best suited for the D810 when it comes time to add to your collection.

- **Chapter 4:** This chapter explores all your options for fine-tuning exposure with the Nikon D810. You'll learn when to use—and not use—each of the camera's metering modes, how to work with histograms, and the rationale for choosing the built-in HDR feature, or whether to capture high dynamic range images "manually." I'm also going to explode the myth of the 18-percent gray card.
- **Chapter 5:** As autofocus features are added, this useful capability often becomes more confusing, even for veteran photographers. I'm going to show you exactly how autofocus works so you can better understand the strengths and limitations of each mode. You'll discover how to select the mode—including the new Group mode—that will give you tack-sharp focus time after time, and learn how to use fine-tuning (with the included focus chart) to correct lenses with front- and back-focus problems.
- **Chapter 6:** Here you'll find discussions of some more advanced techniques, including how to make people "invisible" with long exposures, getting the most from the D810's continuous shooting capabilities, and some clever ways to create multiple exposures.
- **Chapter 7:** Whether you call it Lens Lust, Lens Acquisition Syndrome, or simply a particular creative affliction that calls for lenses that are longer, wider, faster, or more versatile, this chapter will help you. Although most D810 owners will already have a good understanding of the lenses available for their camera, I'm going to provide you with my "second opinion," introduce you to some options you might not have known about, and add in a refresher course that may open your eyes to the possibilities that reside in the old DX lenses that ended up in a closet once you switched to FX. I've moved all the entry-level "lens basics" discussions to the bonus chapter, Appendix B.

4

Nailing the Right Exposure

When you bought your Nikon D810, you probably thought your days of worrying about getting the correct exposure were over. To paraphrase an old Kodak tagline dating back to the 19th Century—the goal is, "you press the button, and the camera does the rest." For the most part, that's a realistic objective. The D810 is one of the smartest cameras available when it comes to calculating the right exposure for most situations. You can generally press the mode button and spin the main command dial to switch to Program (P), Aperture-priority (A), or Shutter-priority (S) and shoot away. Even Manual (M) mode doesn't leave you up a creek without a paddle: the D810's analog exposure display at the bottom of the viewfinder provides feedback about how much your selected settings vary from what the D810 *would* have used if you'd opted for one of the semi-automated exposure modes.

But even a camera as smart as the D810 frequently can benefit from intelligent input. For example, when you shoot with the main light source behind the subject, you end up with *backlighting*, which can result in an overexposed background and/or an underexposed subject. The Nikon D810 recognizes backlit situations nicely, and can properly base exposure on the main subject, producing a decent photo. Features like the D810's built in HDR and Active D-Lighting can fine-tune exposure as you take photos, to preserve detail in the highlights and shadows.

But what if you *want* to underexpose the subject, to produce a silhouette effect? Or, perhaps, you might want to flip up the D810's built-in flash unit to fill in the shadows on your subject. The more you know about how to use your D810, the more you'll run into situations where you want to creatively tweak the exposure to provide a different look than you'd get with a straight shot.

This chapter shows you the fundamentals of exposure, so you'll be better equipped to override the Nikon D810's default settings when you want to, or need to. After all, correct exposure is one of the foundations of good photography, along with accurate focus and sharpness, appropriate color balance, freedom from unwanted noise and excessive contrast, as well as pleasing composition.

The Nikon D810 gives you a great deal of control over all of these, although composition is entirely up to you. You must still frame the photograph to create an interesting arrangement of subject matter, but all the other parameters are basic functions of the camera. You can let your D810 set them for you automatically, you can fine-tune how the camera applies its automatic settings, or you can make them yourself, manually. The amount of control you have over exposure, sensitivity (ISO settings), color balance, focus, and image parameters like sharpness and contrast make the D810 a versatile tool for creating images.

In the next few pages, I'm going to give you a grounding in one of those foundations, and explain the basics of exposure, either as an introduction or as a refresher course, depending on your current level of expertise. When you finish this chapter, you'll understand most of what you need to know to take well-exposed photographs creatively in a broad range of situations.

Getting a Handle on Exposure

This section explains the fundamental concepts that go into creating an exposure. If you already know about the role of f/stops, shutter speeds, and sensor sensitivity in determining an exposure, you might want to skip to the next section, which explains how the D810 calculates exposure.

In the most basic sense, exposure is all about light. Exposure can make or break your photo. Correct exposure brings out the detail in the areas you want to picture, providing the range of tones and colors you need to create the desired image. Poor exposure can cloak important details in shadow, or wash them out in glare-filled featureless expanses of white. However, getting the perfect exposure requires some intelligence—either that built into the camera or the smarts in your head—because digital sensors can't capture all the tones we are able to see. If the range of tones in an image is extensive, embracing both inky black shadows and bright highlights, we often must settle for an exposure that renders most of those tones—but not all—in a way that best suits the photo we want to produce.

As the owner of a Nikon D810, you're probably well aware of the traditional "exposure triangle" of aperture (quantity of light, light passed by the lens), shutter speed (the amount of time the shutter is open), and the ISO sensitivity of the sensor—all work proportionately and reciprocally to produce an exposure. The trio is itself affected by the amount of illumination that is available to work with. So, if you double the amount of light, increase the aperture by one stop, make the shutter speed twice as long, or boost the ISO setting 2X, you'll get twice as much exposure. Similarly, you can increase any of these factors while decreasing one of the others by a similar amount to keep the *same* exposure.

Working with any of the three controls always involves trade-offs. Larger f/stops provide less depth-of-field, while smaller f/stops increase depth-of-field (and, especially, with a camera like the D810), decreases sharpness through a phenomenon called diffraction, as discussed in Chapter 7. Shorter shutter speeds do a better job of reducing the effects of camera/subject motion, while longer shutter speeds make that motion blur more likely. Higher ISO settings increase the amount of visual noise and artifacts in your image, while lower ISO settings reduce the effects of noise. (See Figure 4.1.)

To further understand exposure, you need to understand the six aspects of light that combine to produce an image. Start with a light source—the sun, an interior lamp, or the glow from a campfire—and trace its path to your camera, through the lens, and finally to the sensor that captures the illumination. Here's a brief review of the things within our control that affect exposure, listed in "chronological" order (that is, as the light moves from the subject to the sensor):

- **Light at its source.** Our eyes and our cameras—film or digital—are most sensitive to that portion of the electromagnetic spectrum we call *visible light.* That light has several important aspects that are relevant to photography, such as color, and harshness (which is determined primarily by the apparent size of the light source as it illuminates a subject). But, in terms of exposure, the important attribute of a light source is its *intensity.* We may have direct control over intensity, which might be the case with an interior light that can be brightened or dimmed. Or, we might have only indirect control over intensity, as with sunlight, which can be made to appear dimmer by introducing translucent light-absorbing or reflective materials in its path.
- **Light's duration.** We tend to think of most light sources as continuous. But, as you'll learn in Chapter 8, the duration of light can change quickly enough to modify the exposure, as when the main illumination in a photograph comes from an intermittent source, such as an electronic flash.

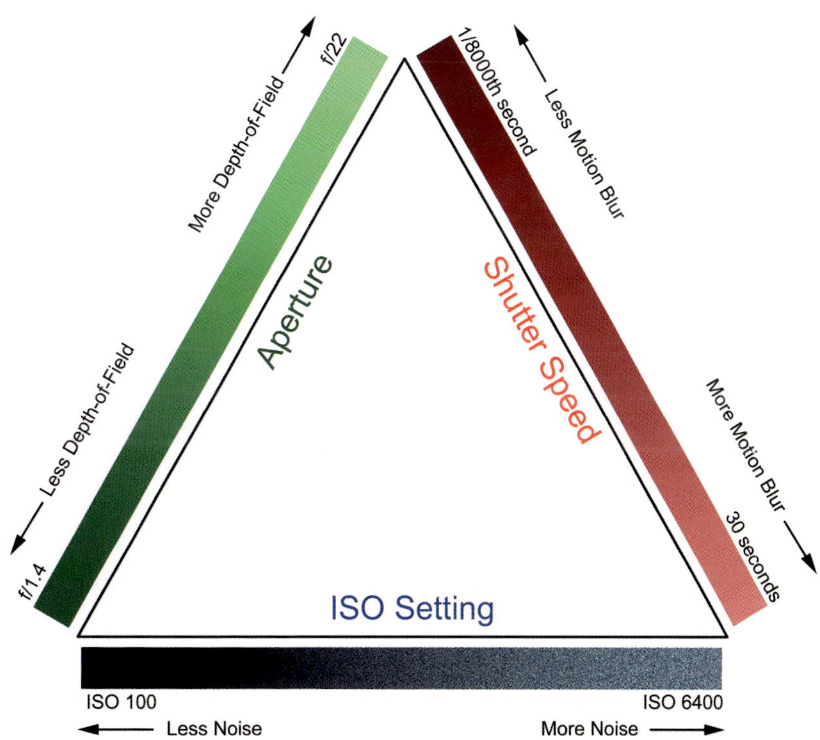

Figure 4.1
The traditional exposure triangle includes aperture, shutter speed, and ISO sensitivity.

- **Light reflected, transmitted, or emitted.** Once light is produced by its source, either continuously or in a brief burst, we are able to see and photograph objects by the light that is reflected from our subjects toward the camera lens; transmitted (say, from translucent objects that are lit from behind); or emitted (by a candle or television screen). When more or less light reaches the lens from the subject, we need to adjust the exposure. This part of the equation is under our control to the extent we can increase the amount of light falling on or passing through the subject (by adding extra light sources or using reflectors), or by pumping up the light that's emitted (by increasing the brightness of the glowing object).
- **Light passed by the lens.** Not all the illumination that reaches the front of the lens makes it all the way through. Filters can remove some of the light before it enters the lens. Inside the lens barrel is a variable-sized diaphragm that produces an opening called an *aperture* that dilates and contracts to control the amount of light that enters the lens. You, or the D810's autoexposure system, can control exposure by varying the size of the aperture. The relative size of the aperture is called the *f/stop*. (See Figure 4.2.)
- **Light passing through the shutter.** Once light passes through the lens, the amount of time the sensor receives it is determined by the D810's shutter, which can remain open for as long as 30 seconds (or even longer if you use the Bulb setting) or as briefly as 1/8,000th second.
- **Light captured by the sensor.** Not all the light falling onto the sensor is captured. If the number of photons reaching a particular photosite doesn't pass a set threshold, no information is recorded. Similarly, if too much light illuminates a pixel in the sensor, then the excess isn't recorded or, worse, spills over to contaminate adjacent pixels. We can modify the minimum and maximum number of pixels that contribute to image detail by adjusting the ISO setting. At higher ISOs, the incoming light is amplified to boost the effective sensitivity of the sensor.

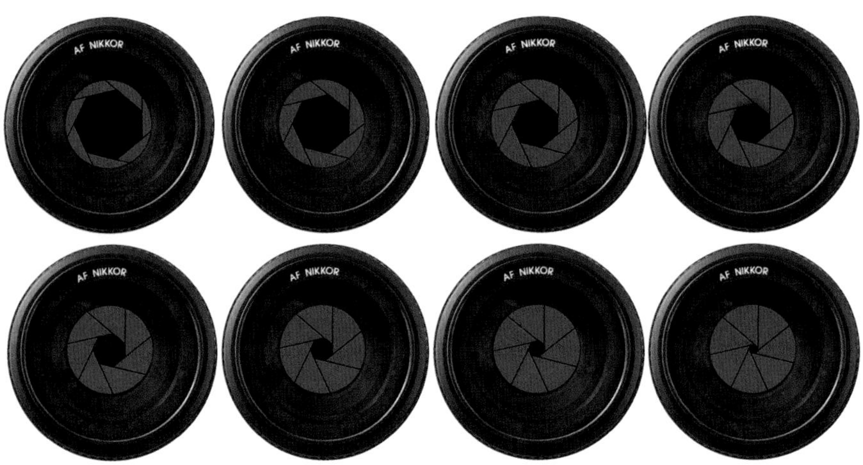

Figure 4.2

Top row (left to right): f/2, f/2.8, f/4, f/5.6; bottom row: f/8, f/11, f/16, f/22.

F/STOPS AND SHUTTER SPEEDS

If you're *really* new to more advanced cameras (and I realize that a few ambitious amateurs do purchase the D810 as their first digital SLR), you might need to know that the lens aperture, or f/stop, is a ratio, much like a fraction, which is why f/2 is larger than f/4, just as 1/2 is larger than 1/4. However, f/2 is actually *four times* as large as f/4. (If you remember your high school geometry, you'll know that to double the area of a circle, you multiply its diameter by the square root of two: 1.4.)

Lenses are usually marked with intermediate f/stops that represent a size that's twice as much/half as much as the previous aperture. So, a lens might be marked: f/2, f/2.8, f/4, f/5.6, f/8, f/11, f/16, f/22, with each larger number representing an aperture that admits half as much light as the one before, as shown in Figure 4.2.

Shutter speeds are actual fractions (of a second), but the numerator is omitted, so that 60, 125, 250, 500, 1,000, and so forth represent 1/60th, 1/125th, 1/250th, 1/500th, and 1/1,000th second. To avoid confusion, Nikon uses quotation marks to signify longer exposures: 2", 2"5, 4", and so forth representing 2.0, 2.5, and 4.0-second exposures, respectively.

Most commonly, exposure settings are made using the aperture and shutter speed, followed by adjusting the ISO sensitivity, if it's not possible to get the preferred exposure (that is, the one that uses the "best" f/stop or shutter speed for the depth-of-field or action stopping we want). Table 4.1 shows equivalent exposure settings using various shutter speeds and f/stops.

When the D810 is set for P mode, the metering system selects the correct exposure for you automatically, but you can change quickly to an equivalent exposure by spinning the main command dial until the desired equivalent exposure combination is displayed. You can use this Flexible Program feature more easily if you remember that you need to rotate the command dial toward the left when you want to increase the amount of depth-of-field or use a slower shutter speed; rotate to the right when you want to reduce the depth-of-field or use a faster shutter speed. The need for more/less DOF and slower/faster shutter speed are the primary reasons you'd want to use Flexible Program. This program shift mode does not work when you're using flash.

Table 4.1 Equivalent Exposures

Shutter speed	f/stop	Shutter speed	f/stop
1/30th second	f/22	1/1,000th second	f/4
1/60th second	f/16	1/2,000th second	f/2.8
1/125th second	f/11	1/4,000th second	f/2
1/250th second	f/8	1/8,000th second	f/1.4
1/500th second	f/5.6		

F/STOPS VERSUS STOPS

In photography parlance, *f/stop* always means the aperture or lens opening. However, for lack of a current commonly used word for one exposure increment, the term *stop* is often used. In the past, EV (Exposure Value) served this purpose, and was used as a measure of the total sensitivity range of a device such as a light meter, but Exposure Value and its abbreviation have since been inextricably intertwined with its use in describing Exposure Compensation. In this book, when I say "stop" by itself (no *f/*), I mean one whole unit of exposure, and am not necessarily referring to an actual f/stop or lens aperture. So, adjusting the exposure by "one stop" can mean both changing to the next shutter speed increment (say, from 1/125th second to 1/250th second) or the next aperture (such as f/4 to f/5.6). Similarly, 1/3 stop or 1/2 stop increments can mean either shutter speed or aperture changes, depending on the context. Be forewarned.

In Aperture-priority (A) and Shutter-priority (S) modes, you can change to an equivalent exposure, but only by either adjusting the aperture (the camera chooses the shutter speed) or shutter speed (the camera selects the aperture). I'll cover all these exposure modes later in the chapter.

How the D810 Calculates Exposure

Although it can make some good guesses based on how the brightness levels vary within a scene, your D810 has no way of knowing for sure what it's pointed at. So, it must make some assumptions and calculate the correct exposure based on its internal rules. One parameter is that the brightness of all—or part—of a scene will average down to a so-called middle gray tone. The conventional wisdom is that this tone is roughly 18-percent gray. Unfortunately, while the traditional 18 percent value is a middle gray in terms of what the eye sees, the D810 is actually calibrated for a slightly darker tone. This section explains how your D810 actually decides on an exposure in one of its semi-automatic (non-manual) modes.

Your D810 calculates exposure by measuring the light that passes through the lens and is bounced up by the mirror to an RGB exposure sensor with roughly 91,000 pixels, located near the focusing surface. The camera's exposure system is said to be able to detect light over a range of –2 to +19 EV at ISO 100, which translates into exposures from 120 seconds at f/8 to 1/8000th second at f/8. In everyday terms, EV –2 represents the illumination you might see outdoors at night under a full moon, while the brightest daytime scene you're likely to encounter (a snow scene in full daylight) would be EV 15. Your D810 is able to *detect* photons under an extremely broad EV span, although its ability to *capture* images is limited to a much smaller range.

The exposure is measured using a pattern you can select (more on that later) and based on the assumption that each area being measured reflects about the same amount of light as a neutral gray card that reflects a "middle" gray of about 12- to 18-percent reflectance. (The photographic "gray cards" you buy at a camera store have an 18-percent gray tone; your camera is calibrated to interpret a somewhat darker 12-percent gray; I'll explain more about this later, too.) That "average" 12- to 18-percent gray assumption is necessary, because different subjects reflect different amounts of light. In a photo containing, say, a white cat and a dark gray cat, the white cat might reflect five times as much light as the gray cat. An exposure based on the white cat will cause the gray cat to appear to be black, while an exposure based only on the gray cat will make the white cat washed out.

This is more easily understood if you look at some photos of subjects that are dark (they reflect little light), those that have predominantly middle tones, and subjects that are highly reflective. The next few figures show a simplified scale with a middle gray 18-percent tone, plus black and white patches, along with a human figure to illustrate how different exposure measurements actually do affect an exposure.

Correctly Exposed

The image shown in Figure 4.3 represents how a photograph might appear if the exposure were calculated by measuring the light reflecting from the middle gray patch, which, for the sake of illustration, we'll assume reflects approximately 12 to 18 percent of the light that strikes it. The exposure meter in the D810 sees an object that it thinks is a middle gray, calculates an exposure based on that, and the patch in the center of the strip is rendered at its proper tonal value. Best of all, because the resulting exposure is correct, the black patch at left and white patch at right are rendered properly as well.

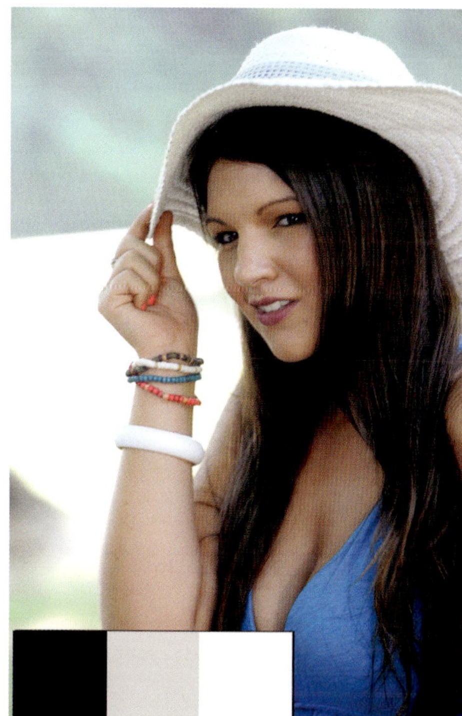

Figure 4.3 When exposure is calculated based on the middle-gray tone in the center of the card, the black and white patches are rendered accurately, too, and our model is properly exposed.

When you're shooting pictures with your D810, and the meter happens to base its exposure on a subject that averages that "ideal" middle gray, then you'll end up with similar (accurate) results. The camera's exposure algorithms are concocted to ensure this kind of result as often as possible, barring any unusual subjects (that is, those that are backlit, or have uneven illumination). The D810 has three different metering modes (described next), each of which is equipped to handle certain types of unusual subjects, as I'll outline.

Overexposed

Figure 4.4 shows what would happen if the exposure were calculated based on metering the leftmost, black patch. The light meter sees less light reflecting from the black square than it would see from a gray middle-tone subject, and so figures, "Aha! I need to add exposure to brighten this subject up to a middle gray!" That lightens the "black" patch, so it now appears to be gray.

But now the patch in the middle that was *originally* middle gray is overexposed and becomes light gray. And the white square at right is now seriously overexposed and loses detail in the highlights, which have become a featureless white. Our human subject is similarly overexposed.

Underexposed

The third possibility in this simplified scenario is that the light meter might measure the illumination bouncing off the white patch, and try to render that tone as a middle gray. A lot of light is reflected by the white square, so the exposure is *reduced*, bringing that patch closer to a middle gray

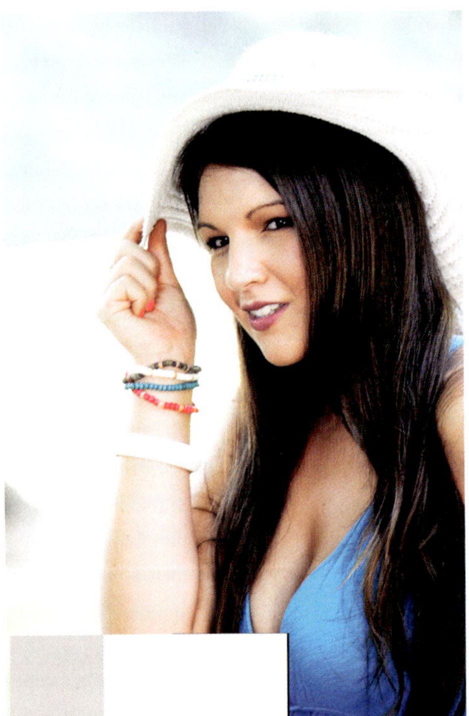

Figure 4.4 When exposure is calculated based on the black square at lower left, the black patch looks gray, the gray patch appears to be a light gray, and the white square is seriously overexposed.

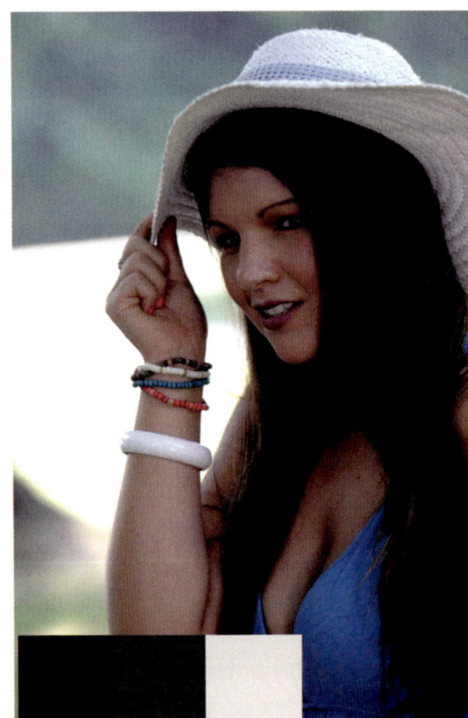

Figure 4.5 When exposure is calculated based on the white patch on the right, the other two patches, and the photo, are underexposed.

tone. The patches that were originally gray and black are now rendered too dark. Clearly, measuring the gray card—or a substitute that reflects about the same amount of light, is the only way to ensure that the exposure is precisely correct. (See Figure 4.5.)

As you can see, the ideal way to measure exposure is to meter from a subject that reflects 12 to 18 percent of the light that reaches it. If you want the most precise exposure calculations, the solution is to use a stand-in, such as the evenly illuminated gray card I mentioned earlier. The standard Kodak gray card reflects 18 percent of the light that reaches it, what is considered to be a middle gray. But, as I said earlier, your D810 is calibrated for a somewhat darker tone than that middle gray, roughly 12-percent gray, so you would need to *add* about one-half stop *more* exposure than the value metered from the card.

Another substitute for a gray card is the palm of a human hand (the backside of the hand is too variable). But a human palm, regardless of ethnic group, is even brighter than a standard gray card, so instead of one-half stop more exposure, you need to add one additional stop. That is, if your meter reading is 1/500th of a second at f/11, use 1/500th second at f/8 or 1/250th second at f/11 instead. (Both exposures are equivalent.)

If you actually wanted to use a gray card, place it in your frame near your main subject, facing the camera, and with the exact same even illumination falling on it that is falling on your subject. Then, use the Spot metering function (described in the next section) to calculate exposure. Of course, in most situations, it's not necessary to do this. Your camera's light meter will do a good job of calculating the right exposure, especially if you use the exposure tips in the next section. But, I felt that explaining exactly what is going on during exposure calculation would help you understand how your D810's metering system works.

To meter properly you'll want to choose both the *metering method* (how light is evaluated) and *exposure method* (how the appropriate shutter speeds and apertures are chosen). I'll describe both in the following sections.

MODES, MODES, AND MORE MODES

Call them modes or methods, the Nikon D810 seems to have a lot of different sets of options that are described using similar terms. Here's how to sort them out:

- **Metering method.** These modes determine the *parts of the image* within the 91,000-segment sensor array that are examined in order to calculate exposure. The D810 may look at many different points within the image, segregating them by zone (Matrix metering), examine the same number of points, but give greater weight to those located in the middle of the frame (Center-weighted metering), or evaluate only a limited number of points in a limited area (Spot metering).
- **Exposure method.** These modes determine *which* settings are used to expose the image. The D810 may adjust the shutter speed, the aperture, or both, or even ISO setting (if Auto ISO is active), depending on the method you choose.

WHY THE GRAY CARD CONFUSION?

Why are so many photographers under the impression that camera light meters are calibrated to the 18-percent "standard," rather than the true value, which may be 12 to 14 percent, depending on the vendor? You'll find this misinformation in an alarming number of places. I've seen the 18-percent "myth" taught in camera classes; I've found it in books, and even been given this wrong information from the technical staff of camera vendors. (They should know better—the same vendors' engineers who design and calibrate the cameras have the right figure.)

The most common explanation is that during a revision of Kodak's instructions for its gray cards in the 1970s, the advice to open up an extra half stop was omitted, and a whole generation of shooters grew up thinking that a measurement off a gray card could be used as-is. The proviso returned to the instructions by 1987, it's said, but by then it was too late. Next to me is a (c)2006 version of the instructions for KODAK Gray Cards, Publication R-27Q (still available in authorized versions from non-Kodak sources). The current directions read (with a bit of paraphrasing from me in italics):

- For subjects of normal reflectance increase the indicated exposure by 1/2 stop.
- For light subjects use the indicated exposure; for very light subjects, decrease the exposure by 1/2 stop. *(That is, you're measuring a subject that's lighter than middle gray.)*
- If the subject is dark to very dark, increase the indicated exposure by 1 to 1-1/2 stops. *(You're shooting a dark subject.)*

EXTERNAL METERS CAN BE CALIBRATED

The light meters built into your D810 are calibrated at the factory and can only be changed using the Fine Tune Optimal Exposure option (Custom Setting b6). But if you use a hand-held incident or reflective light meter, you *can* calibrate it, using the instructions supplied with your meter. Because a hand-held meter can be calibrated to the 18-percent gray standard (or any other value you choose), my rant about the myth of the 18-percent gray card doesn't apply.

Choosing a Metering Method

The D810 has four different schemes for evaluating the light received by its exposure sensors: Matrix (with several variations, depending on what lens you have attached), Center-weighted, Spot, and Highlight-weighted metering. Select the mode you want to use by pressing the metering mode button on the left shoulder of the camera, and rotating the main command dial. You'll be able to see which metering method is selected by noting the symbols shown in the top control panel LCD.

INSTANT SWITCHING

If you frequently use one metering method, but occasionally like to switch to another method on the fly, you can redefine the D810's Fn, Preview, or AE-L/AF-L buttons to shift to your alternate mode instantly. The Fn button can be programmed to provide Matrix metering, Center-weighted metering, or Spot metering (as well as other functions discussed in Chapter 12), using Custom Setting f4. The Preview button can be assigned that role with Custom Setting f5, while the same option is available for the AE-L/AF-L button in Custom Setting f6.

The really cool thing is that you can define one button for, say, Center-weighted metering, another one for Spot metering, and then set the main Metering mode switch to Matrix, and thus be able to switch among those three on a whim. I've done this as a way to compare the exposure settings of the three metering methods while composing a single image in the viewfinder. I've also found the capability useful when I'm, say, working with Matrix metering and want to zero in on a particular area of the frame temporarily using Spot metering. The indicators in the viewfinder will help you remember what metering mode you've switched to.

Here is what you need to know about each metering method:

Matrix Metering

For its various Matrix metering modes, the D810 slices up the frame into 91,000 different zones in an RGB (red/green/blue) array that covers most of the sensor area, shown in Figure 4.6. When Matrix metering is active, an icon appears in the monochrome status LCD (enlarged in the upper-left corner of the figure; in the viewfinder it's actually located at lower left). In all cases, the D810 evaluates the differences between the zones, and compares them with a built-in database of 30,000 actual images to make an educated guess about what kind of picture you're taking. For example, if the top sections of a picture are much lighter than the bottom portions, the algorithm can assume that the scene is a landscape photo with lots of sky. An image that includes most of the lighter portions in the center area may be a portrait. A typical image suitable for Matrix metering is shown in Figure 4.7.

The Nikon D810 also uses information other than brightness to make its evaluation:

- **3D Color Matrix metering III.** This metering mode is used by default when the D810 is equipped with a lens that has a type G, type E, or type D designator in its name, such as the 24-120mm f/4G ED VR AF-S Nikkor lens. The G after the f/4 is the giveaway. (More on lens nomenclature in Chapter 7.) The camera calculates exposure based on brightness, colors of the subject matter (that is, blue pixels in the upper part of the image are probably sky; green pixels in the lower half probably foliage), focus point, and distance information. The D810 is able to use that additional distance data to better calculate what kind of scene you have framed. For example, if you're shooting a portrait with a longer focal-length lens focused to about 5 to 12

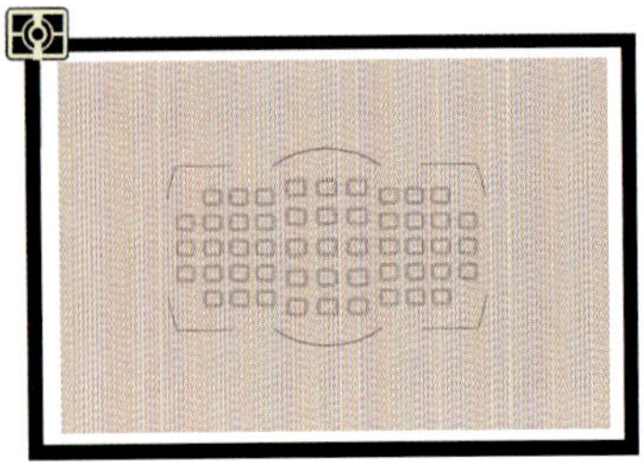

Figure 4.6 Matrix metering calculates exposure based on 91,000 points in the frame.

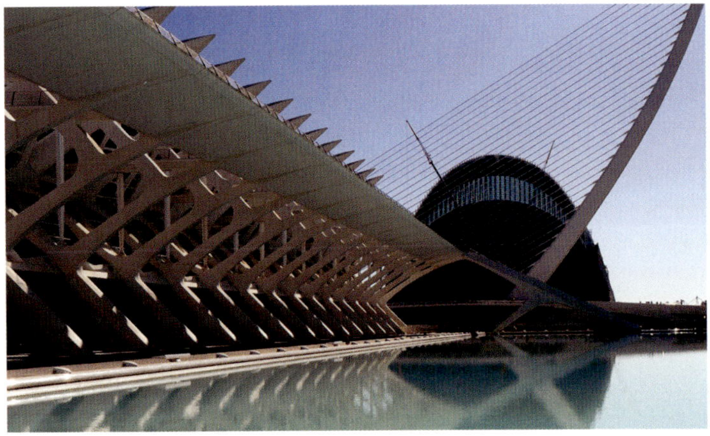

Figure 4.7 Complex scenes lend themselves to the exposure interpretation provided by Matrix metering.

feet from the camera, and the upper half of the scene is very bright, the camera assumes you would prefer to meter for the rest of the image, and discount the bright area. However, if the camera has a wide-angle lens attached and is focused at infinity, the D810 can assume you're taking a landscape photo and take the bright upper area into account to produce better-looking sky and clouds.

- **Color Matrix metering III.** If you have a non-G, non-E, or non-D lens that is equipped with a CPU chip (these are generally older lenses, although chips can sometimes be added to optics that lack them), the distance range is not used. Instead, only focus, brightness, and color information is taken into account to calculate an appropriate exposure.
- **Color Matrix metering.** If you're using a non-CPU lens (such as an older manual focus lens) and have specified the focal length and maximum aperture in the Setup menu (as described in Chapter 13), then the D810 uses plain old color Matrix metering, which evaluates exposure based *only* on brightness and color information detected in the scene.
- **With other lenses.** If you don't specify focal length or maximum aperture for a non-CPU lens, the D810 defaults to Center-weighted metering.

Matrix metering is best for most general subjects, because it is able to intelligently analyze a scene and make an excellent guess of what kind of subject you're shooting a great deal of the time. The camera can tell the difference between low-contrast and high-contrast subjects by looking at the range of differences in brightness across the scene. Because the D810 has a fairly good idea about what kind of subject matter you are shooting, it can underexpose slightly when appropriate to preserve highlight detail when image contrast is high. (It's often possible to pull detail out of shadows that are too dark using an image editor, but once highlights are converted to white pixels, they are gone forever.)

CAUTION

If you're using a strong filter, including a polarizing filter, split-color filter, or neutral-density filter (particularly a graduated neutral-density filter), you should switch from Matrix metering to Center-weighted, because the filter can affect the relationships between the different areas of the frame used to calculate a Matrix exposure. For example, a polarizing filter produces a sky that is darker than usual, hindering the Matrix algorithm's recognition of a landscape photo. Extra dark or colored filters disturb the color relationships used for color Matrix metering, too.

Center-Weighted Metering

In this mode, the exposure meter emphasizes a zone in the center of the frame to calculate exposure, as shown in Figure 4.8. I must apologize for the psychedelic color scheme, but color-coding was the easiest way to see the center-weighted coverage at the four optional spot sizes offered by the D810. About 75 percent of the exposure is based on that central area, and the remaining 25 percent of the exposure is based on the rest of the frame. The center-weighted area can take up as little as 5.8 percent or as much as 36 percent of the entire frame area. Your options are as follows:

- **8mm circle.** This smaller circle size, represented by the orange disc in Figure 4.8, covers 5.8% of the image frame. Use this size if the center area you want to emphasize is relatively small, but not small enough to switch to Spot metering (which has a 4mm metering circle). The distinction is a subtle one, and your choice of this size center-weighted circle will probably come from experience with the kinds of subjects you shoot. I find it useful for shooting plays with multiple performers, when Spot metering may be too narrow and you don't want to bother manipulating the position of the spot metering zone.

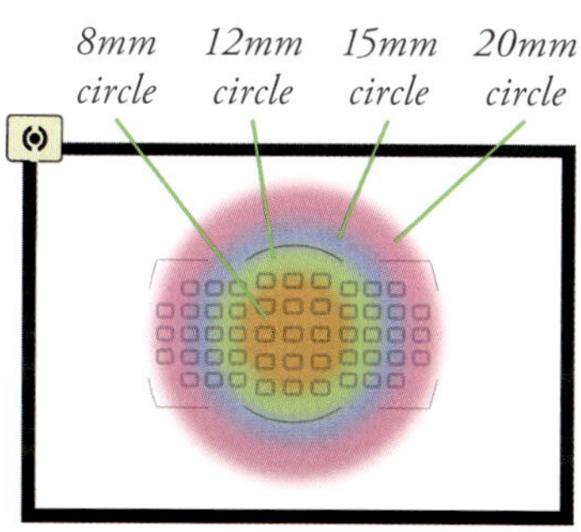

Figure 4.8 Center-weighted metering calculates exposure based on the full frame, but gives 75 percent of the weight to the center area using the circle size you select; the remaining 25 percent of the exposure is determined by the rest of the image area.

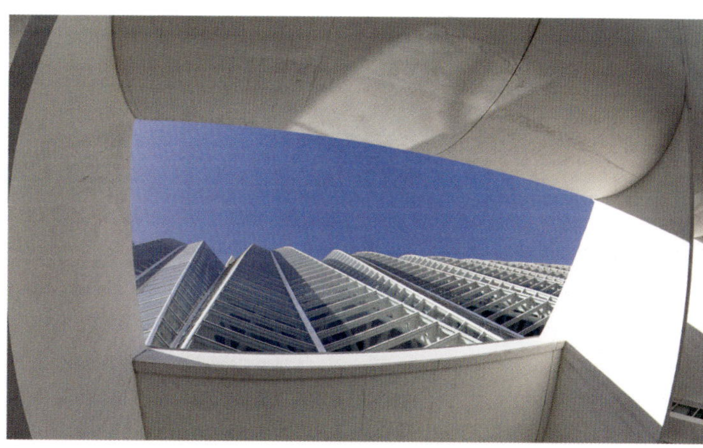

Figure 4.9 Scenes with the main subject in the center, surrounded by areas that are significantly darker or lighter, are perfect for Center-weighted metering.

- **12mm circle.** The default value for the center-weighted metering circle is 12mm, which extends out to the edges of the yellow area of the illustration, roughly 13 percent of the image area. If you're using a non-CPU lens, then this 12mm value is applied even if you've specified an 8mm, 15mm, or 20mm circle. It's a good all-around choice for most subjects that lend themselves to center weighting, like the one shown in Figure 4.9.
- **15mm circle.** This slightly larger circle covers about 20 percent of the frame area, extending out to the blue edges in the illustration. It is a good choice with larger subjects that are in bright or dark surroundings that might confuse Matrix metering.
- **20mm circle.** The largest center-weighted circle covers 36 percent of the frame area, out to the magenta edges of the disc in the figure. I use this when my subject occupies a large area in the viewfinder, but would like to ignore some distracting bright or dark spots at the edges or corners.
- **Averaging.** This setting isn't a center weighting at all, but, instead, averages the illumination of the entire frame to calculate exposure. It's a good choice for evenly lit subjects, without any remarkably bright or dark areas, or when you simply want a decent exposure under varied lighting conditions.

The theory with all center-weighted metering is that, for most pictures, the main subject will be located in the center. So, if the D810 reads the center portion and determines that the exposure for that region should be f/8 at 1/250th second, while the outer area, which is a bit darker, calls for f/4 at 1/125th second, the camera will give the center portion the most weight and arrive at a final exposure of f/5.6 at 1/250th second.

Center-weighting in general works best for portraits, architectural photos, backlit subjects with extra-bright backgrounds (such as snow or sand), and other pictures in which the most important subject is located in the middle of the frame. As the name suggests, the light reading is *weighted* toward the central portion, but information is also used from the rest of the frame. If your main subject is surrounded by very bright or very dark areas, the exposure might not be exactly right. However, this scheme works well in many situations if you don't want to use one of the other modes. This mode can be useful for close-ups of subjects like flowers, or for portraits. You can adjust the size of the center area assigned the greatest weight using Custom Setting b5, as described in Chapter 12. As I noted above, the available circles include 8mm, 12mm, 15mm, 20mm, and "Average" (which in effect, covers the entire screen to produce what is called Average metering).

Spot Metering

Spot metering is favored by those of us who have used a hand-held light meter to measure exposure at various points (such as metering highlights and shadows separately). However, you can use Spot metering in any situation where you want to individually measure the light reflecting from light, midtone, or dark areas of your subject—or any combination of areas.

This mode confines the reading to a limited 4mm area in the viewfinder, making up only 1.5 percent of the image, as shown in Figure 4.10. The circle is centered on the *current focus point* (which can be *any* of the 39 focus points, *not* just the center one shown in Figure 4.10), *but is larger than the focus point*, so don't fall into the trap of believing that exposure is being measured only within the brackets that represent the active focus point. This is the only metering method you can use to tell the D810 exactly where to measure exposure when using the optical viewfinder. However, if a non-CPU lens is mounted, or you have selected Auto-area AF, only the center focus point is used to spot meter.

You'll find Spot metering useful when you want to base exposure on a small area in the frame. If that area is in the center of the frame, so much the better. If not, you'll have to make your meter reading for an off-center subject using an appropriate focus point, and then lock exposure by pressing the shutter release halfway, or by pressing the AE-L/AF-L button. This mode is best for subjects where the background is significantly brighter or darker, as in Figure 4.11, a shot of bluesman Tab Benoit.

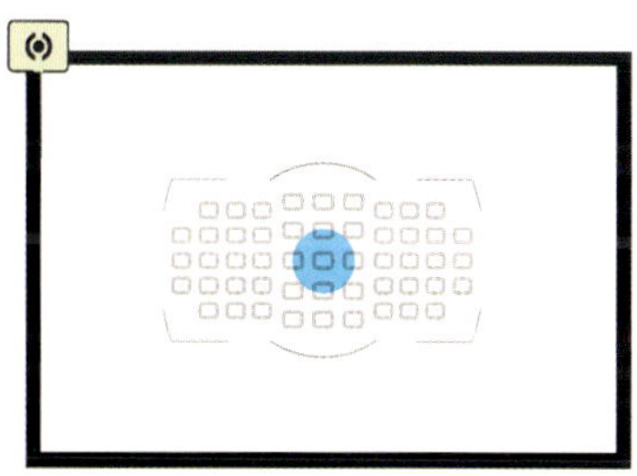

Figure 4.10 Spot metering calculates exposure based on a center spot that's only 1.5 percent of the image area, centered around the current focus point.

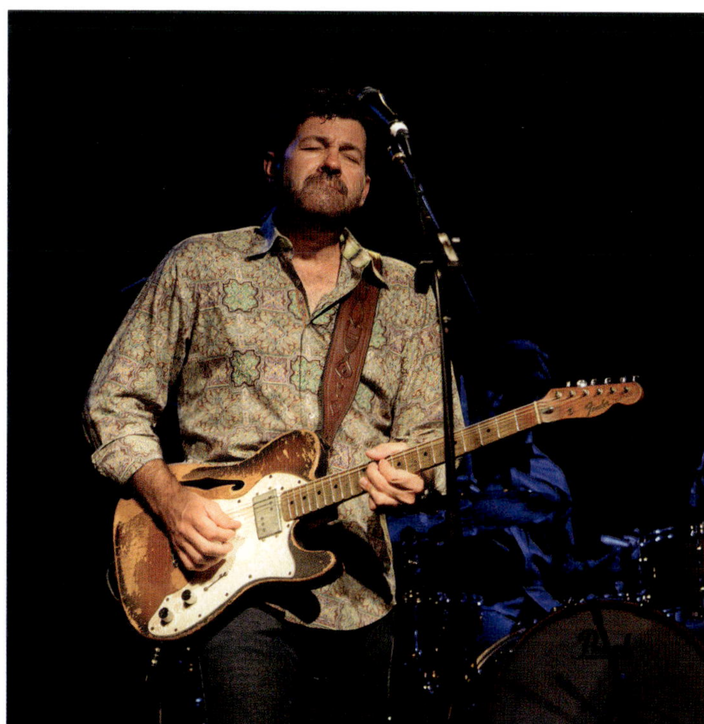

Figure 4.11 Spot metering allowed measuring exposure from the performer's shirt.

Using Spot Metering

Matrix and Center-weighted metering basically have few options to worry about. As I noted earlier, when using Center-weighted, you can vary the size of the center spot from 8mm up to 20mm, or select Averaging, and both Matrix and Center-weighted metering are affected by exposure compensation changes and Custom Setting b6 Fine-Tune Optimal Exposure adjustments. Spot metering, on the other hand, can benefit from your input in selecting the spot used. Here are some considerations to keep in mind:

- **Moving the spot.** Remember that you don't move the metering spot itself; the D810 uses the current focus spot. So, you must be using an AF area mode that allows changing the AF spot, which happens to be any of the AF area modes *except* Auto-area AF. In that mode, or if you are using a non-CPU lens, the center focus point is *always* used as the metering spot, and you cannot change it.
- **Choosing a compatible AF-area mode.** Press the button in the center of the focus mode switch on the front of the camera (just below the lens release button), and rotate the main command dial to switch to AF-C mode, then rotate the sub-command dial to cycle among Single-point, 9-point Dynamic-area, 21-point Dynamic-area, 51-point Dynamic-area, Group-area, or 3D-tracking (but *not* Auto). Use AF-S mode instead, and you can switch *only* between Auto and Single-point. All these AF-area modes except for Auto-area AF will allow you to switch the AF point to any of the 11 or 51 focus points in the viewfinder.
- **Available points.** The Single, 9, 21, and 51 numbers refer *only* to the total number of points centered around the selected point that will be used to determine focus, not the number of zones you can use to locate the focus point. That's determined by Custom Setting a8, where you can select either AF11 or AF51. If you've selected AF11, then your focus point selection is limited to 11 more widely spread AF points, and the metering spot is confined to those same points. I'll explain AF area modes in more detail in Chapter 5; it's necessary to drag an abbreviated discussion of the feature into this chapter only because the spot metering zone is dependent on where the AF point is located. You'll find more detail in the chapter that follows this one.
- **Wrap around.** You'll use the multi selector's directional buttons to move the AF point around within the focus brackets in the viewfinder—and the metering spot with it. The focus point's movement will stop at the left/right/top/bottom edges *unless* you've turned on focus point wrap-around in Custom Setting a7.
- **When using Auto-area AF.** If you've selected Auto-area AF, the center focus point will always be used—*even if the camera selects a different point for the autofocus function*. That's actually a positive: since in Auto-area AF mode you don't know what the focus spot will be until you press the shutter release halfway, it's *good* to know that the D810 will be using the center spot. While Spot metering is most useful when not using Auto-area AF, it still functions, albeit in a less flexible way.

Highlight-Weighted Metering

In this metering mode, the D810 examines your scene using that nifty 91,000-pixel RGB exposure sensor, just as it does using Matrix metering. However, with this new mode, the camera's Expeed 4 processor seeks out highlight areas of your image and bases exposure on a setting that will keep those highlights from being overexposed. Less emphasis ("weight") is given to non-highlight areas.

So, if you're shooting spotlit performers on-stage at a concert or play, the D810 is able to calculate the correct exposure using the performers, and ignoring, for the most part, the dark surroundings. Unlike the other metering modes, I can't offer you a diagram showing the coverage area, as it will vary all over the frame depending on the number and prominence of your subjects. Figure 4.11, earlier, does represent a typical scene that might be metered using this mode. You'd have your choice of measuring exposure in Spot mode, as described in the previous section, placing the metering spot on the dancer's face or shirt; or, you could select Highlight-weighted metering and allow the camera to identify the performer when figuring exposure. Your results might be similar with either, depending on how well you "placed" the Spot area and how cleverly the D810 sorts out your subject from the background. I tend to use Spot mode when the area I want to meter is clearly defined, and Highlight-weighted when there is a range of highlights that I'd like to preserve.

Choosing an Exposure Method

You'll find four methods for choosing the appropriate shutter speed and aperture, when using the semi-automatic/manual modes. (Scene modes, which use their own exposure biases, are described next.) You can choose among Program, Aperture-priority, Shutter-priority, or Manual options by pressing the mode button at top right of the camera, and rotating the main dial until the mode of your choice appears on the top control panel or in the viewfinder. Your decision on which is best for a given shooting situation will depend on things like your need for lots of (or less) depth-of-field, a desire to freeze action or allow motion blur, or how much noise you find acceptable in an image. Each of the D810's exposure methods emphasizes one aspect of image capture or another. This section introduces you to all four.

Aperture-Priority

In A mode, you specify the lens opening used, and the D810 selects the shutter speed. Aperture-priority is especially good when you want to use a particular lens opening to achieve a desired effect. Perhaps you'd like to use the smallest f/stop possible to maximize depth-of-field in a close-up picture. Or, you might want to work with a large f/stop to throw everything except your main subject out of focus, as in Figure 4.12. Maybe you'd just like to "lock in" a particular f/stop because it's the sharpest available aperture with that lens. Or, you might prefer to use, say, f/2.8 on a lens with a maximum aperture of f/1.4, because you want the best compromise between speed and sharpness.

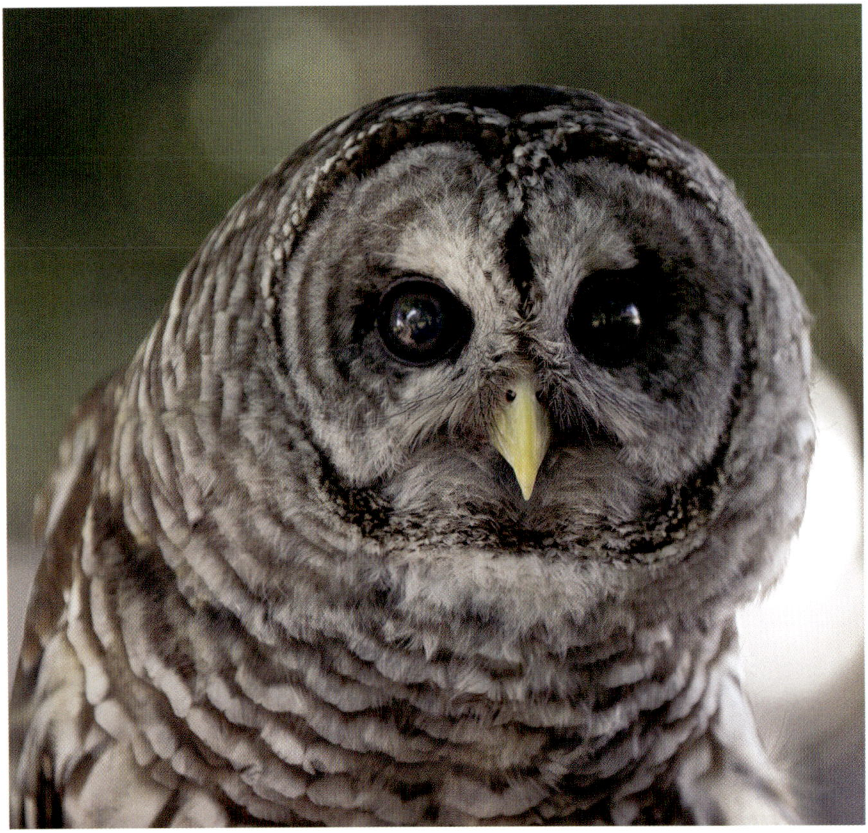

Figure 4.12
Use Aperture-priority to "lock in" a large f/stop when you want to blur the background.

Aperture-priority can even be used to specify a *range* of shutter speeds you want to use under varying lighting conditions, which seems almost contradictory. But think about it. You're shooting a soccer game outdoors with a telephoto lens and want a relatively high shutter speed, but you don't care if the speed changes a little should the sun duck behind a cloud. Set your D810 to A, and adjust the aperture until a shutter speed of, say, 1/1,000th second is selected at your current ISO setting. (In bright sunlight at ISO 400, that aperture is likely to be around f/11.) Then, go ahead and shoot, knowing that your D810 will maintain that f/11 aperture (for sufficient depth-of-field as the soccer players move about the field), but will drop down to 1/750th or 1/500th second if necessary should the lighting change a little.

When the shutter speed indicator in the viewfinder and the top-panel monochrome LCD blink, that indicates that the D810 is unable to select an appropriate shutter speed at the selected aperture and that over- and underexposure will occur at the current ISO setting. That's the major pitfall of using A: you might select an f/stop that is too small or too large to allow an optimal exposure with the available shutter speeds. For example, if you choose f/2.8 as your aperture and the illumination is quite bright (say, at the beach or in snow), even your camera's fastest shutter speed might not be able to cut down the amount of light reaching the sensor to provide the right exposure. Or, if you select f/8 in a dimly lit room, you might find yourself shooting with a very slow shutter speed that can cause blurring from subject movement or camera shake. Aperture-priority is best used by those with a bit of experience in choosing settings. Many seasoned photographers leave their D810 set on A all the time. The exposure indicator scale in the status panel and viewfinder indicate the amount of under- or overexposure.

When to use Aperture-priority:

- **General landscape photography.** The D810 is a great camera for landscape photography, of course, because its high resolution allows making huge, gorgeous prints, as well as smaller prints that are filled with eye-popping detail. Aperture-priority is a good tool for ensuring that your landscape is sharp from foreground to infinity, if you select an f/stop that provides maximum depth-of-field (without running into the D810's *diffraction* bug-a-boo, which I'll discuss in Appendix B).

  If you use A mode and select an aperture like f/11 or f/16, it's your responsibility to make sure the shutter speed selected is fast enough to avoid losing detail to camera shake, or that the D810 is mounted on a tripod. One thing that new landscape photographers fail to account for is the movement of distant leaves and tree branches. When seeking the ultimate in sharpness, go ahead and use Aperture-priority, but boost ISO sensitivity a bit, if necessary, to provide a sufficiently fast shutter speed, whether shooting hand-held or with a tripod.
- **Specific landscape situations.** Aperture-priority is also useful when you have no objection to using a long shutter speed, or, particularly, *want* the D810 to select one. Waterfalls are a perfect example. You can use A mode, set your camera to ISO 100, use a small f/stop, and let the camera select a longer shutter speed that will allow the water to blur as it flows. Indeed, you might need to use a neutral density to get a sufficiently long shutter speed. But Aperture-priority mode is a good start.
- **Portrait photography.** Portraits are the most common applications of selective focus. A medium-large aperture (say, f/5.6 or f/8) with a longer lens/zoom setting (in the 85mm-135mm range) will allow the background behind your portrait subject to blur. A *very* large aperture (I frequently shoot wide open with my 85mm f/1.4D AF Nikkor) lets you apply selective focus to your subject's *face.* With a three-quarters view of your subject, as long as her eyes are sharp, it's okay if the far ear or her hair is out of focus, as in Figure 4.13.
- **When you want to ensure optimal sharpness.** All lenses have an aperture or two at which they perform best, providing the level of sharpness you expect from a camera with the resolution of the D810. That's usually about two stops down from wide open, and thus will vary depending on the maximum aperture of the lens. My 85mm f/1.4 is good wide open, but it's even sharper at f/2.8 or f/4; I shoot my 70-200mm f/2.8 wide open at concerts, but, if I can use f/4 instead, I'll get better results. A relatively slow lens like my favorite travel lens—the super-compact Nikon 28-200mm f/3.5-5.6G ED IF zoom—really needs to be set at f/11 if I crank it out to its maximum focal length. Aperture-priority allows me to use each lens at its very best f/stop.

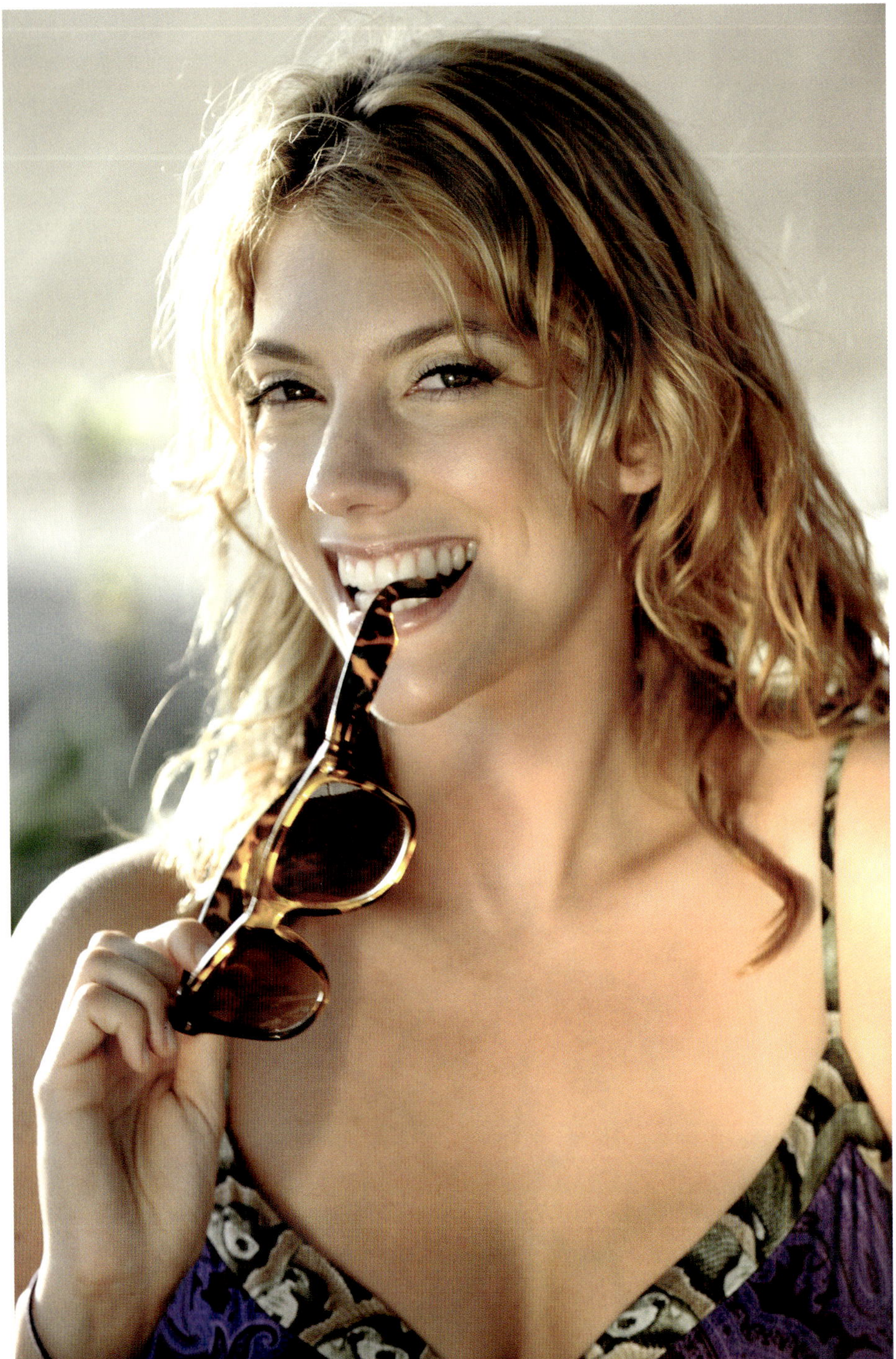

Figure 4.13 A large aperture is useful for portrait photography as long as the eyes are sharp.

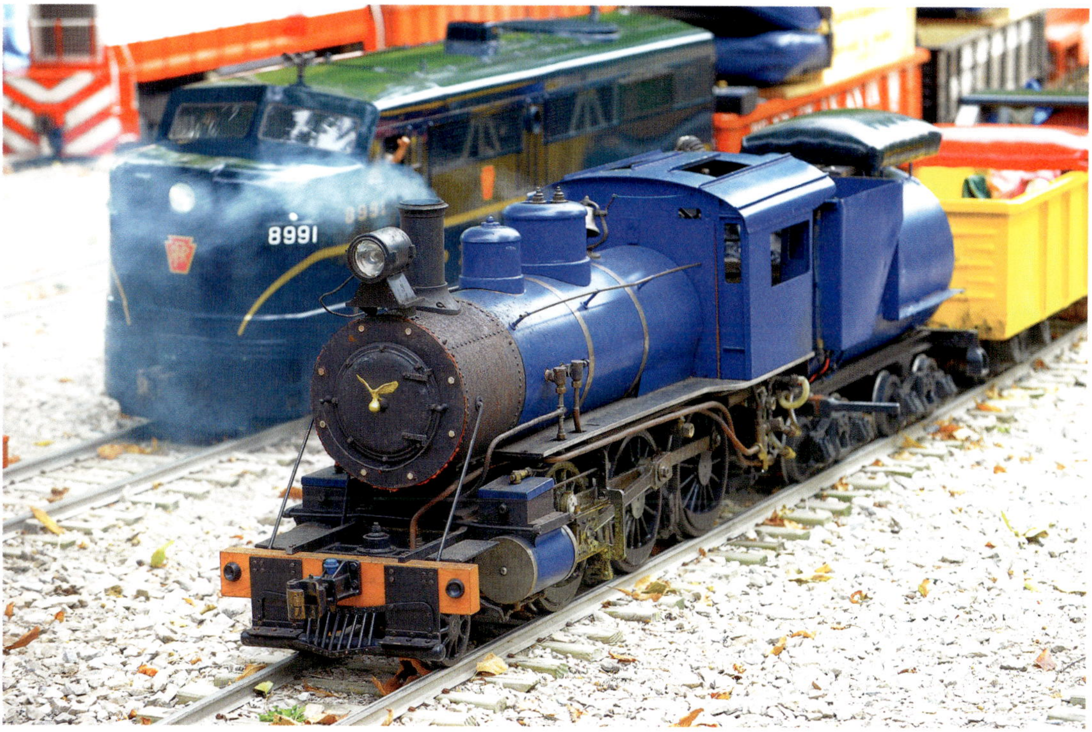

Figure 4.14 Extra depth-of-field came in handy when shooting close-ups of these miniature trains.

- **Close-up/Macro photography.** Depth-of-field is typically very shallow when shooting macro photos, and you'll want to choose your f/stop carefully. Perhaps you need the smallest aperture you can get away with to maximize depth-of-field. Or, you might want to use a wider stop to emphasize your subject, as I did with the photo of the miniature trains in Figure 4.14. A mode comes in very useful when shooting close-up pictures. Because macro work is frequently done with the D810 mounted on a tripod, and your close-up subjects, if not living creatures, may not be moving much, a longer shutter speed isn't a problem. Aperture-priority can be your preferred choice.

Shutter-Priority

Shutter-priority (S) is the inverse of Aperture-priority: you choose the shutter speed you'd like to use, and the camera's metering system selects the appropriate f/stop. Perhaps you're shooting action photos and you want to use the absolute fastest shutter speed available with your camera; in other cases, you might want to use a slow shutter speed to add some blur to an action photo that would be mundane if the action were completely frozen. (See the dancers in Figure 4.15, which was taken while rotating the camera around the lens axis during a 1/8 second exposure.) Shutter-priority mode gives you some control over how much action-freezing capability your digital camera brings to bear in a particular situation.

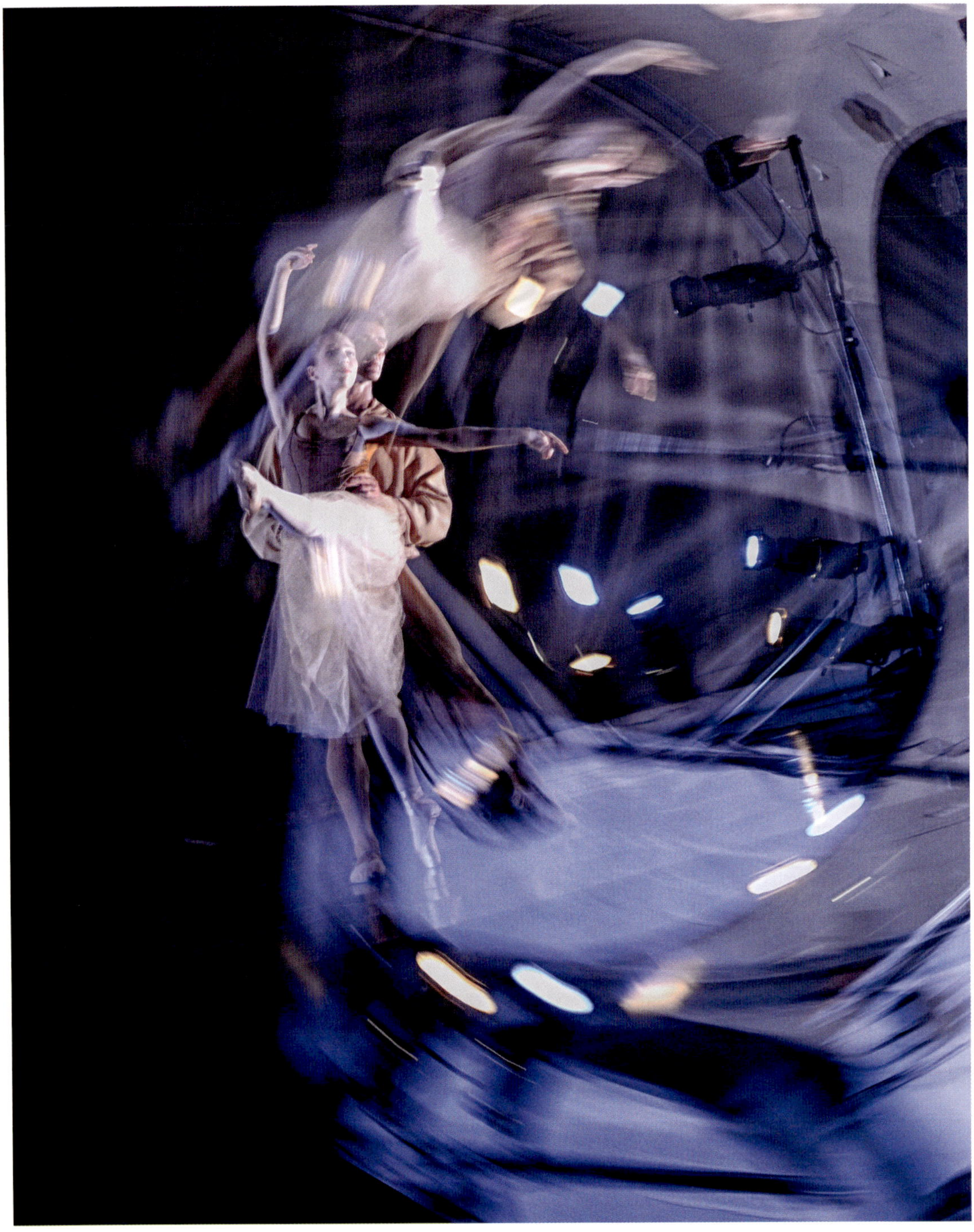

Figure 4.15 Lock the shutter at a specific speed to introduce blur into an action shot.

You'll also encounter the same problem as with Aperture-priority when you select a shutter speed that's too long or too short for correct exposure under some conditions. As in A mode, it's possible to choose an inappropriate shutter speed. If that's the case, the shutter speed indicator in the viewfinder and control panel LCD will blink.

When to use Shutter-priority:

- **To reduce blur from subject motion.** Set the shutter speed of the D810 to a higher value to reduce the amount of blur from subjects that are moving. The exact speed will vary depending on how fast your subject is moving and how much blur is acceptable. You might want to freeze a basketball player in mid-dunk with a 1/1,000th second shutter speed, or use 1/250th second to allow the spinning wheels of a motocross racer to blur a tiny bit to add the feeling of motion.
- **To add blur from subject motion.** There are times when you want a subject to blur, say, when shooting waterfalls with the camera set for a one- or two-second exposure in Shutter-priority mode.
- **To add blur from camera motion when *you* are moving.** Say you're panning to follow a pair of relay runners. You might want to use Shutter-priority mode and set the D810 for 1/60th second, so that the background will blur as you pan with the runners. The shutter speed will be fast enough to provide a sharp image of the athletes, as shown in Figure 4.16.

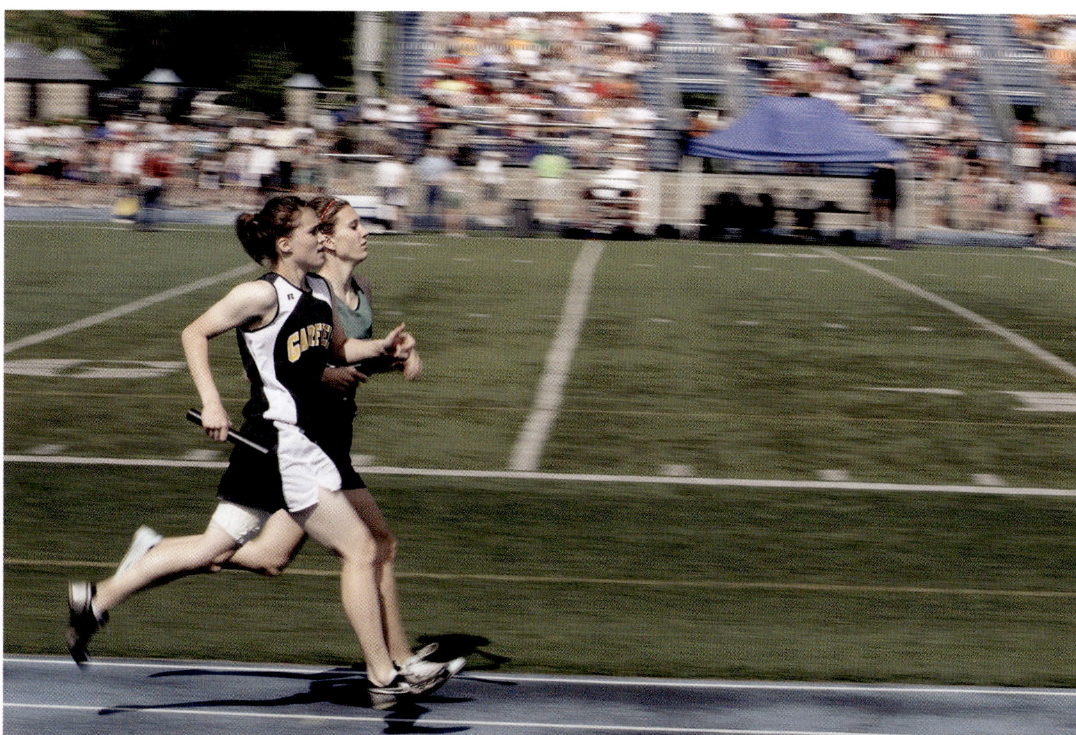

Figure 4.16 Shutter-priority allows you to specify a speed that will render a moving subject sharp as you pan.

- **To reduce blur from camera motion when *you* are moving.** In other situations, the camera may be in motion, say, because you're shooting from a moving train or auto, and you want to minimize the amount of blur caused by the motion of the camera. Shutter-priority is a good choice here, too.
- **Landscape photography hand-held.** If you can't use a tripod for your landscape shots, you'll still probably want the sharpest image possible. Shutter-priority can allow you to specify a shutter speed that's fast enough to reduce or eliminate the effects of camera shake. Just make sure that your ISO setting is high enough that the D810 will select an aperture with sufficient depth-of-field, too.
- **Concerts, stage performances.** I shoot a lot of concerts with my 70-200mm f/2.8 VR Nikkor lens, and have discovered that, when vibration reduction is taken into account, a shutter speed of 1/180th second is fast enough to eliminate camera shake that can result from hand-holding the D810 with this lens, and also to avoid blur from the movement of all but the most energetic performers. I use Shutter-priority and set the ISO so the camera will select an aperture in the f/4-5.6 range.

Program Mode

Program mode (P) uses the D810's built-in smarts to select the correct f/stop and shutter speed using a database of picture information that tells it which combination of shutter speed and aperture will work best for a particular photo. If the correct exposure cannot be achieved at the current ISO setting, the shutter speed and aperture will blink in the viewfinder and control panel. You can then boost or reduce the ISO to increase or decrease sensitivity.

The D810's recommended exposure can be overridden if you want. Use the EV (exposure value) setting feature (described later, because it also applies to S and A modes) to add or subtract exposure from the metered value. And, as I mentioned earlier in this chapter, in Program mode you can rotate the main command dial to change from the recommended setting to an equivalent setting (as shown previously in Table 4.1) that produces the same exposure, but using a different combination of f/stop and shutter speed.

This is called "Flexible Program" by Nikon. Rotate the main command dial left to reduce the size of the aperture (going from, say, f/4 to f/5.6), so that the D810 will automatically use a slower shutter speed (going from, say, 1/250th second to 1/125th second). Rotate the main command dial right to use a larger f/stop, while automatically producing a shorter shutter speed that provides the same equivalent exposure as metered in P mode. An asterisk appears next to the P in the control panel so you'll know you've overridden the D810's default program setting. Your adjustment remains in force until you rotate the main command dial until the asterisk disappears, or you switch to a different exposure mode, or turn the D810 off.

MAKING EV CHANGES

Sometimes you'll want more or less exposure than indicated by the D810's metering system. Perhaps you want to underexpose to create a silhouette effect, or overexpose to produce a high key look. It's easy to use the D810's exposure compensation system to override the exposure recommendations. Press the EV button on the top of the camera (just southeast of the shutter release). Then rotate the main command dial left to add exposure, and right to subtract exposure. The EV change you've made remains for the exposures that follow, until you manually zero out the EV setting. The EV plus/minus icon appears in the viewfinder and control panel to warn you that an exposure compensation change has been entered. You can increase or decrease exposure over a range of plus or minus five stops. (If you've activated Easy Exposure Compensation using Custom Setting b4, as described in Chapter 12, you don't have to hold down the EV button; rotating the main or sub-command dials alone changes the EV value when using Program, Aperture-priority, Shutter-priority, or Manual exposure modes.)

When to use Program mode priority:

- **When you're in a hurry to get a grab shot.** The D810 will do a pretty good job of calculating an appropriate exposure for you, without any input from you.
- **When you hand your camera to a novice.** Set the D810 to P, hand the camera to your friend, relative, or trustworthy stranger you meet in front of the Eiffel Tower, point to the shutter release button and viewfinder, and say, "Look through here, and press this button."
- **When no special shutter speed or aperture settings are needed.** If your subject doesn't require special anti- or pro-blur techniques, and depth-of-field or selective focus aren't important, use P as a general-purpose setting. You can still make adjustments to increase/decrease depth-of-field or add/reduce motion blur with a minimum of fuss.

Manual Exposure

Part of being an experienced photographer comes from knowing when to rely on your D810's automation (with P mode), when to go semi-automatic (with S or A), and when to set exposure manually (using M). Some photographers actually prefer to set their exposure manually, as the D810 will be happy to provide an indication of when its metering system judges your manual settings provide the proper exposure, using the analog exposure scale at the bottom of the viewfinder.

Manual exposure can come in handy in some situations. You might be taking a silhouette photo and find that none of the exposure modes or EV correction features give you exactly the effect you want. Set the exposure manually to use the exact shutter speed and f/stop you need. Or, you might be working in a studio environment using multiple flash units. The additional flash are triggered by slave devices (gadgets that set off the flash when they sense the light from another flash unit, or, perhaps from a radio or infrared remote control). Your camera's exposure meter doesn't compensate for the extra illumination, so you need to set the aperture manually.

METERING WITH OLDER LENSES

Older lenses that lack the CPU chip that tells the Nikon D810 what kind of lens is mounted can be used with Aperture-priority and Manual exposure modes only, assuming you've entered the Non-CPU Lens information in the Setup menu, as described in Chapter 7. If the D810 knows the maximum aperture of the lens, you can set the aperture using the lens's aperture ring, and, in A mode, the camera will automatically select an appropriate shutter speed. In Manual mode, you can set the aperture, and the analog exposure scale in the viewfinder will indicate when you've set the correct shutter speed manually. If a non-CPU lens is mounted and you try to set Program or Shutter-priority modes, the D810 switches to Aperture-priority automatically. The process works because the D810 camera body and other advanced Nikon models (from the old D200 on up through the D4) have a mechanical linkage built into the lens mount that tells the camera when the f/stop has been changed. Less advanced Nikon digital cameras, including the D5100 and D3200, lack this linkage and cannot meter with non-CPU lenses.

Because, depending on your proclivities, you might not need to set exposure manually very often, you should still make sure you understand how it works. Fortunately, the D810 makes setting exposure manually very easy. Just press the mode button and rotate the main command dial to change to Manual mode, and then turn the main command dial to set the shutter speed, and the sub-command dial to adjust the aperture. Press the shutter release halfway or press the AE lock button, and the exposure scale in the viewfinder shows you how far your chosen setting diverges from the metered exposure.

When to use Manual exposure:

- **When working in the studio.** If you're working in a studio environment, you generally have total control over the lighting and can set exposure exactly as you want. The last thing you need is for the D810 to interpret the scene and make adjustments of its own. Use M, and shutter speed, aperture, and (as long as you don't use ISO-Auto) the ISO setting are totally up to you.
- **When using non-dedicated flash.** The Nikon Creative Lighting System (CLS) is cool, and can even be used to coordinate use of your D810's internal flash with external compatible dedicated flash units, like the SB-910. But if you're working with non-CLS flash units, particularly studio flash plugged into the D810's PC/X connector, the camera has no clue about the intensity of the flash, so you'll have to dial in the appropriate aperture manually.
- **If you're using a hand-held light meter.** Determining that appropriate aperture, both for flash exposures and shots taken under continuous lighting, can be determined by a hand-held light meter, flash meter, or combo meter that measures both kinds of illumination. With an external meter, you can measure highlights, shadows, backgrounds, or additional subjects separately, and use Manual exposure to make your settings.

- **When you want to outsmart the metering system.** Your D810's metering system is "trained" to react to unusual lighting situations, such as backlighting, extra bright illumination, or low-key images with murky shadows. In many cases, it can counter these "problems" and produce a well-exposed image. But what if you don't *want* a well-exposed image? Manual exposure allows you to produce silhouettes in backlit situations, wash out all the middle tones to produce a luminous look, or underexpose to create a moody or ominous dark-toned photograph.

Adjusting Exposure with ISO Settings

Another way of adjusting exposures is by changing the ISO sensitivity setting. Sometimes photographers forget about this option, because the common practice is to set the ISO once for a particular shooting session (say, at ISO 200 for bright sunlight outdoors, or ISO 800 when shooting indoors) and then forget about ISO. ISOs higher than ISO 200 or 400 are seen as "bad" or "necessary evils." However, changing the ISO is a valid way of adjusting exposure settings, particularly with the Nikon D810, which produces good results at ISO settings that create grainy, unusable pictures with some other camera models.

Indeed, I find myself using ISO adjustment as a convenient alternate way of adding or subtracting EV when shooting in Manual mode, and as a quick way of choosing equivalent exposures when in Program or Shutter-priority or Aperture-priority modes. For example, I've selected a Manual exposure with both f/stop and shutter speed suitable for my image using, say, ISO 200. I can change the exposure in 1/3 stop increments by holding down the ISO button located on the left shoulder of the camera atop the release mode dial, and spinning the main command dial one click at a time. The difference in image quality/noise at ISO 200 is negligible if I dial in ISO 160 or ISO 125 to reduce exposure a little, or change to ISO 250 or 320 to increase exposure. I keep my preferred f/stop and shutter speed, but still adjust the exposure.

Or, perhaps, I am using S mode and the metered exposure at ISO 200 is 1/500th second at f/11. If I decide on the spur of the moment I'd rather use 1/500th second at f/8, I can press the ISO button and spin the main command dial three clicks left to switch to ISO 100. Of course, it's a good idea to monitor your ISO changes, so you don't end up at ISO 6400 accidentally. An ISO indicator appears in the control panel and in the viewfinder to remind you what sensitivity setting has been dialed in.

ISO settings can, of course, also be used to boost or reduce sensitivity in particular shooting situations. The D810 can use ISO settings from ISO 100 up to ISO 6400, plus Lo 1.0 and Lo 2.0 (ISO 80/ISO 50 equivalent), and Hi 1.0 and Hi 2.0 (ISO 12800 and 25600 equivalent). The camera can also adjust the ISO automatically as appropriate for various lighting conditions. When you choose the Auto ISO setting in the Shooting menu, as described in Chapter 8, the D810 adjusts the sensitivity dynamically to suit the subject matter, based on minimum shutter speed and ISO limits you have prescribed. As I note in Chapter 11, you should use Auto ISO cautiously if you don't want the D810 to use an ISO higher than you might otherwise have selected.

Dealing with Noise

Visual image noise is that random grainy effect that some like to use as a special effect, but which, most of the time, is objectionable because it robs your image of detail even as it adds that "interesting" texture. Noise is caused by two different phenomena: high ISO settings and long exposures.

High ISO noise commonly appears when you raise your camera's sensitivity setting above ISO 400. With the Nikon D810, noise may become visible at ISO 1600, and is often fairly noticeable at ISO 3200. At ISO 6400 and above, noise is usually quite bothersome. Nikon tips you off that settings higher than ISO 12800 may be tools used in special circumstances only by labeling them Hi 0.3, Hi 0.7, Hi 1, and Hi 2 (equivalent to ISO 16000, 21400, 25600, and 51200). You can expect noise and increase in contrast in any pictures taken at these lofty ratings. You can also expect some higher contrast when using the low-end settings below ISO 64: Lo 0.3, Lo 0.7, and Lo 1.0 (ISO 32 equivalent).

High ISO noise appears as a result of the amplification needed to increase the sensitivity of the sensor. While higher ISOs do pull details out of dark areas, they also amplify non-signal information randomly, creating noise. You'll find a High ISO NR choice in the Shooting menu, where you can specify High, Norm, or Low noise reduction, or turn the feature off entirely. Because noise reduction tends to soften the grainy look while robbing an image of detail, you may want to disable the feature if you're willing to accept a little noise in exchange for more details.

A similar noisy phenomenon occurs during long time exposures, which allow more photons to reach the sensor, increasing your ability to capture a picture under low light conditions. However, the longer exposures also increase the likelihood that some pixels will register random phantom photons, often because the longer an imager is "hot," the warmer it gets, and that heat can be mistaken for photons. There's also a special kind of noise that CMOS sensors like the one used in the D810 are potentially susceptible to. With a CCD, the entire signal is conveyed off the chip and funneled through a single amplifier and analog-to-digital conversion circuit. Any noise introduced there is, at least, consistent. CMOS imagers, on the other hand, contain millions of individual amplifiers and A/D converters, all working in unison. Because these circuits don't necessarily all process in precisely the same way all the time, they can introduce something called fixed-pattern noise into the image data.

Fortunately, Nikon's electronics geniuses have done an exceptional job minimizing noise from all causes in the D810. Even so, you might still want to apply the optional long exposure noise reduction that can be activated using Long Exp. NR in the Shooting menu, where the feature can be turned On or Off. This type of noise reduction involves the D810 taking a second, blank exposure, and comparing the random pixels in that image with the photograph you just took. Pixels that coincide in the two represent noise and can safely be suppressed. This noise reduction system, called *dark frame subtraction,* effectively doubles the amount of time required to take a picture, and is used only for exposures longer than one second. Noise reduction can reduce the amount of detail in your picture, as some image information may be removed along with the noise. So, you might want to use this feature with moderation.

You can also apply noise reduction to a lesser extent using Photoshop, and when converting RAW files to some other format, using your favorite RAW converter, or an industrial-strength product like Noise Ninja (www.picturecode.com) to wipe out noise after you've already taken the picture.

Bracketing

Bracketing is a method for shooting several consecutive exposures using different settings, as a way of improving the odds that one will be exactly right. Alternatively, bracketing can be used to create a series of photos with slightly different exposures (or white balances) in anticipation that one of the exposures will be "better" from a creative standpoint. For example, bracketing can supply you with a normal exposure of a backlit subject, one that's "underexposed," producing a silhouette effect, and a third that's "overexposed" to create still another look.

Before digital cameras took over the universe, it was common to bracket exposures, shooting, say, a series of three photos at 1/125th second, but varying the f/stop from f/8 to f/11 to f/16. In practice, smaller than whole-stop increments were used for greater precision, and lenses with apertures that were set manually commonly had half-stop detents on their aperture rings, or could easily be set to a mid-way position between whole f/stops. It was just as common to keep the same aperture and vary the shutter speed, although in the days before electronic shutters, film cameras often had only whole increment shutter speeds available.

Today, cameras like the D810 can bracket exposures much more precisely, and bracket white balance and Active D-Lighting (described later in this chapter) as well. While WB bracketing is sometimes used when getting color absolutely correct in the camera is important, autoexposure bracketing is used much more often. When this feature is activated, the D810 takes a series of consecutive photos: starting with the metered "correct" exposure, then progressing to shots with less exposure, and additional shots with more exposure, using an increment of your choice up to +1/–1 stops. (Choose between increments by setting Custom Setting b2.) In A mode, the shutter speed will change, while in S mode, the aperture will change as the bracketed exposures are made.

ACTIVATING BRACKETING

Once you've set up the type of bracketing you want to use, as described next, taking a bracketed set of exposures is easy. When bracketing is active, to initiate exposing a set just press the Bracketing Burst button. (By default the Fn button, but you can also define the Preview and AE-L/AF-L buttons to perform this function. Use Custom Setting f5, f6, or f7 to define the Bracketing Burst button.) Once the burst button is pressed, all shots in the set will be taken each time you press the shutter release button once.

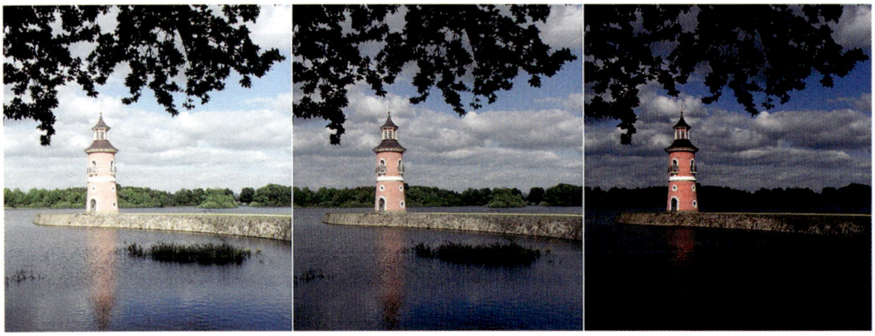

Figure 4.17
Bracketing can give you three different exposures of the same subject.

Setting up autoexposure bracketing parameters is trickier than it needs to be, but you can follow these steps to get results like those shown in Figure 4.17:

1. **Choose type of bracketing.** First, select the type of bracketing you want to do, using Custom Setting e6 (Auto Bracketing Set), as explained in Chapter 12. You can select autoexposure and flash, autoexposure only, flash only, white balance only, and ADL bracketing.

   If you plan on shooting in Manual exposure mode, you can specify how bracketing is performed using Custom Setting e7. Your choices there are flash+shutter speed, flash+shutter speed+aperture, flash+aperture, or flash only. White balance and ADL bracketing are not available in Manual exposure mode.
2. **Choose bracketing order.** With Custom Setting e8 you can select MTR > Under > Over or Under > MTR > Over bracket orders. I prefer the latter order, as it makes certain types of manual HDR exposures easier. You can, for example, shoot nine bracketed exposures, each one stop different from the last, and then delete the even-numbered shots to end up with five bracketed images that are two stops apart. It's easier to drop the correct exposures if you use the Under > MTR > Over bracket order.
3. **Press bracketing setting button.** Press and hold the BKT button on the top-left side of the D810 lens mount housing.
4. **Select number of bracketed exposures.** With the BKT setting button held down, rotate the main command dial to choose the number of shots in the sequence, 0 (which turns bracketing off), 2, 3, 5, 7, or 9 bracketed shots. Rotate the main command dial counterclockwise to center the bracketed shots around the metered exposure (the 2 value is not available if you do this), and rotate it clockwise to choose 2 or 3 bracketed exposures concentrated either over or under the metered exposure. This is the most confusing aspect of bracketing, so I'll explain how this works in more detail next.
5. **Choose bracket increment.** With the setting button still held down, rotate the sub-command dial to choose the exposure increment: 1/3, 2/3, or 1 EV (unless you've redefined the exposure compensation increment to 1/2 or 1 EV in Custom Setting b2).
6. **Frame and shoot.** As you take your photos, the camera will vary exposure, flash level, or white balance for each image, based on the bracketing "program" you selected, and in the order you

specified in Custom Setting e7. In Single-frame mode, you'll need to press the shutter release button the number of times you specified for the exposures in your bracketed burst (2, 3, 5, 7, or 9 shots). I've found it easy to forget that I am shooting bracketed pictures, stop taking my sequence, and then wonder why the remaining pictures in my defined burst are "incorrectly" exposed. To avoid that, I often set the D810 to one of the two continuous shooting modes, so that all my bracketed pictures are taken at once. The D810 does provide indicators on the monochrome LCD (a BKT indicator as well as a bracketing progress indicator), but they may be overlooked.

7. **Turn bracketing off.** When you're finished bracketing shots, remember to press the bracket setting button and rotate the main command dial until the number of shots in the sequence is 0F, and the BKT indicator is no longer displayed.

More on Bracketing

Unless you have previous experience with Nikon's bracketing procedures, the process can seem a little confusing, particularly when it comes time to select the number of bracketed exposures. That's because Nikon combines two functions in one setting: *how many actual shots in the burst* and *where those shots are placed within the overall scheme of exposure.* Both those parameters are set when you hold down the BKT button (on the front of the camera, just fore of the D810 logo) and spin the main command dial. That's an entirely different operation than setting the exposure increment, which, as I said, is accomplished by holding down the BKT setting button and spinning the sub-command dial.

Here's what happens. When you go to set the number of bracketed exposures, there are two "modes" based on which direction you rotate the main command dial:

- **Rotate main command dial counterclockwise.** The number of exposures increases from 0 to 3, 5, 7, or 9 images. In *all* cases, the bracketed exposure values will be evenly spaced on either side of the metered exposure, using the increment you have selected separately (with the sub-command dial). Suppose you have already chosen 1/3 EV as your increment, and then rotate the main command dial counterclockwise. At the 3F 0.3 position, the exposures will be taken at the metered exposure, plus 1/3 stop less and 1/3 stop more (three shots in all). At the 5F 0.3 position, the exposures will be taken at the metered exposure, plus 1/3 stop and 2/3 stop less, as well as 1/3 stop and 2/3 stop more (five shots in all). The bracketed exposures are evenly spread on either side of the metered exposure.
- **Rotate the main command dial clockwise.** In that case, the first setting that appears on the control panel is -2F 0.3, which will tell the D810 to shoot one picture at the measured exposure, and one at 1/3 stop less (two shots). The next click produces a readout of +2F 0.3, which produces one shot at the metered exposure, and one at 1/3 stop *more.* You can also select -3F 0.3 or +3F 0.3. In all cases, the additional bracketed shots are biased either toward under- or over-exposure. That's as far as the clockwise spin to the right will take you. There are no -5F or +5F or larger numeric settings available.

A lot of people find this concept confusing, because the Nikon manual discusses these variations (which it calls "bracketing programs") in the section that follows the description of exposure increments, which are set with the *sub*-command dial. Yes, the exposure increment you select does affect the "program," but the number of shots and distribution of the bracketed exposures is an entirely different concept, and is controlled only by spinning the *main* command dial.

White Balance Bracketing

When you choose white balance bracketing, the D810 does not take multiple exposures. It takes one exposure and saves a series of JPEG images using different color balances. That makes sense, if you think about it. The camera always starts off with a RAW exposure first, no matter whether the camera is set to JPEG, RAW, or RAW+JPEG. If you've selected JPEG-only mode, the camera converts the initial RAW exposure to JPEG format using the settings you've opted for in the camera, and then discards the RAW data. In RAW mode, the camera stores the RAW data as an NEF file, and also creates a Basic JPEG version of the image that is embedded in the RAW file as a thumbnail. That thumbnail is what you're actually looking at on the back-panel LCD when you review your pictures; you never actually see the RAW file itself until you import it into your image editor. Your computer may also use the embedded JPEG file, when it displays a RAW image. Finally, if you save in RAW+JPEG, you end up with two files: the NEF RAW file (with its embedded JPEG image) and a separate JPEG file at the quality level you specify (Fine, Normal, or Basic).

Since the RAW file that the camera initially captures contains all the digital information captured during exposure, when you specify white balance bracketing, the D810 needs to take only one picture—and then save a JPEG file at each of the required white balance settings. One snap, and you get two to nine JPEG files at the quality level you specified, bracketed as you directed. Very slick. As you might guess, WB bracketing is applied only to JPEG files; you can't specify WB bracketing if you've chosen RAW or RAW+JPEG. RAW files created are always unmodified, and will be converted according to the white balance settings you opted for in the camera when the photo is imported into your image editor (if you make no white balance changes during importation).

White balance bracketing produces JPEG files that vary, not by f/stops (which is the case with exposure bracketing), but by units called *mireds* (micro reciprocal degrees) that are used to specify color temperature. You don't really need to understand mireds at all, other than to know that WB bracketing varies the color temperature of your images by 5, 10, or 15 mireds when you select increments of 1, 2, or 3, respectively. Changes are made only in the amber-blue range; bracketing isn't applied to the green-magenta color bias.

As with exposure bracketing, hold down the bracket button and spin the main command dial to select the WB program (for example, off, two shots/amber bias, two shots/blue bias, three shots, amber/+blue bias, and the sub-command dial to choose the increment). The whole process can be a little non-intuitive, so Table 4.2 might be a help.

Table 4.2 White Balance Bracketing Programs

Rotate main command dial to select program	Rotate sub-command dial to select increment	Number of exposures saved	Bias	Bracket order
OF		WB bracketing off	N/A	N/A
b2F	1/2/3 (5/10/15 mireds)	2	Blue	None->1 increment blue
b3f	1/2/3 (5/10/15 mireds)	2	Blue	1 increment blue->None-> 2 increments blue
A2F	1/2/3 (5/10/15 mireds)	2	Amber	None->1 increment amber
a3F	1/2/3 (5/10/15 mireds)	3	Amber	1 increment amber->None-> 2 increment amber
3F	1/2/3 (5/10/15 mireds)	3	Amber/ Blue	None->1 increment amber-> 1 increment blue
5F	1/2/3 (5/10/15 mireds)	5	Amber/ Blue	None->2 increments amber-> 1 increment amber-> 1 increment blue-> 2 increments blue
7F	1/2/3 (5/10/15 mireds)	7	Amber/ Blue	None->3 increments amber-> 2 increments amber-> 1 increment amber-> 1 increment blue-> 2 increments blue-> 3 increments blue
9F	1/2/3 (5/10/15 mireds)	9	Amber/ Blue	None->4 increments amber-> 3 increments amber-> 2 increments amber-> 1 increment amber-> 1 increment blue-> 2 increments blue-> 3 increments blue-> 4 increments blue

ADL Bracketing

Active D-Lighting is a feature that improves the rendition of detail in highlights and shadows when you're photographing high contrast scenes. If you're taking photos in a contrasty environment, Active D-Lighting can automatically improve the apparent dynamic range of your image as you shoot, without additional effort on your part. When shooting non-bracketed ADL images, or bracketed ADL sets, you can specify five different ADL "intensities": Auto, Extra High, High, Normal, or Low. You can read more about how Active D-Lighting works in Chapter 11.

To initiate Active D-Lighting bracketing, select it from Custom Setting e6, Auto Bracketing Set. It's the last entry in the list. Thereafter, press and hold the BKT button you've specified, and follow these steps:

1. **Choose number of shots in sequence.** While holding the BKT button, rotate the main command dial and choose 0 (Off), 2, 3, 4, or 5 shots. At any setting other than 0, an ADL-BKT symbol will appear in the top-panel monochrome display, and BKT will be shown in the D810's viewfinder.
   - **Two shots.** One shot with ADL off and another at the selected value will be taken.
   - **Three shots.** One shot with ADL off, and one shot with Low and one with Normal Active D-Lighting will be taken.
   - **Four shots.** One shot with ADL off, and one each with Low, Normal, and High Active D-Lighting will be taken.
   - **Five shots.** One shot with ADL off, and one each at the Low, Normal, High, and Extra High settings will be captured.
2. **Choose value for a two-shot ADL set.** Selecting 3, 4, or 5 shots in the set uses several different ADL intensities automatically. If you select 2, one shot will have ADL turned off, and you can specify the intensity for the second shot by rotating the sub-command dial. You'll see A, L, N, H, or H+ (for Auto, Low, Normal, High, and Extra High) displayed on the monochrome status LCD.
3. **Take your shots.** Press the shutter release to produce an ADL-bracketed set. If the D810 is set to C_L or C_H the entire bracketed sequence will be taken, and then the camera will stop. Press the shutter release again to take another bracketed set. Note that ADL bracketing is "sticky"; if you switch the camera off before the sequence is complete, the set will resume the next time the D810 is turned on.
4. **Cancel bracketing.** Press the BKT button and rotate the main command dial until 0 is displayed as the number of shots in the sequence.

Working with HDR

High dynamic range (HDR) photography is quite the rage these days, and entire books have been written on the subject. It's not really a new technique—film photographers have been combining multiple exposures for ages to produce a single image of, say, an interior room while maintaining detail in the scene visible through the windows.

It's the same deal in the digital age. Suppose you wanted to photograph a dimly lit room that had a bright window showing an outdoors scene. Proper exposure for the room might be on the order of 1/60th second at f/2.8 at ISO 200, while the outdoors scene probably would require f/11 at 1/400th second. That's almost a 7 EV step difference (approximately 7 f/stops) and well beyond the dynamic range of any digital camera, including the Nikon D810.

Until camera sensors gain much higher dynamic ranges (which may not be as far into the distant future as we think), special tricks like Active D-Lighting and HDR photography will remain basic tools. With the Nikon D810, you can create in-camera HDR exposures, or shoot HDR the old-fashioned way—with separate bracketed exposures that are later combined in a tool like Photomatix or Adobe's Merge to HDR image-editing feature. I'm going to show you how to use both.

Auto HDR

The D810's in-camera HDR feature is simple, not particularly flexible, but still surprisingly effective in creating high dynamic range images. It's also remarkably easy to use. Although it combines only two images to create a single HDR photograph, in some ways it's as good as the manual HDR method I'll describe in the section after this one. For example, it allows you to specify an exposure differential of three stops/EV between the two shots, whereas the D810 shooting bracketed exposures is limited to one EV between shots. (I'll show you how to overcome that limitation easily.)

Figure 4.18 and 4.19 illustrate how the two shots that the D810's HDR feature merges might look. There is a three-stop differential between the underexposed image at left, and the overexposed image at right. The in-camera HDR processing is able to combine the two to derive an image similar to the one shown in Figure 4.20, which has a much fuller range of tones.

To use the D810's HDR feature, just follow these steps. The feature does not work if you have selected RAW or RAW+JPEG formats, or have one of the bracketing features turned on.

1. **Activate the menu.** Press the MENU button and navigate to the Shooting menu, represented by a camera icon. (If you need more help using the D810's menu system, you'll find an introduction at the beginning of Chapter 11.)
2. **Scroll down to HDR.** Press the right multi selector button. The screen shown in Figure 4.21 appears.

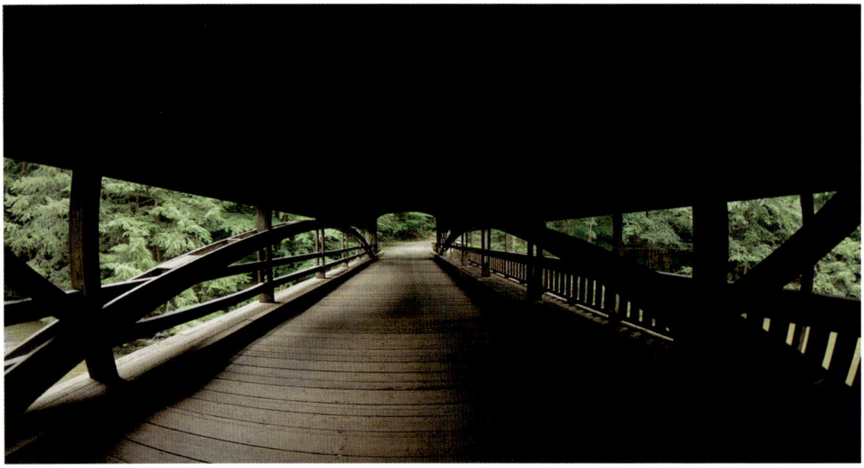

Figure 4.18
The underexposed image can be combined…

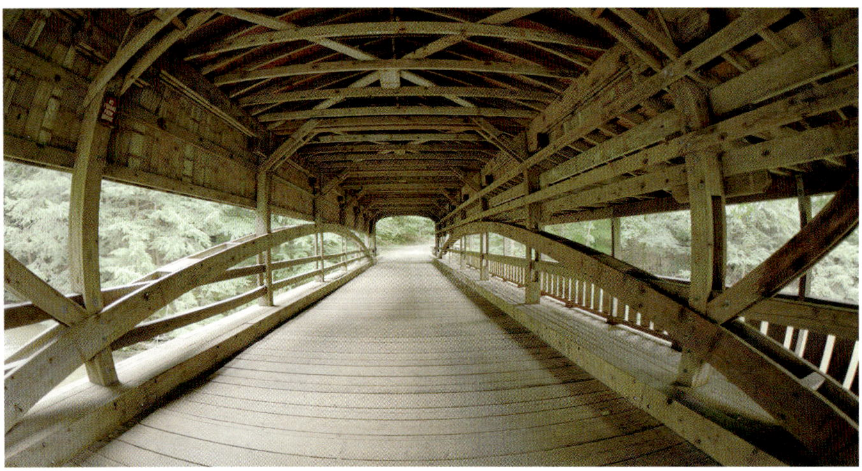

Figure 4.19
…with the overexposed image…

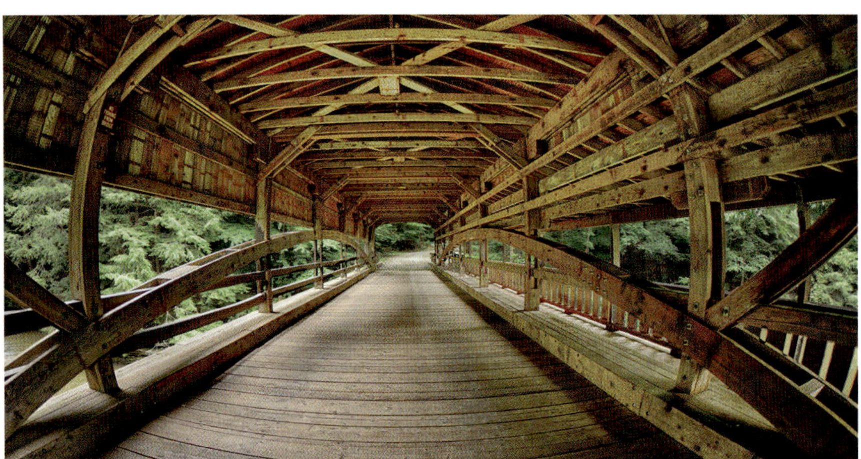

Figure 4.20
…to produce this merged high dynamic range (HDR) image.

3. **Turn on HDR.** Choose HDR Mode, press right, and select either On (series) if you want to shoot multiple HDR photos consecutively, or On (single photo) to take a single HDR image and then shut the feature off. Press OK to confirm.
4. **Set increment.** Choose Exposure Differential, press the right button, and select Auto (the D810 chooses the differential based on how contrasty it deems your scene to be), or 1 EV, 2 EV, or 3 EV. Auto is a good choice for your initial experiments. Or, select a higher EV value for higher contrast subjects, and a lower value for lower contrast subjects. Press OK to confirm.

TIP

You reassign the BKT button to serve as an HDR activate control using Custom Setting f8. That will save you a trip to the main menu. Press the BKT button and rotate the main command dial to select HDR Mode and the sub-command dial to select the Exposure Differential. Smoothing remains as it was last set.

5. **Choose smoothing.** The edges of the areas in your image may have a high contrast, poster-edge like effect in some circumstances. Smoothing adjusts the shading between these edges. You can select High, Normal, or Low. You may need to experiment until you see exactly what kind of results you get with various types of images. Press OK to confirm.
6. **Take your shot.** Although you can shoot HDR hand-held, you'll get the best results with the D810 mounted on a tripod, and with subjects that don't display a lot of motion. (That is, waterfalls are a poor choice.) While the D810 is combining your two shots, the message Job will appear on the monochrome status LCD, and Job Hdr will be shown at the bottom of the viewfinder.

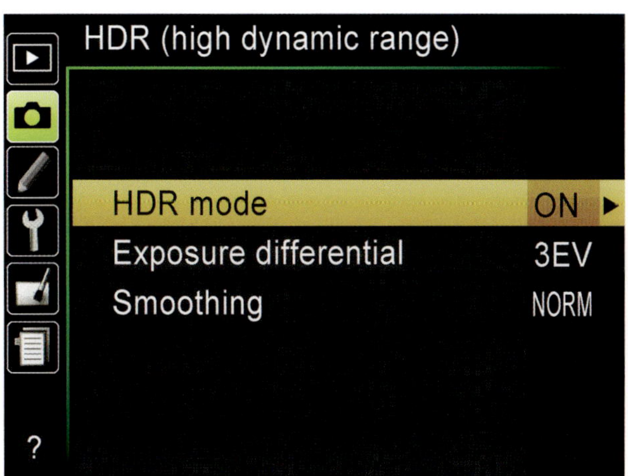

Figure 4.21 Choose HDR parameters.

Bracketing and Merge to HDR

If your credo is "If you want something done right, do it yourself," you can also shoot HDR manually, without resorting to the D810's HDR mode. Instead, you can shoot individual images either by manually bracketing or using the D810's auto bracketing modes, described earlier in this chapter.

While my goal in this book is to show you how to take great photos *in the camera* rather than how to fix your errors in Photoshop, the Merge to HDR Pro feature in Adobe's flagship image editor is too cool to ignore. The ability to have a bracketed set of exposures that are identical except for exposure is key to getting good results with this Photoshop feature, which allows you to produce images with a full, rich dynamic range that includes a level of detail in the highlights and shadows that is almost impossible to achieve with digital cameras.

When you're using Merge to HDR Pro, you'd take several pictures, some exposed for the shadows, some for the middle tones, and some for the highlights. The exact number of images to combine is up to you. Four to seven is a good number. Then, you'd use the Merge to HDR Pro command to combine all of the images into one HDR image that integrates the well-exposed sections of each version. Here's how.

The images should be as identical as possible, except for exposure. So, it's a good idea to mount the D810 on a tripod, use a remote release like MC-30/MC30a, and take all the exposures in one burst. Just follow these steps:

1. **Set up the camera.** Mount the D810 on a tripod.
2. **Set the camera to shoot a bracketed burst with an increment of 1 EV.** The description of how to do this will be found earlier in this chapter. As I noted there, you can set the D810 to shoot up to nine exposures, each one stop/EV apart, and use all nine for your HDR merger. Or, you can go ahead and shoot nine and discard the even numbered shots to arrive at five images spaced two EV apart.
3. **Choose an f/stop.** Set the camera for Aperture-priority and select an aperture that will provide a correct exposure at your initial settings for the series of manually bracketed shots. *And then leave this adjustment alone!* You don't want the aperture to change for your series, as that would change the depth-of-field. You want the D810 to adjust exposure *only* using the shutter speed.
4. **Choose manual focus.** You don't want the focus to change between shots, so set the D810 to manual focus, and carefully focus your shot.
5. **Choose RAW exposures.** Set the camera to take RAW files, which will give you the widest range of tones in your images. (This is an advantage of manually creating HDR files; the D810's Auto HDR feature can't be used when RAW or RAW+JPEG is active.)
6. **Take your bracketed set.** Press the button on the remote (or carefully press the shutter release or use the self-timer) and take the set of bracketed exposures.
7. **Continue with the Merge to HDR Pro steps listed next.** You can also use a different program, such as Photomatix, if you know how to use it.

DETERMINING THE BEST EXPOSURE DIFFERENTIAL

How do you choose the number of EV/stops to separate your exposures? You can use histograms, described at the end of this chapter, to determine the correct bracketing range. Take a test shot and examine the histogram. Reduce the exposure until dark tones are clipped off at the left of the resulting histogram. Then, increase the exposure until the lighter tones are clipped off at the right of the histogram. The number of stops between the two is the range that should be covered using your bracketed exposures.

The next steps show you how to combine the separate exposures into one merged high dynamic range image. The sample images in Figure 4.22 show the results you can get from a three-shot bracketed sequence.

1. **Copy your images to your computer.** If you use an application to transfer the files to your computer, make sure it does not make any adjustments to brightness, contrast, or exposure. You want the real raw information for Merge to HDR Pro to work with.
2. **Activate Merge to HDR Pro.** Choose File > Automate > Merge to HDR Pro.
3. **Select the photos to be merged.** Use the Browse feature to locate and select your photos to be merged. You'll note a checkbox that can be used to automatically align the images if they were not taken with the camera mounted on a rock-steady support. This will adjust for any slight movement of the camera that might have occurred when you changed exposure settings.
4. **Choose parameters (optional).** The first time you use Merge to HDR Pro, you can let the program work with its default parameters. Once you've played with the feature a few times, you can read the Adobe help files and learn more about the options than I can present in this non-software-oriented camera guide.
5. **Click OK.** The merger begins.
6. **Save.** Once HDR merge has done its thing, save the file to your computer.

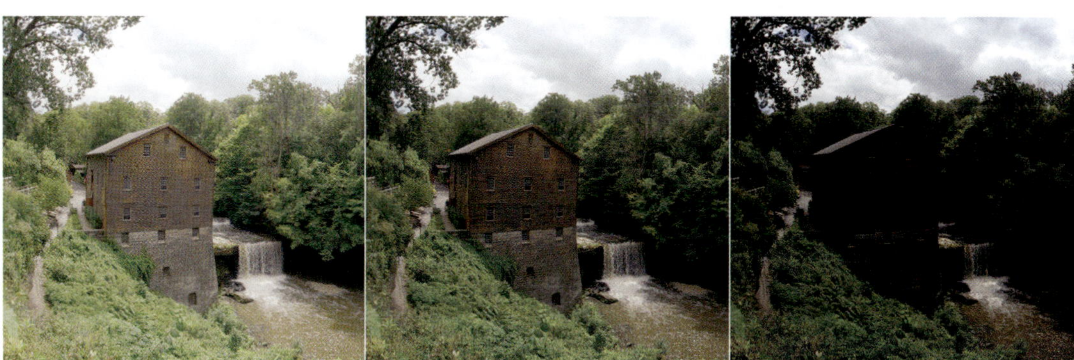

Figure 4.22 Three bracketed photos should look like this.

If you do everything correctly, you'll end up with a photo like the one shown in Figure 4.23.

What if you don't have the opportunity, inclination, or skills to create several images at different exposures, as described? If you shoot in RAW format, you can still use Merge to HDR, working with a *single* original image file. What you do is import the image into Photoshop several times, using Adobe Camera Raw to create multiple copies of the file at different exposure levels.

For example, you'd create one copy that's too dark, so the shadows lose detail, but the highlights are preserved. Create another copy with the shadows intact and allow the highlights to wash out. Then, you can use Merge to HDR to combine the two and end up with a finished image that has the extended dynamic range you're looking for. (This concludes the image-editing portion of the chapter. We now return you to our alternate sponsor: photography.)

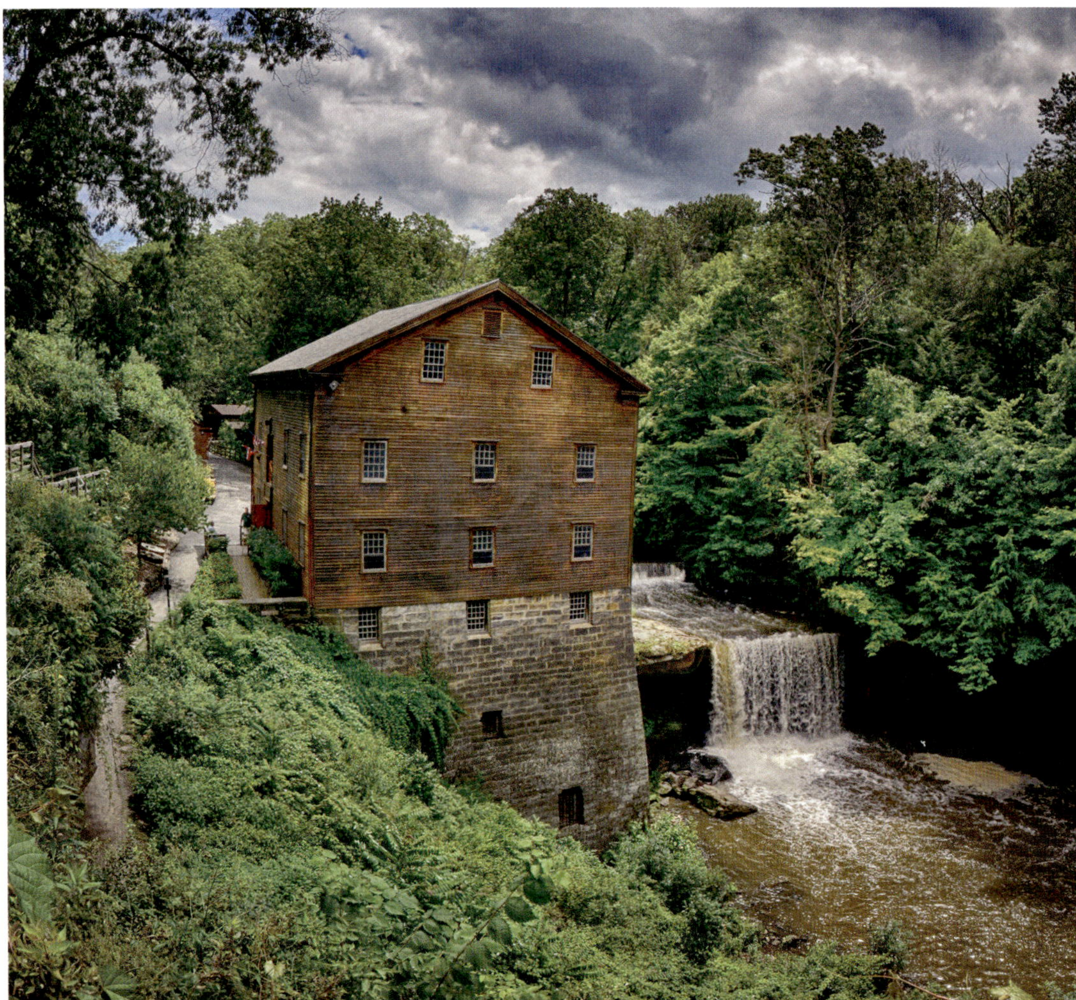

Figure 4.23 You'll end up with an extended dynamic range photo like this one.

Fixing Exposures with Histograms

While you can often recover poorly exposed photos in your image editor, your best bet is to arrive at the correct exposure in the camera, minimizing the tweaks that you have to make in post-processing. However, you can't always judge exposure just by viewing the image on your D810's LCD after the shot is made. Nor can you get a 100 percent accurately exposed picture by using the D810's live view feature. Ambient light may make the LCD difficult to see, and the brightness level you've set can affect the appearance of the playback image.

Instead, you can use a histogram, which is a chart displayed on the D810's LCD that shows the number of tones that have been captured at each brightness level. You must use the information to provide correction for the next shot you take, because no "live" histogram is available. In Playback mode, the D810 offers four histogram variations in two screens: one histogram that shows overall brightness levels for an image (Figure 4.24, left) and an alternate version that also shows brightness, but offers additional histograms that separates the red, green, and blue channels of your image into separate graphs (Figure 4.24, right).

DISPLAYING HISTOGRAMS

To view all the available histograms on your screen, you must have the D810 set up properly. First, you'll need to mark RGB Histograms and Overview using the Playback Display Options entry in the Playback menu, as described in Chapter 11. (Don't forget to select Done and press OK when finished specifying.) That will make the two screens that show Histograms visible when you cycle among the informational screens while pressing the multi selector up/down buttons while an image is displayed.

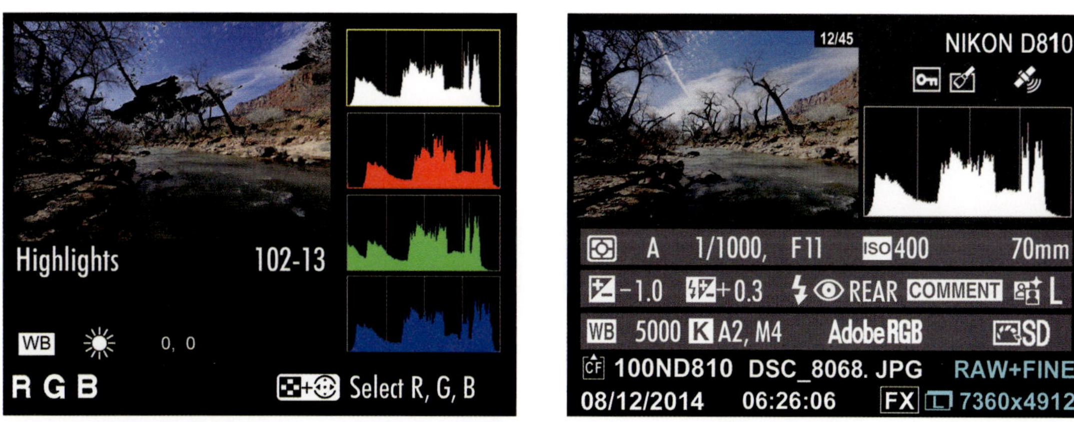

Figure 4.24 Four histograms are available on two different screens during playback.

The most basic histogram is displayed during playback when you press the multi selector up/down buttons to produce the Overview Data screen, as described briefly in Chapter 2. This screen provides a small histogram at the right side that displays the distribution of luminance or brightness. The most useful histogram screen is the RGB Histogram, which displays both a luminance chart and separate red, green, and blue charts.

Tonal Range

Histograms help you adjust the tonal range of an image, the span of dark to light tones, from a complete absence of brightness (black) to the brightest possible tone (white), and all the middle tones in between. Because all values for tones fall into a continuous spectrum between black and white, it's easiest to think of a photo's tonality in terms of a black-and-white or grayscale image, even though you're capturing tones in three separate color layers of red, green, and blue.

Because your images are digital, the tonal "spectrum" isn't really continuous: it's divided into discrete steps that represent the different tones that can be captured. Figure 4.25 may help you understand this concept. The gray steps shown range from 100-percent gray (black) at the left, to 0-percent gray (white) at the right, with 20 gray steps in all (plus white).

Along the bottom of the chart are the digital values from 0 to 255 recorded by your sensor for an image with 8 bits per channel. (8 bits of red, 8 bits of green, and 8 bits of blue equal a 24 bit, full-color image.) Any black captured would be represented by a value of 0, the brightest white by 255, and the midtones would be clustered around the 128 marker. The actual scale may be "finer" and record say, 0 to 4094 for an image captured when the D810 is set to 12 bits per channel in the NEF (RAW) Recording Bit Depth setting of the Shooting menu (see Chapter 11 for more detail on that option).

Grayscale images (which we call black-and-white photos) are easy to understand. Or, at least, that's what we think. When we look at a black-and-white image, we think we're seeing a continuous range of tones from black to white, and all the grays in between. But, that's not exactly true. The blackest

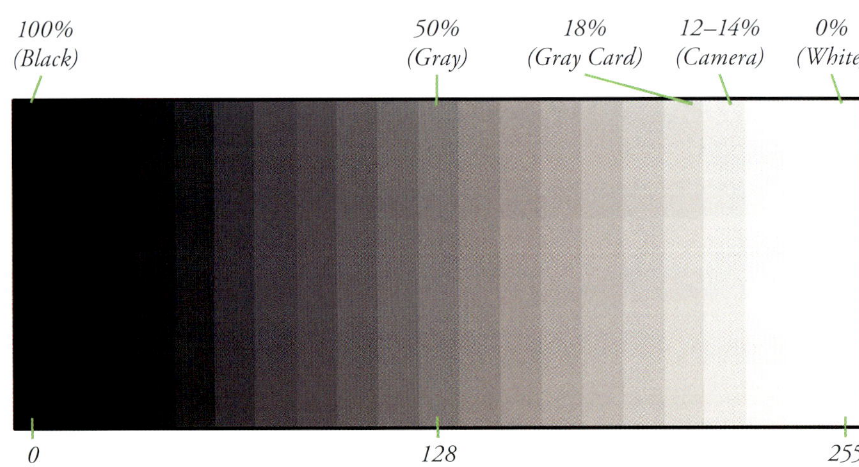

Figure 4.25 A tonal range from black (left) to white (right) and all the gray values in between.

black in any photo isn't a true black, because *some* light is always reflected from the surface of the print, and if viewed on a screen, the deepest black is only as dark as the least-reflective area a computer monitor can produce. The whitest white isn't a true white, either, because even the lightest areas of a print absorb some light (only a mirror reflects close to all the light that strikes it), and, when viewing on a computer monitor, the whites are limited by the brightness of the display's LCD or LEDs picture elements. Lacking darker blacks and brighter, whiter whites, that continuous set of tones doesn't cover the full grayscale tonal range.

The full scale of tones becomes useful when you have an image that has large expanses of shades that change gradually from one level to the next, such as areas of sky, water, or walls. Think of a picture taken of a group of campers around a campfire. Since the light from the fire is striking them directly in the face, there aren't many shadows on the campers' faces. All the tones that make up the *features* of the people around the fire are compressed into one end of the brightness spectrum—the lighter end.

Yet, there's more to this scene than faces. Behind the campers are trees, rocks, and perhaps a few animals that have emerged from the shadows to see what is going on. These are illuminated by the softer light that bounces off the surrounding surfaces. If your eyes become accustomed to the reduced illumination, you'll find that there is a wealth of detail in these shadow images.

This campfire scene would be a nightmare to reproduce faithfully under any circumstances. If you are an experienced photographer, you are probably already wincing at what is called a *high-contrast* lighting situation. Some photos may be high in contrast when there are fewer tones and they are all bunched up at limited points in the scale. In a low-contrast image, there are more tones, but they are spread out so widely that the image looks flat. Your digital camera can show you the relationship between these tones using a *histogram.*

Histogram Basics

Your D810's histograms are a simplified display of the numbers of pixels at each of 256 brightness levels, producing an interesting mountain range effect. Although separate charts may be provided for brightness and the red, green, and blue channels, when you first start using histograms, you'll want to concentrate on the brightness histogram.

Each vertical line in the graph represents the number of pixels in the image for each brightness value, from 0 (black) on the left to 255 (white) on the right. The vertical axis measures that number of pixels at each level.

Although histograms are most often used to fine-tune exposure, you can glean other information from them, such as the relative contrast of the image. Figure 4.26 shows the upper half of the Overview screen, with an image having normal contrast. In such an image, most of the pixels are spread across the image, with a healthy distribution of tones throughout the midtone section of the graph. That large peak at the right side of the graph represents all those light tones in the sky. A normal-contrast image you shoot may have less sky area, and less of a peak at the right side, but

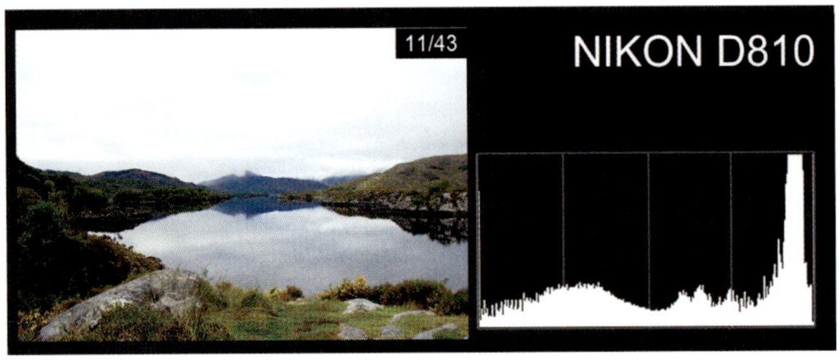

Figure 4.26
This image has fairly normal contrast, even though there is a peak of light tones at the right side representing the sky.

notice that very few pixels hug the right edge of the histogram, indicating that the lightest tones are not being clipped because they are off the chart.

With a lower-contrast image, like the one shown in Figure 4.27, the basic shape of the previous histogram will remain recognizable, but gradually will be compressed together to cover a smaller area of the gray spectrum. The squished shape of the histogram is caused by all the grays in the original image being represented by a limited number of gray tones in a smaller range of the scale.

Instead of the darkest tones of the image reaching into the black end of the spectrum and the whitest tones extending to the lightest end, the blackest areas of the scene are now represented by a light gray, and the whites by a somewhat lighter gray. The overall contrast of the image is reduced. Because all the darker tones are actually a middle gray or lighter, the scene in this version of the photo appears lighter as well.

Going in the other direction, increasing the contrast of an image produces a histogram like the one shown in Figure 4.28. In this case, the tonal range is now spread over the entire width of the chart, but, except for the bright sky, there is not much variation in the middle tones; the mountain "peaks" are not very high. When you stretch the grayscale in both directions like this, the darkest tones become darker (that may not be possible) and the lightest tones become lighter (ditto). In fact, shades that might have been gray before can change to black or white as they are moved toward either end of the scale.

The effect of increasing contrast may be to move some tones off either end of the scale altogether, while spreading the remaining grays over a smaller number of locations on the spectrum. That's exactly the case in the example shown. The number of possible tones is smaller and the image appears harsher.

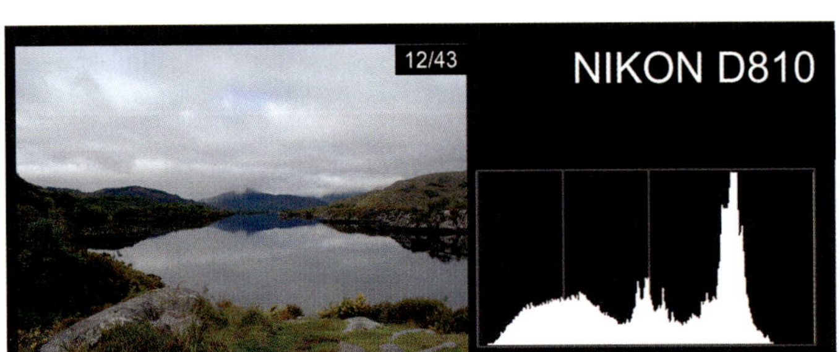

Figure 4.27
This low-contrast image has all the tones squished into one section of the grayscale.

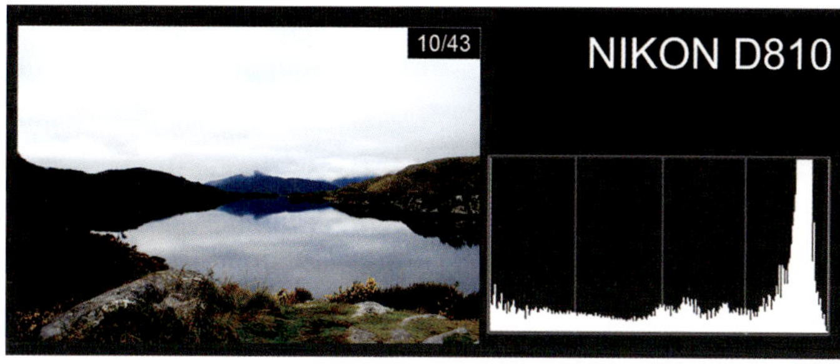

Figure 4.28
A high-contrast image produces a histogram in which the tones are spread out.

Understanding Histograms

The important thing to remember when working with the histogram display in your D810 is that changing the exposure does *not* change the contrast of an image. The curves illustrated in the previous three examples remain exactly the same shape when you increase or decrease exposure. I repeat: The proportional distribution of grays shown in the histogram doesn't change when exposure changes; it is neither stretched nor compressed. However, the tones as a whole are moved toward one end of the scale or the other, depending on whether you're increasing or decreasing exposure. You'll be able to see that in some illustrations that follow.

So, as you reduce exposure, tones gradually move to the black end (and off the scale), while the reverse is true when you increase exposure. The contrast within the image is changed only to the extent that some of the tones can no longer be represented when they are moved off the scale.

To change the *contrast* of an image, you must do one of four things:

- **Change the D810's contrast setting** using the menu system. You'll find these adjustments in your camera's Picture Controls menus, as explained in Chapter 11.
- **Use your camera's shadow-tone "booster."** As previously discussed, Active D-Lighting (or plain old D-Lighting) applied after the fact from the Retouch menu (Chapter 13) can also adjust contrast.
- **Alter the contrast of the scene itself,** for example by using a fill light or reflectors to add illumination to shadows that are too dark.
- **Attempt to adjust contrast in post-processing** using your image editor or RAW file converter. You may use features such as Levels or Curves (in Photoshop, Photoshop Elements, and many other image editors), or work with HDR software to cherry-pick the best values in shadows and highlights from multiple images.

Of the four of these, the third—changing the contrast of the scene—is the most desirable, because attempting to fix contrast by fiddling with the tonal values is unlikely to be a perfect remedy. However, adding a little contrast can be successful because you can discard some tones to make the image more contrasty. However, the opposite is much more difficult. An overly contrasty image rarely can be fixed, because you can't add information that isn't there in the first place.

What you *can* do is adjust the exposure so that the tones *that are already present in the scene* are captured correctly. Figure 4.29 shows the histogram for an image that is badly underexposed. You can guess from the shape of the histogram that many of the dark tones to the left of the graph have been clipped off. There's plenty of room on the right side for additional pixels to reside without having them become overexposed. So, you can increase the exposure (either by changing the f/stop or shutter speed, or by adding an EV value) to produce the corrected histogram shown in Figure 4.30.

Conversely, if your histogram looks like the one shown in Figure 4.31, with bright tones pushed off the right edge of the chart, you have an overexposed image, and you can correct it by reducing exposure. In addition to the histogram, the D810 has its Highlights option, which, when activated, shows areas that are overexposed with flashing tones (often called "blinkies") in the review screen. Depending on the importance of this "clipped" detail, you can adjust exposure or leave it alone. For example, if all the dark-coded areas in the review are in a background that you care little about, you can forget about them and not change the exposure, but if such areas appear in facial details of your subject, you may want to make some adjustments.

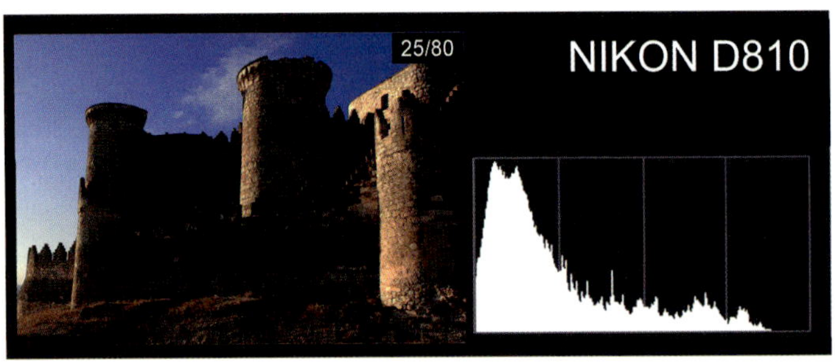

Figure 4.29
A histogram of an underexposed image may look like this.

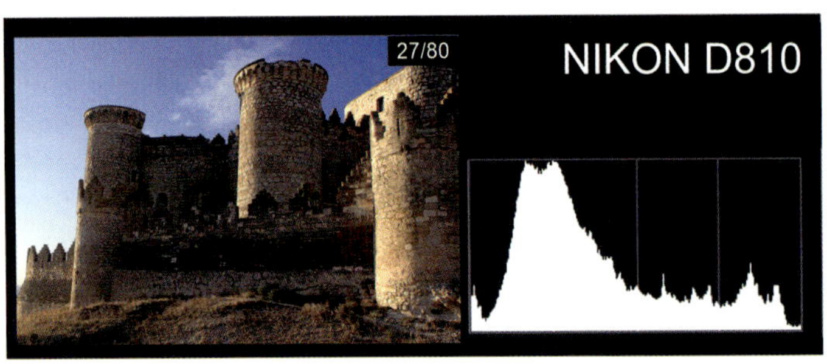

Figure 4.30
Adding exposure will produce a histogram like this one.

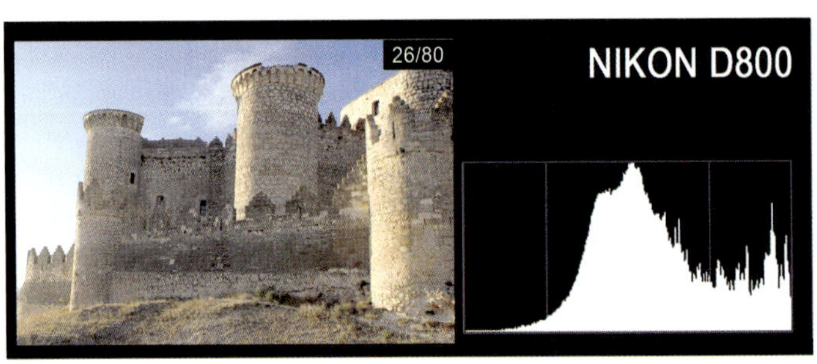

Figure 4.31
A histogram of an overexposed image will show clipping at the right side.

By default, the Highlights display shows "blinkies" for the luminance channel, but you can separately view highlights for the red, green, and blue channels. Just follow these steps:

1. With an image displayed, and the highlights/histogram screen shown, hold down the Zoom In button.
2. Press the multi selector left/right buttons to cycle among RGB (all channels), R, G, and B.
3. When a channel is framed in an orange outline, the highlight information for that channel is shown in the thumbnail image in the upper-left corner. At the bottom left of the screen RGB, R, G, or B will be highlighted to show the currently active channel.

In working with histograms, your goal should be to have all the tones in an image spread out between the edges, with none clipped off at the left and right sides. Underexposing (to preserve highlights) should be done only as a last resort, because retrieving the underexposed shadows in your image editor will frequently increase the noise, even if you're working with RAW files. A better course of action is to expose for the highlights, but, when the subject matter makes it practical, fill in the shadows with additional light, using reflectors, fill flash, or other techniques rather than allowing them to be seriously underexposed.

The more you work with histograms, the more useful they become. One of the first things that histogram veterans notice is that it's possible to overexpose one channel even if the overall exposure appears to be correct. For example, flower photographers soon discover that it's really, really difficult to get a good picture of a red rose, like the one shown in Figure 4.32. The exposure looks okay—but there's no detail in the rose's petals. Looking at the histogram (see Figure 4.33) shows why: the red channel is blown out. If you look at the red histogram, there's a peak at the right edge that indicates that highlight information has been lost. In fact, the green channel has been blown, too, and so the green parts of the flower also lack detail. Only the blue channel's histogram is entirely contained within the boundaries of the chart, and, on first glance, the white luminance histogram at top of the column of graphs seems fairly normal.

Any of the primary channels—red, green, or blue—can blow out all by themselves, although bright reds seem to be the most common problem area. More difficult to diagnose are overexposed tones in one of the "in-between" hues on the color wheel. Overexposed yellows (which are very common) will be shown by blowouts in *both* the red and green channels. Too-bright cyans will manifest as excessive blue and green highlights, while overexposure in the red and blue channels reduces detail in magenta colors. As you gain experience, you'll be able to see exactly how anomalies in the RGB channels translate into poor highlights and murky shadows.

The only way to correct for color channel blowouts is to reduce exposure. As I mentioned earlier, you might want to consider filling in the shadows with additional light to keep them from becoming too dark when you decrease exposure. In practice, you'll want to monitor the red channel most closely, followed by the blue channel, and slightly decrease exposure to see if that helps. Because of the way our eyes perceive color, we are more sensitive to variations in green, so green channel blowouts are less of a problem, unless your main subject is heavily colored in that hue. If you plan on photographing a frog hopping around on your front lawn, you'll want to be extra careful to preserve detail in the green channel, using bracketing or other exposure techniques outlined in this chapter.

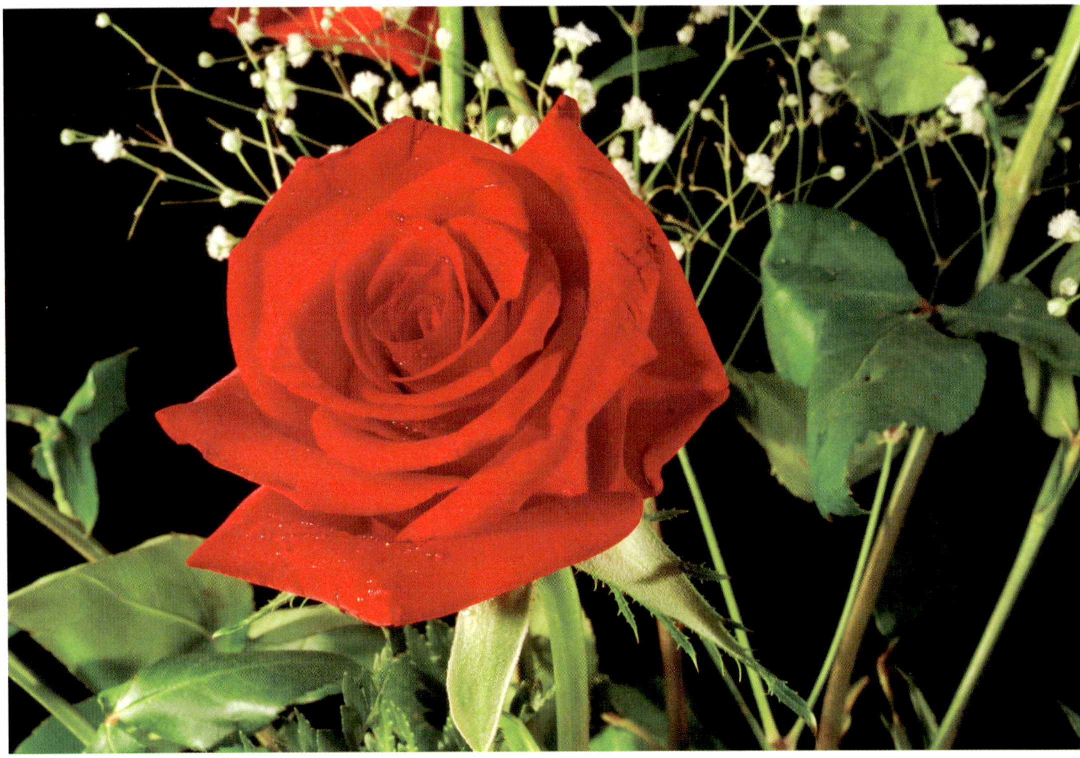

Figure 4.32 It's common to lose detail in bright red flowers because the red channel becomes overexposed even when the other channels are properly exposed.

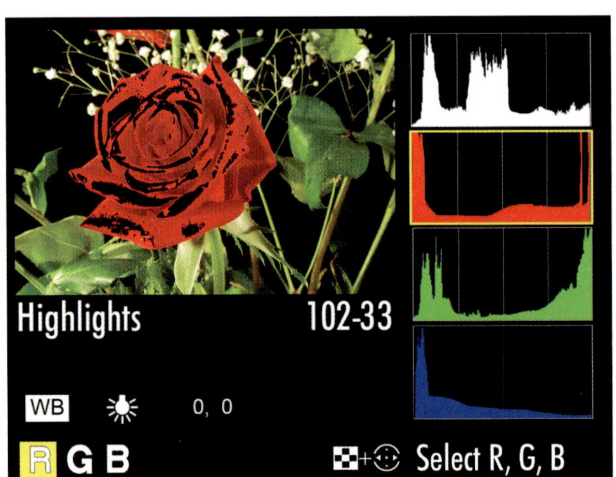

Figure 4.33 The RGB histograms show that both the red and green channels are overexposed.

5

Mastering the Mysteries of Autofocus

One of the most useful and powerful features of modern digital SLR cameras is their ability to lock in sharp focus faster than the blink of an eye. Sometimes. Although autofocus has been with us for more than 20 years, it continues to be problematic. While vendors like Nikon are giving us faster and more precise autofocus systems, with many more options, it's common for the sheer number of options to confuse even the most advanced photographers.

One key problem is that the camera doesn't really know, for certain, what subject you want to be in sharp focus. It may select an object and lock in focus with lightning speed—even though the subject is not the one that's the center of interest of your photograph. Or, the camera may lock focus too soon, or too late. This chapter will help you choose the options available with your Nikon D810 that will help the camera understand what you want to focus, when, and maybe even why.

How Focus Works

Although Nikon added autofocus capabilities in the 1980s, back in the day of film cameras, prior to that focusing was always done manually. Honest. Even though viewfinders were bigger and brighter than they are today, special focusing screens, magnifiers, and other gadgets were often used to help the photographer achieve correct focus. Imagine what it must have been like to focus manually under demanding, fast-moving conditions such as sports photography.

Focusing was problematic because our eyes and brains have poor memory for correct focus, which is why your eye doctor must shift back and forth between sets of lenses and ask "Does that look sharper—or was it sharper before?" in determining your correct prescription. Similarly, manual focusing involves jogging the focus ring back and forth as you go from almost in focus, to sharp focus, to almost focused again. The little clockwise and counterclockwise arcs decrease in size until you've zeroed in on the point of correct focus. What you're looking for is the image with the most contrast between the edges of elements in the image.

The camera also looks for these contrast differences among pixels to determine relative sharpness. There are two ways that sharp focus is determined: phase detection (used when framing your image through the optical viewfinder) and contrast detection (used when shooting stills and movies with live view).

Phase Detection

The 51 autofocus sensors of Nikon's Advanced Multi-CAM 3500FX autofocus module are located in the "floor" of the mirror box, just under the flip-up mirror, which is partially silvered so that most of the light reaching it from the lens is bounced upward to the viewfinder, while some light is directed downward toward the focus sensors. If you lock up the mirror of your camera (using the Lock Mirror Up for Cleaning option in the Setup menu), you can see where these sensors are located. The focus zones cover an area on the center of the viewing frame in FX mode, as shown in Figure 5.1.

In phase detection mode, the autofocus sampling area for each autofocus sensor is divided into two halves by a prism-like optical component in front of the focus sensor, similar to the simplified diagram shown in Figure 5.2. Inside your D810, there are actually two sets of reflective surfaces tucked behind the main mirror. One directs the light that passes through the main mirror downward to the bottom of the mirror box, while the second bounces the light back toward the front of the camera, where the actual focus sensor resides.

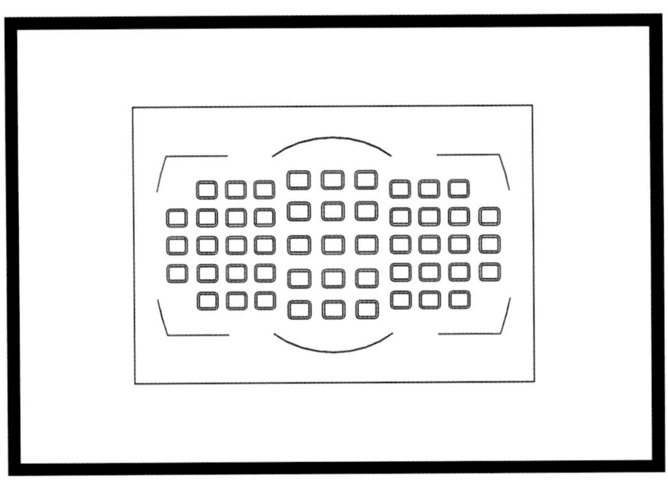

Figure 5.1
The D810's focus sensors cover an area in the center of the frame.

MORE COVERAGE IN DX MODE

The outer rectangle in Figure 5.1 shows the actual frame area when you switch the D810 from FX to DX mode (as described in Chapter 7). One thing that jumps out at you is that, while in FX mode the focus points are concentrated only in the center of the frame, when cropping the image using DX mode, the focus zones now virtually fill the frame, providing more AF area coverage.

This phenomenon is one more reason why you might want to use DX mode for some types of shots where the "expanded" AF area coverage is useful—such as sports. The D810 can more easily locate the important subject matter to zero in on, and you still have a 15MP image to work with even in cropped mode. As a bonus, you pick up a modest frame rate increase in either continuous shooting mode—from 5 fps boosted to 6 or 7 fps (with the MB-D12 pack). Note that you reap these gains *only* if you're shooting in a crop mode—not if you shoot in FX mode and then crop down to DX size in your image editor. Score one for DX mode vs. post processing crops.

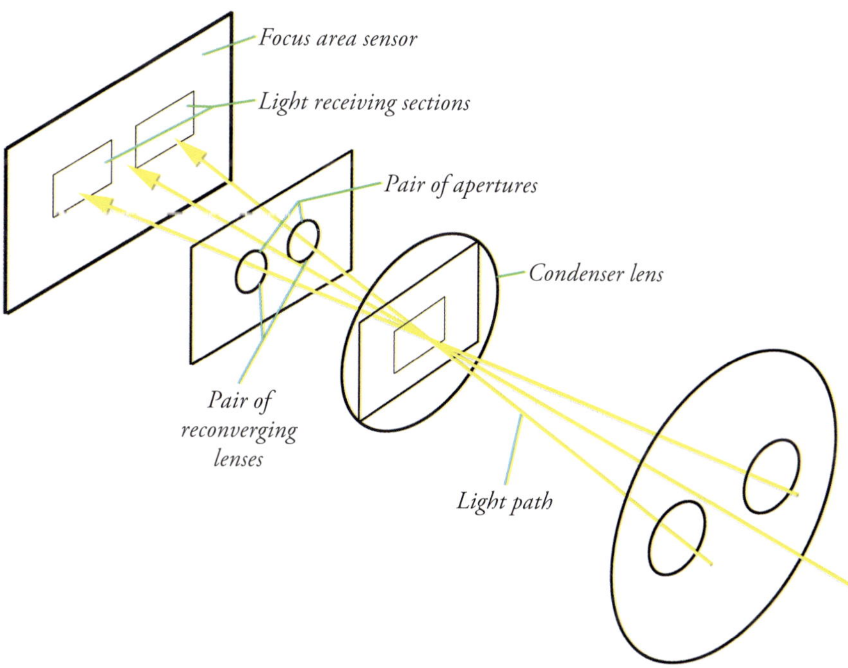

Figure 5.2
The image is split in half before it reaches the AF sensor.

The two halves of the image areas are compared, much like (actually, *exactly* like) a two-window rangefinder used in surveying, weaponry—and non-SLR cameras like the venerable Leica M film models. The relative positions between the two images change as focus is moved in or out, until sharp focus is achieved when the images are "in phase," or lined up. The process can be visualized roughly using Figure 5.3, which shows two image areas being "merged" as the D810 adjusts focus.

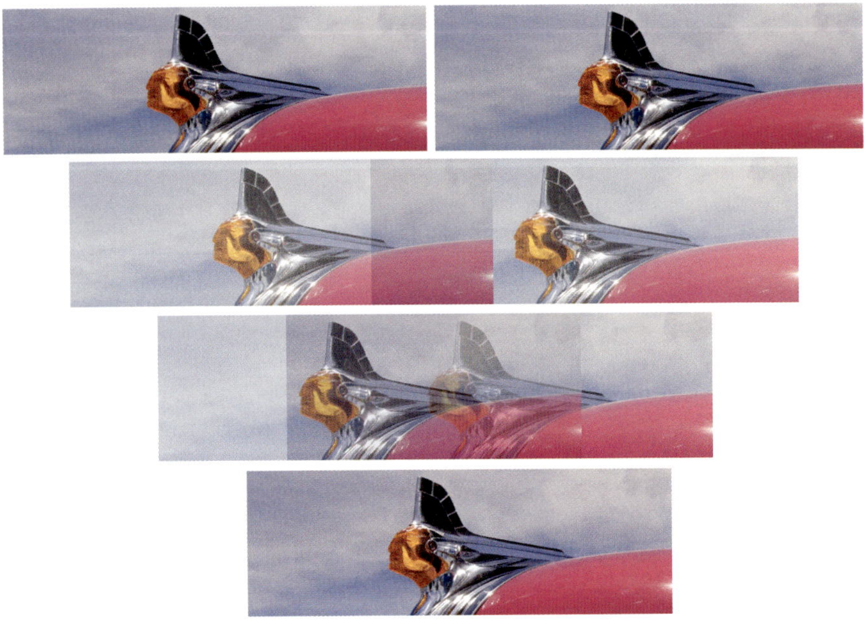

Figure 5.3
The AF sensor tries to match up the two halves of the image.

You can visualize how phase detection autofocus works if you look at Figures 5.4 and 5.5. (However, the action of your camera's actual autofocus sensors don't look *anything* like this; I'm providing a greatly simplified graphical interpretation just for illustration.) In Figure 5.4, a typical horizontally oriented focus sensor is looking at a series of parallel vertical lines in a weathered piece of wood. The lines are broken into two halves by the sensor's rangefinder prism, and you can see that they don't line up exactly; the image is slightly out of focus.

Fortunately, the rangefinder approach of phase detection tells the D810 exactly how out of focus the image is, and in which direction (focus is too near, or too far) thanks to the amount and direction of the displacement of the split image. The camera can quickly and precisely snap the image into sharp focus and line up the vertical lines, as shown in Figure 5.5. Of course, this scenario—vertical lines being interpreted by a horizontally oriented sensor—is ideal. When the same sensor is asked to measure focus for, say, horizontal lines that don't split up quite so conveniently, or, in the worst case, subjects such as the sky (which may have neither vertical nor horizontal lines), focus can slow down drastically, or even become impossible.

Phase detection is the normal mode used by the D810. As with any rangefinder-like function, accuracy is better when the "base length" between the two images is larger. (Think back to your high school trigonometry; you could calculate a distance more accurately when the separation between the two points where the angles were measured was greater.) For that reason, phase detection autofocus is more accurate with larger (wider) lens openings—especially those with maximum f/stops of f/2.8 or better—than with smaller lens openings, and may not work at all when the f/stop is smaller than f/8. As I noted, the D810 is able to perform these comparisons very quickly.

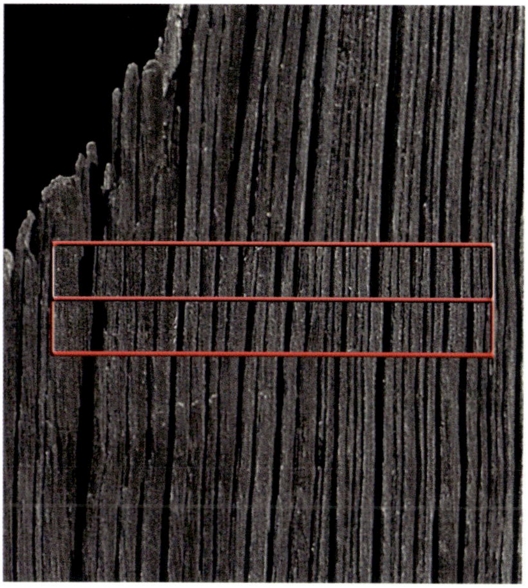

Figure 5.4 When an image is out of focus, the split lines don't align precisely.

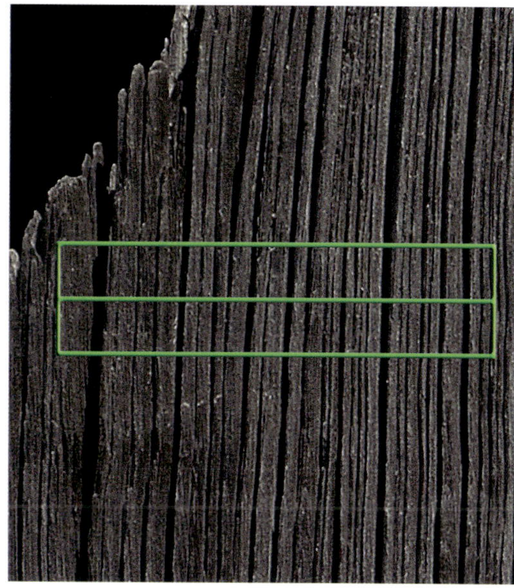

Figure 5.5 Using phase detection mode, the D810 is able to align the features of the image and achieve sharp focus quickly.

Improved Cross-Type Focus Point

One improvement that Nikon D810 owners sometimes overlook is the upgrade to a cross-type focus point at 15 of the 51 center positions, functional with lenses with maximum apertures of f/5.6 or larger; with lenses having an effective maximum aperture of f/8, 11 central sensors are still able to function in cross-type mode. Why is this important? It helps to take a closer look at the phase detection system when presented with a non-ideal subject.

Figure 5.6 shows the same weathered wood pictured earlier, except in this case we've chosen to rotate the camera 90 degrees (say, because we want a vertically oriented composition). In the illustration, the image within the focus sensor's area is split in two and displaced slightly side-to-side, but the amount and direction of the misalignment is far from obvious. A horizontally oriented focus sensor will be forced to look for less obvious vertical lines to match up. Our best-case subject has been transformed into a *worst*-case subject for a horizontal focus sensor.

The value of the cross-type focus sensor, which can interpret contrast in both horizontal and vertical directions, can be seen in Figure 5.7. The horizontal lines are still giving the horizontal portion of the cross sensor fits, but the vertical bar can easily split and align the subject to achieve optimum focus. Cross-type sensors can handle horizontal and vertical lines with equal aplomb and, if you think about it, lines at any diagonal angle as well. In lower light levels, with subjects that were moving, or with subjects that have no pattern and less contrast to begin with, the cross-type sensor not only works faster but can focus subjects that a horizontal- or vertical-only sensor can't handle at all.

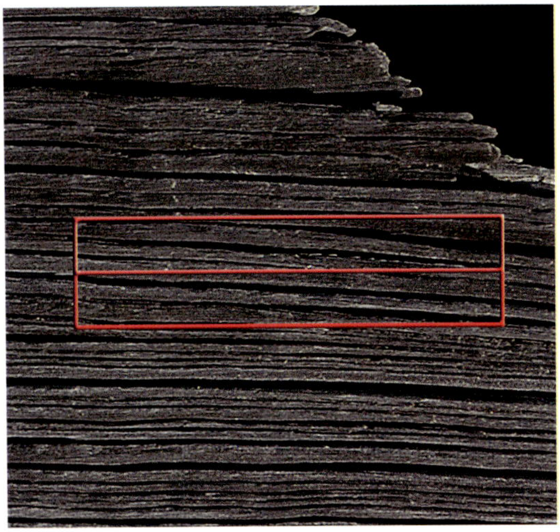

Figure 5.6 A horizontal focus sensor doesn't handle horizontal lines very well.

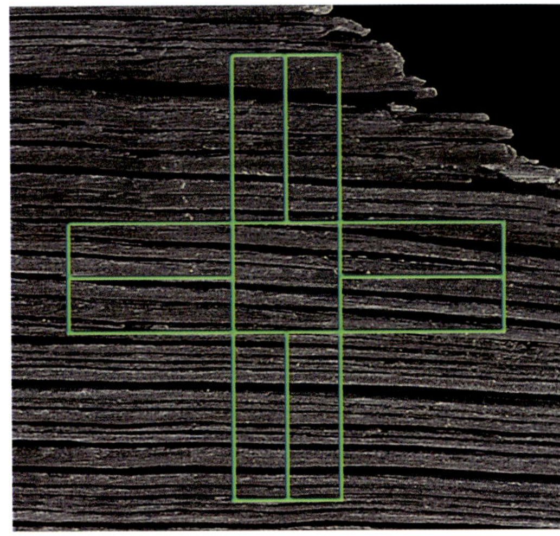

Figure 5.7 Cross-type sensors can evaluate contrast in both horizontal and vertical directions, as well as diagonally.

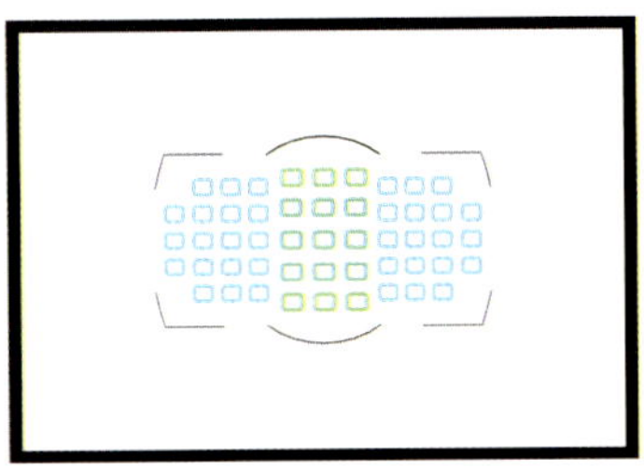

Figure 5.8 With lenses having a maximum aperture of f/5.6 or larger, the 15 central AF sensors, shown here in green, function as cross-type sensors. The remaining 36 sensors (shown in blue) function as line sensors.

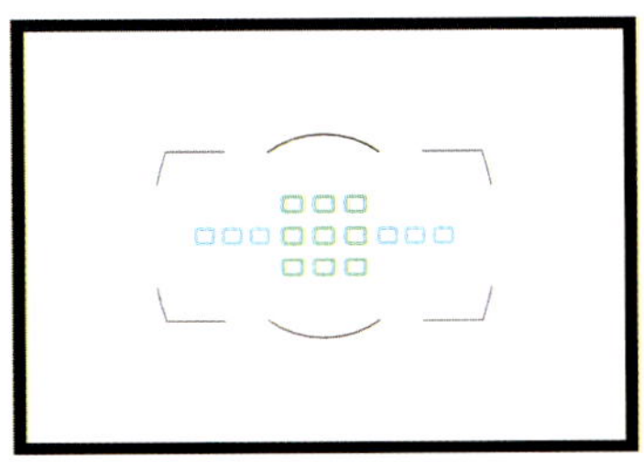

Figure 5.9 With lenses having maximum apertures smaller than f/5.6, but no smaller than f/8, the nine cross-type sensors are located in the middle of the frame (shown in green). The remaining six sensors (shown in blue), function as line sensors.

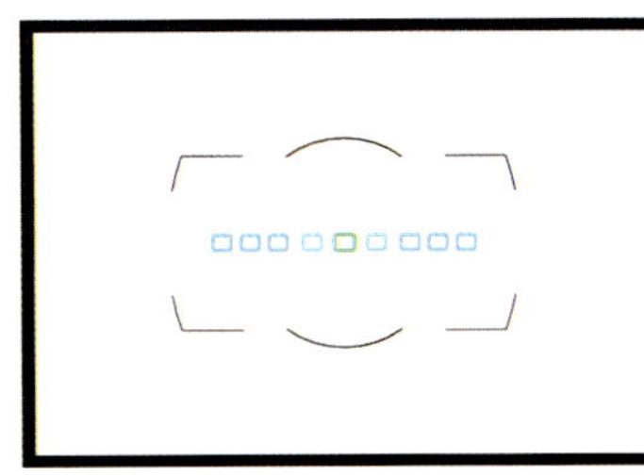

Figure 5.10 If you mount a lens having a maximum aperture of f/8, only the central focus point functions as a cross sensor; the six remaining sensors act as line sensors. If your lens has a maximum aperture that's smaller than f/8, autofocus is not possible.

So, you can see that having a center cross-type focus sensor that is extra-sensitive with faster lenses is a definite advantage. The location of the D810's cross-type focus sensors is shown in Figures 5.8 and 5.9. With lenses having an effective maximum aperture (that is, taking into account any light loss from teleconverters, automatic extension tubes, etc.) of f/5.6 or faster, 15 central focus points function as cross-type sensors; the rest act as line sensors. If you're using a lens with a maximum aperture a tad smaller than f/5.6 and not quite as small as f/8 (in other words, f/5.7 to f/7.9), nine central AF points function as cross-type sensors, while the six sensors flanking them still act as line sensors. With lenses having an effective maximum aperture of f/8, only the central focus point acts as a cross-type sensor, but the remaining six function as line sensors. (See Figure 5.10.)

Contrast Detection

This is a slower mode, suitable for static subjects, and used by the D810 in live view and movie modes. It's a bit easier to understand, and is illustrated by Figure 5.11. At top in the figure, the transitions between the edges found in the image are soft and blurred because of the low contrast between them. Although the illustration uses the same vertical lines used with the phase detection example, the orientation of the features doesn't matter. The focus system looks only for contrast between edges, and those edges can run in any direction.

At the bottom of Figure 5.11, the image has been brought into sharp focus, and the edges have much more contrast; the transitions are sharp and clear. Although this example is a bit exaggerated so you can see the results on the printed page, it's easy to understand that when maximum contrast in a subject is achieved, it can be deemed to be in sharp focus. Although achieving focus with contrast detection is generally quite a bit slower, there are several advantages to this method:

- **Works with more image types.** Contrast detection doesn't require subject matter rotated 90 degrees from the sensor's orientation to operate optimally. Any subject that has edges will work.
- **Focus on any point.** While phase detection focus can be achieved *only* at the points that fall under one of the nine autofocus sensors, with contrast detection, any portion of the image can be used. Focus is achieved with the actual sensor image, so focus point selection is simply a matter of choosing which part of the sensor image to use. As you'll learn in Chapter 14, you can move the focus frame around on the screen when working with live view.
- **Potentially more accurate.** Phase detection can fall prey to the vagaries of uncooperative subject matter: if suitable lines aren't available, the system may have to hunt for focus or achieve less than optimal focus. Contrast detection is more clear-cut. The camera can clearly see when the highest contrast has been achieved, as long as there is sufficient light to allow the camera to examine the image produced by the sensor. (The focus assist lamp can help when shooting subjects close enough to the camera for the focus assist illumination to provide extra contrast, approximately 1 ft. 8 in. to 9 ft. 10 in.)

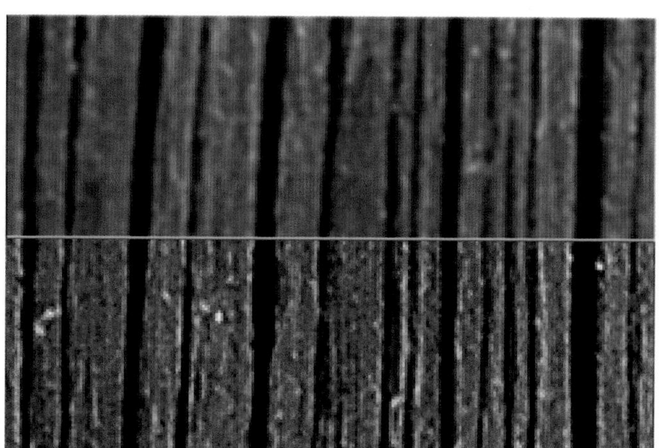

Figure 5.11
Focus in contrast detection mode evaluates the increase in contrast in the edges of subjects, starting with a blurry image (top) and producing a sharp, contrasty image (bottom).

The D810's autofocus mechanism, like all such systems found in SLR cameras, evaluates the degree of focus, but, unlike the human eye, it is able to remember the progression perfectly, so that autofocus can lock in much more quickly and, with an image that has sufficient contrast, more precisely. Unfortunately, while the D810's focus system finds it easy to measure degrees of apparent focus at each of the focus points in the viewfinder, it doesn't really know with any certainty *which* object should be in sharpest focus. Is it the closest object? The subject in the center? Something lurking *behind* the closest subject? A person standing over at the side of the picture? Many of the techniques for using autofocus effectively involve telling the Nikon D810 exactly what it should be focusing on, by choosing a focus zone or by allowing the camera to choose a focus zone for you. I'll address that topic shortly.

Adding Circles of Confusion

But there are other factors in play, as well. You know that increased depth-of-field brings more of your subject into focus. But more depth-of-field also makes autofocusing (or manual focusing) more difficult because the contrast is lower between objects at different distances. So, autofocus with a 200mm lens (or zoom setting) may be easier than at a 28mm focal length (or zoom setting) because the longer lens has less apparent depth-of-field. By the same token, a lens with a maximum aperture of f/1.8 will be easier to autofocus (or manually focus) than one of the same focal length with an f/4 maximum aperture, because the f/4 lens has more depth-of-field *and* a dimmer view. That's why lenses with a maximum aperture smaller than f/8 can give your D810's autofocus system fits.

To make things even more complicated, many subjects aren't polite enough to remain still. They move around in the frame, so that even if the D810 is sharply focused on your main subject, it may change position and require refocusing. An intervening subject may pop into the frame and pass between you and the subject you meant to photograph. You (or the D810) have to decide whether to lock focus on this new subject, or remain focused on the original subject. Finally, there are some kinds of subjects that are difficult to bring into sharp focus because they lack enough contrast to allow the D810's AF system (or our eyes) to lock in. Blank walls, a clear blue sky, birds-in-flight, or other subject matter may make focusing difficult.

If you find all these focus factors confusing, you're on the right track. Focus is, in fact, measured using something called a *circle of confusion.* An ideal image consists of zillions of tiny little points, which, like all points, theoretically have no height or width. There is perfect contrast between the point and its surroundings. You can think of each point as a pinpoint of light in a darkened room. When a given point is out of focus, its edges decrease in contrast and it changes from a perfect point to a tiny disc with blurry edges (remember, blur is the lack of contrast between boundaries in an image). (See Figure 5.12.)

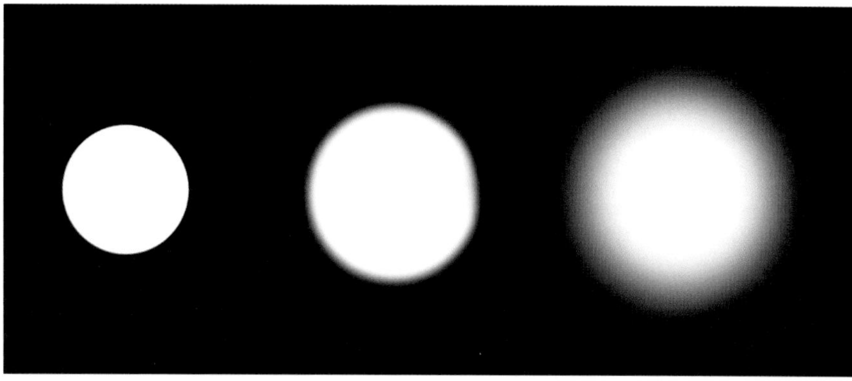

Figure 5.12
When a pinpoint of light (left) goes out of focus, its blurry edges form a circle of confusion (center and right).

If this blurry disc—the circle of confusion—is small enough, our eye still perceives it as a point. It's only when the disc grows large enough that we can see it as a blur rather than a sharp point that a given point is viewed as out of focus. You can see, then, that enlarging an image, either by displaying it larger on your computer monitor or by making a large print, also enlarges the size of each circle of confusion. Moving closer to the image does the same thing. So, parts of an image that may look perfectly sharp in a 5 × 7-inch print viewed at arm's length, might appear blurry when blown up to 11 × 14 and examined at the same distance. Take a few steps back, however, and it may look sharp again.

To a lesser extent, the viewer also affects the apparent size of these circles of confusion. Some people see details better at a given distance and may perceive smaller circles of confusion than someone standing next to them. For the most part, however, such differences are small. Truly blurry images will look blurry to just about everyone under the same conditions.

Technically, there is just one plane within your picture area, parallel to the back of the camera (or sensor, in the case of a digital camera), that is in sharp focus. That's the plane in which the points of the image are rendered as precise points. At every other plane in front of or behind the focus plane, the points show up as discs that range from slightly blurry to extremely blurry (see Figure 5.13). In practice, the discs in many of these planes will still be so small that we see them as points, and that's where we get depth-of-field. Depth-of-field is just the range of planes that include discs that we perceive as points rather than blurred splotches. The size of this range increases as the aperture is reduced in size and is allocated roughly one-third in front of the plane of sharpest focus, and two-thirds behind it. The range of sharp focus is always greater behind your subject than in front of it.

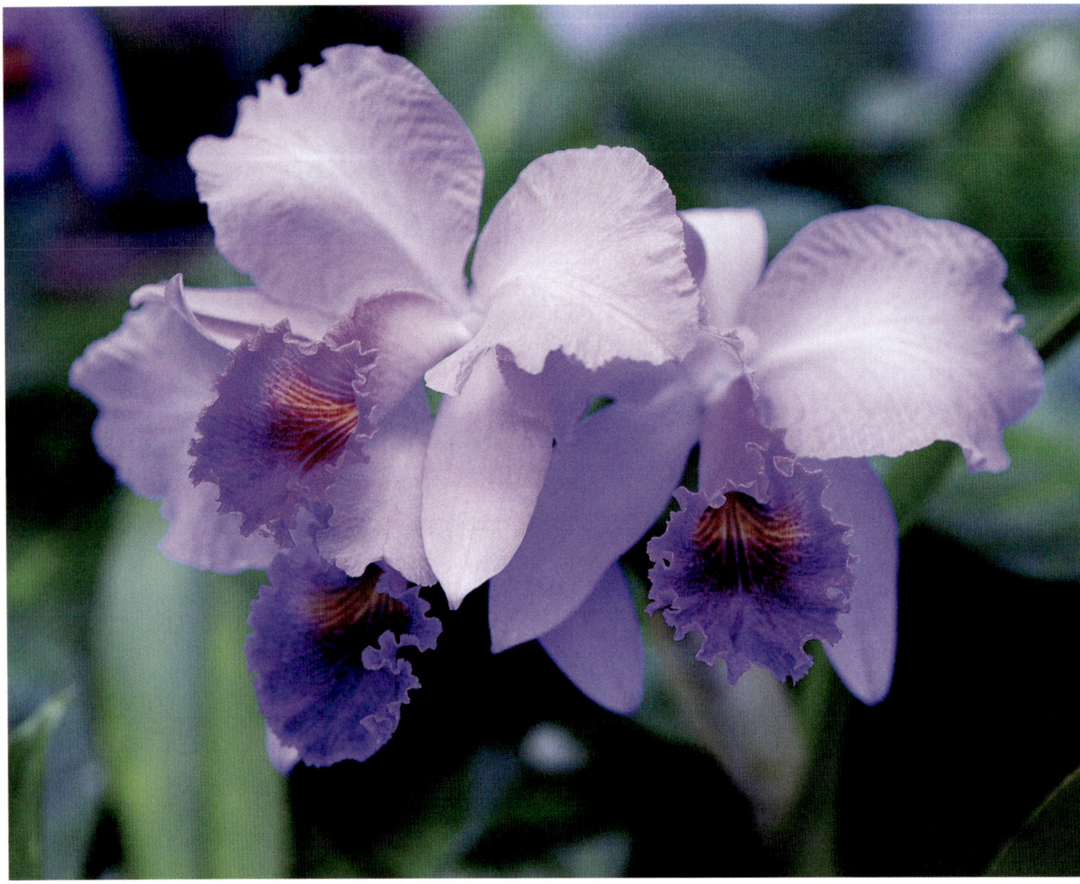

Figure 5.13 Only the blossoms in the foreground are in focus—the area behind them appears blurry because the depth-of-field is limited.

Using Autofocus

Autofocus can sometimes be frustrating for the new digital SLR photographer, especially those coming from the point-and-shoot world. That's because correct focus plays a greater role among your creative options with a dSLR, even when photographing the same subjects. Many non-dSLR digital cameras have sensors that are much tinier than the sensor in the D810. Those smaller sensors require shorter focal lengths, which have, effectively, more depth-of-field.

The bottom line is that with the average point-and-shoot camera, *everything* is in focus from about one foot to infinity and at virtually every f/stop. Unless you're shooting close-up photos a few inches from the camera, the depth-of-field is prodigious, and autofocus is almost a non-factor. The D810, on the other hand, is a full-frame camera that uses longer focal length lenses to achieve the same field of view with its larger sensor, so there is less depth-of-field. That's a *good* thing, creatively, because you have the choice to use selective focus to isolate subjects. But it does make the correct use of autofocus more critical. To maintain the most creative control, you have to choose three attributes:

- **How much is in focus.** Generally, by choosing the f/stop used, you'll determine the *range* of sharpness/amount of depth-of-field. The larger the DOF, the "easier" it is for the autofocus system's locked-in focus point to be appropriate (even though, strictly speaking, there is only one actual plane of sharp focus). With less depth-of-field, the accuracy of the focus point becomes more critical, because even a small error will result in an out-of-focus shot.
- **What subject is in focus.** The portion of your subject that is zeroed in for autofocus is determined by the autofocus zone that is active, and which is chosen either by you or by the Nikon D810 (as described next). For example, when shooting portraits, it's actually okay for part of the subject—or even part of the subject's face—to be slightly out of focus as long as the eyes (or even just the *nearest* eye) appear sharp.
- **When focus is applied.** For static shots of objects that aren't moving, *when* focus is applied doesn't matter much. But when you're shooting sports, or birds in flight, or children, the subject may move within the viewfinder as you're framing the image. Whether that movement is across the frame or headed right toward you, timing the instant when autofocus is applied can be important.

Autofocus Simplifies Our Lives... Doesn't It?

Manual focus is tricky, requires judgment, and fast reflexes. So, we're all better off now that autofocus has become almost universal, right? On the one hand, AF does save time and allows us to capture subjects (particularly fast-moving sports) that are difficult to image sharply using manual focusing (unless you have training and know certain techniques). On the other hand, learning to apply the Nikon D810's autofocus system most effectively requires a bit of study and some practice. Then, once you're comfortable with autofocus, you'll know when it's appropriate to use the manual focus option, too.

The important thing to remember is that focus isn't absolute. For example, some things that look in sharp focus at a given viewing size and distance might not be in focus at a larger size and/or closer distance. In addition, the goal of optimum focus isn't always to make things look sharp. Not all of an image will be or should be sharp. Controlling exactly what is sharp and what is not is part of your creative palette. Use of depth-of-field characteristics to throw part of an image out of focus while other parts are sharply focused is one of the most valuable tools available to a photographer. But selective focus works only when the desired areas of an image are in focus properly. For the digital SLR photographer, correct focus can be one of the trickiest parts of the technical and creative process.

The D810 now uses Nikon's 51-zone Advanced Multi-CAM 3500FX autofocus system. (The "Advanced" part of the nomenclature refers to some improvements made since the original D800 was introduced, such as the Group-area AF option I'll describe shortly.) The D810 deploys an intelligent array of cross-type sensors and horizontal sensors in the viewing system. All 51 autofocus sensors can be used individually or in groups of 9, 21, or all 51 focus zones. The AF system uses the color and light values, as measured by the 91,000 pixel RGB exposure sensor to accurately track moving objects, and to classify subjects.

Like all camera autofocus sensors, those in your D810 require a minimum amount of light as well as a minimum aperture size to operate, which is why autofocus capabilities are possible only with lenses having an f/8 or larger maximum aperture. While there's not a lot you can do to "fix" a lens that has a maximum aperture that's too small, if your subject's focus is difficult to evaluate because of waning light levels, the AF assist beam built into the D810 (usually of minimal aid because it is relatively weak) and the assist beams of Nikon's dedicated flash units provide additional light that helps assure enough illumination for autofocus under some circumstances.

SUPERIOR FACE TRACKING

If you're using Auto-area AF (discussed later in this chapter), the D810 has enough resolution in its exposure system to identify faces, and use that information to track your human subjects. That's a powerful capability for anyone shooting sports or other fast-moving subjects. Face detection is, by default, active all the time, but can be disabled. Don't look for the switch under the D810's AF options; it's located under Custom Setting b5 Matrix Metering. (Face detection is also used in calculating exposure.)

Bringing the Advanced Multi-CAM 3500FX AF System into Focus

I've explained individual bits and pieces of the Nikon D810's autofocus system earlier in this book, particularly in the "roadmap" sections that showed you where all the controls were located, and the "setup" chapters that explained the key autofocus options. Now it's time to round out the coverage as we tie everything together. There are three aspects of autofocus that you need to understand to use this essential feature productively. They apply—in slightly different ways—to both autofocus when using the optical viewfinder, and in live view/movie modes. For now, we're going to concentrate on the optical viewfinder/phase detection system's most important features:

- **Autofocus point selection.** This aspect controls how the D810 selects which areas of the frame are used to evaluate focus. Point selection allows the camera (or you) to specify a subject and lock focus in on that subject.

- **Autofocus mode and priority.** This governs *when* during the framing and shooting process autofocus is achieved. Should the camera focus *once* when activated, or *continue* to monitor your subject and refocus should the subject move? Is it okay to take a picture even if sharp focus isn't yet achieved, or should the camera lock out the shutter release until the image is sharp?
- **Autofocus activation.** When should the autofocus process begin, and when should it be locked? This aspect is related to the autofocus mode, but uses controls that you can specify to activate and/or lock the autofocus process.

Autofocus Point Selection Overview

I'm discussing this aspect of autofocus first, because, in many ways, it is the most important. If your D810 isn't focusing on the correct subject, autofocus speed and activation are pretty much wasted effort. As you've learned, the D810 has up to 51 different points on the screen that can be individually selected by you or the camera as the active focus zone.

The number and type of autofocus sensors in use can affect how well the system operates. The focus sensors can consist of lines of pixels (oriented either vertically or horizontally), cross-shapes, and/or a mixture of these types within a single camera, as with the D810. The more AF points available, the more easily the camera can differentiate among areas of the frame, and the more precisely you can specify the area you want to be in focus if you're manually choosing a focus spot.

But, there's another side of the coin. There is such a thing as *too many* focus zones for some types of subjects. For example, when using 51 focus points to select a zone for large, evenly illuminated subjects, you can waste a lot of time thumbing the multi selector among the four-dozen (plus) focus points. That's why Custom Setting a8 lets you switch the D810 to a more widely spaced set of 11 focus zones that you can select quickly. Figure 5.14 shows the distribution of the active focus points when in 51-point mode (top) or 11-point mode (bottom).

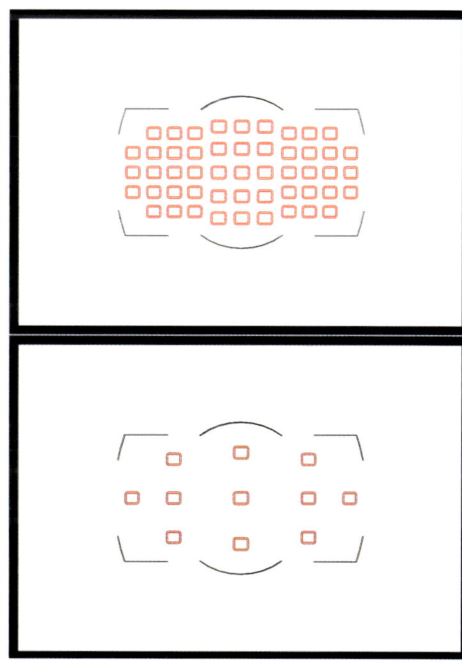

Figure 5.14 The D810 can use a dense set of 51 focus points (top), or a wider array of 11 points (bottom).

As the camera collects contrast information from the sensors, it then evaluates the data to determine whether the desired sharp focus has been achieved. The calculations may include whether the subject is moving, and whether the camera needs to "predict" where the subject will be when the shutter release button is fully depressed and the picture is taken.

(Predictive focus tracking kicks in when the camera is set to AF-C continuous autofocus. I'll explain these modes in more detail in the next section.)

The speed with which the camera is able to evaluate focus and then move the lens elements into the proper position to achieve the sharpest focus determines how fast the autofocus mechanism is. Although your D810 will almost always focus more quickly than a human, there are types of shooting situations where that's not fast enough. For example, if you're having problems shooting sports because the D810's autofocus system manically follows each moving subject, a better choice might be to switch autofocus modes or shift into manual and prefocus on a spot where you anticipate the action will be, such as a goal line or soccer net. At night football games, for example, when I am shooting with a telephoto lens almost wide open, I often focus manually on one of the referees who happens to be standing where I expect the action to be taking place (say, a halfback run or a pass reception). I also use *trap focus*, which is a technique discussed in a sidebar later in this chapter.

Choosing Autofocus Point Selection Mode

The D810 has only three different focus point selection modes. I'm going to describe each of the three modes, and explain how to use them. To set any of the three point selection modes, rotate the focus mode selector switch, located on the front of the camera (under the lens release button) to the AF position. Then, hold down the button in the center of that switch (seen in Figure 5.15) and rotate the sub-command dial. The selected AF mode will appear in the viewfinder briefly as you make your selection, and on top of the camera in the control panel. It will also be shown on the back-panel LCD when the shooting settings screen is active. (See Figure 5.16.)

Single-Point AF

In this mode, you always select the focus point manually, using the multi selector button (which, helpfully, will respond to your thumb presses not only in the left/right and up/down directions, but diagonally, as well). The D810 evaluates focus based solely on the point you select, making this a good choice for subjects that don't move much. As I mentioned earlier, you can use Custom Setting

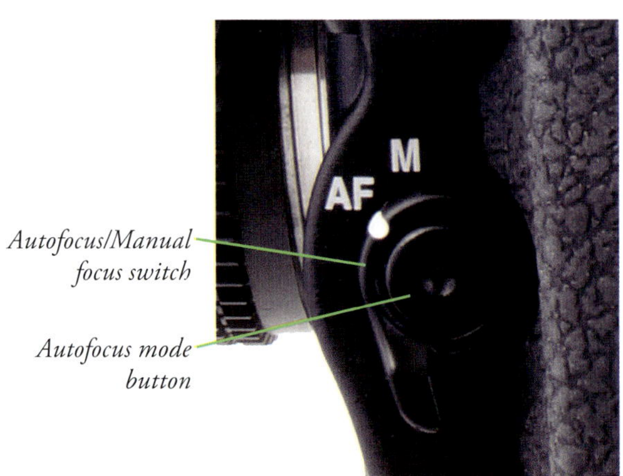

Figure 5.15
The Autofocus mode selector switch is used to choose autofocus settings.

a8 to choose whether the selected focus point resides in an 11-point widely spaced distribution, or within the full 51-point array. In either Single-point AF or Dynamic-area AF, if you want to lock the focus point you've selected for a series of shots, rotate the focus selector lock lever surrounding the multi selector back to the L position. You can also temporarily lock the focus point by partially depressing the shutter release, or pressing the AE-L/AF-L button (unless you've redefined this behavior to some other controls in the Custom Settings menu).

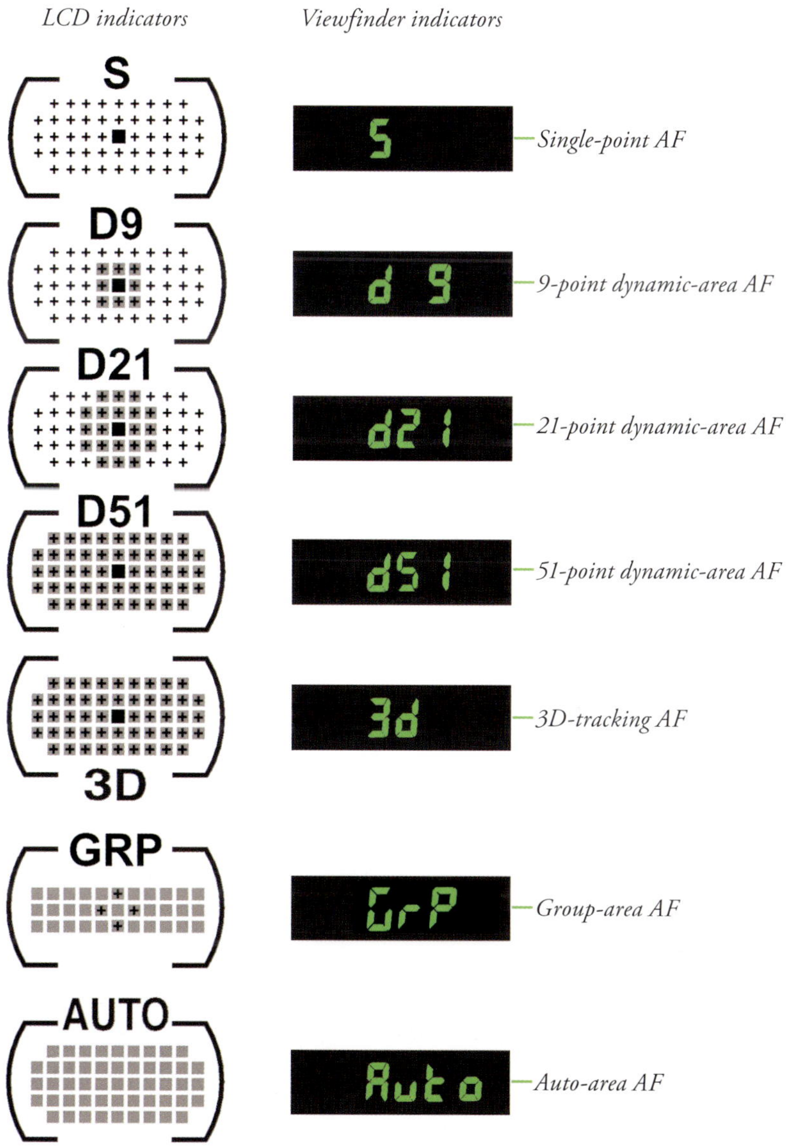

Figure 5.16
Autofocus point selection modes.

Dynamic-Area AF

In this mode, you still select the focus point yourself using the multi selector button, and when using Single-servo autofocus (AF-S, discussed later), the D810 will evaluate focus solely based on that point. In that respect, the D810 behaves exactly as it does in Single-point AF mode. However, if you have chosen Continuous-servo autofocus (AF-C), the D810's "smarts" spring to life if your subject leaves the selected focus zone. When that happens, the camera re-evaluates focus based on the other focus points surrounding the one you chose. To recap, you can set the D810 so that it will use 9, 21, or 51 points. You can view what pattern is currently being used by pressing the Info button and viewing the autofocus array representation in the screen that pops up.

- **9 points.** Only eight focus points surrounding the selected point will be used, allowing the D810 to respond quickly to subjects that are moving in a predictable way.
- **21 points.** Should the subject leave the selected focus point, the D810 will refocus based on information from 20 surrounding focus points. This mode is best for subjects that are moving erratically. Autofocus may take slightly longer because more points are considered. I prefer this mode most of the time.

Note

The active focus points surrounding the red highlighted focus zone will shift around the array as you move the manually chosen focus point.

- **51 points.** Should the subject leave your selected focus point, the camera will refocus based on information from all 50 surrounding focus points, which may be best for fast moving subjects.
- **51 point (3D-tracking).** Should the subject leave your selected focus zone, the camera uses distance information to calculate the path of the subject and select a new focus point. Nikon recommends using this setting to focus subjects that move erratically from side to side, because the camera can use the distance information to differentiate the original subject from objects that are closer or farther away. The camera uses pattern recognition to keep track of your actual subject, based on information from multiple focus points—it knows the "shape" of your subject, and thus can follow it more reliably. In AF-C focus mode, the camera tracks subjects that leave the selected focus point and chooses new focus points as needed.

3D-Tracking

All 51 points are used, and you can select the focus point as described for the other modes. Should the subject leave your selected focus zone, the D810 uses distance information to calculate the path of the subject and select a new focus point. Nikon recommends using this setting to focus subjects that move erratically from side to side (say, a child at play or a basketball player moving around the court on defense), because the camera can use the distance information to differentiate the original subject from objects that are closer or farther away. Tracking will abort if your subject leaves the viewfinder entirely; in that case, release the shutter button and reframe your image with your subject in the selected focus point.

Group-Area AF

The D810 uses a group of focus points that you select, thereby enlarging the focus area compared to single-point focus. Faces that are detected when using AF-S focus mode will be given priority. This point selection mode is helpful for focusing on subjects that are difficult to track, such as fast-moving children.

Automatic-Area AF

In this mode, autofocus point selection is out of your hands; the D810 performs the task for you using its own intelligence. If you are using a type G or D lens, the camera can even work with the supplied distance information to distinguish humans from their background, so a person standing at the side of the frame will be detected and used to evaluate focus, while the camera ignores the background area in the frame.

The D810 tends to keep the active focus point somewhat of a mystery (although it will be displayed during picture review if you've activated that option). In AF-S mode, the active focus point is highlighted in the viewfinder for about one second after focus is achieved. In AF-C mode, the active focus point is not shown. This is the mode that allows face-tracking using the 91,000 point RGB exposure sensor. The D810 will find faces in your image and use the sensor's data to track focus on that subject as it moves within the frame.

Store by Orientation

Some types of shooting call for different ways of choosing a focus point's orientation. For example, say you're shooting a sport like basketball that lends itself to both horizontal and vertical framing. You may rotate your camera constantly as the action unfolds, but want the focus point to remain in the upper portion of your horizontal or vertical frame. That won't happen if you are shooting with a D810 in its default mode. Your chosen focus point will stay fixed relative to the other points and "rotate" along with the camera, as shown at top in Figure 5.17. The same focus point in the camera's array is used regardless of the D810's orientation.

With the D810, however, you have another option, tucked away in Custom Setting a9, Store by Orientation. Set to Off, the camera behaves exactly like the D810 and as shown in the upper half of Figure 5.17. However, you can also choose Focus Point or Focus Point and AF-Area Mode, which allow *different* focus points to be selected for each of the three likely camera orientations (ignoring the possible, but less likely upside-down horizontal position).

When either of the latter two options are selected, simply rotate the camera to any of the three configurations, and select the focus point you want. Repeat, if you like, for the other two. (It's best to do this during a lull in the action, although you can reselect points on the fly if you like.) Then, as you shoot you'll notice the focus point shifting in the viewfinder as you rotate the camera. You don't need to keep the point in the same relative position in the frame (as I just described). You can select any focus point for any of the three orientations if, for example, you're shooting architecture and want to focus on a different position in the frame as you vary camera orientation.

It gets better. Select Focus Point and AF-Area mode, and you can choose a different AF-Area mode for *each* orientation, using Single Point, Dynamic Area, or Automatic Area selection, depending on how you hold the camera.

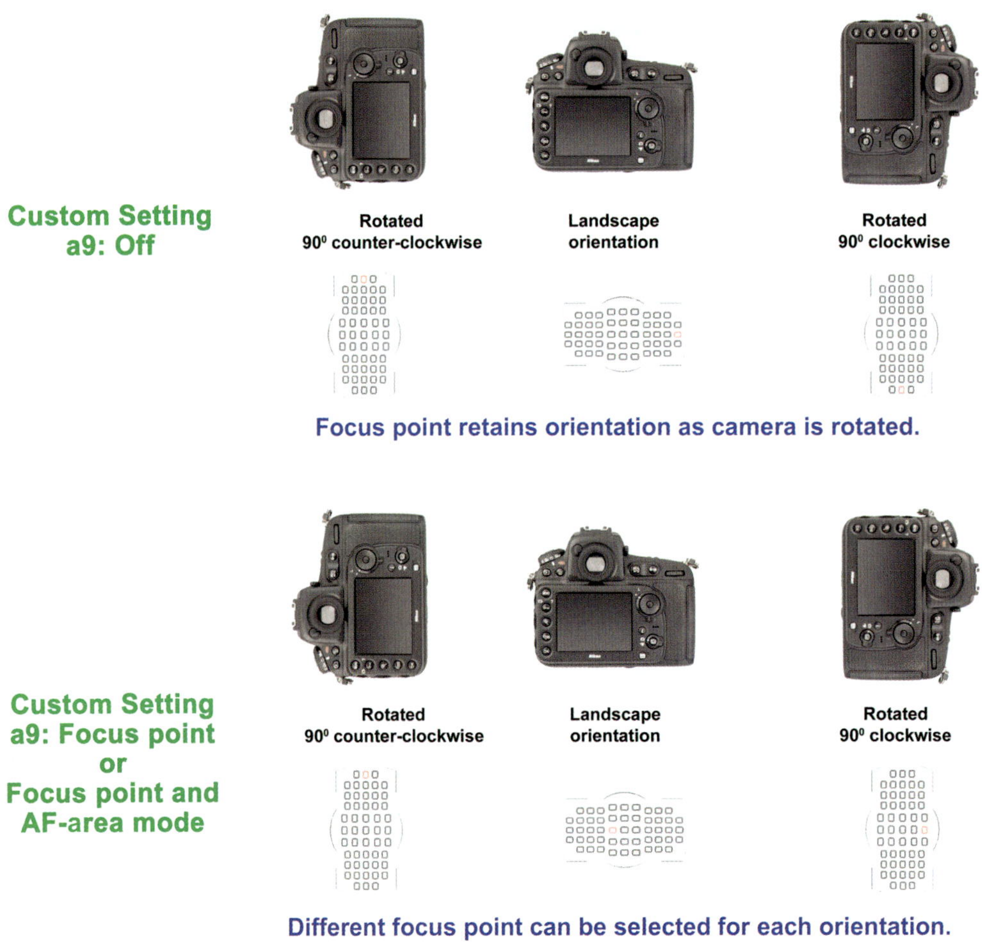

Figure 5.17 Store AF points by orientation—or not.

Restricting Modes

If you have certain AF-area modes or Autofocus modes that you don't use much, you can lock them out so they can't be selected by holding down the AF-Mode button and rotating the main and sub-command dials. Chapter 12 shows you how to use Custom Setting option a11 to disable any of the AF-area modes (except for Single-point AF), or disable either AF-S or AF-C modes (described next).

Autofocus Mode and Priority

Choosing the right autofocus mode (AF-S, AF-C, or Manual) is another key to focusing success. To save battery power, your D810 doesn't start to focus the lens until you partially depress the shutter release or press the AE-L/AF-L button on the back of the camera or on the MB-D12 battery pack/grip (unless you've reprogrammed the button for some other function or have specified another control to activate autofocus, as described in Chapter 12). But, autofocus isn't some mindless beast out there snapping your pictures in and out of focus with no feedback from you after you press that button. There are several settings you can modify that return at least a modicum of control to you. Your first decision should be whether you set the D810 to AF-S, AF-C, or Manual.

To set any of the three modes, with the AF mode switch in the AF position, hold down the center button of the focus mode selector switch on the front of the camera (under the lens release button, and seen earlier in Figure 5.15) and rotate the main command dial. The selected AF mode will appear in the viewfinder briefly as you make your selection, and on top of the camera in the control panel. It will also be shown on the back-panel LCD monitor when the shooting settings screen is active.

Autofocus Mode

This choice determines *when* your D810 starts to autofocus, and what it does when focus is achieved. Automatic focus is not something that happens all the time when your camera is turned on.

Single-Servo Autofocus (AF-S)

In this mode, also called *AF-S*, focus is set once and remains at that setting until the button is fully depressed, taking the picture, or until you release the shutter button without taking a shot. For non-action photography, this setting is usually your best choice, as it minimizes out-of-focus pictures (at the expense of spontaneity). The drawback here is that you might not be able to take a picture at all while the camera is seeking focus; you're locked out until the autofocus mechanism is happy with the current setting. As described in Chapter 12, you can set AF-S mode to use either focus-priority (the default) or release-priority using Custom Setting a2.

When sharp focus is achieved, the selected focus point will flash red in the viewfinder, and the focus confirmation light at the lower left will flash green. If you're using Matrix metering, the exposure will be locked at the same time. By keeping the shutter button depressed halfway, you'll find you can reframe the image while retaining the focus (and exposure) that's been set. You can also use the AE-L/AF-L button if you've defined that button (as described in Chapter 12) to lock focus when pressed. Because of the small delay while the camera zeroes in on correct focus, you might experience slightly more shutter lag. AF-S mode uses less battery power.

Continuous-Servo Autofocus (AF-C)

This mode, also known as *AF-C*, is the mode to use for sports and other fast-moving subjects. In this mode, once the shutter release is partially depressed, the camera sets the focus but continues to monitor the subject, so that if it moves or you move, the lens will be refocused to suit. Focus and exposure aren't really locked until you press the shutter release down all the way to take the picture. You'll find that AF-C produces the least amount of shutter lag of any autofocus mode when set to release priority: press the button and the camera fires. It also uses the most battery power, because the autofocus system operates as long as the shutter release button is partially depressed.

Continuous-servo autofocus uses a technology called *predictive tracking AF*, which allows the D810 to calculate the correct focus if the subject is moving toward or away from the camera at a constant rate. It uses either the automatically selected AF point (in Auto-area AF mode) or the point you select manually to set focus. As described in Chapter 12, you can set AF-C mode to use release-priority (the default), or focus priority using Custom Setting a1.

If you want to lock the focus point you've selected for a series of shots, rotate the focus selector lock lever up to the L position. You can also temporarily lock the focus point by partially depressing the shutter release, or pressing the AE-L/AF-L button (unless you've redefined this behavior to some other controls in the Custom Settings menu).

Manual Focus

With manual focus activated by sliding the switch on the lens to the M position, or rotating the switch on the camera body near the lens mount to M, your D810 lets you set the focus yourself. (Both the camera and lens settings must agree if you want to use an autofocus mode; when either is set to Manual, then only manual focus is possible.) There are some advantages and disadvantages to this approach. While your batteries will last longer in manual focus mode, it will take you longer to focus the camera for each photo, a process that can be difficult. Modern digital cameras, even dSLRs, depend so much on autofocus that the viewfinders are no longer designed for optimum manual focus. Pick up any film camera and you'll see a bigger, brighter viewfinder with a focusing screen that's a joy to focus on manually.

WARNING

Do not use a lens marked AF (rather than AF-S) when the focus mode switch on the lens is set to M and the switch on the camera is set to AF. As you'll learn in Chapter 7, non-AF-S lenses do not have a built-in focus motor, and are focused by a motor in the camera body instead. When you set up the lens/camera in this conflicting configuration, it's possible the camera's internal motor may try to focus the lens (which has been set for manual focus only) and, with some lenses, damage can occur to the camera's focus motor. With AF-S lenses, the lens and body switches should agree, but no damage should occur if you have a mismatch; if *either* switch is set to M, then manual focus is what you will get.

If the lens mounted on your camera has a maximum f/stop of f/5.6 or larger, you can use the D810's *electronic rangefinder* feature to assist in focusing manually. Just follow these steps:

1. **Activate manual focus.** Set the lens *and* camera focus mode to M (see the warning above). If you happen to be using an old non-autofocus (manual focus) lens, you're all set—it won't autofocus under any circumstances.
2. **Select a focus point.** With the focus point selector lock off, select one of the 51 focus points using the multi selector.
3. **Press the shutter release button halfway.** This activates the D810's autofocus system, which continues to function even though the camera's ability to adjust the focus of the lens has been disabled.
4. **Rotate the lens's focus ring.** Adjust until the in-focus indicator at the lower left of the viewfinder display illuminates continually. Arrows on either side of the indicator will illuminate to help you focus in the correct direction.
5. **Confirm.** Visually evaluate whether you're actually in sharp focus—the in-focus indicator is sometimes wrong, because it doesn't really know the exact plane you want to be in focus!

Autofocus Activation... and More

The final considerations in using autofocus are the control or controls used to activate and lock autofocus, plus a few odds and ends. I'll cover them in ample detail in Chapter 12, which explains all the options, but here are some cross references if you feel you need some review. I'm also going to continue the discussion of focusing in Chapter 14, which explains live view and movie making, and some special focus options the D810 has when using those two modes.

- **Focus tracking with lock on.** Intervening subjects passing in front of your main area of interest can interfere with autofocus. Set a delay time before the camera refocuses using Custom Setting a3, as described in Chapter 12.

- **Focus Point illumination.** This option lets you choose to have the active focus point displayed in manual focus mode all the time, or only during focus point selection; display the selected focus point and surrounding focus points in dynamic-area AF mode; or display active focus points as boxes or dots when using Group-area AF. This maze of possibilities for Custom Setting a5 will be explained in Chapter 12.
- **AF point illumination.** Do you want the *active* autofocus point illuminated when that is an option? Look up Custom Setting a6 in Chapter 12. You can have the point highlighted in red only when necessary to contrast with a background; on all the time; or off.
- **Focus point wrap around.** Do you want the focus point to wrap around to the opposite side during manual selection? Use Custom Setting a7.
- **AF-assist illuminator.** Need to turn off the autofocus assist illuminator for your built-in flash? Use Custom Setting a10.
- **Autofocus Mode Restrictions.** If there is an autofocus mode you want to lock out, you can disable AF-S *or* AF-C, or allow both when using the optical viewfinder to frame your image by selecting the mode(s) you want to use.
- **Which controls activate/lock autofocus.** You can use a half-press of the shutter release or a press of the AE-L/AF-L button (or both), or another button. See the instructions for Custom Settings f4, f5, and f6 in Chapter 12 for your options.
- **Center/show focus point.** You can program the multi selector center button to either jump the active focus point to the center or to highlight the active focus point, using Custom Setting f2, as described in Chapter 12.

Focusing in Live View

When you're not using the optical viewfinder, and instead using the D810's live view mode on the back panel color monitor, available modes differ slightly. Instead of using phase detection autofocus (or the human eye's contrast detection system when focusing manually), the D810 puts contrast detection to work full-time. The camera evaluates the focus of the image as seen by the sensor, and makes adjustments from there.

This section will explain your live view focus options.

Focus Mode

Activate live view for still or movie mode by rotating the Lv switch to either Still or Movie modes, and then pressing the Lv button on the back of the D810. Then press the information edit button to view the information edit screen. You can then adjust the focus mode by pressing the focus mode button and rotating the main command dial. The available modes differ slightly from those possible when not shooting in live view mode, and your selection will appear at the top of the live view screen (highlighted in yellow when initially set):

- **AF-S.** This single autofocus mode, which Nikon calls single-servo AF, locks focus when the shutter release is pressed halfway. This mode uses *focus-priority;* the shutter can be fully released to take a picture only if the D810 is able to achieve sharp focus.
- **AF-F.** This mode is roughly the equivalent of AF-C. Nikon calls it full-time servo AF. The D810 focuses and refocuses continually as you shoot stills in live view mode or record movies. Unlike AF-C, this mode also uses focus-priority. You can't release the shutter unless the camera has achieved sharp focus.

Focus Area

With the focus mode button depressed, you can also choose the D810's AF-area mode for live view by rotating the sub-command dial. Your choices are as follows:

- **Face-priority AF.** The camera automatically detects faces, and focuses on subjects facing the camera, as when you're shooting a portrait. You can't select the focus zone yourself. Instead, a double yellow border will be displayed on the LCD monitor when the camera detects a face. You don't need to press the shutter release to activate this behavior. (Up to five faces may be detected; the D810 focuses on the face that is closest to the camera.) When you press down the shutter release halfway, the camera attempts to focus the face. As sharp focus is achieved, the border turns green (see Figure 5.18). If the camera is unable to focus, the border blinks red. Focus may also be lost if the subject turns away from the camera and is no longer detectable by Face-priority.
- **Wide-area AF.** This is the mode to use for non-portrait subjects, such as landscapes, as you can select the focus zone to be used manually. It's good for shooting hand-held, because the subjects may change as you reframe the image with a hand-held camera, and the wide-area zones are forgiving of these changes. The focus zone will be outlined in red. You can move the focus zone around the screen with the multi selector buttons. When sharp focus is achieved, the focus zone box will turn green. (See Figure 5.19.)
- **Normal-area AF.** This mode uses smaller focus zones, and so is best suited for tripod-mounted images where the camera is held fairly steady. As with Wide-area AF, the focus zone will be outlined in red. You can move the focus zone around the screen with the multi selector buttons. When sharp focus is achieved, the focus zone box will turn green. (See Figure 5.20.)
- **Subject-tracking AF.** This mode allows the camera to "grab" a subject, focus, and then follow the subject as it moves within the frame. You can use this mode for subjects that don't remain stationary, such as small children. When using Subject-tracking AF, a white border appears in the center of the frame, and turns yellow when focus is locked in (as described in the section that follows). To activate focus or refocus, press the multi selector up button. I'll explain Subject-tracking in more detail next. (See Figure 5.21.)

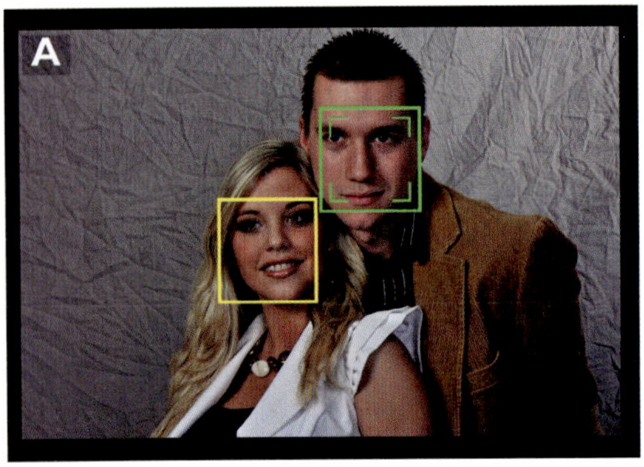

Figure 5.18 Face-priority AF attempts to focus on the face that's closest to the camera.

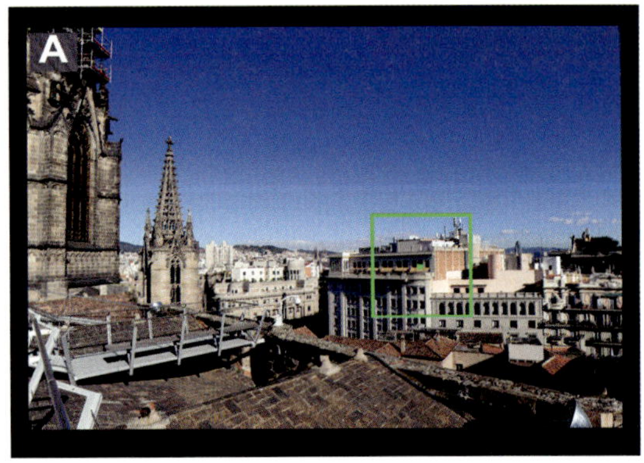

Figure 5.19 Wide-area AF is best for landscapes and other subjects with large elements.

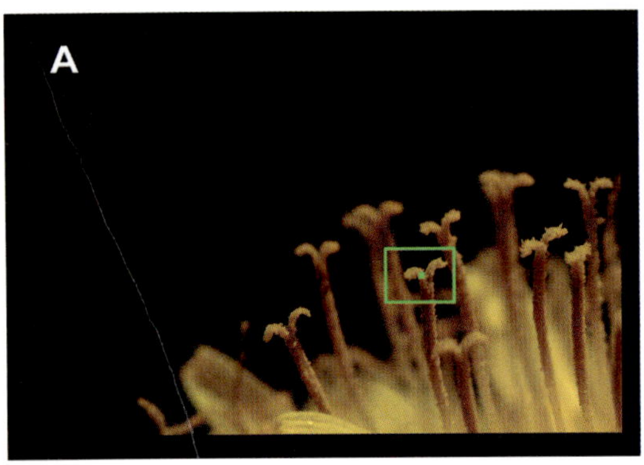

Figure 5.20 Normal-area AF allows you to zero in on a specific point of focus.

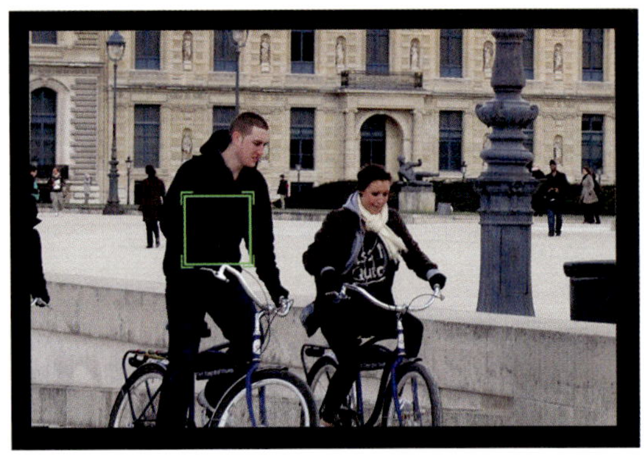

Figure 5.21 Subject-tracking can keep focus as it follows your subject around in the frame.

- **Manual focus.** In this non-automatic focus mode, which you have to select by setting the focus mode switch on the camera and lens to M, you can select the focus zone to use with the multi selector buttons, press the shutter release halfway, and then adjust focus manually by rotating the focus ring on the lens. When sharp focus is achieved, the focus confirmation indicator at the lower left of the viewfinder will turn a steady green.

Introducing Subject-Tracking

The useful Subject-tracking autofocus feature is one of those features that can be confusing at first, but once you get the hang of it, it's remarkably easy to use. Face-priority, in comparison, is almost intuitive to learn. Here's the quick introduction you need to Subject-tracking.

- **Ready, aim…** When you've activated Subject-tracking, a white border appears in the center of the frame. Use that border to "aim" the camera until the subject you want to focus on and track is located within the border.

- **...Focus.** When you've pinpointed your subject, press the OK button to activate the D810's contrast detection autofocus feature. The focus frame will turn yellow and the camera will emit a beep (unless you've disabled the beep within the Setup menu) when locked in.
- **Reframe as desired.** Once the focus frame has turned yellow, it seemingly takes on a life of its own, and will "follow" your subject around on the monitor as you reframe your image. (See Figure 5.21.) (In other words, the subject being tracked doesn't have to be in the center of the frame for the actual photo.) Best of all, if your subject moves, the D810 will follow it and keep focus as required.
- **Tracking continues.** The only glitches that may pop up might occur if your subject is small and difficult to track, or is too close in tonal value to its background, or if the subject approaches the camera or recedes sufficiently to change its relative size on the monitor significantly.
- **Grab a new subject.** If you want to refocus or grab a new subject, press the OK button again.

Focus Stacking

If you are doing macro (close-up) photography of flowers, or other small objects at short distances, the depth-of-field often will be extremely narrow. In some cases, it will be so narrow that it will be impossible to keep the entire subject in focus in one photograph. Although having part of the image out of focus can be a pleasing effect for a portrait of a person, it is likely to be a hindrance when you are trying to make an accurate photographic record of a flower, or small piece of precision equipment. One solution to this problem is focus stacking, a procedure that can be considered like HDR translated for the world of focus—taking multiple shots with different settings, and, using software as explained below, combining the best parts from each image in order to make a whole that is better than the sum of the parts. Focus stacking requires a non-moving object, so some subjects, such as flowers, are best photographed in a breezeless environment, such as indoors.

For example, see Figures 5.22 through 5.24, in which I took photographs of three colorful crayons. As you can see from these images, the depth-of-field was extremely narrow, and only a small part of the subject was in focus for each shot.

Now look at Figure 5.25, in which the entire subject is in reasonably sharp focus. This image is a composite, made up of the three shots above, as well as 10 others, each one focused on the same scene, but at very gradually increasing distances from the camera's lens. All 13 images were then combined in Adobe Photoshop using the focus stacking procedure. Here are the steps you can take to combine shots for the purpose of achieving sharp focus in this sort of situation:

1. **Set the camera firmly on a solid tripod.** A tripod or other equally firm support is absolutely essential for this procedure.
2. **Attach a remote release, such as the MC-30.** You want to be able to trigger the camera without moving it.
3. **Set the camera to manual focus mode.** Use the procedure described in the previous section to activate manual focus.

4. **Set the exposure, ISO, and white balance manually.** Use test shots if necessary to determine the best values. This step in the Shooting menu will help prevent visible variations from arising among the multiple shots that you'll be taking. You don't want the D810 to change the ISO setting or white balance between shots.
5. **Set the quality of the images to NEF (RAW) + JPEG FINE.** Use the Shooting menu to make this adjustment. Having both formats will give you flexibility when combining the images.

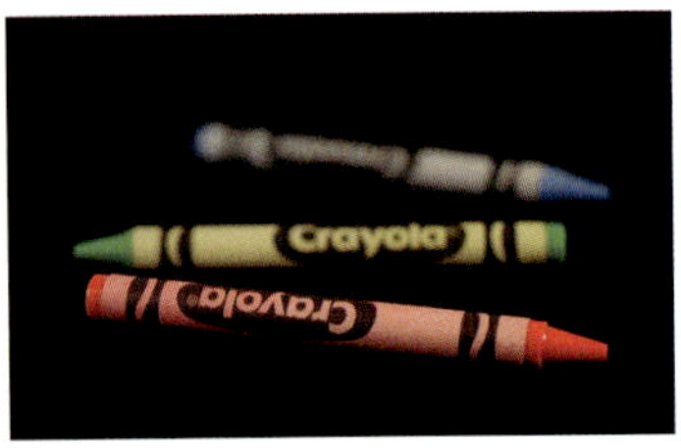

Figure 5.22

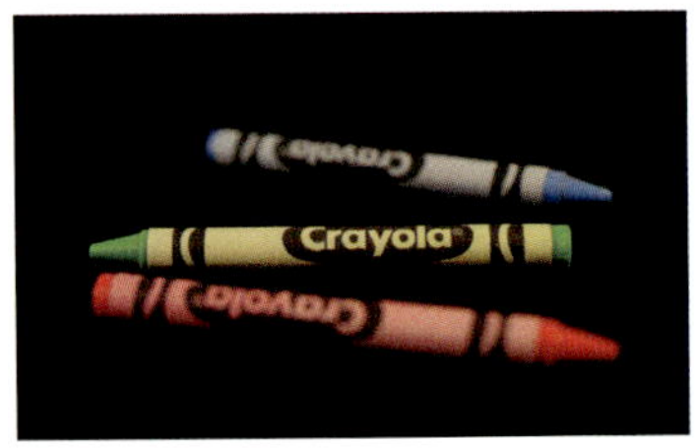

Figure 5.23

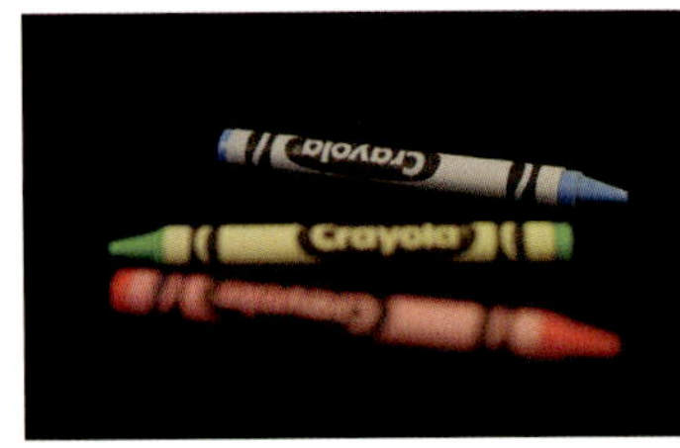

Figure 5.24

These three shots were all focused on different distances within the same scene. No single shot could bring the entire subject into sharp focus.

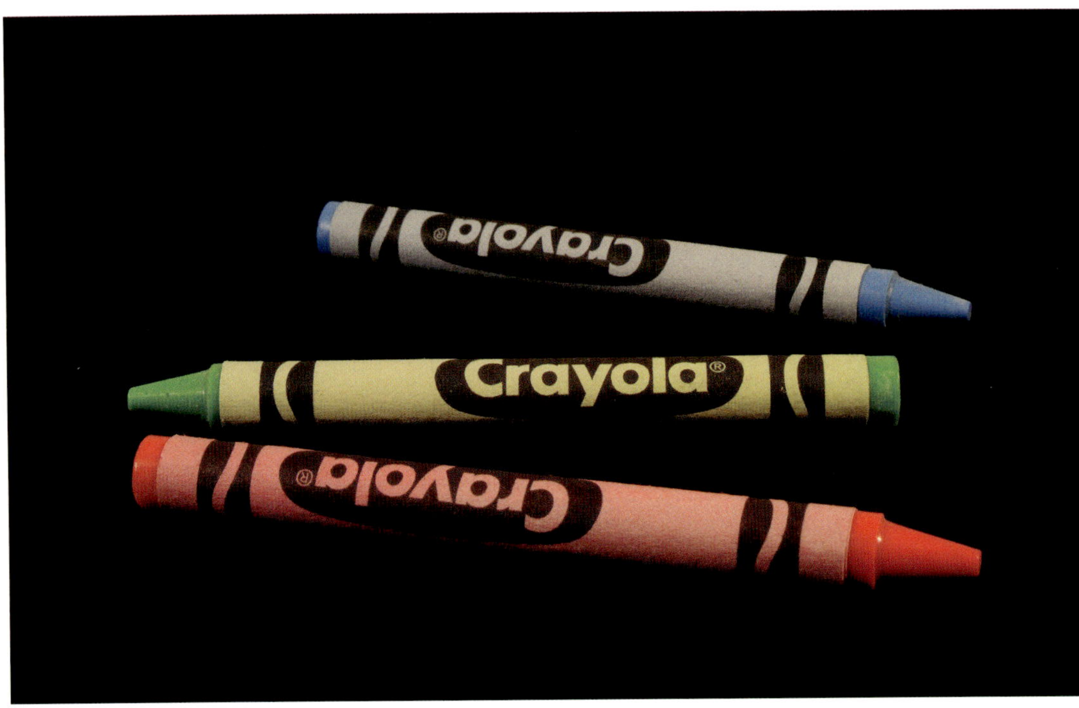

Figure 5.25 Three partially out-of-focus shots have been merged, along with ten others, through a focus stacking procedure in Adobe Photoshop, to produce a single image with the entire subject in focus.

6. **Turn off image stabilization.** Use the VR switch on your lens to disable vibration reduction, if that feature is available with that particular lens. You don't need it when the camera is securely mounted on a tripod, and disabling VR will keep the D810 from making any sort of image adjustment between exposures.
7. **Focus manually on the very closest point of the subject to the lens.** Rotate the multi selector dial to change the focus.
8. **Trip the shutter.** Use the remote.
9. **Carefully refocus.** Gently rotate the focus ring on the lens to focus on a point slightly farther away from the lens and trip the shutter again.
10. **Continue taking photographs** in this way until you have covered the entire subject with in-focus shots.

The next step is to process the images you've taken in Photoshop. Transfer the images to your computer, and then follow these steps:

1. In Photoshop, select File > Scripts > Load Files into Stack. In the dialog box that then appears, navigate on your computer to find the files for the photographs you have taken, and highlight them all.
2. At the bottom of the next dialog box that appears, check the box that says, "Attempt to Automatically Align Source Images," then click OK. The images will load; it may take several minutes for the program to load the images and attempt to arrange them into layers that are aligned based on their content.
3. Once the program has finished processing the images, go to the Layers panel and select all of the layers. You can do this by clicking on the top layer and then Shift-clicking on the bottom one.
4. While the layers are all selected, in Photoshop go to Edit > Auto-Blend Layers. In the dialog box that appears, select the two options, Stack Images and Seamless Tones and Colors, then click OK. The program will process the images, possibly for a considerable length of time.
5. If the procedure worked well, the result will be a single image made up of numerous layers that have been processed to produce a sharply focused rendering of your subject. If it did not work well, you may have to take additional images the next time, focusing very carefully on small slices of the subject as you move progressively farther away from the lens.

Although this procedure can work very well in Photoshop, you also may want to try it with programs that were developed more specifically for focus stacking and related procedures, such as Helicon Focus (www.heliconsoft.com), PhotoAcute (www.photoacute.com), or CombineZM (www.hadleyweb.pwp.blueyonder.co.uk).

Trap (Auto) Focus

For some unknown reason, Nikon removed the ability to use trap focus with the original D4 and D800/D800e. That oversight has been fixed through a firmware update for the D4 and D800-series, and in the later D810 and D4s. This technique comes in handy when you know where the action is going to take place (such as at the finish line of a horse race), but you don't know exactly *when.* The solution is to prefocus on the point where the action will occur, and then tell your camera not to actually take the photo until something moves into the prefocus spot (see Figure 5.26). It's a good technique for sports action when you know that, say, a runner is going to pass by a certain position. You can also use trap focus for hand-held macro shots—set focus for a particular distance and then move the camera toward your subject. The shutter will trip automatically when your subject comes into focus.

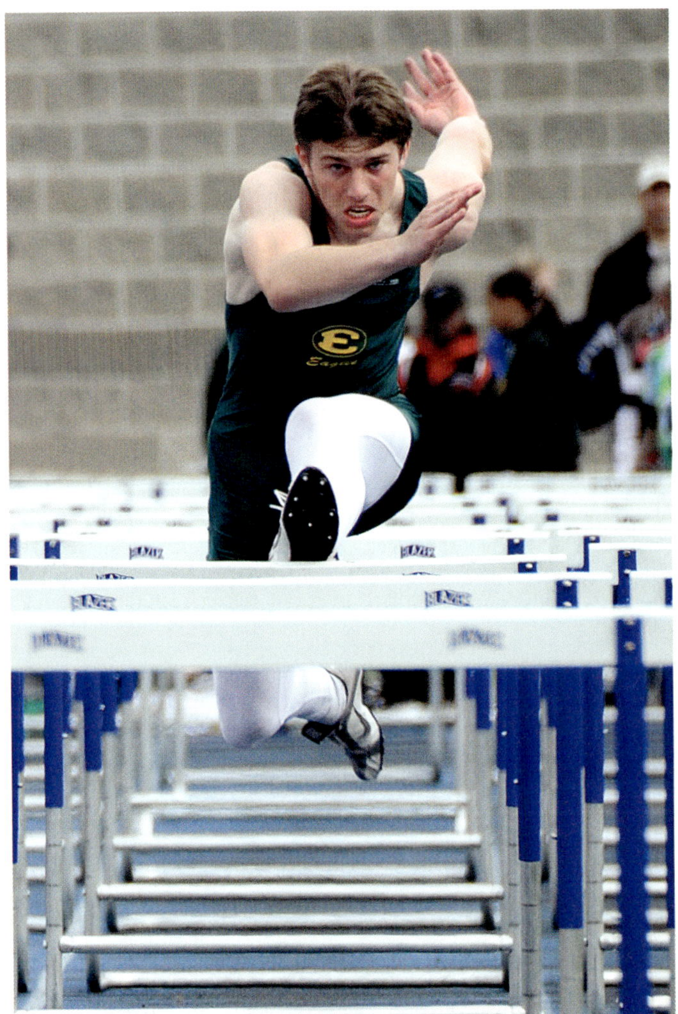

Figure 5.26
By prefocusing on one of the hurdlers, trap focus captured this athlete the instant he moved into the point of focus.

Trap focus isn't as difficult as you might think. The key is to decouple the focusing operation from the shutter release function. Just follow these steps:

1. **Set Custom Setting a4 to AF-ON Only.** At that setting, pressing the shutter release halfway down does *not* activate autofocus. That happens *only* when you press the AF-ON button.
2. **Set Custom Setting a2 to Focus Priority.** The shutter will trip only when your subject is in focus.
3. **Set focus mode to AF-S.**
4. **Set your point selection mode to Single Area.**
5. **Make sure your lens is set to autofocus (either A or M/A).**
6. **Prefocus on the spot where the action will occur, or an equivalent distance.** You can use the AE-L/AF-L button to activate focus.
7. **Reframe your picture, if necessary, so that nothing is at the prefocused distance.** (If an object occupies that spot, the D810 will take the photo immediately when you press the shutter release.)
8. **Press and hold down the shutter release all the way.** The camera will not refocus, because you've disconnected the autofocus function from the shutter release.
9. **The picture will be taken** when a subject moves into the prefocused area.

DANGER, WILL ROBINSON!

If you don't use trap focus often, or don't work with the AF-ON button as your primary autofocus start control regularly, don't make the mistake I did. One time I forgot that I had followed the steps above, and used a different camera (my Nikon D4) in the interim. The next time I picked up my D810, it "refused" to autofocus—at least when I pressed the shutter release halfway. Much consternation followed until I remembered what I had done a few days earlier, pressed the AF-ON button, and found that the AF function was just fine. I had simply "turned off" the shutter release as an AF start control.

Fine-Tuning the Focus of Your Lenses

In this section, I'll show you how to calibrate your lenses using the D810's AF Fine Tune feature.

Why is the focus "off" for some lenses in the first place? There are lots of factors, including the age of the lens (an older lens may focus slightly differently), temperature effects on certain types of glass, humidity, and tolerances built into a lens's design that all add up to a slight misadjustment, even though the components themselves are, strictly speaking, within specs. A very slight variation in your lens's mount can cause focus to vary slightly. With any luck (if you can call it that) a lens that doesn't focus exactly right will at least be consistent. If a lens always focuses a bit behind the subject, the symptom is *back focus.* If it focuses in front of the subject, it's called *front focus.*

As I noted, you're almost always better off sending such a lens in to Nikon to have them make it right. But that's not always possible. Perhaps you need your lens recalibrated right now, or you purchased a gray market lens that Nikon isn't willing to fix. If you want to do it yourself, the first thing to do is determine whether or not your lens has a back focus or front focus problem.

For a quick-and-dirty diagnosis (*not* a calibration; you'll use a different target for that), lay down a piece of graph paper on a flat surface, and place an object on the line at the middle, which will represent the point of focus (we hope). Then, shoot the target at an angle using your lens's widest aperture and the autofocus mode you want to test. Mount the camera on a tripod so you can get accurate, repeatable results.

If your camera/lens combination doesn't suffer from front or back focus, the point of sharpest focus will be the center line of the chart, as you can see in Figure 5.27. If you do have a problem, one of the other lines will be sharply focused instead. Should you discover that your lens consistently front or back focuses, it needs to be recalibrated. Unfortunately, it's only possible to calibrate a lens for a single focusing distance. So, if you use a particular lens (such as a macro lens) for close-focusing, calibrate for that. If you use a lens primarily for middle distances, calibrate for that. Close-to-middle distances are most likely to cause focus problems, anyway, because as you get closer to infinity, small changes in focus are less likely to have an effect.

Lens Tune-up

The key tool you can use to fine-tune your lens is the AF Fine Tune entry in the Setup menu, shown in Figure 5.28. You'll find the process easier to understand if you first run through this quick overview of the menu options:

- **AF fine tune (On/Off).** This option enables/disables AF fine-tuning for all the lenses you've defined using the menu entry. If you discover you don't care for the calibrations you make in certain situations (say, it works better for the lens you have mounted at middle distances, but is less successful at correcting close-up focus errors) you can deactivate the feature as you require. You should set this to On when you're doing the actual fine-tuning.
- **Saved value.** This setting lets you tune the autofocus calibration for the current CPU-chipped lens (virtually all Nikon-brand autofocus lenses) mounted on the D810. When you first fine-tune a lens, the saved value will be 0 (zero). You can press the multi selector up/down buttons to choose a value between +20 and –20. Positive numbers move the focal point farther from the camera, and would be used if your lens consistently suffers from front focus problems. Negative numbers move the focal point closer to the camera, and would be used if your lens is plagued with consistent back focus. The value is relative, and doesn't correlate to any particular distance or percentage.

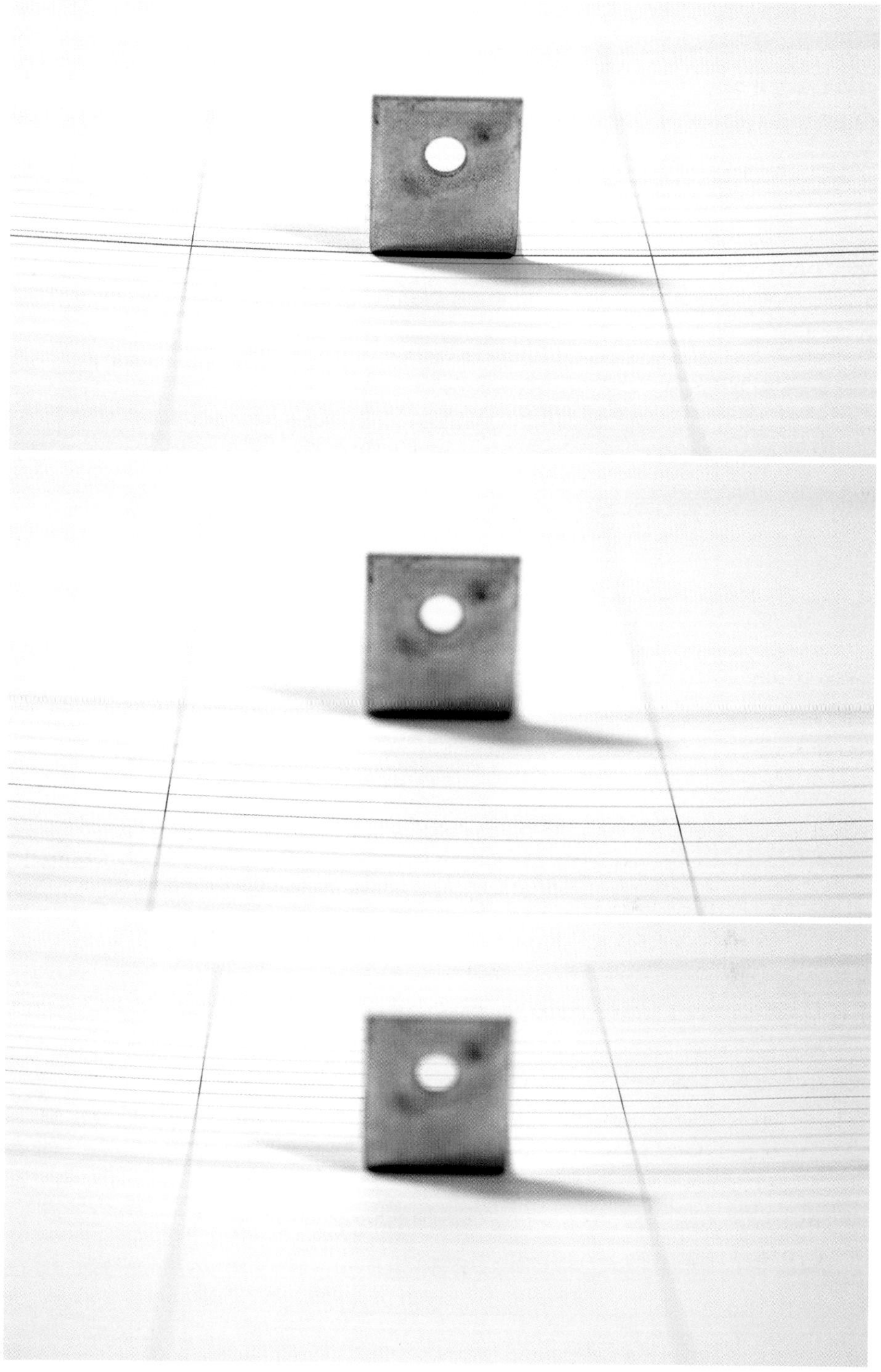

Figure 5.27 Correct focus (top), front focus (middle), and back focus (bottom).

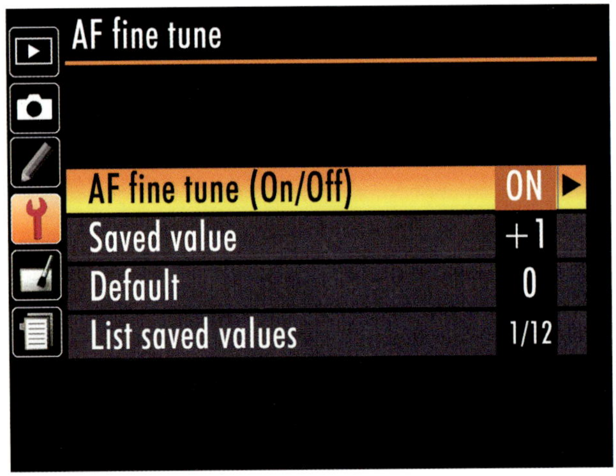

Figure 5.28
The AF Fine Tune menu.

- **Default.** This entry often confuses. It is a value that is applied to *every* lens mounted on the camera that doesn't already have a customized saved value associated with it. That is, if your D810 has consistent front or back focus problems with *all* lenses, you can enter a value here, and the camera will apply the correction to each CPU lens you use. This default setting can be overridden by saved values you've stored for particular lenses. So, you can change the default focal plane for all lenses, and still further fine-tune specific lenses that need more autofocus correction. My recommendation is that if your camera and lenses are so out of whack that you need global correction and individual fine-tuning, you *really* ought to consider shipping the whole kit off to Nikon for proper calibration.
- **List saved values.** This screen shows you the saved fine-tuning values for all lenses. If the currently mounted lens has a stored value, it will be marked with a solid black box icon. You can delete lenses from this list by highlighting them and pressing the Trash button. You can also change the number (a two-digit number from 00-99) used to identify a particular lens.

Evaluate Current Focus

The first step is to capture a baseline image that represents how the lens you want to fine-tune autofocuses at a particular distance. You'll often see advice for photographing a test chart with millimeter markings from an angle, and the suggestion that you autofocus on a particular point on the chart. Supposedly, the markings that actually *are* in focus will help you recalibrate your lens. The problem with this approach is that the information you get from photographing a test chart at an angle doesn't actually tell you what to do to make a precise correction. So, your lens back focuses three millimeters behind the target area on the chart. So what? Does that mean you change the Saved Value by –3 clicks? Or –15 clicks? Angled targets are a "shortcut" that don't save you time.

Instead, you'll want to photograph a target that represents what you're actually trying to achieve: a plane of focus locked in by your lens that represents the actual plane of focus of your subject. For that, you'll need a flat target, mounted precisely perpendicular to the sensor plane of the camera.

Then, you can take a photo, see if the plane of focus is correct, and if not, dial in a bit of fine-tuning in the AF Fine Tuning menu, and shoot again. Lather, rinse, and repeat until the target is sharply focused.

You can use the focus target shown in Figure 5.29, or you can use a chart of your own, as long as it has contrasty areas that will be easily seen by the autofocus system, and without very small details that are likely to confuse the AF. Download your own copy of my chart from www.dslrguides.com/FocusChart.pdf. (The URL is case-sensitive.) Then print out a copy on the largest paper your printer can handle. (I don't recommend just displaying the file on your monitor and focusing on that; it's unlikely you'll have the monitor screen lined up perfectly perpendicular to the camera sensor.) Then, follow these steps:

1. **Position the camera.** Place your Nikon D810 on a sturdy tripod with a remote release attached, positioned at roughly eye-level at a distance from a wall that represents the distance you want to test for. Keep in mind that autofocus problems can be different at varying distances and lens focal lengths, and that you can enter only *one* correction value for a particular lens. So, choose a distance (close-up or mid range) and zoom setting with your shooting habits in mind.
2. **Set the autofocus mode.** Choose the autofocus mode (AF-C or AF-S) you want to test.
3. **Level the camera (in an ideal world).** If the wall happens to be perfectly perpendicular, you can use a bubble level, plumb bob, or other device of your choice to ensure that the camera is level to match. Many tripods and tripod heads have bubble levels built in. Avoid using the center column, if you can. When the camera is properly oriented, lock the legs and tripod head tightly. Using an actual level will give you more accurate results than the D810's built-in virtual horizon feature.
4. **Level the camera (in the real world).** If your wall is not perfectly perpendicular, use this old trick. Tape a mirror to the wall, and then adjust the camera on the tripod so that when you look through the viewfinder at the mirror, you see directly into the reflection of the lens. Then, lock the tripod and remove the mirror.
5. **Mount the test chart.** Tape the test chart on the wall so it is centered in your camera's viewfinder.
6. **Photograph the test chart using AF.** Allow the camera to autofocus, and take a test photo, using the remote release to avoid shaking or moving the camera.
7. **Make an adjustment and rephotograph.** Make a fine-tuning adjustment and photograph the target again. Follow the instructions in the next section. I've separated the fine-tuning adjustments from these steps because some people may want to just tweak the focus at a later time without going through all these evaluation steps. Repeat steps 1-8 in the section that follows this one to make evaluation images at a range of corrections, say, –5 through +5.

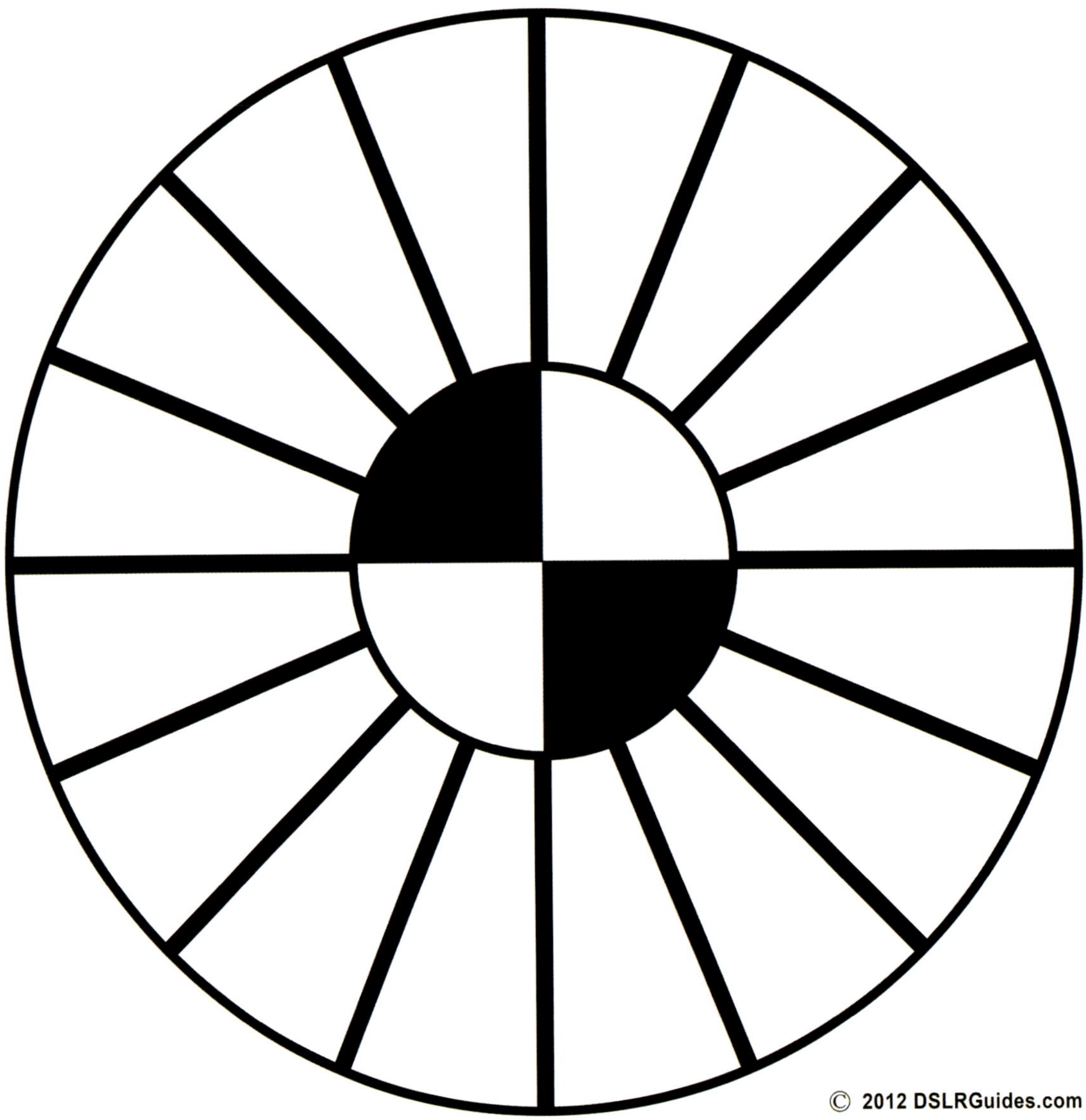

Figure 5.29 Use this focus test chart, or create one of your own.

8. **Evaluate the image.** If you have the camera connected to your computer with a USB cable and Camera Control Pro or other linkup software such as Nikon Transfer, or through a Wi-Fi connection, so much the better. You can view the image after it's transferred to your computer. Otherwise, *carefully* open the camera card door and slip the memory card out and copy the images to your computer.
9. **Evaluate focus.** Which image is sharpest? That's the setting you need to use for this lens. If your initial range doesn't provide the correction you need, repeat the steps between –20 and +20 until you find the best fine-tuning.

Changing the Fine-Tuning Setting

Adjust the fine-tuning for the lens you have mounted on the camera by following these steps:

1. If you haven't been running the test described previously, mount the CPU-equipped lens you want to fine-tune on the Nikon D810. The camera will automatically recognize the lens you are using during the "calibration" process and display its name on the screen.
2. If you haven't already done so, choose AF Fine Tune (On/Off) and turn it ON.
3. Select Saved Value.
4. Press the multi selector up/down buttons to tell the D810 to adjust the autofocus from +20 (move the focal point away from the camera to fix front focus problems) to –20 values (move the focal point toward the camera to fix back focus). (See Figure 5.30.)
5. Press OK when the value you want is entered. You may have to run the test described above several times and use some trial and error to determine the correct adjustment.

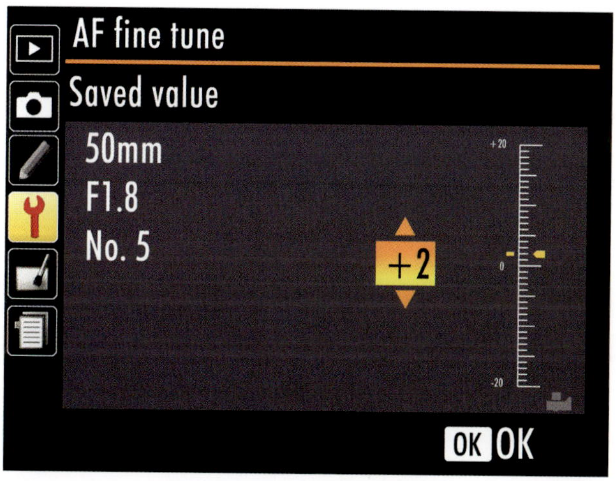

Figure 5.30 Change a Saved Value for a particular lens.

6. Choose List Saved Values to see the lenses you've fine-tuned. (See Figure 5.31.)
7. Assign a lens identifier from 00 to 99 to the lens you've just calibrated. This identifier can be used to differentiate a particular lens from other lenses of the same type, if you own, say, some duplicate lenses. That's not as far-fetched as you might think. Some organizations, such as newspapers, allow their photographers to use favorite lenses exclusively, but may need to share other optics among several photographers. If you don't know which of the pooled AF-S Nikkor 600mm f/4G ED VR lenses you'll be using on any particular day, you can calibrate your camera separately for each of them. (See Figure 5.32.)
8. Press MENU to exit.

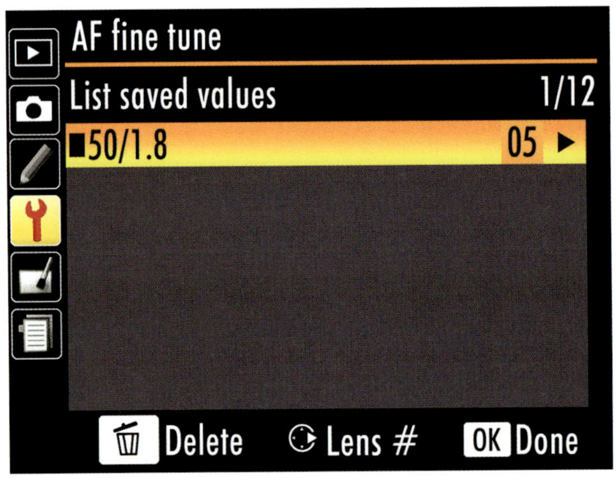

Figure 5.31
List the Saved Values you've stored.

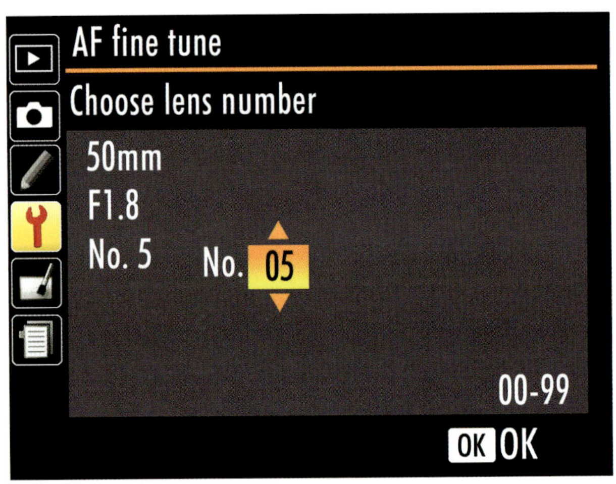

Figure 5.32
Assign a lens number, if necessary, to differentiate a particular lens from other lenses of the same type you may use.

Set Default Value

If you want to set a default value for lenses that aren't in your Saved Values list (say, because your camera always back or front focuses slightly), choose the Default setting from the AF Fine Tune menu, and adjust as shown in Figure 5.33.

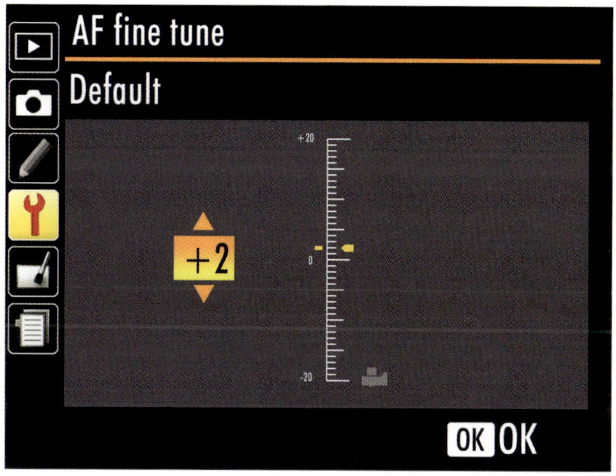

Figure 5.33
Choose a default value to be applied to all lenses not already fine-tuned.

6

Advanced Techniques

I've saved some of my favorite advanced techniques for this chapter, which devotes a little extra space to some special features of the Nikon D810. This chapter covers GPS techniques and special exposure options, including time-lapse photography, very long, and very short exposures. You'll even find an introduction to infrared photography.

Continuous Shooting

The Nikon D810's pair of continuous shooting modes reminds me how far digital photography has brought us. The first accessory I purchased when I worked as a sports photographer some years ago was a motor drive for my film SLR. It enabled me to snap off a series of shots in rapid succession, which came in very handy when a fullback broke through the line and headed for the end zone. Even a seasoned action photographer can miss the decisive instant when a crucial block is made, or a baseball superstar's bat shatters and pieces of cork fly out. Continuous shooting simplifies taking a series of pictures, either to ensure that one has more or less the exact moment you want to capture or to capture a sequence that is interesting as a collection of successive images.

The D810's "motor drive" capabilities are, in many ways, much superior to what you get with a film camera. For one thing, a motor-driven film camera can eat up film at an incredible pace, which is why many of them are used with cassettes that hold hundreds of feet of film stock. At three frames per second (typical of film cameras), a short burst of a few seconds can burn up as much as half of an ordinary 36 exposure roll of film. Digital cameras, in contrast, have reusable "film," so if you waste a few dozen shots on non-decisive moments, you can erase them and shoot more.

The increased capacity of digital memory cards gives you a prodigious number of frames to work with. At a game I covered earlier this year, I took more than 1,000 images in a couple hours. Yet, even shooting JPEG Fine I could fit more than 1,400 images on a single 32GB memory card. Even at the top speed of 5 frames per second that the D810 is capable of in FX mode, that's a lot of shooting. Given an average burst of about eight frames per sequence (nobody really takes 15-20 shots or more of one play), I was able to capture hundreds of different sequences before I needed to swap cards. Even a halfback's 8-yard gain seemed more exciting when captured in a sequence of shots, as in Figure 6.1.

I use continuous shooting a *lot*—and not just for sports. The up side is that I may be able to capture an image or a sequence that I could never grab in single shot mode. The down side is that I end up with many shots to wade through to find the "keepers." I know that sounds like I am using my Nikon like a machine gun, and hoping that I capture a worthwhile moment through sheer luck, but that's not really the case. Here are some types of scenes where the rapid fire capabilities of the D810 pay big dividends.

- **Action.** Of course. If you're shooting a fast-moving sport, continuous shooting is your only option. But it's important to remember that lightning-quick bursts don't replace good timing. A 90 mph fastball moves about 16 feet between frames when you're shooting at 5 fps. A ball making contact with a bat is *still* likely to escape capture. Continuous shooting may provide its best advantages in capturing sequences, so that each shot tells part of the story.
- **Bracketing.** I almost always set my camera to continuous shooting when bracketing. My goal is not to capture a bunch of different moments, each slightly different from the last but, rather, to grab virtually the *same* moment, at different exposures (or, less frequently, with different white balance or Active D-Lighting settings). I can then choose which of the nearly identical shots has the exposure I prefer, or can assemble some of them into a high dynamic range. The high burst rate of the D810 makes bracketing and hand-held HDR entirely practical. Software that combines such images does an excellent job of aligning images that are framed slightly differently when creating the final HDR version.

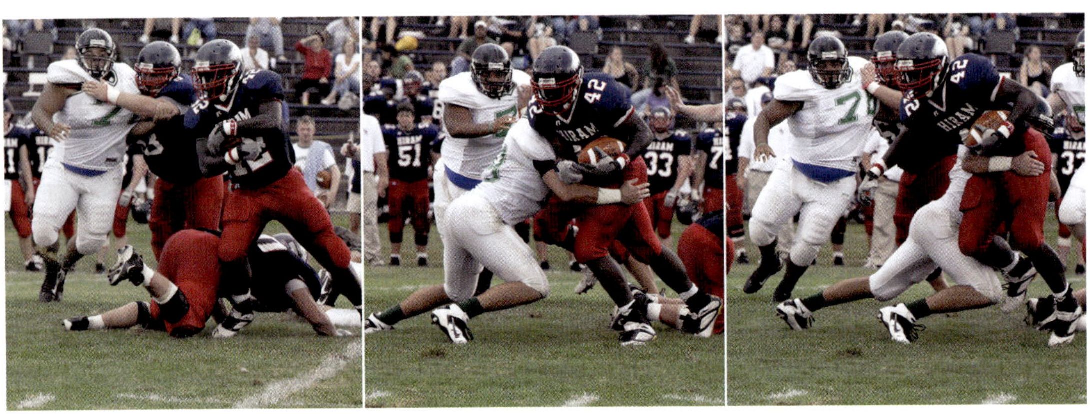

Figure 6.1 Continuous shooting allows you to capture an entire sequence of exciting moments as they unfold.

- **Ersatz vibration reduction.** I shoot three or four concerts a month, most of them with my beloved 70-200mm f/2.8 VR Nikkor, always hand-held, and always with VR turned on. I usually add a little simulated vibration reduction by shooting in continuous mode. While I have a fairly steady hand, I find that the *middle* exposures of a sequence are often noticeably sharper than those at the beginning, because my motions have "settled down" after initially depressing the shutter release button. My only caution for using this tool is to limit your shots during quiet passages, and avoid continuous shooting during acoustic concerts. The rat-a-tat-tat of a Nikon D810 will earn you no friends.
- **Variations on a theme.** Some subjects benefit from sequences more than others, because some aspect changes between shots. Cavorting children, emoting concert performers (as described above), fashion models, participants at weddings or other events all can look quite different within the span of a few seconds.

To use the D810's continuous shooting modes, hold down the release mode dial's unlock button and rotate the dial until either C_L or C_H appear. When you partially depress the shutter button, the viewfinder will display at the right side a number representing the maximum number of shots you can take at the current quality settings. The large buffer in the D810 will generally allow you to take as many as 100 JPEG Fine shots in a single burst, or 47 RAW photos (at 12-bit color depth).

To increase this number, reduce the image-quality setting by switching to a lower JPEG quality setting, such as JPEG Normal, or by reducing the camera's resolution from L to M or S (or RAW Small). You can also switch to a crop mode using the Image Area entry in the Shooting menu. Select the field-sports-friendly DX mode, to boost your frame rate and the number of shots you can cram into the buffer, and transform the effective field-of-view of your lens to that of a lens with 1.5X the focal length. (There's more on the "crop factor" in Chapter 7.) Other crops, including 1.2X and 5:4 proportions can also be chosen.

This internal "smart" buffer can suck up photos much more quickly than the memory card and, indeed, some memory cards are significantly faster or slower than others. When the buffer fills, you can't take any more continuous shots until the D810 has written some of them to the card, making more room in the buffer. You should keep in mind that faster memory cards write images more quickly, freeing up buffer space faster. Today, SD cards are speed-rated using a "Class" figure, with Class 4 (4 megabits per second transfer speed) being the slowest units commonly available. CF cards are rated using megabits per second transfer rates (for example, 15mb/sec to 90mb/sec) or the old-fashioned convention of comparing the card's speed to that of CD-ROM drives, giving 133X, 400X, 600X, or even 1000X ratings.

The frame rate you select will depend on the kind of shooting you want to do. For example, when shooting multiple exposures, if you're carefully planning and composing each individual exposure, you might not want to shoot continuously at all. But if your subject is moving, your double exposure might be more effective if you select a frame rate that matches the speed of motion of your target. Here are some guidelines:

- **6/7 fps.** The max rate of 6 fps is available when using Continuous High mode, DX cropping, and the MB-D12 grip with EN-EL18 battery installed. (The maximum frame rate is also available when working on AC power.) Use this for sports and other subjects where you want to optimize your chances of capturing the decisive moment. Of course, the DX crop will give your lens a 50 percent bump in apparent magnification, so your fast 50mm f/1.4 lens becomes the equivalent of a 75mm f/1.4 short telephoto.

  Perhaps you're shooting some active kids and want to grab their most appealing expressions. This fast frame rate can improve the odds. However, there is no guarantee that even at 6 fps the crucial instant won't occur *between* frames. (A ball pitched at 90 miles per hour travels 15 feet between each frame when you're shooting at 6 fps.) For example, when shooting major league baseball games, if I want to shoot a batter, I keep both eyes open, and keep one of them on the pitcher. Then, I start taking my sequence just as the pitcher releases the ball. My goal is to capture the batter making contact with the ball. But even at 6 fps, I find that a hitter connects between frames. I usually must take pictures of a couple dozen at-bats to get a shot of bat and ball connecting.
- **4.0-5.0 fps.** When using DX or 1.2X crop modes, a "naked" D810 can shoot 5 fps at the Continuous H release setting. Or, you can choose a minimum of 1-5 fps in FX mode or any cropped mode for Continuous L, using Custom Setting d2. A slightly slower rate can be useful for activities that aren't quite so fast moving. But, there's another benefit. Using the fastest frame rate means that your camera may fill up its buffer and won't be ready for the next sequence. If you don't want to miss any sequences, using a moderately slower frame rate can help prevent buffer overload.
- **1.0-3.0 fps.** You can set Continuous L mode to use a relatively pokey frame rate, too. Use these rates when you just want to be able to take pictures quickly, and aren't interested in filling up your memory card with mostly duplicated images. At 1 fps you can hold down the shutter release and fire away, or ease up when you want to pause. At higher frame rates, by the time you've decided to stop shooting, you may have taken an extra three or four shots that you really don't want. Slow frame rates are good for bracketing, too. Set the D810 to take a three-frame bracket burst, and you can take all three with one press of the shutter release. You'll find that slower frame rates also come in handy for subjects that are moving around in interesting ways (photographic models come to mind) but don't change their looks or poses quickly enough to merit a 6 fps burst.

BURSTS NOT JUST FOR ACTION

I often use continuous shooting mode even when I'm not busy shooting action. As I've mentioned before, bursts make sense when you're shooting HDR, bracketing, or doing multiple exposure tricks. But here's a technique you might not have thought of—continuous shooting can give you sharper images!

When I'm photographing concerts, I most frequently use my 70-200mm f/2.8 VR zoom, hand-held, with vibration reduction turned on, and using the highest continuous frame rate at my disposal. I enjoy greater mobility by not using a monopod (and a tripod would be even more of a ball-and-chain, even if not forbidden by the venue). I'm generally shooting at around 1/180th second, which is usually fast enough to eliminate blur from the performers' motion. VR has no effect on stopping *their* movement, of course, and it does a fairly good job of eliminating camera/photographer shake. However, I invariably find that if I shoot in Continuous H mode, one of the middle frames in a sequence will be sharpest. Even the most seasoned photographer will add a little bump to the camera when they squeeze (not stab) the shutter release.

A Tiny Slice of Time

Exposures that seem impossibly brief can reveal a world we didn't know existed. In the 1930s, Dr. Harold Edgerton, a professor of electrical engineering at MIT, pioneered high-speed photography using a repeating electronic flash unit he patented called the *stroboscope*. As the inventor of the electronic flash, he popularized its use to freeze objects in motion, and you've probably seen his photographs of bullets piercing balloons and drops of milk forming a coronet-shaped splash.

Electronic flash freezes action by virtue of its extremely short duration—as brief as 1/50,000th second or less. Although the D810's built-in flash unit can give you these ultra-quick glimpses of moving subjects, an external flash, such as one of the Nikon Speedlights, offers even more versatility. You can read more about using electronic flash to stop action in Chapter 9.

Of course, the D810 is fully capable of immobilizing all but the fastest movement using only its shutter speeds, which range all the way up to 1/8,000th second. Indeed, you'll rarely have need for such a brief shutter speed in ordinary shooting. (For the record, I don't believe I've *ever* used a shutter speed of 1/8,000th second, except when testing a camera's ISO 25800 or equivalent setting outdoors in broad daylight.) But at more reasonable sensitivity settings, say, to use an aperture of f/1.8 at ISO 200 outdoors in bright sunlight, a shutter speed of 1/8,000th second would more than do the job. You'd need a faster shutter speed only if you moved the ISO setting to a higher sensitivity (but why would you do that, outside of testing situations like mine?). Under less than full sunlight, 1/8,000th second is more than fast enough for any conditions you're likely to encounter.

Most sports action can be frozen at 1/2,000th second or slower, as you can see in the high jump image in Figure 6.2; I caught the leaper at the peak of the action, so 1/800th second was easily fast enough to freeze her in mid-air. At ISO 100, I used f/5.6 on my 70-200mm lens to allow the distracting background to blur.

Of course, in many sports a slower shutter speed is actually preferable—for example, to allow the wheels of a racing automobile or motorcycle, or the rotors on a helicopter to blur realistically, as shown in Figure 6.3. At top, a 1/1,000th second shutter speed effectively stopped the rotors of the helicopter, making it look like a crash was impending. At bottom, I used a slower 1/250th second shutter speed to allow enough blur to make this a true action picture.

But if you want to do some exotic action-freezing photography without resorting to electronic flash, the D810's top shutter speed is at your disposal. Here are some things to think about when exploring this type of high-speed photography:

- **You'll need a lot of light.** Very high shutter speeds cut extremely fine slices of time and sharply reduce the amount of illumination that reaches your sensor. To use 1/8,000th second at an aperture of f/6.3, you'd need an ISO setting of 1600—even in full daylight. To use an f/stop smaller than f/6.3 or an ISO setting lower than 1600, you'd need *more* light than full daylight

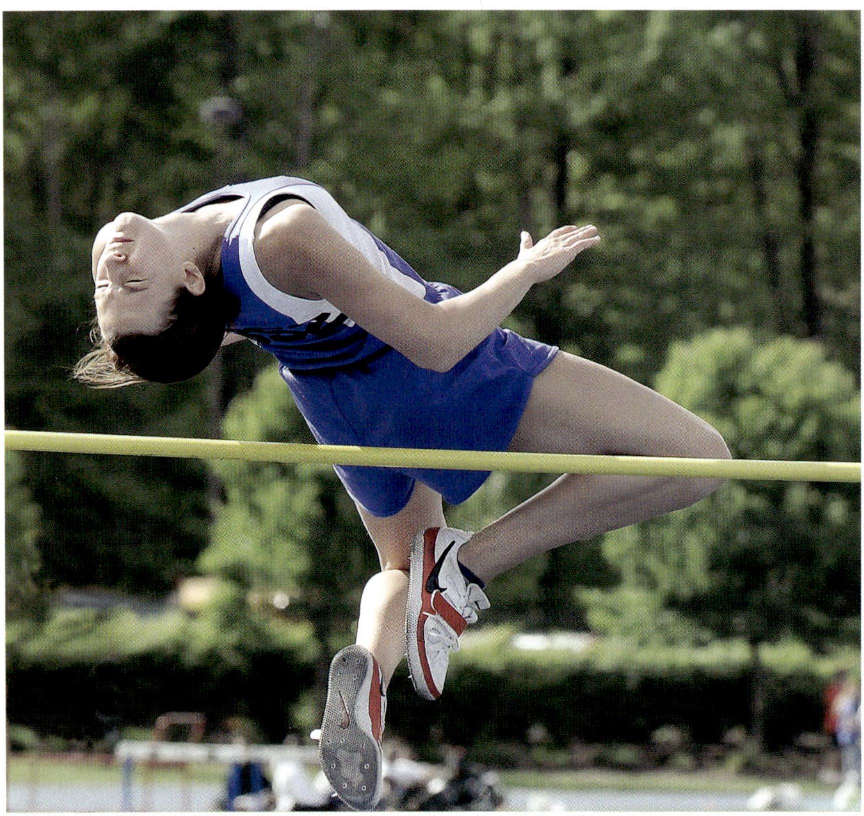

Figure 6.2
A shutter speed of 1/800th second was fast enough to stop this action.

provides. (That's why electronic flash units work so well for high-speed photography when used as the sole illumination; they provide both the effect of a brief shutter speed and the high levels of illumination needed.)

- **Forget about reciprocity failure.** If you're an old-time film shooter, you might recall that very brief shutter speeds (as well as very high light levels and very *long* exposures) produced an effect called *reciprocity failure,* in which given exposures ended up providing less than the calculated value because of the way film responded to very short, very intense, or very long exposures of light. Solid-state sensors don't suffer from this defect, so you don't need to make an adjustment when using high shutter speeds (or brief flash bursts).
- **High shutter speeds with electronic flash.** You might be tempted to use an electronic flash with a high shutter speed. Perhaps you want to stop some action in daylight with a brief shutter speed and use electronic flash only as supplemental illumination to fill in the shadows. Unfortunately, under ordinary conditions you can't use flash in subdued illumination with your D810 at any shutter speed faster than 1/250th or 1/320th second. Those are the fastest speeds at which the camera's focal plane shutter is fully open: at shorter speeds, the "slit" described above comes into play, so that the flash will expose only the small portion of the sensor exposed by the slit throughout its duration. (Check out "High Speed Sync" in Chapter 9 if you want to see how you *can* use shutter speeds shorter than 1/250th or 1/320th second, albeit at much-reduced effective flash power levels.)

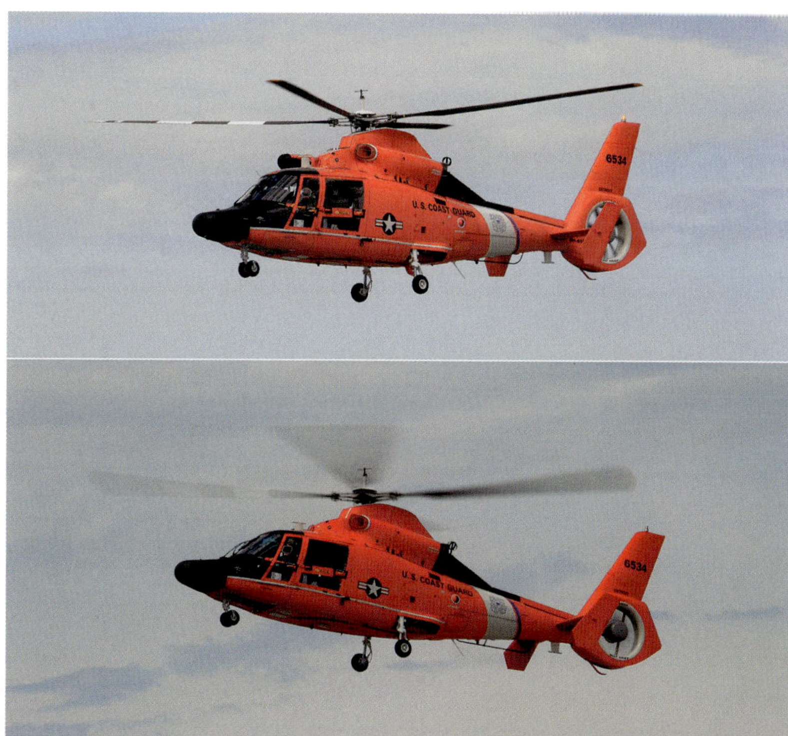

Figure 6.3
A little blur can be a good thing, as these shots of a helicopter at 1/1000th second (top) and 1/250th second (bottom) show.

Working with Short Exposures

You can have a lot of fun exploring the kinds of pictures you can take using very brief exposure times, whether you decide to take advantage of the action-stopping capabilities of your built-in or external electronic flash or work with the Nikon D810's faster shutter speeds. Here are a few ideas to get you started:

- **Take revealing images.** Fast shutter speeds can help you reveal the real subject behind the façade, by freezing constant motion to capture an enlightening moment in time. Legendary fashion/portrait photographer Philippe Halsman used leaping photos of famous people, such as the Duke and Duchess of Windsor, Richard Nixon, and Salvador Dali to illuminate their real selves. Halsman said, "*When you ask a person to jump, his attention is mostly directed toward the act of jumping and the mask falls so that the real person appears.*" Try some high-speed portraits of people you know in motion to see how they appear when concentrating on something other than the portrait. Figure 6.4 provides an example. It's not an electronic flash shot; in the original image you can see how blurry the model's feet are.

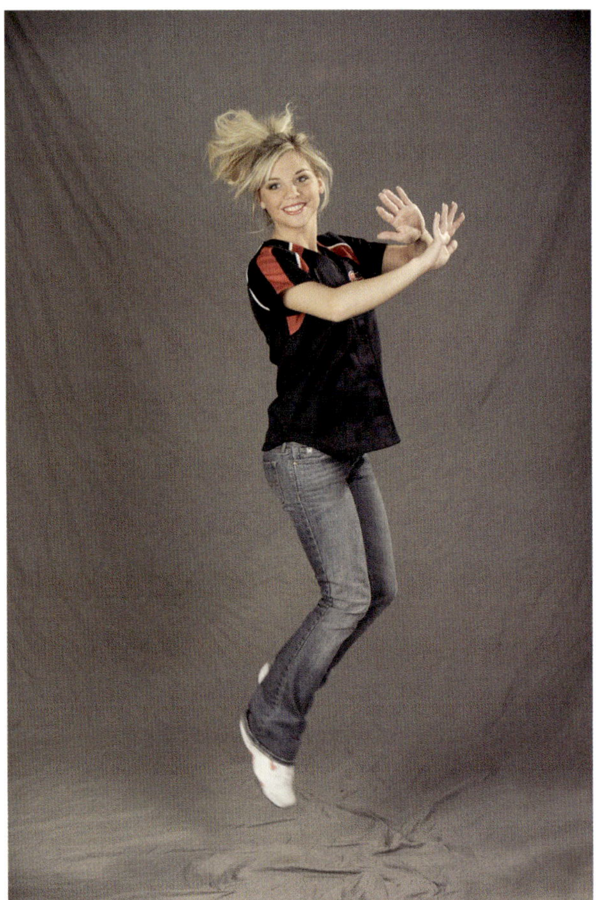

Figure 6.4
Shoot your subjects leaping and see what they look like when they're not preoccupied with posing.

- **Create unreal images.** High-speed photography can also produce photographs that show your subjects in ways that are quite unreal. A motocross cyclist leaping over a ramp, but with all motion stopped so that the rider and machine look as if they were frozen in mid-air, make for an unusual picture. When we're accustomed to seeing subjects in motion, seeing them stopped in time can verge on the surreal.
- **Capture unseen perspectives.** Some things are *never* seen in real life, except when viewed in a stop-action photograph. Edgerton's balloon bursts were only a starting point. Freeze a hummingbird in flight for a view of wings that never seem to stop. Or, capture the splashes as liquid falls into a bowl, as shown in Figure 6.5. No electronic flash was required for this image. Instead, two high-intensity lamps with green gels at left and right and an ISO setting of 1600 allowed the D810 to capture this image at 1/2,000th second.

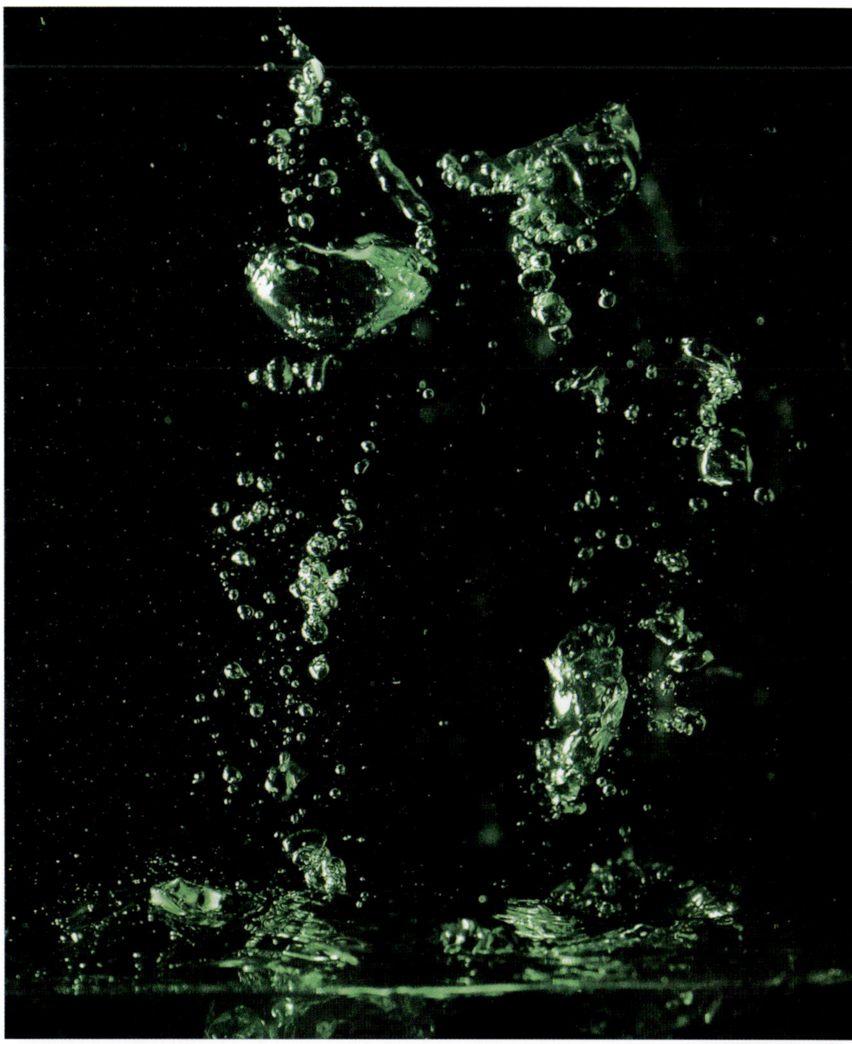

Figure 6.5
A large amount of artificial illumination and an ISO 1600 sensitivity setting allowed capturing this shot at 1/2,000th second without use of an electronic flash.

- **Vanquish camera shake and gain new angles.** Here's an idea that's so obvious it isn't always explored to its fullest extent. A high enough shutter speed can free you from the tyranny of a tripod, making it easier to capture new angles, or to shoot quickly while moving around, especially with longer lenses. I tend to use a monopod or tripod frequently when I'm not using an image-stabilized lens, and I end up missing some shots because of a reluctance to adjust my camera support to get a higher, lower, or different angle. If you have enough light and can use an f/stop wide enough to permit a high shutter speed, you'll find a new freedom to choose your shots. I have a favored 170mm-500mm lens that I use for sports and wildlife photography, almost invariably with a tripod, as I don't find the "reciprocal of the focal length" rule particularly helpful in most cases. I would *not* hand-hold this hefty lens at its 500mm setting with a 1/500th second shutter speed under most circumstances. Nor, if you want to account for the crop factor, would I use 1/750th second. However, at 1/2,000th second or faster, it's entirely possible for a steady hand to use this lens without a tripod or monopod's extra support, and I've found that my whole approach to shooting animals and other elusive subjects changes in high-speed mode. Selective focus allows dramatically isolating my prey wide open at f/6.3, too. Of course, at such a high shutter speed, you may need to boost your ISO setting—even when shooting outdoors.

Long Exposures

Longer exposures are a doorway into another world, showing us how even familiar scenes can look much different when photographed over periods measured in seconds. At night, long exposures produce streaks of light from moving, illuminated subjects like automobiles or amusement park rides. Extra-long exposures of seemingly pitch-dark subjects can reveal interesting views using light levels barely bright enough to see by. At any time of day, including daytime (in which case you'll often need the help of neutral-density filters to make the long exposure practical), long exposures can cause moving objects to vanish entirely, because they don't remain stationary long enough to register in a photograph.

Three Ways to Take Long Exposures

There are actually three common types of lengthy exposures: *timed exposures*, *bulb exposures*, and *time exposures*. The D810 offers only the first two (although time exposures are possible with certain remote releases), but once you understand all three, you'll see why Nikon made the choices it did. Because of the length of the exposure, all of the following techniques should be used with a tripod to hold the camera steady.

- **Timed exposures.** These are long exposures from 1 second to 30 seconds, measured by the camera itself. To take a picture in this range, simply use Manual or S modes and use the main command dial to set the shutter speed to the length of time you want, choosing from preset speeds of 1.0, 1.5, 2.0, 3.0, 4.0, 6.0, 8.0, 10.0, 15.0, 20.0, or 30.0 seconds (if you've specified 1/2 stop increments for exposure adjustments), or 1.0, 1.3, 1.6, 2.0, 2.5, 3.2, 4.0, 5.0, 6.0, 8.0,

10.0, 13.0, 15.0, 20.0, 25.0, and 30.0 seconds (if you're using 1/3 stop increments). The advantage of timed exposures is that the camera does all the calculating for you. There's no need for a stopwatch. If you review your image on the monitor and decide to try again with the exposure doubled or halved, you can dial in the correct exposure with precision. The disadvantage of timed exposures is that you can't take a photo for longer than 30 seconds.

- **Bulb exposures.** This type of exposure is so-called because in the olden days the photographer squeezed and held an air bulb attached to a tube that provided the force necessary to keep the shutter open. Traditionally, a bulb exposure is one that lasts as long as the shutter release button is pressed; when you release the button, the exposure ends. To make a bulb exposure with the D810, set the camera on Manual mode and use the main command dial to select the shutter speed immediately after 30 seconds—Bulb. Then, press the shutter to start the exposure, and press it again to close the shutter. If you'd like to simulate a time exposure (described below), you can use the Nikon MC-30 control.
- **Time exposures.** This is a setting found on some cameras to produce longer exposures. With cameras that implement this option, the shutter opens when you press the shutter release button, and remains open until you press the button again. With the Nikon D810, you can produce this effect with a locking cable release, such as the Nikon MC-30/MC-30a, as I did for the shot in San Juan, Puerto Rico shown in Figure 6.6. You can press the shutter release button, go off for a few minutes, and come back to close the shutter (assuming your camera is still there). The disadvantages of this mode are exposures must be timed manually, and with shorter exposures it's possible for the vibration of manually opening and closing the shutter to register in the photo. For longer exposures, the period of vibration is relatively brief and not usually a problem.

Figure 6.6
A locking release cord can give you long time exposures, such as this 60 second shot in San Juan, Puerto Rico.

Working with Long Exposures

Because the D810 produces such good images at longer exposures, and there are so many creative things you can do with long exposure techniques, you'll want to do some experimenting. Get yourself a tripod or another firm support and take some test shots with long exposure noise reduction both enabled and disabled (to see whether you prefer low noise or high detail) and get started. Here are some things to try:

- **Make people invisible.** One very cool thing about long exposures is that objects that move rapidly enough won't register at all in a photograph, while the subjects that remain stationary are portrayed in the normal way. That makes it easy to produce people-free landscape photos and architectural photos at night or, even, in full daylight if you use a neutral-density filter (or two) (or three) to allow an exposure of at least a few seconds. At ISO 100, f/22, and a pair of 8X (three-stop) neutral-density filters, you can use exposures of nearly two seconds; overcast days and/or even more neutral-density filtration would work even better if daylight people-vanishing is your goal. They'll have to be walking *very* briskly and across the field of view (rather than directly toward the camera) for this to work. At night, it's much easier to achieve this effect with the 20- to 30-second exposures that are possible, as you can see in Figure 6.7. At left, with an exposure of several seconds, the crowded street is fully populated. At right, with a 20-second exposure, the folks moving slowly (at left) show up as blurs; those standing still (at right) are portrayed normally, and the fast-moving walkers in the foreground are barely perceptible blurs.
- **Create streaks.** If you aren't shooting for total invisibility, long exposures with the camera on a tripod can produce some interesting streaky effects. Even a single 8X ND filter will let you shoot at f/22 and 1/6th second in daylight. Indoors, you shouldn't have a problem using long shutter speeds to get shots like the one shown in Figure 6.8.

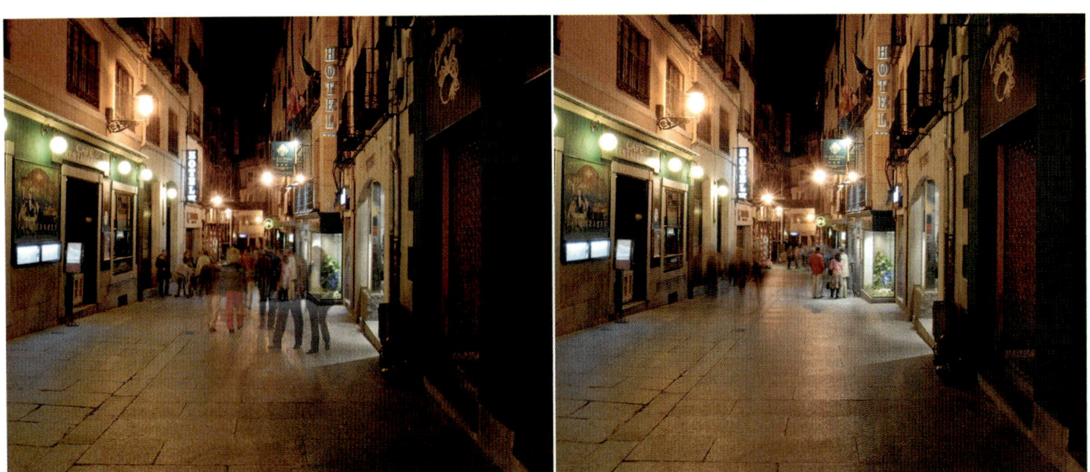

Figure 6.7 This European alleyway is thronged with people (left), but with the camera on a tripod, a 20-second exposure rendered most of the passersby almost invisible.

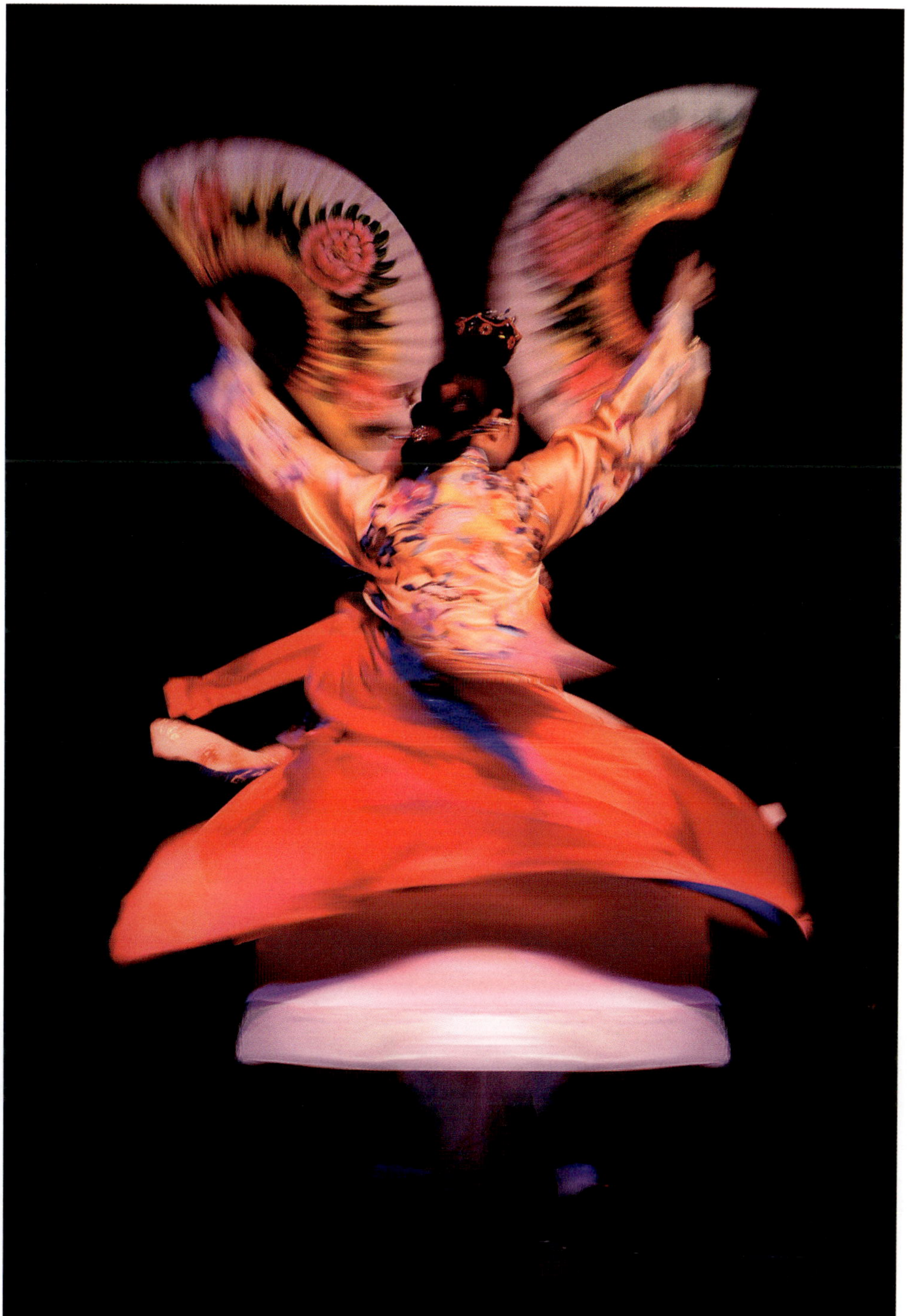

Figure 6.8 Long exposures can turn a dancer into a swirling image.

- **Produce light trails.** At night, car headlights and taillights and other moving sources of illumination can generate interesting light trails, as shown in Figure 6.9. Your camera doesn't even need to be mounted on a tripod; hand-holding the D810 for longer exposures adds movement and patterns to your streaky trails. If you're shooting fireworks, a longer exposure may allow you to combine several bursts into one picture.
- **Blur waterfalls, etc.** You'll find that waterfalls and other sources of moving liquid produce a special type of long-exposure blur, because the water merges into a fantasy-like veil that looks different at different exposure times, and with different waterfalls. Cascades with turbulent flow produce a rougher look at a given longer exposure than falls that flow smoothly. Although blurred waterfalls have become almost a cliché, there are still plenty of variations for a creative photographer to explore. (See Figure 6.10.)
- **Show total darkness in new ways.** Even on the darkest, moonless nights, there is enough starlight or glow from distant illumination sources to see by, and, if you use a long exposure, there is enough light to take a picture, too.

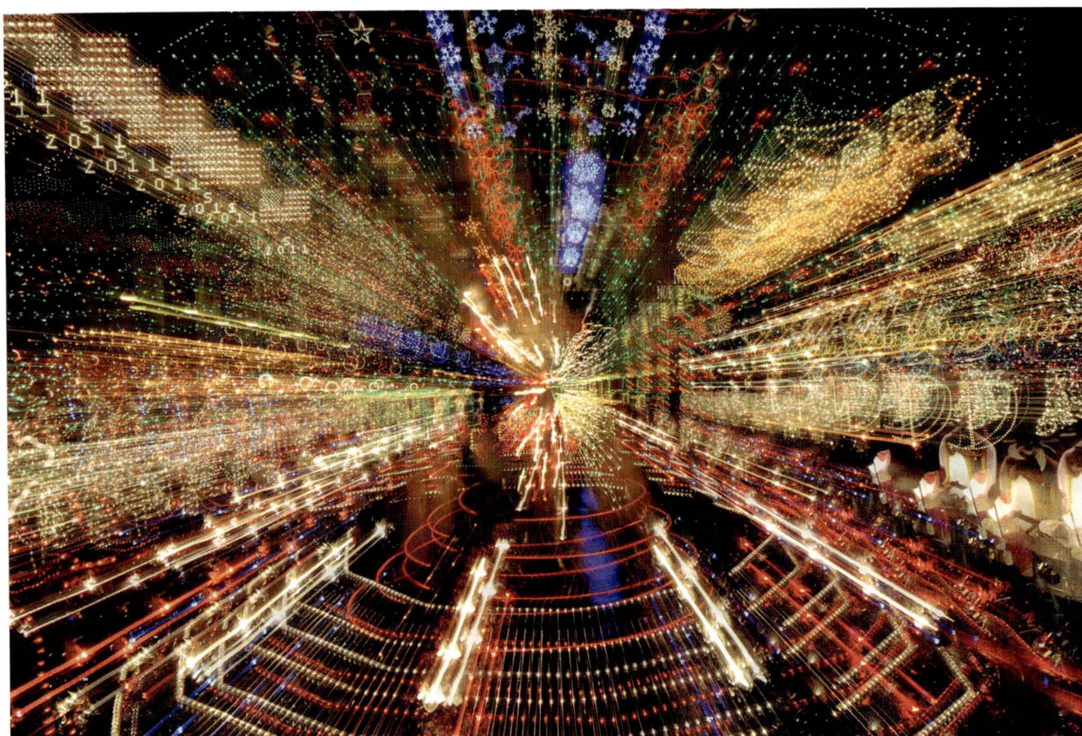

Figure 6.9 Zoom during a long exposure for an interesting effect.

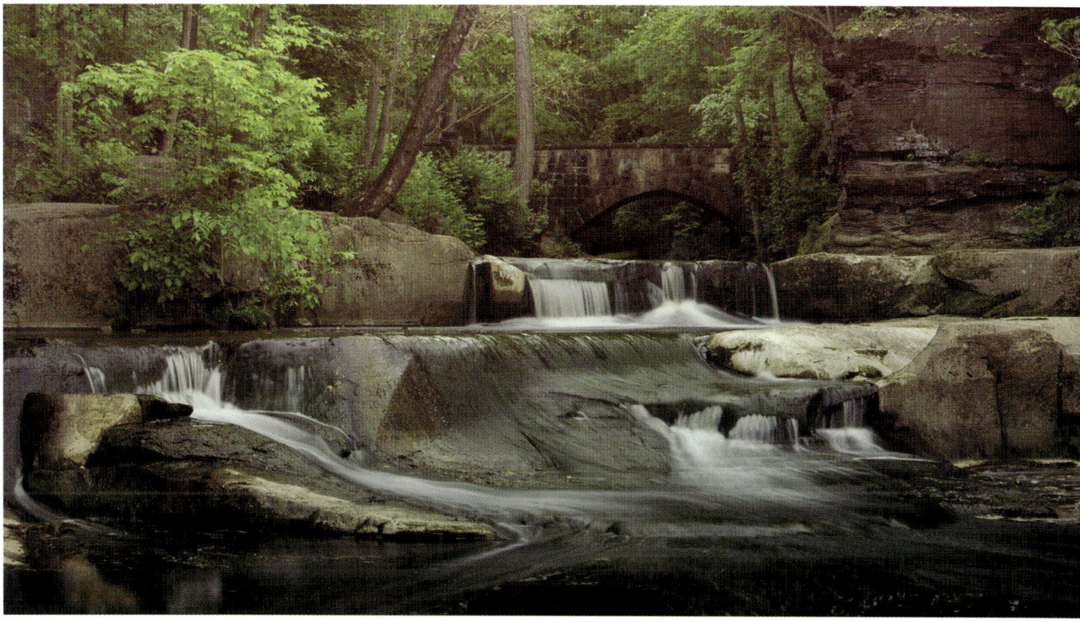

Figure 6.10 A three-second exposure blurred this cascade of flowing water.

Delayed Exposures

Sometimes it's desirable to have a delay of some sort before a picture is actually taken. Perhaps you'd like to get in the picture yourself, and would appreciate it if the camera waited 10 seconds after you press the shutter release to actually take the picture. Maybe you want to give a tripod-mounted camera time to settle down and damp any residual vibration after the release is pressed to improve sharpness for an exposure with a relatively slow shutter speed. It's possible you want to explore the world of time-lapse photography. The next sections present your delayed exposure options.

Self-Timer

The D810 has a built-in self-timer with a user-selectable delay. Activate the timer by rotating the release mode dial to the self-timer icon. Press the shutter release button halfway to lock in focus on your subjects (if you're taking a self-portrait, focus on an object at a similar distance and use focus lock). When you're ready to take the photo, continue pressing the shutter release the rest of the way. The lamp on the front of the camera will blink slowly for eight seconds (when using the 10-second timer) and the beeper will chirp (if you haven't disabled it in the Custom Settings menu, as described in Chapter 12). During the final two seconds, the beeper sounds more rapidly and the lamp remains on until the picture is taken. It's a good idea to close the viewfinder eyepiece shutter if you're not using live view or shooting in Manual exposure mode, to prevent light from the viewing window getting inside the camera and affecting the automatic exposure.

You can customize the settings of the self-timer. Your adjustments are "sticky" and remain in effect until you change them. Your options include:

- **Self-timer delay.** Choose 2, 5, 10, or 20 seconds, using Custom Setting c3. If I have the camera mounted on a tripod or other support and am too lazy to dig around for my wired remote, I can set a two-second delay that is sufficient to let the camera stop vibrating after I've pressed the shutter release. An alternative is to use the Exposure Delay Mode, Custom Setting d4, which allows setting delays of 1, 2, or 3 seconds. A longer delay time of 20 seconds is useful if you want to get into the picture and are not sure you can make it in 10 seconds.
- **Number of shots.** After the timer finishes counting down, the D810 can take from 1 to 9 different shots. This is a godsend when shooting photos of groups, especially if you want to appear in the photo itself. You'll always want to shoot several pictures to ensure that everyone's eyes are open and there are smiling expressions on each face. Instead of racing back and forth between the camera to trigger the self-timer multiple times, you can select the number of shots taken after a single countdown. For small groups, I always take at least as many shots as there are people in the group—plus one. That gives everybody a chance to close their eyes.
- **Interval between shots.** If you've selected 2 to 9 as your number of shots to be snapped off, you can use this option to space out the different exposures. Your choices are 0.5 seconds, 1, 2, or 3 seconds. Use a short interval when you want to capture everyone saying "Cheese!" The 3-second option is helpful if you're using flash, as 3 seconds is generally long enough to allow the flash to recycle and have enough juice for the next photo.

Tip

Another way to simulate a longer self-timer is with the Mup mirror lockup. This is something you might want to do if you're shooting close-ups, landscapes, or other types of pictures using the self-timer only to trip the shutter in the most vibration-free way possible. Forget to bring along your tripod, but still want to take a close-up picture with a precise focus setting? That happened to me when I encountered this colorful plant (see Figure 6.11) in a greenhouse when picking up some potted plants. I wheeled a planting cart over to the blossom, rested the D810 on a soft bag of potting soil (a beanbag would have been better!), carefully focused, and let the self-timer trip the shutter at the appropriate moment. In such situations, the camera might teeter back and forth for a second or three (rendering the Exposure Delay Mode option less than optimal), but it will settle back to its original position before the self-timer activates the shutter. The self-timer remains the active mode until you turn it off—even if you power down the D810—so remember to turn the release mode dial back to Single frame mode when you're finished.

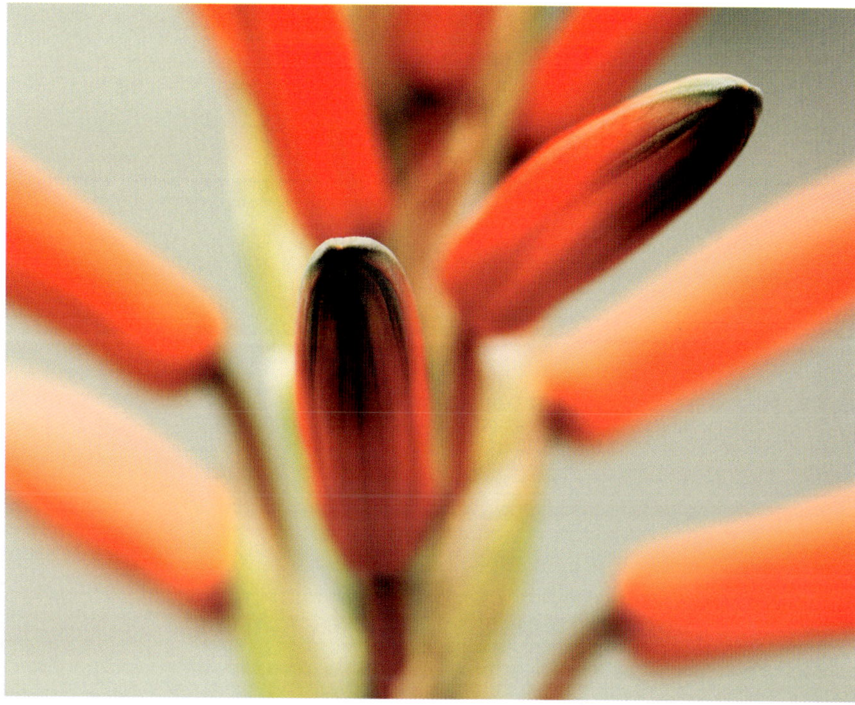

Figure 6.11
With the camera resting on a bag of potting soil on a cart, the self-timer triggered this vibration-free image of a bud about to open.

Time-Lapse/Interval Photography

Who hasn't marveled at a time-lapse photograph of a flower opening, a series of shots of the moon marching across the sky, or one of those extreme time-lapse picture sets showing something that takes a very, very long time, such as a building under construction.

You probably won't be shooting such construction shots, unless you have a spare D810 you don't need for a few months (or are willing to go through the rigmarole of figuring out how to set up your camera in precisely the same position using the same lens settings to shoot a series of pictures at intervals). However, other kinds of time-lapse photography are entirely within reach.

The D810 can take time-lapse/interval photographs all by itself, using the Interval Timer Shooting entry found in the Shooting menu. You'll find step-by-step instructions for using this feature in Chapter 11. If you're willing to tether the camera to a computer (a laptop will do) using the USB cable, you can take time-lapse photos using the optional extra-cost Nikon Camera Control Pro.

Here are the essential tips for effective time-lapse photography:

- **Use AC power.** If you're shooting a long sequence, consider connecting your camera to an AC adapter, as leaving the D810 on for long periods of time will rapidly deplete the battery.
- **Make sure you have enough storage space.** Unless your memory card has enough capacity to hold all the images you'll be taking, you might want to change to a higher compression rate or reduced resolution to maximize the image count.

- **Make a movie.** While time-lapse stills are interesting, you can increase your fun factor by compiling all your shots into a motion picture using your favorite desktop movie-making software.
- **Protect your camera.** If your camera will be set up, make sure it's protected from weather, earthquakes, animals, young children, innocent bystanders, and theft.
- **Vary intervals.** Experiment with different time intervals. You don't want to take pictures too often or less often than necessary to capture the changes you hope to image.

Multiple Exposures

Some of my very first images captured when I was a budding photographer at age 11 were double exposures. Some were unintentional, as my box camera, using 620-size film, could take several pictures on one frame if you forgot to wind it between shots. But my initial foray into special effects as a pre-teen were shots of my brother throwing a baseball to himself, serving as both pitcher and batter thanks to a multiple exposure.

The D810's multiple exposure feature is remarkably flexible. It allows you to combine two to ten exposures into one image without the need for an image editor like Photoshop and can be an entertaining way to return to those thrilling days of yesteryear, when complex photos were created in the camera itself. In truth, prior to the digital age, multiple exposures were a cool, groovy, far-out, hep/hip, phat, sick, fabulous way of producing composite images. Today, it's more common to take the lazy way out, snap two or more pictures, and then assemble them in an image editor like Photoshop, or use the D810's Image Overlay feature in the Retouch menu.

However, if you're willing to spend the time planning a multiple exposure (or are open to some happy accidents), there is a lot to recommend the multiple exposure capability that Nikon has bestowed on the D810. For one thing, the camera is able to combine two to ten images using the RAW data from the sensor, producing photos that are blended together more smoothly than is likely for anyone who's not a Photoshop guru. To take your own multiple exposures, just follow these steps (although it's probably a good idea to do a little planning and maybe even some sketching on paper first):

1. **Access Multiple Exposure setting.** Navigate to the option in the Shooting menu.
2. **Select Number of Shots.** Choose a value from two to ten with the multi selector up/down buttons, and press OK.
3. **Choose Auto Gain.** Specify either On (the default) or Off. When On is selected, the D810 will divide the total exposure of the image by the number of shots specified; for example, applying 1/3 of the exposure time to each shot in a three-image series. Choose Off, and the full exposure is applied to each picture. You'd want to use Off when using a dark background that would allow successive exposures to add details, and On to avoid the risk of overlapping images washing each other out. Press OK to set the gain.
4. **Finish.** Move the cursor up to Multiple Exposure Mode and select On. The multiple exposure icon appears in the monochrome control panel.

5. **Take the multiple exposures.** Press the shutter release button multiple times until all the exposures in the series have been taken. (In continuous shooting mode, the entire series will be shot in a single burst.) The blinking multiple exposure icon vanishes when the series is finished. Note: if you've selected Series mode, you'll need to disable the Multiple Exposure feature once you've finished taking a series; it does not shut off automatically in that mode, until you turn the camera off, do a reset, you delete photos, or your battery dies. If you choose On (Single Photo) instead, the D810 exits multiple exposure mode after taking that one picture.

Keep in mind if you wait longer than 30 seconds between any two photos in the series, the sequence will terminate and combine the images taken so far. If you want a longer elapsed time between exposures, go to the Playback menu and make sure On has been specified for Image Review, and then extend the monitor display time using Custom Setting c4 to an appropriate maximum interval. The Multiple Exposure feature will then use the monitor-off delay as its maximum interval between shots. Figure 6.12 shows triple exposure of Eddie Perez, guitarist for Dwight Yoakam and alt-country band the Mavericks.

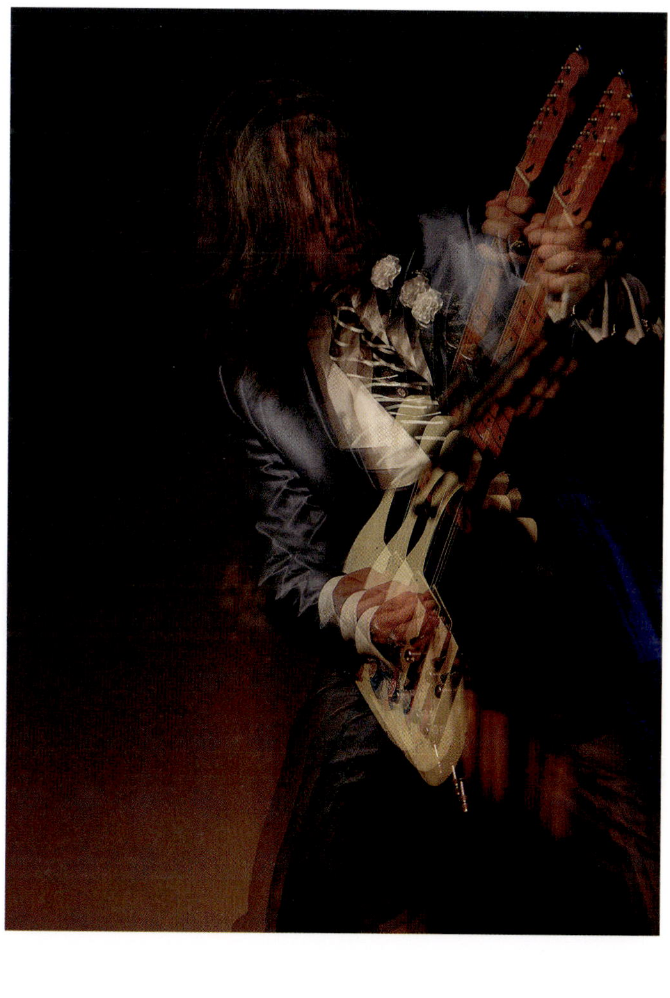

Figure 6.12
The D810's Multiple Exposure capability allows combining images without an image editor.

Infrared Photography

The D810 is not an ideal camera for infrared, because Nikon has been fairly successful in limiting its sensor's IR sensitivity. (My ideal camera is my Nikon D3200, converted to full-time infrared use by Lifepixel [www.lifepixel.com].) However, I've successfully taken some IR images with my D810, and, once you get past the investment of up to $100 in an IR filter, you can have a lot of fun.

IR photography captures an image primarily using the infrared light that bounces off your subject matter, resulting in an eerie monochrome or false-color photograph featuring white foliage and dark skies, like the image shown in Figure 6.13. Because everyday objects reflect infrared in proportions that differ sharply than that of visible light, the tonal relationships are wildly unexpected.

Scenic photos lend themselves to the IR treatment for a number of reasons. People photographed by infrared light often look pale and ghastly (or, at times, interesting!). Landscapes, on the other hand, take on an other-worldly look that's fascinating.

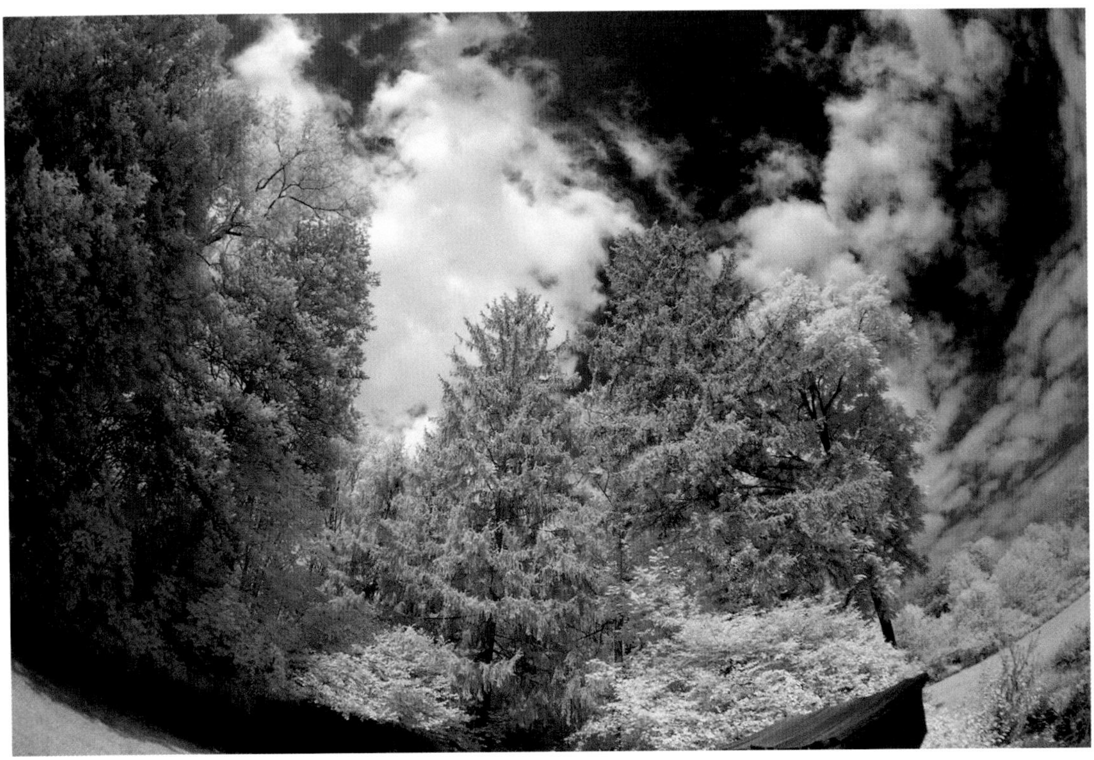

Figure 6.13 Infrared photography produces weird black-and-white landscape photos.

What You Need

The unadorned sensors found in digital cameras generally are sensitive to infrared light in the range of 700-1200 nanometers, which is a good thing if you want to take infrared pictures, and not so good if you don't want infrared illumination to spoil your non-infrared photographs. So, most digital cameras like the D810 now include a filter or "hot mirror" that specifically blocks IR light from the sensor. Some IR still gets through to the sensor, so if you block the visible light and let only that residual IR reach the D810's sensor, you can take infrared photographs, after a fashion, albeit with very long exposure times.

You'll need an IR filter to block the visible light from your sensor. Find a Wratten #87 filter to fit your lens. You can also use a Wratten 87C, Hoya R72 (#87B), or try #88A and #89B filters. A simpatico camera store may let you try out several filters to see which one works best with your camera. These filters aren't necessarily cheap, easily costing $60 to $100, depending on the diameter. Some can be purchased for less than $30, however.

It's likely that you're using a bunch of pro lenses with your D810, and those generally have a standard 77mm filter thread, so expect to pay at the high end of the filter range. I use a 77mm Marumi HB700 filter, which wasn't too pricey at $60. I elected not to go for a high-end filter because most of my IR shots are made with a converted camera (which needs no IR filter at all). The figure in the filter name represents the visible light cutoff point, specifically 700 nanometers with my HB700 filter. Marumi also offers HM830, which blocks virtually *all* visible light, creating *really* long exposure times, and eliminates the possibility of producing false-color IR images. (You end up with monochrome-only renditions.) Table 6.1 shows the cut-off point of visible light for some typical filters:

Once you're equipped, you have to learn to contend with the quirks and limitations of IR photography. These include:

- **Light loss.** The IR filter blocks the visible illumination, leaving you with an unknown amount of infrared light to expose by. Typically, you'll lose 5 to 7 f/stops, and will have to boost your exposure by that much to compensate. A tripod and long exposures, even outdoors, may be in your future.

Table 6.1 Light Blocked by Red/Infrared Filters

Filter Number	50% blockage	Filter Number	50% blockage
Wratten #25	600nm	Wratten #87	800nm
Wratten #29	620nm	Wratten #87C	850nm
Wratten #70	680nm	Wratten #87B	940nm
Wratten #89B	720nm	Wratten #87A	1050nm
Wratten #88A	750nm		

- **Difficulty metering.** Exposure systems are set up to work with visible illumination. The amount of IR reflected by various subjects differs wildly, so two scenes that look similar visually can call for quite different exposures under IR. Manual exposure may be your best bet.
- **Difficulty seeing.** Because the visual light is eliminated, you'll be in a heap of trouble trying to view an infrared scene through the D810's optical viewfinder. However, live view on the LCD monitor works well, as the D810 amplifies the signal just enough to make it visible.
- **Focus problems.** Infrared light doesn't focus at the same point as visible light, so manual focus is often easiest. You may have to experiment to determine how to best focus your D810 for infrared photos. If you're shooting landscapes, setting the lens to the infinity setting probably will work (even though *infrared infinity* is at a different point than visible light infinity). Some older lenses have markings that help adjust visible light focus for infrared photography.
- **Spotty images.** Some lenses include an anti-IR coating that produces central bright spots in IR images. Test your lens for this problem before blaming the artifacts on your filter or sensor. I had absolutely terrible results with my 17-35mm f/2.8 AF-S Nikkor—a bright spot showed up on every single image. My 14-24mm f/2.8 AF-S Nikkor wasn't an option, because it doesn't take filters. My best wide-angle shots were with the 24-70mm f/2.8 AF-S Nikkor, which showed no bright spots at all.

Fixing White Balance

Unfortunately, none of your D810's white balance settings will match the "color" balance of infrared illumination. An infrared photo taken using Auto or Daylight settings will have a distinct red cast, as you can see at left in Figure 6.14. When white balance has been set properly for infrared, you'll get the results shown at right in the figure, producing the basic brick-and-cyan look. Images of this type can be converted to other looks, including straight black-and-white, channel-swapped false color, and other variations.

Although you might actually want to work with a red-saturated image for creative reasons, and you can manipulate an uncorrected IR image in post-processing, most of the time you'll want to capture infrared photos with the proper white balance, if only because the non-reddish version is much easier to evaluate on the camera's monitor after exposure.

The goal is to set the white balance based on the IR reflectance of an object, and the best way to do that is to measure white balance from a subject that reflects a lot of infrared. Most experienced shooters use the grass or leafy trees as their "neutral" WB target. To set a preset white balance for infrared, follow these steps:

1. **Choose reference subject.** I do this outdoors, finding a patch of grass or other greenery under the lighting I want to measure.
2. **Change to Preset white balance.** Hold down the WB button on the top-left panel of the camera and rotate the main command dial until you see PRE and d-0 displayed in the monochrome control panel.

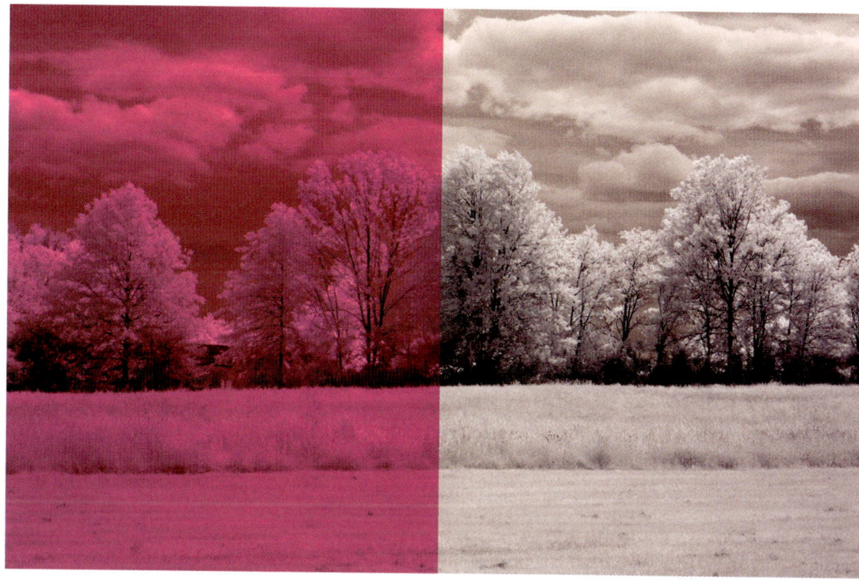

Figure 6.14
With the default Daylight white balance, an IR photo has a reddish cast. Setting the white balance correctly produces a more traditional infrared look.

3. **Activate capture mode.** Release the WB button for a moment, then press and hold it again until the PRE icon on the control panel begins a flashing cycle of about six seconds.
4. **Capture white balance of reference.** While the PRE icon is flashing, take a picture of the reference object.
5. **Confirm successful capture of white balance.** If the camera successfully measured white balance, Good will flash on the control panel for about six seconds, and Gd will appear in the bottom line of the viewfinder. Otherwise, you'll see no Gd on the monitor and viewfinder. White balance measurement can fail when the reference object is too brightly or poorly illuminated. In that case, repeat steps 2-5 until the measurement is successful.
6. **Use captured white balance.** You can immediately begin taking pictures using the captured white balance, until you hold down the WB button again and switch to one of the other white balance settings, such as Tungsten, or Fluorescent. You can assign a name to the captured balance, such as Infrared, to help you identify it the next time you use it.

Channel Swapping

Channel swapping does nothing more than *exchange* the color values found in the red channel for those in the blue channel (leaving the green channel alone). For most landscape and nature-oriented infrared photos, exchanging the browns found in the sky, water, and similar elements for blue, while swapping the bluish/cyan tones of foliage for browns, produces a more "realistic" image, as shown earlier in Figure 6.13.

You can swap channels using Photoshop's Channel Mixer. Just follow these steps:

1. Load the photograph you want to use with swapped channels.
2. Choose Image > Adjustments > Channel Mixer.
3. Select the Red channel from the Output Channel drop-down list. Place the cursor in the box to the right of the Red slider. Type in the value 0.
4. Place the cursor in the box to the right of the Blue slider and type in 100.
5. Select the Red channel from the drop-down list. Place the cursor in the box to the right of the Blue slider. Type in the value 0.
6. Place the cursor in the box to the right of the Red slider and type in 100.
7. Click OK. That's all there is to it.

Geotagging with the Nikon GP-1a

A swarm of satellites in geosynchronous orbits above the Earth became a big part of my life even before I purchased the Nikon D810. I use the GPS features of my iPhone and iPad and the GPS device in my car to track and plan my movements. When family members travel without me—most recently to Europe—I can use the Find my iPhone feature to see where they are roaming and vicariously accompany them with Google Maps' Street View features. And, since the introduction of the Nikon GP-1a accessory, GPS has become an integral part of my shooting regimen, too.

I do own and use a Garmin eTrex 20 hand-held GPS device, which can link to the D810 using a Nikon MC-35 cable plugged into the camera's 10-pin connector on the front of the camera, and mated with the cable provided by Garmin. However, it's much more convenient and less Rube Goldberg-ish to just clip the GP-1a to the top of the D810 and shoot away.

The GP-1a unit makes it easy to tag your images with the same kind of longitude, latitude, altitude, and time stamp information that is supplied by the GPS unit you use in your car. (Don't have a GPS? Photographers who get lost in the boonies as easily as I do *must* have one of these!) The geotagging information is stored in the metadata space within your image files, and can be accessed by Nikon View NX2, or by online photo services such as mypicturetown.com and Flickr.

Geotagging can also be done by attaching geographic information to the photo after it's already been taken. This is often done with online sharing services, such as Flickr, which allow you to associate your uploaded photographs with a map, city, street address, or postal code. When properly geotagged and uploaded to sites like Flickr, users can browse through your photos using a map, finding pictures you've taken in a given area, or even searching through photos taken at the same location by other users. Of course, in this day and age it's probably wise not to include GPS information in photos of your home, especially if your photos can be viewed by an unrestricted audience.

Having this information available makes it easier to track where your pictures are taken. That can be essential, as I learned from a trip out West recently, where I found the red rocks, canyons, and arroyos of Nevada, Utah, Arizona, and Colorado all pretty much look alike to my untrained eye. I find the capability especially useful when I want to return to a spot I've photographed in the past and am not sure how to get there. I can enter the coordinates shown into my hand-held or auto GPS (or an app in my iPad or iPhone) and receive instructions on how to get there. That's handy if you're returning to a spot later in the same day, or months later.

Like all GPS units, the Nikon GP-1a obtains its data by triangulating signals from satellites orbiting the Earth. It works with the Nikon D810, as well as many other Nikon cameras. At about $312, it's not cheap, but those who need geotagging—especially for professional mapping or location applications—will find it to be a bargain.

The GP-1a (see Figure 6.15) slips onto the accessory shoe on top of the Nikon D810. It connects to the GPS port on the camera using the Nikon GP1-CA10 cable, which plugs into the connector marked CAMERA on the GP-1a.

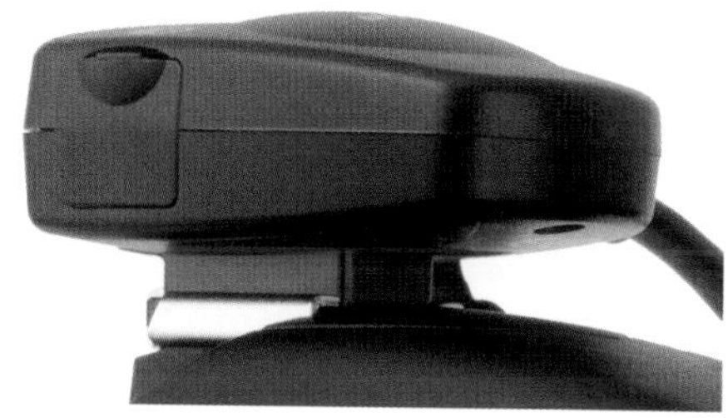

Figure 6.15 Nikon GP-1a geotagging unit.

EXTRA REMOTE

Ordinarily, D810 users who happen to own the Nikon MC-DC2 remote control (which is used with other Nikon cameras, such as the Nikon D3200) cannot connect that device to their camera. However, the GP-1a has a port labeled with a remote control icon, so you can plug in the Nikon MC-DC2 remote release, and it will work just fine.

A third connector connects the GP-1a to your computer using a USB cable. Nikon has released a utility for Windows and Mac operating systems that allows you to read GPS data from the GP-1a directly in your computer—no camera required. I tried the driver, and discovered that the GP-1a couldn't "see" any satellites from inside my office (big surprise). I plan on trying it with my netbook outdoors, in a car, or in some other more satellite-accessible location. Once attached, the device is very easy to use. You need to activate the Nikon D810's GPS capabilities in the GPS choice within the Setup menu, as described in Chapter 13.

The first step is to allow the GP-1a to acquire signals from at least three satellites. If you've used a GPS in your car, you'll know that satellite acquisition works best outdoors under a clear sky and out of the "shadow" of tall buildings, and the Nikon unit is no exception. It takes about 40-60 seconds for the GP-1a to "connect." A red blinking LED means that GPS data is not being recorded; a green blinking LED signifies that the unit has acquired three satellites and is recording data. When the LED is solid green, the unit has connected to four or more satellites, and is recording data with optimum accuracy.

Next, set up the camera by selecting the GPS option found under the Setup menu on the Nikon D810. There are three choices:

- **Auto meter-off.** You can choose Enable or Disable. Enabling reduces battery drain by allowing the D810 to turn off exposure meters while using the GP-1a after the time specified in Custom Setting c2 (Standby timer, discussed in Chapter 11) has elapsed. When the meters turn off, the GP-1a becomes inactive and must reacquire at least three satellite signals before it can begin recording GPS data once more. When you choose Disable, the exposure meters remain on while using the GP-1, so that GPS data can be recorded at any time, despite increased battery drain.
- **Position.** This is an information display, rather than a selectable option. It appears when the GP-1a is connected and receiving satellite positioning data. It shows the latitude, longitude, altitude, and Coordinated Universal Time (UTC) values for your current location. I've found this feature to be more valuable than I expected. If I don't have my eTrex 20 with me and someone wants to know exactly where I am, say, to meet up, I can check this readout, make a quick phone call, and tell them to set their own GPS (car, hand-held, whatever) for those coordinates, and then make a beeline for me.
- **Use GPS to set camera clock.** Select Yes or No. When enabled, your D810's internal camera clock will be set using UTC values whenever the GP-1a is attached to the camera. If you use the device frequently, this will ensure that your camera's clock is always set accurately, and won't require a manual update periodically.

Once the unit is up and running, you can view GPS information using photo information screens available on the color monitor (and described in Chapter 2). The GPS screen, which appears only when a photo has been taken using the GPS unit, looks something like Figure 6.16.

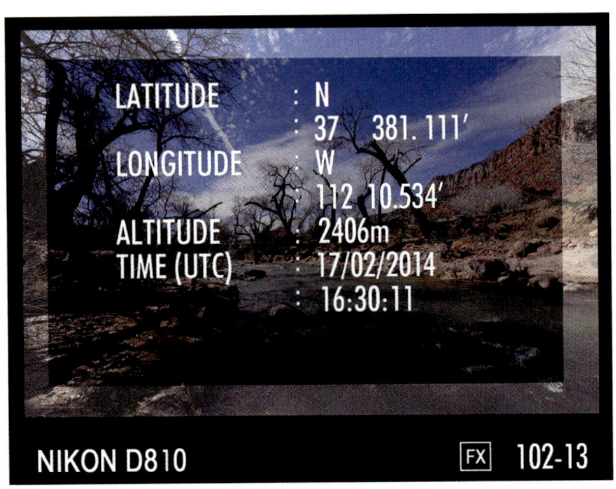

Figure 6.16
Captured GPS information can be displayed when you review the image.

7

Working with Lenses

In most of my previous Nikon books, I included discussions of the essentials of choosing lenses in the same chapter as more advanced topics and specific recommendations. For this Nikon D810 book, however, I've moved most of the basics, such as discussions of the kinds of effects you can expect from various focal lengths and zoom ranges, to my Part VI "bonus" section. If you need some background on lenses and their use, jump there. This chapter is aimed at those with more experience with optics, and Nikon lenses in particular.

By the time this book is published, Nikon will have announced the production of its 90 millionth Nikkor lens. However, as a D810 owner, you probably will be happy owning just a dozen or two of the available optics. With the introduction of Nikon's 36-megapixel digital SLR, your options and considerations for selecting and using lenses became a great deal more complicated.

For most of us, the old approach was to select FX lenses if we were using an FX camera, and to choose DX lenses if we were working with a cropped-sensor model. Within each lens type (FX or DX), we looked for optics with appropriate focal length range, aperture speed, image quality, and physical characteristics like weight and build quality. And price.

There were some exceptions to this conventional wisdom, of course. Those who planned to someday upgrade from DX format to FX tried to hedge their bets by emphasizing full-frame-friendly lenses even if they were using a DX camera. Owners of DX models discovered that, sometimes, an FX lens offered something not available with the DX lens variety, such as an f/1.4 maximum aperture or shift/tilt capabilities. Conversely, owners of Nikon D700 or D3-series models occasionally found a unique DX lens (in my case a Tokina 10-17mm fisheye zoom) that was worth the limitations of using a lens intended for cropped sensor cameras on a full-frame model.

That was then; this is now. With 36 megapixels of resolution, the D810 makes virtually any Nikon-compatible lens a viable option. Your camera can be used in FX mode at full resolution with all your full-frame lenses, as you expect. But the D810 also includes, in effect, a "free" DX-sensor camera that has a quite usable 15MP of resolution. Any DX lenses you might own, want to own, or can borrow/rent will work quite well on the D810. Earlier Nikon full-frame models gave you only a barely tolerable 5, 8, or 10 megapixels of resolution in DX mode (with 12-, 16-, and 24-megapixel sensors, respectively). The D810 makes swapping FX and DX lenses a whole new ballgame. You can now use *thousands* of current and older lenses introduced by Nikon and third-party vendors since 1959 (although lenses made before 1977 may need an inexpensive modification). You have a huge choice in selecting optics that can give you a wider view, bring distant subjects closer, let you focus closer, shoot under lower light conditions, or provide a more detailed, sharper image for critical work. Other than the sensor itself, the lens you choose for your dSLR is the most important component in determining image quality and perspective of your images.

Of course, there are some downsides that you might not have had to consider before. With so many pixels to fill up, the Nikon D810 can highlight any deficiencies in your lenses. A few lenses that outresolved your 16-megapixel full-frame cameras may not be up to snuff when 36 megapixels of resolution are in play. In addition, loss of sharpness at the smallest f/stops, due to a phenomenon known as *diffraction*, is more critical with the D810. Where you might have shot close-ups at f/22 or f/32 with your macro lens in the past, those apertures might cost you more sharpness than gains you get from the 36-megapixel sensor.

This chapter provides information for several types of Nikon D810 owners. Those who are new to FX photography, new to Nikon, or new to digital SLRs will find some information on general lens concepts, such as crop factor, and what lenses are compatible with the D810. More seasoned photographers may appreciate my recommendations on specific lenses and "kits" for particular types of photography. If you're looking for basics, including the best uses of wide-angle, "normal," telephoto, and special-purpose lenses, check out Appendix B at the end of this book.

Surprising Benefits of the Crop Factor

> The so-called *crop factor,* and the differences between the FX, DX, 1.2x, and 5:4 image areas available with the D810 still confuse some. If you're in that number, or need a refresher, you'll want to at least skim through this following section, which explains the crop factor and some of its unexpected benefits.

If you've moved up to the full-frame Nikon D810 from one of Nikon's DX models specifically to escape from the effects of the "crop" factor, I have some good news for you. D810 owners are the first generation of FX camera owners who are *not* entirely at the mercy of the differences between full-frame (FX) and cropped-frame (DX) sensors. Owners of DX-format models have always been able to use virtually *any* Nikon lens ever produced; previous FX users had to make some sacrifices to put the full range of available optics to work. While lenses designed for DX use will *fit* on your D810, the images they produce won't completely fill that precious full frame, at least, not at all focal lengths. To deploy these lenses in the way they were designed, you'll have to switch to the D810's DX mode, which, with the D810, happily provides a 15-megapixel image. Even though you're essentially wasting a lot of your sensor's photosites, cropping the image isn't a tremendous sacrifice. After all, a 15MP image is very close, in terms of resolution, to what you get with the top-of-the-line Nikon D4s model.

The *crop factor*, also called a *lens multiplier factor*, lives on. Both are misleading and inaccurate terms used to describe the same phenomenon: the fact that cameras like any of Nikon's DX models provide a field of view that's smaller and narrower than that produced by full-frame, FX models like the D810 and D4s.

Figure 7.1 quite clearly shows the phenomenon at work. The outer rectangle, marked 1X, shows the field of view you might expect with a 50mm lens mounted on a D810 or another one of Nikon's FX cameras. The area marked 1.5X shows the field of view you'd get with that 50mm lens installed on a DX model. It's easy to see from the illustration that the 1X rendition provides a wider, more expansive view, while the inner field of view is, in comparison, *cropped*.

The cropping effect is produced because the sensors of DX cameras are smaller than the sensors of the D810, D4, or earlier Nikon FX models. These "full-frame" cameras have a sensor that's the size of the standard 35mm film frame, 24mm × 36mm. Any DX sensor does *not* measure 24mm × 36mm; instead, it specs out at approximately 23.6mm × 15.8mm. You can calculate the relative field of view by multiplying the actual focal length by 1.5 (or, in the case of the D810's 1.2X crop, by 1.2).

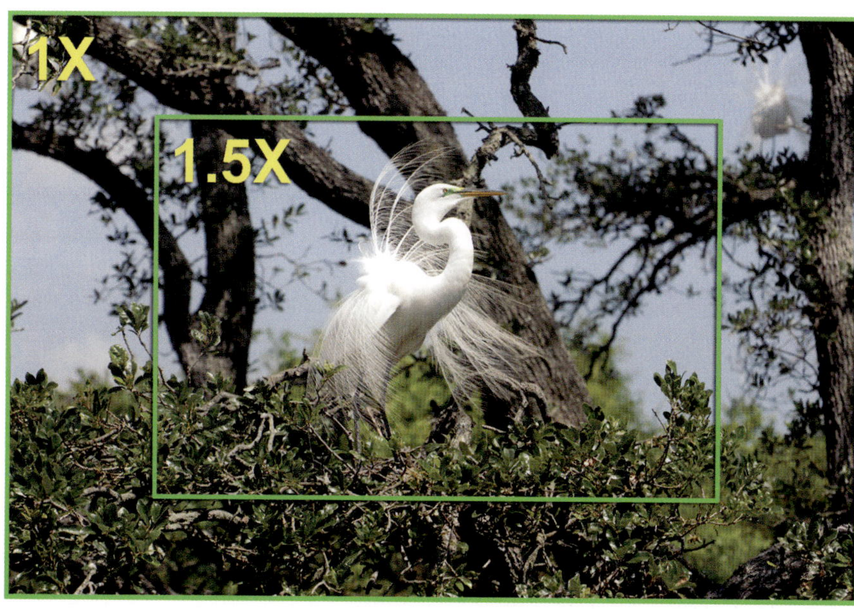

Figure 7.1
Nikon offers digital SLRs with full-frame (1X) crops, as well as 1.5X.

This translation is generally necessary only if you're using your D810 accompanied by a DX model, or are working with any lens in the D810's DX crop mode, and want to know how a familiar lens will perform. I strongly prefer *crop factor* over *lens multiplier*, because nothing is being multiplied; a 100mm lens doesn't "become" a 150mm lens—the depth-of-field and lens aperture remain the same for all practical purposes (despite what you may be reading about f/stop *equivalency* on several blogs and web sites). Only the field of view is cropped. But *crop factor* isn't much better, as it implies that the 24mm × 36mm frame is "full" and anything else is "less." I get e-mails all the time from photographers who point out that they own full-frame cameras with 36mm × 48mm sensors (like the Mamiya 645ZD or Hasselblad H3D-39 medium-format digitals). By their reckoning, the "half-size" sensors found in cameras like the Nikon D810 are "cropped."

If you need to work with both types, you might find it helpful to use the crop factor "multiplier" to translate a lens's real focal length into the full-frame equivalent, even though, as I said, nothing is actually being multiplied. Throughout most of this book, I've been using actual focal lengths and not equivalents, except when referring to specific wide-angle or telephoto focal length ranges and their fields of view.

Lenses designed for the DX format may or may not be usable for full-frame images on your D810. The image circle produced by a DX lens is generally smaller than the area of a full frame, at least at the widest focal length setting. Figure 7.2 shows the approximate coverage of a particular DX lens at a wide-angle setting. It covers the inner DX rectangle (just barely; some lenses exhibit darkening, or *vignetting* in the corners of the frame for this reason). But there is severe darkening at the corners of the full FX frame. Zoom the same lens in to a longer focal length setting, however, and the image coverage circle enlarges so that the lens is *almost* acceptable for full-frame use. (See Figure 7.3.)

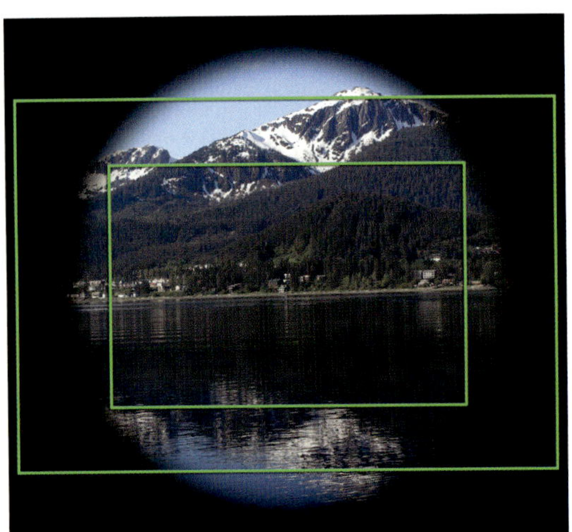

Figure 7.2 At a wide-angle setting, the image circle of a typical DX lens won't cover the full D810 frame.

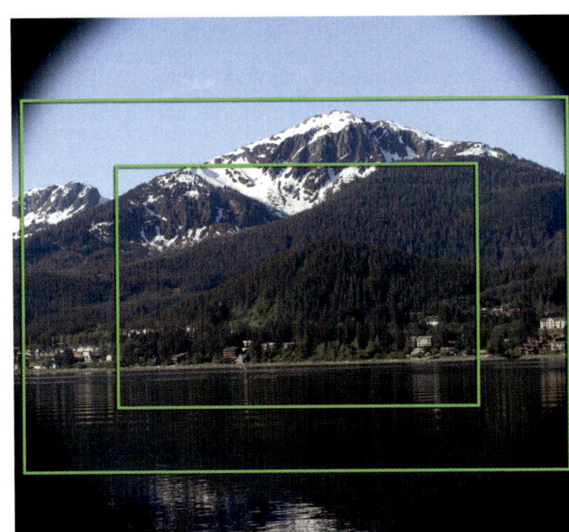

Figure 7.3 Zoom in, and the image circle enlarges, making the lens acceptable for full-frame coverage.

D810 owners who have certain DX lenses to test will see this phenomenon in action. When I mount my 10-24mm f/3.5-4.5 DX zoom on my D810, the image is a dark-cornered circle at 10mm, but when I zoom in to just shy of 15mm, the lens covers the full frame. I can use it as a 15-24mm zoom in FX mode, although there's no guarantee that the corners, while not vignetted, will be as sharp as I'd like. My older 12-24mm f/4 DX Nikkor covers the full FX frame at 18-24mm. My 55-200mm f/4-5.6 DX zoom fills the full FX frame at all focal lengths (although it is not very sharp, corner-to-corner, at any of them). If you do own a selection of DX lenses, you have several alternatives:

- **Give it a go.** Try them out on your D810 to see if they cover the full frame at various focal lengths and provide enough sharpness at the edges to be useful.
- **Keep as DX/backup lens.** If you own a backup camera in the DX format, you can still use your old DX lenses on that camera. It may be a pain carrying around lenses that you can't use on all your cameras, but the pain will be less than if you must sell those lenses for hundreds of dollars less than you paid for them.
- **Use DX mode.** You can tell the D810 to automatically switch to DX crop mode when a DX lens is mounted and recognized, using the Auto DX Crop option within the Image Area entry of the Shooting menu. The camera may not identify non-Nikon DX lenses, but you can select the Choose Image Area entry and set either FX or DX mode manually, as I have to do when working with my Tokina 10-17mm fisheye zoom lens.
- **Try one of the other cropped modes.** The D810 has a 5:4 ratio crop mode (30mm × 24mm) that is smaller than the full frame, and *may* provide enough of a crop to allow your DX lens to fill the remaining image area. It also has a 1.2X crop mode (30mm × 20mm) that I've found works quite well with some DX format lenses. You'll find these options all tucked away in the Image Area entry of the Shooting menu.
- **Use your DX lenses as a compact alternate kit.** This one's a bit of a stretch, but it might work out for some who own a particular set of lenses. When I am traveling overseas, I like to carry along more compact lenses to reduce the weight slung around my neck while tromping through European cities all day. Nikon's 10-24mm and 18-200mm DX zooms are a lot smaller and lighter than their FX 14-24mm and 28-300mm field-of-view counterparts. (The 28-300mm FX lens alone weighs almost as much as the two DX lenses.) The substitution would work only if you happened to own the lenses in question (possibly unlikely, because the DX lenses cost in the neighborhood of $1,000 each) and were willing to accept the reduction to 15 megapixels in DX mode.
- **Dump and replace.** Nikon has shown with its recent camera introductions that it won't be dumping the DX format anytime soon. So, your old DX lenses have retained a lot of their value on the used market. Instead of taking a bath when you sell them, you might have to endure little more than a splash in the face.

What You See Is What You Get

The usual way of illustrating the crop modes available with the Nikon D810 is to provide an example similar to the first three in this chapter: a full-frame shot with brackets marking the effective image area. But, of course, that's not what you see when you load your pre-cropped photos into your image editor. Figure 7.4 offers an easier-to-visualize illustration of what you see and what you get in a finished shot.

At upper left is a full-frame image, taken of the ancient section of Salamanca, Spain from across the Rio Tormes with a 28mm wide-angle lens. At upper right, you can see the same image in 5:4 crop mode. Details in the image are the same size as in the original shot, but the scene is cropped to the same proportions as a 4 × 5, 8 × 10, or 16 × 20 print. The 5:4 crop mode is useful if your final destination is a print using those proportions. Of course, you can tell from the example that a 5:4 crop is certainly not the best proportion for this panorama-worthy view.

At lower left you can see the same image taken using the D810's 1.2X crop. It retains the same 1.5:1 proportions as the full-frame shot, but the top, bottom, and sides are clipped off, providing that 1.2X magnification. This cropping is a useful compromise, and may allow you to use some DX

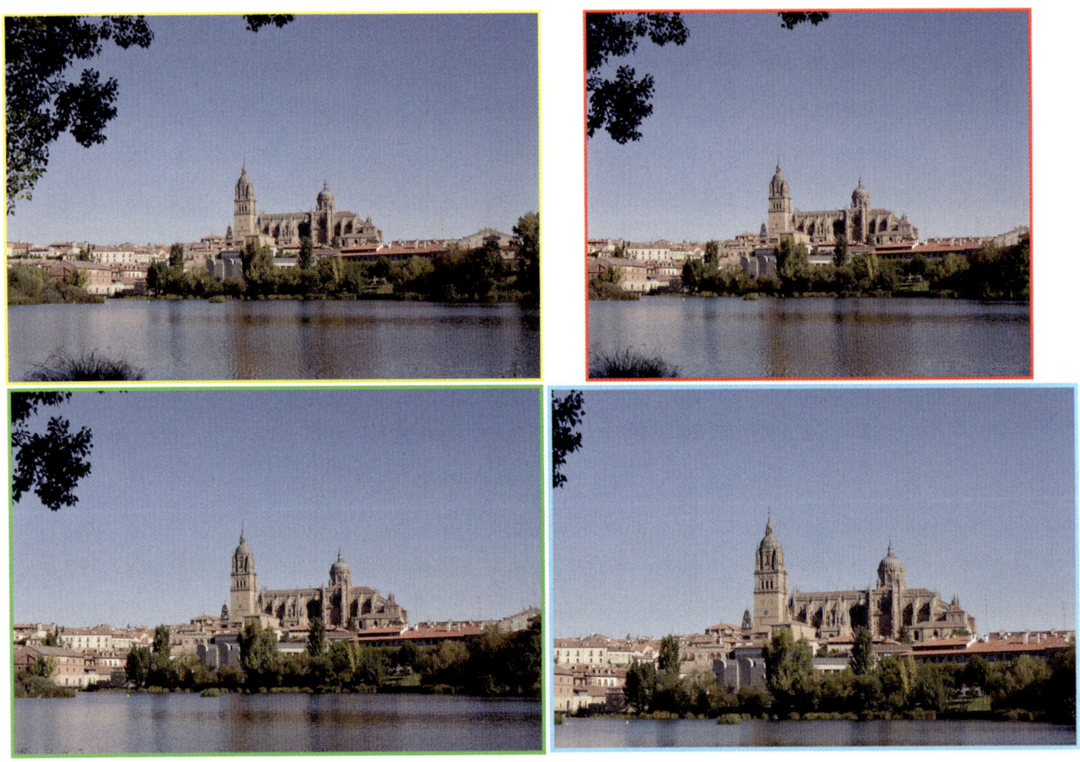

Figure 7.4 Full frame (upper left); 5:4 crop (upper right); 1.2X crop (lower left); and 1.5X crop (lower right).

lenses that don't quite fill the FX frame at certain focal lengths, but which do a decent job with this crop. At lower right is the original image with the standard DX crop with the 1.5X effective magnification, and the advantages I'll discuss in the next section.

Free Inside! A DX Camera!

For many photographers, the choice of an FX or DX camera is serious business. The D810 gives you both, at no additional cost. Wildlife and sports photographers appreciate having their longer lenses "boosted" 1.5X when using a DX model (as I discuss next), while landscape and architectural photographers need wide-angle optics that provide a truly wide field of view. DX mode does reduce the wide-angle effect of any given lens. There's a lot of debate over the "advantages" and "disadvantages" of using a camera in "cropped" sensor mode, versus using the "full-frame" sensor.

Do you really get a "free" 1.5X teleconverter? The D810's DX mode magically transforms any telephoto lens you have into a longer lens, which can be useful for sports, wildlife photography, and other endeavors that benefit from more reach. Yet, your f/stop remains the virtually the same. That is, a 300mm f/4 becomes a very fast 450mm f/4 lens (although some have produced some complicated mathematical formulas and test results that say this isn't strictly true; in practice, you'll rarely notice any difference). Nikon's AF-S Nikkor 500mm f/4G ED VR lens has a price tag in the $8,000 range. It has VR built-in, but weighs eight and a half pounds. In contrast, the $1,400 AF-S Nikkor 300mm f/4D ED-IF lens in DX mode has roughly the same field of view, the same maximum f/stop, and weighs more than five pounds less. It lacks vibration reduction, but you're more likely to be able to hand-hold a three pound lens than an eight pound monster.

Is VR really worth $6,000? The 500mm f/4 makes a lot of sense for some, such as serious wildlife photographers who want to fill a 36-megapixel frame at 500mm. But the average photographer would find the 300mm f/4 lens in DX mode entirely acceptable. If vibration reduction *is* important to you and your budget is large, Nikon offers the $5,500 AF-S VR Nikkor 300mm f/2.8G IF-ED that *does* have VR built in, and is even more versatile. Add a $550 *actual* teleconverter, like the AF-S Teleconverter TC-17E II (which multiplies the focal length by 1.7X, as discussed later in this chapter) and you can shoot in full FX mode with the equivalent of a 510mm f/4.5 telephoto, or in DX mode as a whopping 765mm f/4.5 lens! Decisions, decisions (if you have either $6,000 or $8,000 burning a hole in your pocket).

Some discount the "free teleconverter" aspect, pointing out that the exact same field of view can be had by taking a full-frame image, and trimming it to the 1.5X equivalent. So, they say, why bother to shoot in DX mode? Simply shoot in FX mode all the time and crop as needed.

Yes, it's true that shooting full-frame and then cropping in your image editor makes sense for everyday, casual shooting, but it is not the best option for many specific types of shooting. For example, if you're shooting sports or any type of subject where autofocus is critical and you want to take advantage of the extra "reach" of crop mode anyway, then DX mode has an advantage. The 51 AF sensors virtually fill the DX frame, so autofocus has nearly edge-to-edge coverage, with no special effort on your part. In FX mode, only the center portion of your image has AF coverage. Of course, if you intend to crop to just the DX portion later, the net effect is the same; AF coverage for a DX mode shot and the DX part of an FX shot is identical.

There's a benefit to DX mode if you're using live view. The D810 scales the live view image such that the monitor is filled with the DX view. That's an advantage over the optical viewfinder, which just provides a black box crop outline. As discussed in Chapter 5, the D810 uses Contrast Detect AF in live view mode, so if your intent is truly to use only the DX area, then DX mode simplifies moving the box around to choose a zone, and limits face detection to the area of interest.

Finally, if I am shooting 1,000 to 1,200 pictures of a sports contest or other event, the last thing I need is the "freedom" to crop later in an image editor. I tend to compose my images in the camera rather than in Photoshop, so it makes sense to end up with a thousand photos already cropped the way I want them than to have to manually crop each one.

BATCH CROPPING IN LIGHTROOM

If you use Adobe Lightroom, one way to get the best of both worlds is to shoot in FX mode, and then use Lightroom to crop every single image to DX format (or any other format or cropping you choose). You avoid the tedium of manually cropping all the images after the shoot, but retain the flexibility of having the original shot available should you *want* to do some cropping outside the default area.

What Lenses Can You Use?

If you're new to FX photography or to the Nikon system, you're probably wondering which lenses from the vast array of available optics can be added to your growing collection (trust me, it will grow). You need to know which lenses are suitable and, most importantly, which lenses are fully compatible with your Nikon D810.

With the D810 and Nikon's other FX cameras, the compatibility issue is a simple one: you can use in full-frame format any modern-era non-DX Nikon lens with the AF-S or AF designation, with full availability of all autofocus, auto aperture, autoexposure, tilt-shift, and image-stabilization features (if present). As I noted earlier, DX lenses must be used in one of the D810's crop modes if you want some assurance that the entire image area will be filled. Spotting DX lenses is easy: Nikon's versions all have the letters DX in their names.

The process is a bit more complicated when it comes to third-party manufacturers. Tamron uses the Di (Digitally integrated) designation for its lenses that are compatible with full-frame digital (and film) cameras, and applies the Di II label to lenses suitable only for cropped-sensor models. With Sigma lenses, DG is used for lenses suitable for both FX and DX cameras, and DC indicates a DX-only model. Tokina seems to use the D (for FX) and DX (for DX) nomenclature. All three vendors have been making lenses for (full-frame) film cameras for many years, well before the digital/DX factor became a factor, so when purchasing one of their lenses you may not see a special designation, but, if the lens was introduced prior to about 2004, it's almost certainly a full-frame model.

That's the case with Nikon's older lenses, too, such as the Nikon AI, AI-S, or AI-P lens, which are manual focus lenses produced starting in 1977 and effectively through the present day, because Nikon continues to offer a limited number of manual focus lenses for those who need them. All are full-frame models.

Nikon lenses produced prior to 1977 must have a minor conversion done to be used safely with the D810, because cameras other than certain Nikon entry-level models (such as the D40/D40x, D60, D3000-series, and D5000-series) have an indexing pin on the lens mount that can be damaged by an older, unmodified lens. This pin is lacking on the entry level Nikon cameras, and can be flipped up out of the way with the retro Nikon Df. John White at www.aiconversions.com will do the work for about $35 to allow these older lenses to be safely used on any Nikon digital camera.

Ingredients of Nikon's Alphanumeric Soup

Nikon has always been fond of appending cryptic letters and descriptors onto the names of its lenses. Some of the first Nikon lenses I purchased had names like 35mm f/2 Auto Nikkor-O, 85mm f/1.8 Auto Nikkor-H, 105mm Auto Nikkor-P, and 200mm f/4 Auto Nikkor-Q. At the time, I didn't know what the funny letters represented, but I did know that the "Auto" portion of the name was not for Autofocus or Autoexposure. It meant that, when you pressed the shutter release button, the lens would actually *stop down automatically* to the aperture you'd selected for the exposure. Don't laugh. Many lenses required rotating a ring manually after focusing and before taking the picture in order to close the lens down to the so-called *pre-set* aperture.

I actually still own all those lenses, because they work just fine on my Nikon digital camera bodies, including my beloved D810. And I now know that the funny letters stood for the number of elements in the lens, which was apparently a more important attribute for a photographer to know than it is today. P stood for *penta* (five elements); H represented *hexa* (six elements); S stood for *septa* (seven elements); and so on through *octa*, *nona*, and *deca* (eight, nine, and ten). I'd finally found a use for my high school Latin, even though Nikon substituted *penta* for *quinta*, because Q was already taken by *quadra* (four elements).

In the years since, Nikon lens nomenclature has become considerably more complex. Even the basic name of the company's lenses can be a source of confusion. Today, *Nikkor* is still officially part of the name of each lens produced by Nikon, with the exception of the company's "budget" line of 30 years go, which were called *Nikon Lens Series E* to differentiate them from all the other "top of the line" lenses. But it's become more common to informally refer to a Nikon lens without fear of being corrected.

Here's an alphabetical list of lens terms you're likely to encounter, either as part of the lens name or in reference to the lens's capabilities. Not all of these are used as parts of a lens's name, but you may come across some of these terms in discussions of particular Nikon optics:

- **AF, AF-D, AF-I, AF-S.** In all cases, AF stands for *autofocus* when appended to the name of a Nikon lens. An extra letter is added to provide additional information. A plain-old AF lens is an autofocus lens that uses a slot-drive motor in the camera body to provide autofocus functions (and so cannot be used in AF mode on the Nikon D40, D40x, D60, D3000-series, or D5000-series, which lack the camera body motor). The D means that it's a D-type lens (described later in this listing); the I indicates that focus is through a motor inside the lens; and the S means that a super-special (Silent Wave) motor in the lens provides focusing. (Don't confuse a Nikon AF-S lens with the AF-S [Single-servo autofocus mode].) Nikon is currently upgrading its older AF lenses with AF-S versions, but it's not safe to assume that all newer Nikkors are AF-S, or even offer autofocus. For example, the PC-E Nikkor 24mm f/3.5D ED perspective control lens must be focused manually, and Nikon offers a small collection of other manual focus lenses to meet specialized needs.
- **AI, AI-S.** All Nikkor lenses produced after 1977 have either automatic aperture indexing (AI) or automatic indexing-shutter (AI-S) features that eliminate the previous requirement to manually align the aperture ring on the camera when mounting a lens. When AI/AI-S was introduced, Nikon included the designation in the lens name and offered a service to convert most older lenses to the new configuration. Within a few years, all Nikkors had this automatic aperture indexing feature (except for G-type lenses, which have no aperture ring at all), including Nikon's budget-priced Series E lenses, so the designation was dropped at the time the first autofocus (AF) lenses were introduced. The most important difference between AI and AI-S lenses is that the aperture action of the AI-S versions is *linear*, theoretically allowing for more efficient shutter-priority and programmed exposure metering on cameras of the time. Current models make no distinction between AI and AI-S lenses. These lenses can be used for Aperture-priority and Manual mode metering on the Nikon D810 and other Nikon mid-range and pro bodies.
- **AI-P.** A lens with an AI-P designation is an AI lens that has the CPU chip included, which allows the transfer of basic lens information to the camera. It was possible to add an appropriate chip to most AI and AI-S lenses, upgrading them to AI-P status, but there are few companies offering this service anymore. "Chipped" AI/AI-S/AI-P lenses are manual focus optics that can be used with the full range of metering options, the same as with autofocus lenses.
- **CRC (Close Range Correction).** The so-called "floating element" system allowed lens elements to shift position to reduce curvature of field and spherical aberrations at close-focusing distances. It is available with certain lenses, including the AF Micro-Nikkor 60mm f/2.8D, which was replaced by the AF-S Micro-Nikkor 60mm f/2.8G ED.

- **E.** The E designation was used for Nikon's budget-priced E Series optics, five prime and three zoom manual focus lenses built using aluminum or plastic parts rather than brass, the preferred material in those days, so they were less rugged. All are effectively AI-S lenses. They do have good image quality, which makes them a bargain for those who treat their lenses gently and don't need the latest autofocus features. They were available in 28mm f/2.8, 35mm f/2.5, 50mm f/1.8, 100mm f/2.8, and 135mm f/2.8 focal lengths, plus 36-72mm f/3.5, 75mm-150mm f/3.5, and 70-210mm f/4 zooms. (All these would be considered fairly "fast" today.)
- **D.** Appended to the maximum f/stop of the lens (as in f/2.8D), a D Series lens is able to send focus distance data to the camera, which uses the information for flash exposure calculation and 3D Color Matrix II matrix metering.
- **DC.** The DC stands for defocus control, which allows managing the out-of-focus parts of an image to produce better-looking portraits and close-ups.
- **DX.** The DX lenses are designed for use with digital cameras using the APS-C–sized sensor having the 1.5X crop factor. Their image circle isn't large enough to fill up a full 35mm frame at all focal lengths, but they can be used on Nikon's full-frame models using the automatic/manual DX crop mode. Theoretically, these lenses can be built smaller and lighter than their full-frame counterparts, but there are some hefty DX lenses available, including the AF-S DX Zoom-Nikkor 17-55mm f/2.8G IF-ED.
- **ED (or LD/UD).** The ED (extra low dispersion) designation indicates that some lens elements are made of a special hard and scratch-resistant glass that minimizes the divergence of the different colors of light as they pass through, thus reducing chromatic aberration (color "fringing") and other image defects. A gold band around the front of the lens indicates an optic with ED elements. You sometimes find LD (low dispersion) or UD (ultra-low dispersion) designations.
- **FX.** When Nikon introduced the Nikon D3 full-frame camera, it coined the term "FX," representing the 24mm × 35.9mm sensor format as a counterpart to "DX," which was used for its 15.6mm × 23.7mm APS-C-sized sensors. Although FX hasn't been officially applied to any Nikon lenses as part of the model name so far, expect to see the designation used more often to differentiate between lenses that are compatible with any Nikon digital SLR (FX) and those that operate only on DX-format cameras, or in DX mode when used on an FX camera like the D810.
- **G.** G-type lenses have no aperture ring, and you can use them at other than the maximum aperture only with electronic cameras like the D810 that set the aperture automatically or by using the command dial while the exposure compensation/aperture button is depressed. This includes all Nikon digital dSLRs.

- **IF.** Nikon's *internal focusing* lenses change focus by shifting only small internal lens groups with no change required in the lens's physical length, unlike conventional double helicoid focusing systems that move all lens groups toward the front or rear during focusing. IF lenses are more compact and lighter in weight, provide better balance, focus more closely, and can be focused more quickly.
- **IX.** These lenses were produced for Nikon's long-discontinued Pronea 6i and S APS film cameras. While the Pronea could use many standard Nikon lenses, IX lenses cannot be mounted on any Nikon digital SLR.
- **Micro.** Nikon uses the term *micro* to designate its close-up lenses. Most other vendors use *macro* instead.
- **N (Nano Crystal Coat).** Nano Crystal lens coating virtually eliminates internal lens element reflections across a wide range of wavelengths, and is particularly effective in reducing ghost and flare peculiar to ultra-wide-angle lenses. Nano Crystal Coat employs multiple layers of Nikon's extra-low refractive index coating, which features ultra-fine crystallized particles of nano size (one nanometer equals one millionth of a mm).
- **NAI.** This is not an official Nikon term, but it is widely used to indicate that a manual focus lens is *Not-AI*, which means that it was manufactured before 1977, and therefore cannot be used safely on modern digital Nikon SLRs without modification.
- **NOCT (Nocturnal).** Used primarily to refer to the prized Nikkor AI-S Noct 58mm f/1.2, a "fast" (wide aperture) prime lens, with aspherical elements, capable of taking photographs in very low light.
- **PC (Perspective Control).** A PC lens is capable of shifting the lens from side to side (and up/down) to provide a more realistic perspective when photographing architecture and other subjects that otherwise require tilting the camera so that the sensor plane is not parallel to the subject. Older Nikkor PC lenses offered shifting only, but more modern models, such as the PC-E Nikkor 24mm f/3.5D ED lens introduced early in 2008 allow both shifting and tilting.
- **UV.** This term is applied to special (and expensive) lenses designed to pass ultra-violet light.
- **UW.** Lenses with this designation are designed for underwater photography with Nikonos camera bodies, and cannot be used with Nikon digital SLRs.
- **VR.** Nikon has an expanding line of vibration reduction (VR) lenses, including several very affordable models, which shift lens elements internally to counteract camera shake. The VR feature allows using a shutter speed up to four stops slower than would be possible without vibration reduction. You can expect to see variations, such as VR, VR II, or VR III depending upon how recently the lens was introduced.

Expanding Your Lens Kit

There is really only one advantage to using just a single lens, and that's the creativity forced on you by having only a single lens available. Keeping one set of optics mounted on your D810 all the time forces you to be especially imaginative in your approach to your subjects. I once visited Europe with only a single camera body and a 35mm f/2 lens. The experience was actually quite exciting, because I had to use a variety of techniques to allow that one lens to serve for landscapes, available light photos, action, close-ups, portraits, and other kinds of images.

Of course, it's more likely that your single lens is actually a zoom, which is, in truth, many lenses in one, taking you from, say, 28mm to 300mm (or some other range) with a rapid twist of the zoom ring. You'll still find some creative challenges when you stick to a single zoom lens's focal lengths.

It's more likely that you'll succumb to the malady known as *Lens Lust* or *Nikon Acquisition Syndrome*, which is defined as an incurable disease marked by a significant yen for newer, better, longer, faster, sharper, anything-er optics for your camera. (And, it must be noted, this disease can *cost* you significant yen—or dollars, or whatever currency you use.) In its worst manifestations, sufferers find themselves with lenses that have overlapping zoom ranges or capabilities, because one or the other offers a slight margin in performance or suitability for specific tasks. When you find yourself already lusting after a new lens before you've really had a chance to put your latest purchase to the test, you'll know the disease has reached the terminal phase.

In this final part of the chapter, I'm going to discuss some specific Nikon lenses that I have experience with, and provide some recommendations. That's not to say that I use only Nikon lenses; I absolutely love my Sigma 15mm f/2.8 fisheye, and couldn't afford a zoom that reaches all the way out to 500mm if I hadn't been able to pick up my 170-500mm Sigma full-frame zoom lens secondhand for an excellent price. But there are so many lens options available that it makes more sense to confine my comments to the true-blue Nikkors that I've had experience with.

Your Best Do-Everything Option?

Virtually all the lenses in the rest of this chapter will be full-frame, FX-friendly optics. However, Nikon has introduced a revised version of its AF-S DX Nikkor 18-300mm f/3.5-5.6G ED VR II zoom, with an incredible 16.7X zoom range, but which is relatively light and compact, focuses close, and has image stabilization built in. Although it's not a stellar performer from 200mm-300mm, it's a reasonable walk-around lens on DX format cameras for those who find 15MP is plenty, and do want the 27mm-450mm equivalent focal length range (for sports and wildlife). I kept my copy of the original version of this lens for about six months before selling it (which is why it is pictured in Figure 7.5 mounted on my original Nikon D800).

My "crop factor" discussion earlier in this chapter explains why I like using this 18mm-300mm lens in DX mode, rather than just cropping the image. And I don't own a 27mm-450mm zoom. Perhaps you wouldn't want to buy this lens exclusively for use on full-frame cameras, but if you also own a DX model, you'll find that Nikon's wide-to-supertele zoom can easily do double duty.

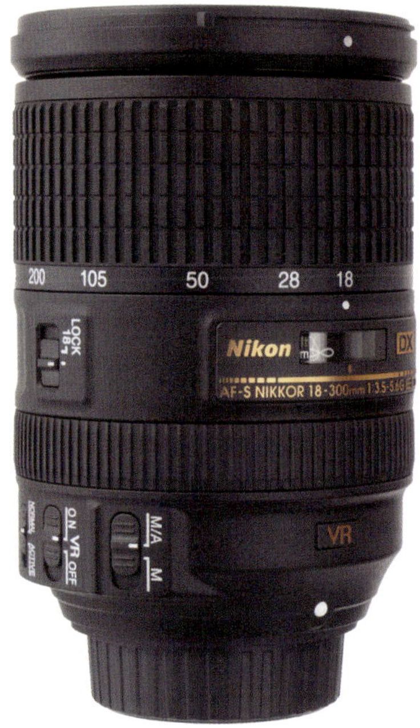

Figure 7.5
Could Nikon's improved 18-300mm DX lens find a home on your D810?

Check these aspects out:

- **Ultra-long zoom range.** Used in DX mode on your D810, this lens provides the equivalent field of view as a full-frame 27mm-400mm lens. That's sort of wide to supertelephoto, without the need to swap lenses. That versatility is important when shooting stills, of course, especially with sports and other rapidly changing scenes. But if you're shooting movies, the 18-300mm focal lengths come in especially handy. You can capture a wide establishing shot to set the scene, switch to a medium shot to draw viewer attention to your main subjects, then capture an extreme close-up. Even if you're collecting short clips, the action may be continuing between "takes," so if you had to switch lenses you might miss something. Not so with this lens. You can change field of view between each shot as quickly as you can rotate the zoom ring. The lens's long range has some possibilities for those mind-boggling quick zooms in or out *during* video capture, too. (Use with restraint!)
- **But forget about FX mode.** Unlike many of Nikon's wide-angle DX lenses, this one doesn't really fill the frame at *any* focal length—even when you remove the lens hood. I tried it out at various zoom settings, but vignetting is severe until about 45mm-50mm, and then the dark corners come back at *longer* focal lengths, too. Although it works great in DX mode, with the FX non-crop and 1.2X partial crop the dark corners are obvious.
- **Vibration reduction.** It's so common to have VR in telephoto lenses these days, especially those with equivalent or actual focal lengths of 400mm or more that you might not stop to think how rare image stabilization is at the other end. Nikon's 24-120mm f/4, 16-35mm f/4 full-frame, and 24-85mm VR lenses (discussed later in this chapter) along with DX lenses (the

18-55mm kit lenses, 16-85mm f/3.5-5.6G, and 18-200mm f3.5-5.6) are *it* in the Nikon product line. While it's arguable that VR is less essential in a wide-angle lens because camera shake blur is less of a problem, having a lens that starts wide and goes all the way to supertelephoto with optical image stabilization built in is a definite plus.

- **Compact size.** Although it replaces a half-dozen or more lenses, the 18-300mm zoom measures just 3.3 × 4.7 inches and weighs 1 pound, 13 ounces, which is svelte for a 300mm lens (even if a bit large for an 18mm wide angle). Your do-everything walk around lens compares favorably to its 18-200mm predecessor (3 × 3.8, 1 pound, four ounces), takes pro-standard 77mm filters (vs 72mm for the older model), and has a lock to totally prevent dreaded zoom creep, to boot. Mine doesn't exhibit creep even with the lock off, however.
- **Close focusing.** The ability to focus down to 1.48 feet at 300mm, gives you a 1:3.2X maximum reproduction ratio (about one-third life-size in DX format). The 18-300mm is not a true macro lens, but when you're venturing out with a single lens on your D810, the ability to focus that closely at 300mm is the next best thing.

The Magic Three

If you cruise the forums, you'll find the same three lenses mentioned over and over, often referred to as "The Trinity," "The Magic Three," or some other affectionate nickname. They are the three lenses you'll find in the kit of just about every serious Nikon photographer (including me). They're fast, expensive, heavier than you might expect, and provide such exquisite image quality that once you equip yourself with the Trinity, you'll never be happy with anything else.

In recent years, Nikon has replaced the original members of the Magic Three with new lenses. I've been fortunate enough to own both, and will describe them for you lovingly. They're now divided into two kits, the original trio, which I describe as the Affordable Magic Three—because all of them are still readily available, and at much lower prices than the new, reigning magic lineup.

The Original Magic Three

For a significant number of years, the most commonly cited "ideal" lenses for "serious" Nikon digital SLRs were the 17-35mm f/2.8, 28-70mm f/2.8, and 70-200mm f/2.8 VR. (See Figure 7.6.) The trio share a number of attributes. All three are non-DX lenses that (theoretically) work equally well on film cameras, the full-frame models like the D810 and D4, as well as advanced DX cameras for those who could justify their cost, making for a sound investment in optics that could be used on any Nikon SLR, past or future. Indeed, I owned all three well before I bought my first full-frame digital Nikon, as my purchases predated the introduction of the original Nikon D3 and D700 models.

All three incorporate internal Silent Wave motors and focus incredibly fast. They all have f/2.8 maximum apertures that are *constant*; they don't change as the lens is zoomed in or out. All three are internal focusing (IF) models that don't change length as they focus, and include extra-low dispersion (ED) elements. And, all three are expensive, at $1,000 to $1,600 each, whether you

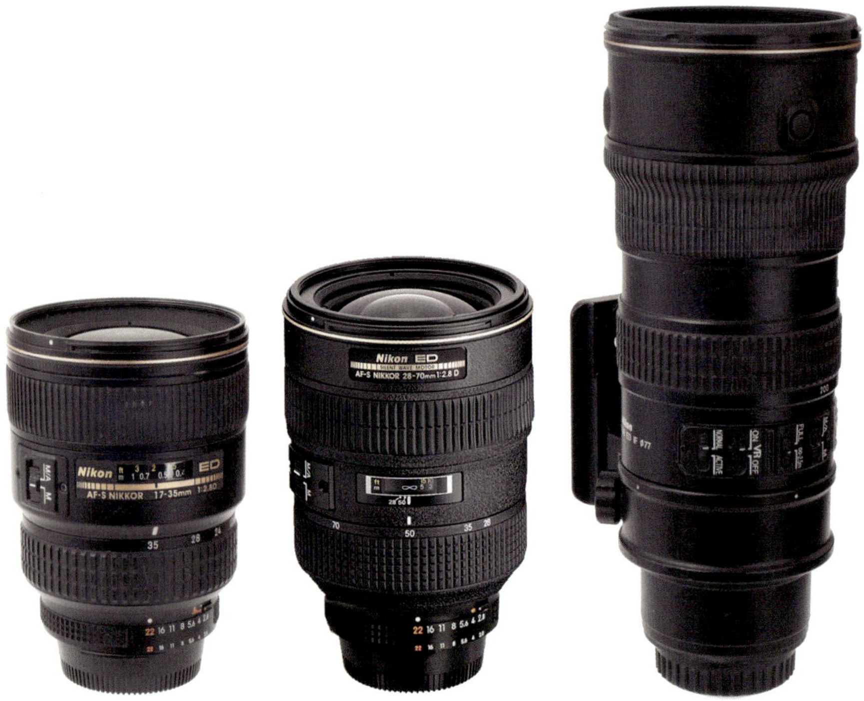

Figure 7.6
The "affordable" Magic Three lenses.

manage to find one new or, more likely, in mint used condition. But, as I discovered when I added this set, once you have them, you don't need any other lenses unless you're doing field sports like football or soccer, extreme wide-angle, or close-up photography. When these three were my primary lenses, I took them with me everywhere, adding another lens or two as required for specialized needs. If you can't find a new AF-S VR Zoom-Nikkor 70-200mm f/2.8G IF-ED of the VR I variety, Nikon has introduced an f/4 version that, too, is available for an affordable price, and I'll describe it later in this chapter.

- **AF-S Zoom-Nikkor 17-35mm f/2.8D IF-ED.** When I am shooting landscapes, doing street photography, or some types of indoor sports, this lens can go on my D810 and never come off, even though I also own its nominal replacement, the AF-S Nikkor 14-24mm f/2.8G ED. Its actual direct replacement, in terms of focal length range and size, is the AF-S Nikkor 16-35mm f/4G ED VR. The newer lens is slower at f/4 instead of f/2.8, but adds VR as an equalizer. The 17-35mm is known to have autofocus motor problems (although my copy has been trouble-free), so if you buy this lens used and find one with a motor that has been recently replaced, that's a plus. I kept this lens after I got the 14-24mm zoom, because I find I need its 24-35mm focal length range more often than I need the 14-17mm range of the latter lens. I don't need to swap out for a longer lens as often, and, as a bonus, the 17-35mm lens accepts 77mm filters if I need them, and has an actual old-school aperture ring. I'll keep this member of the Affordable Magic Three forever.

- **AF-S Zoom-Nikkor 28-70mm f/2.8D IF-ED.** Nicknamed "The Beast" because of its size and weight, this lens, too, is wonderfully sharp, and well suited for anything from sports to portraiture that falls within its focal length lens. I know many photographers who aren't heavily into landscapes who use this lens as their main lens. With its impressive lens hood mounted, The Beast is useful for terrifying small children, too. I eventually sold mine and replaced it with the newer 24-70mm f/2.8 lens described later, primarily because my job requires me to keep up to date on the latest Nikon lenses. This one is just as good as its replacement, and it, too, sports an aperture ring that's not really essential these days.
- **AF-S VR Zoom-Nikkor 70-200mm f/2.8G IF-ED.** This legendary lens is perfect for some indoor and many outdoor sports, on a monopod, or hand-held, and can be used for portraiture, street photography, wildlife (especially with the 1.4X teleconverter), and even distant scenics. I use it for concerts, too, alternating between this lens and my 85mm f/1.4. It takes me in close to the performer, and can be used wide-open or at f/4 with good image quality. The only time I leave it behind is when I need to travel light (although it's not really that huge). This is the only lens of the magic trio that lacks an aperture ring, but you probably won't be using it with a bellows extension, anyway.

The original AF-S VR Zoom-Nikkor 70-200mm f/2.8G IF-ED, is typical of the VR lenses Nikon offers. Like the newer model, it has the basic controls shown in Figure 7.7, top, to adjust focus range (full, or limited to infinity down to 2.5 meters); VR On/Off; and Normal VR/Active VR (the latter an aggressive mode used in extreme situations, such as a moving car). Not visible (it's over the horizon, so to speak) is the M/A-M focus mode switch, which allows changing from autofocus (with manual override) to manual focus. There's also a focus lock button near the front of the lens (see Figure 7.7, bottom). I often use the rotating tripod mount collar, which helps take some stress off the camera lens mount, as a grip for the lens when shooting hand-held, and, as you can see in Figure 7.8, I've replaced the factory tripod mounting foot with Kirk's Arca-Swiss-compatible quick release mount foot.

FULL-FRAME FOLLY?

The only "problem" with the original 70-200mm lens is that it produces noticeable vignetting and reduced sharpness in the corners at many focal lengths when used on a full-frame camera like the D810. These characteristics tend to vanish when the lens is used in DX mode or with a 1.4X teleconverter. To be honest, I've had wonderful results with this lens with my full-frame cameras. I don't shoot landscapes or brick walls with 70mm to 200mm focal lengths, and for the portrait and fashion work I do, the corners aren't important. You should keep this "shortcoming" of the original 70-200mm zoom in mind. And, unlike the newer 70-200mm f/2.8 VR II lens, it doesn't "breathe" (a trait I'll discuss later).

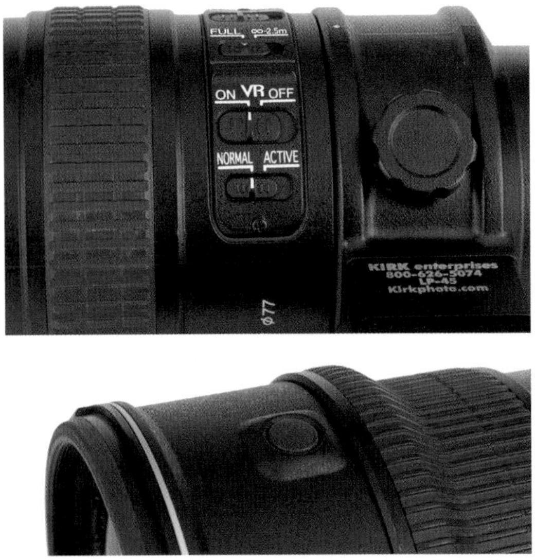

Figure 7.7 On the Nikon 70-200mm VR zoom you'll find (top): the focus limit switch, VR on/off switch, and Normal/Active VR adjustment. The lens also includes an autofocus lock button that can be activated while holding the lens (bottom).

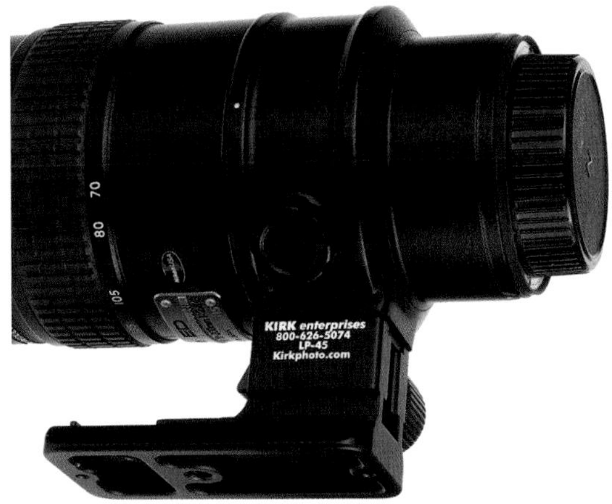

Figure 7.8 The rotating collar allows mounting the lens/camera to a tripod in vertical or horizontal orientations—or anything in-between.

The Reigning Magic Three

When Nikon introduced the D3 and the original D300, it also debuted two new lenses, an AF-S Nikkor 14-24mm f/2.8G ED, and an AF-S Nikkor 24-70mm f/2.8G ED lens. Both are G-type lenses (they lack an aperture ring), have AF-S focusing, and have constant f/2.8 apertures. In 2009, Nikon announced a replacement for the 70-200mm VR lens, rounding out the Magic Trio with an all new lineup. Like the original big three, these are all full-frame lenses that work with any DX or FX-format Nikon camera. (See Figure 7.9.)

Other than some minor (and major) sharpness tweaks, one chief advantage of the new lineup (if you can call it that) is that there is no overlap. You can go from 14-24mm to 24-70mm to 70-200mm with no gaps in coverage. I don't find that an overwhelming advantage, because there are lots of situations in which the 17-35mm range of my existing lens is exactly what I need; if I used the "new" trio exclusively, I'd find myself swapping lenses whenever I needed more than a 24mm focal length.

So, I now own both the new 14-24mm f/2.8 zoom *and* the old 17-35mm f/2.8 lens—and I use them both about equally. The 14-24mm gives me a bit more wide-angle perspective than the 17-35mm lens, and it is fabulously sharp. I use the 17-35mm lens when I think I'll need the longer focal length, when I want to shoot semi-macro pictures of, say, flowers, and when I am traveling light. For example, when shooting in Europe I take along the 17-35mm lens (which is *much* smaller than the 14-24mm, and can be used with polarizing filters, to boot) and my 28-200mm zoom (described later).

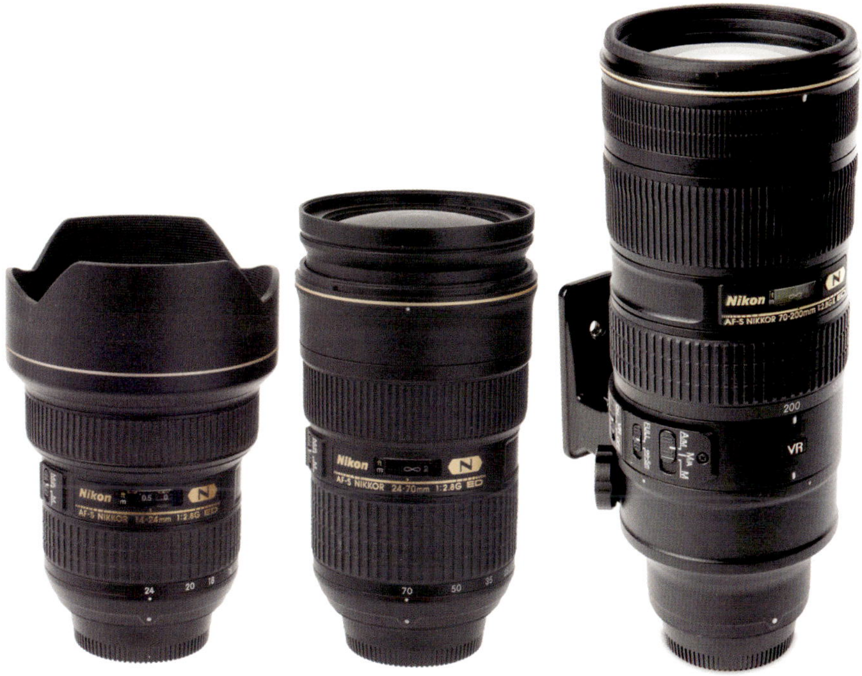

Figure 7.9
The reigning Magic Three.

Carefully consider the focal lengths you need before deciding which "magic" triad is best for you. The new lineup looks like this:

- **AF-S Nikkor 14-24mm f/2.8G ED.** I own this lens, and its image quality is incredible, with very low barrel distortion (outward bowing at the edges) and very little of the chromatic aberrations common to lenses this wide. Because it has full-frame coverage, it's immune to obsolescence. It focuses down to 10.8 inches, allowing for some interesting close-up/wide-angle effects. The downside? The outward curving front element precludes the use of most filters, although I haven't tried this lens with add-on Cokin-style filter holders, including one very expensive ($400) Lee Kit-SW150 Super Wide Filter Holder, which uses 150mm × 170mm and 150mm × 150mm filters. Usually, lack of filter compatibility isn't a fatal flaw for D810 users, as the use of polarizers, in particular, would be problematic at wider focal lengths. The polarizing effect would be highly variable because of this lens's extremely wide field of view.
- **AF-S Nikkor 24-70mm f/2.8G ED.** This lens seems to provide even better image quality than the legendary Beast, especially when used wide open or in flare-inducing environments. (You can credit the new internal Nano Crystal Coat treatment for that improvement.) My recommendation is that if you already own The Beast, or can get one used for a good price ($1,200 or less), you don't sacrifice much going with the older 28-70mm lens, and may find the overlap with the 14-24mm lens useful. But if you have the cash and opportunity to purchase this newer lens, you won't be making a mistake. Some were surprised when it was introduced without the

VR feature, but Nikon has kept the size of this useful lens down, while maintaining a reasonable price for a "pro" level lens. Some have reported a light leakage problem in the lens barrel, associated with the transparent focus scale window. Nikon will fix it for you, but a temporary fix is to cover the window with black tape.

- **AF-S VR II Zoom-Nikkor 70-200mm f/2.8G IF-ED.** Not a lot to be added about the latest version of this lens, which is a worthy representative of the telephoto zoom range in this "ideal" trio of lenses. It does have better performance in the corners on full-frame cameras, but most of its other attributes remain the same. One aspect that is different is the tendency of this lens to "breathe" when focused at close distances and long focal lengths, as I'll describe next.

Lenses that Breathe

One difference between the older VR I and newer VR II versions of Nikon is that the newer lens has a tendency to exhibit focus breathing. That is, the effective focal length of the lens changes as you focus closer and closer. This is not a phenomenon that's unique to the 70-200mm f/2.8 VR II lens; some lens designs breathe, and some don't. The original 70-200mm f/2.8 VR I lens exhibited much less of this effect, so those who are upgrading to the newer lens may be in for a surprise.

By convention, the advertised focal length of a lens is measured when the lens is focused at infinity. The effective focal length of the original VR I lens when cranked all the way to its maximum and focused at infinity is 196mm, so it's assigned a nominal focal length of 200mm (just as 2 × 4 lumber doesn't really measure 2 × 4 inches). The VR II lens at its maximum zoom setting has an effective focal length of 192mm, so it, too, qualifies for the 200mm designation. At their minimum zoom settings, both lenses are close enough to 70mm that either can be described as 70-200mm zooms. This happens to be true whether either lens is focused at infinity or at their closest focusing distances.

However, at the 200mm setting, when either lens is focused at its minimum focus distance, something interesting happens. The original VR I lens has an effective focal length of 182mm—but the VR II lens's magnification drops to the equivalent of a 135mm lens. (The original lens focuses down to 4.9 feet, while the newer one focuses slightly closer at 4.6 feet.) At the same distance, that's quite a difference. Most people don't shoot these lenses at their maximum zoom setting and minimum focus distance—but I do, and I prefer the older lens for a lot of my work. If I'm shooting very close to my subject, I want and expect a lens that performs more like a 200mm telephoto (even if it's effectively 182mm) than one that acts like a 135mm medium tele. Figure 7.10 shows the difference.

New Affordable Honorary Magic Three Entry

Nikon has made things even more interesting with an additional "affordable" replacement for the original 70-200mm f/2.8 zoom. The Nikkor AF-S 70-200mm f/4G ED VR lens, priced at about $1,400, is a slower, lower-cost zoom with the same zoom range. It does focus down to 3.3 feet, but, unlike virtually all of Nikon's "pro" lenses, takes 67mm filters instead of the standard 77mm diameter filters. Plan to buy yourself a 67mm-77mm step-up ring.

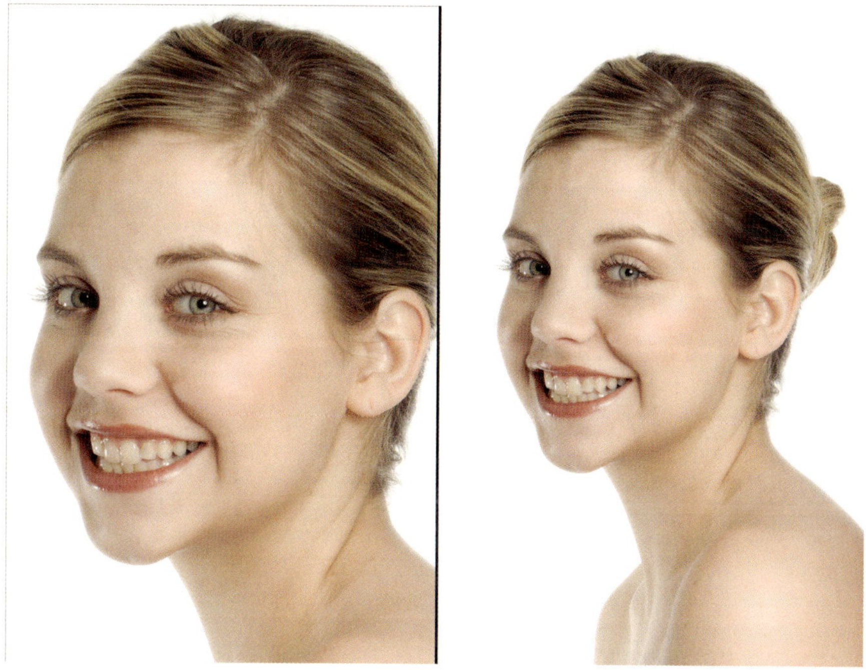

Figure 7.10
The Nikon 70-200mm f/2.8 VR I lens at its maximum zoom setting and closest focus distance (left); the 70-200mm f/2.8 VR II lens at the same zoom setting and focus distance.

This has proved to be a very good lens, indeed. It has the Nano Crystal Coat and Super Integrated multilayer coating, which should reduce ghosting, flare, and internal reflections, along with three extra-low dispersion (ED) elements. The lens has a newer VR system, with a claimed *five* stop improvement in camera stabilization, meaning that, theoretically, you could shoot at, say, the 200mm zoom setting with a shutter speed of 1/30th second and achieve the same camera steadiness that you would have gotten at 1/1000th second. Nikon must be confident about the lens's VR capabilities, as it's not even furnished with a tripod collar. That's an optional accessory; the Nikon RT-1 tripod mount ring is priced at around $225. I recommend that; it's always wisest to center a long lens to your tripod or monopod instead of the camera's tripod socket, even if you're using a camera like the D810 with an extra sturdy lens mount flange that can accommodate the extra weight.

Nikon's Lens Roundup

The following section represents my personal recommendations on Nikon lenses, based on the more than four dozen lenses I owned in the past and the more than 30 lenses that remain in my collection today. What follows are just my opinions, and descriptions of what has worked for me. If you want lens testing and more detailed qualitative/quantitative data, you're better off visiting one of the websites devoted to providing up-to-date information of that type. I recommend Bjørn Rørslett's original Nature Photograph website (which no longer receives updates, but has a lot of information about older lenses) at www.naturfotograf.com, and the newer www.nikongear.com, as well as DPReview at www.dpreview.com.

Here, my goal is simply to let you know the broad range of optics available and help you narrow down your choices from the vast array of lenses offered. Not all of the lenses I mention will be currently available new from Nikon, but all can be readily found in mint used condition.

Generally, I'm not going to cover non-Nikon lenses, primarily because I have stuck to Nikon products for most of my career. While Nikon lenses aren't always the best in their focal length/speed ranges, they are always near the top and have proved to be dependable and consistent. I'm not going to provide a lot of exact pricing information, as you can easily Google that, and prices have been trending upward for some time. One of my favorite lenses, which I purchased new for $1,300 now lists at $1,800!

Wide Angles

Nikon has an interesting collection of wide-angle prime lenses and zooms, both old and new, that range in price from a few hundred dollars to around $2,000. Here's a list of some of the key lenses that are readily available. I'll describe the zooms and prime lenses separately.

Wide Zooms

These lenses include the widest zooms Nikon offers, along with a set of three prime lenses that cover roughly the same focal length range. These zoom lenses are as follows:

- **14-24mm f/2.8G ED AF-S.** Simply the sharpest wide-angle zoom ever made (don't take my word for it: Google), this is a hefty lens that produces an exquisite rectilinear image (virtually no bowed lines), and it's fast, to boot. Its chief drawback is that it doesn't take conventional filters, although Lee makes an expensive adapter for square filters, as I mentioned earlier in this chapter. Expect to pay at least $2,000 for this lens, and, if you depend on gradient ND for your landscape photos, you'll need to add a second wide-angle lens that does accept filters. Or rely on the D810's HDR capabilities.
- **17-35mm f/2.8D IF-ED.** This member of the "affordable" Magic Three is still offered, and, unless you find a mint used copy, isn't even that affordable. I described its positives earlier. As I said, I use it in tandem with the 14-24mm f/2.8.
- **16-35mm f/4G ED VR AF-S.** A tiny bit slower with a constant f/4 maximum aperture, this lens includes VR. For hand-held shots, that means you won't miss f/2.8 at all. Instead of 1/60th second at f/2.8, you can shoot at 1/30th second at f/4 and expect the same sharpness.
- **18-35mm f/3.5-4.5G ED AF-S.** This is a $750 ultra-wide-angle zoom lens for those who don't want to spend the bucks for the 17-35mm and 16-35mm VR optics. It's small and light (at just under 14 ounces), and has three aspherical and two ED elements for great image quality.

- **18-35mm f/3.5-4.5D AF IF-ED.** Although replaced by the lens above in 2013, this older lens is still available, and much less than the other three wide-to-35mm zooms. It lacks an internal Silent Wave motor and focuses a bit more slowly, and does not have a constant aperture. The maximum f/stop ranges from f/3.5 at the 18mm focal length setting to f/4.5 at 35mm. Many shooters have found this to be an excellent lens for building a modest collection of FX optics on a budget.

Wide Prime Lenses

Many photographers build a nice kit of lenses using only primes rather than zoom lenses. Most of these lenses are compact, light in weight, and fast, with an f/2.8 or better maximum aperture. A large number of us grew up using only prime lenses—we're the folks you might have seen a few decades ago with two and three cameras around our neck, each outfitted with a different prime lens. We learned quickly how to use "sneaker zoom" to move in closer or to back up to change our field of view without swapping optics. Not all of these lenses are ancient; Nikon has introduced an affordable 28mm f/1.8 lens, and two wide-angle f/1.4 lenses in 24mm and 35mm focal lengths are fairly recent additions.

- **14mm f/2.8D ED AF.** This lens has been largely supplanted by the 14-24mm f/2.8 zoom. It's not much cheaper, weighs two-thirds as much, isn't quite as sharp—and doesn't zoom. It does take rear-mounted gelatin filters, however.
- **20mm f/2.8D AF / 24mm f/2.8D AF / 28mm f/2.8D AF.** This is a trio of affordable (around $300-$600 each) wide prime lenses, all with f/2.8 maximum apertures and AF (non-AF-S) focusing. You won't need all three, but you might like to pair the 20mm and 28mm lenses to give you a decent wide-angle range, or stake out the middle ground with the 24mm version.
- **24mm f/1.4G AF-S ED.** Oh, the howls of anguish and outrage could be heard world-wide, especially among photojournalists, when the predecessor of this lens, a 28mm f/1.4D AF optic, was discontinued without a replacement some years back. The old lens had a list price of about $2,000, and reportedly cost Nikon a lot more than that to make (which is why it was axed), and soon sold for up to $4,000 on the used market. This new, sharp, fast lens is a worthy successor, and a must-have for architectural photographers, photojournalists, and street shooters. Its roughly $2,200 price tag seems cheap compared to the prices commanded by the old 28mm f/1.4 lens.
- **28mm f/1.8G AF-S.** If a maximum aperture of f/1.8 is fast enough for you, this brand-new lens is an amazing bargain at roughly one-third the price of the wider/faster 24mm f/1.4 optic. It's got all the latest features including the Nano Crystal lens coating found on most other recently introduced Nikkors, for reduced flaring and ghost effects. Light in weight at 11 ounces, it focuses down to less than one foot. Unfortunately, unlike most of Nikon's "pro" lenses, it takes 67mm filters instead of 77mm filters. You may be able to find a very thin step-up ring that allows you to mount the larger filters without vignetting.

- **35mm f/1.4G AF-S.** If you need a fast f/1.4 aperture and a slightly narrower field of view, this lens should fill the bill. It, too, takes 67mm filters, and is priced a few hundred dollars south of $2,000. Most photojournalists you know, and more than a few architectural photographers probably own this lens.
- **35mm f/1.8G AF-S.** Only one-half stop slower than the f/1.4 version above, this one is a lot more affordable at about $600, and is a wise choice if you want to add a fast wide-angle prime to your arsenal. It includes one aspheric and one ED element to provide excellent image quality, and focuses down to about 10 inches. Its chief drawback is the odd-ball 58mm filter size; if you want to avoid buying yet another polarizer or neutral density filter set, you'll need an adapter ring that doesn't cause vignetting with your current filters. Don't confuse this with the older, less expensive 35mm f/1.8G AF-S DX Nikkor, which is not a full-frame lens.
- **35mm f/2D AF.** This inexpensive lens was my full-frame mainstay back in the film days, and I once visited Europe with only a single body and this lens. It's not especially sharp wide open, but at 2 inches long and 7 ounces it's super compact.

Wide to Medium/Long Zooms

There aren't too many "do everything" walk-around lenses for full-frame cameras like the D810, but this sextet offers some useful alternatives.

- **24-120mm f/4G ED AF-S VR.** I love the newest version of this lens, and frequently use it as a walk-around lens on my D4s (see Figure 7.11, left), D810, and Df (although it makes the Df a bit front-heavy). But, caveat emptor! Nikon has offered *three* different lenses in this focal length range, and this latest model is the good one. Accept no substitute! The original 24-120mm f/3.5-5.6 AF-D lens was produced from 1996 through 2002, and was replaced in 2003 with a version having similar specs, but an internal AF-S motor and vibration reduction. Neither lens was the sharpest optic in the drawer, but they were popular because of their useful focal length range. This latest version has a constant f/4 aperture, and produces much better image quality, with the VR making it an excellent walk-about lens for hand-held exposures. Priced in the $1,300 range, it's almost a bargain for what it does: giving you everything from moderate wide angle to short telephoto focal lengths.

  Last winter, when I moved my office to the Florida Keys to escape the brutal weather, I found myself unexpectedly needing to do some product photography on a seamless background. I was amazed to find that this lens functioned quite handily as a macro lens. It was even more versatile than I'd thought.
- **24-85mm f/2.8-4D AF IF.** This older AF lens was recently replaced by a new AF-S 24-85mm f/3.5-4.5 zoom with vibration reduction. However, this lens can often be picked up used for a few hundred dollars, and it has long been an acceptable substitute for the 28-70mm "Beast" and current 24-70mm f/2.8 "magic" lens, at a third or less the price. It has an aperture that varies from f/2.8 at the wide end to a respectable f/4 at the telephoto end. It's even a tad longer than the 24/28-70mm zooms, making it a decent portrait lens for everything from full figures to head-and-shoulders.

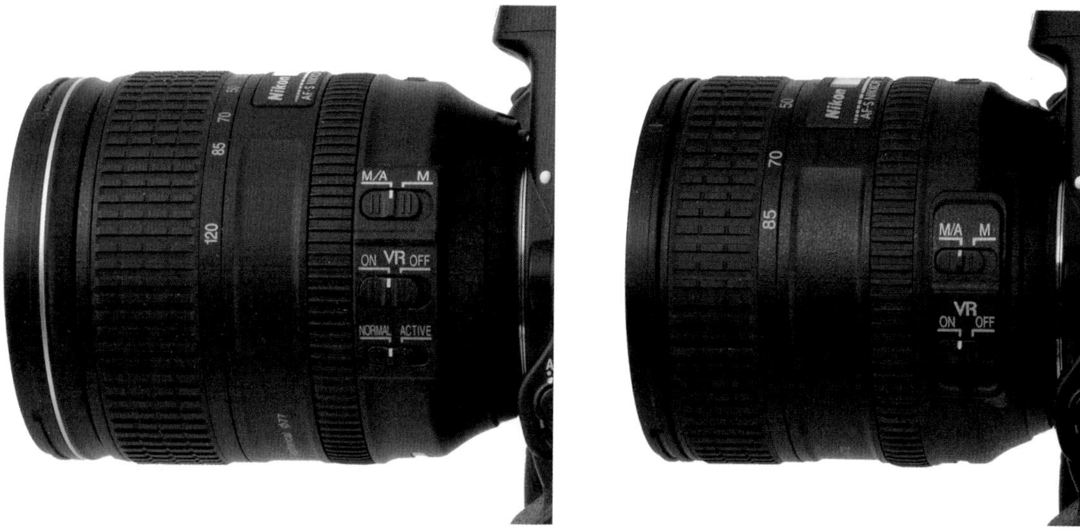

Figure 7.11 The Nikon 24-120mm f/4G ED AF-S VR (left) and Nikon 24-85mm f/3.5-5.6 zooms are affordable mid-range lenses, with the added benefit of vibration reduction.

- **24-85mm f/3.5-4.5G AF-S ED VR.** Introduced in June 2012 with a very affordable $600 price tag, and intended as a "cheap" full-frame lens for Nikon's new low-end FX cameras like the D610, this zoom works just fine on an upscale model like the D4/D4s. (See Figure 7.11, right.) I received mine as I was writing my earlier Nikon D800 book, and find myself using it frequently as a walk-around lens in preference to my much heavier 24-70mm f/2.8 "Magic Three" optic. This new lens has a slightly longer zoom range (up to 85mm), and it's slower. It's shorter and lighter than the 24-120mm zoom, as you can see from the figure.

  Its low price may leave you with some extra cash to buy another lens, or that SB-910 Speedlight you've been lusting after. The best thing about this lens—other than its price—is the auto tripod detection feature, which means you can leave VR switched on when the camera is mounted on the tripod, and still receive specialized VR shake camera movement protection during both video and still shooting. As a full-frame lens, this one is suitable for everything from landscapes to portraits. When I'm just out casually shooting, the VR (which the 24-70mm f/2.8 lacks) comes in very handy.
- **24-70mm f/2.8G ED AF-S.** Not a lot to add about this lens. It's the one to buy if you care enough to shoot the very best. Some early copies had "light leaks" around the distance scale panel that could affect image quality when photographing under very bright lighting conditions, but Nikon fixed the problems for free. Test yours by taking a photo with an external flash unit aimed at the distance scale panel, and see if there is anomalous brightening along the upper edge of the photo. A piece of black electrician's tape will solve the problem until you can send the lens to Nikon for the fix.

- **28-300mm f/3.5-5.6G AF-S ED VR.** This is the closest thing Nikon offers to an "all around" lens. It's shy of two pounds at 28 ounces, fairly compact, and features the second edition of Nikon's vibration reduction technology. At a little over $1,000, it's fairly affordable, too. As a full-frame lens, it's my recommendation when you want to use all the megapixels the camera puts at your disposal. But the ancient lens I'm describing next is my all-time fav walk-around optic.
- **28-200mm f/3.5-5.6G AF ED IF.** This remarkable lens was one of the best purchases I ever made. When I travel overseas, it's one of only two lenses I carry with me. It's compact, about three inches long and three inches in diameter, weighs just 12 ounces, focuses down to 1.3 feet, and is super sharp. And I paid $330 for mine. Unfortunately, it was introduced just as Nikon was phasing out full-frame film cameras in favor of DX digital cameras and, as the company had no FX digital models to sell, when the 18-200mm f/3.5-5.6G AF-S ED VR DX lens was introduced, this one was scrapped. It had a shorter range, no VR, and no Silent Wave motor. But, in terms of image quality and versatility, it was better than its "replacement" in every way. You may be able to find one used for roughly the original price, but they're not as easy to find as you might expect. I wouldn't sell mine for double what I paid for it. (See Figure 7.12.) The earlier D model, with an aperture ring, is not bad, but this one is better. It does take an oddball 62mm filter size, but I have step-up rings that let me use either 67mm or 77mm filters with it. (I have a complete set in both sizes.)

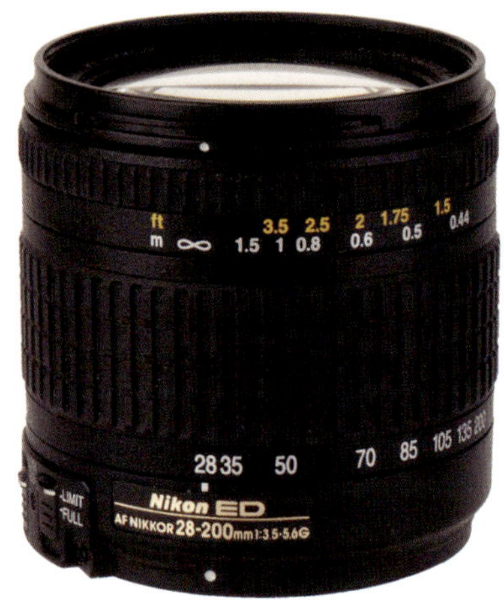

Figure 7.12 The Nikon 28-200mm f/3.5-5.6G ED IF Autofocus Nikkor Zoom Lens, although discontinued, ironically makes one of the best all-around basic lenses for the Nikon D810.

Normal to Medium Telephoto

The "normal" to medium telephoto range is useful for photojournalism and street photography in situations where you have room to back up and don't want the apparent distortion that wider lenses can add when some elements are particularly close to the lens. Wide-angle and perspective distortion is just fine when you want to use it as a creative element, but if not, you'll want to consider one of these lenses. They're also good for portraits for the same reason: objects that are closer to the lens (such as human noses) aren't rendered disproportionately large, with more distant objects (ears) too small (which can be the case with wide-angle lenses). Humans look more natural when photographed with lenses in this range, as longer lenses (150mm and above), tend to "flatten" faces and make them appear wider.

Normal Lenses

"Normal" is defined as focal lengths roughly equivalent to the diagonal of the image frame, which in the case of the Nikon D810 is about 45mm (43.3mm precisely). This field of view is said to look most natural for general subject matter, as opposed to the stretched-out appearance that wide-angle lenses can have, and the compressed look found in telephoto lenses. Nikon actually has just two normal lenses in its lineup (not counting the 60mm f/2.8 Micro-Nikkor), but I'm going to describe five options for you to consider.

- **50mm f/1.2 AI-S.** I'm including this older design, manual focus lens because quite a mystique has developed around so-called "super speed" optics, including the remarkable (and remarkably expensive) Nikon 58mm f/1.2 Noct (which can cost upward of $3,000 on the used market). While the Noct was sensational wide open, this one is merely good at f/1.2, but it's quite usable (and really sharpens up by f/2) and a *lot* more affordable at around $700. If you *must* have the fastest lens available consider this one. Given the very shallow depth-of-field at wide apertures, you probably would want to focus this one manually, anyway.
- **50mm f/1.4D AF.** Only a shade slower with an f/1.4 maximum aperture, this discontinued lens can be found for about half the price of its manual focus f/1.2 counterpart. It offers autofocus through the D810's body screw-drive, and includes an aperture ring, which can be important if you plan to use it for macro photography on a bellows attachment that lacks electronic contacts (all the inexpensive, old-school bellows like my old Nikon PB-4 do).
- **50mm f/1.4G AF-S.** This is the replacement for the D-version of this lens. It's not appreciably sharper, lacks an aperture ring, and costs more at around $500, but offers faster AF-S focusing. If you have a large collection of 52mm filters (which fit many old and new Nikon prime lenses), they won't fit on this lens without a step-down ring. It takes the larger 58mm variety.
- **58mm f/1.4G AF-S.** If you think that eight extra millimeters of focal length can't possibly make this lens worth $1,200 more than its 50mm f/1.4 cousin described above, you're missing the point. This one is, quite simply, one of the sharpest lenses Nikon offers, even wide open, besting its 24mm, 35mm, 50mm, and 85mm f/1.4 stablemates at maximum aperture. *That's* what you'll be paying roughly $1,700 for, and if you're a photojournalist or wedding photographer, you'll think it's worth it. Although it's an AF-S lens, autofocus is a bit on the slow side. I already own an old 58mm f/1.4 manual focus Nikkor, and the two lenses have nothing in common—including filter size. My 1960s-era 58mm takes Nikon's then standard 52mm filters, and this one has a 72mm filter thread (not Nikon's 77mm "pro" size).
- **50mm f/1.8D AF.** I have touted this lens as the bargain of the Nikon line in all my Nikon guidebooks dating back to 2005. At around $100-$135, it was likely to be the sharpest and most versatile lens, per dollar spent, of any you owned. Usable at f/1.8, it makes a good lens for photojournalism, can be used for portraits with the D810 in DX mode (as a 75mm equivalent optic), great for indoor sports like basketball (although focus is a tad slow), and wonderful as a macro lens. It focuses down to 1.5 feet without accessories, and you can use it with automatic or manual extension tubes. Attach a BR2a reversing ring, and you can mount it with the front

of the lens facing the sensor for extra magnification and sharpness when doing extreme close-ups. Its aperture ring allows setting f/stop manually in this mode (or on a bellows).

- **50mm f/1.8G AF-S.** Nikon updated the D-version of this lens, adding an internal Silent Wave motor for faster focusing, deleting the useful aperture ring, and almost doubling the price. This version makes sense for entry-level Nikon cameras that lack an autofocus motor in the body, but I won't be replacing my 50mm f/1.8D lens with this one anytime soon.

Medium to Long

I tend to shoot either ultra-wide, with fisheyes or lenses like the 14-24mm f/2.8 (for landscapes, interiors, exteriors, street photography, and for perspective exaggeration) or use this medium-to-long telephoto focal length range (for portraits, sports, fashion, and isolating subjects using selective focus). Probably 80 percent of my images are made using lenses in one of those two categories. So, I tend to lump all the lenses in this group together in my mind. They all do about the same thing and, surprisingly, almost all equally well. Here are some brief descriptions of your choices:

- **70-300mm f/4-5.6G AF.** This is the low-end, bargain lens in the group, which can be found for a couple hundred bucks. It's slow, lacks VR, but you can't beat the versatility it gives you at this price.
- **70-300mm f/4.5-5.6G AF-S VR.** Another bargain, in the $600 range, this lens is a better choice for most, as it adds AF-S focus and vibration reduction.
- **70-200mm f/2.8 AF-S VR / 70-200mm f/2.8G ED AF-S VR II.** Anyone who can afford either of these lenses will never regret their purchase. I've described both earlier in this chapter.
- **80-200mm f/2.8D AF ED.** This older lens has long been the "low cost" non-VR version of Nikon's 70-200mm f/2.8 telephoto zoom. It has almost the same range, the same f/2.8 maximum aperture, and is known for being exceptionally sharp. It can be found for as little as half the price of either of the two 70-200mm AF-S lenses.
- **80-400mm f/4.5-5.6D AF VR ED.** Compact and lightweight (and only in a 400mm lens would 3 pounds be considered lightweight), this lens competes almost directly with Nikon's 70-300mm VR. The latter is shorter and more compact, and about a third the price of this lens, so you'll need to decide how much you really need the 300mm–400mm range before you decide to pay a premium (around $1,850) for this superb optic. Prices may change rapidly now that this lens's replacement (described next) has become available. More than a dozen years ago it was the first Nikkor to boast vibration reduction.
- **80-400mm f/4.5-5.6G ED AF-S VR.** If you're looking at the older 80-400mm zoom and have an extra $1,000 you don't need, Nikon may tempt you with this optically improved version with better VR, more road-hugging weight in its larger frame (55 vs. 47 ounces), closer focusing (about 5 feet vs. 7.5 feet), and flare-thwarting Super Nano Coat. Those in the prime of life willing to sling 6 pounds of D810 and lens around their necks will find this to be a supremely versatile optic.

Medium Telephoto Prime

One advantage of medium telephoto prime lenses is that they are all quite fast, with maximum apertures of f/1.4 to f/4, which makes them an excellent choice for portraits, sports, animals, and other subjects that don't call for a really long lens. Their large f/stops are great for selective focus and allow you to use faster shutter speeds for hand-held shooting.

- **85mm f/1.4D AF IF.** You know a lens has to be legendary when it has its own nickname. This lens is universally known as the "Cream Machine" because of the exquisite quality bokeh produced by its nine-bladed aperture. This is absolutely the perfect portrait lens. You can use it wide open or stopped down a notch to throw the background out of focus (see Figure 7.13). This is another lens that's a permanent part of my collection. My biggest beef with it is that it takes a screw-in lens hood rather than a bayonet-mount hood. I tend to leave the hood on all the time, and forget about it.
- **85mm f/1.4G AF-S.** In its never-ending quest to upgrade its older AF lenses to AF-S, Nikon introduced this rated-G version of the Cream Machine. It's excellent, and offers a bit more autofocus speed, but if you own the older lens, there's no pressing reason to upgrade.
- **85mm f/1.8D AF / 85mm f/1.8G AF-S.** Those looking for a fast 85mm portrait lens at an affordable price need look no further. Both the original D-version and the brand-new G-version with AF-S focus are priced in the $500 range. Nikon claims that the replacement has been optimized for digital shooting, which usually means that the angle of the light rays approaching the sensor has been tweaked so that the illumination is collected by the sensor efficiency, and photons don't bounce back and reflect off the rear of the lens to reduce contrast. In practice, either one of these lenses will do an excellent job.
- **180mm f/2.8D AF IF-ED.** This older design is noted for being sharp, even wide open, and relatively low in price (currently about $1,000). The venerable 180mm f/2.8 is an excellent sports lens for those who don't need zoom or vibration reduction.
- **300mm f/4D AF-S IF-ED.** This lens isn't really a "medium" telephoto, but it is a prime lens, and I didn't want to toss it in with the more exotic lenses in the section that follows this one. I love this lens. Although I once shot sports professionally full-time, I only manage two or three events for each of my favorite sports these days (soccer, football, basketball, motor sports, hockey, volleyball, baseball, and track), and can't justify keeping the wonderful 300mm f/2.8 lens in my collection. This one is a more reasonably priced ($1,000–$1,500) alternative. It works fine with my Nikon teleconverters, so I can transform it into a 420mm f/5.6 (with the 1.4X converter), or 510mm f/6.3 (1.7x teleconverter) with ease. You'll probably use this lens mounted on a tripod or monopod most of the time, and, if so, you should be aware that the factory tripod mount flexes. I replaced mine with an improved mount from Kirk, and get sharp images even though this lens lacks VR.

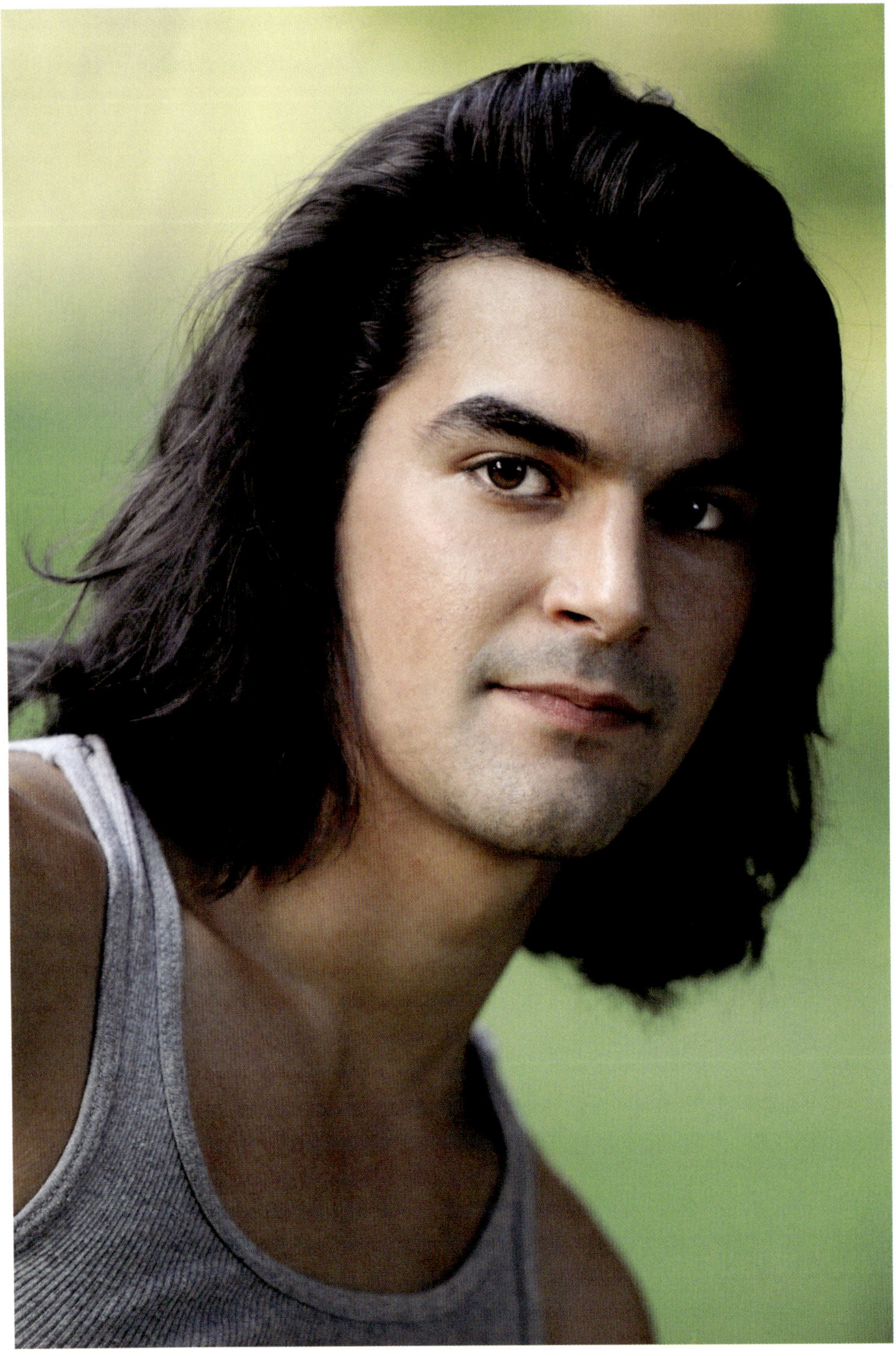

Figure 7.13 Nikon's 85mm f/1.4 lens has amazing bokeh and is perfect for portrait photography.

- **105mm f/2D AF DC/135mm f/2D AF DC.** These two $1,000-plus lenses feature defocus control, and are prized for both their speed and use in portraiture. They focus to three and four feet (respectively), and feature rounded diaphragms for excellent bokeh. However, each features a defocus ring, which allows you to further refine the bokeh by controlling the amount of spherical aberration in the lens. Set the ring to zero, and the lens functions as a non-defocus control optic. Dial in more "correction" and the out-of-focus highlights become even more diffuse.

BOKEH AND SPHERICAL ABBERATION

The characteristics of out-of-focus discs in your image are affected both by the number of blades in the aperture (rounder is better; sharp-sided polygons are worse), and the evenness of illumination of those discs. Highlights may be brighter on the edges and darker in the center, because the lens doesn't focus light passing through the edges of the lens exactly as it does light going through the center. That's bad.

Other kinds of spherical aberration generate circles of confusion (see Appendix B for more on CoC) that are brightest in the center and fade out at the edges, producing a smooth blending effect. Ironically, when no spherical aberration is present at all, the discs are a uniform shade, which, while better than the doughnut effect, is not as pleasing as the bright center/dark edge rendition. Defocus controls allow you to adjust the amount of spherical aberration to refine the bokeh produced by DC lenses.

Exotic Long Lenses

These are the lenses that most of us borrow, or lust after, and usually end up purchasing a car or a house with the funds instead. I see photographer friends hefting the 500mm f/4 or 600mm f/4 around sporting events all the time, and as I watch them huff and puff my envy evaporates. But if you're heavily involved in wildlife photography, sports, or double-naught spy activities, you can probably justify at least one of these. All are very fast, with constant maximum apertures of f/4 *or better,* feature the latest internal Silent Wave focus motors, and VR. All are priced at a minimum of $5,000, and one tops the $10,000 price point.

- **200-400mm f/4G AF-S ED VR II.** This is an amazing lens, and one that a great many photographers who probably couldn't justify a copy end up mortgaging their houses to buy (at around $7,000). At least, that's what I glean from the forum postings by photographers who are agonizing over being forced to sell this lens to keep the wolf at bay. It's sharp, more than 14 inches long and seven pounds in heft, and one of the most versatile lenses in this group for wildlife and sports photographers. And, it's one of the few Nikon lenses that comes with its own "protective" filter, what Nikon calls a "dedicated protective glass" (which itself is furnished with a separate case). You can slip actual 52mm filters into a slot in the rear of the lens, though. The newest version, introduced in 2010, has the nano coating for reduced flare. This is another lens that almost demands a third-party replacement for the factory tripod collar. This lens is heavy enough that you'll be using it on a tripod or monopod most of the time.

- **200mm f/2G AF-S ED VR II / 300mm f/2.8G AF-S VR II IF-ED.** This pair of lenses is fast and primarily useful for sports photography under waning light conditions (both are a bit too short for wildlife in the wild). Priced in the $6,000 range, both are fast enough to be used with Nikon's 1.4x, 1.7x, or 2x teleconverters.
- **400mm f/2.8G AF-S FL ED VR / 500mm f/4G ED VR / 600mm f/4G AF-S ED VR / 800mm f/5.6G ED VR.** A set of these four lenses will deduct at least $40,000 from your wallet, but they are the ultimate sports or wildlife lenses, or for capturing images of the Great Wall of China from the International Space Station.

Perspective Control/Special Lenses

My first perspective control lens was a 35mm f/3.5 PC-Nikkor that I still own. It was manual focus, manual exposure, manual aperture, shifted but didn't tilt, and I had to machine down part of the sliding mechanism so it wouldn't bump against the metering head of my Nikon film camera. In those days, PC lenses were used primarily for architectural photography and some product photography to allow keeping the focal plane of the camera parallel with a subject to avoid a tilted/distorted effect.

Things have changed! Today shift/tilt photography is so popular that Nikon and other vendors are building a faux perspective/focus control capability right into the camera as a "Miniature Effect" retouching aid. While lenses like Nikon's PC-E line are still useful for their original purpose—perspective control—I've seen some absolutely brilliant portrait and wedding photography that uses tilt/shift capabilities as a dreamy focus control. Wedding guru Parker Pfister comes to mind (although he's a Canon guy; don't hold it against him), but you can find this tool used everywhere you look. The three lenses currently in the Nikon lineup are listed next, along with one additional "special" lens, an oddball fisheye that fit nowhere else in this chapter's discussions.

VIRTUAL HORIZON TOOL IDEAL FOR PC-E LENSES

The D810's virtual horizon tool is often overlooked as a perfect complement to perspective control lenses. If you've set the camera so the Fn button activates the viewfinder virtual horizon, you can use it to synchronize your camera's pitch and roll with the tilting/shifting effects of your PC-E lens.

- **24mm f/3.5D PC-E ED.** When applied to architectural applications, the wider the shift/tilt lens the better. Priced in the $2,000 range (like all Nikon's PC-E optics), this 24mm lens shifts plus or minus 11mm from side to side and plus or minus 8.5 degrees tilt. The mechanism rotates 90 degrees in two directions so you can apply the corrections/distortions from virtually any angle. It focuses down to about eight inches, so you can use its effects for close-ups and product/model photography. The big surprise for those who aren't old-timers is that this can be used as a *pre-set* lens. You set the f/stop you want to use on a ring, and can focus with the lens wide open. Then, when you're ready to shoot, press the aperture button and the lens stops down to the selected f/stop. However, Nikon has included an electronic autoaperture mechanism that can set to provide automatic stop-down with the D810. The shifting/tilting mechanism precludes autofocus.
- **45mm f/2.8 PC-E ED Micro Nikkor.** With the same amount of shifting/tilting available, this lens (and its 85mm counterpart, next) is classified as a macro lens, focusing down to about 10 inches and providing a half-life-size image on the sensor.
- **85mm f/2.8D PC-E Micro Nikkor.** This is the PC-E lens you'd want to use for your dreamy wedding portraits. It shifts and tilts the same amount as the other, and focuses down to 1.3 feet.
- **16mm f/2.8D AF Fisheye-Nikkor.** Okay, I admit I'm the world's most avid fisheye user. I owned Nikon's exotic 7.5mm f/5.6 fisheye back in the days of film, and would have it today except that the lens required locking up the mirror and using an auxiliary viewfinder in a mode quite incompatible with any of Nikon's digital cameras. (Nikon later introduced fisheyes that didn't require mirror lock-up.) I still own Nikon's 16mm f/3.5 manual focus/pre-AI fisheye, as well as a Tokina 10-17mm fisheye zoom, and a Sigma 15mm f/2.8 fisheye. This full-frame (non-circular image) autofocus model, which can be purchased for about $600, is probably the most practical of the bunch. It fills the FX frame with lines that exhibit a gloriously frightful amount of barrel distortion. When I travel overseas, I take along my two "main" lenses (17-35mm f/2.8 and 28-200G zoom) and a fisheye "fun" lens like this one.

Macro Lenses

Nikon makes a range of lenses that are officially designated as macro lenses for full-frame use. The most popular include:

- **AF-S Micro-Nikkor 60mm f/2.8G ED.** This type G lens supposedly replaces the type D lens listed next, adding an internal Silent Wave autofocus motor that should operate faster, and which is also compatible with Nikon's entry-level cameras that lack a body motor. It also has ED lens elements for improved image quality. However, because it lacks an aperture ring, you can control the f/stop only when the lens is mounted directly on the camera or used with automatic extension tubes. Should you want to reverse a macro lens (which can improve image quality) or mount it on a bellows, you're better off with a lens having an aperture ring.

- **AF Micro-Nikkor 60mm f/2.8D.** This older lens's aperture ring gives it a little more versatility but, realistically, only fanatical close-up shooters actually use the Nikon BR-2a lens reversing ring (which can improve image quality) or mount the lens on a bellows. I happen to belong in that camp, so I am hanging onto mine.
- **AF-S VR Micro-Nikkor 105mm f/2.8G IF-ED.** This G-series lens did replace a similar D-type, non-AF-S version that also lacked VR. I own the older lens, too, and am keeping it for the same reasons described above—but also because I find VR a rather specialized tool for macro work. Some 99 percent of the time, I shoot close-ups with my D810 mounted on a tripod or, at the very least, on a monopod, so camera vibration is not much of a concern. Indeed, *subject* movement is a more serious problem, especially when shooting plant life outdoors on days plagued with even slight breezes. Because my outdoor subjects are likely to move while I am composing my photo, I find both VR and autofocus not very useful. I end up focusing manually most of the time, too. This lens provides a little extra camera-to-subject distance, so you'll find it very useful, but consider the older non-G, non-VR version, too, if you're in the market.
- **AF Micro-Nikkor 200mm f/4D IF-ED.** With a price tag of about $1,800, you'd probably want this lens only if you planned a great deal of close-up shooting at greater distances. It focuses down to 1.6 feet, but provides enough magnification to allow interesting close-ups of subjects that are farther away. A specialized tool for specialized shooting.

Part III

Working with Light

Unless you're extraordinarily lucky, or supremely observant, great lighting, like most things of artistic value, doesn't happen by accident. It's entirely possible that you'll randomly encounter a scene or subject that's bathed in marvelous lighting, illumination that perfectly sculpts an image in highlights and shadows. But how often can you count on such luck? Ansel Adams is often quoted as saying (although he probably didn't) that "The harder I work, the luckier I get."

The great photographer *was* known for his patience in seeking out the best lighting for a composition, and he *did* actually say, "A good photograph is knowing where to stand." My own take on excellence in illumination is that you have to possess the ability to *recognize* effective lighting when it is already present, and have the skill to manipulate the light when it is not.

This part will launch you down the road to being able to put your D810 to work using the light that is present, manipulate it when necessary to achieve the effects you want, and to create good lighting from scratch using the electronic flash and other tools available. The next three chapters include:

- **Chapter 8:** Although most of the emphasis in this section of the book is on the use of electronic flash, this chapter, which helps you understand how continuous, "available" forms of illumination work with your D810, can actually help you use flash better. After all, in many ways, continuous illumination is just flash with a very, very long duration!
- **Chapter 9:** This chapter shows you how your D810's built-in flash works, and explains the basics of optional external flash units, like the Nikon SB-700 and SB-910 Speedlights.
- **Chapter 10:** An entire book could be devoted to more advanced external flash techniques, but I'm going to summarize the most important things you really need to know in this chapter.

8

Making Light Work for You

Successful photographers and artists have an intimate understanding of the importance of light in shaping an image. Rembrandt was a master of using light to create moods and reveal the character of his subjects. Late artist Thomas Kinkade's official tagline was "Painter of Light." Dean Collins, co-founder of Finelight Studios, revolutionized how a whole generation of photographers learned and used lighting. Photo guru Ed Pierce conducted seminars called "Captivated by the Light," that reveal his secrets for portrait lighting. It's impossible to underestimate how the use of light adds to—and how misuse can detract from—your photographs.

All forms of visual art use light to shape the finished product. Sculptors don't have control over the light used to illuminate their finished work, so they must create shapes using planes and curved surfaces so that the form envisioned by the artist comes to life from a variety of viewing and lighting angles. Painters, in contrast, have absolute control over both shape and light in their work, as well as the viewing angle, so they can use both the contours of their two-dimensional subjects and the qualities of the "light" they use to illuminate those subjects to evoke the image they want to produce.

Photography is a third form of art. The photographer may have little or no control over the subject (other than posing human subjects) but can often adjust both viewing angle *and* the nature of the light source to create a particular compelling image. The direction and intensity of the light sources create the shapes and textures that we see. The distribution and proportions determine the contrast and tonal values: whether the image is stark or high key, or muted and low in contrast. The colors of the light (because even "white" light has a color balance that the sensor can detect), and how much of those colors the subject reflects or absorbs, paint the hues visible in the image.

As a Nikon D810 photographer, you must learn to be a painter and sculptor of light if you want to move from *taking* a picture to *making* a photograph. This chapter provides an introduction to using *continuous* lighting (such as daylight, incandescent, or fluorescent sources), but it's useful to first consider how that form of illumination compares to the brief, but brilliant snippets of light we call *electronic flash.*

Because Nikon doesn't offer continuous lighting gear, this chapter is a bit more generic than I'd like in a book that is tightly focused on the Nikon D810. However, you'll find the concepts presented here useful in the next two chapters, which deal with using Nikon Speedlights.

Continuous Illumination versus Electronic Flash

Continuous lighting is exactly what you might think: uninterrupted illumination that is available all the time during a shooting session. Daylight, moonlight, and the artificial lighting encountered both indoors and outdoors count as continuous light sources (although all of them can be "interrupted" by passing clouds, solar eclipses, a blown fuse, or simply by switching a lamp off). Indoor continuous illumination includes both the lights that are there already (such as incandescent lamps or overhead fluorescent lights indoors) and fixtures you supply yourself, including photoflood lamps or reflectors used to bounce existing light onto your subject.

Electronic flash is notable because it can be much more intense than continuous lighting, lasts only a brief moment, and can be much more portable than supplementary incandescent sources. It's a light source you can carry with you and use anywhere. There are advantages and disadvantages to each type of illumination. Here's a quick checklist of pros and cons:

- **Lighting preview—Pro: continuous lighting.** With continuous lighting, you always know exactly what kind of lighting effect you're going to get and, if multiple lights are used, how they will interact with each other. Figure 8.1 shows a portrait taken in the simplest of environments, an industrial-type loft converted to a studio, with a large frosted glass window located to the left and slightly behind the subject providing all the illumination. A white piece of foamcore to the right of the camera filled in the shadows, and an aperture of f/4 assured that the rough white wall in the background would be featureless and out of focus.
- **Lighting preview—Con: electronic flash.** With flash, the general effect you're going to see may be a mystery until you've built some experience, and you may need to review a shot on the LCD monitor, make some adjustments, and then reshoot to get the look you want. (In this sense, a digital camera's review capabilities replace the Polaroid test shots pro photographers relied on in decades past.) An image like the one in Figure 8.1 would have been difficult to achieve with an off-camera battery-powered flash unit, because it would be tricky to preview exactly how the shadows would fall without a true continuous modeling light.

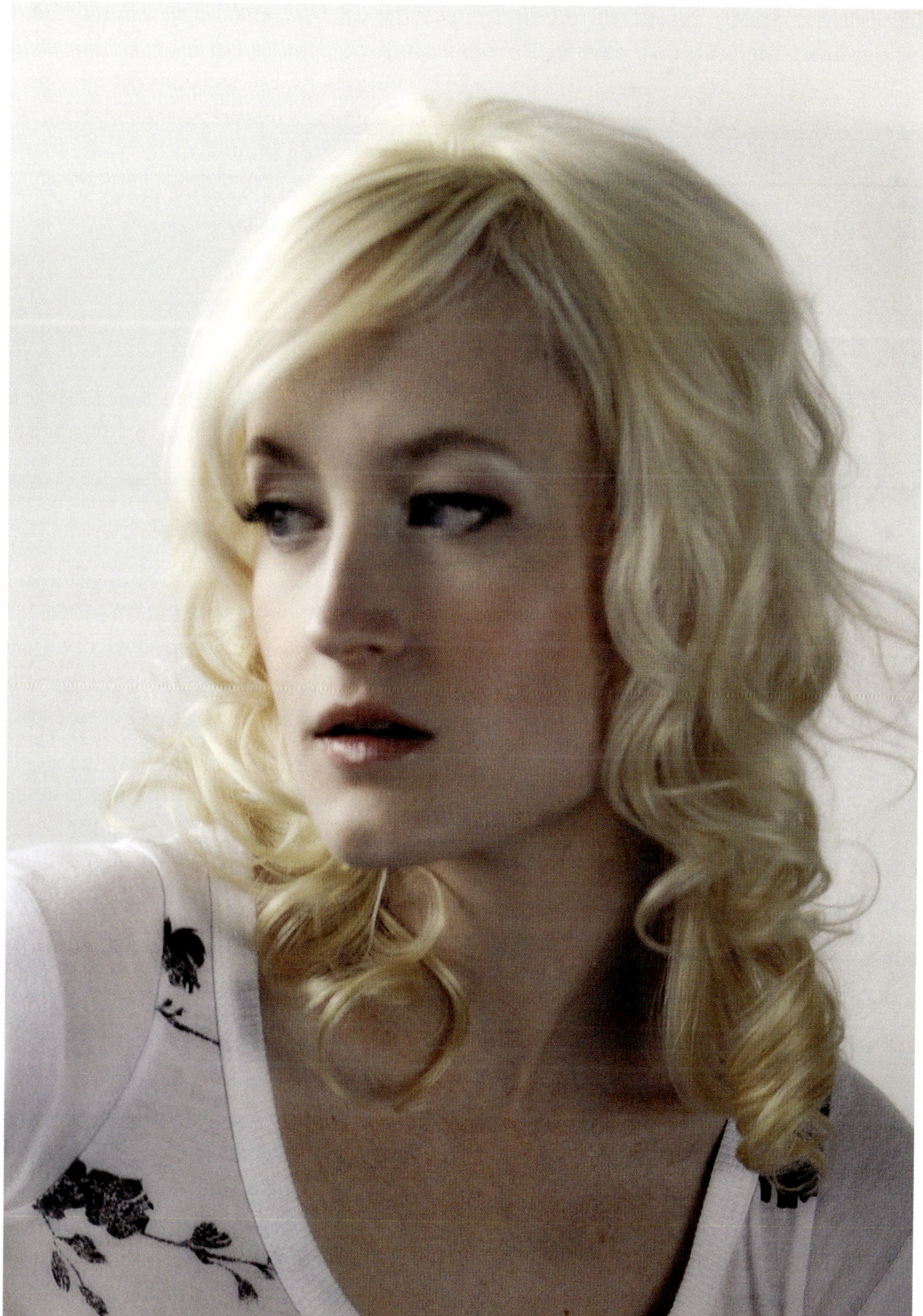

Figure 8.1 You always know how the lighting will look when using continuous illumination.

- **Exposure calculation—Pro: continuous lighting.** Your D810 has no problem calculating exposure for continuous lighting, because it remains constant and can be measured through the 91,000-pixel sensor that interprets the light reaching the viewfinder. The amount of light available just before the exposure will, in almost all cases, be the same amount of light present when the shutter is released. The D810's Spot metering mode can be used to measure and compare the proportions of light in the highlights and shadows, so you can make an adjustment (such as using more or less fill light) if necessary. You can even use a hand-held light meter to measure the light yourself.
- **Exposure calculation—Con: electronic flash.** Electronic flash illumination doesn't exist until the flash fires, and so can't be measured by the D810's exposure sensor when the mirror is flipped up at the moment of exposure. Instead, the light must be measured by metering the intensity of a *pre-flash* triggered an instant before the main flash, as it is reflected back to the camera and through the lens. A less attractive alternative, available with higher-end Nikon flash units like the SB-910, is to use a sensor built into the external flash itself and measure reflected light that bounces back, but which has not traveled through the lens. If you have a do-it-yourself bent, there are hand-held flash meters, too, including models that measure both flash and continuous light, so you need only one meter for both types of illumination.
- **Evenness of illumination—Pro/con: continuous lighting.** Of the continuous light sources, daylight, in particular, provides illumination that tends to fill an image completely, lighting up the foreground, background, and your subject almost equally. Shadows do come into play, of course, so you might need to use reflectors like the one used for Figure 8.1, or fill in additional light sources to even out the illumination further. But, barring objects that block large sections of your image from daylight, the light is spread fairly evenly. Indoors, however, continuous lighting is commonly less evenly distributed. The average living room, for example, has hot spots near the lamps and overhead lights, and dark corners located farther from those light sources. But on the plus side, you can easily *see* this uneven illumination and compensate with additional lamps.
- **Evenness of illumination—Con: electronic flash.** Electronic flash units, like continuous light sources such as lamps that don't have the advantage of being located 93 million miles from the subject, suffer from the effects of their proximity. The *inverse square law*, first applied to both gravity and light by Sir Isaac Newton, dictates that as a light source's distance increases from the subject, the amount of light reaching the subject falls off proportionately to the square of the distance. In plain English, that means that a flash or lamp that's twelve feet away from a subject provides only one-quarter as much illumination as a source that's six feet away (rather than half as much). (See Figure 8.2.) This translates into relatively shallow "depth-of-light."
- **Action stopping—Pro: electronic flash.** When it comes to the ability to freeze moving objects in their tracks, the advantage goes to electronic flash. The brief duration of electronic flash serves as a very high "shutter speed" when the flash is the main or only source of illumination for the photo. Your D810's shutter speed may be set for 1/250th second during a flash exposure,

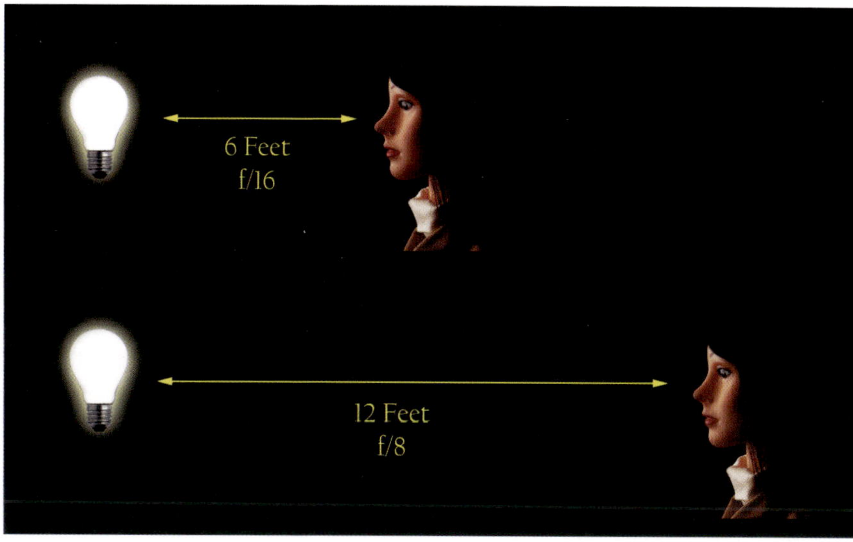

Figure 8.2
A light source that is twice as far away provides only one-quarter as much illumination.

but if the flash illumination predominates, the *effective* exposure time will be the 1/1,000th to 1/50,000th second or less duration of the flash, as you can see in Figure 8.3, because the flash unit reduces the amount of light released by cutting short the duration of the flash. The only fly in the ointment is that, if the ambient light is strong enough, it may produce a secondary, "ghost" exposure, as I'll explain later in this chapter.

- **Action stopping—Con: continuous lighting.** Action stopping with continuous light sources is completely dependent on the shutter speed you've dialed in on the camera. And the speeds available are dependent on the amount of light available and your ISO sensitivity setting. Outdoors in daylight, there will probably be enough sunlight to let you shoot at 1/2,000th second and f/6.3 with a non-grainy sensitivity setting for your D810 of ISO 400. That's a fairly useful combination of settings if you're not using a super-telephoto with a small maximum aperture. But inside, the reduced illumination quickly has you pushing your D810 to its limits. For example, if you're shooting indoor sports, there probably won't be enough available light to allow you to use a 1/2,000th second shutter speed (although I routinely shoot indoor basketball with my D810 at ISO 1600 and 1/500th second at f/4). The D810 is not my favorite indoor sports camera—that's not what it was designed for—but it works surprisingly well. But in many indoor sports situations, due to the lack of available light, and the D810's increased visual noise at settings of ISO 6400 and above, you may find yourself limited to 1/500th second or slower.
- **Cost—Pro: continuous lighting.** Incandescent or fluorescent lamps are generally much less expensive than electronic flash units, which can easily cost several hundred dollars. I've used everything from desktop high-intensity lamps to reflector flood lights for continuous illumination at very little cost. There are lamps made especially for photographic purposes, too. Maintenance is economical, too: many incandescent or fluorescents use bulbs that cost only a few dollars.

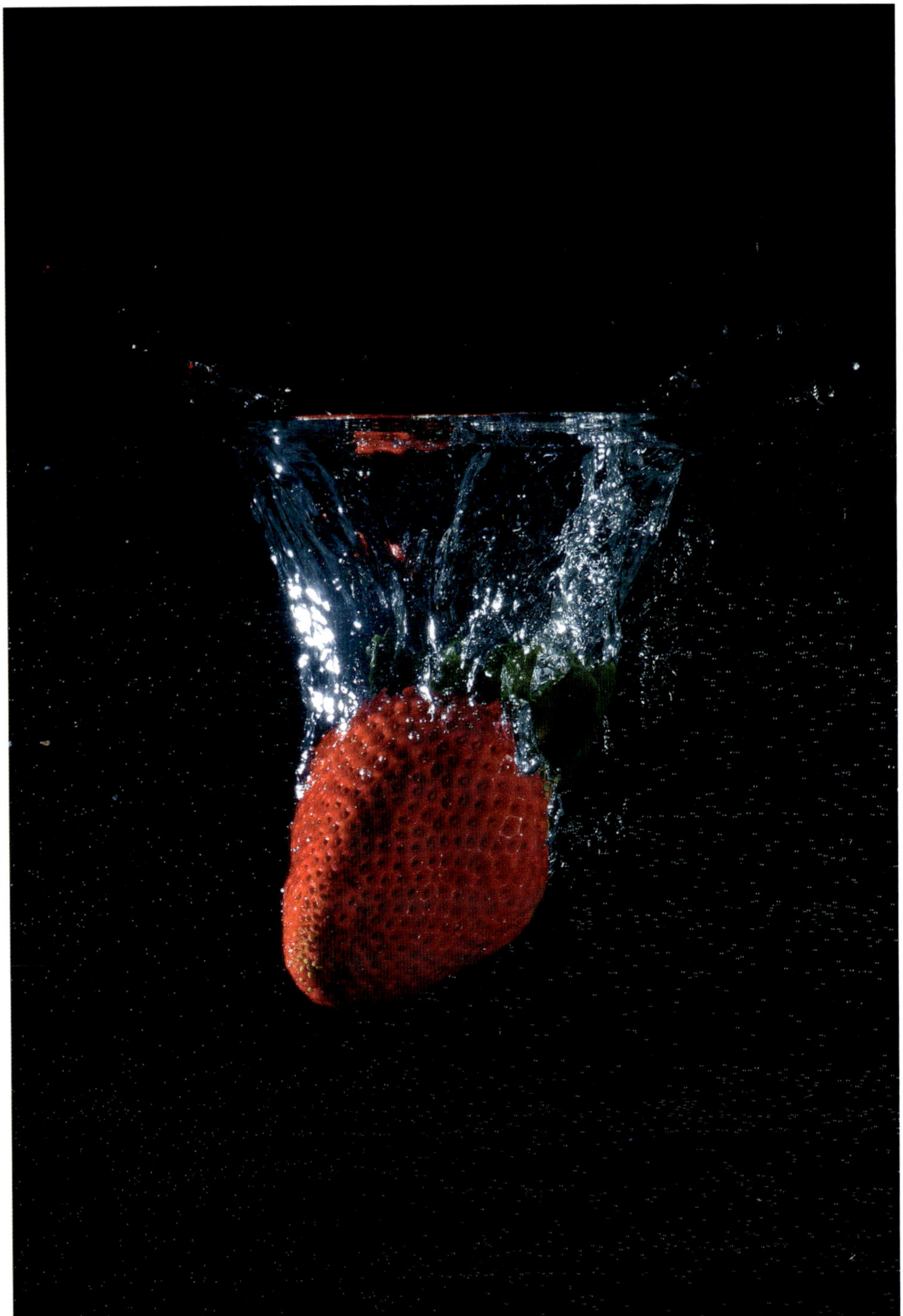

Figure 8.3 Electronic flash can freeze almost any action.

- **Cost—Con: electronic flash.** Electronic flash units aren't particularly cheap. The lowest-cost dedicated flash designed specifically for the Nikon dSLRs is about $150, and that SB-300 is probably not one that will be favored by many D810 owners. Such units are limited in features, however, and intended for those with entry-level cameras like the D3200. Plan on spending some money to get the features that a sophisticated electronic flash offers. I paid more than $500 for my SB-910, and only a little less for its "mate," an SB-900 that I purchased a couple years ago. I've got nearly $1,000 sunk into just two battery-operated strobes, and also invested that much—and more—in studio flash units.
- **Flexibility—Pro: electronic flash.** Electronic flash's action-freezing power allows you to work without a tripod in the studio (and elsewhere), adding flexibility and speed when choosing angles and positions. Flash units can be easily filtered, and, because the filtration is placed over the light source rather than the lens, you don't need to use high-quality filter material. For example, Roscoe or Lee lighting gels, which may be too flimsy to use in front of the lens, can be mounted or taped in front of your flash with ease.
- **Flexibility—Con: continuous lighting.** Because incandescent and fluorescent lamps are not as bright as electronic flash, the slower shutter speeds required (see "Action stopping," above) mean that you may have to use a tripod more often, especially when shooting portraits. The incandescent variety of continuous lighting gets hot, especially in the studio, and the side effects range from discomfort (for your human models) to disintegration (if you happen to be shooting perishable foods like ice cream). The heat also makes it more difficult to add filtration to incandescent sources.

Continuous Lighting Basics

While continuous lighting and its effects are generally much easier to visualize and use than electronic flash, there are some factors you need to take into account, particularly the color temperature of the light, how accurately a given form of illumination reproduces colors (we've all seen the ghastly looks human faces assume under mercury-vapor lamps outdoors), and other considerations.

One important aspect is color temperature. Of course, color temperature concerns aren't exclusive to continuous light sources, but the variations tend to be more extreme and less predictable than those of electronic flash, which output relatively consistent daylight-like illumination.

Living with Color Temperature

Nikon has been valiant in its efforts to help us tame the color balance monster. Some earlier Nikon pro cameras (the last one being the Nikon D2Xs) had a bindi-like white dot on their "foreheads" which measured ambient color temperature. Although this special sensor was abandoned by Nikon long before the D810 was introduced, the technology lives on in the form of ExpoDisc filter/caps (see Figure 8.4) and their ilk (www.expoimaging.com), which allow the camera's built-in custom white balance measuring feature to evaluate the illumination that passes through the disc/cap/filter/Pringle's can lid, or whatever neutral-color substitute you employ. (A white or gray card also works.) To help us tangle with the many different types of non-incandescent/non-daylight sources, Nikon has provided the D810 with seven different presets for fluorescents, sodium-vapor, and mercury vapor illumination. If those aren't enough, you can select a specific color temperature, or capture and save up to six white balance settings for retrieval later.

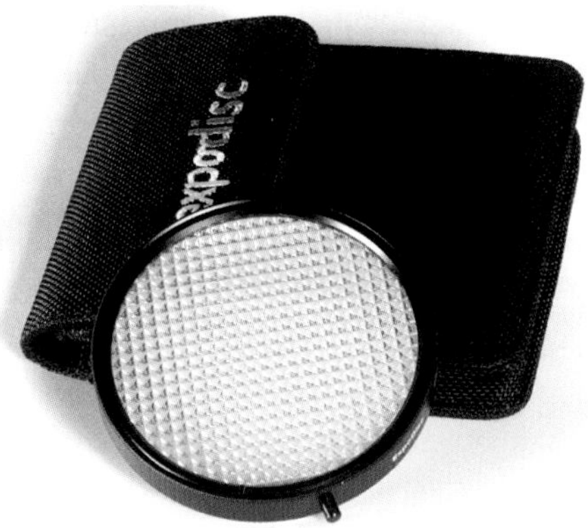

Figure 8.4 The ExpoDisc is placed on a lens and used as a neutral subject for measuring white balance.

In practical terms, color temperature, is how "bluish" or how "reddish" the light appears to be to the digital camera's sensor. Indoor illumination is quite warm, comparatively, and appears reddish to the sensor. Daylight, in contrast, seems much bluer to the sensor. Our eyes (our brains, actually) are quite adaptable to these variations, so white objects don't appear to have an orange tinge when viewed indoors, nor do they seem excessively blue outdoors in full daylight. Yet, these color temperature variations are real and the sensor is not fooled. To capture the most accurate colors, we need to take the color temperature into account in setting the color balance (or *white balance*) of the D810—either automatically using the camera's smarts or manually using our own knowledge and experience. You'll find a lot about setting and adjusting white balance and color temperature in Chapter 4. Table 8.1 provides a summary of what you need to know, and where you can look for explanations.

The only time you need to think in terms of actual color temperature is when you're making adjustments using the Choose Color Temp. setting in the White Balance entry within the Shooting menu which, as I'll describe in Chapter 11, allows you to dial in exact color temperatures, if known. You can also shift and bias color balance along the blue/amber and magenta/green axes, and bracket white balance.

In most cases, however, either of the two Auto settings in the Shooting menu's White Balance entry (Normal, or Keep Warm Lighting Colors) will do a good job of calculating white balance for you. Auto can be used as your choice most of the time. Use the preset values (Auto1 for normal or Auto2 for warmer images) or set a custom white balance that matches the current shooting conditions when you need to.

Remember that if you shoot RAW, you can specify the white balance of your image when you import it into Photoshop, Photoshop Elements, or another image editor using Nikon Capture NX 2, Capture NX-D, Adobe Camera Raw, or your preferred RAW converter. While color-balancing filters that fit on the front of the lens exist, they are primarily useful for film cameras, because film's color balance can't be tweaked as extensively as that of a sensor.

Table 8.1 White Balance Adjustment Options

Type of Adjustment	Options	Location	Explanation
Color balance presets	Auto (two options); Incandescent; Fluorescent (seven options); Sunlight (three options); Flash	Shooting Menu	Chapter 11
Choose color temperature	2,500-10,000K	Shooting Menu	Chapter 11
Fine Tune color balance	Adjust white balance along blue/amber, magenta/green axes, or both	Shooting Menu	Chapter 11
Manual color balance	Capture white balance or use existing photo's white balance	Shooting Menu	Chapter 11
White balance bracketing/Bracket order	2, 3, 5, 7, or 9 bracketed images using three increments	Custom Settings Menu, BKT button/command dials	Chapter 4, Chapter 12

White Balance Bracketing

As I explained in Chapter 4, with WB bracketing the D810 takes a single shot, and then saves 2, 3, 5, 7, or 9 (your choice) JPEG copies, each with a different color balance. It's not necessary to capture multiple shots, as the camera uses the raw information retrieved from the sensor for the single exposure and then processes it to generate the multiple different versions. The bracketing adjustments are made only on the amber/blue axis (no bracketing in the magenta/green bias is possible), but you can select whether the bracketed shots are spread in the blue *or* amber directions (that is, each one bluer/less blue or yellower/less yellow) or balanced to provide both blue and amber-oriented brackets.

Making these adjustments are the only times you're likely to be confused by a seeming contradiction in how color temperatures are named: warmer (more reddish) color temperatures (measured in degrees Kelvin) are the *lower* numbers, while cooler (bluer) color temperatures are *higher* numbers. It might not make sense to say that 3,400K is warmer than 6,000K, but that's the way it is. If it helps, think of a glowing red ember contrasted with a white-hot welder's torch, rather than fire and ice.

The confusion comes from physics. Scientists calculate color temperature from the light emitted by a mythical object called a black body radiator, which absorbs all the radiant energy that strikes it, and reflects none at all. Such a black body not only *absorbs* light perfectly, but it *emits* it perfectly when heated (and since nothing in the universe is perfect, that makes it mythical).

At a particular physical temperature, this imaginary object always emits light of the same wavelength or color. That makes it possible to define color temperature in terms of actual temperature in degrees on the Kelvin scale that scientists use. Incandescent light, for example, typically has a color temperature of 3,200K to 3,400K. Daylight might range from 5,500K to 6,000K. Each type of illumination we use for photography has its own color temperature range—with some cautions.

Daylight

Daylight is produced by the sun, and so is moonlight (which is just reflected sunlight). Daylight is present, of course, even when you can't see the sun. When sunlight is direct, it can be bright and harsh. If daylight is diffused by clouds, softened by bouncing off objects such as walls or your photo reflectors, or filtered by shade, it can be much dimmer and less contrasty.

Daylight's color temperature can vary quite widely. It is highest in temperature (most blue) at noon when the sun is directly overhead, because the light is traveling through a minimum amount of the filtering layer we call the atmosphere. The color temperature at high noon may be 6,000K. At other times of day, the sun is lower in the sky and the particles in the air provide a filtering effect that warms the illumination to about 5,500K for most of the day. Starting an hour before dusk and for an hour after sunrise, the warm appearance of the sunlight is even visible to our eyes when the color temperature may dip to 5,000-4,500K, as shown in Figure 8.5.

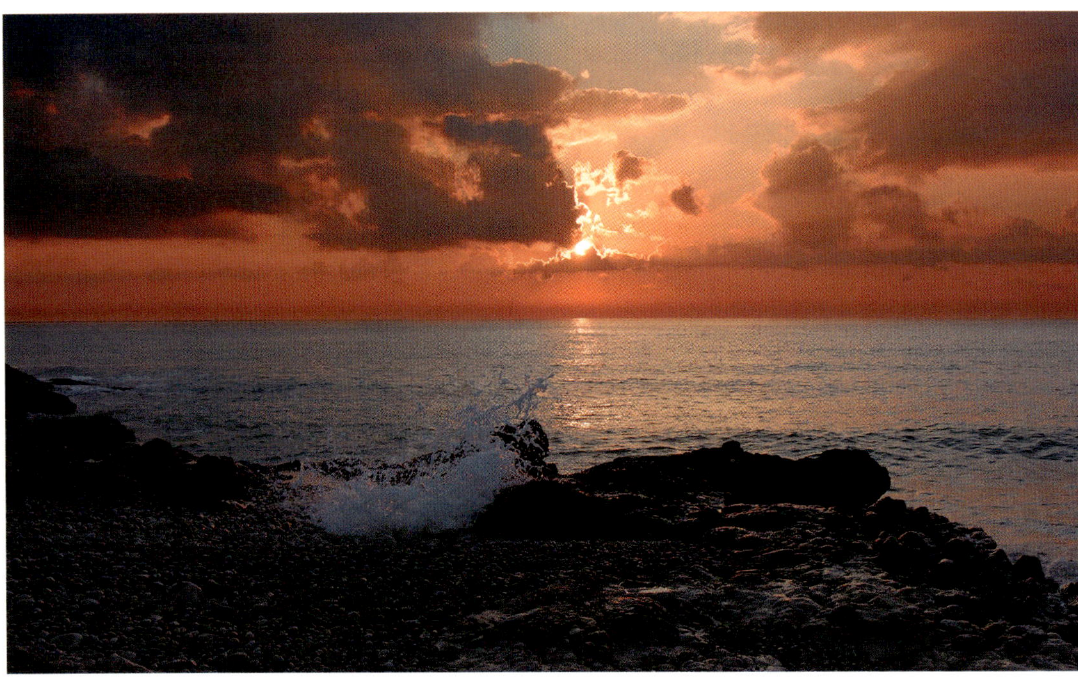

Figure 8.5 At dawn and dusk, the color temperature of daylight may dip as low as 4,500K.

Because you'll be taking so many photos in daylight, you'll want to learn how to use or compensate for the brightness and contrast of sunlight, as well as how to deal with its color temperature. I'll provide some hints later in this chapter.

Incandescent/Tungsten Light

The term incandescent or tungsten illumination is usually applied to the direct descendents of Thomas Edison's original electric lamp. Such lights consist of a glass bulb that contains a vacuum, or is filled with a halogen gas, and contains a tungsten filament that is heated by an electrical current, producing photons and heat. Tungsten-halogen lamps are a variation on the basic light bulb, using a more rugged (and longer-lasting) filament that can be heated to a higher temperature, housed in a thicker glass or quartz envelope, and filled with iodine or bromine ("halogen") gases. The higher temperature allows tungsten-halogen (or quartz-halogen/quartz-iodine, depending on their construction) lamps to burn "hotter" and whiter. Although popular for automobile headlamps today, they've also been used for photographic illumination.

Although incandescent illumination isn't a perfect black body radiator, it's close enough that the color temperature of such lamps can be precisely calculated and used for photography without concerns about color variation (at least, until the very end of the lamp's life).

Of course, old-style tungsten lamps are on the way out, eventually to be replaced either by compact fluorescent lights (CFL) or newer, more energy efficient (and expensive) tungsten lights. Although government regulations that would have put restrictions on tungsten lamps were eventually tabled, as a practical matter such bulbs can't be phased out completely, because CFLs don't work in all fixtures and for all applications, such as dimmers (even if you purchase special "dimmable" CFLs), electronic timer or "dusk-to-dawn" light controllers, some illuminated wall switches, or with motion sensors. Only certain types of CFLs (cold cathode models) operate outside in cold weather; they emit IR signals that can confuse the remote control of your TV, air-conditioner, etc.

The other qualities of this type of lighting, such as contrast, are dependent on the distance of the lamp from the subject, type of reflectors used, and other factors that I'll explain later in this chapter.

Fluorescent Light/Other Light Sources

Fluorescent light has some advantages in terms of illumination, but some disadvantages from a photographic standpoint. This type of lamp generates light through an electro-chemical reaction that emits most of its energy as visible light, rather than heat, which is why the bulbs don't get as hot. The type of light produced varies depending on the phosphor coatings and type of gas in the tube. So, the illumination fluorescent bulbs produce can vary widely in its characteristics.

That's not great news for photographers. Different types of lamps have different "color temperatures" that can't be precisely measured in degrees Kelvin, because the light isn't produced by heating. Worse, fluorescent lamps have a discontinuous spectrum of light that can have some colors missing entirely. A particular type of tube can lack certain shades of red or other colors (see Figure 8.6), which is why fluorescent lamps and other alternative technologies such as sodium-vapor illumination can produce ghastly looking human skin tones. Their spectra can lack the reddish tones we associate with healthy skin and emphasize the blues and greens popular in horror movies.

Vendors, such as GE and Sylvania, may actually provide a figure known as the *color rendering index* (or CRI), which is a measure of how accurately a particular light source represents standard colors, using a scale of 0 (some sodium-vapor lamps) to 100 (daylight and most incandescent lamps). Daylight fluorescents and deluxe cool white fluorescents might have a CRI of about 79 to 95, which is perfectly acceptable for most photographic applications. Warm white fluorescents might have a CRI of 55. White deluxe mercury vapor lights are less suitable with a CRI of 45, while low-pressure sodium lamps can vary from CRI 0-18.

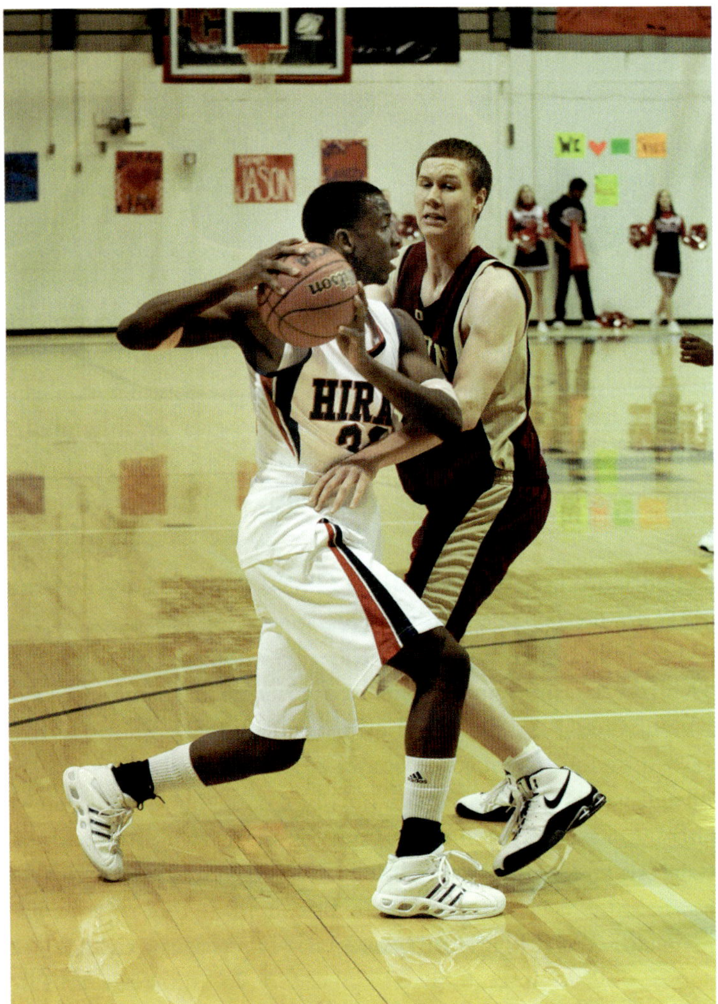

Figure 8.6
The uncorrected fluorescent lighting in the gym added a distinct greenish cast to this image when exposed with a daylight white balance setting.

Also gaining in popularity are LED light sources, particularly for movies, in the form of compact units that clip onto the camera and provide a continuous beam of light to fill in shadows indoors or out, and/or to provide the main illumination when shooting video inside.

Other Lighting Accessories

Once you start working with light, you'll find there are plenty of useful accessories that can help you. Here are some of the most popular that you might want to consider. These all work well with both continuous lighting, discussed in this chapter, as well as with electronic flash, which will be our focus in the chapter that follows.

Do-It-Yourself Lighting

The cool thing about continuous lighting is that anything that lights up can be used as a lighting tool for your D810. Flashlights (for "painting with light" techniques), shop work lights, or even desktop high-intensity lamps, like the one seen in Figure 8.7, can be pressed into service at little or no cost (if you already happen to own something that will work). I used that desk lamp to shoot the image seen in Figure 8.8, simply because the lamp was bright enough to let me use a small f/stop to maximize depth-of-field, and it was really easy to see the lighting effect and move the lamp an inch or two to get different effects.

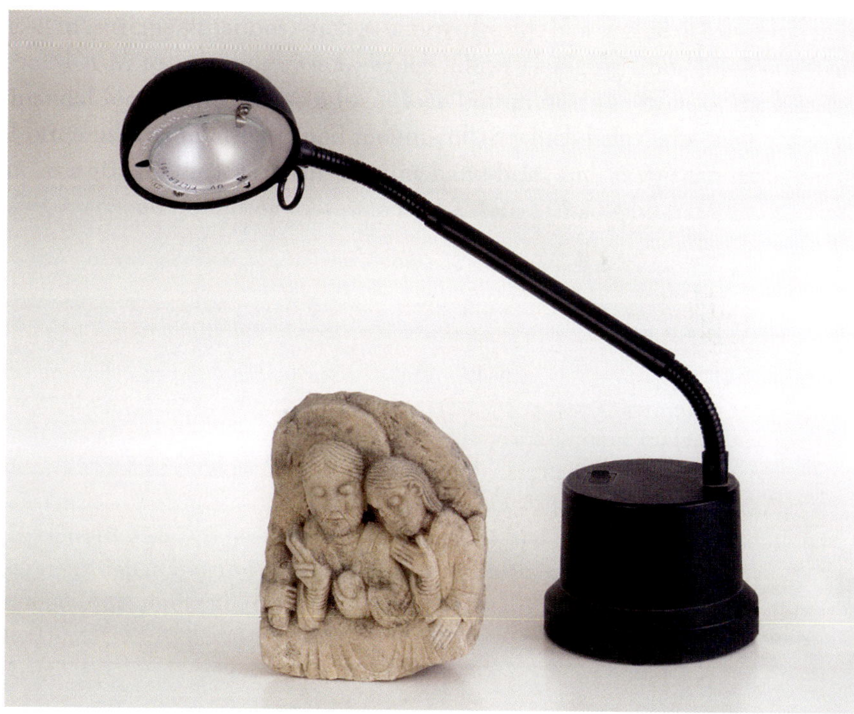

Figure 8.7
A desk lamp can be pressed into service as a light source for tabletop and macro photography.

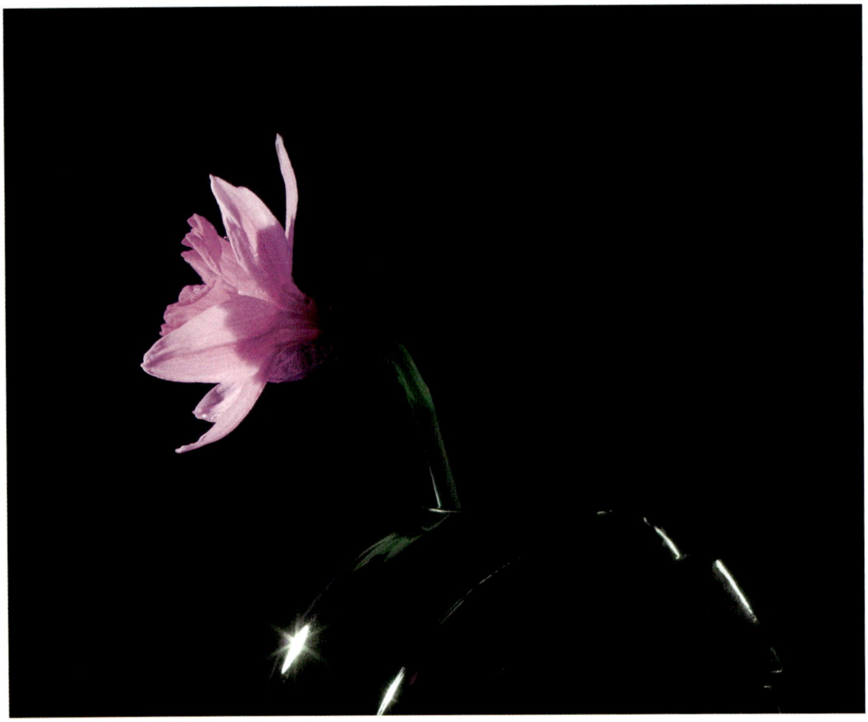

Figure 8.8
It was easy to move the desk lamp a few inches to get the exact lighting effect I wanted.

Umbrellas

Umbrellas are just what you might think, a variation on those trusty shields-on-a-stick that protect us from the ravages of sun, rain, snow, or other elements of nature. Whether we know them as parasols (for the sun) or paraguas (for the water) on the Costa del Sol; as parapluies/ombrelles on the Riviera; or Sonnenschirme/Regenschirme (gotta love those Germans!); these inexpensive accessories are just as versatile for reflecting light as blocking it.

Indeed, you can use umbrellas in multiple roles:

- **Light reflector.** A silver umbrella can provide a softer, but not *too* soft light source, or a much softer source of illumination is produced when a non-shiny white umbrella is used. The quality and quantity of the light that your D810 sees can be further adjusted simply by moving the umbrella closer to your subject (for a softer illumination) or farther away (for more contrast).
- **Light diffuser.** A white umbrella diffuses and softens light, but a translucent white umbrella (of the "shoot-through" variety) can be reversed so that the illumination passes through the fabric and becomes even more soft and diffuse.

- **Light blocker.** Some umbrellas have a white or silver interior surface, and a black cover that prevents any light from leaking through the umbrella. Those models can be used to *block* light from other sources of illumination—even outdoors in daylight—to allow you to create subtle lighting effects.
- **Light colorizer.** Umbrellas may have a shiny golden, silver, or blue interior surface (as do many flat reflectors), and so can be used to add a rich warm tone, neutral sheen, or cold bluish cast to an image or shadows. You can use umbrella "colorizing" to create an effect or balance multiple light sources.
- **Soft box in an instant.** Many umbrellas can be fitted with a cover over their front that transforms them into a soft box. This conversion is more practical for use with electronic flash (covered in the next chapter) than for some kinds of continuous lighting, because of heat build-up. "Colder" forms of continuous lighting, such as fluorescent lights designed specially for photographic applications, can be used in soft box mode, however. Figure 8.9 shows both an umbrella and a soft box.

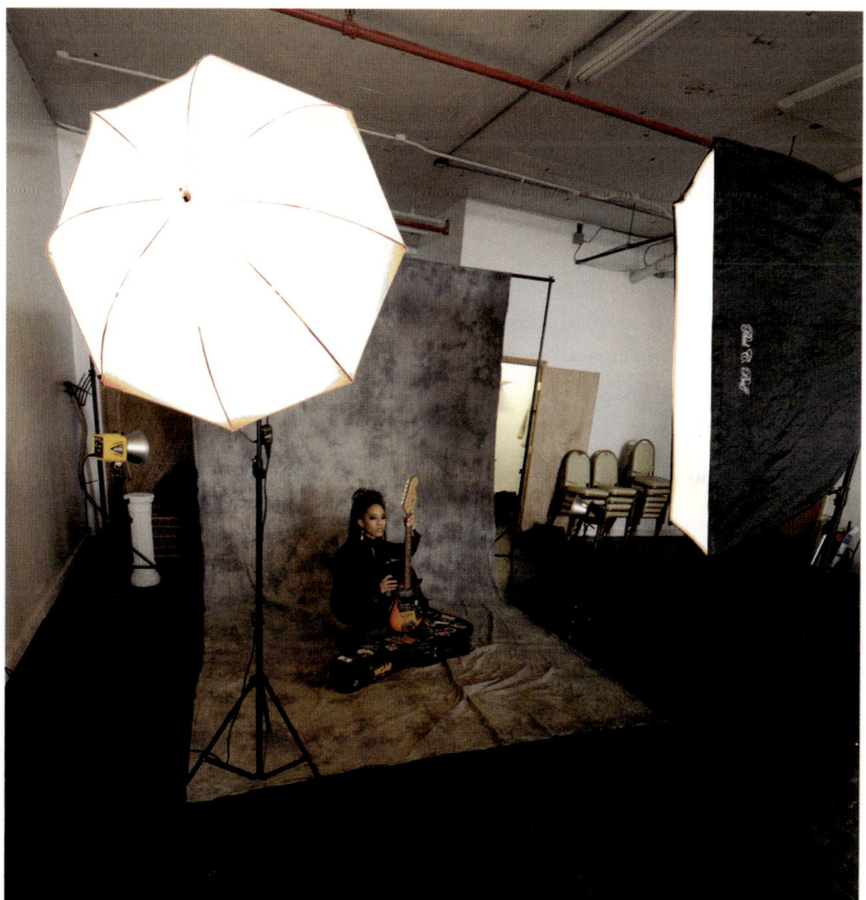

Figure 8.9
Umbrellas, like the one at left, and soft boxes (right) can provide a soft, diffuse light source.

Tents

Tents, like the one seen in Figure 8.10, are useful for photographing shiny objects or any subject where you want to reduce the shadows and reflections to a minimum. The fabric of the tent is translucent, so you place the light sources around the sides or above, and a soft glow filters through to illuminate the image. You can still maintain subtle lighting effects by choosing to light up—or not light up—individual sides of the cube.

The lens of the D810 protrudes through a hole or slit in the tent, so you can photograph the shiniest subject without having you or your camera show up in the final picture.

Soft Boxes

Soft boxes are also handy for photographing shiny objects. They not only provide a soft light, but if the box itself happens to reflect in the subject (say you're photographing a chromium toaster), the box will provide an interesting highlight that's indistinct and not distracting.

You can buy soft boxes or make your own. Some lengths of friction-fit plastic pipe and a lot of muslin cut and sewed just so may be all that you need. Soft boxes are large square, rectangular (or round or octagonal) devices that may resemble an umbrella with a front cover, and produce a similar lighting effect. They can extend from a few feet square to massive boxes that stand five or six feet tall—virtually a wall of light. With a light source or two inside a soft box, you have a very large, semi-directional light source that's very diffuse and very flattering for portraiture and other people photography.

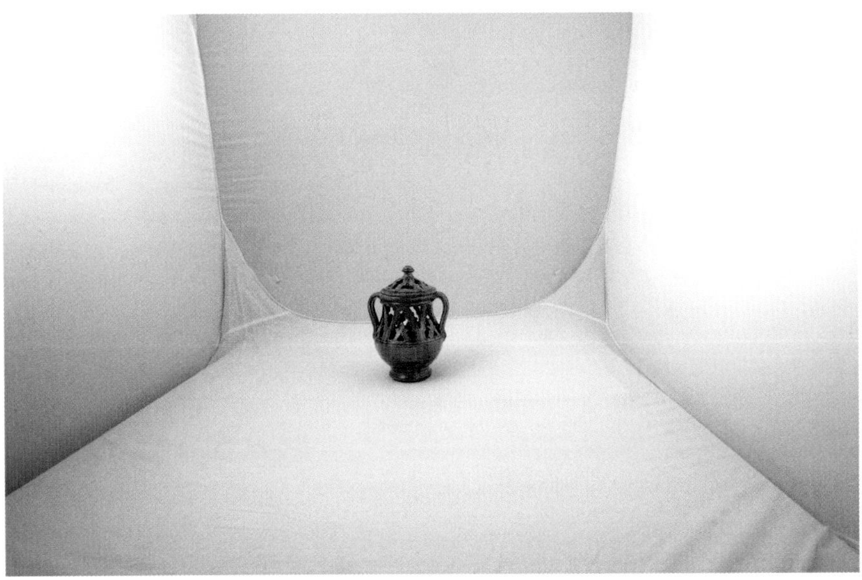

Figure 8.10
Tents provide almost shadowless lighting for photographing shiny objects.

Light Stands

Both electronic flash and incandescent lamps can benefit from light stands. These are lightweight, tripod-like devices (but without a swiveling or tilting head) that can be set on the floor, tabletops, or other elevated surfaces and positioned as needed. Light stands should be strong enough to support an external lighting unit, up to and including a relatively heavy flash with soft box or umbrella reflectors. You want the supports to be capable of raising the lights high enough to be effective. Look for light stands capable of extending six to seven feet high. The nine-foot units usually have larger, steadier bases, and extend high enough that you can use them as background supports. You'll be using these stands for a lifetime, so invest in good ones. I bought my light stands when I was in college, and I have been using them for decades.

Backgrounds

Backgrounds can be backdrops of cloth, sheets of muslin you've painted yourself using a sponge dipped in paint, rolls of seamless paper, or any other suitable surface your mind can dream up. Backgrounds provide a complementary and non-distracting area behind subjects (especially portraits) and can be lit separately to provide contrast and separation that outlines the subject, or which helps set a mood.

I like to use plain-colored backgrounds for portraits, and white or gray seamless paper backgrounds for product photography. You can usually construct these yourself from cheap materials and tape them up on the wall behind your subject, or mount them on a pole stretched between a pair of light stands.

Snoots and Barn Doors

These fit over the flash unit and direct the light at your subject. Snoots are excellent for converting a light source into a hair light, while barn doors give you enough control over the illumination by opening and closing their flaps that you can use another flash as a background light, with the capability of feathering the light exactly where you want it on the background.

9

Electronic Flash with the Nikon D810

The term "professional camera" doesn't always mean a lot, except to those who aren't professional photographers, and who enjoy drawing distinctions among various camera categories. A real pro chooses photographic tools by what features and capabilities are needed to do a paying job. In some cases, one of the components that *isn't* needed is a built-in flash. Although handy in many cases, a built-in unit, while economical (it comes "free" with the camera) has some limitations that can be easily overcome by using an external flash. That's why Nikon's flagship "pro" dSLRs (currently the Nikon D4) have traditionally come without any built-in flash at all. Other vendors, most notably Canon, followed suit and eschewed a built-in flash not only in their top-of-the-line cameras, but their mid-line models (such as the 5D Mark III).

Fortunately, Nikon has taken a more reasonable approach for the more compact versions of its full-frame cameras—first, the Nikon D700, and now the D810. Both include a flip-up internal flash unit, which, while certainly not a total flash solution for creative photography, *does* provide extra flexibility even if you elect not to carry or use an external flash unit.

Until you delve into the flash situation deeply enough, it might appear that serious photographers have a love/hate relationship with electronic flash. You'll often hear that flash photography is less natural looking, and that the built-in flash in most cameras should never be used as the primary source of illumination because it provides a harsh, garish look.

In truth, however, the bias is against *bad* flash photography. Indeed, flash has become the studio light source of choice for many pro photographers, because it's more intense (and its intensity can be varied to order by the photographer), freezes action, frees you from using a tripod (unless you want to use one to lock down a composition), and has a snappy, consistent light quality that matches daylight. (While color balance changes as the flash duration shortens, some Nikon flash units can communicate to the camera the exact white balance provided for that shot.) And even pros will cede that the built-in flash of the Nikon D810 has some important uses as an adjunct to existing light, particularly to fill in dark shadows or to serve as a wireless trigger for additional, off-camera strobes.

But electronic flash isn't as inherently easy to use as continuous lighting. As I noted in Chapter 8, electronic flash units are more expensive, don't show you exactly what the lighting effect will be (unless you use a second source or mode called a *modeling light* for a preview), and the exposure of electronic flash units is more difficult to calculate accurately.

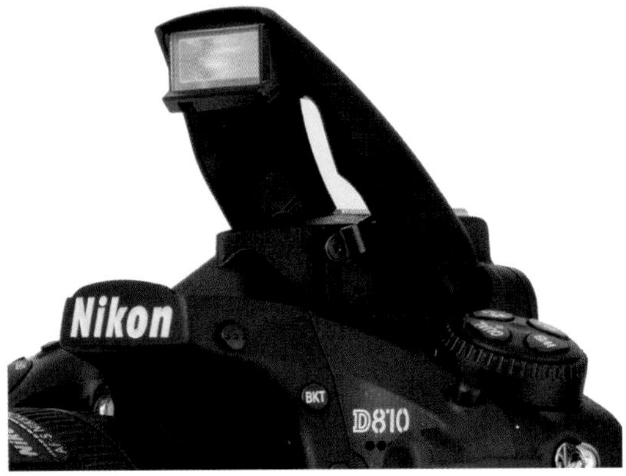

Figure 9.1 One form of light that's always available is the flip-up flash on your Nikon D810.

This chapter and the next will show you how to manage all the creative and technical challenges, using both the D810's internal flash (shown in Figure 9.1) and external flash units. First, we'll look at the basics of working with both types and then, in Chapter 10, explore the world of wireless flash photography.

Electronic Flash Basics

The bursts of light we call electronic flash are produced by a flash of photons generated by an electrical charge that is accumulated in a component called a *capacitor* and then directed through a glass tube containing xenon gas, which absorbs the energy and emits the brief flash. For the pop-up flash built into the D810, the full burst of light lasts about 1/1,000th of a second when the unit is set to full power, and provides enough illumination to shoot a subject 10 feet away at f/4 using the ISO 100 setting. In a more typical situation you'd bump the sensitivity up to ISO 200, and use f/5.6 to f/8 to photograph something 8 to 10 feet away. As you can see, the built-in flash is somewhat limited in range; you'll see why external flash units are often a good idea later in this chapter.

Fire When Ready!

Once the capacitor is charged, the burst of light that produces the main exposure can be initiated by a signal from the D810 that commands the internal or connected flash units to fire. External strobes can be linked to the D810 in several different ways:

- **Camera mounted/hardwired external dedicated flash.** Units offered by Nikon or other vendors that are compatible with Nikon's Creative Lighting System—CLS—can be clipped onto the accessory "hot" shoe on top of the camera or linked through a wired system such as the Nikon SC-28/SC-29 cables. I'll describe CLS later in this chapter.

- **Wireless dedicated flash.** A CLS-compatible unit can be triggered by signals produced by a pre-flash (before the main flash burst begins), which offers two-way communication between the camera and flash unit. The triggering flash can be the D810's built-in unit, a CLS flash unit in Master mode, or a wireless non-flashing accessory, such as the Nikon RU-800, which does nothing but "talk" to the external flashes. You'll find more on this mode in Chapter 10.
- **Wired, non-intelligent mode.** The PC/X connector on the front of the camera (located under a rubber cover, above the 10-pin connector, as shown in Figure 9.2) is a non-intelligent camera/flash link that sends just one piece of information, one way: it tells a connected flash to fire. There is no other exchange of information between the camera and flash. The PC/X connector can be used to link the Nikon D810 with non-dedicated/non-CLS-friendly strobes, which can be studio flash units, manual non-CLS flash, flash units from other vendors that can use a PC cable, or even Nikon brand Speedlights that you elect to connect to the D810 in a non-CLS, "unintelligent" mode.
- **Infrared/radio transmitter/receivers.** Another way to link flash units to the D810 is through a wireless infrared or radio *transmitter*, like a Pocket Wizard, Radio Popper, or the Paul C. Buff CyberSync trigger shown in Figure 9.3. These are generally mounted on the accessory shoe of the D810, and emit a signal when the D810 sends a command to fire through the hot shoe. The simplest of these function as a wireless PC/X connector, with no other communication between the camera and flash (other than the instruction to fire). However, sophisticated units have their own built-in controls and can send additional commands to the receivers when connected to compatible flash units. I use one to adjust the power output of my Alien Bees studio flash from the camera, without the need to walk over to the flash itself.

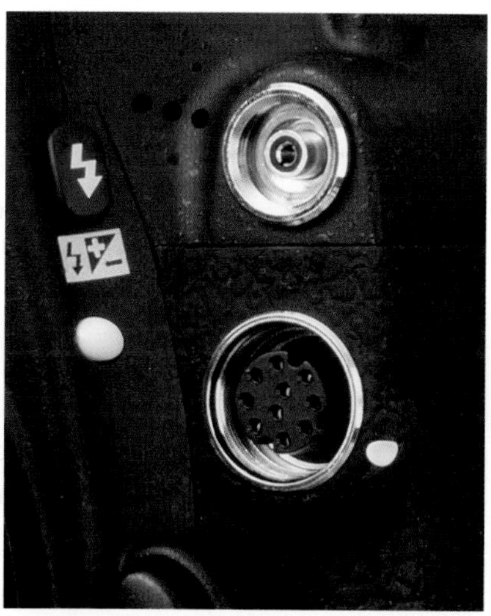

Figure 9.2 The PC/X connector (top) can trigger flash units non-intelligently.

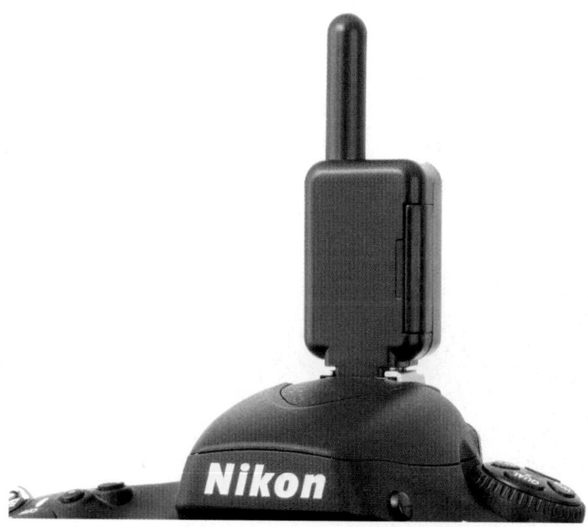

Figure 9.3 A wireless trigger can command external flash units to fire.

- **Simple slave connection.** In the days before intelligent wireless communication, the most common way to trigger off-camera, non-wired flash units was through a *slave* unit. These can be small external triggers connected to the remote flash (or built into the flash itself), and set off when the slave's optical sensor detects a burst initiated by the camera itself. When it "sees" the main flash (from the D810's built-in flash, or another flash) the slave flash units are triggered quickly enough to contribute to the same exposure. The main problem with this type of connection—other than the lack of any intelligent communication between the camera and flash—is that the slave may be fooled by any pre-flashes that are emitted by the other strobes, and fire too soon. Modern slave triggers have a special "digital" mode that ignores the pre-flash and fires only from the main flash burst.

The Moment of Exposure

The D810 has a vertically traveling shutter that consists of two curtains. Just before the flash fires, the first curtain opens and moves down to the opposite side of the frame, at which point the shutter is completely open. The flash can be triggered at this point (so-called *first-curtain* or *front-curtain sync*), making the flash exposure. Then, after a delay that can vary from 30 seconds to 1/250th second (or faster when *high-speed sync,* discussed later, is used), a second curtain begins moving down the sensor plane, covering up the sensor again. If the flash is triggered just before the second curtain starts to close, then *second-curtain* (or *rear-curtain*) *sync* is used. In both cases, though, a shutter speed of 1/250th second is the maximum that can be used to take a photo, unless you're using the high-speed 1/320th second sync.

Figure 9.4 illustrates how this works, with a fanciful illustration of a generic shutter (your D810's shutter does *not* look like this). Both curtains are tightly closed at upper left. At upper right, the first curtain begins to move downward, starting to expose a narrow slit that reveals the sensor behind the shutter. At lower left, the first curtain moves downward farther until, as you can see at lower right in the figure, the sensor is fully exposed.

Here's a more detailed look at what happens when you take a photo using electronic flash, either the unit built into the Nikon D810 or an external flash like the Nikon SB-910, all within a few milliseconds of time. The following list assumes you are using the optical viewfinder rather than live view. The sequence is similar when using live view, except that the mirror isn't flipping up and down as described below:

1. **Sync mode.** After you've selected a shooting mode, choose the flash sync option available in that mode by holding down the Flash button (on the front left side of the pentaprism housing, marked with a lightning bolt) and rotating the main command dial until the icon representing the choice you want is displayed in the monochrome control panel. (See Figure 9.5.) I'll describe the sync modes later in this chapter.
2. **Metering method.** Choose the metering method you want, from Matrix, Center-weighted, Spot, or Highlight-weighted metering.

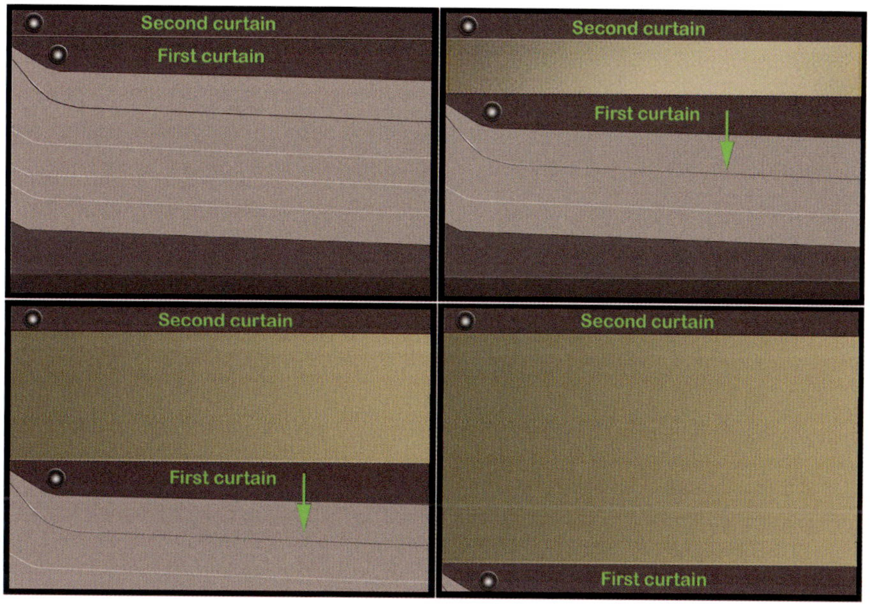

Figure 9.4
A focal plane shutter has two curtains, the lower, or first curtain, and an upper, second curtain.

3. **Activate flash.** Press the flash pop-up button to flip up the built-in flash, if necessary, or mount (or connect with a cable) an external flash and turn it on. A ready light appears in the viewfinder and on the back of an external dedicated flash when the unit is ready to take a picture.
4. **Check exposure.** Select a shutter speed when using Manual, Program, or Shutter-priority modes; select an aperture when using Aperture-priority and Manual exposure modes.
5. **Preview lighting.** If you want to preview the lighting effect, press the depth-of-field button to produce a modeling flash burst (unless you've redefined this control in the Custom Settings menu as described in Chapter 12).
6. **Lock flash setting (if desired).** Optionally, if the main subject is located significantly off-center, you can frame so the subject is centered, lock the flash at the exposure needed to illuminate that subject, and then reframe using the composition you want. Lock the flash level using the Flash Value Lock button (which is, by default, the Fn button, but can also be assigned to the Fn, Preview, or AE-L/AF-L buttons in Custom Settings menu choices f4, f5, or f6). Press the FV lock button, and the flash will emit a pre-flash to determine the correct flash level, and then the D810 will lock the flash at that level until you press the FV lock button again to release it. FV lock icons appear in the monochrome control panel and the viewfinder.
7. **Take photo.** Press the shutter release down all the way.
8. **D810 receives distance data.** A D- or G-series lens now supplies focus distance to the D810.
9. **Pre-flash emitted.** The internal flash, if used, or external dedicated flash sends out one or two pre-flash bursts. One burst can be used to control additional wireless flash units in Commander mode, while the other is used to determine exposure.

10. **Exposure calculated.** The pre-flash bounces back and is measured by the 91,000-pixel RGB sensor in the viewfinder. It measures brightness and contrast of the image to calculate exposure. If you're using Matrix metering, the D810 evaluates the scene to determine whether the subject may be backlit (for fill flash), a subject that requires extra ambient light exposure to balance the scene with the flash exposure, or classifies the scene in some other way. The camera to subject information as well as the degree of sharp focus of the subject matter is used to locate the subject within the frame. If you've selected Spot metering, only standard i-TTL (without balanced fill flash) is used.
11. **Mirror up.** The mirror flips up. At this point exposure and focus are locked in.

> **Tip**
>
> Cool trick: If you want to confirm that the pre-flash fires before the mirror flips up, set the D810 to Mup (Mirror Up) mode using the release mode dial. (This separates the firing of the pre-flash from the flash used to make the exposure.) Press the shutter release as you look through the viewfinder. You'll see the pre-flash fire, and *then* the mirror will flip up, obscuring your view. Press the shutter release a second time to take the actual picture. Only *then* will the main flash fire.

12. **First curtain opens.** With the D810, this first curtain can take two forms:
    - **Physical curtain.** The exposure by ambient light begins when the physical shutter curtain is fully open. This is the traditional way flash pictures are taken.
    - **Electronic first curtain.** Available only in Mup mode, the electronic first curtain shutter commences the actual exposure a fraction of a second after the physical first curtain has opened (and its vibration ceases) to expose the sensor.
13. **Flash fired.** At the correct triggering moment (depending on whether front or rear sync is used), the camera sends a signal to one or more flashes to start flash discharge. The flash is quenched as soon as the correct exposure has been achieved.
14. **Shutter closes.** The shutter closes and the mirror flips down. You're ready to take another picture. Remember to press the FV lock button again to release the flash exposure if your next shot will use a different composition.
15. **Exposure confirmed.** Ordinarily, the full charge in the flash may not be required. If the flash indicator in the viewfinder blinks for about three seconds after the exposure, that means that the entire flash charge was required, and it *could* mean that the full charge wasn't enough for a proper exposure. Be sure to review your image on the monitor to make sure it's not underexposed, and, if it is, make adjustments (such as increasing the ISO setting of the D810) to remedy the situation.

Determining Exposure

Calculating the proper exposure for an electronic flash photograph is a bit more complicated than determining the settings for continuous light. The right exposure isn't simply a function of how far away your subject is (which the camera can figure out based on the autofocus distance that's locked in just prior to taking the picture). Various objects reflect more or less light at the same distance so, obviously, the camera needs to measure the amount of light reflected back and through the lens. Yet, as the flash itself isn't available for measuring until it's triggered, the D810 has nothing to measure.

The solution is to fire the flash twice. The initial shot is a *monitor pre-flash* that can be analyzed, then followed virtually instantaneously by a main flash (to the eye the bursts appear to be a single flash) that's given exactly the calculated intensity needed to provide a correct exposure. As a result, the primary flash may be longer in duration for distant objects and shorter in duration for closer subjects, depending on the required intensity for exposure. This through-the-lens evaluative flash exposure system is called i-TTL (intelligent Through The Lens), and it operates whenever you use the built-in flash or have attached a Nikon dedicated flash unit to the D810.

The amount of light emitted by the flash is changed in an interesting way—interrupting the flash as the charge flows from the capacitor through the flash tube. When full power is required, either to supply the correct exposure in i-TTL mode or because you're using the flash in Manual mode at the full power (1/1) setting, then all the energy in the capacitor flows through the flash tube. However, if less than full power is needed, the energy is stopped partway through the exposure by opening the circuit with a solid-state switch. In the olden days this was always done using a component called a *thyristor,* but today a component called an *insulated-gate bipolar transistor*, or IGBT is more common.

Because the current is interrupted before the full power of the capacitor is used, the resulting burst becomes shorter as the power output is reduced. For example, with some Nikon flash units you might see a burst lasting about 1/1,000th second at full power, but only a little longer than 1/10,000th second at 1/16th power, or 1/40,000th second at 1/128th power. This behavior is nifty when you want to freeze really fast action, such as falling water droplets—just use a lower power output level and/or work extremely close to your subject.

Because the full contents of the capacitor are not used with these partial flashes, the Speedlight is able to recycle more quickly, or even use the retained energy to fire multiple times in Repeating flash mode (described later in this chapter). The only downside is that shorter flash exposures tend to take on a bluish tinge as the duration decreases. That's because the burst starts out with a very cool color temperature and ends up much warmer at the end of the burst, averaging out to a hue that's pretty close to daylight in color balance. When you trim off the reddish end of the flash, your resulting image may be noticeably more blue. That's why the Flash color balance of the D810 doesn't always produce a pleasing color rendition. You may have to fine-tune the white balance, as described in Chapter 11, or shoot RAW and correct in your image editor.

Those of you using studio flash units may be interested to know that your non-automatic strobes produce their varying power levels in a different way. With the typical studio flash, the capacitor is *always* fully discharged each time you take a picture, and then recharged *to the level you specify* for the next shot. It happens very quickly because you're using AC power or a high-voltage battery pack instead of low-capacity alkaline or rechargeable cells.

If you set the flash for ½ power, the capacitor (or capacitors—studio flash may use several of them) is charged only half-filled; at ¼ power it's only replenished to 25 percent of its capacity. Then, when you take the photo, the full contents of the capacitor is sent through the flash tube. That's why you need to "dump" your studio flash when you reduce the power output from a higher level. The capacitor retains the charge that was in there before, and can't fire at the reduced capacity you want until the existing power is dumped and then replenished to the level you specify. Because of the way studio flash store and release their power, they can be designed to be more consistent at different power levels than your typical Nikon flash unit. Of course, wild color variations from flash units aren't a huge problem, but just something you should be aware of.

So, to summarize, with CLS-compatible flash units, your automatic exposure is calculated by measuring a pre-flash and determining an appropriate exposure from that. There are other exposure modes than i-TTL available from Nikon external flash units, and I'll get into them later in this chapter, but this section has described the process in a nutshell.

Guide Numbers

Guide numbers, usually abbreviated GN, were originally developed as a way of calculating exposure manually, but today are more useful as a measurement of the power of an electronic flash unit. A GN is usually given as a pair of numbers for both feet and meters that represent the range at ISO 100. For example, the Nikon SB-910 has a GN in i-TTL mode of 48/157 (meters/feet) at ISO 200 when using the coverage needed for a 35mm lens (the flash has a *zoom head* to spread/narrow the light for a range of focal lengths). To calculate the right exposure at that ISO setting, you'd divide the guide number by the distance to arrive at the appropriate f/stop.

Using the SB-910 as an example, at ISO 200 with its GN of 156, if you wanted to shoot a subject at a distance of 10 feet, you'd use f/15.6 (or, f/16). At 5 feet, an f/stop of f/32 would be used. Some quick mental calculations with the GN will give you any particular electronic flash's range. Many years ago Nikon offered a 45mm GN lens that could couple the f/stop setting of the lens with the focus distance. You specified the guide number of the flash using a scale on the lens itself, and as you focused closer or farther away the f/stop was reduced or increased to match.

Today, guide numbers are most useful for comparing the power of various flash units, rather than actually calculating what exposure to use. You don't need to be a math genius to see that an electronic flash with a GN in feet of, say, 157 (like the SB-910) would be *a lot* more powerful than the built-in flash of a camera like the Nikon D810, which has a guide number of about 55. At ISO 200, you could use f/8 instead of f/2.8 at 20 feet, an improvement of about 3.5 stops.

Choosing a Flash Sync Mode

The Nikon D810 has five flash sync modes, plus a sixth (High Speed Sync, described later) that comes into play in some circumstances. The five main modes are selected by holding down the Flash button while rotating the main command dial. (See Figure 9.5 for the icons.) Those modes (which I've listed in logical order, so the explanation will make more sense, rather than the order in which they appear during the selection cycle) are as follows:

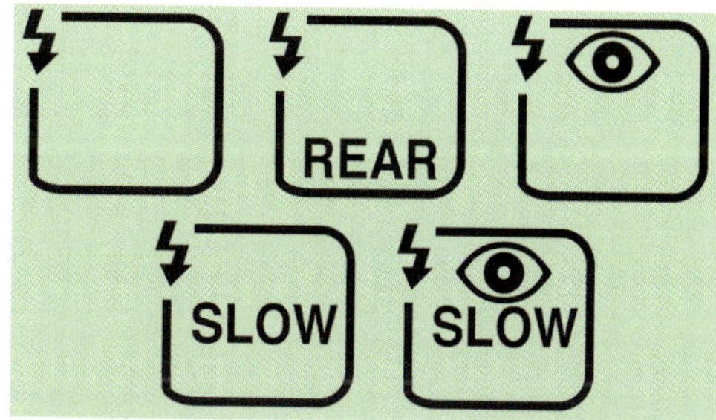

Figure 9.5 Icons for flash sync modes include front sync (top left), rear sync (top middle), red-eye reduction (top right), slow sync (lower left), and slow sync with red-eye reduction (lower right).

- **Front-curtain sync (available in PSAM modes).** This setting, available in all exposure modes, should be your default setting. In this mode the flash fires as soon as the front curtain opens completely. The shutter then remains open for the duration of the exposure, until the rear curtain closes. If the subject is moving and ambient light levels are high enough, the movement will cause a secondary "ghost" exposure that appears in front of the flash exposure.
- **Rear-curtain sync (available in PSAM modes).** With this setting, which can be used with Program, Shutter-priority, Aperture-priority, or Manual exposure modes, the front curtain opens completely and remains open for the duration of the exposure. Then, the flash is fired and the rear curtain closes. If the subject is moving and ambient light levels are high enough, the movement will cause a secondary "ghost" exposure that appears behind the flash exposure (trailing it). You'll find more on "ghost" exposures next. In Program and Aperture-priority modes, the D810 will combine rear-curtain sync with slow shutter speeds (just like slow sync, discussed below) to balance ambient light with flash illumination. (It's best to use a tripod to avoid blur at these slow shutter speeds.)
- **Red-eye reduction (available in PSAM modes).** In this PSAM-compatible mode, there is a one-second lag after pressing the shutter release before the picture is actually taken, during which the D810's red-eye reduction lamp lights, causing the subject's pupils to contract (assuming they are looking at the camera), and thus reducing potential red-eye effects. Don't use with moving subjects or when you can't abide the delay.
- **Slow sync (available in P or A modes).** This setting allows the D810 in Program and Aperture-priority modes to use shutter speeds as slow as 30 seconds with the flash to help balance a background illuminated with ambient light with your main subject, which will be lit by the electronic flash. You'll want to use a tripod at slower shutter speeds, of course. As shown in Figure 9.6, it's common that the ambient light will be incandescent illumination that's much warmer than the electronic flash's "daylight" balance, so, if you want the two sources to match, you may want to use a warming filter on the flash. That can be done with a gel if you're using an external flash like the SB-910, or by taping an appropriate warm filter over the D810's built-

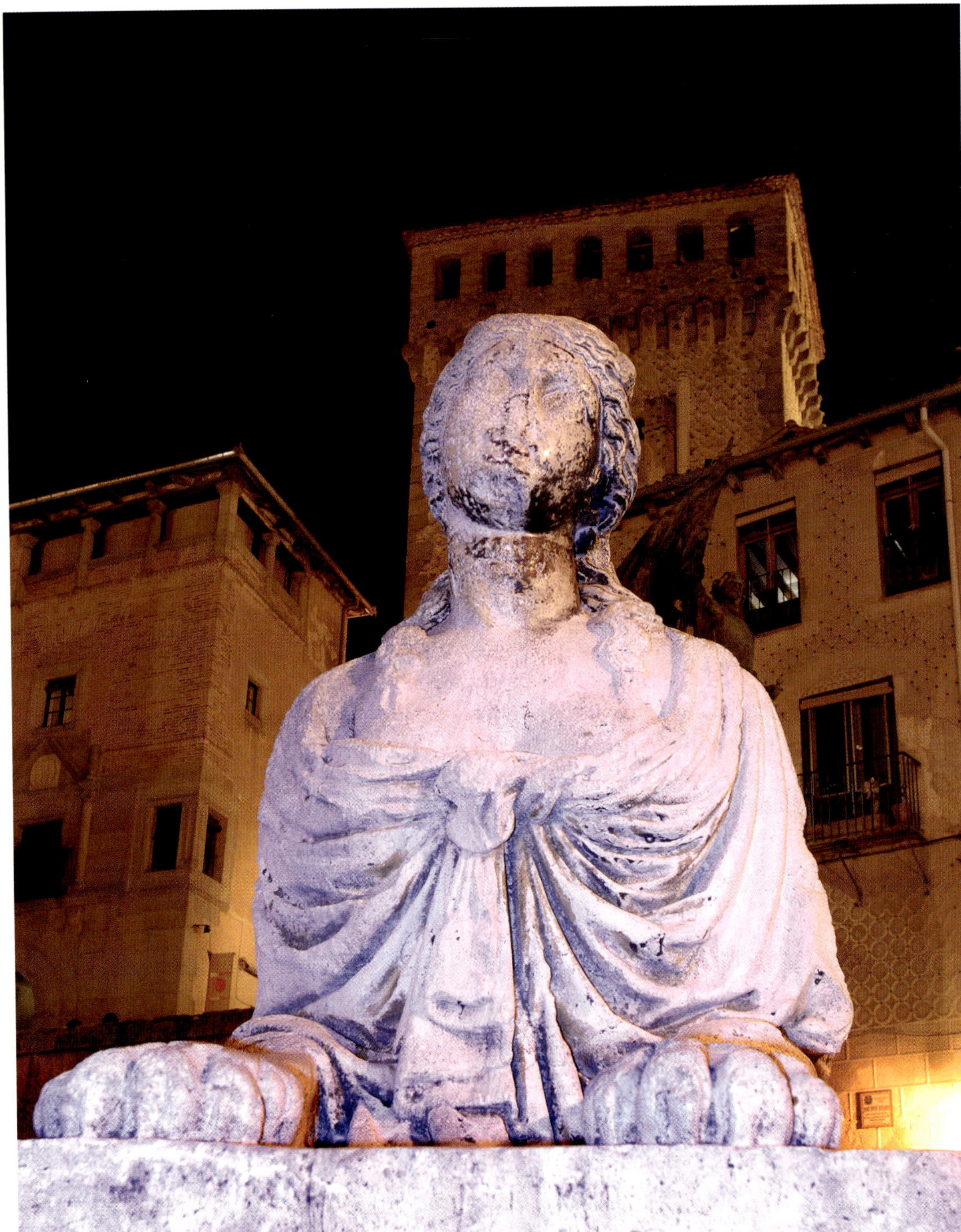

Figure 9.6 I deliberately used flash and slow sync to separate this Roman sphinx sculpture (limned in bluish light from the flash) from the background illuminated by warmer incandescents.

in flash. (That's not a convenient approach, and many find the warm/cool mismatch unobjectionable and don't bother with filtration.)

- **Red-eye reduction with slow sync (available in P or A modes).** This mode combines slow sync with the D810's red-eye reduction behavior when using Program or Aperture-priority modes.

As a reminder, note that in Shutter-priority and Manual exposure modes, you can select only the following three flash synchronization settings:

- **Front-curtain sync/fill flash.** This setting should be your default setting. This mode is also available in Program and Aperture-priority mode, as described above, and, with high ambient light levels, can produce ghost images, discussed below.
- **Red-eye reduction.** This mode, with its one-second lag and red-eye lamp flash, is described above.
- **Rear-curtain sync.** As noted previously, in this sync mode, the front curtain opens completely and remains open for the duration of the exposure. Then, the flash is fired and the rear curtain closes. If the subject is moving and ambient light levels are high enough, the movement will cause that "ghost" exposure that appears to be trailing the flash exposure.

Ghost Images

The difference might not seem like much, but whether you use first curtain sync (the default setting) or rear-curtain sync (an optional setting) can make a significant difference to your photograph *if the ambient light in your scene also contributes to the image.* At faster shutter speeds, particularly 1/250th second, there isn't much time for the ambient light to register, unless it is very bright. It's likely that the electronic flash will provide almost all the illumination, so first-curtain sync or second-curtain sync isn't very important.

However, at slower shutter speeds, or with very bright ambient light levels, there is a significant difference, particularly if your subject is moving, or the camera isn't steady. In any of those situations, the ambient light will register as a second image accompanying the flash exposure, and if there is movement (camera or subject), that additional image will not be in the same place as the flash exposure. It will show as a ghost image and, if the movement is significant enough, as a blurred ghost image trailing in front of or behind your subject in the direction of the movement.

As I mentioned earlier, when you're using front-curtain sync, the flash goes off the instant the shutter opens, producing an image of the subject on the sensor. Then, the shutter remains open for an additional period (which can be from 30 seconds to 1/250th second). If your subject is moving, say, toward the right side of the frame, the ghost image produced by the ambient light will produce a blur on the right side of the original subject image. That makes it look as if your sharp (flash-produced) image is chasing the ghost (see Figure 9.7, left), which looks unnatural to those of us who grew up with lightning-fast superheroes (rather than modern dancers) who always left a ghost trail *behind them* (see Figure 9.7, right).

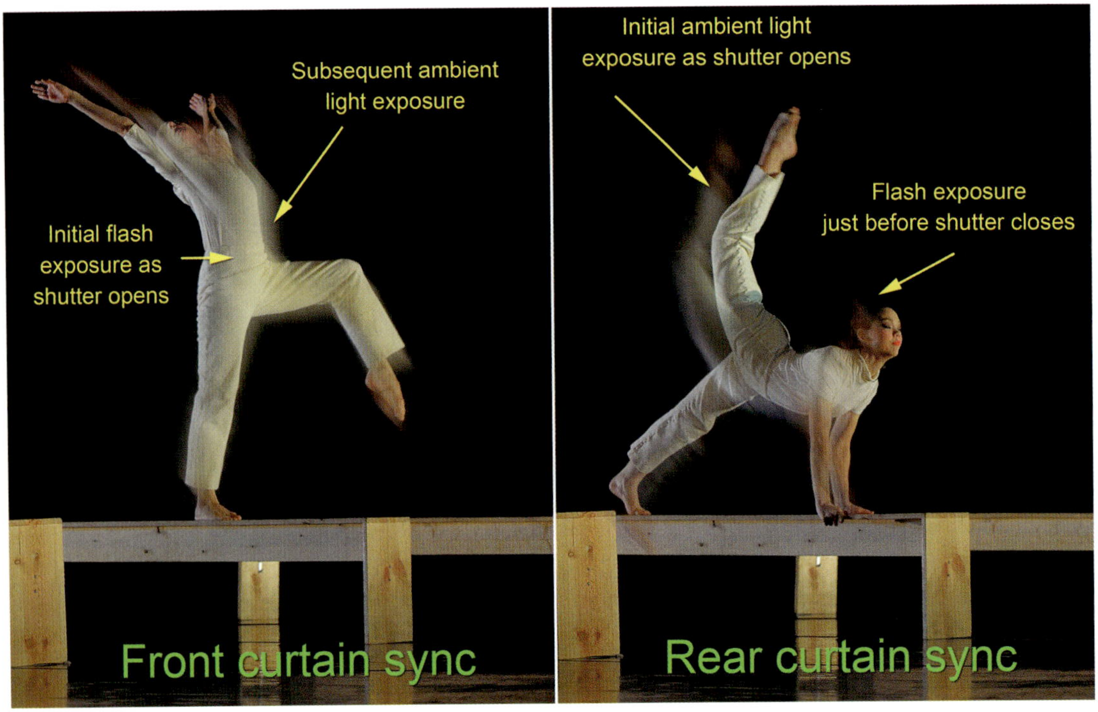

Figure 9.7 Front-curtain sync produces an image that trails in front of the flash exposure (left), while rear-curtain sync creates a more "natural looking" trail behind the flash image (right).

So, Nikon provides rear (second) curtain sync to remedy the situation. In that mode, the shutter opens, as before. The shutter remains open for its designated duration, and the ghost image forms. If your subject moves from the left side of the frame to the right side, the ghost will move from left to right, too. *Then*, about 1.5 milliseconds before the second shutter curtain closes, the flash is triggered, producing a nice, sharp flash image *ahead* of the ghost image. Voilà! We have monsieur *le Flash* outrunning his own trailing image.

EVERY WHICH WAY, INCLUDING UP

Note that, although I describe the ghost effect in terms of subject matter that is moving left to right in a horizontally oriented composition, it can occur in any orientation, and with the subject moving in *any* direction. (Try photographing a falling rock, if you can, and you'll see the same effect.) Nor are the ghost images affected by the fact that modern shutters travel vertically rather than horizontally. Secondary images are caused between the time the first curtain fully opens, and the second curtain begins to close. The direction of travel of the shutter curtains, or the direction of your subject, does not matter.

Avoiding Sync Speed Problems

Using a shutter speed faster than 1/250th second can cause problems. Triggering the electronic flash only when the shutter is completely open makes a lot of sense if you think about what's going on. To obtain shutter speeds faster than 1/250th second, the D810 exposes only part of the sensor at one time, by starting the second curtain on its journey before the first curtain has completely opened, as shown in Figure 9.8. That effectively provides a briefer exposure as a slit of the shutter passes over the surface of the sensor. If the flash were to fire during the time when the first and second curtains partially obscured the sensor, only the slit that was actually open would be exposed.

You'd end up with only a narrow band, representing the portion of the sensor that was exposed when the picture is taken. For shutter speeds *faster* than 1/250th second, the second curtain begins moving *before* the first curtain reaches the bottom of the frame. As a result, a moving slit, the distance between the first and second curtains, exposes one portion of the sensor at a time as it moves from the top to the bottom. Figure 9.8 shows three views of our typical (but imaginary) focal plane shutter. At left is pictured the closed shutter; in the middle version you can see the first curtain has moved down about 1/4 of the distance to the top; and in the right-hand version, the second curtain has started to "chase" the first curtain across the frame toward the bottom.

If the flash is triggered while this slit is moving, only the exposed portion of the sensor will receive any illumination. You end up with a photo like the one shown in Figure 9.9. Note that a band across the bottom of the image is black. That's a shadow of the second shutter curtain, which had started to move when the flash was triggered. Sharp-eyed readers will wonder why the black band is at the *bottom* of the frame rather than at the top, where the second curtain begins its journey. The answer is simple: your lens flips the image upside down and forms it on the sensor in a reversed position. You never notice that, because the camera is smart enough to show you the pixels that make up your photo in their proper orientation during picture review. But this image flip is why, if your sensor gets dirty and you detect a spot of dust in the upper half of a test photo, if cleaning manually, you need to look for the speck in the *bottom* half of the sensor.

I generally end up with sync speed problems only when shooting in the studio, using studio flash units rather than my D810's built-in flash or a Nikon dedicated Speedlight. That's because if you're using either type of "smart" flash, the camera knows that a strobe is attached, and remedies any

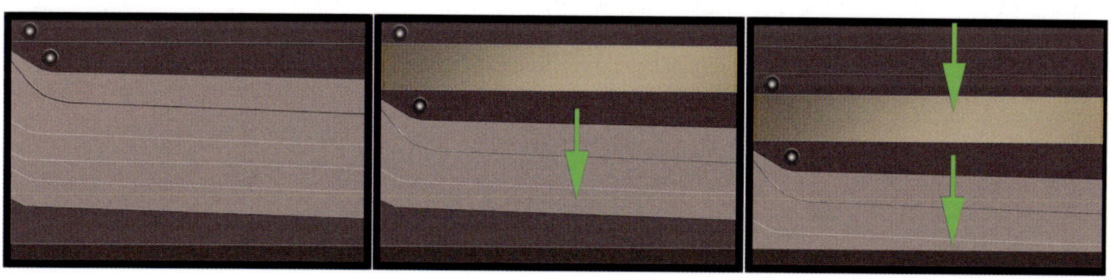

Figure 9.8 A closed shutter (left); partially open shutter as the first curtain begins to move downward (middle); only part of the sensor is exposed as the slit moves (right).

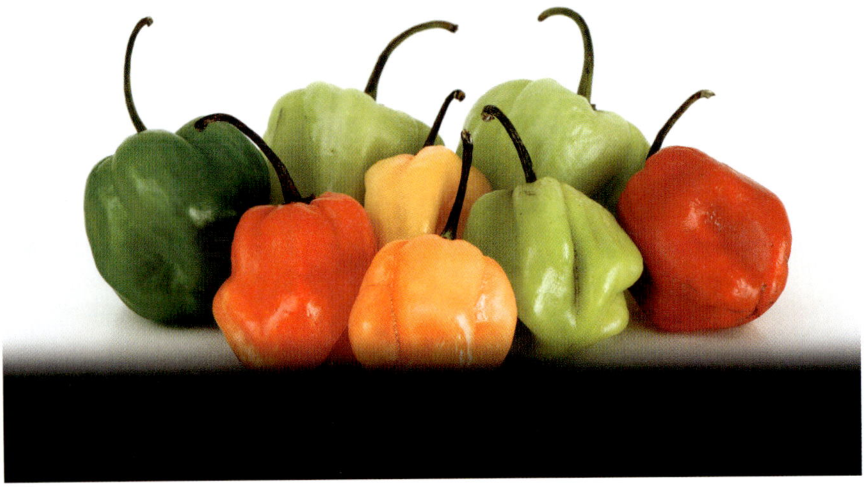

Figure 9.9
If a shutter speed faster than 1/250th second is used, you can end up photographing only a portion of the image.

unintentional goof in shutter speed settings. If you happen to set the D810's shutter to a faster speed in S or M mode, the camera will automatically adjust the shutter speed down to 1/250th second as soon as you flip up the flash (or prevent you from choosing a faster speed if the flash is already up). In A, or P modes, where the D810 selects the shutter speed, it will never choose a shutter speed higher than 1/250th second when using flash. In P mode, shutter speed is automatically set between 1/60th to 1/250th second when using flash.

But when using a non-dedicated flash, such as a studio unit plugged into the front flash sync terminal, the camera has no way of knowing that a flash is connected, so shutter speeds faster than 1/250th second can be set inadvertently. To avoid that problem with studio flash, I strongly recommend setting your camera to Manual exposure, and using the x250 shutter speed, which is located *past* the Bulb speed when rotating the main command dial all the way to the left. You won't have to worry as much about accidentally changing the shutter speed to an unusable setting; there is no speed *beyond* x250th second, and if you nudge the main command dial to the right, you'll get a Bulb exposure, which will immediately become evident.

High-Speed (FP) Sync

Note that the D810 can use a feature called *high-speed sync,* which allows shutter speeds faster than 1/250-1/320th second with certain external dedicated Nikon flash units. When using high-speed sync, the flash fires a continuous serious of bursts at reduced power for the entire duration of the exposure, so that the illumination is able to expose the sensor as the slit moves. HS sync is set using the controls that adjust the compatible external flash. You don't need to make any special settings on the flash; the D810 takes care of the details for you, as I'll describe in this section.

As I said earlier, triggering the electronic flash only when the shutter is completely open makes a lot of sense if you think about what's going on. To obtain shutter speeds faster than 1/250th second, the D810 exposes only part of the sensor at one time, by starting the second curtain on its journey before the first curtain has completely opened. That effectively provides a briefer exposure as a slit of the shutter passes over the surface of the sensor. If the flash were to fire during the time when the first and second curtains partially obscured the sensor, only the area defined by the slit that was actually open would be exposed.

However, the D810 and certain Nikon flashes provide a partial solution, called *high-speed sync* or *FP sync* (focal plane sync). Those flash units can fire a series of flashes consecutively in rapid succession, producing the illusion of a longer continuous flash, although at reduced intensity. These multiple flashes have a duration long enough to allow exposing the area of the sensor revealed by the traveling slit as it makes its full pass. However, the reduced intensity means that your flash's range is greatly reduced.

This technique is most useful outdoors when you need fill-in flash, but find that 1/250th second is way too slow for the f/stop you want to use. For example, at ISO 200, an outdoors exposure is likely to be 1/250th second at, say, f/14, which is perfectly fine for an ambient/balanced fill-flash exposure if you don't mind the extreme depth-of-field offered by the small f/stop. But, what if you'd rather shoot at 1/1,600th second at f/5.6? High-speed sync will let you do that, and you probably won't mind the reduced flash power, because you're looking for fill flash, anyway. This sync mode offers more flexibility than, say, dropping down to ISO 100.

High-speed sync is also useful when you want to use a larger f/stop to limit the amount of depth-of-field. Select a shutter speed higher than 1/250th second, and the faster sync speed automatically reduces the effective light of the flash, without other intervention from you.

To use Auto FP sync with units like the Nikon SB-910/SB-900, SB-700, SB-R200 units and a few discontinued Speedlights like the SB-800 and SB-600, there is no setting to make on the flash itself. You need to use Custom Setting e1 to specify either 1/320 s (Auto FP) or 1/250 s (Auto FP). When either of those settings is activated, when using P or A exposure modes, the shutter speed will be set to 1/320th or 1/250th second (respectively) when a compatible external flash is attached. Higher shutter speeds than 1/320th or 1/250th second—all the way up to 1/8,000th second—can then be used with full synchronization, at reduced flash output. There are also situations in which you might want to set flash sync speed to *less* than 1/250th second, say, because you *want* ambient light to produce secondary ghost images in your frame. You can choose the following settings:

- **1/320 s (Auto FP).** This setting allows using compatible external flash units with high-speed synchronization at 1/320th second or faster, and activates auto FP sync when the camera selects a shutter speed of 1/320th second or faster in programmed and Aperture-priority modes. Other flash units, including the built-in flash, will be used at speeds no faster than 1/250th second.

- **1/250 s (Auto FP).** This similar setting allows using the named external flash units with high-speed synchronization at 1/250th second or faster, and activates auto FP sync when the camera selects a shutter speed of 1/250th second or faster in programmed and Aperture-priority modes. Other flash units, including the flip-up internal flash, will be used at speeds no faster than 1/250th second.
- **1/250 s.** At this default setting, only shutter speeds up to 1/250th second can be used with flash, both internal and external. Note: To lock in shutter speed at 1/250th second, rotate the main control dial in M or S modes to choose the x250 setting located after the 30s and bulb speeds.
- **1/200 s-1/60 s.** You can specify a specific shutter speed from the range of speeds 1/200th second to 1/60th second to be used as the synchronization speed for external flash units. Forcing a slower shutter speed produces a "slow sync" effect. For example, when 1/60th second has been set as the maximum flash shutter speed, ambient light is more likely to contribute to the exposure. (See Figure 9.10.) That can help balance the flash exposure with available light falling on the background (use a tripod or VR to minimize ghost images). Or, that slow shutter speed can help generate ghost images when you intentionally want them to appear in your image, say, to create a feeling of motion.

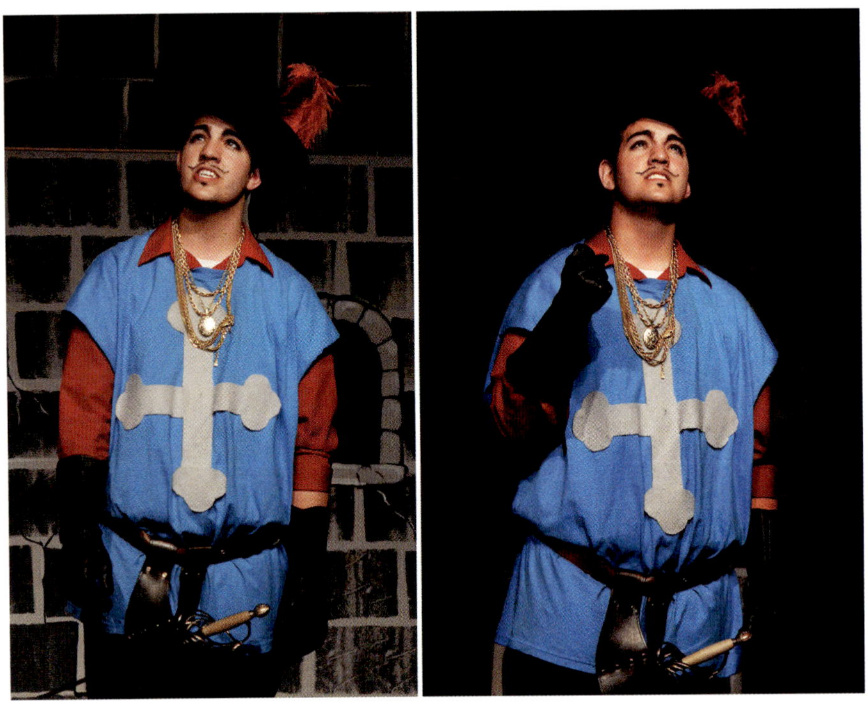

Figure 9.10
At 1/60th second, the ambient light behind the actor provided detail in the background (left). With a shutter speed of 1/250th second, the background is dark (right).

Using the Nikon D810's Built-in Flash

The D810's internal flash unit is part of a larger system that includes external Speedlights and other flash components. I'm referring to the Nikon Creative Lighting System (CLS), which was introduced in July, 2003 when the company unveiled the Speedlight SB-800, a flash unit compatible with early professional digital SLRs, such as the Nikon D2h/D2hs, and, within a few months, more affordable models like 2004's Nikon D70 and all subsequent dSLRs from the company. CLS has the following features, although not all of these are supported by every Nikon camera:

- **i-TTL.** Intelligent through-the-lens exposure control calculates exposure based on a monitor pre-flash that is fired a fraction of a second before the main burst, and then evaluated by the same RGB exposure sensor used for continuous light measurements. The system's intelligence allows sophisticated adjustments, such as balancing the flash exposure with the ambient light exposure, say, when you shoot in full daylight, to provide fill in the shadows.
- **Advanced wireless lighting.** A system that uses the same pre-flash concept to communicate triggering and exposure information to external flash units that aren't physically linked to the camera, and located within a reasonable distance (say, about 30 feet). Not all Nikon cameras support AWL for their built-in flashes (and some cameras, like the D4, have no built-in flash at all). You can still use wireless lighting with such models by having a compatible external flash or trigger device serve as the "master." Depending on whether you're using the D810's built-in flash or an external flash, you may be able to divide multiple flash units into up to three different "groups," and communicate with them using your choice of any of four "channels" (to avoid having your flash units triggered by the master flash of another Nikon photographer in the vicinity). I'll explain AWL in more detail in Chapter 10.
- **FV Lock.** A *flash value* locking system that allows you to fix in place the current flash exposure so that you can, for example, measure flash exposure for a subject that is not in the center of the frame, and then reframe while using that value for subsequent exposures.
- **Auto FP high-speed sync.** Focal plane HS sync allows synchronizing an external flash while using shutter speeds faster than 1/250th or 1/320th second (with the D810; other Nikon cameras may have different maximum sync speeds of 1/200th or even 1/500th second). With a compatible flash and a camera like the D810, shutter speeds up to 1/8000th second can be used, although only a part of the flash's illumination is used and flash range is reduced (sometimes to as little as a few feet).
- **Focus assist.** Although Nikon cameras themselves may have focus assist illumination built-in, the CLS system allows including wide-area AF-assist illumination to be built into the front of the flash unit, or into a flash connecting cable.

- **Zoom coverage.** Some CLS-compatible flash units have a powered zoom head built in to allow changing the area covered by the flash to match the focal length of the lens in use, as communicated by the camera to the flash itself. Zooming can also be done manually.
- **Flash color information communication.** The exact color temperature of the light emitted by a CLS-compatible flash can vary, based on the duration of the flash burst. The flash is initially rather blue in color, and becomes redder as the burst continues. The Speedlight is able to send information to the camera to allow adjusting white balance in AWB mode based on the true color information of the flash exposure.

The Nikon D810's built-in flash has a guide number of 12/39 (meters/feet) at ISO 100 and must be activated by manually flipping it up. This flash is powerful enough to provide primary direct flash illumination when required, but can't be angled up for diffuse bounce flash off the ceiling. It's useful for balanced fill flash (more on that later) and for use in Commander mode, which allows the built-in flash to trigger one or more off-camera flash units in up to four separate groups wirelessly. You can use Custom Setting e3 to dial down the intensity of the built-in flash manually to 1/128 power so that, in Commander mode, it will activate off-camera flash units but not contribute much (if at all) to the exposure. The built-in flash can also be set to fire only as a pre-flash that will trigger external units, without setting off its main burst. The built-in flash has useful modeling light and repeating flash modes, which will be described later in this chapter.

Because the built-in flash draws its power from the D810's battery, extensive use will reduce the power available to take pictures. For that reason alone, use of an external flash unit can be a good idea when you plan to take a lot of flash pictures. The following sections describe the basics of using the built-in flash, although many of the settings/controls also apply to external Speedlights, which are discussed later in this chapter.

If you want to temporarily disable the built-in flash (and any attached external flash), a handy way to do this is to assign the Flash Off function to the Fn button, using Custom Setting f4, as described in Chapter 12. Then, when you press the Fn button, the built-in flash (if elevated) and any external flash attached and powered up will not fire while the Fn button is held down. This is useful if you want to temporarily disable the flash, say, to take a picture or two by available light, and then return to normal flash operation.

Using Flash Exposure Compensation

If the exposure produced by your flash isn't satisfactory, you can manually add or subtract exposure to the flash exposure calculated by the D810. Just press the Flash button on the camera (located just below the flash pop-up button) and rotate the sub-command dial until the amount of exposure compensation you want appears on the monochrome control panel and in the viewfinder. You can make adjustments from –3EV to +1EV in 1/3 EV increments (or using some other increment, either ½ or 1 EV, selected by you with Custom Setting b3).

As with ordinary exposure compensation, the adjustment you make remains in effect until you zero it out by pressing the Flash button and rotating the sub-command dial until 0 appears on the monochrome control panel and in the viewfinder. To view the current flash exposure compensation setting, press the Flash button. When compensation is being used, an icon will be displayed in the viewfinder and on the control panel.

To change the size of the compensation increment, access Exp./Flash Comp. Step Value, Custom Setting b3 and select 1/3, 1/2, or 1 EV steps. Your change will adjust the size of the increment for *both* flash and ordinary exposure compensation, which I prefer. It's always best to have your D810 use the same size "jumps" when making these exposure adjustments, which are set separately in Custom Setting b2.

Specifying Flash Shutter Speed

This is another way of specifying the shutter speed the D810 will use when working with flash. Unlike Custom Setting e1 described earlier, this setting determines the *slowest* shutter speed that is available for electronic flash synchronization when you're not using a "slow sync" mode. When you want to avoid ghost images from a secondary exposure, you should use the highest shutter speed that will synchronize with your flash. This setting prevents programmed or Aperture-priority modes (which both select the shutter speed for you) from selecting a shutter speed that captures ambient light along with the flash.

With Custom Setting e2, select a value from 30 s to 1/60 s, and the D810 will avoid using speeds slower than the one you specify with electronic flash if you don't override that decision by deliberately choosing slow sync, slow rear-curtain sync, or red-eye reduction with slow sync. If you think you can hold the D810 steady, a value of 1/30 s is a good compromise; if you have shaky hands, use 1/60 s or higher. Those with extraordinarily solid grips or a lens with vibration reduction can try the 1/15 s setting. Remember that this setting only determines the slowest shutter speed that will be used, not the default shutter speed, which is set with Custom Setting e1.

Built-in Flash Control

Use Custom Setting e3 to choose one of four modes for the built-in flash. These options, which I'll describe in more detail later, are also available for external flash units.

- **TTL.** When the built-in flash is triggered, the D810 first fires a pre-flash and measures the light reflected back and through the lens to calculate the proper exposure when the full flash is emitted a fraction of a second later.
- **Manual.** You can set the level of the built-in flash from full power to 1/128 power.

- **Repeating flash.** The flash fires multiple bursts, producing an interesting stroboscopic lighting effect. When you choose repeating flash you'll be asked to select Output (flash power level), Times (the number of times the flash is fired at the output level you specify), and Frequency (how often the flash fires per second). Note that these factors are interdependent. For example, if you tell the flash to fire at 1/8 output power, you can select from 2 to 5 flashes, at a rate of 1 to 50 flashes per second. That's because the flash has only enough power for a maximum of 5 flashes at the 1/8 output setting. At 1/128 power, there's enough juice for 2 to 35 individual flashes, at a rate of no more than 50 flashes per second.
- **Commander mode.** If you never use external flash, you can safely ignore this setting. If you do, you'll want to set up the D810 for your most frequently used options, to avoid having to fiddle with the camera if you decide to pull your SB-910 out of your bag for some impromptu multi-flash shooting. In Commander mode, the built-in flash emits pre-flashes that can be used to wirelessly control one or more remote external flash units.

Previewing Your Flash Effect

The Nikon D810's built-in flash and compatible external units, including the SB-910, SB-700, and some earlier models, can simulate a modeling light, in the form of a set of repeated bursts of light that allow you to pre-visualize the effect the strobe will provide when fired for the main exposure. While this modeling flash, turned on or off using Custom Setting e4, is not a perfect substitute for a real incandescent or fluorescent modeling lamp, it does assist in seeing how your subject will be illuminated, so you can spot any potential problems with shadows.

When this feature is activated, pressing the depth-of-field button on the D810 briefly triggers the modeling flash for your preview. Selecting Off disables the feature. You'll generally want to leave it On, except when you anticipate using the depth-of-field preview button for depth-of-field purposes (imagine that) and do *not* want the modeling flash to fire when the flash unit is charged and ready. Some external flash units, such as the SB-910, have their own modeling flash buttons.

Activating Bracketing

I discussed exposure bracketing in Chapter 4. This useful tool can also be applied to flash exposures. If you want to be able to use flash exposure bracketing in semi-automatic (Program, Shutter-priority, or Aperture-priority) modes, activate the feature using Custom Setting e6, where you can choose whether bracketing is used for both automatic exposure *and* flash (AE & flash), automatic exposure only (AE), or flash bracketing only (Flash only). Additional bracketing modes for white balance and Active D-Lighting are also available. Either of those two settings disables flash and exposure bracketing.

Bracketing is available when using Manual exposure mode, too. Configure your options using Custom Setting e7. If your flash is used and has been activated for bracketing, the flash will be factored in, as well. Your choices include:

- **Flash/Speed.** With this default value, the D810 will vary the shutter speed to produce bracketed exposures and, if flash bracketing is available, will vary flash output as well. Use this option to lock your aperture set at the f/stop you choose for selective focus.
- **Flash/Speed/Aperture.** The D810 will vary both shutter speed and aperture from your manual settings, and adjust flash output if flash bracketing is available. This setting is useful when creating a large bracket set, up to nine different exposures, because you'll rarely want to vary shutter speed or aperture alone over such a large range of shots. The Flash/Speed/Aperture option spreads the variation over a combination of shutter speeds and apertures. You would not want to use this option for HDR photography, which works best when bracketing is accomplished *only* by adjusting shutter speed.
- **Flash/Aperture.** The D810 will use the aperture to bracket your photos taken by ambient light, and if flash bracketing is available, will use flash output as well. This option is best if you're shooting sports with manual exposure and want to lock in a specific shutter speed. As with Flash/Speed, this setting works best when the number of exposures in your bracket set is limited to 2 to 5 exposures; otherwise, the f/stop selected can vary wildly.
- **Flash Only.** The D810 will bracket only flash exposure.

If you want to change the order in which bracketed exposures are taken (from Metered to Under to Over or Under to Metered to Over), use Custom Setting e7 as described in Chapter 12.

Working with Nikon Flash External Units

Nikon offers several external flash units that are compatible with CLS, ranging from the top-of-the-line SB-910 to the entry-level SB-300. In addition, there are a number of older units that have been officially or unofficially discontinued, such as the SB-600, SB-800, and SB-900, which are still available, in both new and used condition. I'm going to concentrate on the current models only in the following sections, with the most emphasis on the SB-700 and SB-910 that are the most practical for owners of high-end Nikon dSLRs like the D810. The new Nikon SB-500 unit was not available before this book went to press. It's a compact electronic flash with a built-in LED that provides continuous illumination for movie-making and close-up still photography.

Nikon SB-300

This entry-level Speedlight, at about $150, is the smallest and most basic of the Nikon series of Speedlights. The SB-300 has a limited, easy-to-use feature set suited for point-and-shoot photography and some slightly more advanced techniques. Do note however that it does not support wireless off-camera flash. The SB-300 has a moderate guide number of 18/59 at ISO 100. Its main advantage, then, is to provide some additional elevation of the flash above the camera to provide an improved coverage angle and less chance of red-eye effects. Its flash head tilts up to 120 degrees, with click stops at 120, 90, 75, and 60 degrees when the flash is pointed directly ahead. It has a zoom flash head. The SB-300 is lighter in weight at 3.4 ounces than the SB-400 it replaces, and uses two AAA batteries.

Nikon SB-400

Recently discontinued, but still widely available new from many retailers, this entry-level Speedlight (see Figure 9.11) was, until the SB-300 was unveiled, the smallest and most basic of the series. The SB-400 has a limited, easy-to-use feature set suited for point-and-shoot photography and some slightly more advanced techniques. Do note however that, like the SB-300, it does not support wireless off-camera flash. The 4.5-ounce SB-400 has a moderate guide number of 21/69 at ISO 100 when the zooming head (which can be set to either 18mm or 27mm) is at the 18mm position. It tilts up to 90 degrees, allowing you to bounce the light off of a ceiling, but it cannot be rotated to the side.

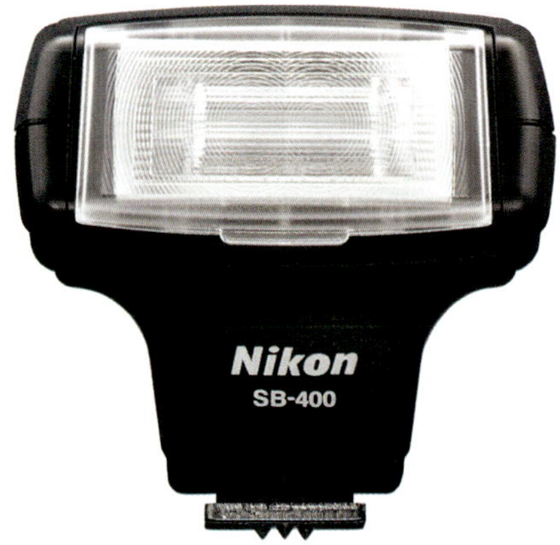

Figure 9.11 The Nikon SB-400 is an entry-level flash best suited for Nikon's entry-level dSLRs.

Nikon SB-700

This affordable (about $330) unit (see Figure 9.12) has a guide number of 28/92 (meters/feet) at ISO 100 when set to the 35mm zoom position. It has many of the top-model SB-910's features, including zoomable flash coverage equal to the field of view of a 16-56mm lens on the D810 (24-120mm settings with a full-frame camera), and 14mm with a built-in diffuser panel. It has a built-in modeling flash feature, a wireless Commander mode, and automatic detection of DX format when mounted on non-FX camera models.

But the SB-700 lacks some important features found in the SB-910. Depending on how you use your Speedlight, these differences may or may not be important to you. They include:

- **No repeating flash mode.** You can't shoot interesting stroboscopic effects with the SB-700, as you can with the D810's built-in flash (which is less than an ideal light source in RPT mode), or the SB-910.
- **No accessory filters or flash diffuser dome included.** You can purchase these separately, and probably should, as they are very useful. You'll pay $30 to $50 for a set, although enterprising third parties offer substitutes for the Nikon accessories.

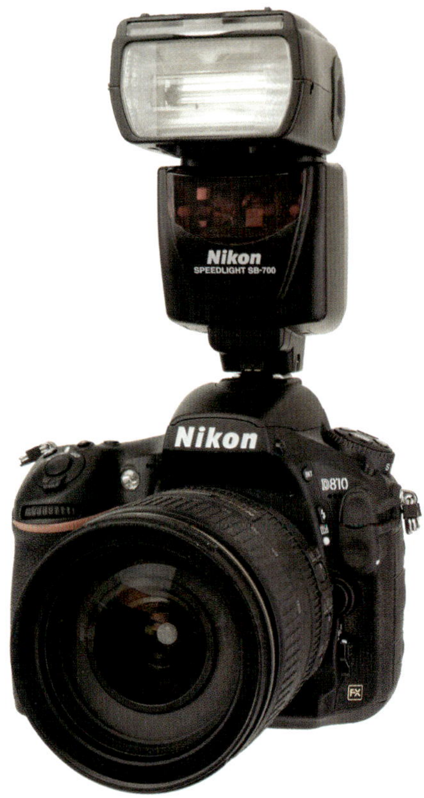

Figure 9.12 The Nikon SB-700 has most features a D810 owner might want.

- **No port for external power pack.** Using an external battery pack, like those available from Quantum and others can be important for wedding and event photographers who want to fire off a bunch of shots quickly, while avoiding frequent changes of the AA batteries the SB-700 uses. An external pack has another benefit: more exposures before the Speedlight slows down to prevent overheating. External batteries don't generate heat inside the flash as internal batteries do.
- **No external PC/X sync socket.** This option, not found on the SB-700, is of limited use for those who want to attach an off-camera flash to the camera. The D810 has a built-in PC/X connector, so the lack of one on the SB-700 is no big deal.
- **Limited zoom range.** The SB-700's zoom head is limited to 24-120mm, plus 14mm with the diffuser panel. The SB-910 allows adjustments for 17-200mm focal lengths, plus 12mm with its diffuser panel. The ability to match the zoom head to the focal length you're using can match the coverage to the field of view, so the flash's output isn't wasted illuminating areas that aren't within the actual frame.

Nikon SB-R200

One oddball flash unit in the Nikon line is the SB-200. This is a specialized wireless-only flash (see Figure 9.13) that's especially useful for close-up photography, and is often purchased in pairs for use with the Nikon R1 and R1C1 Wireless Close-Up Speedlight systems. Its output power is low at 10/33 (meters/feet) for ISO 100 as you might expect for a unit used to photograph subjects that are often inches from the camera. It has a fixed coverage angle of 78 degrees horizontal and 60 degrees vertical, but the flash head tilts down to 60 degrees and up to 45 degrees (with detents every 15 degrees in both directions). In this case, "up" and "down" has a different meaning, because the SB-R200 can be mounted on the SX-1 Attachment Ring mounted around the lens, so the pair of flash units are on the sides and titled toward or away from the optical axis. It supports i-TTL, D-TTL, TTL (for film cameras), and Manual modes.

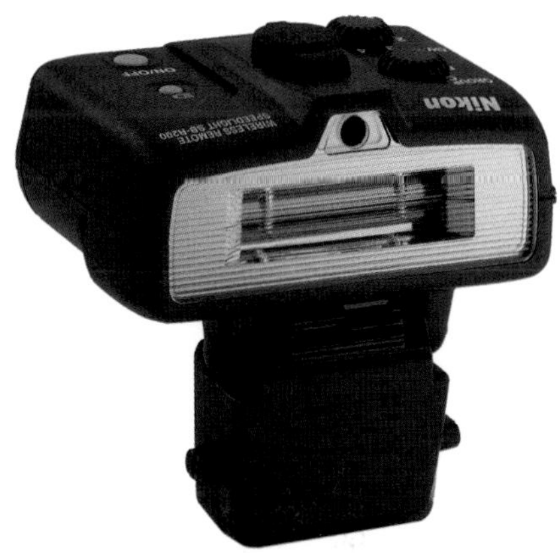

Figure 9.13 The Nikon SB-R200 is a wireless macro-only flash supplied with the Nikon R1 and R1C1 Wireless Close-Up Speedlight systems.

Nikon SB-910

The Nikon SB-910 is currently the flagship of the Nikon flash line up, and has a guide number of 34/111.5 (meters/feet) when the "zooming" flash head (which can be set to adjust the coverage angle of the lens) is set to the 35mm position. It has all the features of the D810's built-in flash unit, including Commander mode, repeating flash, modeling light, and selectable power output, along with some extra capabilities.

The SB-910 is basically a slight reboot of the older SB-900, which gained a bad reputation for overheating and then shutting down after a relatively small number of consecutive exposures (as few as a dozen or so shots). The SB-910 also can overheat, but features a different thermal protection system. Instead of disabling the flash as it begins warming up, the SB-910 instead increases the recycle time between flashes, giving the unit additional time to cool a bit before the next shot. While this "improvement" is not a real fix, it does encourage you to slow your shooting pace a bit to stretch out the number of flashes this Speedlight produces before it must be shut down for additional cooling.

Nikon estimates that you should be able to get 190 flashes from the SB-910 when using AA 2600 mAh rechargeable batteries, if firing the Speedlight at full output once every 30 seconds, with a minimum recycling time of 2.3 seconds (which gradually becomes longer as the flash heats up and the thermal protection kicks in). To get the maximum number of shots from your batteries, Nikon figures that AF-assist illumination, power zoom, and the LCD panel illumination are switched off.

There are some improvements, such as illuminated buttons and a restyled soft case, but, in general, the SB-910 is very similar to the SB-900 that we Nikon photographers have learned to know and fear. For example, you can angle the flash and rotate it to provide bounce flash. It includes additional, non-through-the-lens exposure modes, thanks to its built-in light sensor, and can "zoom" and diffuse its coverage angle to illuminate the field of view of lenses from 12mm to 200mm on a D810 in FX mode. (In DX mode, coverage ranges from 8mm to 200mm.)

The SB-910/SB-900 also has its own powerful focus assist lamp to aid autofocus in dim lighting, and has reduced red-eye effects simply because the unit, even when attached to the D810 and not used off-camera, is mounted in a higher position that tends to eliminate reflections from the eye back to the camera lens.

Figure 9.14 shows the SB-910 fastened to the optional Nikon SC-7 bracket, and linked to the D810 through the available SC-29 cable. There are a couple advantages to this configuration. First, the side-mounting moves the flash even farther from the axis of the lens, providing additional red-eye protection. You can still tilt the flash for bounce effects. I find this setup easier to hold, and not as awkward because you don't have a top-heavy flash unit mounted above the camera.

But, best of all, it's easy to uncouple the flash/SC-29 from the bracket and use both off-camera. There's no need to fuss with wireless modes, channels, groups, or other settings; the SB-910 thinks that it's still connected directly to the D810—which it is, of course. Another nine-foot cable, the SC-28, is available but does not have the SC-29's built-in focus assist illuminator. I own both, but like having the SC-29's focus-assist lamp on top of the camera, so that it is aimed at my subject should the D810 need a bit of extra illumination for focusing. Although the SB-910 has its own focus lamp, it may or may not be pointed at your subject when it comes time to use it.

I power my SB-910 with Sanyo Eneloop AA nickel metal hydride batteries, seen in Figure 9.15. These are a special type of rechargeable battery with a feature that's ideal for electronic flash use. The Eneloop cells, unlike conventional batteries, don't self-discharge over relative short periods of time. Once charged, they can hold onto their juice for a year or more. That means you can stuff

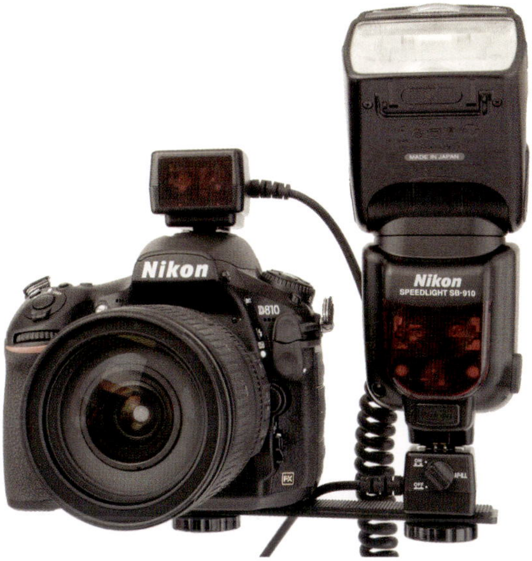

Figure 9.14 The Nikon SB-910 is currently the flagship of the Nikon electronic flash line up.

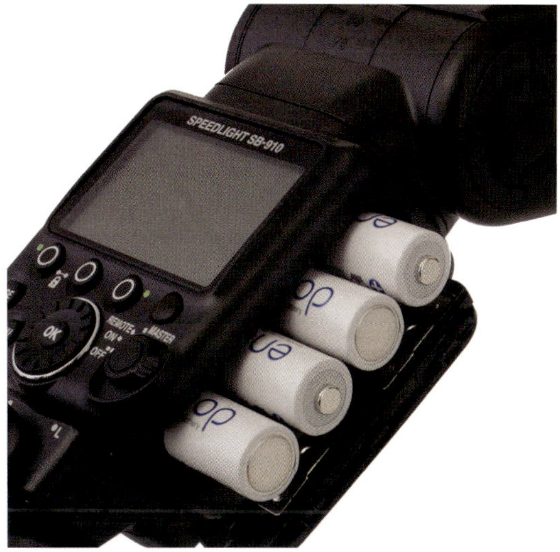

Figure 9.15 Sanyo's Eneloop AA batteries are a perfect power source for Nikon Speedlights.

some of these into your Speedlight, along with a few spares in your camera bag, and not worry about whether the batteries have retained their power between uses. There's nothing worse than firing up your strobe after not using it for a month, and discovering that the batteries are dead.

Note that the SB-910, like your camera, contains firmware that can be updated. The custom settings readouts on the flash itself will tell you what firmware version you currently have. If an update is required, you'll need to download the firmware module from the Nikon website. Load it onto a memory card, and then mount the flash on your D810 and power it up. You'll find a fourth entry in the Firmware section of the Setup menu, marked S (for Speedlight or Strobe). The SB-910's firmware can be updated through the camera/flash connection just like the camera's own firmware. I'll provide more information on firmware updates in Appendix D.

Light Modifiers

The SB-910 has a better array of included light modifying tools than other Speedlights in the Nikon line. The standard pop-up white "card" slides out of the flash head, as shown in Figure 9.16, to bounce a little fill illumination toward your subject when the flash is tilted to bounce off a ceiling or rotated and tilted to bounce off a wall or other surface. A wide-angle diffuser also slides out and rotates to cover the front of the flash and spread the light to cover lenses with focal lengths as wide as 12mm. The included diffuser dome (see Figure 9.17) provides softer illumination for direct flash, with the SB-910 pointed at your subject, or something of a "bare bulb" effect when pointed upward. (The "bare bulb" concept dates back to film days when an electronic flash, flashbulb (!), or even an incandescent lamp was used without a reflector or shade to provide a flood of soft illumination that spread out in all directions from the source.)

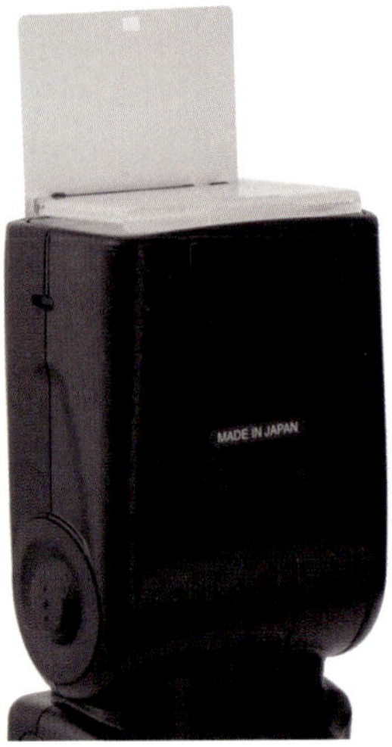

Figure 9.16 The slide-out bounce card adds a kicker of light to fill in shadows or provide a catch light in the eyes of human (or others).

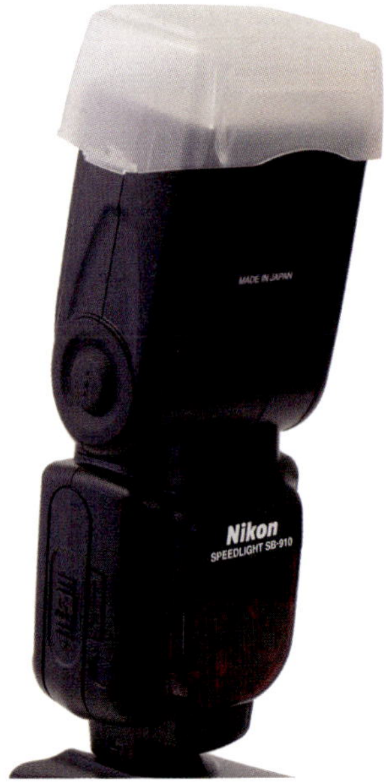

Figure 9.17 The included diffuser dome produces a soft, flattering light.

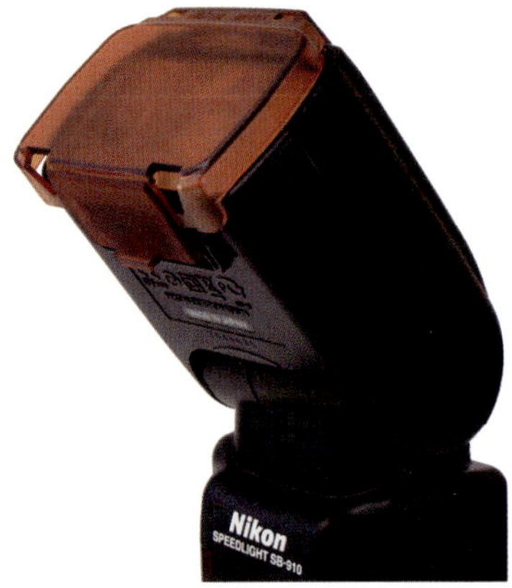

Figure 9.18 The SZ-2TN incandescent filter warms the flash's illumination to match tungsten lighting.

Various filters are available for the SB-910 (and other Nikon strobes) to change the color of the light source. Two are included with the unit, the SZ-2TN incandescent filter (shown in Figure 9.18), and the SZ-2FL fluorescent filter. The SJ-3 color filter set is 20 gelatin filters in eight different colors, including blue, yellow, red, and amber. The incandescent filter is most useful, because it changes the Speedlight's illumination to match typical indoor lamps, so you can use both to light a scene without encountering a nasty mixed lighting situation. The nifty thing about the SZ-series filters is that they include a type of bar code that can be read by a sensor underneath the SB-910's flash head, so the strobe (and your D810) "know" that a particular filter has been fitted.

Other Accessories

The SB-910 comes with the AS-21 Speedlight Stand, which lets you give the strobe a broad "foot" that can rest on any flat surface when working in wireless mode. The stand has a tripod-type socket underneath, so you can also mount the flash on a tripod or light stand without needing to purchase a special adapter.

Not included with the SB-910 are things like the WG-AS3 Water Guard, a $35 shield used when the flash is mounted on the D810, to protect the hot shoe contact from moisture or (more likely) driving rain in sports photography situations. Well-heeled photographers who shoot weddings or events and don't already own a Quantum battery pack may be interested in the SD-9 High Performance Battery pack ($255), which holds up to eight AA batteries; or the (now discontinued)

SK-6 Power Bracket, which could be outfitted with four AA batteries and provides a side-mounted handle as well as auxiliary power source.

Using Zoom Heads

External flash zoom heads can adjust themselves automatically to match lens focal lengths in use reported by the D810 to the flash unit, or you can adjust the zoom head position manually if you want to use a setting that doesn't correspond to the automatic setting the flash will use. With older flash units, like the discontinued SB-600, automatic zoom adjustment wastes some of your flash's power, because the flash unit assumes that the focal length reported comes from a full-frame camera. Because of the 1.5X crop factor the D810 is used in DX mode, so the flash coverage when the flash is set to a particular focal length will be wider than is required by the D810's cropped image.

You can manually adjust the zoom position yourself, using positions built-into the flash unit that more closely correspond to your D810's field of view when using a flash that does not, like the SB-910 and SB-900, automatically take into account the difference between FX (full-frame) and DX (APS-C) coverage. Table 9.1 shows the actual focal length of a lens (or focal length position of a zoom lens) in the left column, with the closest zoom head position on the flash unit in the right column.

To set the zoom position manually to a position of your choice (even if it doesn't match the actual focal length in use), follow one of these steps:

- **SB-910.** Press the Function 1 button to select the Zoom function, and then rotate the selector dial to set the zoom head position. A clockwise turn increases the value, while counterclockwise rotation decreases the zoom setting. Alternatively, you can press the Function 1 button repeatedly to increase the zoom value; it will wrap around to the widest position once you reach the maximum. To restore Power Zoom operation, press the Function 1 button to display Zoom, then press the Function 2 button. An "M" appears on the LCD above the Zoom indicator to show that the zoom setting has been made manually. An FX or DX indicator appears to the left, just above the Zoom indicator to show that the SB-910 is set for FX or DX coverage. Figure 9.19 shows the controls on the back of the SB-910 at left.

Table 9.1 Focal Length Equivalents for Zoom Heads

Lens Focal Length	Zoom head position	Lens Focal Length	Zoom head position
14mm	20mm	35mm	50mm
18mm	24mm	50mm	50mm
20mm	28mm	70mm	85mm
24mm	35mm	85mm	105mm
28mm	50mm		

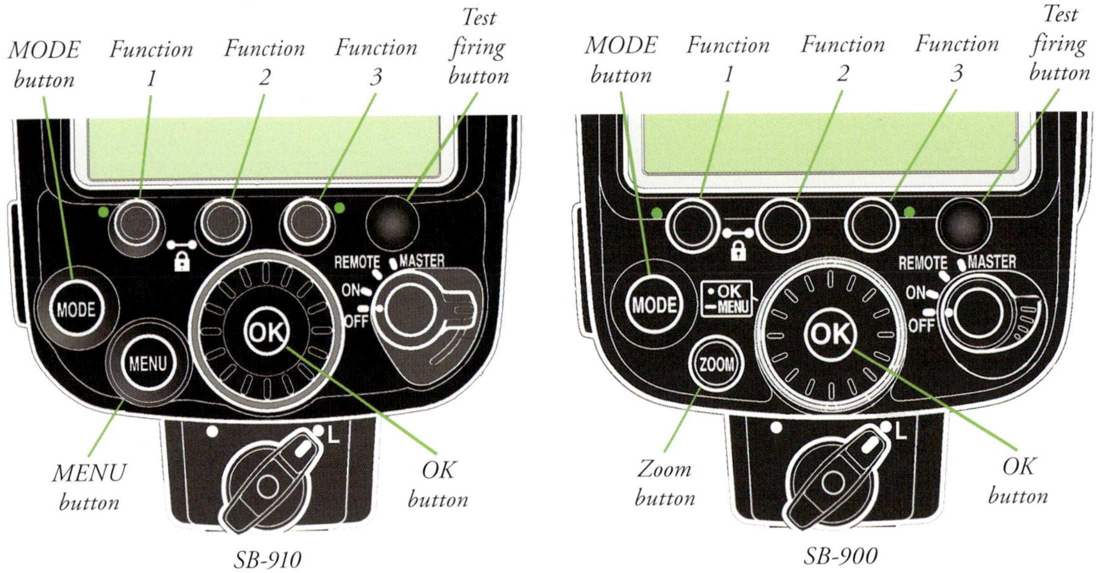

Figure 9.19 Flash head zoom settings can be set manually using the controls on the back of the SB-910 (left) and SB-900 (right).

- **SB-900.** Manually setting the zoom position is slightly different with the older SB-900 Speedlight. Press the Zoom button (located southwest of the selector dial/OK button pad) once, release it, and then rotate the selector dial until the zoom setting you want appears on the LCD. An "M" appears on the LCD above the Zoom indicator to show that the zoom setting has been made manually. An FX or DX indicator appears to the left, just above the Zoom indicator to show that the SB-900 is set for FX or DX coverage. You can also change the zoom setting by pressing the Zoom button repeatedly, in which case the focal length setting will jump from one increment to the next, wrapping around at 200mm back to the 12mm setting. Figure 9.19 shows the controls on the back of the SB-900 at right.
- **SB-700.** Press the Zoom button to the left of the selector dial to highlight Zoom on the flash's LCD screen. Then, rotate the control dial to the zoom position you want. Press the center OK button on the selector dial to confirm your setting. (You can also cycle through the available zoom settings by pressing the Zoom button repeatedly.) An M appears above the Zoom indicator on the LCD to show you've set the zoom value manually. To switch back to power zoom, press the Zoom button until the power zoom icon appears (it's the word "zoom" with a back-looping arrow). Then press the Sel (Select) button to confirm.
- **SB-600.** Press the Zoom button and adjust zoom position manually. M appears above Zoom in the LCD. To cancel manual zoom, press the zoom button until it matches the focal length set on the lens.

Flash Modes

The external flash units have various flash modes included, which are available or not available with different camera models, categorized into nine different groups that embrace the latest model dSLRs, some really ancient digital SLRs, and even more aged film cameras. A table showing most of the groups is included in the manuals for the external flash units, but the table is irrelevant for D810 users (unless you happen to own an older digital or film SLR, as well).

For digital cameras, there are two main groups: digital cameras *not* compatible with the Nikon Creative Lighting System (Nikon D1-series cameras, and the Nikon D100), and digital cameras that *are* compatible with CLS (including the D810). Groups I through VII, which support various combinations of features, consist of various film SLRs. You can ignore those options, unless you're using your external flash with an older film camera.

To change flash mode with the SB-910 or SB-900, press the MODE button on the back left edge, then release it and rotate the selector dial until the mode you want appears on the LCD. The TTL automatic flash modes available for the SB-910/SB-900 are described next. (The SB-700 has a sliding mode selector switch to the left of the Speedlight's LCD with positions for TTL, Manual, and GN settings. Those are the only modes available with that flash when you're using it as a Master. However, when the SB-700 is used as a remote flash triggered by a Master Commander flash, it can operate in Repeating mode.)

- **iTTL Automatic Balanced Fill Flash.** In both Matrix and Center-weighted camera exposure modes, the camera and flash balance the exposure so that the main subject and background are well exposed. A TTL BL indicator appears on the LCD. However, if you switch to Spot metering, the flash switches to standard iTTL, described next.
- **Standard iTTL.** In this mode, the exposure is set for the main subject, and the background exposure is not taken into account. A TTL indicator appears on the LCD. In either iTTL Automatic Balanced Fill Flash or Standard iTTL modes, if the full power of the flash is used, the ready light indicator on the flash and in the camera viewfinder will blink for three seconds. This is your cue that perhaps even the full power of the flash might not have been enough for proper exposure. If that's the case, an EV indicator will display the amount of underexposure (–0.3 to –3.0 EV) on the LCD while the ready light indicator flashes.
- **AA: Auto Aperture flash.** An A indicator next to an icon representing a lens opening/aperture is shown on the LCD when this mode is selected. The SB-910/SB-900 uses a built-in light sensor to measure the amount of flash illumination reflected back from the subject, and adjusts the output to produce an appropriate exposure based on the ISO, aperture, focal length, and flash compensation values set on the D810. This setting on the flash can be used with the D810 in Program or Aperture-priority modes.
- **A: Non-TTL auto flash.** To work with this mode, you must set the SB-910/SB-900 for its use using the flash's (not the camera's) Custom Settings menu. Press the OK button in the center of the flash unit's selector dial for about one second, and when the Custom Settings menu appears, rotate the selector dial to choose A. Press OK again, and you can choose from among

four variations, Auto Aperture Flash (described above) with or without monitor pre-flash, or Non-TTL auto flash, with or without monitor pre-flash. (Note that the manual calls these options "modeling illumination" instead.) In this mode, the Speedlight's sensor measures the flash illumination reflected back from the subject, and adjusts the output to provide an appropriate exposure, without the feedback about the aperture setting of the camera that's used with AA mode. This setting on the flash can be used when the D810 is set to Aperture-priority or Manual modes. You can use this setting to manually "bracket" exposures, as adjusting the aperture value of the lens will produce more or less exposure; the flash has no idea what aperture you've changed to.

- **GN: Distance priority manual.** You enter a distance value, and the SB-910/SB-900 adjusts light output based on distance, ISO, and aperture to produce the right exposure in either Aperture-priority or Manual exposure modes. Press the MODE button on the flash and rotate the selector dial until the GN indicator appears (the GN option appears only when the flash is pointed directly ahead, or is in the downward bounce position). Then press the OK button to confirm your choice. After that, you can specify a shooting distance by pressing Function 2 button, and then rotating the selector dial until the distance you want is indicated on the LCD. Press the OK button to confirm. The SB-910/SB-900 will indicate a recommended aperture, which you then set on the lens mounted on the D810 in Manual exposure mode.
- **M: Manual flash.** The flash fires at a fixed output level. Press the MODE button and rotate the selector dial until M appears on the LCD panel. Press the OK button to confirm your choice. Press the Function 1 button and rotate the selector dial to dial in the power output level you want. Calculate the correct f/stop to use, either by taking a few test photos, with a flash meter, or by the seat of your pants. Then, set the D810 to Aperture-priority or Manual exposure and choose the f/stop you've decided on. (You can also use manual flash with the D810's built-in unit by choosing a flash level in Custom Setting e3, as described in Chapter 12, and calculating the appropriate aperture.) (Good luck. I use test shots to calculate the f/stop, myself.)
- **RPT: Repeating flash.** The flash fires repeatedly to produce a multiple flash strobing effect. To use this mode, set the D810's exposure mode to Manual. Then set up the number of repeating flashes per frame, frequency, and flash output level, as described in Chapter 12. When using the D810's built-in flash, use Custom Setting e3; with the SB-910/SB-900, press the MODE button and rotate the selector dial to display RPT. Set the flash output level with Function 1 button and the selector dial, and choose the number of flashes with the Function 2 button and the selector dial. Finally, press Function 3 button and rotate the selector dial to choose the frequency. If you don't have a flash meter, the best way to decide what aperture to use on the camera in repeating mode is to take a few test shots.

Repeating Flash

Repeating flash is a function that can be used with the D810's built-in flash, as well as with external flashes like the SB-910 and SB-900. It can be used with a single flash, or in Advanced Wireless Lighting (AWL) mode, as described in Chapter 10. This section will introduce you to single-flash RPT mode. Just follow these steps:

1. **Set flash for RPT mode.** You can activate either the built-in unit or your external flash. For the D810's built-in flash, navigate to Custom Setting e3 and choose RPT: Repeating Flash and press OK to confirm. With the SB-910/SB-900, press the MODE button and rotate the selector dial until RPT is shown at upper left on the LCD. Then press the OK button to confirm.
2. **Choose Flash Output Level.** With either type of flash, you must specify the power level of the flash. That level will determine the range of the number of flashes you can expect from the capacitor's charge. With the built-in flash, Output is selected from the left column of the Repeating Flash screen (see Figure 9.20). With the SB-910/SB-900, press the Function 2 button (on the SB-910) or Function 1 button (on the SB-900) until the number of flashes is highlighted on the LCD (to the immediate right of the RPT indicator), and rotate the selector dial. Choose a power level from 1/4 to 1/128 (with the D810 built-in flash) or 1/8 to 1/128 power with the SB-910/SB-900.
3. **Select number of shots.** Next choose the number of shots in your series. With the built-in flash, the number is selected from the center column of the Repeating Flash screen. With the SB-910, highlight the option by pressing the Function 3 button; it's the Function 2 button on the SB-900. The number of shots you can specify varies depending on the shutter speed and firing frequency (specified next).
4. **Choose frequency: how many shots per second.** This determines how quickly the series is taken. The frequency is selected from the third column of the Repeating Flash screen when using the D810's built-in flash. With the SB-910, highlight the option by pressing the Function 3 button; it's the Function 2 button on the SB-900.

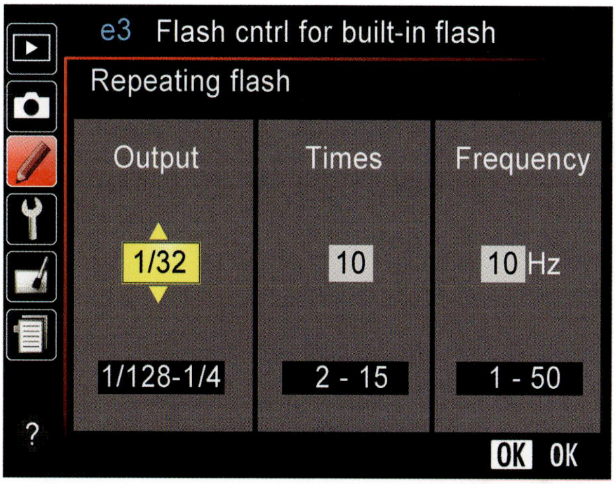

Figure 9.20
Set parameters for flash output level, number of shots, and frequency.

The maximum number of shots in a series varies, depending on the shutter speed, output level, and frequency you select. The multiple flashes can be emitted only while the shutter is completely open, so a faster shutter speed limits the number of bursts that can be fired off at a given frequency. High output levels and high frequency settings both deplete the capacitor more quickly. So, the number of possible bursts will depend on the combination you choose. With the SB-910, the maximum number of shots you can expect is about 90 (at 1/64 or 1/128 power), and frequencies of from 1-3 bursts per second. That's a large number of firings over a long period of time (30 seconds or more).

If you want very rapid bursts, expect fewer total flashes: the SB-910 will give you 24 firings at 1/128th power and 20-100 firings per second. Still, that's quite a bit of flexibility if you think about it. You can get 24 bursts in just a bit more than one second (at the 20 Hz setting) or over five seconds (at the 100Hz setting). With the built-in flash, your options are more limited: expect 2 firings at 1/4 power and up to 35 firings at 1/128th power.

BURN OUT

When using repeating flash with the built-in flash or the SB-910/SB-900 or SB-700, or *any* large number of consecutive flashes in any mode (more than about 15 shots at full power), allow the flash to cool off (Nikon recommends a 10-minute time out) to avoid overheating the flash. The SB-910 increases the recycling time to extend the useful period, while both the SB-910/SB-900 and SB-700 will signal you when it's time for a cooling-off period. The flash will actually disable itself, if necessary, to prevent damage.

10

Wireless and Multiple Flash

As I mentioned in the last chapter, one of the chief objections to the use of electronic flash is the stark, flat look of direct/on-camera flash, as you can see in Figure 10.1. But as flash wizard Joe McNally, author of *The Hotshoe Diaries*, has proven, small flash units can produce amazingly creative images when used properly.

An on-camera flash is useful for fill light or as a master flash to trigger other units; the real key to effective flash photography is to get the flash off the camera, so its illumination can be used to paint your subject in interesting and subtle ways from a variety of angles.

Of course, often, using a cable to liberate your external flash from the accessory shoe isn't enough. Nor is the use of just a single electronic flash always the best solution; two or more units can be combined in interesting ways to sculpt with light. What we have really needed is a way to trigger one—or more—flash units wirelessly, giving us the freedom to place the electronic flash anywhere in the scene and, if our budgets and time allow, to work in this mode with multiple flashes.

Nikon shooters have long had wireless flash capabilities, ever since the creation of the Nikon Creative Lighting System, described in Chapter 9. Like the i-TTL exposure system, the Advanced Wireless Lighting (AWL) system uses pre-flashes that fire before the main exposure to transmit triggering and exposure information to external flash units that aren't actually connected to the D810. Depending on whether you're using the D810's built-in flash or an external flash, you may be able to divide multiple flash units into up to three different "groups," and communicate with them using your choice of any of four "channels" (to avoid interference from other Nikon photographers within range of your flash units who might be using the same channel).

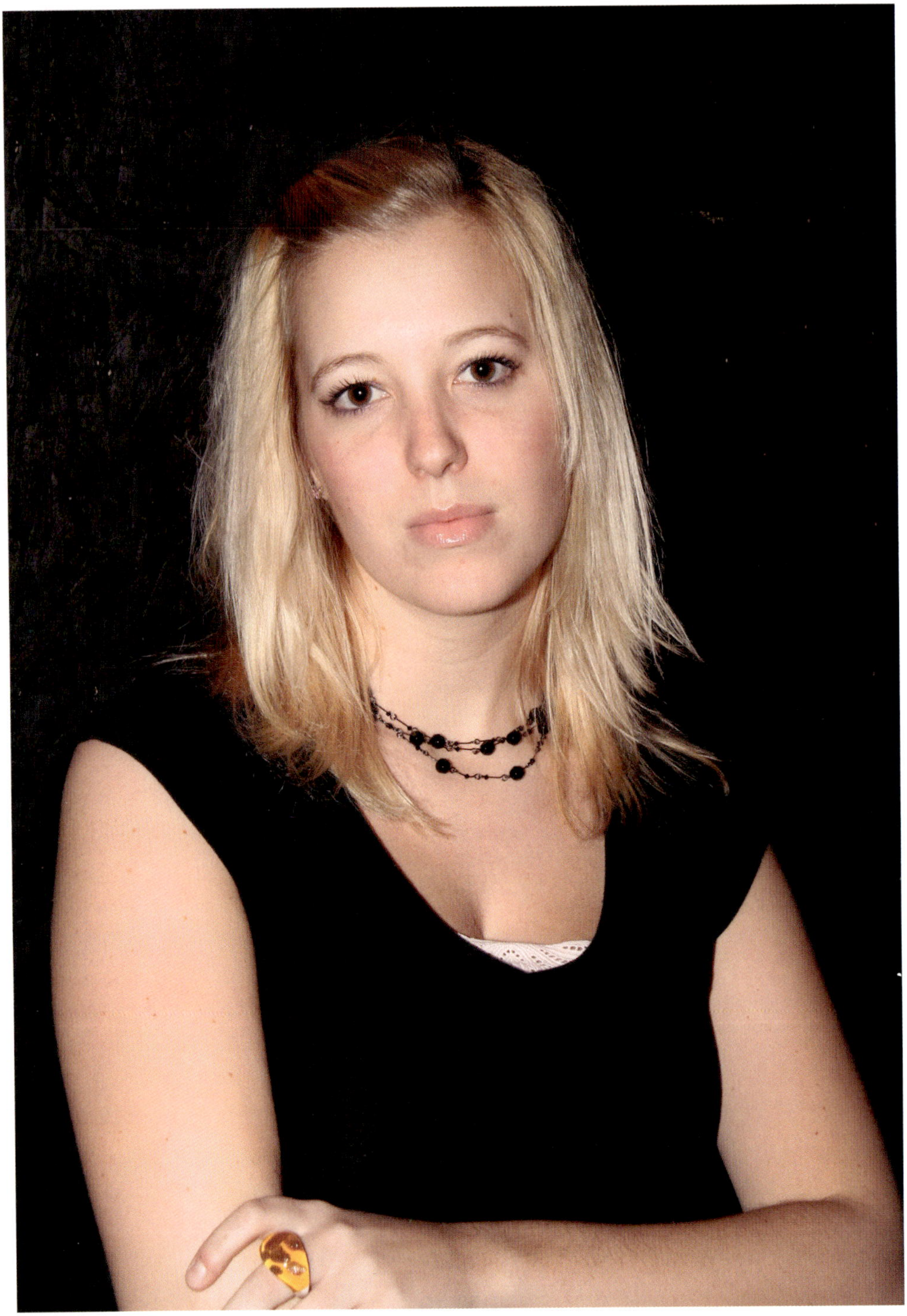

Figure 10.1 On-camera flash is often harsh and unflattering.

It's not possible to cover every aspect of wireless flash in one chapter. There are too many permutations involved. For example, you can use the D810's internal flash, an external flash like the SB-700 or SB-910/SB-900, an SU-800 wireless trigger, or a Pocket Wizard-type device as the master. You may have one external "slave" flash, or use several. It's possible to control all your wireless flash units as if they were one multi-headed flash, or you can allocate them into "groups" that can be managed individually. You may select one of four "channels" to communicate with your strobes. These are all aspects that you'll want to explore as you become used to working with the D810's wireless capabilities.

What I hope to do in this chapter is provide the introduction to the basics that you won't find in the other camera-based guidebooks, so you can learn how to operate the D810's wireless capabilities quickly, and then embark on your own exploration of the possibilities.

Elements of Wireless Flash

Here are some of the key concepts to electronic flash and wireless flash that I'll be describing in this chapter:

- **Master flash.** The *master* is the flash (or other device) that commands each of the additional flashes when using Commander mode.
- **Remote flashes.** For wireless operation, you need at least one more flash unit in addition to the master.
- **Channel controls.** Nikon's wireless flash system offers users the ability to determine on which of four possible channels the flash units can communicate.
- **Groups.** Nikon's wireless flash system lets you designate multiple flash units in separate groups (as many as three groups). You can then have flash units in one group fire at a different output than flash units in another group. This lets you create different styles of lighting for portraits and other shots.
- **Using flash ratios.** You can control the power of multiple off-camera Speedlights to adjust each unit's relative contribution to the image, for more dramatic portraits and other effects.

Master Flash

The master flash is the commander that tells all the other units in a setup what to do, including when to fire, and at what intensity. It communicates with your D810, and then, when the firing parameters are determined by the camera (or you, manually), passes along the information to the individual remote flash units.

Your master flash can be one of the following:

- **The Nikon D810's built-in flash.** Your camera's pop-up flash can be used as a master to trigger all the other units operating on the same channel. The D810's flash can contribute to the exposure (perhaps as fill light), or can be set to transmit *only* exposure/triggering information to the remote flash units.
- **An external flash with Commander capabilities.** Use a Nikon SB-910, SB-700, or compatible earlier units to communicate with the remote Speedlights. When used as a master flash, the external strobe must be physically connected to the D810. You can mount the flash on the camera's accessory hot shoe, or mount it on a cable, such as the SC-28 or SC-29, and then connect the other end of the cable to the D810's accessory shoe. (See Figure 10.2.) As with the built-in flash, the master flash can be set so that it does or does not contribute to the exposure, although, because it can be used off-camera, the latter mode offers more advantages.
- **The Nikon SU-800.** This device is an expensive non-flash (about $340) that does nothing but serve as a commander for CLS-compatible flash units. It mounts on the hot shoe of the camera (see Figure 10.3) and emits infrared signals (rather than monitor pre-flashes) to trigger the remote flash units. It otherwise functions exactly like a "real" master flash, communicating to

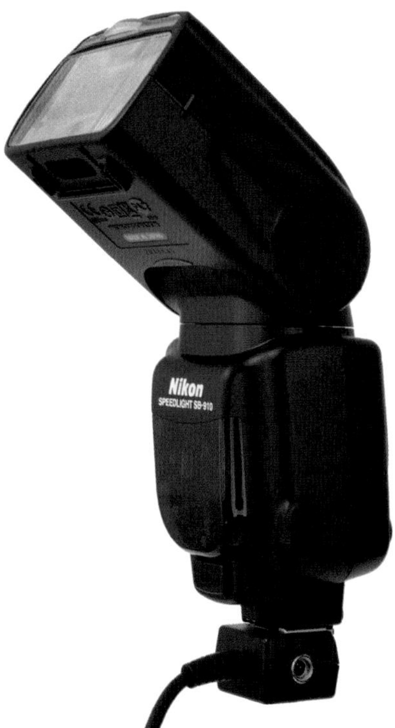

Figure 10.2 An external flash can be used as an off-camera master when connected to a cable that links it to the camera.

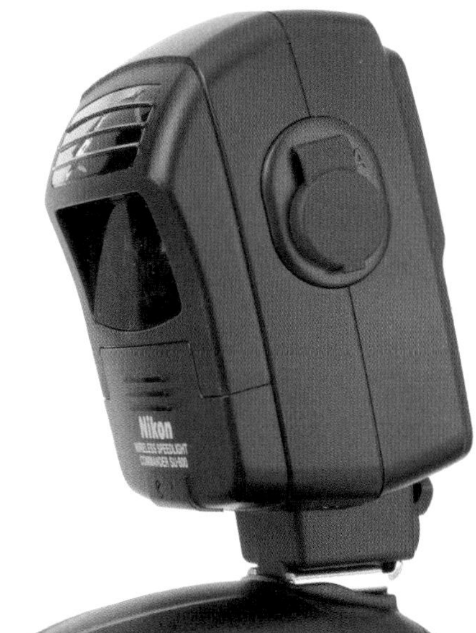

Figure 10.3 The Nikon SU-800 can serve as a master unit.

groups of Speedlights over the same channels, and allowing i-TTL exposure control. It has two main uses. One application is as a commander for Nikon's wireless "macro" lights, the SB-R200 units. In that mode, it's ideal for any Nikon dSLR, as it serves as a trigger for models without the built-in flash that the D810 has (such as the D4, D4s, D3, D3s, or D3x, and some earlier models). It's also a more convenient close-range substitute for the built-in flash of Nikon cameras like the D810 that include one.

I like to use mine for off-camera flash with no need to fuss with a cable connection or camera-mounted master flash unit. The owl shown at left in Figure 10.4 was perched on the limb of a fir tree, deep in shade. For the shot at right in the figure, a helper held my SB-910 flash eight feet off to the left while I concentrated on catching the bird's reactions. The SU-800's infrared control has an impressive 66-foot range under these conditions (that is, not under direct sunlight). It helped me capture the little owl using the off-camera flash (which provided a nice catchlight in the creature's eye) as the primary illumination.

- **Compatible third-party triggering devices.** These include models from PocketWizard and Radio Popper. The advantage of these devices is that, unlike the optical system used by Nikon's CLS products (limited to about 30 feet), third-party devices use radio control to extend your remote "reach" to as far as 1,500 feet or more. Their transmitters/receivers can work in concert with your own master flash, which controls the remote flashes normally when they're in range, with the radio control taking over when the transmitter senses that the remote flash isn't responding to the master's instructions.

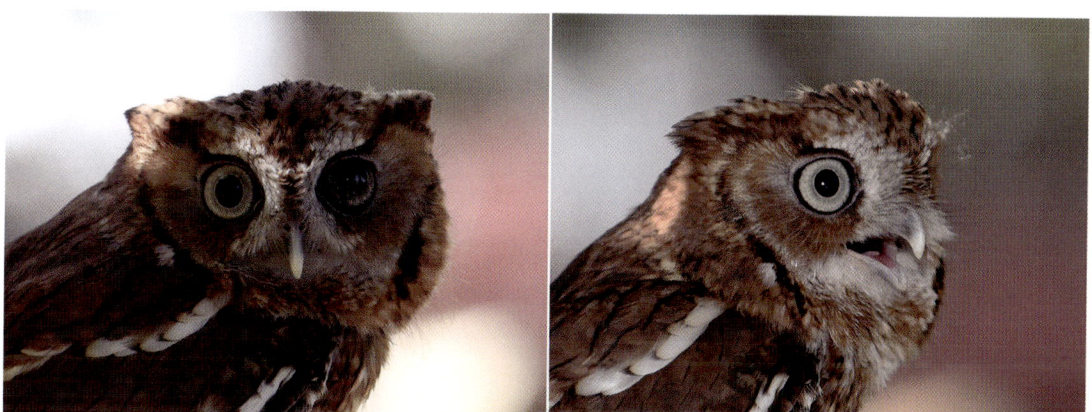

Figure 10.4 A flash can provide the predominant illumination outdoors in the shade.

POCKET WIZARDRY

I'm generally covering only Nikon-branded products in this book, because there are so many third-party devices that it's difficult to sort out all the options. However, one product line that stands head and shoulders above the rest and deserves special mention is the PocketWizard transmitters and receivers (www.pocketwizard.com). These devices attach to your camera (generally by mounting on the hot shoe) and connect to your flash to allow one or more flashes to communicate with the D810. The company makes several products specifically for Nikon cameras, including a transmitter, which locks onto the camera's accessory shoe (a shoe-mount flash can be mounted on top of the transmitter, if you wish). Your remote flash units can use PocketWizard transceivers.

The transmitter interprets the i-TTL data from the camera and converts it into a digital radio signal to command your remote flash units. Note that this radio control system is more versatile than the pulsed light pre-flashes and infrared communications the Speedlights and SU-800 use (respectively), working through walls and in bright daylight. The PocketWizard ControlTL system switches to high-speed sync mode automatically when you choose a fast shutter speed.

Remote Flashes

To use the Advanced Wireless System, you'll want to work with at least one remote, or slave flash unit. You can use units that are compatible with CLS or, with the (now discontinued) SU-4 accessory. The remote flash can be any unit compatible with the Creative Lighting System, including the current SB-910 and SB-700, or simpatico discontinued models, such as the SB-900, SB-800, or SB-600. (Of these, the SB-600 can't function as a master flash on its own.) You'll need to set the auxiliary Speedlights to remote mode, as I'll describe later.

Channels

Channels are the discrete lines of communication used by the master flash to communicate with each of the remote units. The pilots, ham radio operators, or scanner listeners among you can think of the channels as individual communications frequencies.

If you're working alone, you'll seldom have to fuss with channels. Just remember that all the Speedlights you'll be triggering must be using the same channel, exactly like a CB radio or walkie-talkie. (Google these terms if you're younger than 40.) If every flash isn't set for the same channel, they will be unable to "talk" to each other, good buddy. I'll show you how to adjust channels shortly.

The channel ability is most important when you're working around other photographers who are also using the same Nikon CLS system. Each photographer sets his or her flash units to a different channel as to not accidentally trigger other users' strobes. (At big events with more than four photographers using Nikon flash, you may need to negotiate.) Don't worry about Canon or Sony photographers at the same event. Their wireless flash systems use different communication systems that won't interfere with yours.

It's always a good idea to double-check your flash units before you set them up to make sure they're all set to the same channel, and this should also be one of your first troubleshooting questions if a flash doesn't fire the first time you try to use it wirelessly.

Groups

Each flash unit can be assigned to one of three groups, labeled A, B, and C. All the flashes in a particular group perform together as if they were one big flash, using the same output level and flash compensation values. That means you can control the relative intensity of flashes in each group, compared to the intensity of flashes assigned to a different group. A particular group needs at least one flash unit, but can have more.

For example, you could assign one (or more) flash to Group A, and use as the main light in your setup. Group B could be used as the fill light, and Group C designated as a hair or background light. The power output of each group could be set individually, so your main light(s) in Group A might be two or three times as intense as the light(s) in Group B (used for fill), while another power level could be set for the Group C auxiliary lights. You don't *have* to use all three groups, but it is an option.

But there's a lot more you can do if you've splurged and own two or more compatible external flash units (some photographers I know own five or six Nikon Speedlights). Nikon wireless photography lets you collect individual strobes into *groups*, and control all the Speedlights within a given group together. You can operate as few as two strobes in two groups or three strobes in three groups, while controlling more units if desired. You can also have them fire at equal output settings versus using them at different power ratios. Setting each group's strobes to different power ratios gives you more control over lighting for portraiture and other uses.

This is one of the more powerful options of the Nikon wireless flash system. I prefer to keep my Speedlights set to different groups normally. I can always set the power ratio to 1:1 if I want to operate the flash units all at the same power. If I change my mind and need to make adjustments, I can just change the wireless flash controller and then be able to manipulate the different groups' output as desired.

Remember that with whatever equipment you are using, outdoors you must have a clear line-of-sight between the master flash or SU-800 unit and sensors on the front of the slave flash units. Indoors, this requirement isn't as critical because the pre-flash and IR signals bounce off walls and other surroundings.

Lighting Ratios

Lighting ratios are the relative proportions of the illumination among the groups, as I just described. To get the most from the CLS system, you'll want to understand how ratios work. That's a topic that deserves a chapter of its own, but many Nikon D810 owners will already be familiar with the concept. If not, there are plenty of good books and online tutorials available.

Setting Your Master Flash

Nikon's wireless flash system gives you a number of advantages that include the ability to use directional lighting, which can help bring out detail or emphasize certain aspects of the picture area. It also lets you operate multiple strobes (although most of us won't own more than two Nikon Speedlights). You can set up complicated portrait or location lighting setups. Since the top-of-the line Nikon Speedlight SB-910 pumps out a lot of light for a shoe mount flash, a set of these units can give you near studio-quality lighting. Of course, the cost of these high-end Speedlights approaches that of some studio monolights—but the Nikon battery-powered units are more portable and don't require an external AC power source.

This chapter builds on the information in Chapter 9 and shows how to take advantage of the D810's wireless capabilities. While it may seem complicated at first, it really isn't. Learning the D810's controls takes a lot of effort, and once you get the hang of it, you'll be able to make changes quickly.

Since it's necessary to set up both the camera and the strobes for wireless operation, this guide will help you with both, starting with prepping the camera. To configure your camera for wireless flash, just follow these steps. (I'm going to condense them a bit, because many of these settings have been introduced in previous chapters.) I'm going to assume that you're using either your D810's built-in flash as your CLS master, or are using an external flash connected to the D810 as a master strobe.

Setting Commander Mode for the D810's Built-in Flash

Setting Commander mode for the built-in flash unit is confusing only because there are so many options. I'll run through each of them individually so you can see that it's easier than it looks. Here are the instructions you need to use the built-in flash as the Commander unit, with each of the external flashes set up individually as remotes.

1. **Access Flash Control for Built-In Flash.** Navigate to Custom Setting e3, and choose Commander Mode. A screen like the one shown in Figure 10.5 appears.
2. **Choose Built-in Flash.** Use the multi selector left/right buttons to highlight Mode in the Built-in Flash row, then press the up/down buttons to choose the mode you want to use. Select from:
   - **TTL.** This activates i-TTL exposure calculation; the D810 will initiate pre-flashes for the built-in flash plus any linked flashes using the same channel, and then set the exposure, taking into account any Flash Exposure Compensation you specify in the Comp. column for the built-in flash.
   - **M (Manual).** If you select Manual, the Comp column changes to indicate power ratios, from 1/1 (full power) to 1/128th power.
   - **-- (Flash disabled).** The built-in flash will not emit a main burst (contributing to the overall exposure), but will instead only fire the pre-flashes needed to measure/set exposure of the external Speedlights, and to trigger their main bursts. In effect, this disables the built-in flash, but allows it to function as a commander for the other strobes on that channel.

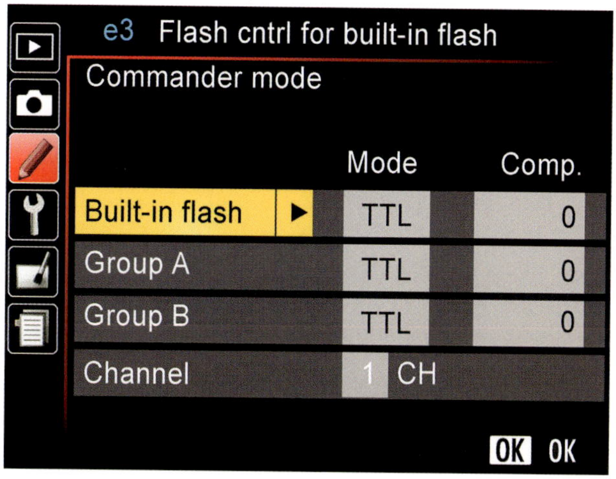

Figure 10.5 Commander mode for the built-in flash can be set in the Custom Settings menu.

3. **Dial in Flash Exposure Compensation.** Next, use the multi selector right button to highlight the Comp. parameter in the third column. If you choose TTL, you can select exposure compensation from –3 to +3.0 in increments of 1/3 EV; choose M, and you can set flash output from 1/1 to 1/128; choose - - and the pre-flashes will still be used to control any remote units in use, but the built-in flash will not fire to contribute to the exposure.
4. **Set mode for Group A external flashes.** Use the multi selector right button to move down to Group A to select TTL, Manual, or - - exposure (to deactivate that group), plus an additional choice, AA, which is Auto Aperture mode, which switches exposure control from i-TTL to measurement using the external flash's own (non-through-the-lens) light sensor. The external flash evaluates the amount of light reflecting from the subject and adjusts the flash's output to produce an appropriate exposure based on the ISO, aperture, focal length, and flash compensation values set on the D810. This setting on the flash can be used with the D810 in Program or Aperture-priority modes.
5. **Set Group A Flash Exposure Compensation.** Move to the right in the Group A row and set any exposure compensation you want in the Comp. column. The options for TTL and AA modes are the same as when using TTL with the built-in flash. The M and - - options are the same, too.
6. **Set mode and Flash Exposure Compensation for Group B (if used).** If you elect to use a second group, you can set the mode and exposure compensation for Group B in the same way as for Group A. Just repeat Steps 4 and 5 for the additional group. Note that when using the built-in flash as the commander, you can select only Group A and Group B. Group C is not available (actually, the built-in flash itself is Group C, although Nikon doesn't tell you that).

7. Use the multi selector right button to highlight the Channel setting, and use the up/down buttons to select the channel, from 1 to 4, that all the flash units will communicate over. Most of the time you can select a channel once, and then forget about it. You'll need to switch to another channel only when you want to avoid interference with other nearby Nikon photographers.
8. Press OK when finished.

Setting Commander Modes for the SB-910 or SB-900

Setting Commander modes for the SB-910/SB-900 has been greatly simplified, compared to some previous Nikon Speedlights. If you'd rather use an attached flash as the master, just rotate the On/Off/Wireless mode switch to the Master position.

As with the D810's built-in flash, you'll want to tell the SB-910/SB-900 which channel it is using to communicate with the other Speedlights. You'll need to do this separately for each of the SB-910/SB-900 units you are working with, if you're using more than one. Here are the steps to follow. (I recommend doing several dry runs to see how setting up multiple flashes works before trying it "live.") The steps are almost identical between the SB-910 and SB-900 (shown at the bottom of Figure 10.6), differing primarily in the Function buttons used. In each case, the buttons numbered 1 through 3 are the first three buttons just south of the LCD panel starting from left to right.

1. **Set master flash to Commander mode.** On the master flash, rotate the power switch to the Master position, holding down the center lock release button of the switch so that it will move to the Master position. (This extra step is needed because Nikon knows you won't want to accidentally change from Master to Remote.)
2. **Access Mode.** Press the Function 2 button (Function 1 button on the SB-900) to highlight M on the LCD. (Note: M in this case stands for Master, not Manual.)
3. **Select Mode.** Press the MODE button and then spin the selector dial to choose the flash mode you want to use for that flash unit, from among TTL, A (Auto Aperture), M (Manual), or - -. Then, press OK.

Reminder

At the - - setting, the master flash is disabled; it will trigger the other units, but its flash won't contribute to the exposure—except if you're shooting very close to the subject using a high ISO setting. If an external flash is the master, try tilting or rotating the flash head away from your subject to minimize this spill-over effect.

4. **Set Flash Exposure Compensation.** Press the Function 3 button (Function 2 button on the SB-900), and rotate the selector dial to choose the flash compensation level (–3 to +3) or manual power level (1/1 to 1/128). The amount of EV correction appears at the right side, opposite the master flash's mode indicator.
5. **Specify group.** Press the Function 2 button (Function 1 button on the SB-900) to move on to the Group Selection option. Press OK to choose Group A, or rotate the selector dial to choose Group B or C, then press OK to confirm the group you've chosen.

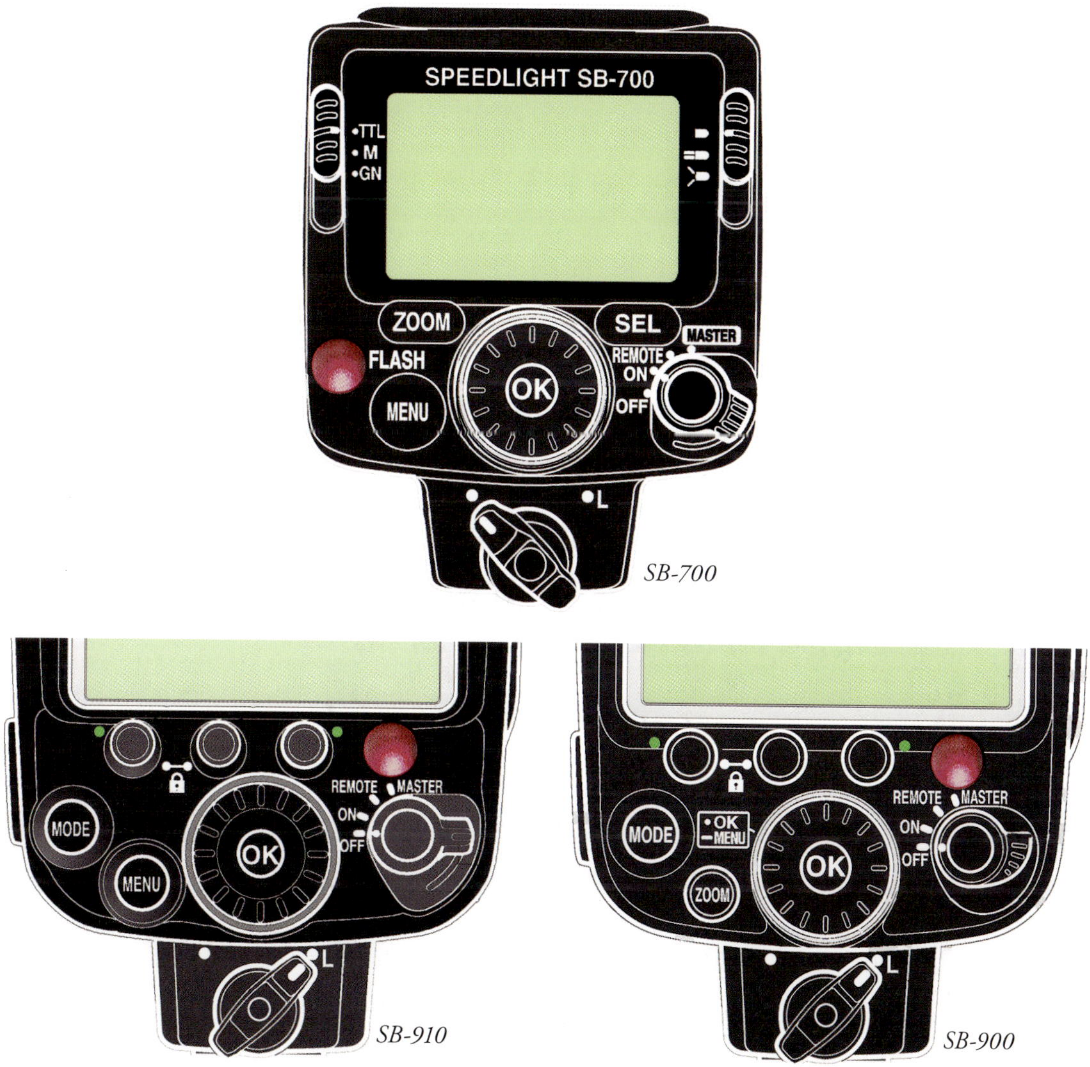

Figure 10.6 Location of the control buttons on the SB-700, SB-910, and SB-900 Speedlights.

6. **Set modes for group.** Once a group is highlighted, select the mode for that group. Press the MODE button and then spin the selector dial to choose the flash mode you want to use for that flash unit, from among TTL, A (Auto Aperture), M (Manual), or - -. Then, press OK.
7. **Set Flash Exposure Compensation for group.** Press the Function 3 button (Function 2 button on the SB-900), and rotate the selector dial to choose the flash compensation level for the current group as you did in Step 3. The amount of EV correction appears at the right side, opposite the group's mode indicator.
8. **Repeat for other groups.** If you're using Group B and Group C, repeat steps 4-6 to set the mode and Flash Exposure Compensation for the additional groups.
9. **Specify channel.** Once the modes and compensation for all the groups have been set on the master flash, press the Function 3 button (Function 2 button on the SB-900) and rotate the selector dial to set a channel number that the master flash will use to control its groups.
10. **Set up remote flashes.** Now take each of the remote flash units and set the correct group and channel number you want to use for each of them. I'll describe this step later.

Setting Commander Modes for the SB-700

Setting Commander modes for the SB-700 is similar in concept to the settings for the SB-910 or SB-900. The controls for the SB-700 are shown at top in Figure 10.6. If you want to use an attached SB-700 as the master flash, follow these steps:

1. **Set master flash to Commander mode.** On the master flash, rotate the power switch to the Master position, holding down the center lock release button of the switch so that it will move to the Master position.
2. **Choose mode.** There's a sliding switch on the left side of the SB-700. You can choose TTL, M (Manual), or GN modes.
3. **Set Flash Exposure Compensation.** Press the SEL button to select the master flash, then choose a flash compensation value/output level using the selector dial. Press OK to confirm.
4. **Specify group.** Press the SEL button to move on to the Group Selection option. Press OK to choose Group A, or rotate the selector dial to choose Group B. (Group C is not available with the SB-700.) Set the flash exposure compensation value for each group using the selector dial. Then press OK to confirm.
5. **Specify channel.** Once the modes and compensation for all the groups have been set on the master flash, press the SEL button to highlight the Channel, then rotate the selector dial to set a channel number that the master flash will use to control its groups.
6. **Set up remote flashes.** Now take each of the remote flash units and set the correct group and channel number you want to use for each of them. I'll describe this step next.

Setting Remote Modes

Each of the external remote flash units must be set to Remote mode, whether you are using the D810's built-in flash as the master, or another external flash as the commander. Here's how to set up the Nikon SB-700, SB-900, and SB-910 Speedlights as remote slave flash units. Note that you don't need to specify compensation/output level; that's handled by the master/commander flash. You just need to set the flash to Remote, then choose Group, Channel, and Zoom head function.

1. **Switch flash to remote mode.** With the SB-900/SB-910 or SB-700, rotate the power switch to the Remote position, holding down the center lock release button of the switch so that it will move to the Remote position.
2. **Select group.** With the SB-910, press the Function 2 button (Function 1 button on the SB-900) and choose Group A with the selector dial, and press OK. With the SB-700, press the SEL button to highlight the group, then press OK. Repeat for Group B or (with the SB-900/SB-910 only) Group C.
3. **Set channel.** Press the Function 2 button to highlight the channel. If you're using the SB-700, press the SEL button until the channel is highlighted. Then, rotate the selector dial to choose the channel number. Make sure you choose the same channel number you set earlier on the master flash. Press OK to confirm.
4. **Choose zoom head position.** With the SB-910, press the the Function 1 button (or the Zoom button on the SB-900 or SB-700) to highlight Zoom Head Position, and choose a zoom head setting with the selector dial. Press OK to confirm. With the SB-900 and SB-700 push the Zoom button multiple times to change zoom settings.
5. **Repeat for each remote flash.** If you're using more than one remote/slave flash, repeat Steps 1-4 for each of the additional CLS-compatible units.

Part IV

Configuring Your Nikon D810

The next three chapters are devoted to helping you dig deeper into the customization capabilities of your Nikon D810, so you can exploit all those cool features that your previous camera lacked. Chapters 11, 12, and 13 list every setting and option found in the Playback, Shooting, Custom Settings, Setup, and Retouch menus, and My Menu. Your setup options include:

- **Chapter 11:** With a camera that sports two memory card slots, it's important to be able to specify which card and which folder of images is displayed during image review. I'll show you how with the Playback menu. You'll discover an easy way to specify exactly which information screens are displayed, and my advice on copying images from one card to another. Then, we'll move on to the Shooting menu, with its important tools including HDR, vignetting and distortion control, multiple exposures, and Picture Controls.
- **Chapter 12:** You'll find a mind-boggling 65 Custom Setting entries in seven different categories (and many of those have three or more sub-options) that let you fine-tune everything from autofocus and metering to the functions assigned to various buttons and dials. If your D810 doesn't behave exactly as you'd like, you can probably tweak it with one of the recommendations I provide in this chapter.
- **Chapter 13:** In the Setup and Retouch menus and My Menu, you'll be able to fine-tune your D810's autofocus, work with an optional GPS attachment, manage monitor brightness, and manipulate your images *after* they are stored on your memory card. If you don't like the Nikon D810's menu layout, you can create your own menu system, too.

11

Playback and Shooting Menus

My job is to be your guide on a wild trip down the rabbit hole, where Menuland rivals Wonderland in its possibility to confuse and confound you. Under that thicket of choices is the kind of versatility that makes the Nikon D810 one of the most customizable, tweakable, and fine-tunable cameras Nikon has ever offered. If your camera doesn't behave in exactly the way you'd like, chances are you can make a small change in the Playback, Shooting, Custom Settings, and Setup menus that will tailor the D810 to your needs.

However, just telling you what your options are and what they do doesn't really give you the information you need to use your camera to its fullest. What you really want to know is *why* you would want to choose a particular option, and *how* making a particular change will help improve your photographs in a given situation. That's a big job, and I'm going to devote three entire chapters to demystifying the D810 menu choices for you.

This chapter will help you sort out the settings for the Playback and Shooting menus, which determine how the D810 displays images on review, and how it uses many of its shooting features to take a photo. The following chapters will focus on the Custom Settings menu (Chapter 12), and Setup, Retouch, and My Menu options (Chapter 13).

As I've mentioned before, this book isn't intended to replace the manual you received with your D810, nor have I any interest in rehashing its contents. You'll still find the original manual useful as a standby reference that lists every possible option in exhaustive (if mind-numbing) detail—without really telling you how to use those options to take better pictures. There is, however, some unavoidable duplication between the Nikon manual and the next three chapters, because, like the

Nikon book, I'm going to explain all the key menu choices and the options you may have in using them. You should find, though, that I will give you the information you really require in a much more helpful format, with plenty of detail on why you should make some settings that are particularly cryptic.

I'm not going to waste a lot of space on some of the more obvious menu choices in these chapters. For example, you can probably figure out that the Beep option in Custom Setting d1 deals with the solid-state beeper in your camera that sounds off during various activities (such as the self-timer countdown). You can certainly decipher the import of the two options available for the Beep entry (Volume and Pitch). In this chapter, I'll devote no more than a sentence or two to the blatantly obvious settings and concentrate on the more confusing aspects of the D810 setup, such as automatic exposure bracketing. I'll start with an overview of using the D810's menus themselves.

Anatomy of the Nikon D810's Menus

If you used any Nikon digital SLR before you purchased your Nikon D810, you're probably already familiar with the basic menu system. The menus consist of a series of screens with entries, as shown in the illustration of the Playback menu (discussed next) in Figure 11.1. Navigating among the various menus is easy and follows a consistent set of rules:

- **View menu.** Press the MENU button on the left side of the back of the camera to display the main menu screens.
- **Navigate main menu headings.** Use the multi selector's left/right/up/down buttons to navigate among the menu entries to highlight your choice. Moving the highlighting to the left column lets you scroll up and down among the six top-level menus. From the top in Figure 11.1, they are Playback, Shooting, Custom Settings, Setup, Retouch, and My Menu, with Help access represented by a question mark at the bottom of the column.
- **Choose a top-level menu.** A highlighted top-level menu's icon will change from black-and-white to yellow highlighting. Use the multi selector's right button to move into the column containing that menu's choices. The selected top-level menu's icon will change from yellow to a color associated with that menu (blue for Playback, green for Shooting, red for Custom Settings, orange for Setup, purple for Retouch, and gray for My Menu).
- **Select a menu entry.** Use the up/down buttons to scroll among the entries. If more than one screen full of choices is available, a scroll bar appears at the far right of the screen, with a position slider showing the relative position of the currently highlighted entry.
- **Choose options.** To work with a highlighted menu entry, press the OK button at lower left on the back of the D810 or, more conveniently, just press the right button on the multi selector. Any additional screens of choices will appear. You can move among them using the same multi selector movements.

- **Confirm your choice.** You can activate a selection by pressing the OK button or, frequently, by pressing the right button on the multi selector once again. Some functions require scrolling to a Done menu choice, or include an instruction to Set a choice using some other button.
- **Exit menus.** Pressing the multi selector left button usually backs you out of the current screen, and pressing the MENU button again usually does the same thing. You can exit the menu system at any time by tapping the shutter release button.
- **Returning to an entry.** The Nikon D810 "remembers" the top-level menu and specific menu entry you were using (but not any submenus) the last time the menu system was accessed, so pressing the MENU button brings you back to where you left off. So, if you were working with an entry in the Custom Settings menu's Metering/Exposure section, then decided to take a photo, the next time you press the MENU button the Custom Settings menu and the Metering/Exposure entry will be highlighted, but not the specific submenu (b1 through b7) that you might have selected.
- **Accessing a frequently used entry.** If you use the same menu items over and over, you can create a My Menu listing of those entries. Or, if you'd rather have a rotating listing of the last 20 menu items you accessed, you can convert My Menu to a Recent Settings menu instead. I'll show you exactly how to do that in Chapter 13.

As I noted, the top-level menus are color-coded with accents within the menu itself, most notably a half-frame that underlines the menu title and runs down the left side of the menu entries. The colors are: Playback menu (blue); Shooting menu (green); Custom Settings menu (red); Setup menu (orange); Retouch menu (purple); and My Menu (gray). The Custom Settings menu has seven submenus that are themselves color-coded to help you keep track of where you are located in the menu system. You'll learn about the Custom Settings, Setup, Retouch, and My Menu options in Chapters 12 and 13.

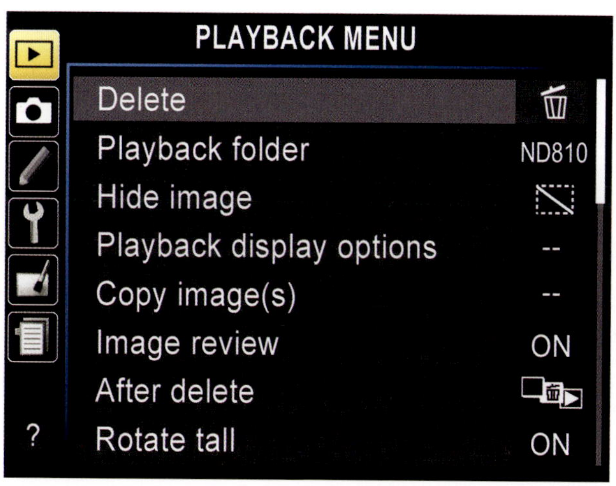

Figure 11.1
The multi selector's navigational buttons are used to move among the various menu entries shown here.

Playback Menu Options

The blue-coded Playback menu, shown previously in Figure 11.1, has ten entries where you select options related to the display, review, transfer, and printing of the photos you've taken. The choices you'll find include the following entries (the last two, Slide Show and Print Set [DPOF], are not pictured in Figure 11.1, and don't appear until you scroll the listing on the screen to the bottom):

- Delete
- Playback Folder
- Hide Image
- Playback Display Options
- Copy Image(s)
- Image Review
- After Delete
- Rotate Tall
- Slide Show
- DPOF Print Order

Delete

Choose this menu entry and you'll be given two choices: Selected and All. If you choose All, then all the pictures in the folder currently selected for playback will be removed. When two memory cards are in the camera and have photos, you can choose which card to use to select images for removal (as described next). To delete only some pictures from a folder, choose Selected, and you'll see an image selection screen. Then, follow these instructions:

1. **Choose card and folder.** If you have pictures on both the CF and SD cards, you can choose the card to delete images from. When the screen like the one shown in Figure 11.2 appears, press the Zoom Out/Index button, and a dialog box will pop up allowing you to select a card.
2. **Select image.** Use the multi selector cursor keys to scroll among the available images.
3. **Evaluate image.** When you highlight an image you think you might like to delete, press the Zoom In button to temporarily enlarge that image so you can evaluate it further. When you release the button, the selection screen returns.

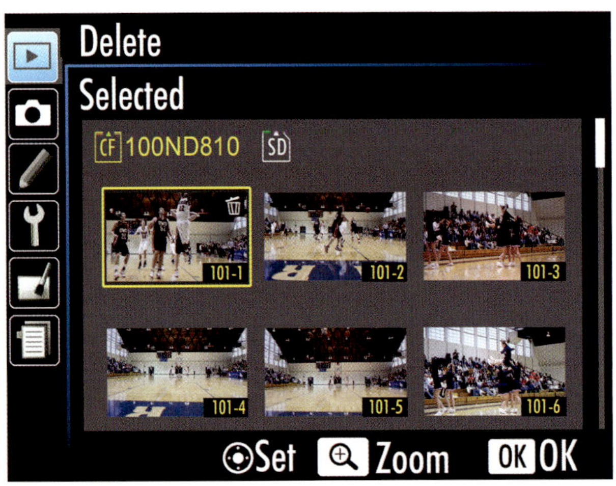

Figure 11.2
Select images to delete.

4. **Mark images.** To mark an image for deletion, press the multi selector center button (*not* the Trash button). A trash can icon will appear overlaid on that image's thumbnail. To unmark an image, press the multi selector center button again.
5. **Delete images.** When you've finished marking images to delete, press OK. A final screen will appear asking you to confirm the removal of the image(s). Choose Yes to delete the image(s) or No to cancel deletion, and then press OK. If you selected Yes, then you'll return to the Playback menu; if you chose No, you'll be taken back to the selection screen to mark/unmark images.
6. **Exit Delete menu.** To back out of the selection screen, press the MENU button.

Using this menu to delete images will have no effect on images that have been marked as protected with the Protect key. Keep in mind that deleting images in this way is slower than just wiping out the whole card with the Format command, so using Format is generally much faster than choosing Delete: All, and also is a safer way of returning your memory card to a fresh, blank state.

Playback Folder

Your Nikon D810 will create folders on your memory card to store the images that it creates. It assigns the first folder a number, like 100ND810, and when that folder fills with 999 images, the camera automatically creates a new folder numbered one higher, such as 101ND810. If you use the same memory card in another camera, that camera will also create its own folder. Thus, you can end up with several folders on the same memory card, until you eventually reformat the card and folder creation starts anew.

This menu item allows you to choose which folders are accessed when displaying images using the D810's Playback facility. Your choices are as follows:

- **ND810.** The camera will use only the folders on your memory card created by the D810 and ignore those created by other cameras. Images in all the D810's folders will be displayed. This is the default setting.
- **All.** All folders containing images that the D810 can read will be accessed, regardless of which camera created them. You might want to use this setting if you swap memory cards among several cameras and want to be able to review all the photos (especially when considering reformatting the memory card). You will be able to view images even if they were created by a non-Nikon camera if those images conform to the Design Rule for Camera File system (DCF) specifications.
- **Current.** The D810 will display only images in the current folder. For example, if you have been shooting heavily at an event and have already accumulated more than 999 shots in one folder (or an image has been stored that's numbered 9999) and the D810 has created a new folder for the overflow, you'd use this setting to view only the most recent photos, which reside in the current folder. You can change the current folder to any other folder on your memory card using the Active Folder option in the Shooting menu, described later in this chapter.

Hide Image

Use this menu option to protect *and* hide images. When you choose Hide Image, you'll be given a choice to select/set images (using a selection screen almost identical to the one used to delete images, as shown earlier in Figure 11.2) or the option of deselecting all hidden images.

Unlike the Protect option, which just *marks* images to keep them from accidental deletion, this selection also hides them from view using the regular Playback functions. Pictures that have been hidden can only be viewed from the selection screen. I use this facility in two different ways:

- **Hide non-relevant images.** Sometimes I have a memory card filled with images and I want to show some of the images, perhaps as a slideshow, or sometimes just by handing the camera to someone and asking them to browse through the photos. I can hide the non-relevant images so only the relevant pictures appear.
- **Bury your mistakes.** Hiding images is a good way to make your real stinkers invisible from the eyes of those who otherwise respect your work, if you haven't quite made up your mind to delete them. Tuck them out of view until you move them to your computer, or get up the courage to nuke them forever.

Remember that if you "unhide" an image you are also removing the Protect attribute. If you want the photo to be visible, but still protected, press the Protect button (it has a key icon as a label) while viewing the image on the LCD monitor. The key icon will be superimposed on the image, showing you that it is now protected from accidental erasure. Reformatting the card removes the Hidden and Protected attributes, of course—because it removes those images as well!

Playback Display Options

You'll recall from Chapter 2 that a great deal of information, available on multiple screens, can be displayed when reviewing images. This menu item helps you reduce/increase the clutter by specifying which information and screens will be available. To activate or deactivate an info option, scroll to that option and press the right multi selector button to add a check mark to the box next to that item. Press the right button to unmark an item that has previously been checked. Important: when you're finished, you must scroll up to Done and press OK or the right multi selector button to confirm your choices. Exiting the Display mode menu any other way will cause any changes you may have made to be ignored. Your info options include:

- **Focus point.** Activate this option to display the active focus point(s) with red highlighting, as shown in Figure 11.3.
- **None.** A screen with the image only and no photo information will be displayed.
- **Highlights.** When enabled, overexposed highlight areas in your image will blink with a black border during picture review. That's your cue to consider using exposure compensation to reduce exposure, unless a minus-EV setting will cause loss of shadow detail that you want to preserve. You can read more about correcting exposure in Chapter 4.

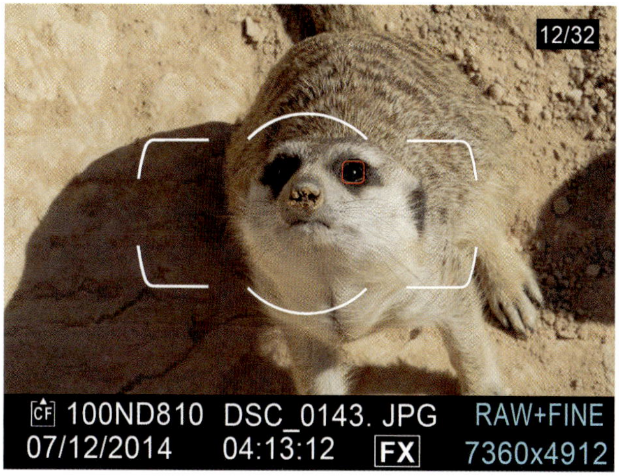

Figure 11.3
Use the Display Mode menu entry to activate data display, like the focus point shown in this reviewed image.

- **RGB histogram.** Displays both luminance (brightness) and RGB histograms on a screen that can be displayed using the up/down multi selector buttons, as shown in Chapter 2. If you're viewing this histogram with the Highlights display enabled, you can change the Highlights focus from the luminance histogram to any of the three RGB channels by holding down the Thumbnail button and pressing the multi selector right button until the channel you want is selected. I explained the use of this feature in Chapter 4.
- **Shooting Data.** Activates the pages of shooting data shown in Chapter 2.
- **Overview.** Activates the overview screen shown in Chapter 2.

Copy Image(s)

The ability to work with two memory cards simultaneously ranked as my absolutely favorite new feature when the first Nikons to offer dual slots were introduced in 2007. One of the best uses for two cards is to make back-up images while traveling, or at any other time that your computer isn't easily accessible. Here are some examples of what I do:

- **Shoot to two cards simultaneously.** This gives you an instant backup in case pictures on your primary card become corrupt or erased. Ideally, your two cards should be equal in storage size.
- **Make a copy.** Use this Copy Image(s) facility to make a copy of images you shot on one card to your second card. Instead of shooting on two cards at once (which does slow down the D810 a bit), use only one card when you take photos, then make a backup onto a second card at the end of the day. You can copy all or only some of the photos you've shot.
- **Make copies to distribute.** I bought a bunch of 8GB memory cards for $5.98 each, and find it's quick and easy to make multiple copies of photos, not for backup, but for distribution either on the spot, say, to provide models I've hired with some raw (not RAW) images or to send by snail mail to colleagues, friends, or family that I want to share photos with. No computer required!

- **Leave your laptop or external storage at home.** Since I've begun using Nikon cameras with dual memory card slots, I leave my hard disk/personal storage device with its built-in reader or my laptop at home more often. If I am going to be gone for only a day or two, it's easier to just make copies in the camera, and not bother with another external device.

To copy images from one card to another, just follow these steps (which are available only when two memory cards are present in the camera):

1. **Access copy menus.** Choose Copy Image(s) from the Playback menu. There are four choices that may be available to you: Select Source; Select Image(s); Select Destination Folder; and Copy Image(s)?.
   - If you have images on only one card, all other choices will be grayed out, and the card containing images will be selected. In the Copy Image(s) menu, Select Image(s) will be preselected for you.
   - If there are images on both cards already, you can choose Select Source to specify either the SD or CF card slot as the source to copy from or you can Select Image(s) if the source displayed is satisfactory. (See Figure 11.4, left.)
   - If you have already marked some images previously, then all four choices will be available.
2. **Select Source or copy.** Press the right button on the multi selector to perform the task of your choice:
   - Choose Select Source, then highlight SD or CF and press OK.
   - Choose Select Image(s) and continue to Step 3.
   - Choose Select Destination Folder and continue to Step 3.
   - If you've chosen source, destination, and images, choose Copy Image(s)? and skip to Step 4.
3. **Select destination folder or images.** Perform one or both of these tasks.
   - If you are choosing a destination folder, you can select by folder number (either a current folder number or one you create by specifying a number for the new folder), or choose from a list of existing folders. Press OK when finished to return to the Copy Image(s) menu.
   - If you are selecting images (as shown in Figure 11.4, right), you can Deselect All images to cancel previous selections (and then proceed to mark individual images with the Thumbnail/Zoom Out button); Select All Images to view a screen similar to the one shown previously in Figure 11.2, where you can mark and unmark specific thumbnails (Hidden images cannot be copied); or Select Protected Images to choose from among images you've previously marked with the Protect key (located just under the MENU button). Press OK when finished to return to the Copy Image(s) menu.
4. **Start copying.** When you choose Copy Image(s)? you'll see a confirmation screen. Highlight Yes, press OK, and a progress screen with a green progress bar appears while the copying is underway. You'll see a Copy Complete message when the task is finished. Press OK, and then the MENU button twice to back out of the menus; or just tap the shutter release button.

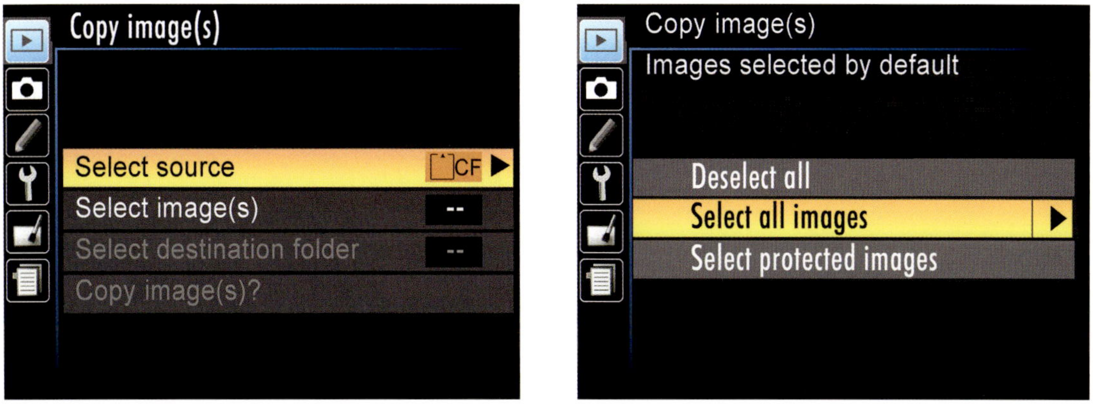

Figure 11.4 Choose a source slot for the images to be copied (left), or select images (right).

> **Tip**
>
> The Copy command will ask for confirmation before overwriting images on the destination card that have the same name as the source images. You can choose Replace Existing Image, Replace All, Skip, or Cancel the rest of the copying operation.

Image Review

There are certain shooting situations in which it's useful to have the picture you've just shot pop up on the monitor automatically for review. Perhaps you're fine-tuning exposure or autofocus and want to be able to see whether your most recent image is acceptable. Or, maybe you're the nervous type and just want confirmation that you actually took a picture. Instant review has saved my bacon a few times; for example, when I was shooting with studio flash in Manual mode and didn't notice that the shutter speed had been set to a (non-syncing) 1/500 second by mistake.

A lot of the time, however, it's a better idea to *not* automatically review your shots in order to conserve battery power (the LCD monitor is one of the major juice drains in the camera) or to speed up or simplify operations. For example, if you've just fired off a burst of eight shots during a football game, do you *really* need to have each and every frame display as the camera clears its buffer and stores the photos on your memory card? This menu operation allows you to choose which mode to use:

- **On.** Image review is automatic after every shot is taken.
- **Off.** Images are displayed only when you press the Playback button. Nikon, in its wisdom, has made this the default setting.

TIP

When I am shooting concerts and performances where the audience area is darkened, I always make two settings changes: I turn off Image Review so my LCD monitor isn't lighting up after every shot and annoying people. Then, I pop over to the Monitor Brightness entry in the Setup menu and select Manual Brightness set to –5. This produces a very dark screen, which is unlikely to annoy those around me. It also makes it difficult to judge my exposure from the monitor alone (*that's what the histogram is for!*). But it does make it possible for me to access menus and other screens during the performance without illuminating those behind me with LCD glare.

After Delete

When you've deleted an image, you probably will want to do one of three things: have the D810 display the next picture (in the order shot); show the *previous* picture; or show either the next *or* previous picture, depending on which way you were scrolling during picture review. Your D810 lets you select which action to take:

- **Show next.** It's likely that you'll want to look at the picture taken after the one you just deleted, so Nikon makes this the default action.
- **Show previous.** I use this setting a lot when shooting sports with a continuous shooting setting. After the sequence is taken, I press the Playback button to see the last picture in the series and sometimes discover that the whole sequence missed the boat. I sometimes go ahead and press the Trash button twice to delete the offending image, then continue moving backward to delete the five or six or eleven other pictures in the wasted sequence. You'll often find yourself with time on your hands at football games, and the urge to delete some stinker series to save your time reviewing back at the computer, while freeing up a little space on your card.
- **Continue as before.** This setting actually makes a lot of sense: if you were scrolling backward or forward and deleting photos as you go, you might want to continue in the same direction weeding out bad shots. Use this setting to set your Nikon D810 to behave that way.

Rotate Tall

When you rotate the D810 to photograph vertical subjects in portrait (tall), rather than landscape (wide) orientation, you probably don't want to view them tilted onto their sides later on, either on the camera monitor or within your image viewing/editing application on your computer. The D810 is way ahead of you. It has a directional sensor built in that can detect whether the camera was rotated when the photo was taken and hide this information in the image file itself. (This is the same sensor used to determine camera tilt in Virtual Horizon mode.)

The orientation data is applied in two different ways. It can be used by the D810 to automatically rotate images when they are displayed on the camera's monitor, or you can ignore the data and let the images display in non-rotated fashion (so you have to rotate the camera to view them in their proper orientation). Your image-editing application, such as Adobe Photoshop Elements, can also use the embedded file data to automatically rotate images on your computer screen.

Rotation works only if you've set Auto Image Rotation to On in the Setup menu (I'll show you how to do that later in this chapter). Once you've done that, the D810 will embed information about orientation in the image file, and your image editor (such as Adobe Photoshop or Photoshop Elements) will rotate the images for you as the files are loaded.

This menu choice deals only with whether the image should be rotated when displayed on the *camera LCD monitor.* (If you deactivate this option, your image-editing software can still read the embedded rotation data and properly display your images.) When Rotate Tall is turned off, the Nikon D810 does not rotate pictures taken in vertical orientation, displaying them as shown in Figure 11.5. The image is large on your LCD screen, but you must rotate the camera to view it upright.

When Rotate Tall is turned on, the D810 rotates pictures taken in vertical orientation on the monitor screen so you don't have to turn the camera to view them comfortably. However, this orientation also means that the longest dimension of the image is shown using the shortest dimension of the monitor, so the picture is reduced in size, as you can see in Figure 11.6.

So, turn this feature On (as well as Auto Image Rotation in the Setup menu) if you'd rather not turn your camera to view vertical shots in their natural orientation, and don't mind the smaller image. Turn the feature Off if, as I do, you'd rather see a larger image and are willing to rotate the camera to do so.

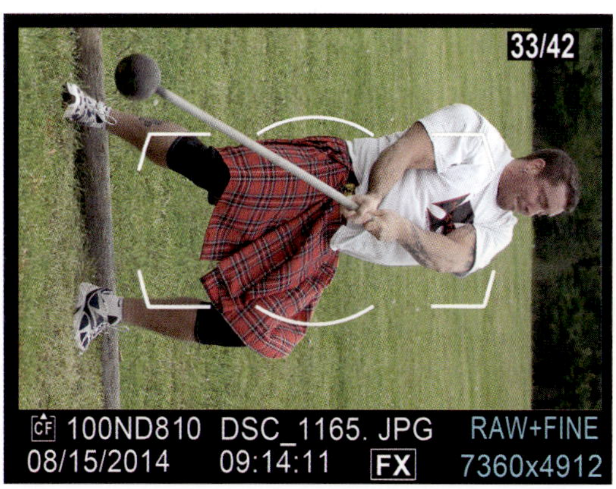

Figure 11.5 With Rotate Tall turned off, vertical images appear large on the monitor, but you must turn the camera to view them upright.

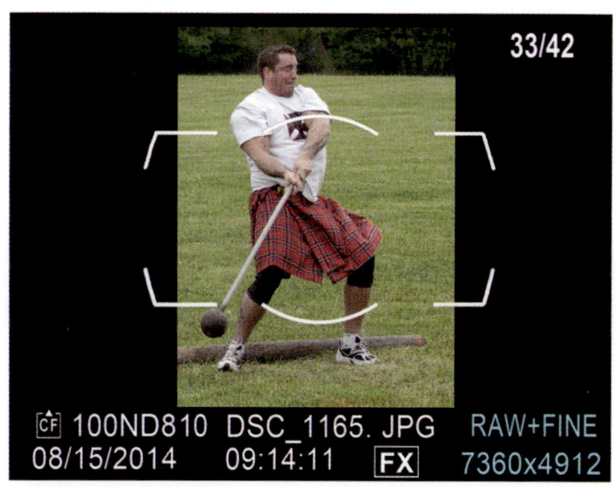

Figure 11.6 With Rotate Tall turned on, vertical images are shown in a smaller size, but oriented for viewing without turning the camera.

Slide Show

The D810's Slide Show feature is a convenient way to review images in the current playback folder one after another, without the need to manually switch between them. If you've recorded voice memos for some or all of the images you display in your slide show, you can opt to have them played back as narration. Redirect the output of your camera's video to an HDTV television, and you've got an instant camera-based large-screen audiovisual extravaganza. Your options include:

- **Start.** To activate a slide show, just choose Start from this entry in the Playback menu. During playback, you can press the OK button to pause the "slide show." When the show is paused, a menu pops up, as shown in Figure 11.7, with choices to restart the show (by pressing the OK button again); change the interval between frames; or to exit the show entirely.
- **Image Type.** You can choose to display both still images and movies, still images only, or movies only.
- **Frame interval.** If you like, you can choose Frame Interval before commencing the show in order to select an interval of either 2, 3, 5, or 10 seconds between "slides."

As the images are displayed, press the up/down multi selector buttons to change the amount of information presented on the screen with each image. For example, you might want to review a set of images and the settings used to shoot them. At any time during the show, press the up/down buttons until the informational screen you want is overlaid on the images.

As the slide show progresses, you can press the left/right multi selector buttons to move back to a previous frame or jump ahead to the next one. The slide show will then proceed as before. Press the MENU button to exit the slide show and return to the menu, or press the Playback button to exit the menu system totally. As always, while reviewing images you can tap the MENU button to exit

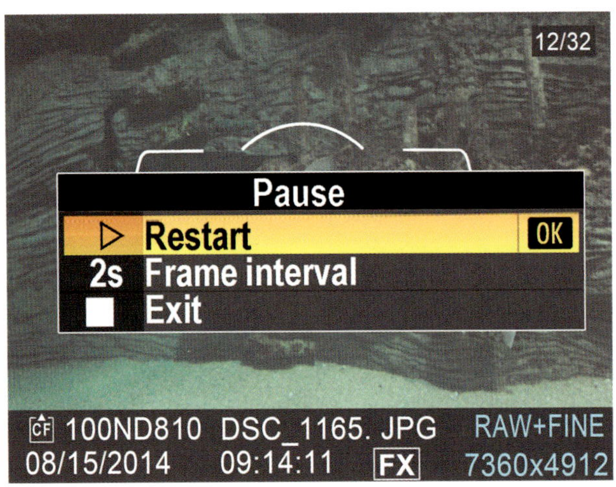

Figure 11.7
Press the OK button to pause the slide show, change the interval between slides, or to exit the presentation.

the show and return to the menus, or tap the shutter release button if you want to remove everything from the screen and return to shooting mode.

At the end of the slide show, as when you've paused it, you'll be offered the choice of restarting the sequence, changing the frame interval, or exiting the Slide Show feature completely.

DPOF Print Order

The Nikon D810 supports the DPOF (Digital Print Order Format) that is now almost universally used by digital cameras to specify which images on your memory card should be printed, and the number of prints desired of each image. This information is recorded on the memory card and can be interpreted by a compatible printer when the camera is linked to the printer using the USB cable (using the Direct Print facility, discussed in the next section), or when the memory card is inserted into a card reader slot on the printer itself. Photo labs are also equipped to read this data and make prints when you supply your memory card to them.

When you choose this menu item, you're presented with a set of screens that look very much like the Delete photos screens described earlier, only you're selecting pictures for printing rather than deleting them. The button sequences are slightly different, however:

1. **Select/Set or Deselect All.** The first screen allows you to quickly deselect any images that may have already been marked for printing, or to proceed directly to the Select/Set screen.
2. **Review images.** Use the multi selector cursor keys to scroll among the available images. **Note:** press the Zoom Out/Thumbnail button if you want to change to a different memory card or folder.
3. **Evaluate image.** When you highlight an image you might want to print, press the Zoom In button to temporarily enlarge that image so you can evaluate it further. When you release the button, the selection screen returns.
4. **Mark for printing.** To mark an image for printing, press the Protect button and hold it down while pressing the multi selector up and down buttons to choose the number of prints you want, up to 99 per image. A printer icon and the number specified will appear overlaid on that image's thumbnail. (See Figure 11.8.)
5. **Unmark unwanted images.** To unmark an image for printing, highlight and hold down the Protect button while pressing the down button until the number of prints reaches zero. The printer icon will vanish.
6. **Exit image selection.** When you've finished marking images to print, press OK.

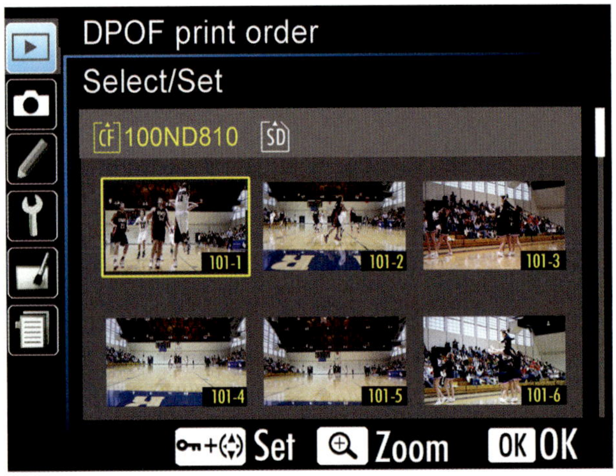

Figure 11.8
Select images for printing.

7. **Choose imprint options.** A final screen will appear in which you can request a data imprint (shutter speed and aperture) or imprint date (the date the photos were taken). Use the up/down buttons to select one or both of these options, if desired, and press the left/right buttons to mark or unmark the check boxes. When a box is marked, the imprint information for that option will be included on *all* prints in the print order.
8. **Complete print order.** Scroll up to Done when finished, and press OK or the right cursor button.

Direct Printing

Direct printing from your D810 to a PictBridge-compatible printer is not one of the Playback menu options; the PictBridge menu appears when the camera is connected to a PictBridge printer using the USB cable. In that mode, you can print any images you've selected using the Print Set (DPOF) menu entry in the Playback menu, or you can print directly. Just follow these steps to print a single image:

1. Connect the camera to the PictBridge printer using the USB cable; do not connect through a USB hub.
2. Turn the camera back on. The PictBridge display will appear.
3. Use the left/right directional buttons on the multi selector to browse among available images. You can press the Zoom In button and rotate the main command dial to zoom in and out of a frame being viewed. (Press the Playback button to return to full frame view.)
4. Press the multi selector center button to view up to six thumbnails at once. Press the button a second time to view a highlighted picture in full frame mode.
5. When you've highlighted a picture you want to print, press OK to view the PictBridge printing options.

6. Use the up/down directional buttons to highlight an option, and the right directional button to select it. Your choices are:
   - **Page size.** Choose from your printer's default page size, 3.5 × 5 in., 5 × 7 in., or A4 sizes.
   - **No. of copies.** Choose from 1 to 99 copies, and press OK.
   - **Border.** Select from Printer Default (the border setting already stored in your printer), Print With Border, or No Border. Press OK to return to the menu.
   - **Time stamp.** Select from Printer Default (the time stamp setting already stored in your printer), Print Time Stamp, or No Time Stamp. Press OK to return to the menu.
   - **Cropping.** A dialog box will appear, and you can rotate the main command dial to zoom cropping in or out, and the multi selector directional buttons to position the cropping frame.
7. When ready to print, select Start Printing. Once printing has begun, press OK to cancel before all the copies have been output. Press OK to return to the menu.

To print multiple images, follow these steps:

1. Press the MENU button in the PictBridge playback display.
2. Select one of the following:
   - Choose Print Select to choose the images now that you want to print.
   - Choose Print (DPOF) to print the images that you have previously marked using the Playback menu's Print Set (DPOF) menu.
   - Choose Index Print to create an index print of all the JPEG images on the memory card.
3. If you've chosen Print Select, choose the images to be printed, using the left/right directional buttons, the Protect button to mark them, and the up/down buttons to select the number of prints from 1 to 99 copies.
4. Press the OK button to display PictBridge printing options, as in Step 8 above, except that only Page Size, Border, and Time Stamp may be specified.
5. When ready to print, select Start Printing. Once printing has begun, press OK to cancel before all the copies have been output. Press OK to return to the menu.

Shooting Menu Options

The various direct setting buttons and dials on the D810, for image quality, autofocus mode, white balance, release mode, ISO sensitivity, metering mode, and flash, along with exposure compensation (EV) adjustments, are likely to be the most common settings changes you make, with changes during a particular session fairly common. You'll find some of these duplicated in the Shooting menu (see Figure 11.9), along with options that you access second-most frequently when you're using your Nikon D810, such as specifying noise reduction for long exposures or high ISO settings. You might make such adjustments as you begin a shooting session, or when you move from one type of subject to another. Nikon makes accessing these changes very easy.

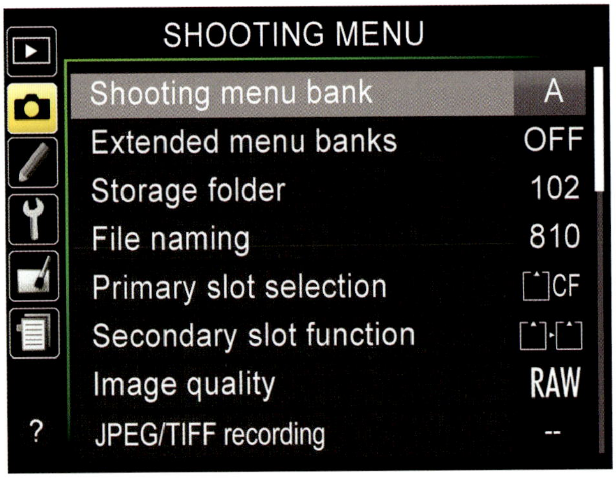

Figure 11.9
Common shooting settings can be changed in this menu.

This section explains the options of the Shooting menu and how to use them. The options you'll find in these green-coded menus include:

- Shooting Menu Bank
- Extended Menu Banks
- Storage Folder
- File Naming
- Primary Slot Selection
- Secondary Slot Function
- Image Quality
- JPEG/TIFF Recording
- NEF (RAW) Recording
- Image Area
- White Balance
- Set Picture Control
- Manage Picture Control
- Color Space
- Active D-Lighting
- HDR (High Dynamic Range)
- Vignette Control
- Auto Distortion Control
- Long Exposure NR
- High ISO NR
- ISO Sensitivity Settings
- Multiple Exposure
- Interval Timer Shooting
- Time-Lapse Photography
- Movie Settings

Shooting Menu Bank

The Nikon D810's Shooting menu banks are four groups named, initially, A, B, C, and D that store specific collections of Shooting menu settings that you can recall at any time by switching to the bank containing the preferences you want to use. These banks are one of the primary reasons why the D810 is more versatile than Nikon's entry-level dSLRs, which lack the ability to change shooting specifications *en masse* using a simple menu command. The Shooting menu banks A, B, C, and D should not be confused with the four similarly named Custom Settings menu banks A, B, C, and D, which provide similar, but *separate* storage of your Custom Settings. You can use your Shooting menu banks and Custom Settings menu banks in any combination. That is, you can use Shooting menu bank A and Custom Settings menu bank C at the same time.

In addition to the standard menu banks, the D810 has the ability to store additional information in what Nikon calls Extended menu banks. They aren't really different banks; when you activate extended banks, the A, B, C, and D banks simply include exposure mode and exposure settings information in those banks, as I'll explain in the section that follows this one.

The D810 uses bank A by default. To switch to another bank:

- **Navigate to the Shooting menu.** Press MENU and select the Shooting menu.
- **Choose the menu bank option.** Scroll to Shooting Menu Bank and press the multi selector right button.
- **Select the bank to activate.** Scroll to the bank you want to use with the multi selector up/down buttons, and press OK to confirm, or press the multi selector right button to assign a name (other than the default A, B, C, or D), as described below.
- **Exit menus.** The Shooting menu appears again. Press the MENU button to back out of the menu, or simply tap the shutter release.

Any changes you make to one menu bank do not affect the other banks, except for the following exceptions: changes made to Interval Timer Shooting, Multiple Exposure, Time-Lapse Photography, and Extended Menu Banks settings, along with any changes you make to customize Picture Controls carry across *all* four menu banks. All other Shooting menu changes you make are confined *only* to the bank that is active when you make those adjustments. For example, if you change Image Quality to RAW in bank A, then the Image Quality setting in bank B will not be modified.

Because the settings for each bank are more or less independent of the others, you can set each one up with the settings you like to use in particular situations. For example, you could use bank A for sports, bank B for landscapes, bank C for portraits, and bank D for general shooting. Or, if you're a specialist, one bank could be dedicated to indoor sports (with high ISO settings and tungsten or fluorescent light balance) and another for outdoor sports (normal ISO and daylight white balance), with both specifying JPEG FINE capture only, because RAW or RAW+JPEG can slow down continuous shooting. You could even tailor a D810's operation using parameters other than typical shooting sessions. For example, a wedding photography studio that shares a pool of Nikon D810 cameras among several photographers could have one bank named Peter, another named Paul, and a third dedicated to shooter Mary. The currently selected bank is indicated in the monochrome control panel, and in the shooting information display.

Entering Text on the Nikon D810

Customized names of up to 20 characters each can be used to replace the generic A, B, C, and D designations. Highlight the bank you want to label in the Shooting Menu Bank screen, and select Rename by pressing the right directional button. You can then use the standard Nikon text entry screen to specify the name you want to use. Now is a good time to master text entry, because you can use it to enter comments, rename folders, and perform other functions.

The Nikon D810 uses a fairly standardized text entry screen to name files, Picture Controls, create new folder names, enter image comments, and other text. You'll be using text entry with other functions that I'll describe later in this book. The screen looks like the one shown in Figure 11.10, with some variations (for example, some functions have a less diverse character set, or offer more or fewer spaces for your entries). To name a menu bank, just use the multi selector navigational buttons to scroll around within the array of alphanumerics. Then, enter your text:

- **Highlight a character.** Use the multi selector keys to scroll around within the array of characters.
- **Insert highlighted character.** Press the multi selector center button to insert the highlighted character. The cursor will move one place to the right to accept the next character.
- **Non-destructively backspace.** Hold down the Thumbnail/Zoom Out button and use the left/right buttons to move the cursor within the line of characters you've entered. This allows you to backspace and replace a character without disturbing the others you've entered.
- **Erase a highlighted character.** To remove a character you've already input, move the cursor to highlight that character, and then press the Trash button.
- **Confirm your entry.** When you're finished entering text, press the OK button to confirm your entry, then press the left button twice to return to the Shooting menu, or just tap the shutter release to exit the menu system entirely.

As you work with menu banks, keep in mind that while changes you make to a particular bank don't effect the other banks, they are "sticky" within that bank once you've made them. That is, if you've set up a "sports" menu bank to use a high ISO sensitivity setting, and then during a session change the value to ISO 200, that's what you'll get the next time you access that menu bank (unless you remember to change it back to your preferred value at the end of the session). So, at best, your customized banks are preset for you *only* to the extent that you don't change those settings while you use them.

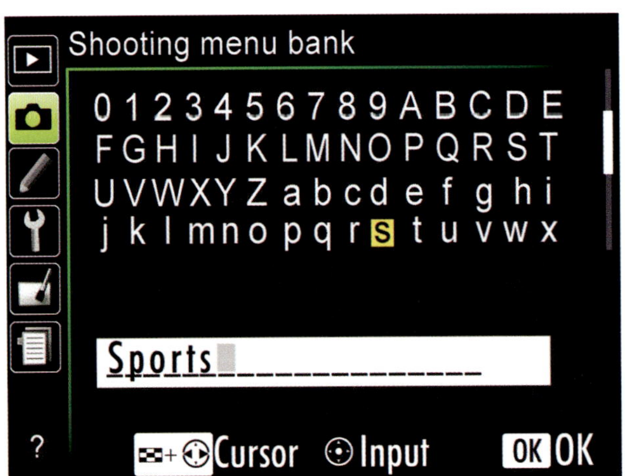

Figure 11.10
Use this D810 screen to enter text.

In Chapter 3, I provided a list of recommended Shooting menu bank settings for typical photo environments, from sports and landscapes to portraits and macros.

Reset Shooting Menu

Earlier Nikon cameras had a separate entry for reverting the settings of the current menu bank to the factory default settings. However, by placing this option at the top level of the Shooting menu, it was easy to overlook the fact that this reset applied *only* to the currently active bank, and not to all banks. To reset the A, B, C, and D banks to their factory defaults, you must reset each bank individually. Nikon has moved the option into the Shooting Menu Bank entry, where it is a choice (along with Rename) for whichever menu bank is highlighted.

Don't feel bad over being confused about what this menu item does. The Nikon D810 has, in effect, *three* different kinds of resets. This is one of them.

- **Shooting menu reset.** Use this option to reset the values of the currently selected Shooting menu bank *except for image quality, image size, white balance, and ISO sensitivity* to their default values. When you select this option by pressing the Trash button in the Shooting Menu Bank screen, your choices are Yes and No. As I said earlier, kindly note that the defaults are restored *only* for the menu bank that is active, and not any of the other three Shooting menu banks, except for multiple exposure and interval timer shooting settings, which are reset for all four banks. A reset has no effect on the four settings noted above.
- **Custom Settings menu reset.** This option, which I'll describe in Chapter 12, is used to reset any of the four Custom Settings menu banks. It has no effect on camera settings or Shooting menu banks.
- **Two-button reset.** The Nikon D810's two-button reset (holding down the QUAL and Exposure Compensation buttons [on the top of the camera at the left and right sides, respectively] simultaneously for more than two seconds) will *not* reset your Shooting menu banks or Custom Settings menu banks. This particular reset is for basic settings, such as focus point, exposure mode, flexible program, exposure/flash compensation, autoexposure hold, bracketing, flash mode, flash value lock, and multiple exposure settings.

Table 11.1 shows the default values that are set using Reset Shooting menu option. If you don't know what some of these settings are, I'll explain them later in this section.

Extended Menu Banks

The Nikon D810 has the ability to add several additional parameters—exposure mode, shutter speed, and aperture—to the values stored in a particular Shooting menu bank. So, if you have a Sports mode especially for action photography and always begin a sports session using Shutter-priority and a shutter speed of 1/1,000th second, you can include that information in each of your shooting menu banks. Or, perhaps you have a bank set up for portraits, and you like to use Aperture-priority with an f/stop of f/5.6 to reduce depth-of-field. The extended menu banks can keep that information on file, too.

Table 11.1 Default Shooting Menu Values

Function	Value
Extended menu banks	Off
File naming	DSC
Primary Slot selection	SD card slot
Secondary Slot function	Overflow
Image quality	JPEG normal
JPEG/TIFF recording	
Image size	Large
JPEG compression	Size Priority
NEF (RAW) recording	
Image Size	Raw L (Large)
Type	Lossless compressed
NEF (RAW) bit depth	14-bit
Image area	
Choose image area	FX (36 × 24)
Auto DX crop	On
White balance	Auto>Normal
Fine tuning	A-B:0, G-M:0
Choose color temp	5000K
Preset manual	d-1
Set Picture Control	Standard
Color space	sRGB
Active D-Lighting	Off
HDR (High Dynamic Range)	
HDR mode	Off
Exposure differential	Auto
Smoothing	Normal
Vignette control	Normal
Auto distortion control	Off
Long exp. NR	Off
High ISO NR	Normal
ISO sensitivity settings	
ISO sensitivity	100
Auto ISO sensitivity control	Off
Multiple exposure	
Multiple exposure mode	Off
Number of shots	2
Auto gain	On
Interval timer shooting	Off
Start Options	Now
Interval	1 min.
No. intervals x shots/ interval	0001x1
Exposure smoothing	Off
Time-lapse photography	Off
Interval	5s
Shooting time	25 min.
Exposure smoothing	On
Movie settings	
Frame size/rate	1920 × 1080; 60p
Movie Quality	Normal
Microphone sensitivity	Auto sensitivity (A)
Frequency response	Wide range
Wind noise reduction	Off
Destination	SD card slot
Movie ISO sensitivity	
ISO sensitivity (mode M):	100
Auto ISO control (mode M):	Off
Maximum sensitivity:	12800

When would you *not* want to use extended menu banks? You'd probably want to switch this feature off if you change exposure modes frequently and don't want a particular shutter speed or aperture to be preset for you when you change to a particular menu bank. (Keep in mind that, once a bank has been loaded, you can always change to a different mode or setting, and that your new setting will become the default for that bank when you reload it in the future.)

With this option set to Off (the default), the D810 will not store exposure mode, f/stop, or shutter speed in a menu bank. If you select On, then exposure mode *will* be stored. If the exposure mode that is stored is Shutter-priority or Manual, then the shutter speed will be remembered as well. If the exposure mode is Aperture-priority or Manual, the aperture will be remembered.

Storage Folder

If you want to store images in a folder other than the one created and selected by the Nikon D810, you can switch among available folders on your memory card, or create your own folder. Remember that any folders you create will be deleted when you reformat your memory card.

Why create your own folders? Perhaps you're traveling and have a high-capacity memory card and want to store the images for each day (or for each city that you visit) in a separate folder. Maybe you'd like to separate those wedding photos you snapped at the ceremony from those taken at the reception. As I mentioned earlier, the Nikon D810 automatically creates a folder on a newly formatted memory card with a name like 100ND810, and when it fills with 999 images, it will automatically create a new folder with a number incremented by one (such as 101ND810). To create your own folder or select an existing folder:

1. **Access active folder entry.** Choose Storage Folder in the Shooting menu, and press the right multi selector button.
2. **Choose selection method.** Highlight either Select Folder by Number or Select Folder from List (to choose a folder that you know already exists). Press the right directional button to confirm your choice. One of two screens appears, with the card in the currently active slot highlighted. Perform the tasks in *either* Step 3 or Step 4.
3. **Select Folder by Number/New Folder Number.** If you've chosen this option, a screen appears with three digits representing the possible folder numbers from 100-999, as shown in Figure 11.11. Use the left/right buttons to move between the digits, and the up/down buttons to increase or decrease the value of the digit. If a folder already exists with the number you dial in, an icon appears showing the folder is empty, partially full, or has 999 or a picture numbered 9999 and can contain no more images. Press OK to create the new folder and make it the active folder. You'd want to use this option to create a new folder *or* when you don't know whether a folder by a particular number already exists. If a folder with that number already resides on the memory card, you can use it (if it is not full); if it doesn't exist, you can create it.

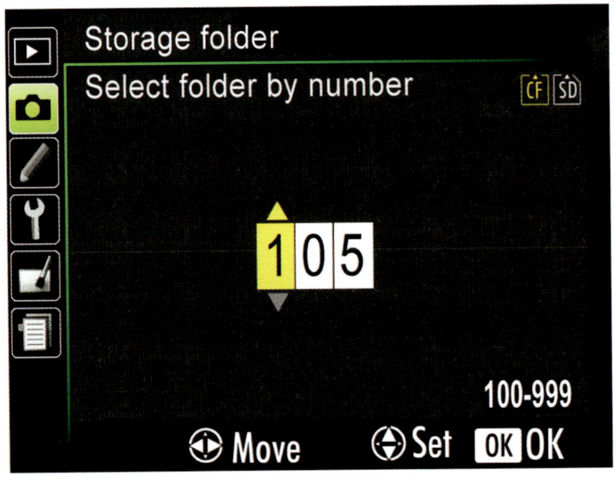

Figure 11.11
Create a new folder or select an existing folder number.

4. **Select Folder from List/Select Folder.** From among the available folders shown, scroll to the one that you want to become active for image storage and playback. This feature is handy when you want to display a slide show located in a particular folder. Use this option if you know that the folder you want to use already resides on the memory card. Press OK to confirm your choice and make the folder active.
5. **Exit menus.** Press the MENU button or tap the shutter release to exit.

File Naming

The D810, like other cameras in the Nikon product line, automatically applies a name like _DSC0001.jpg or DSC_0001.nef to your image files as they are created. You can use this menu option to change the names applied to your photos and associated voice memos—but only within certain strict limitations. In practice, you can change only three of the eight characters, the *DSC* portion of the filename. The other five are mandated either by the Design Rule for Camera File System (DCF) specification that all digital camera makers adhere to or to industry conventions.

DCF limits filenames created by conforming digital cameras to a maximum of eight characters, plus a three-character extension (such as .jpg, .tif, .nef, or .wav in the case of audio files) that represents the format of the file. The eight-plus-three (usually called 8.3) length limitation dates back to an evil and frustrating computer operating system that we older photographers would like to forget (its initials are D.O.S), but which, unhappily, lives on as the wraith of a filenaming convention.

Of the eight available characters, four are used to represent, in a general sense, the type of camera used to create the image. By convention, one of those characters is an underline, placed in the first position (as in _DSCxxxx.xxx) when the image uses the Adobe RGB color space (more on color spaces later), and in the fourth position (as in DSC_xxxx.xxx) for sRGB and RAW (NEF) files. That leaves just three characters for the manufacturer (and you) to use. Nikon, Sony, and some other vendors use DSC (which may or may not stand for Digital Still Camera, depending on who you ask), while Canon prefers IMG. The remaining four characters are used for numbers from 0000 to 9999, which is why your D810 "rolls over" to DSC_0000 again when the 9999 number limitation is reached.

When you select File Naming in the Shooting menu, you'll be shown the current settings for both sRGB (and RAW) and Adobe RGB. Press the right multi selector button, and you'll be taken to the (mostly) standard Nikon text entry screen (go back to Figure 11.10 if you've forgotten what it looks like) and allowed to change the DSC value to something else. In this version of the text entry screen, however, only the numbers from 0 to 9 and characters A-Z are available; the filename cannot contain other characters. As always, press the OK button to confirm your new setting.

Because the default DSC characters don't tell you much, don't hesitate to change them to something else. I use 800 for my D810 and ND4 for my Nikon D4. If you don't need to differentiate between different camera models, you can change the three characters to anything else that suits your purposes, including your initials (DDB_ or JFK_ for example) or even customize for particular shooting sessions (EUR_, GER_, FRA_, and JAP_ when taking vacation trips). You can also use the filename flexibility to partially overcome the 9999 numbering limitation. You could, for example, use the template 801_ to represent the first 10,000 pictures you take with your D810, and then 802_ for the next 10,000, and 803_ for the 10,000 after that.

That's assuming that you don't rename your image files in your computer. In a way, filenaming verges on a moot consideration, because, they apply *only* to the images as they exist in your camera. After (or during) transfer to your computer you can change the names to anything you want, completely disregarding the 8.3 limitations (although it's a good idea to retain the default extensions). If you shot an image file named DSC_4832.jpg in your camera, you could change it to Paris_EiffelTower_32.jpg later on. Indeed, virtually all photo transfer programs, including Nikon Transfer and Photoshop Elements Transfer, allow you to specify a template and rename your photos as they are moved or copied to your computer from your camera or memory card.

I usually don't go to that bother (I generally don't use transfer software; I just drag and drop images from my memory card to folders I have set up), but renaming can be useful for those willing to take the time to do it.

Primary Slot Selection

This menu entry allows you to specify which of the two slots in your D810 is the primary slot. Nikon's default is the SD slot (perhaps they are trying to tell us something), but you can, as I do, choose the CF card slot instead. There are many reasons why I prefer to use my CF card as my primary storage. Although I use 64GB cards in both slots (almost a must with a 36-megapixel camera), my preferred CF card is a 600X with a read/write speed of 90 megabits/second, while my Class 10 SDXC card is in practice a tad slower. (It's difficult to compare read/write speeds of CF and SD-class cards directly, because the way in which those speeds are reported is different. CF card ratings give a *maximum* speed under ideal conditions, while SDXC speed ratings are the *minimum* you can expect.)

Secondary Slot Function

This menu entry allows you to specify the function of the second memory card slot in the Nikon D810, choosing to use the secondary slot to accept overflow images when the primary card fills up; create a backup of all the files stored on the primary card; or to split your RAW+JPEG files between primary and secondary slots. The D810's Movie Settings functions (explained later in this chapter) offer a fourth option: you can select which slot is used to store your movie clips (and can therefore choose the largest memory card or fastest memory card for your movies).

As I've mentioned before, the second memory card slot, introduced to the Nikon world with the original D3 (Canon has had this feature on its high-end dSLRs for some time) is one of my favorite features. I'll explain your choices for secondary slot functions—and the importance of each of them—in the next sections.

Overflow

In this case, when the memory card in the primary slot fills up, the D810 automatically switches over to the card in the secondary slot. The changeover happens quickly, and you're not even likely to notice, unless you have your eye on the "slot" indicators on the top control panel or the monitor's shooting information display. There are dozens of ways to use this capability:

- **"Limitless" Capacity.** My standard operating procedure is to put one 64GB memory card in each slot. As a practical matter, that means I can shoot all day without changing memory cards, even if I am shooting landscapes and bracketing everything with three- or five-shot sets (either to optimize exposure, or, when the camera is mounted on a tripod, to capture files for later HDR processing). Or, I might be shooting sports/photojournalism, where the practice is to change memory cards when your media is 80 percent full to eliminate the possibility of missing anything important due to a card change at an inopportune time.
- **Small/fast—with backup.** For some sports, if you are shooting continuously, you may want your fastest memory card in the primary slot to maximize write speed out of the camera's buffer, but the real speed demons in the memory card world can be expensive. So, instead of an affordable 64GB medium-speed card, you may put a (per gigabyte) more expensive 8GB or 16GB high speed card in the primary slot, and back it up with a slightly slower (and cheaper) 16GB or 32GB card. You can capture images with the fastest card you've got, yet not have to worry about missing shots, because you have a backup card installed in the secondary slot.

- **Put smaller cards to use.** If you don't think you'll need the overflow capacity, but still want to have it just in case, put a smaller card that you don't use much anymore in the secondary slot. If your large card that you didn't think would fill *does* come up short, you won't lose any shots. They'll be directed to that old 8GB card you put in the secondary slot for insurance. I sometimes do this when I am using several cameras and have a limited number of large cards at my disposal. I'll save the big cards for primary use, knowing that any overflow shots will be stored on the small backup cards if necessary. I own two 64GB CF and SD cards, five 32GB CF cards, two 32GB SD cards, and a gazillion 16GB SD cards, so I am able to use the smallest and slowest cards as my overflow storage as I keep feeding the largest/fastest cards into my primary slot.
- **Stretch your budget.** Your D810 produces files that are at least two or three times as large as your old 16 or 12 megapixel model, but after spending an arm and a leg for a 36-megapixel camera, you'd like to avoid replacing your old fast but limited-capacity 8GB memory cards for a little while. (Perhaps you're waiting for those new 128GB cards to come down in price.) With one 8GB card in each slot, you can double your shooting before it's time to swap cards.

Backup

In this case, each photograph you take is recorded on the memory cards in both the primary slot and secondary slot. The write process takes slightly longer (so it may not be your best option when shooting sports), but it's otherwise a seamless way to create a backup copy of each and every image you take. If you're shooting RAW+JPEG, both files associated with each image are recorded on both slots. I absolutely love this feature, as I've mentioned before in this book. In Backup mode, the camera always shows the number of exposures remaining on the card with the least amount of free space remaining, so you'll know when the backup process will come to an end. The shutter release is locked when either card is full. Here are some of my favorite applications:

- **Critical shots backed up instantly.** When I was a photojournalist, a lot of the images I took, particularly of spot news events, were literally once-in-a-lifetime shots that couldn't be duplicated under any circumstances. I also shot weddings, and while it was sometimes possible to restage a particular setup or pose, that was never a satisfactory option, even if done on the day of the nuptials. So, there was always a degree of trepidation until the film was processed or digital files backed up. With dual-slot backup capabilities, backup files can be made instantly, as you shoot. What a relief!
- **Great when there's No-Fi.** Many pros (and more than a few amateurs) rely on in-camera Wi-Fi connectivity (using Nikon's WT-4a accessory) to beam backups to a nearby laptop computer for safekeeping, or, at events, so that an assistant can be processing some images while photography continues. But, sometimes that's not possible, or, perhaps, you don't own the necessary equipment. Making a backup in your camera is a great alternative when wireless capabilities are unavailable or impractical. You can even shuttle that secondary slot card to an assistant at intervals while retaining the "main" copy of your images in the camera.

- **Leave your PSD at home.** When I travel overseas, I like to pack light, with only a carry-on bag that holds my camera gear and some of my clothing, with the rest of my apparel relegated to the second tote that qualifies as a "personal" item. But I've always carried two card reader/personal storage devices so I can make backup copies of my images while I travel. I've found that my dual-card Nikon cameras can easily replace the PSD. I can back up each image as it's shot automatically, or shoot on one card (to allow faster capture) and make a duplicate with a card-to-card copy back in my hotel room in the evening. Or I can use the D810's Copy Image(s) feature to make an extra copy of only the images I want.
- **Instant copy to share.** Want to give a traveling companion copies of all the images you shoot? Create a backup as you take the photos and hand over the copy on the spot. (Again, if you want to share only *some* of your pictures, you can use the Copy Image(s) feature instead.)

RAW, the Primary Slot—JPEG, the Secondary Slot

In this mode, when you're shooting RAW+JPEG, the NEF (RAW) files are saved to the card in the primary slot, and the JPEG files are saved to the card in the secondary slot. When you're using any other Quality setting (any JPEG option, or TIFF), the images are stored in the primary slot, until that card fills; then the photos overflow to the secondary slot. (This is effectively the same as the Backup option.) You'll find this mode useful under the following conditions:

- **Separate RAW and JPEG.** Perhaps you like to store your RAW and JPEG files in separate locations. This mode makes it easy to do that. Copy the card containing the RAW files to one destination on your computer, and the JPEG files from the other card to a second destination. The only complication is that the memory card in the primary slot is likely to fill up more quickly than the card with the smaller JPEG files in the secondary slot, so if you shoot to the capacity of the card in the primary slot, you'll need to replace it more often than you will the card with the JPEG files. Or, if you want the two cards to be mirror images of each other (but in different formats), you can swap them both out at the same time, with the secondary slot card only partially full. With the D810, you have the ability to select either the RAW L (standard RAW) or RAW S (Small) option. RAW S helps even out the size difference between RAW and JPEG files.
- **Faster backup of RAW+JPEG.** If you shoot RAW+JPEG, using the Backup option (described earlier) means that you're saving *four* files each time you press the shutter release. That can slow you down in some situations if you're rapid-firing a sequence of images. Storing RAW files on one card, and JPEG files on the other is a faster way of capturing a backup, because only two files are saved per click. If you have a problem with one of your JPEG files, you can easily produce a new JPEG from the RAW file. (Nikon Capture NX 2 has a batch mode that simplifies creating JPEGs from NEFs *en masse,* in fact.) The reverse is not true, however. If your NEF file gets munged, your RAW information is lost forever, even though you still have the JPEG version. So, use this option carefully if your RAW files are especially important for a particular shooting session.

Image Quality

As I noted in Chapter 2, you can choose the image quality settings used by the D810 to store its files. The quickest way to do that is to hold down the QUAL button embedded on the release mode dial at left on the camera's top panel, and spin the main command dial until the quality setting you want is shown. You can also use this menu option to make the quality settings using the bigger, brighter 3.2-inch color monitor. You have three choices to make:

- **JPEG compression.** To reduce the size of your image files and allow more photos to be stored on a given memory card, the D810 uses JPEG compression to squeeze the images down to a smaller size. This compacting reduces the image quality a little, so you're offered your choice of Fine (a 1:4 reduction), Normal (1:8 reduction), and Basic (1:16) compression. You can see an exaggerated version of the effects of JPEG compression in Figure 11.12. There is a further tweak you can make, specifying whether JPEG compression should be optimized for the smallest possible image size at a given compression level, or whether you'd prefer to sacrifice some compression for optimal quality. You won't find those options in this menu entry; instead, use the JPEG Compression menu item, described later in this section.

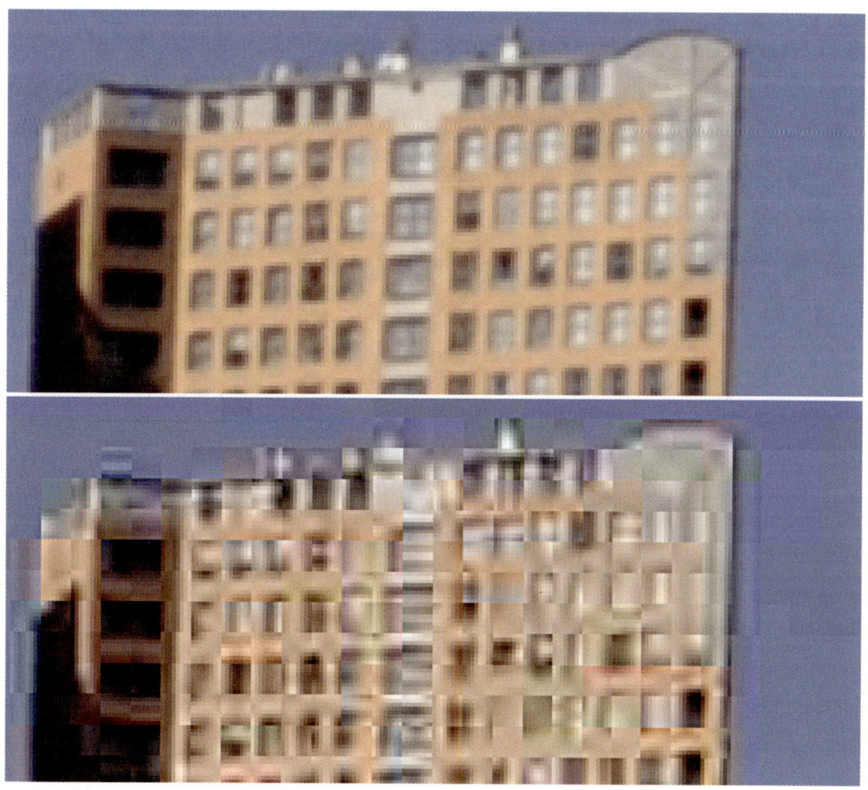

Figure 11.12
At low levels of JPEG compression, the image looks sharp even when you enlarge it enough to see the actual pixels (top); when using extreme JPEG compression (bottom) an image obviously loses quality.

- **JPEG, RAW, or both.** You can elect to store only JPEG versions of the images you shoot, or you can save your photos as RAW files, which consume more than twice as much space on your memory card. Or, you can store both at once as you shoot (and store them to different memory cards, if you like, using the secondary slot function described previously). Many photographers elect to save *both* JPEG and a RAW, so they'll have a JPEG version that might be usable as-is, as well as the original "digital negative" RAW file in case they want to do some processing of the image later. You'll end up with two different versions of the same file: one with a .jpg extension, and one with the .nef extension that signifies a Nikon RAW file.
- **TIFF.** The TIFF format is a lossless uncompressed 8-bit format (at least, in its Nikon incarnation) that is preferred for some applications, such as stock photography. TIFFs are several times larger than RAW files, however, and it takes a long time to store a TIFF file on a memory card (a second or two, at least), so most photographers don't create TIFFs in the camera. It's usually a better idea to produce a TIFF file from a RAW file, which, because it can contain up to 14 bits of information (instead of the Nikon TIFF format's 8 bits), has potentially a wider range of colors captured.

Tip

The D810 always saves a full-resolution RAW L 7360 × 4912 pixel or RAW S 3680 × 2456 pixel image even if you choose a smaller image size (resolution) for the JPEG version (such as Medium (M) or Small (S)). I'll show you how to choose between RAW L or RAW S with the NEF (RAW) Recording entry shortly.

To choose the combination you want, access the Shooting menu, scroll to Image Quality, and select it. A screen similar to the one shown in Figure 11.13 will appear. Scroll to highlight the setting you want, and either press OK or push the multi selector right button to confirm your selection.

In practice, you'll probably use the JPEG Fine and RAW+JPEG Fine selections most often. Why so many choices, then? There are some limited advantages to using the JPEG Normal and JPEG Basic settings, either at full resolution (Large) or when using the Medium and Small resolution settings. Settings that are less than max allow stretching the capacity of your memory card so you can shoehorn quite a few more pictures onto a single memory card. That can come in useful when on vacation and you're running out of storage, or when you're shooting non-critical work that doesn't require 36 megapixels of resolution (such as photos taken for real estate listings, web page display, photo ID cards, or similar applications). Some photographers like to record RAW+JPEG Basic so they'll have a moderate quality JPEG file for review only and no intention of using for editing purposes, while retaining access to the original full-resolution/uncompressed RAW file for serious editing.

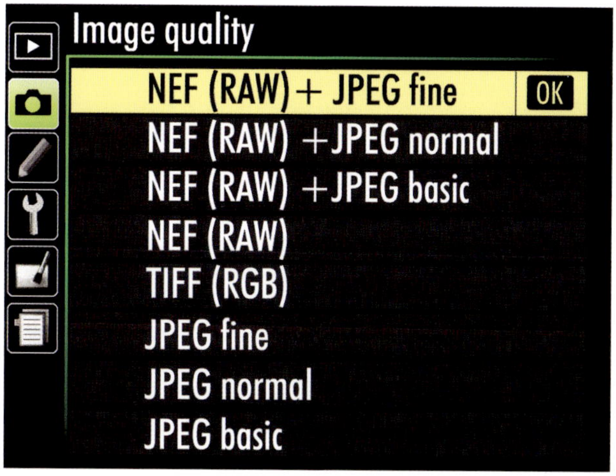

Figure 11.13 You can choose RAW, JPEG, RAW+JPEG, or TIFF formats here.

For most work, using lower resolution and extra compression is false economy. You never know when you might actually need that extra bit of picture detail. Your best bet is to have enough memory cards to handle all the shooting you want to do until you have the chance to transfer your photos to your computer or a personal storage device.

However, reduced image quality can sometimes be beneficial if you're shooting sequences of photos rapidly, as the D810 is able to hold more of them in its internal memory buffer before transferring to the memory card. Still, for most sports and other applications, you'd probably rather have better, sharper pictures than longer periods of continuous shooting. Do you really need 20 or 30 shots of a pass reception in a football game, or a dozen or two slightly different versions of your local basketball star driving in for a lay-up?

JPEG vs. RAW

You'll sometimes be told that RAW files are the "unprocessed" image information your camera produces, before it's been modified. That's nonsense. RAW files are no more unprocessed than your camera film is after it's been through the chemicals to produce a negative or transparency. A lot can happen in the developer that can affect the quality of a film image—positively and negatively—and, similarly, your digital image undergoes a significant amount of processing before it is saved as a RAW file. Nikon even applies a name (EXPEED) to the digital image processing (DIP) chip used to perform this magic.

A RAW file is more similar to a film camera's processed negative. It contains all the information, captured in 12-bit or 14-bit channels per color (and stored in a 16-bit space), with no sharpening and no application of any special filters or other settings you might have specified when you took the picture. Those settings are *stored* with the RAW file so they can be applied when the image is converted to a form compatible with your favorite image editor. However, using RAW conversion software such as Adobe Camera Raw or Nikon Capture NX, you can override those settings and apply settings of your own. You can select essentially the same changes there that you might have specified in your camera's picture-taking options.

RAW exists because sometimes we want to have access to all the information captured by the camera, before the camera's internal logic has processed it and converted the image to a standard file format. Even Compressed RAW doesn't save as much space as JPEG. What it does do is preserve all the information captured by your camera after it's been converted from analog to digital form.

So, why don't we always use RAW? Some photographers avoid using Nikon's RAW NEF files on the misguided conviction that they don't want to spend time in post-processing, forgetting that, if the camera settings you would have used for JPEG are correct, each RAW image's default attributes will use those settings and the RAW image will not need much manipulation. Post-processing in such cases is *optional*, and overwhelmingly helpful when an image needs to be fine-tuned.

Although some photographers do save *only* in RAW format, it's more common (and frequently more convenient) to use RAW plus one of the JPEG options, or, if you're confident about your settings, just shoot JPEG and eschew RAW altogether. In some situations, working with a RAW file can slow you down a little. RAW images take longer to store on the memory card, and must be converted from RAW to a format your image editor can handle, whether you elect to go with the default settings in force when the picture was taken, or make minor adjustments to the settings you specified in the camera.

As a result, those who depend on speedy access to images or who shoot large numbers of photos at once may prefer JPEG over RAW. Wedding photographers, for example, might expose several thousand photos during a bridal affair and offer hundreds to clients as electronic proofs for inclusion in an album. Wedding shooters take the time to make sure that their in-camera settings are correct, minimizing the need to post-process photos after the event. Given that their JPEGs are so good, there is little need to get bogged down shooting RAW.

Sports photographers also avoid RAW files. I visited a local Division III college one sunny September afternoon. I covered the first half of a football game, trotted down a hill to shoot a women's soccer match later that afternoon, and ended up in the adjacent field house shooting a volleyball invitational tournament an hour later. I managed to shoot 1,920 photos, most of them using continuous shooting, in about four hours. I certainly didn't have any plans to do post-processing on very many of those shots, and firing the camera at its maximum frame rate didn't allow RAW shooting, so carefully exposed and precisely focused JPEG images were my file format of choice that day.

JPEG was invented as a more compact file format that can store most of the information in a digital image, but in a much smaller size. JPEG predates most digital SLRs and was initially used to squeeze down files for transmission over slow dial-up connections. Even if you were using an early dSLR with 1.3 megapixel files for news photography, you didn't want to send them back to the office over a modem at 1,200 bps.

But, as I noted, JPEG provides smaller files by compressing the information in a way that loses some image data. JPEG remains a viable alternative because it offers several different quality levels. At the highest quality Fine level, you might not be able to tell the difference between the original RAW file and the JPEG version.

In my case, I shoot virtually everything at RAW+JPEG Fine. Most of the time, I'm not concerned about filling up my memory cards, even when shooting in dual-slot Backup mode, as I usually have my 64GB CF and SDXC cards, and a minimum of five 32GB memory cards with me. I also use a MacBook Air with an external 1TB hard drive, and (as I mentioned earlier) for short trips, rely on my D810's capability of copying directly from one memory card to the other in the camera. When shooting sports I'll shift to JPEG Fine (with no RAW file) to squeeze a little extra speed out of my camera's continuous shooting mode, and to reduce the need to wade through eight-photo bursts taken in RAW format.

You may notice that I am not going into the TIFF option in any detail. To oversimplify things, for most of us, TIFF provides the worst of both worlds: it has heftier storage space requirements than the "worst" case RAW file. Those who don't mind waiting up to four or five seconds for a single image to be stored to the memory card, and who have prodigious skills at getting their in-camera settings correct the first time, can use TIFF if necessary. The main reason to use TIFF is because of its ability to include an embedded ICC color profile. The format itself doesn't provide much in the way of perceptible quality improvement, and if the image requires extensive editing, it may actually limit the quality of the photo.

HIDDEN JPEGS

You may not be aware that your RAW file contains an embedded JPEG file, hidden inside in the JPEG Basic format. It's used to provide thumbnail previews of JPEG files, which is why you may notice an interesting phenomenon when loading a RAW image into a program like Nikon Capture NX 2 or Adobe Lightroom. When the software first starts interpreting the RAW image, it may immediately display this hidden JPEG view which has, as you might expect, all the settings applied that you dialed into the camera. Then, as it finishes loading the RAW file, the application (Lightroom in particular) uses its own intelligence to fine-tune the image and display what it thinks is a decent version of the image, replacing the embedded JPEG. That's why you may see complaints that Lightroom or another program is behaving oddly: the initial embedded JPEG may look better than the final version, so it looks as if the application is degrading the image quality as the file loads. Of course, in all cases, once the RAW file is available, you can make your own changes to optimize it to your taste.

There is a second use for these hidden JPEG files. If you shoot RAW without creating JPEG files and later decide you want a JPEG version, there are dozens of utility programs that will extract the embedded JPEG and save it as a separate file. (Google "JPEG extractor" to locate a freeware program that will perform this step for your Mac, PC, or other computer.)

JPEG/TIFF Recording

The next menu command in the Shooting menu lets you select the resolution, or number of pixels captured as you shoot with your Nikon D810 for both JPEG and TIFF format files, as well as the type of compression for JPEG images. (The basic *amount* of compression is specified using the Fine, Normal, Basic JPEG options under Image Quality, described previously.) You have two options.

Image Size

Your choices range from Large (L), Medium (M), and Small (S). On the D810, those resolutions correspond to 7360 × 4912 pixels/36 megapixels (L); 5520 × 3680/20 megapixels (M); and 3680 × 2456/9 megapixels (S) sizes. These figures are all for the full-frame FX image area, which Nikon calls (36 × 24) 1.0x in the Image Area entry of the Shooting menu. Resolutions and megapixels depart from those values when using DX format (24 × 16) 1.5x, 5:4 format (30 × 24), and (on the D810) 1.2x, which is called (30 × 20) 1.2x.

Select image sizes by holding down the QUAL button on top of the release mode dial, while rotating the sub-command dial to change resolution among Large (L), Medium (M), or Small (S). Or, you can use this menu to perform the task (usually because you find the color monitor easier to view under the particular circumstances). There are no additional options available from the Image Size menu screen.

JPEG Compression

This menu entry is a simple one, offering you the choice of specifying either Size Priority (variable compression) or Optimal Quality (minimal compression) when the D810 creates JPEG files. I'll explain image compression in more detail in the next section.

- **Size priority.** When this option is selected, the D810 will create files that are fairly uniformly sized at roughly 16.3MB for a JPEG Fine image. Because some photos have content that is more easily compressible (for example, plain areas of sky can be squeezed down more than areas filled with detail), to maintain the standard file size the camera must apply more compression to some images, and less to others. As a result, there may be a barely noticeable loss of detail in the more heavily compressed images. The uniform file size also means that the D810's buffer will hold the maximum number of shots during continuous shooting, allowing you to shoot longer sequences without the need to pause and wait for some images to be written to the memory card.
- **Optimal quality.** Choose this option if you want to maintain the best image quality possible at a particular JPEG setting (Fine, Normal, or Basic) and don't care if the file size varies. Because the D810 will use only the minimum amount of compression required at each JPEG setting, file size will vary depending on scene content, and your buffer may hold fewer images during continuous shooting.

NEF (RAW) Recording

This is the first entry on the second page of the Shooting menu, as shown in Figure 11.14. Unfortunately, Nikon's chosen nomenclature can be a bit confusing. You have three main categories of settings to work with here:

- **Image Size.** This is a *separate* option from the Image Size choice under JPEG/TIFF Recording, explained above. It allows you to specify whether the camera saves the traditional full-size RAW images (7360 × 4912, totaling 36.2 megapixels), or a new type called RAW Small, which are 3680 × 2456 pixels/9 megapixels). You might want to opt for RAW S when you simply have no need for high-resolution images (say, you're shooting for a web page), but want to retain the RAW file's ability to manipulate settings that are locked in place in the camera when shooting JPEG.
- **NEF (RAW) Compression.** Here you can specify the type of compression used on your RAW files; lossless compressed, compressed, or uncompressed, all discussed below.
- **NEF (RAW) Bit Depth.** Choose from 12-bit or 14-bit color. I'll explain these options later, as well.

NEF (RAW) Compression

Compression is a mathematical technique for reducing the size of a collection of information (such as an image; but other types of data or even programs can be compressed, too) in order to reduce the storage requirements and/or time required to transmit or transfer the information. Some compression algorithms arrange strings of bits that are most frequently used into a table, so that a binary number like, say, 1001011011100111 (16 digits long) doesn't have to be stored as two 8-bit bytes every time it appears in the image file. Instead, a smaller number that points to that position in the

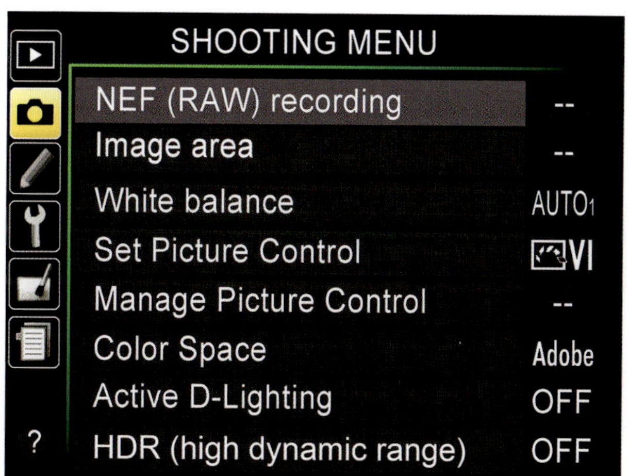

Figure 11.14 NEF (RAW) Recording is the first entry on the second page of the Shooting menu.

table can be used. The more times the pointer is used rather than the full number, the more space is saved in the file. Such a compression scheme can be used to reproduce exactly the original string of numbers, and so is called *lossless* compression.

Other types of compression are more aggressive and actually discard some of the information deemed to be redundant from a visual standpoint, so that, theoretically, you won't *notice* that details are missing, and the file can be made even more compact. The Nikon D810's RAW storage routines can use this kind of size reduction, which is called *lossy* compression, to reduce file size by up to about half with very little effect on image quality. JPEG compression can be even more enthusiastic, resulting in images that are 15X smaller (or more) and which display noticeable loss of image quality.

Under Type in the NEF (RAW) Recording menu, you can select from:

- **Lossless compressed.** This is the default setting, and uses what you might think of as reversible algorithms that discard no image information, so that the image can be compressed from 20-40 percent for a significantly smaller file size. The squeezed file can always be restored to its original size precisely, with no effect on image quality.
- **Compressed.** Use this setting if you want to store more images on your memory card and are willing to accept a tiny potential loss in image quality in the highlights, after significant editing (I've never been able to detect any effect at all). The D810 can achieve from 40-55 percent compression with this option. It uses a two-step process, first grouping some very similar tonal values in the mid-tone and lighter areas of the image together, and then storing each group as a single value, followed by a lossless compression scheme that is applied to the dark tones, further reducing the file size. The process does a good job of preserving tones in shadow areas of an image, with only small losses in the midtone and lighter areas. The differences may show up only if you perform certain types of extensive post-processing on an image, such as image sharpening or some tonal corrections.
- **Uncompressed.** At this setting, RAW images are not compressed at all, increasing the time needed to transfer these slightly larger files to your memory card. The files are identical to those produced by the lossless compressed option. The only real difference is that some software can handle uncompressed NEF files more readily than lossless compressed files. If you use an up-to-date RAW converter, there's no real reason to use this format.

Bit Depth

The Bit Depth setting is another option that looks good on paper but, in the real world, is less useful than you might think. For most applications, the default value that produces 12-bit image files is probably your best choice, unless you're exposing images that will be combined using HDR (high dynamic range) software later on. In that case, you can definitely gain some extra exposure "headroom" using 14-bit processing.

As you may know, bit depth is a way of measuring the amount of color data that an image file can contain. What we call "24-bit color" actually consists of three channels of information—red, green, and blue—with one 8-bit bit assigned to each channel, so a 24-bit image contains three 8-bit channels (each with 256 different shades of red, green, or blue). A 24-bit color image can contain up to 16.8 million different colors (256 × 256 × 256; you do the math). Because each of the red, green, and blue channels always is stored using the same number of bits, it's become the custom to refer only to the channel bit depth to describe the amount of color information that can be collected.

So, when we're talking about 12-bit color, what we really mean are three 12-bit RGB channels, each capable of recording colors from 000000000000 to 111111111111 hues in a particular channel (in binary), or 4,096 colors per channel (decimal) and a total of 68,719,476,736 (68.7 billion) different hues. By comparison, 14-bit color offers 16,384 colors per channel and a total of 4,398,046,511,104 (4.4 trillion) colors.

The advantage of having such a humongous number of colors for an image that will, in the end, be boiled down to 16.8 million hues in Photoshop or another image editor is that, to simplify things a little, there is a better chance that the mere millions of colors you end up with have a better chance of being the *right* colors to accurately represent the image. For example, if there are subtle differences in the colors of a certain range of tones that represent only, say, 10 percent of a channel's colors, there would be only 26 colors to choose from in an 8-bit channel, but 410 colors in a 12-bit channel, and a whopping 1,638 colors in a 14-bit channel. The larger number of colors improves the odds of ending up with accurate hues.

It's not quite that simple, of course, because bit depth also improves the chances of having the right number of colors to choose from after the inevitable loss of some information due to noise and other factors. But in the real world, the difference between 26 colors and 410 colors is significant (which is why digital cameras always capture at least 12 bits per channel), and the difference between 12 bits and 14 bits (410 and 1,638 colors, respectively in our example) is less significant. Because there is a penalty in terms of file size and the amount of time needed to process the image as it is recorded to your memory card, 14 bits per channel is not always your best option. Your two choices look like this:

- **12 bit.** Images are recorded at 12 bits per channel in the RAW file, and end up with 12 bits of information per channel that is translated during conversion for your image editor either into 12 bits within a 16-bits-per-channel space or interpreted down to 8 bits per channel.
- **14 bit.** This is the default bit depth for the Nikon D810. At this setting, the D810 grabs 16,384 colors per channel instead of 4,096, ending up as 14 bits in a 16-channel space or reduced to 256 colors by the RAW conversion software that translates the image for your image editor. You'll find that such 14-bit files end up almost one-third larger than 12-bit files. 14-bit images are great for HDR photography.

Image Area

You have two options, Auto DX Crop and Choose Image Area:

- **Auto DX Crop.** You can switch this feature On or Off. When activated, the D810 will detect when a Nikon-brand DX lens is mounted and automatically crop the image to produce a frame filled with the DX coverage area, reducing the resolution of the photo to 15 megapixels. The camera may not detect DX-format lenses from other vendors, in which case you'll need to use the manual image area option described next. Turn Auto DX Crop off, and the camera always captures the full frame. You'd want to use that option if you don't mind the vignetting that a DX lens can produce in full-frame mode, or if you're using a lens that you know will cover the full frame acceptably at the focal length you plan to use.
- **Choose Image Area.** You can manually specify the image area to be used, which the D810 will apply regardless of what type of lens is mounted on the camera. Use this option to force the image area issue (as when you're using a DX-format lens that the D810 can't detect automatically), or to use a particular image area for all your shots in a session. Your choices include:
  - **FX format (36 × 24).** This is the full FX image format area, roughly 36mm × 24mm.
  - **1.2X (30 × 20).** This image area produces an image that fills the frame with a 3:2 aspect ratio (the same proportions as the full-frame image area), but with a 1.2X crop factor. I like to use this setting with some DX-format lenses that don't quite cover the full 36mm × 24mm frame, but which do fill up the entire 30mm × 20mm image area. For example, I have a 10-17mm fisheye zoom lens that I like to use on my full-frame cameras, and I can get an acceptable 15-megapixel image with my D810 in DX mode. However, when I switch to the 1.2X crop mode, I lose a little bit of the fisheye effect, but get corner-to-corner coverage in an even more usable 25-megapixel image file.
  - **DX format (24 × 16).** This fills the image frame with the image in the center 24mm × 16mm of the sensor, creating a 1.5X *crop factor.* (See Chapter 7 for more about the crop factor and lenses.)
  - **5:4 (30 × 24).** Images are captured using a 5:4 aspect ratio, the same as a 4 × 5 or 8 × 10-inch print.

White Balance

This menu entry allows you to choose one of the white balance values from among Auto, Incandescent, seven varieties of Fluorescent illumination, Direct Sunlight, Flash, Cloudy, Shade, a specific color temperature of your choice, or a preset value taken from an existing photograph, or a measurement you make. Some of the settings you make here can be duplicated using the WB button on top of the camera's release mode dial and main and sub-command dials, but the menus offer even more choices, as you'll see. Your white balance settings can have a significant impact on the color rendition of your images, as you can see in Figure 11.15.

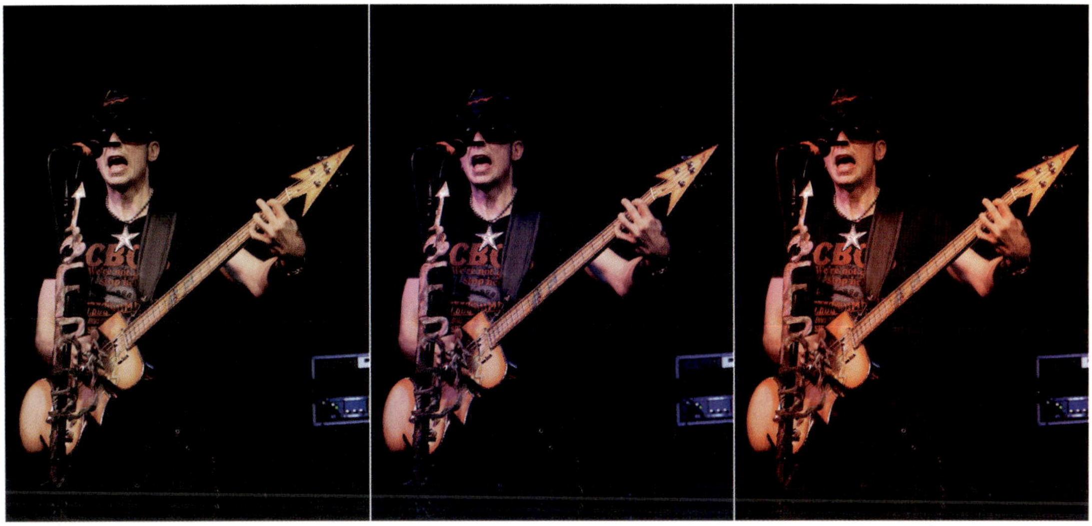

Figure 11.15 Adjusting color temperature can provide different results of the same subject at settings of 3,400K (left), 5,000K (middle), and 2,800K (right).

When you select the White Balance entry on the Shooting menu, you'll see an array of choices like those shown in Figure 11.16. (Two additional choices, K Choose Color Temp. and PRE Preset Manual are not visible until you scroll down to them.) If you choose Fluorescent, you'll be taken to another screen that presents seven different types of lamps, from sodium-vapor through warm-white fluorescent down to high temperature mercury-vapor. If you know the exact type of non-incandescent lighting being used, you can select it, or settle on a likely compromise.

The Choose Color Temp. selection allows you to select from an array of color temperatures in degrees Kelvin (more on this in Chapter 8) from 2,500K to 10,000K, and then further fine-tune the color bias using the fine-tuning feature described below. Select Preset Manual to record or recall custom white balance settings suitable for environments with unusual lighting or mixed lighting, as described later in this section.

For all other settings (Auto, Incandescent, Direct Sunlight, Flash, Cloudy, or Shade), highlight the white balance option you want, then press the multi selector right button (or press OK) to view the fine-tuning screen shown in Figure 11.17 (and which uses the incandescent setting as an example). The screen shows a grid with two axes, a blue/amber axis extending left/right, and a green/magenta axis extending up and down the grid. By default, the grid's cursor is positioned in the middle, and a readout to the right of the grid shows the cursor's coordinates on the A-B axis (yes, I know the display has the end points reversed) and G-M axis at 0,0.

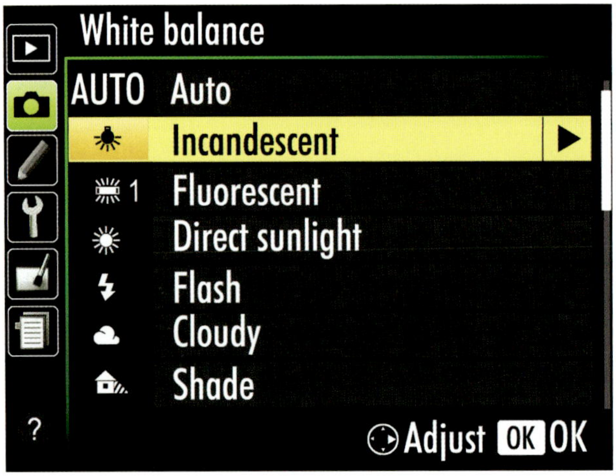

Figure 11.16
The White Balance menu has predefined values, plus the options of setting color temperature and presets you measure yourself.

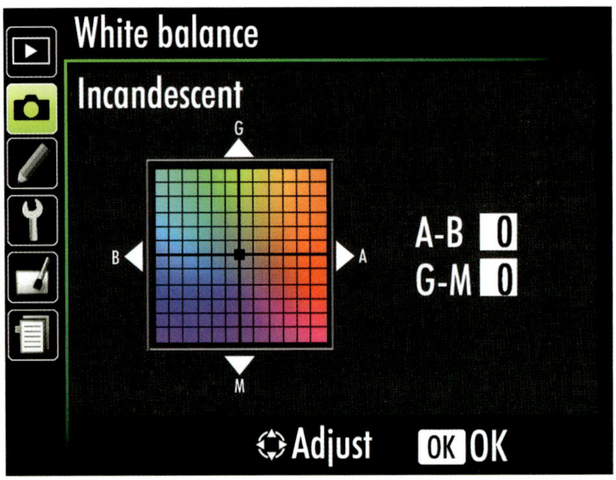

Figure 11.17
Specific white balance settings can be fine-tuned by changing their bias in the amber/blue, magenta/green directions—or along both axes simultaneously.

You can use the multi selector's up/down and right/left buttons to move the cursor to any coordinate in the grid, thereby biasing the white balance in the direction(s) you choose. The amber-blue axis makes the image warmer or colder (but not actually yellow or blue). Similarly, the green-magenta axis preserves all the colors in the original image, but gives them a tinge biased toward green or magenta. Each increment equals about five mired units, but you should know that mired values aren't linear; five mireds at 2,500K produces a much stronger effect than five mireds at 6,000K. If you really want to fine-tune your color balance, you're better off experimenting and evaluating the results of a particular change.

When you've fine-tuned white balance, either using the Shooting menu options or the WB button, left/right triangles appear in the white balance section of the control panel at lower right to remind you that this tweaking has taken place.

Using Preset Manual White Balance

If automatic white balance or one of the predefined settings available aren't suitable, you can set a custom white balance using the Preset Manual menu option. You can apply the white balance from a scene, either by shooting a new picture on the spot and using the resulting white balance (Direct Measurement) or using an image you have already shot (Copy from Existing Photograph). To perform direct measurement from your current scene using a reference object (preferably a neutral gray or white object), follow these steps:

1. **Use gray or white reference.** Place the neutral reference, such as a white piece of paper, or a gray card, under the lighting you want to measure. You can also use one of those white balance caps that fit on the front of your lens like a lens cap, such as the ExpoDisc.
2. **Choose Preset Manual.** Hold down the WB button on the release mode dial and rotate the main command dial until PRE is displayed in the lower-right corner of the monochrome LCD control panel. The number of the "slot" (from d-1 through d-6) where the white balance setting will appear is displayed at the top of the control panel and in the viewfinder.
3. **Select your "slot."** Press the WB button again and rotate the sub-command dial to choose d-1 through d-6. Note that you can "protect" a given slot from being overwritten with a new value, in which case **Prt** will appear on the control panel and in the viewfinder.
4. **Start measurement.** Release the WB button for a moment, then press and hold it again until the PRE icon on the monochrome LCD and in the viewfinder begins a flashing cycle of about six seconds.

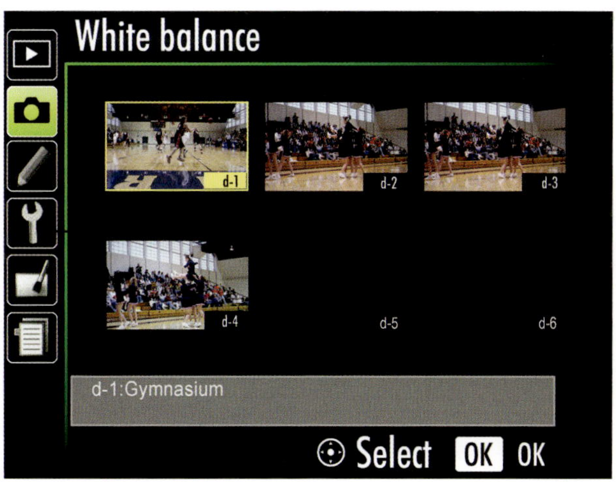

Figure 11.18
When you capture a scene's white balance, it will be stored in the selected slot.

5. **Capture white balance.** While the PRE icon is flashing, take a picture of the reference object. No photo is actually taken, so the preset slot appears to be blank.
6. **Confirm capture.** If the camera successfully measured white balance, **Good** will flash on the control panel for about six seconds, and **Gd** will appear in the bottom line of the viewfinder. Otherwise, you'll see **no Gd** on the LCD and viewfinder. White balance measurement can fail when the reference object is too brightly or poorly illuminated. In that case, repeat steps 2-5 until the measurement is successful.

The preset value you've captured will remain in the slot until you replace that white balance with a new captured value. It can be summoned at any time (press the WB button on the top left of the camera and dial it in by rotating the sub-command dial until the desired white balance slot is displayed on the control panel). You can also choose an existing image or protect a captured white balance from being overwritten:

1. Choose Preset Manual from the White Balance menu.
2. A screen of thumbnails appears, showing the four "slots" numbered d-1 to d-6. Use the multi selector buttons to highlight one of the four thumbnail slots, and press the multi selector center button.
3. The next screen that appears (see Figure 11.19) has four options: Fine-tune, Edit Comment, Select Image, and Protect.
   - Choose Fine-tune to fine-tune the amber/blue/magenta/green white balance of an image already stored in one of the four user slots.
   - Choose Edit Comment to add or change the comment applied to d-1 to d-6. The comment can be used as a label to better identify the white balance information in the slot, with terms like Gymnasium Daytime or Rumpus Room. (The standard D810 Edit Comment screen, as in Figure 11.10, appears.)
   - Choose Select Image to view the D810's standard image selection screen (see Figure 11.8 again) and highlight and choose the existing image you want to use. Press the multi selector center button to confirm your choice and copy the white balance of the selected image to the slot you selected in Step 2.
   - Choose Protect to lock the white balance setting currently stored in the selected slot. Use this to preserve a captured white balance setting.
4. Press OK to confirm your white balance setting.

A WHITE BALANCE LIBRARY

Consider dedicating a low-capacity memory card to stow a selection of images taken under a variety of lighting conditions. If you want to "recycle" one of the color temperatures you've stored, insert the card and load one of those images into your choice of preset slots d-1 to d-6, as described above.

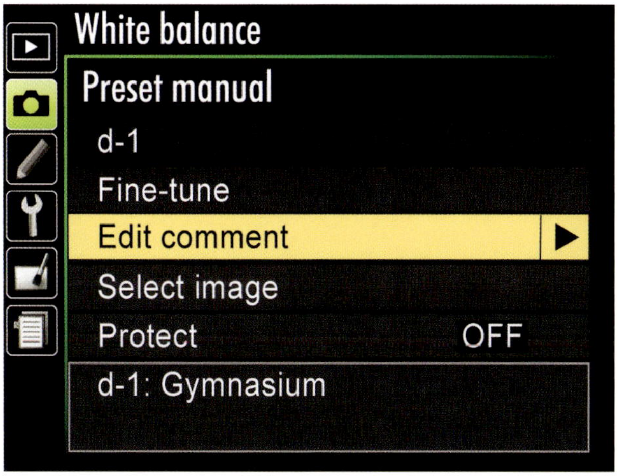

Figure 11.19
The Preset Manual screen lets you fine-tune preset white balance settings, label them with a comment, select an image to use as a white balance reference, and protect captured settings.

Set Picture Control

Nikon's Picture Control styles allow you to choose your own sharpness, contrast, color saturation, and hue settings applied to your color images and movies, with an additional attribute, clarity (described below), available for still photographs. There are only seven predefined styles offered, which Nikon calls Original Picture Controls: Standard, Neutral, Vivid, Monochrome, Portrait, Landscape, and Flat. The characteristics of the first six are self explanatory; Flat is a control that retains as much detail as possible in both shadows and highlights. While you may not prefer Flat images as they come out of the camera, the rendition lends itself to fine-tuning in your image editor, as you end up with a wealth of detail to work with. In addition, you can *edit* the settings of any of those styles so they better suit your taste.

But that's only the beginning; the D810 also offers *nine* (count 'em) user-definable Picture Control styles, which follow the seven predefined styles in the listing after you create them. You can edit these styles to your heart's content, assign descriptive names, and deploy at the press of a few buttons. Even better, you can *copy* these styles to a memory card, edit them on your computer, and reload them into your camera at any time. So, effectively, you can have a lot more than nine custom Picture Control styles available: the nine in your camera, as well as a virtually unlimited library of user-defined styles that you have stored on memory cards or create using Capture NX 2/NX-D or View NX2.

Moreover, Nikon insists that these styles have been standardized to the extent that if you reuse a style created for one camera (say, your D810) and load it into a different compatible camera (such as a Nikon D4), you'll get substantially the same rendition. In a way, Picture Control styles are a bit like using a particular film. Do you want the look of Kodak Ektachrome or Fujifilm Velvia? (Even if you've never *used* these films, but have seen the results they produced.) Load the appropriate style created by you—or anyone else.

Using and managing Picture Control styles is accomplished using two different menu entries, Set Picture Control, which allows you to *choose* an existing style and to edit the predefined styles that Nikon provides, and Manage Picture Control, discussed in the next section, which gives you the capability of creating and editing user-defined styles.

Choosing a Picture Control Style

To choose from one of the predefined styles (Standard, Neutral, Vivid, Monochrome, Portrait, Landscape, or Flat) or select a user-defined style (numbered C-1 to C-9), follow these steps:

1. Choose Set Picture Control from the Shooting menu. The screen shown in Figure 11.20 appears. Note that Picture Controls that have been modified from their standard settings have an asterisk next to their name.
2. Scroll down to the Picture Control you'd like to use.
3. Press OK to activate the highlighted style. (Although you can usually select a menu item by pressing the multi selector right button; in this case, that button activates editing instead.)
4. Press the MENU button or tap the shutter release to exit the menu system.

Editing a Picture Control Style

You can change the parameters of any of Nikon's predefined Picture Controls, or any of the nine user-defined styles you create. You can use the quick adjust/fine-tune facility to modify a Picture Control with a few sliders. To make quick adjustments to any Picture Control except the Monochrome style, follow these steps:

1. Choose Set Picture Control from the Shooting menu.
2. Scroll down to the Picture Control you'd like to edit.
3. Press the multi selector right button to produce the adjustment screen shown in Figure 11.21.
4. Use the Quick Adjust slider to exaggerate the attributes (Quick Adjustments are not available with Neutral, Monochrome, or Flat styles).

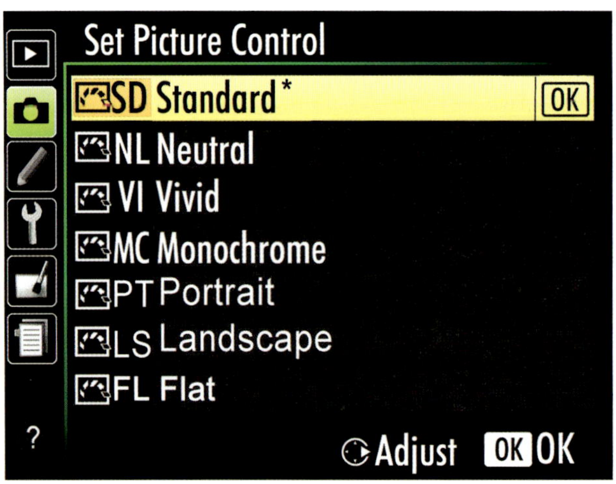

Figure 11.20
You can choose from the seven predefined Picture Controls shown here.

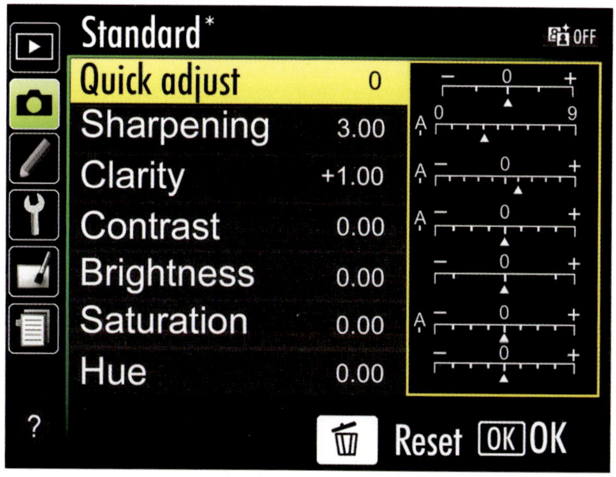

Figure 11.21
Sliders can be used to make quick adjustments to your Picture Control styles.

5. Scroll down to the Sharpening, Clarity, Contrast, Brightness, Saturation, and Hue sliders with the multi selector up/down buttons, then use the left/right buttons to decrease or increase the effects. The directional buttons move the indicators in whole increments; use the sub-command dial instead for fine-tuning with .25 increments.

   Note: The new Clarity control provides extra sharpness around the edges of objects. Beware of applying this attribute too heavily, as it can produce shadows around bright objects, and halos around dark objects. The Clarity control is not applied to movies.

6. A line will appear under the original setting in the slider whenever you've made a change from the defaults. Unlike some previous Nikon models, you *can* adjust contrast and brightness when Active D-Lighting (discussed later in this chapter) is active. But ADL will affect your images on top of the changes made by Picture Controls. So, a helpful icon at upper right in the dialog box will alert you when ADL is enabled.
7. Instead of making changes with the slider's scale, you can move the cursor to the far left and choose A (for auto) instead when working with the Sharpening, Clarity, Contrast, and Saturation sliders. The D810 will adjust these parameters automatically, depending on the type of scene it detects. You can quickly switch back and forth between auto and manual adjustments by pressing the Zoom In button.
8. Press the Trash button to reset the values to their defaults.
9. Press OK when you're finished making adjustments.

Editing the Monochrome style is similar, except that the parameters differ slightly. Sharpening, Clarity, Contrast, and Brightness are available, but, instead of Saturation and Hue, you can choose a filter effect (Yellow, Orange, Red, Green, or none) and a toning effect (black-and-white, plus seven levels of Sepia, Cyanotype, Red, Yellow, Green, Blue Green, Blue, Purple Blue, and Red Purple). (Keep in mind that once you've taken a JPEG photo using a Monochrome style, you can't convert the image back to full color.)

FILTERS VS. TONING

Although some of the color choices seem to overlap, you'll get very different looks when choosing between Filter Effects and Toning. Filter Effects add no color to the monochrome image. Instead, they reproduce the look of black-and-white film that has been shot through a color filter. That is, Yellow will make the sky darker and the clouds will stand out more, while Orange makes the sky even darker and sunsets more full of detail. The Red filter produces the darkest sky of all and darkens

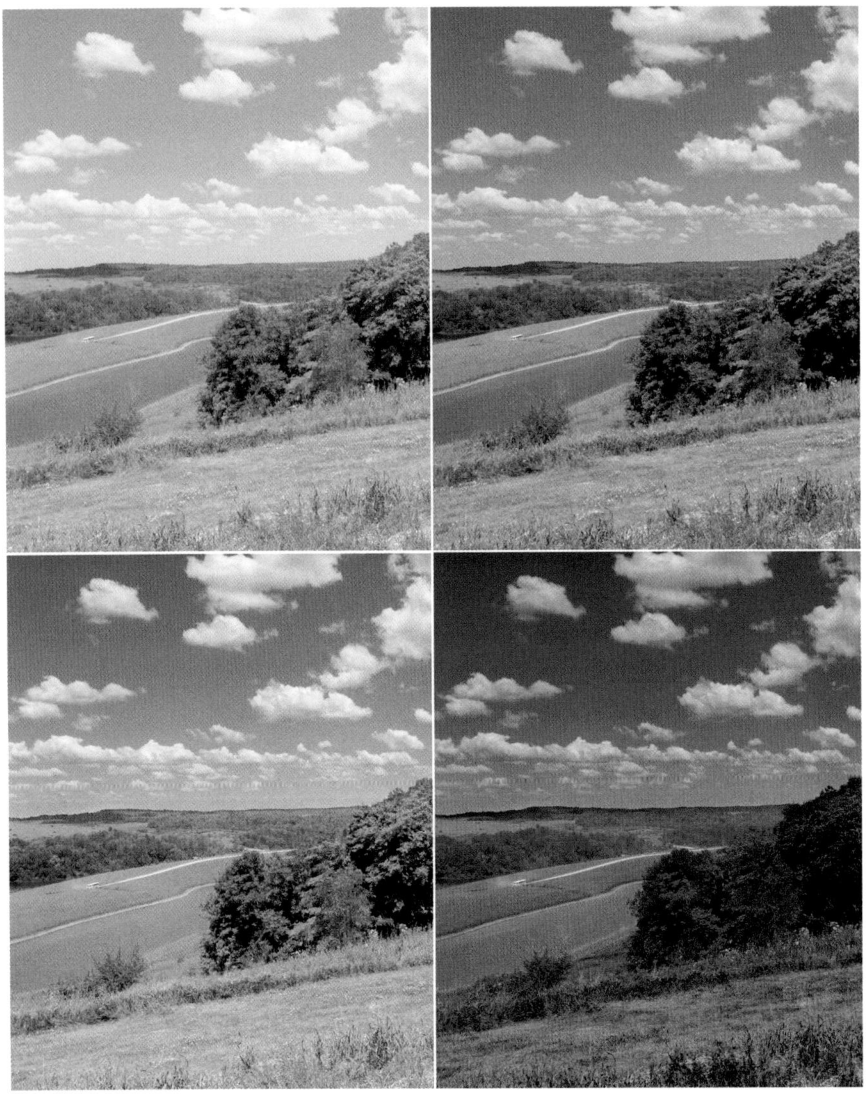

Figure 11.22
Color filter effects: No filter (upper left); yellow filter (upper right); green filter (lower left); and red filter (lower right).

green objects, such as leaves. Human skin may appear lighter than normal. The Green filter has the opposite effect on leaves, making them appear lighter in tone. Figure 11.22 shows the same scene shot with no filter, then Yellow, Green, and Red filters.

The Sepia, Blue, Green, and other toning effects, on the other hand, all add a color cast to your monochrome image. Use these when you want an old-time look or a special effect, without bothering to recolor your shots in an image editor. Toning is shown in Figure 11.23.

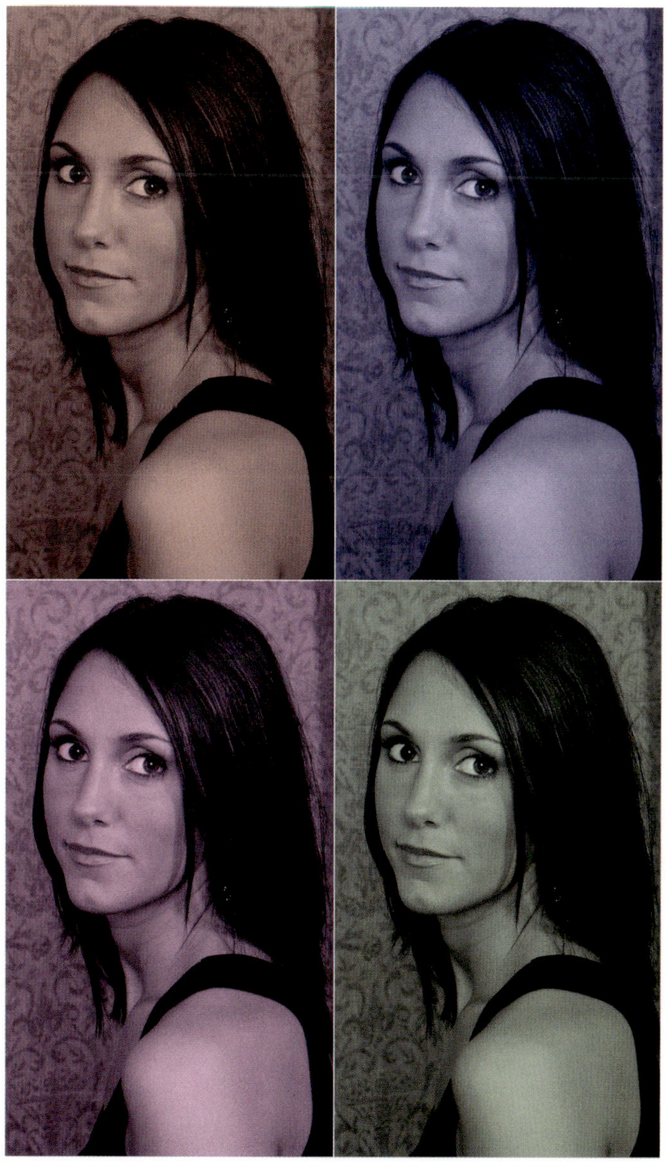

Figure 11.23
Toning effect: Sepia (upper left); Purple Blue (upper right); Red Purple (lower left); and Green (lower right).

Manage Picture Control

The Manage Picture Control menu entry can be used to create new styles, edit existing styles, rename or delete them, and store/retrieve them from the memory card. Here are the basic functions of this menu item, which can be found on the Shooting menu directly below the Set Picture Control entry:

- **Make a copy.** Choose Save/Edit, select from the list of available Picture Controls, and press OK to store that style in one of the user-defined slots C-1 to C-9 (with slots C-1 to C-7 shown in Figure 11.24).
- **Save an edited copy.** Choose Save/Edit, select from the list of available Picture Controls, and then press the multi selector right button to edit the style, as described in the previous section. Press OK when finished editing, and then save the modified style in one of the user-defined slots C-1 to C-9.
- **Rename a style.** Choose Rename, select from the list of user-defined Picture Controls (you cannot rename the default styles), and then enter the text used as the new label for the style, using the standard D810 text entry screen shown earlier in Figure 11.10. You may use up to 19 characters for the name.
- **Remove a style.** Select Delete, choose from the list of user-defined Picture Controls (you can't remove one of the default styles), press the multi selector right button, then highlight Yes in the screen that follows, and press OK to remove that Picture Control.
- **Store/retrieve style on card.** Choose Load/Save, then select Copy to Camera to locate a Picture Control on your memory card and copy it to the D810; Delete from Card to select a Picture Control on your memory card and remove it; or Copy to Card to duplicate a style currently in your camera onto the memory card. This last option allows you to create and save Picture Controls in excess of the nine that can be loaded into the camera at one time. Once you've copied a style to your memory card, you can modify the version in the camera, give it a new name, and, in effect, create a whole new Picture Control.

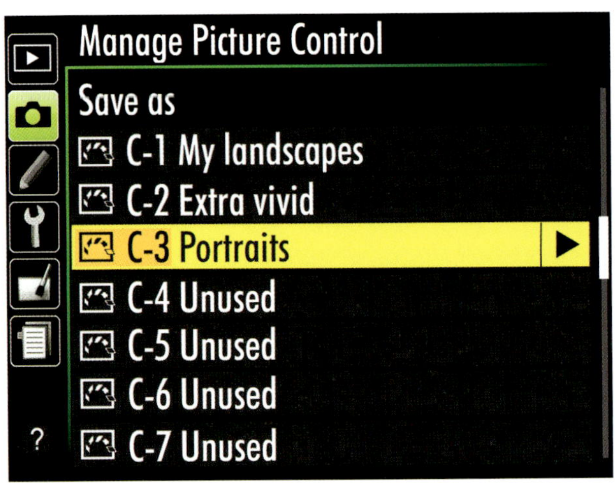

Figure 11.24 Picture Controls that you define can be stored in your D810's settings.

Color Space

The Nikon D810's Color Space option gives you two different color spaces (also called *color gamuts*), named Adobe RGB (because it was developed by Adobe Systems in 1998), and sRGB (supposedly because it is the *standard* RGB color space). These two color gamuts define a specific set of colors that can be applied to the images your D810 captures.

You're probably surprised that the Nikon D810 doesn't automatically capture *all* the colors we see. Unfortunately, that's impossible because of the limitations of the sensor and the filters used to capture the fundamental red, green, and blue colors, as well as that of the phosphors used to display those colors on your camera and computer monitors. Nor is it possible to *print* every color our eyes detect, because the inks or pigments used don't absorb and reflect colors perfectly.

On the other hand, the D810 does capture quite a few more colors than we need. A basic 12-bit RAW image contains a possible 4.3 *billion* different hues (4,096 colors per red, green, or blue channel), which are condensed down to a mere 16.8 million possible colors when converted to a 24-bit (eight bits per channel) image. While 16.8 million colors may seem like a lot, it's a small subset of 4.3 billion captured, and an even smaller subset of all the possible colors we can see. A 14-bit RAW image has even more possible colors—16,384 per color channel, or 281 *trillion* hues.

The set of colors, or gamut, that can be reproduced or captured by a given device (scanner, digital camera, monitor, printer, or some other piece of equipment) is represented as a color space that exists within the larger full range of colors. That full range is represented by the odd-shaped splotch of color shown in Figure 11.25, as defined by scientists at an international organization back in 1931. The colors possible with Adobe RGB are represented by the larger, black triangle in the figure, while the sRGB gamut is represented by the smaller white triangle.

Regardless of which triangle—or color space—is used by the D810, you end up with some combination of 16.8 million different colors that can be used in your photograph. (No one image will contain all 16.8 million! To require that many, only about two pixels of any one color could be the same in a 36-megapixel image!) But, as you can see from the figure, the colors available will be *different.*

Adobe RGB is an expanded color space useful for commercial and professional printing, and it can reproduce a wider range of colors. It can also come in useful if an image is going to be extensively retouched, especially within an advanced image editor, like Adobe Photoshop, which has sophisticated color management capabilities that can be tailored to specific color spaces. As an advanced user, you don't need to automatically "upgrade" your D810 to Adobe RGB, because images tend to look less saturated on your monitor and, it is likely, significantly different from what you will get if you output the photo to your personal inkjet. (You can *profile* your monitor for the Adobe RGB color space to improve your on-screen rendition.)

While both Adobe RGB and sRGB can reproduce the exact same 16.8 million absolute colors, Adobe RGB spreads those colors over a larger portion of the visible spectrum, as you can see in the figure. Think of a box of crayons (the jumbo 16.8 million crayon variety). Some of the basic crayons

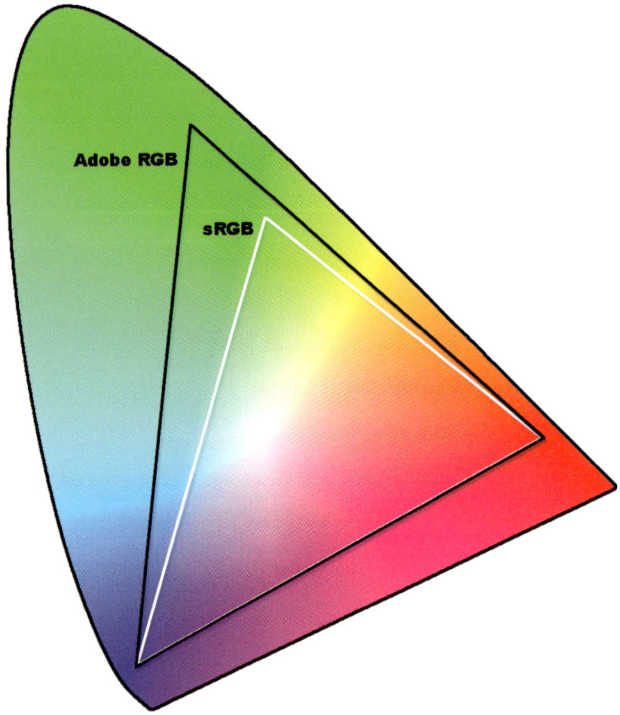

Figure 11.25
The outer figure shows all the colors we can see; the two inner outlines show the boundaries of Adobe RGB (black triangle) and sRGB (white triangle).

from the original sRGB set have been removed and replaced with new hues not contained in the original box. Your "new" box contains colors that can't be reproduced by your computer monitor, but which work just fine with a commercial printing press. For example, Adobe RGB has more "crayons" available in the cyan-green portion of the box, compared to sRGB, which is unlikely to be an advantage unless your image's final destination are the cyan, magenta, yellow, and black inks of a printing press.

The other color space, sRGB, is recommended for images that will be output locally on the user's own printer, as this color space matches that of the typical inkjet printer fairly closely. You might prefer sRGB, which is the default for the Nikon D810 and most other cameras, as it is well suited for the range of colors that can be displayed on a computer screen and viewed over the Internet. If you plan to take your image file to a retailer's kiosk for printing, sRGB is your best choice, because those automated output devices are calibrated for the sRGB color space that consumers use.

BEST OF BOTH WORLDS

If you plan to use RAW+JPEG for most of your photos, go ahead and set sRGB as your color space. You'll end up with JPEGs suitable for output on your own printer, but you can still extract an Adobe RGB version from the RAW file at any time. It's like shooting two different color spaces at once—sRGB and Adobe RGB—and getting the best of both worlds.

Of course, choosing the right color space doesn't solve the problems that result from having each device in the image chain manipulating or producing a slightly different set of colors. To that end, you'll need to investigate the wonderful world of *color management*, which uses hardware and software tools to match or *calibrate* all your devices, as closely as possible, so that what you see more closely resembles what you capture, what you see on your computer display, and what ends up on a printed hardcopy. Entire books have been devoted to color management, and most of what you need to know doesn't directly involve your Nikon D810, so I won't detail the nuts and bolts here.

To manage your color, you'll need, at the bare minimum, some sort of calibration system for your computer display, so that your monitor can be adjusted to show a standardized set of colors that is repeatable over time. (What you see on the screen can vary as the monitor ages, or even when the room light changes.) I use Datacolor's Spyder 4 color correction system for my computer's main 26-inch wide-screen LCD display (see Figure 11.26), as well as for the matching 26-inch wide-screen and a 24-inch third display. The unit checks room light levels every five minutes, and reminds me to recalibrate every week or two, using the small sensor device shown which attaches temporarily to the front of the screen, and interprets test patches that the software displays during calibration. The rest of the time, the sensor sits in its stand, measuring the room illumination and adjusting my monitors for higher or lower ambient light levels.

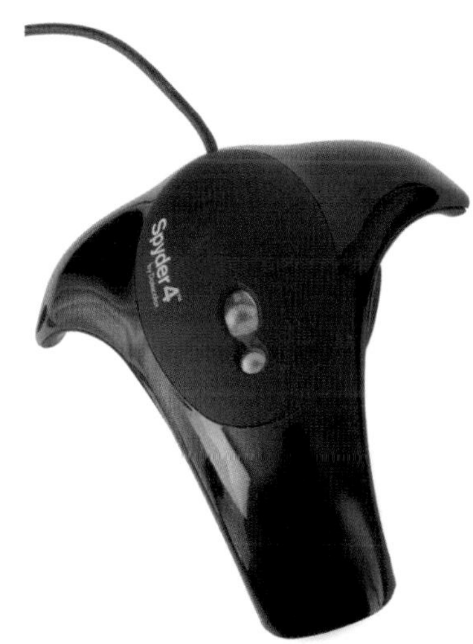

Figure 11.26 Datacolor Spyder 4 color correction system.

If you want more advanced capabilities for adjustments for accurate color and making prints, you might want a more sophisticated system (up to $500) like the various other Spyder products from Datacolor (www.datacolor.com), or Colormunki from X-Rite (www.colormunki.com).

Active D-Lighting

Active D-Lighting is a feature that improves the rendition of detail in highlights and shadows when you're photographing high contrast scenes. It's been available as an internal retouching option in Nikon's lower-end cameras (by that I mean the Coolpix point-and-shoot line) for some time, and gradually worked its way up through the company's dSLR products, eventually reaching advanced cameras like the D810. You'll find the "non-active" D-Lighting feature in the Retouch menu, which I'll describe in Chapter 13.

Active D-Lighting, unlike the Retouch menu post-processing feature, applies its tonal improvements *while you are actually taking the photo.* That's good news and bad news. It means that, if you're taking photos in a contrasty environment, Active D-Lighting can automatically improve the apparent dynamic range of your image as you shoot, without additional effort on your part. However, you'll need to disable the feature once you leave the high contrast lighting behind, and the process does take some time. You wouldn't want to use Active D-Lighting for continuous shooting of sports subjects, for example. There are many situations in which the selective application of D-Lighting using the Retouch menu is a better choice.

You have six choices: Auto, Extra High, High, Normal, Low, and Off. You may need to experiment with the feature a little to discover how much D-Lighting you can apply to a high contrast image before the shadows start to darken objectionably. Note that when this feature is activated, brightness and contrast Picture Control settings cannot be changed. Figure 11.27 shows some examples of Active D-Lighting applied. By the time the sample images shown have been half-toned and rendered to the printed page, the differences may be fairly subtle. For that reason, I'm not illustrating the effects of the Auto setting (which varies, of course, depending on the scene) or the Extra High setting. Look at the amount of detail in the overhanging rock in the upper-right area of each version.

For best results, use your D810's Matrix metering mode, so the Active D-Lighting feature can work with a full range of exposure information from multiple points in the image. Active D-Lighting works its magic by subtly *underexposing* your image so that details in the highlights (which would normally be overexposed and become featureless white pixels) are not lost. At the same time, it adjusts the values of pixels located in midtone and shadow areas so they don't become too dark because of the underexposure. Highlight tones will be preserved, while shadows will eventually be allowed to go dark more readily. Bright beach or snow scenes, especially those with few shadows (think high noon, when the shadows are smaller) can benefit from using Active D-Lighting.

It's important to *always* keep in mind that Active D-Lighting not only adjusts the contrast automatically of your image (that's why you can't adjust the brightness/contrast of a Picture Control when Active D-Lighting is turned on), it modifies exposure for both existing light and flash as well, as I've noted. Exposure for both is reduced from about 1/3 stop (at the Low setting) to as much as 1 full stop less at the Extra High setting.

Nikon gives you a lot of flexibility in using Active D-Lighting. You can choose the setting yourself, or let the camera *vary* the amount of tweaking by using Active D-Lighting Bracketing. You'll find this is a useful feature, if used with caution.

Tip

In Manual exposure mode, Active D-Lighting does not adjust the exposure of your image; it simply shifts the center (zero) point of the analog exposure indicator in the viewfinder/control panel.

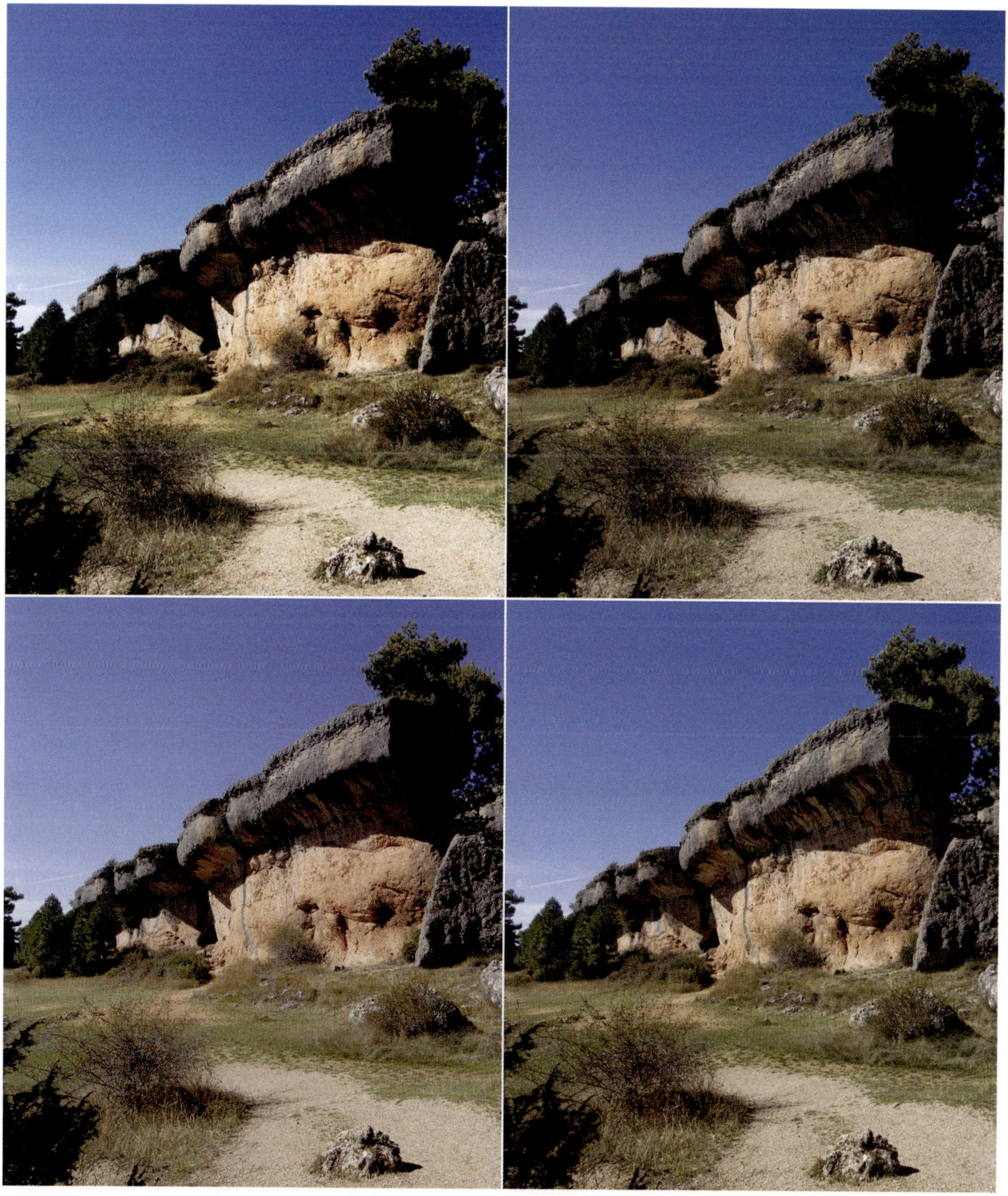

Figure 11.27 No D-Lighting (upper left); low (upper right); normal (lower left); and high (lower right).

HDR (High Dynamic Range)

I was surprised at how well the D810's in-camera HDR worked, because there are two stumbling blocks that, at least theoretically, should lead to less-than-awesome results. First, when your camera can perform HDR for you on the fly, there is the tendency to put the feature to work under non-optimal conditions; specifically, impromptu hand-held situations. If you've done any traditional HDR, you know that the technique works best when the camera is mounted on a tripod, so that the bracketed exposures are virtually identical except for the exposure itself. Although all HDR software can correct for slight camera movement and align images that are slightly out of register, the results I've gotten have not been great. I expected hand-held HDR with the D810's auto HDR feature to be comparable.

The second theoretical weakness of the D810's HDR feature is the limitation of combining just two shots to arrive at the final image. The best traditional HDR photos I've produced have involved at least three shots, and more frequently five or more, each separated by a stop of exposure. The D810 takes two shots, total, and combines them. Despite these speedbumps, I've been pleased with my results.

I was prowling around a decommissioned railroad roundhouse, exploring some rolling stock that was being repaired and preserved by a group of enthusiasts who'd taken over the railyard. The engine shown in Figure 11.28 was cloaked in near-darkness, except for a large spot of light from a hanging bulb seen at left. I decided to try out the D810's HDR. With the camera set to ISO 3200

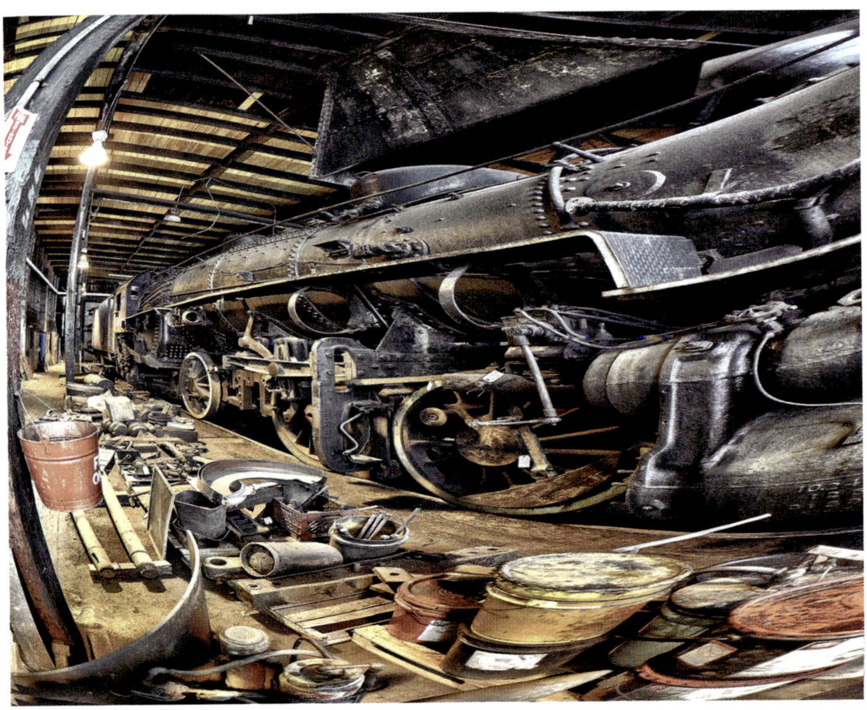

Figure 11.28
The D810's built-in HDR feature can produce good results even when the camera is hand-held.

and a base exposure of 1/125th second at f/2.8 and an exposure differential of 3 EV, and a fisheye lens mounted, the camera conjured up the image you see. Not bad for a grab shot.

I'm continuing to play with this feature to see what it can do, and suggest you do the same. The steps, originally outlined in Chapter 4, are easy enough to follow.

1. **Turn off conflicting features.** Disable bracketing if active, and choose JPEG as your image format.
2. **Access the HDR entry.** Navigate to the Shooting menu and select HDR (high dynamic range).
3. **Turn on HDR.** Choose HDR Mode, press right, and select either On (series) if you want to shoot multiple HDR photos consecutively or On (single photo) to take a single HDR image and then shut the feature off. Press OK to confirm.
4. **Choose an increment.** Choose Exposure Differential, press the right button, and select Auto (the D810 chooses the differential based on how contrasty it deems your scene to be), or 1 EV, 2 EV, or 3 EV. Auto is a good choice for your initial experiments. Or, select a higher EV value for higher contrast subjects, and a lower value for lower contrast subjects. Press OK to confirm.
5. **Select smoothing.** The edges of the areas in your image may have a high-contrast, poster-edge like effect in some circumstances. If you don't like the effect, you can use smoothing to adjust the shading between these edges. Press OK to confirm.
6. **Take your shot**. As with all HDR photography, you'll want to use Aperture-priority so the depth-of-field and focus won't change between the two shots. As I noted, you'll get the best results with the D810 mounted on a tripod, and with subjects that don't display a lot of motion, but hand-held shots are possible.
7. **Wait for the results.** After you make the exposure, the D810 will merge your two shots. The message **Job** will appear on the control panel, and **Job Hdr** will be shown at the bottom of the viewfinder.

Vignette Control

This is the first entry in the third page of the Shooting menu (see Figure 11.29). Some lenses may not be up to the challenge of covering the full FX frame evenly, producing darkening in the corners of your images at certain focal lengths. That was the chief beef many FX users had with the otherwise superb original version of the Nikon 70-200 f/2.8 VR zoom. (It's since been replaced with a new VR II version that does a better job of avoiding vignetting effects.)

If you consistently encounter vignetting, this option may help. It reduces darkening at the periphery of images when using non-DX/non-perspective control lenses of the G and D type. (I explained the nomenclature of Nikon's lens alphabet soup in Chapter 7.) You can choose from High, Normal, Low, and Off. It's difficult to quantify exactly how much corner-brightening each setting provides. Your best bet is to shoot some blank walls of a single color with lenses that seem to have this problem, and try a few at each of the settings. Then select the value that best seems to counter vignetting with your particular lenses.

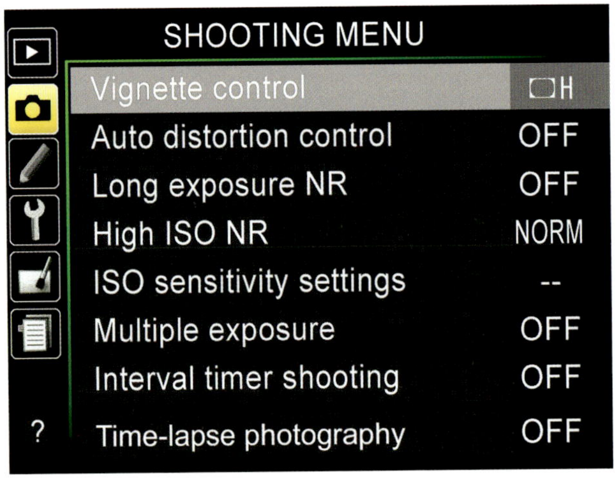

Figure 11.29
Vignette Control is the first entry on the third page of the D810 Shooting menu.

Auto Distortion Control

As I explained in Chapter 7, wide-angle lenses are prone to barrel distortion, in which straight lines appear to bow outward, especially near the edges of the frame. Telephoto lenses often have the opposite problem: lines may bend inward, producing pincushion distortion. Both these types of distortion can be easily corrected in your image editor, but your D810's digital image processing chip has similar algorithms built in and can do the job for you. Your choices are easy: just select On or Off to enable or disable this feature.

For the process to work, the lenses have to be of a type that are able to communicate electronically with the camera to let the D810 know what type lens it is working with, so that means you should be using a G or D type optic. The camera will warp the photo before saving it to your memory card, cropping a bit if necessary to exclude some areas of the image. If you're working with DX lenses, either choose Auto DX Crop: On or manually select DX (24 × 16) 1.5x (if you're using a DX-type lens that might not be recognized as such by the D810) to avoid distortion outside the intended DX image area.

Long Exp. NR

Visual noise is that awful graininess caused by long exposures and high ISO settings, and which shows up as multicolored specks in images. This setting helps you manage the kind of noise caused by lengthy exposure times. In some ways, noise is like the excessive grain found in some high-speed photographic films. However, while photographic grain is sometimes used as a special effect, it's rarely desirable in a digital photograph. There are easier ways to add texture to your photos.

Some noise is created when you're using shutter speeds longer than eight seconds to create a longer exposure. Extended exposure times allow more photons to reach the sensor, but increase the likelihood that some photosites will react randomly even though not struck by a particle of light. Moreover, as the sensor remains switched on for the longer exposure, it heats, and this heat can be mistakenly recorded as if it were a barrage of photons. This menu setting can be used to activate the D810's long exposure noise-canceling operation performed by the EXPEED 4 digital signal processor.

- **Off.** This default setting disables long exposure noise reduction. Use it when you want the maximum amount of detail present in your photograph, even though higher noise levels will result. This setting also eliminates the extra time needed to take a picture caused by the noise reduction process. If you plan to use only lower ISO settings (thereby reducing the noise caused by ISO amplification), the noise levels produced by longer exposures may be acceptable. For example, you might be shooting a waterfall at ISO 50 or ISO 100 with the camera mounted on a tripod, using a neutral-density filter and a long exposure to cause the water to blur. (Try exposures of 2 to 16 seconds, depending on the intensity of the light and how much blur you want.) (See Figure 11.30.) To maximize detail in the non-moving portions of your photos for the exposures that are eight seconds or longer, you can switch off long exposure noise reduction.

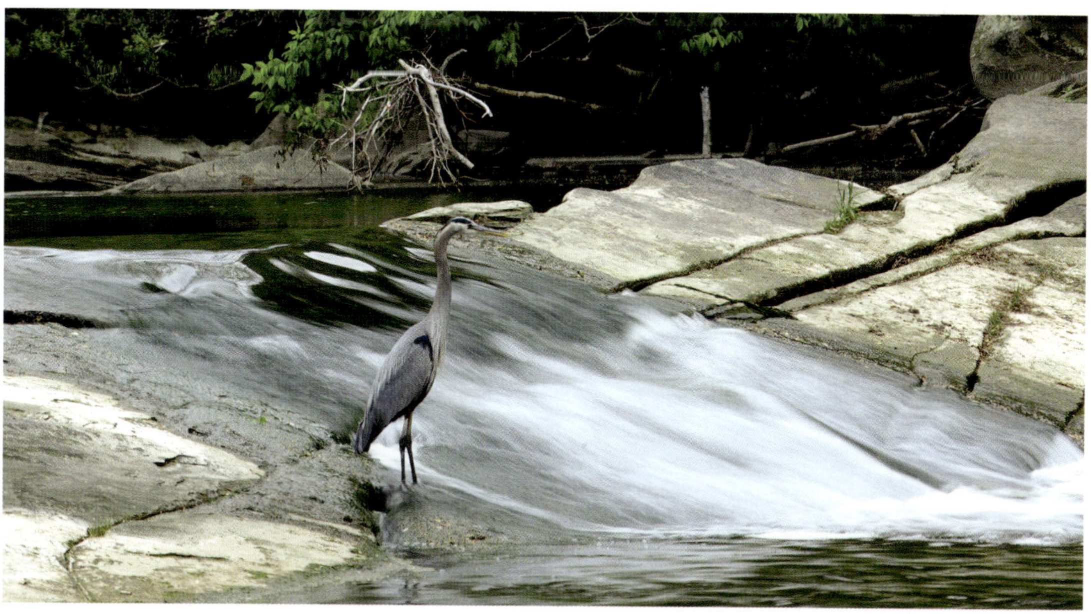

Figure 11.30 A long exposure with the camera mounted on a tripod produces this traditional moving water photo.

- **On.** When exposures are eight seconds or longer, the Nikon D810 takes a second, blank exposure to compare that to the first image. (While the second image is taken, the warning Job nr appears on the monochrome control panel and in the viewfinder.) Noise (pixels that are bright in a frame that *should* be completely black) in the "dark frame" image is subtracted from your original picture, and only the noise-corrected image is saved to your memory card. Because the noise-reduction process effectively doubles the time required to take a picture, you won't want to use this setting when you're rushed. Some noise can be removed later on, using tools like the noise reduction features built into Nikon Capture NX 2/NX-D.

High ISO NR

Noise can also be caused by higher ISO sensitivity settings, and the Nikon D810, which offers direct settings up to ISO 6400 and extended settings that go even higher, including Hi 1 (ISO 12800 equivalent) and Hi 2 (ISO 25600 equivalent). Although it costs you some detail, High ISO noise reduction, which can be set with this menu option, may be a good option in many cases. You can choose Off when you want to preserve detail at the cost of some noise graininess, and the D810 will apply high ISO NR only at the "boosted" settings of Hi 0.3, Hi 0.5, Hi 0.7, Hi 1, and Hi 2. Or, you can select Low, Normal, and High noise reduction, which is applied when ISO sensitivity has been set to ISO 800 or higher.

The effects of high ISO noise are something like listening to a CD in your car, and then rolling down all the windows. You're adding sonic noise to the audio signal, and while increasing the CD player's volume may help a bit, you're still contending with an unfavorable signal to noise ratio that probably mutes tones (especially higher treble notes) that you really want to hear.

The same thing happens when the analog image signal is amplified: You're increasing the image information in the signal, but boosting the background fuzziness at the same time. Tune in a very faint or distant AM radio station on your car stereo. Then turn up the volume. After a certain point, turning up the volume further no longer helps you hear better. There's a similar point of diminishing returns for digital sensor ISO increases and signal amplification as well.

As the captured information is amplified to produce higher ISO sensitivities, some random noise in the signal is amplified along with the photon information. Increasing the ISO setting of your camera raises the threshold of sensitivity so that fewer and fewer photons are needed to register as an exposed pixel. Yet, that also increases the chances of one of those phantom photons being counted among the real-life light particles, too.

Fortunately, the Nikon D810's CMOS sensor and its EXPEED 4 digital processing chip are optimized to produce the low noise levels, so ratings as high as ISO 12800 can be used routinely (although there will be some noise, of course), and even ISO 6400 can generate good results. I regularly shoot concerts at ISO 3200, and indoor sports at ISO 6400 with my D810. Some kinds of subjects may not require this kind of noise cancellation, particularly with images that have a texture of their own that tends to hide or mask the noise.

ISO Sensitivity Settings

This menu entry has two parts, ISO Sensitivity and ISO Sensitivity Auto Control. The former is simply a screen that allows you to specify the ISO setting, just as you would by spinning the main command dial while holding down the ISO button on the top-left panel of the D810. The available settings range from LO 1 (ISO 32 equivalent) through ISO 12800 to Hi 2 (ISO 51200 equivalent). The available settings are determined by the size of the increment you've specified in Custom Setting b1: 1/3, 1/2, or 1 step values. Use the ISO Sensitivity menu when you find it more convenient to set ISO using the three-inch color LCD.

The ISO Sensitivity Auto Control menu entry lets you specify how and when the D810 will adjust the ISO value for you automatically under certain conditions. This capability can be potentially useful, although experienced photographers tend to shy away from any feature that allows the camera to change basic settings like ISO that have been carefully selected. Fortunately, you can set some boundaries so the D810 will use this adjustment in a fairly intelligent way.

When Auto ISO is activated, the camera can bump up the ISO sensitivity, if necessary, whenever an optimal exposure cannot be achieved at the current ISO setting. Of course, it can be disconcerting to think you're shooting at ISO 400 and then see a grainier ISO 1600 shot during LCD review. While the D810 provides a flashing ISO-Auto alert in the viewfinder and control panel, the warning is easy to miss. Here are the important considerations to keep in mind when using the options available for this feature:

- **Off.** Set ISO Sensitivity Auto Control to Off, and the ISO setting will not budge from whatever value you have specified. Use this setting when you don't want any ISO surprises, or when ISO increases are not needed to counter slow shutter speeds. For example, if the D810 is mounted on a tripod, you can safely use slower shutter speeds at a relatively low ISO setting, so there is no need for a speed bump. On the other hand, if you're hand-holding the camera and the D810 set for Program (P) or Aperture-priority (A) mode wants to use a shutter speed slower than, say, 1/30 second, it's probably a good idea to increase the ISO to avoid the effects of camera shake. If you're using a longer lens, a shutter speed of 1/125 second or higher might be the point where an ISO bump would be a good idea. In that case, you can turn the ISO sensitivity auto control on, or remember to boost the ISO setting yourself.
- **Maximum sensitivity.** Use this parameter to indicate the highest ISO setting you're comfortable having the D810 set on its own. You can choose the max ISO setting the camera will use from ISO 80 to 12800 up to Hi 1 and Hi 2 (ISO 25600 and ISO 51200 equivalent). Use a low number if you'd rather not take any photos at a high ISO without manually setting that value yourself. Dial in a higher ISO number if getting the photo at any sensitivity setting is more important than worrying about noise.

- **Minimum shutter speed.** This setting allows you to tell the D810 how slow the shutter speed must be before the ISO boost kicks in, either Auto or within the range 30 seconds to 1/4000th second. The default value is Auto. For most shooters in most situations, any shutter speed longer than 1/30 is to be avoided, unless you're using a tripod, monopod, or looking for a special effect. If you have steady hands, or the camera is partially braced against movement (say, you're using that monopod), a slower shutter speed, down to 1 full second, can be specified. Similarly, if you're working with a telephoto lens and find even a relatively brief shutter speed "dangerous," you can set a minimum shutter speed threshold of 1/250 second. When the shutter speed is faster than the minimum you enter, Auto ISO will not take effect.

Multiple Exposure

This option lets you combine two exposures into one image without the need for an image editor like Photoshop and can be an entertaining way to return to those thrilling days of yesteryear, when complex photos were created in the camera itself. In truth, prior to the digital age, multiple exposures were a cool, groovy, far-out, hep/hip, phat, sick, fabulous way of producing composite images. Today, it's more common to take the lazy way out, snap two or more pictures, and then assemble them in an image editor like Photoshop.

However, if you're willing to spend the time planning a multiple exposure (or are open to some happy accidents), there is a lot to recommend the multiple exposure capability that Nikon has bestowed on the D810. For one thing, the camera is able to combine two or more images using the RAW data from the sensor, producing photos that are blended together more smoothly than is likely for anyone who's not a Photoshop guru. In addition, Nikon has eliminated one annoying aspect of the feature in some previous incarnations: it's no longer necessary to return to the menu to activate multiple exposure for each and every set. If you want to take a series of pictures, you can set it once, and forget it. (But don't forget to turn it off when you're done!)

To take your own multiple exposures, just follow these steps (although it's probably a good idea to do a little planning and maybe even some sketching on paper first):

1. **Activate the feature.** Choose Multiple Exposure from the Shooting menu.
2. **Choose exposures per frame.** Select Number of Shots, choose a value from 2 to 10 with the multi selector up/down buttons, and press OK.
3. **Specify ratio of exposure between frames.** Choose Auto Gain and specify either On (the default) or Off. When On is selected, the D810 will divide the total exposure of the image by the number of shots specified; for example, applying 1/4 of the exposure time to each shot in a four-image series. Choose Off, and the full exposure is applied to each picture. You'd want to use Off when using a dark background that would allow successive exposures to add details, and On to avoid the risk of overlapping images washing each other out.
4. **Confirm gain setting.** Press OK to set the gain.

5. **Choose Multiple Exposure mode.** Select Multiple Exposure Mode. A submenu appears with three choices:
   - **On (series).** The Multiple Exposure feature remains active even after you've taken a complete set of exposures for the number of shots you specified. Use this if you want to shoot several multiple exposures in a row. Remember to turn it off when you're done.
   - **On (single photo).** Once you've taken a single set of multiple exposures, the feature turns itself off.
   - **Off.** Use this option to cancel multiple exposures.
6. **Shoot your multiple exposure set.** Take the photo by pressing the shutter release button multiple times until all the exposures in the series have been taken. (In continuous shooting mode, the entire series will be shot in a single burst.) The blinking multiple exposure icon vanishes when the series is finished. Reminder: you'll need to reactivate the Multiple Exposure feature once you've finished taking a set, unless the D810 is set to On (single photo); it shuts off automatically.

Keep in mind if you wait longer than 30 seconds between any two photos in the series, the sequence will terminate and combine the images taken so far. If you want a longer elapsed time between exposures, go to the Playback menu and make sure On has been specified for Image Review, and then extend the monitor display time using Custom Setting c2 (Auto meter-off delay) to an appropriate maximum interval. The camera will grant you an additional 30 seconds beyond that. The Multiple Exposure feature will then use the monitor-off delay as its maximum interval between shots. Figure 11.31 shows an odd multiple exposure created of energetic Dwight Yoakam/Mavericks guitarist Eddie Perez.

Interval Timer Photography

Nikon D810's built-in time-lapse photography feature allows you to take still pictures for up to 9999 intervals in bursts of as many as nine shots, with a delay of up to 23 hours and 59 minutes between shots/bursts, and an initial start-up time of as long as 23 hours and 59 minutes from the time you activate the feature. That means that if you want to photograph a rosebud opening and would like to photograph the flower once every two minutes over the next 16 hours, you can do that easily. If you like, you can delay the first photo taken by a couple hours so you don't have to stand there by the camera waiting for the right moment.

Or, you might want to photograph a particular scene every hour for 24 hours to capture, say, a landscape from sunrise to sunset to the following day's sunrise again. The D810 can do that, too, and, in fact, offers most of the features of the expensive ($130) Nikon MC-16 Multi-Function Remote control. Nikon has done us all a huge favor by including this functionality essentially for free! I will offer two practical tips right now, in case you want to run out and try interval timer shooting immediately: *use a tripod, and for best results over longer time periods, plan on connecting your camera to an external power source!*

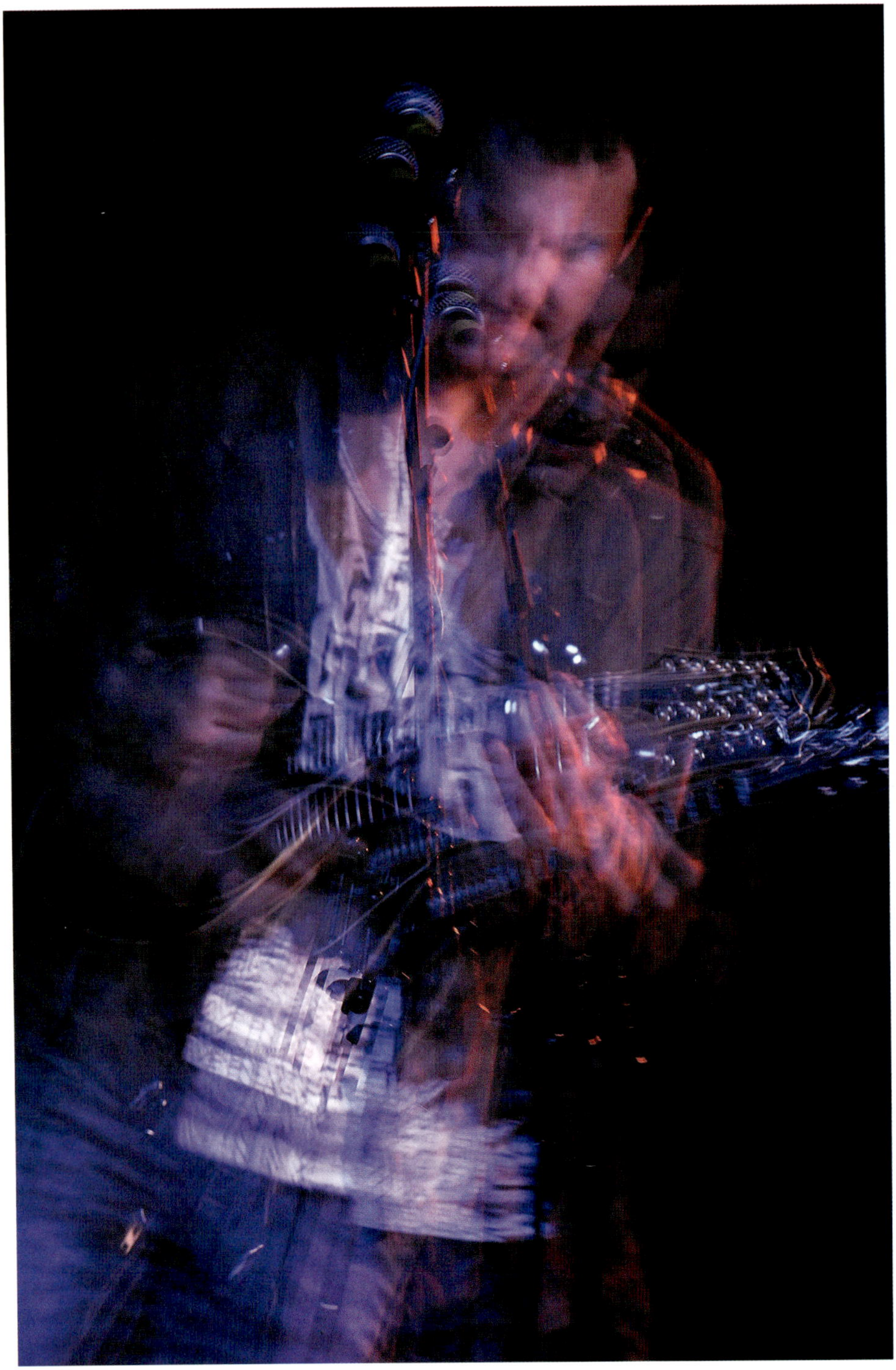

Figure 11.31 The D810's Multiple Exposure capability allows combining images without an image editor.

Before you start:

1. **Check your time.** The D810 uses its internal clock to activate, so make sure the time has been set accurately in the Setup menu before you begin.
2. **Choose release mode.** If you want to shoot bursts of images each time an interval elapses, set the release mode dial to **C$_L$** (low speed continuous; pictures will be taken at the rate specified in Custom Setting d5) or C$_H$ (high speed continuous). If you prefer to take one picture per interval, set the release mode dial to S. However, you can still specify multiple shots per interval when using S; the D810 will use the frame rate specified in Custom Setting d2 just as if you had set the release mode to C$_L$. You can't use the Self-timer or Mup release mode with interval timing.
3. **Set up optional bracketing.** If you'd like to bracket exposures during interval shooting, set up bracketing prior to beginning. (You learned how to bracket in Chapter 4.)
4. **Position camera.** Mount the camera on a tripod or other secure support.
5. **Fully charge the battery.** You might want to connect the D810 to the optional Nikon AC Adapter if you plan to shoot long sequences. Although the camera more or less goes to sleep between intervals, some power is drawn, and long sequences with bursts of shots can drain power even when you're not using the interval timer feature.
6. **Make sure the camera is protected** from the elements, accidents, and theft, and that the viewfinder is covered (use the eyepiece shutter if necessary) if you need to keep strong ambient light from entering the viewfinder and affecting exposure.

When you're ready to go, set up the D810 for interval shooting:

1. **Access feature.** Choose Interval Timer Shooting from the Shooting menu.
2. **Specify a starting time.** You must choose a start time before the camera will let you set other parameters. Highlight either Now or Choose Start Day and Start Time and press the multi selector right button. If you choose Now, the interval shooting will begin approximately three seconds after you've finished setting the parameters beginning with Step 5. If you select Choose Start Day and Start Time, you'll be able to enter a specific date and time, as described in Steps 3 and 4.
3. **Select initial delay.** When the Start Time sub-screen appears, use the multi selector left/right buttons to highlight the date field, or hours/ minutes, and the up/down buttons to increase or decrease the entries. The 24-hour clock is used, so you can specify a time from 00:00 (midnight) to 23:59 (one minute to midnight). When both date and hours/minutes have been set, press the OK button to move the highlighting to the Interval section of the sub-screen.
4. **Set the interval between exposures.** You can use the left/right buttons to move among hours, minutes, and seconds, and use the up/down buttons to choose an interval from one second to 24 hours. Press the OK button when finished to move down to the number of intervals/shots per interval sub-screen.

> **Tip**
>
> The interval cannot be shorter than the shutter speed; for example, you cannot set one second as the interval if the images will be taken at two seconds or longer.

5. **Set number of intervals and shots per interval.** Highlight No. of Intervals x shots/intervals and press the right button to move to the next screen. Then, use the left/right buttons to highlight the number of intervals, the number of shots taken after each interval has elapsed, and the total number of shots to be exposed overall. You can highlight each number column separately, so that to enter, say, 250 intervals you can set the 100s, 10s, and 1s columns individually (rather than press the up button 250 times!). You can select up to 9999 intervals, and 9 shots per interval.
6. **Exposure smoothing.** Turn this option On to allow the D810 to adjust the exposure between shots so that they more or less match as lighting conditions change. This feature works in P, S, and A modes, as well as in M mode if Auto ISO is active (in M mode, shutter speed and aperture will remain the same, and only ISO will be adjusted). Press OK to confirm.
7. **Activate shooting.** When all the parameters have been entered, highlight Start and the series will commence at the specified time (if you selected Choose Start Day and Start Time), or in about three seconds (if you selected Now as your Start option). Once you activate interval shooting, a message is displayed on the monitor one minute before each series of shots begins, and an INTVL icon will flash on the control panel.
8. **See progress.** The control panel's shutter speed display will show the number of intervals remaining, and the aperture display will show the number of shots remaining for the current interval. Between intervals, you can also view this information by pressing the shutter release button halfway; the information will appear on the control panel until the standby timer elapses. You can review pictures taken so far between intervals; the monitor will shut off automatically about four seconds before the next image in the series is due to be captured. If you change camera settings while interval photography is underway, the series may end.

PAUSE OR CANCEL INTERVAL SHOOTING

Press the MENU button between intervals (but not when images are still being recorded to the memory card), choose the Interval Timer Shooting menu entry, and select Pause. Interval shooting can also be paused by turning the camera on or off (useful if you want to swap batteries or memory cards), or by rotating the release mode dial to Live View, Self-timer, or Mup positions. To resume the Interval Timer Shooting menu again, press the multi selector left button, and choose Restart. You may also select Off to stop the shooting entirely.

Time-Lapse Photography

This menu entry is basically the same as interval shooting with a similar setup menu and options, except that the frames captured will be assembled into a time-lapse motion picture rather than saved as a series of still shots. The feature uses the settings specified in the Movie Settings entry (described next). One difference between time-lapse and interval shooting is that the maximum movie capture time is 7 hours and 59 minutes. Time-lapse photography is not possible when using live view or interval timer shooting, while bracketing, taking multiple or HDR exposures, or when the shutter speed is set to Bulb. To shoot a time-lapse movie, just follow these steps:

1. **Access feature.** Choose Time-Lapse Photography from the Shooting menu.
2. **Choose an interval.** Highlight the Interval setting and press the right directional button to select an interval between shots. The default value is 5 seconds. As with interval timer shooting, the interval must be longer than the slowest shutter speed you can expect. That is, if you will be shooting a time-lapse photo at night with a shutter speed of 5 seconds, the interval must be longer than 5 seconds. Press OK to confirm.
3. **Select a shooting time.** Use the right directional button to move down one line and choose the shooting time. The maximum length is 7 hours and 59 minutes. Press OK to confirm.
4. **Choose Exposure Smoothing.** You can specify exposure smoothing, as described in Step 6 earlier.
5. **Start shooting.** Move the highlighting to the top of the screen to highlight Start, and press OK to begin capture. Actual capture begins three seconds after you select On. To end time-lapse photography, return to this menu and choose Off. Press OK to confirm.
6. **See progress.** An INTVL icon will flash in the control panel while time-lapse photography is underway. The remaining time appears in the shutter speed display just before each frame is recorded. You can also view this information by pressing the shutter release halfway.

Tip

Remember, the interval cannot be shorter than the shutter speed; for example, you cannot set one second as the interval if the images will be taken at two seconds or longer.

Time-lapse movies cannot be captured when using live view, bracketing, HDR, multiple exposure, or interval timer photography, nor when Bulb is selected as the shutter speed. The self-timer is disabled during capture.

While capturing, INTVL is displayed as a blinking icon and the time-lapse recording indicator is shown on the monochrome control panel. The time remaining in hours and minutes is shown just before each frame is recorded; if you want to know at other times, press the shutter release halfway.

Movie Settings

This menu entry on the last Shooting menu page (not shown; it's the only entry) allows you to choose four movie-making parameters for the D810, which I'll discuss in much more detail in Chapters 15 and 16. The three are as follows:

- **Frame size/Frame rate.** Choose from 1920 × 1080 at 60, 50, 30, 25, or 24 fps; 1280 × 720 at 60, 50, 30, or 25 fps. I'll show you how to select the best settings in Chapter 15.
- **Movie Quality.** Choose High Quality or Normal Quality.
- **Microphone Sensitivity.** Select from Auto Sensitivity and Manual Sensitivity settings with levels from 1-20.
- **Frequency Response.** This entry lets you specify a Wide Range or Vocal Range response.
- **Wind noise reduction.** This setting allows you to turn your microphone's wind noise canceling circuitry on or off. I'll explain more about wind noise in Chapter 15.
- **Destination.** Choose the slot containing the memory card you want to store your movies on; generally, use the slot containing the fastest memory card. The default value is the SD card.
- **Movie ISO sensitivity settings.** This entry allows you to choose ISO sensitivity in Manual exposure mode from ISO 64 to Hi 2, and turn Auto ISO On or Off while shooting movies in Manual exposure mode.

12

The Custom Settings Menu

Unlike the Shooting menu options, which you are likely to modify frequently as your picture-taking environment changes, Custom Settings are slightly more stable sets of preferences that let you tailor the behavior of your camera in a variety of different ways for longer-term use.

Some options are minor tweaks useful for specific shooting situations. You can turn off the autofocus assist lamp, the back-panel monitor's shooting information display, and the D810's built-in beeper when you are shooting an acoustic music concert, when you'd rather not disrupt the environment. Others make the camera more convenient to use. Perhaps you'd like to assign a frequently used feature to the Fn button, or turn on the viewfinder grid display to make it easier to align vertical or horizontal shapes.

Best of all are the settings that actually *improve* the way the D810 operates. Custom Setting b7, for example, provides a way to fine-tune the exposures your camera calculates for each of the metering modes: Matrix, Center-weighted, Spot, and Highlight-weighted. If you find that one or the other consistently over- or underexposes more than you like, it's easy to dial in a permanent correction. Should you feel that the D810 is taking a few pictures that are out of focus, Custom Settings a1 and a2 can be used to tell it not to fire until optimum focus is achieved.

This chapter concentrates on explaining all the options of the Custom Settings menu and, most importantly, when and why you might want to use each setting.

Custom Settings Menu Layout

There are 65 different Custom Settings, arranged in seven different categories, as shown in Figure 12.1: Autofocus, Metering/Exposure, Timers/AE Lock, Shooting/Display, Bracketing/Flash, Controls, and Movie. Some of those may seem to be an odd match. What does bracketing have to do with flash? Oh, wait! You can *bracket* flash (as well as non-flash) exposures. The category system

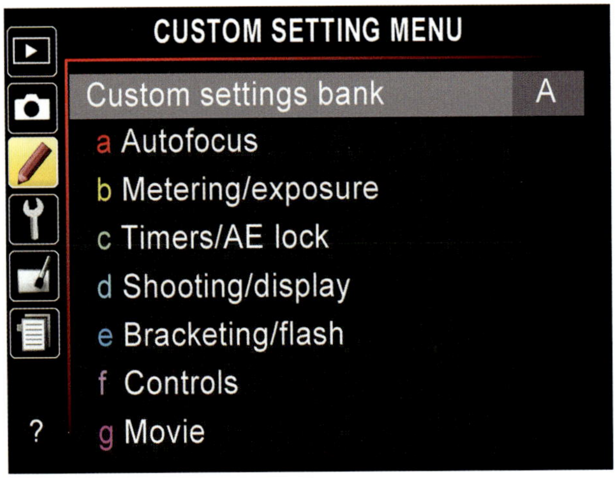

Figure 12.1
These seven categories include 65 different entries in the Custom Settings menu.

does have an advantage. Once you're familiar with what settings are available within each category, you can select the Custom Settings menu, scroll down to the specific category you want, press the right button, and enter the Custom Settings system at that point, skipping the other entries.

However, once you get past the main Custom Settings screen, the entries are one long scrolling list, so if you've guessed wrong about where you want to start, you can enter the list at any point and then scroll up or down until you find the entry you want. Or, press the left directional key to get back to the main screen, then move down to another entry point and re-enter. The Custom Settings menu items are all color- and letter-coded: **a** (red) for autofocus functions; **b** (orange) for metering/exposure; **c** (green) for timers and AE lock features; **d** (light blue) for shooting/display functions; **e** (dark blue) for bracketing/flash; **f** (purple) for adjustments to the D810's controls; and **g** (magenta) to assign Movie mode functions to the Fn, Preview, AE-L/AF-L, and shutter buttons.

For simplicity, in this book I have been consistently referring to the Custom Settings menu entries by their letter/names, so that you always know that when I mention Custom Setting option a10, I am describing the eighth entry in the Autofocus menu. That terminology makes it easy to jump quickly to the specific entry. Note that for simplicity's sake, in the figures that illustrate each of the separate Custom Settings categories in this chapter, that category's entries are shown on as few screens as possible. In practice, as you scroll through the listings, the entries for a particular category may be spread over several different screens.

You can select a Custom Settings function as you do any menu entry, by pressing the multi selector right button, and navigating through the screen that appears with the up/down (and sometimes left/right) buttons. Confirming an option is usually done by pressing the OK button, pushing the multi selector right button, or sometimes by choosing Done when a series of related options have been chosen.

At the top level, you'll see these entries:

- Custom Settings Bank
- a. Autofocus
- b. Metering/Exposure
- c. Timers/AE Lock
- d. Shooting/Display
- e. Bracketing/Flash
- f. Controls
- g. Movie

Custom Settings Bank

The Custom Settings menu has four banks, counterparts to the A, B, C, and D banks in the Shooting menu, that store specific collections of Custom Settings. As with the Shooting menu banks, you can recall any of the four at any time. As I mentioned in Chapter 3, the Custom Settings banks A, B, C, and D should not be confused with the four similarly named Shooting menu banks A, B, C, and D, which provide storage of separate sets of options. You can use your Shooting menu banks and Custom Settings menu banks in any combination.

The D810 uses bank A by default. To switch to another bank:

- Press MENU and select the Custom Settings menu.
- Scroll to Custom Settings bank and press the multi selector right button.
- Scroll to the bank you want to use with the multi selector up/down buttons, and press OK to confirm your choice. (Pressing the right button takes you to the bank renaming screen.)
- The Custom Settings menu appears again. Press the MENU button to back out of the menu, or simply tap the shutter release.

If you've changed a bank from its default values, the active bank's letter will be shown in the control panel and the shooting information display. As with Shooting menu banks, any changes you make to one menu bank do not affect the other banks, so you can set one up with the settings you like to use in particular situations, and assign each of them customized names of up to 20 characters to replace the generic A, B, C, and D designations. As with the Shooting menu banks, use the standard Nikon text-entry screen to enter the name you want to use.

- Press MENU and select the Custom Settings menu.
- Scroll to the Custom Settings menu bank entry and press the multi selector right button.
- Scroll down to the bank you want to rename, and press the multi selector right button to activate the text entry screen.
- Use the multi selector navigational buttons to scroll around within the array of alphanumerics, as described in Chapter 11. Press the multi selector's center button to insert the highlighted character; hold down the Thumbnail/Zoom Out button and use the left/right buttons to move the cursor within the line of characters; remove a character by highlighting the character and pressing the Trash button. Press OK when finished, then press the left button twice to return to the Custom Settings menu, or just tap the shutter release to exit the menu system entirely.

Reset Custom Settings

You can restore the settings of the Custom Settings banks to their default values by choosing a particular menu bank under the Custom Settings Bank entry, and pressing the trash button. Only the currently active bank is reset; the other three are untouched. In Chapter 3, I provided a list of recommended Custom Settings menu bank settings for typical photo environments. Tables 12.1–12.6 show the default values as the Nikon D810 comes from the factory, and after a reset. If you don't know what some of these settings are, I'll explain them later in this chapter. Be careful when changing any of your carefully tailored customized settings back to the defaults.

Table 12.1 Default Custom Settings Bank Values: Autofocus

Function	Option	Default
a1	AF-C priority selection	Release
a2	AF-S priority selection	Focus
a3	Focus tracking with lock-on	3 (Normal)
a4	AF activation	Shutter/AF-ON
a5	Focus point illumination	
	Manual focus mode	On
	Continuous mode	On
	Focus point brightness	Normal
	Dynamic-area AF display	Off
	Group-area AF illumination	Squares
a6	AF point illumination	
a7	Focus point wrap-around	No wrap
a8	Number of focus points	51 points
a9	Store by orientation	Off
a10	Built-in AF-assist illuminator	On
a11	Limit AF-area mode selection	All active
a12	Autofocus mode restrictions	Off

Table 12.2 Default Custom Settings Bank Values: Metering/Exposure

Function	Option	Default
b1	ISO sensitivity step value	1/3 step
b2	EV steps for exposure cntrl.	1/3 step
b3	Exp/flash comp. step value	1/3 step
b4	Easy exposure compensation	Off
b5	Matrix metering	Face detection on
b6	Center-weighted area	12mm
b7	Fine-tune optimal exposure	
	Matrix metering	0
	Center-weighted metering	0
	Spot metering	0

Table 12.3 Default Custom Settings Bank Values: Timers/AE Lock

Function	Option	Default
c1	Shutter release button AE-L	Off
c2	Standby timer	6 seconds
c3	Self-timer	
	Self-timer delay	10s
	Number of shots	1
	Interval between shots	0.5s
c4	Monitor off delay	
	Playback	10s
	Menus	1 min.
	Information display	10s
	Image review	4s
	Live view	10 min.

Table 12.4 Default Custom Settings Bank Values: Shooting/Display

Function	Option	Default
d1	Beep	
	Volume	Off
	Pitch	High
d2	CL mode shooting speed	3 fps
d3	Max. Continuous release	200
d4	Exposure delay mode	Off
d5	Electronic front-curtain shutter	Off
d6	File number sequence	On
d7	Viewfinder grid display	Off
d8	ISO display and adjustment	
	Rear control panel	ISO sensitivity
	Viewfinder display	Frame count
d9	Screen tips	On
d10	Information display	Auto
d11	LCD illumination	Off
d12	MB-D12 battery type	LR6 (AA alkaline)
d13	Battery order	Use MB-D12 batteries first

Table 12.5 Default Custom Settings Bank Values: Bracketing/Flash

Function	Option	Default
e1	Flash sync speed	1/250 second
e2	Flash shutter speed	1/60 second
e3	Flash cntrl for built-in flash	TTL
e4	Exposure comp. for flash	Entire frame
e5	Modeling flash	On
e6	Auto bracketing set	AE & Flash
e7	Auto bracketing (Mode M)	Flash/speed
e8	Bracketing order	MTR>under>over

Table 12.6 Default Custom Settings Bank Values: Controls

Function	Option	Default
f1	Illuminator switch	LCD backlight
f2	Multi selector center button	
	Shooting mode	Select center focus point
	Playback mode	Thumbnail on/off
	Live view	Select center focus point
f3	Multi selector	Do nothing
f4	Assign Fn Button	
	FUNC. button press	Viewfinder virtual horizon
	FUNC. button + command dials	None
f5	Assign preview button	
	Preview button press	Preview
	Preview + command dials	None
f6	Assign AE-L/AF-L button	
	AE-L/AF-L button press	AE/AF Lock
	AE-L/AF-L + command dials	None
f7	Shutter spd & aperture lock	
	Shutter speed lock	Off
	Aperture lock	Off
f8	Assign BKT button	Auto bracketing
f9	Customize command dials	
	Reverse rotation	Exposure Compensation: Off Shutter speed/Aperture: Off
	Change main/sub	Off
	Aperture setting	Sub-command dial
	Menus and Playback	Off
f10	Release button to use dial	No
f11	Slot empty release lock	Enable release
f12	Reverse indicators	-/+
f13	Assign movie record button	AF-ON

Table 12.6 Default Custom Settings Bank Values: Controls (continued)

Function	Option	Default
f14	Live view button options	Enable
f15	Assign MB-D12 AF-ON	AF-ON
f16	Assign remote (WR) Fn button	None
f17	Lens focus function buttons	AF Lock Only

Table 12.7 Default Custom Settings Bank Values: Movie

Function	Option	Default
g1	Assign Fn Button	
	Fn button press	None
g2	Assign preview button	
	Preview button press	Index marking
g3	Assign AE-L/AF-L button	
	AE-L/AF-L button press	AE/AF Lock
g4	Assign shutter button	Take photos

a. Autofocus

The red-coded Autofocus options (see Figure 12.2) deal with some of the potentially most vexing settings available with the Nikon D810. After all, incorrect focus is one of the most damaging picture killers of all the attributes in an image. You may be able to compensate for bad exposure, partially fix errant color balance, and perhaps even incorporate motion blur into an image as a creative element. But if focus is wrong, the photograph doesn't look right, and no amount of "I meant to do that!" pleas are likely to work. The D810's autofocus options enable you to choose how and when focus is applied (using the AF-S or AF-C focus mode you selected on the camera body), the controls used to activate the feature, and the way focus points are selected from the available 51 zones.

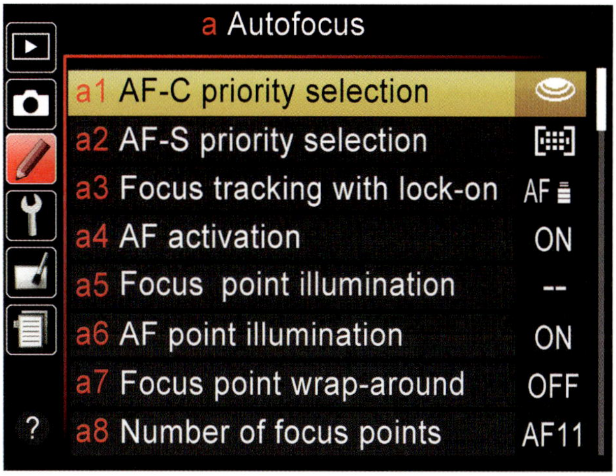

Figure 12.2
The Autofocus options menu.

a1 AF-C Priority Selection

As you learned in Chapter 5, when not using live view, the Nikon D810 has two primary autofocus modes, continuous-servo autofocus (AF-C) and single-servo autofocus (AF-S). This menu entry allows you to specify what takes precedence when you press the shutter release all the way down to take a picture: focus (called *focus-priority*) or the release button (called *release-priority*). You can choose from:

- **Release.** When this option is selected (the default), the shutter is activated when the release button is pushed down all the way, even if sharp focus has not yet been achieved. Because AF-C focuses and refocuses constantly when autofocus is active, you may find that an image is not quite in sharpest focus. Use this option when taking a picture is more important than absolute best focus, such as fast action or photojournalism applications. (You don't want to miss that record-setting home run, or the protestor's pie smashing into the Governor's face.) Using this setting doesn't mean that your image won't be sharply focused; it just means that you'll get a picture even if autofocusing isn't quite complete. If you've been poised with the shutter release pressed halfway, the D810 probably has been tracking the focus of your image.
- **Release+focus.** The shutter is released when the button is pressed, but the frame rate is reduced slightly to give the D810 more time to autofocus every shot in the sequence when AF-C mode is used. (In non-live view modes, the D810 is able to autofocus *only* between shots when the mirror is down and the autofocus sensors can interpret the incoming light.) You would not want to use this setting if the highest possible continuous shooting rates are important to you.
- **Focus.** The shutter is not activated until sharp focus is achieved. This is best for subjects that are not moving rapidly. AF-C will continue to track your subjects' movement, but the D810 won't take a picture until focus is locked in. You might miss a few shots, but you will have fewer out-of-focus images.

a2 AF-S Priority Selection

This is the counterpart setting for single-servo autofocus mode.

- **Release.** The shutter is activated when the button is depressed all the way, even if sharp focus is not quite achieved. Keep in mind that, unlike AF-C, the D810 focuses only *once* when AF-S mode is used. So, if you've partially depressed the shutter release, paused, and then pressed the button down all the way, it's possible that the subject has moved and release-priority will yield more out-of-focus shots than release-priority with AF-C. This setting is most viable if you're using a fast lens with a speedy internal focus motor (designated AF-S, which is *not* the same as the AF-S focus mode).
- **Focus.** This default prevents the D810 from taking a picture until focus is achieved and the in-focus indicator in the viewfinder glows a steady green. If you're using single-servo autofocus mode, this is probably the best setting. Moving subjects really call for AF-C mode in most cases.

a3 Focus Tracking with Lock-on

Sometimes new subjects interject themselves in the frame temporarily. Perhaps you're shooting an architectural photo from across the street and a car passes in front of the camera. Or, at a football game, a referee dashes past just as a receiver is about to make a catch. This setting lets you specify how quickly the D810 reacts to these transient interruptions that would cause relatively large changes in focus before refocusing on the "new" subject matter. You can specify a long delay, so that the interloper is ignored, a shorter delay, or turn off lock-on completely so that the D810 immediately refocuses when a new subject moves into the frame. The D810 provides intermediate settings between long/normal and normal/short, and numbers each of the settings. In the labels below, the D810's number system is shown first. The options are as follows:

- **AF 5/Long.** The longest delay causes the D810 to ignore the intervening subject matter for a significant period of time. Use this setting when shooting subjects, such as sports, in which focus interruptions are likely to be frequent and significant.
- **AF 4.** A slightly shorter delay (Nikon does not provide the exact timings).
- **AF 3/Normal.** This default setting provides an intermediate delay before the camera refocuses on the new subject. It's usually the best choice when shooting sports in either of the continuous shooting modes, as the long delay can throw off autofocus accuracy at higher fps settings.
- **AF 2.** A slightly shorter delay than Normal.
- **AF 1/Short.** Choose this setting to tell the D810 to wait only a moment before refocusing. Very high frame rates may work better when you allow refocusing to take place rapidly, without a lock-on delay.
- **Off.** Turn off focus lock-on if you want the D810 to refocus immediately. This may be the best choice for general subjects, because it allows the camera to smoothly follow focus on a moving subject with no delay.

a4 AF Activation

This setting lets you change which controls are used to activate autofocus, either the shutter release button *and* the AF-ON button or the AF-ON button only. Most of us learned to use a half-press of the shutter release button to activate autofocus at the same time the exposure is calculated, but if you're willing to retrain yourself to use the AF-ON button, there are some nifty things you can do. For example, the AF-ON button can be used to lock in focus separately from exposure and taking the picture, and to produce the effect called *trap focus* in which you pre-focus at a certain point, press the shutter release, and the D810 doesn't take a picture until your subject (say, a horse crossing the finish line) moves into the pre-focused position. I described trap focus in more detail in Chapter 5, but you can learn the basic use of this custom setting now.

- **Shutter/AF-ON.** With this default setting, you can use either the shutter release button or the AF-ON button to initiate focus. For example, you could press the AF-ON button to start the autofocus operation as you initially frame the image, then press the shutter release when you're ready to take the picture to meter the scene. Or, without changing anything, you could press the shutter release button to perform autofocus and metering at the same time.
- **AF-ON only.** This setting decouples metering from autofocus activation. You must press AF-ON to start autofocus, and you must press the shutter release to start metering. So, you can activate and reactivate autofocus at any time. For example, suppose you're photographing a field goal attempt in a football game. Press AF-ON to lock in focus on the player who will be holding the ball for the kicker. When the play begins, focus will remain locked on the holder, even if defenders suddenly burst into the frame. As the kicker goes into motion, press the shutter release button to meter the scene and take the picture, confident that the focus you've set will not change. (In fast-moving situations, this is obviously more precise than manually focusing.) As a bonus, you don't have to worry about autofocus lag; the D810 will snap the picture virtually instantly. AF-ON can also be used in sneaky ways with the AE-L/AF-L button, and I covered those in Chapter 5.

a5 Focus Point Illumination

It's usually helpful to have the active focus point highlighted in red in the viewfinder. This setting lets you specify when/if this highlighting happens. You can choose to have the active focus point displayed in manual focus mode all the time, or only during focus point selection; display the selected focus point and surrounding focus points in Dynamic-area AF mode; or display active focus points as boxes or dots when using group-area AF.

- **Manual focus mode.** Select On to show the active focus point when you're focusing manually. Choose Off, and the focus point is displayed only when you're selecting a specific focus point. Why bother with focus points when focusing manually? Keep in mind that your D810 can monitor your focusing efforts and confirm when sharp focus is achieved *for the selected focus point* using the green focus confirmation indicator in the viewfinder. Even though you are focusing visually, this additional help can prove useful.

- **Dynamic-area AF display.** In Dynamic-area focus point selection mode, both the selected focus point and surrounding focus points are used to determine focus. If you want to see what those points are as you shoot, choose On. When 3D tracking is active, a dot will be shown in the center focus point. If you'd rather not have the distraction, select Off.
- **Group-area AF illumination.** You can choose how the active focus points are displayed when using Group-area AF focus, selecting from boxes or smaller points, depending on your preference.

a6 AF Point Illumination

Do you want the *active* autofocus point illuminated when that is an option? You can have the point highlighted in red only when necessary to contrast with a background; on all the time; or off.

- **Auto.** This is the default. The D810 will evaluate the scene and illuminate the active autofocus point to contrast with the background if required.
- **On.** Active point illumination is always used. Select this option if you like to know what focus point is being used.
- **Off.** Active point illumination is never used. This setting switches off the active point display if you find it distracting.

a7 Focus Point Wrap-Around

This setting is purely a personal preference parameter. When you press the multi selector left/right and up/down buttons to choose a focus point, the D810 can be told to stop when the selection reaches the edge of the 51-point array—or, it can continue, wrapping around to the opposite edge, like Pac-Man leaving the playing area on one side or top/bottom to re-emerge on the other. (I hope I'm not revealing my age, here.) Your choices are simple; decide which behavior you prefer:

- **Wrap.** Pressing the left/right or up/down buttons when you've reached the edge of the focus point display wraps the selection to the opposite side, still moving in the same direction.
- **No Wrap.** The focus point selection stops at the edge of the focus zone array.

a8 Number of Focus Points

You can choose the number of focus points available when you manually select a zone using the multi selector up/down and left/right buttons. Your choices, shown in Figure 12.3, are as follows:

- **51 points.** This is the default. All 51 focus points can be selected.
- **11 points.** A more widely spaced array of points is available. This can be the best choice for faster focus point selection when taking pictures of relatively large, evenly illuminated subject matter such that choosing precise focus zones is not particularly beneficial. I often use the 11-point option when photographing basketball games.

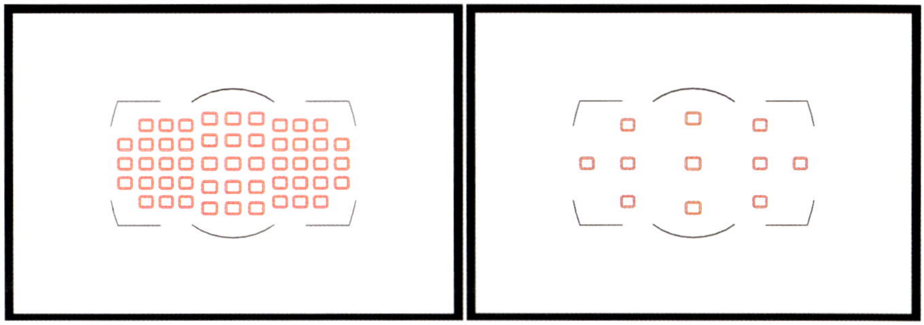

Figure 12.3
Select from all 51 focus points (left), or 11 more widely spaced points (right).

a9 Store by Orientation

This is the first entry on the second page of the Autofocus menu. (See Figure 12.4.) Here you can choose whether separate focus points can be selected for landscape and portrait orientations of the camera, and whether you can select different AF-area modes in these orientations, as explained in Chapter 5.

When you choose Off, the focus point will maintain the same relative position as you rotate the camera, and the AF-area mode will remain exactly the same. Select Focus Point, and you can choose a different focus point when the camera is set to horizontal orientation, rotated 90 degrees clockwise from horizontal, or rotated 90 degrees counterclockwise from horizontal. Select Focus Point and AF-Area Mode, and you can specify a different AF-area method for each of those three orientations.

This is a very cool feature, and best visualized using the illustrations I supply in Chapter 5 where Store by Orientation is explained in detail.

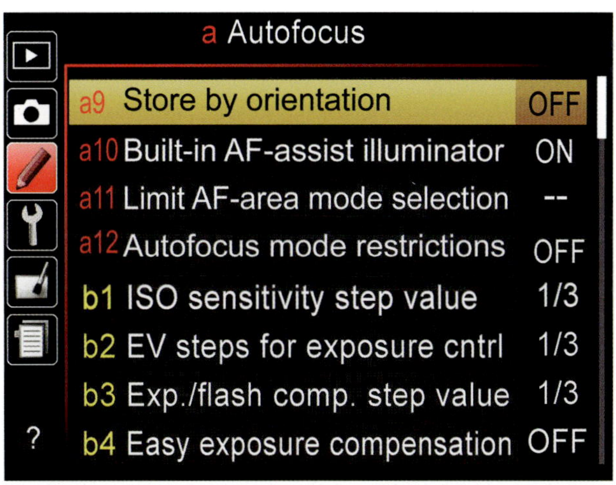

Figure 12.4
The second page of the Autofocus menu.

a10 Built-in AF-Assist Illuminator

Use this setting to control whether to use the AF-assist lamp built into the Nikon D810, or rely on the more powerful AF-assist lamp built into Nikon electronic flash units (like the Nikon SB-910) and the Nikon SC-29 coiled remote flash cord (for firing the flash when not mounted on the camera).

- **On.** This default value will cause the AF-assist illuminator lamp to fire when lighting is poor, but only if single-servo autofocus (AF-S) is active, or you have selected the center focus point manually and either Single-point or Dynamic-area autofocus (rather than Auto-area autofocus) has been chosen.
- **Off.** Use this to disable the AF-assist illuminator. You'd find that useful when the lamp might be distracting or discourteous (say, at a religious ceremony or acoustic music concert), or your subject is located closer than one foot, eight inches or farther than about 10 feet. Turning off the illuminator can be important in stage and dance performances, because performers often use a point of light in the audience area to orient themselves as they spin or turn. I've been asked specifically at ballet dress rehearsals to make sure my camera emitted no illumination from the front to prevent disorienting the performers.

It's important to note that AF-assist illumination is not available with all lenses, most commonly because the lenses themselves are so large that they block the AF illuminator. The lenses affected are as follows:

- **Lenses longer than 200mm.** Because the AF illumination is good only out to about 10 feet, it should be obvious that long lenses that aren't typically used at such close focusing distances (or may not even focus that close) are not practical for focus-assist. Nikon specifically states that neither the VR I or VR II versions of its 200mm f/2 and 200-400mm f/4 zoom lenses can be used with focus-assist.
- **Lenses that are usable from 2 feet, 4 inches to 10 feet.** Some lenses are large enough that they block the AF-assist illuminator at close focusing distances (2 feet 4 inches or less). FX lenses on this list are the 16-35mm f/4G VR; the 24-70mm/28-70mm f/2.8 medium zooms; Nikon's 24-120mm f/3.5-5.6 VR lens; and the 200mm f/4 Micro-Nikkor. In addition, the 17-55mm f/2.8 and 18-200mm f/3.5 f5.6 DX format lenses also fall into this category.
- **Lenses that can be used from 3 feet, 7 inches to 10 feet.** The D810's built-in AF illuminator is blocked by the 24-120mm f/4 lens and 28-300mm f/3.5-5.6 VR lenses, and the DX format 55-200mm f/4-5.6 DX zoom.
- **Lenses that can be used from 4 feet, 11 inches to 10 feet.** These include a group of FX lenses, including the 14-24mm f/2.8 super-wide, both VR I and VR II versions of Nikon's 70-200mm f/2.8 zooms, both the AF and AF-S versions of the company's 80-200mm f/2.8 zoom, and the 70-300 f/4-5.6 telephoto zoom. Nikon's 80-400mm f/4.5-5.6 VR zoom blocks the AF illuminator at any distance closer than 7 feet, 7 inches, so you can chalk that one off your focus-assist list as well.

a11 Limit AF-Area Mode Selection

AF-area modes are chosen by holding down the AF-mode button (just underneath the lens release button) and rotating the sub-command dial. If there are certain area modes that you don't use, you can disable them (for viewfinder photography only; live view is not affected) using this menu item.

Single-point AF area mode is always available, but you can highlight any of the others and press the right directional button to remove the check box next to that mode's label to disable it. You can thus enable Single-point AF, plus any combination of Dynamic-area AF (9, 21, or 51 points), 3D-tracking, Group-area AF, or Auto-area AF. I explained this feature in Chapter 5.

a12 Autofocus Mode Restrictions

Use this to enable/disable AF-S, AF-C, or provide no restrictions.

b. Metering/Exposure

The orange-coded Metering/Exposure Custom Settings (see Figure 12.5) let you define seven different parameters that affect exposure metering in the Nikon D810.

b1 ISO Sensitivity Step Value

This setting determines the size of the "jumps" it should use when making ISO adjustments—either one-third or one full stop. At the 1/3 stop setting, typical ISO values would be 200, 250, 320, 400, 500, 640, 800, 1000, 1250, 1600, and so forth. Choose 1/2 stop settings, and your choices would be 200, 280, 400, 560, 500, 800, 1100, and 1600 over the same range. For really large increments, set the full-stop option, and choose 200, 400, 800, and 1600, and so forth. The larger

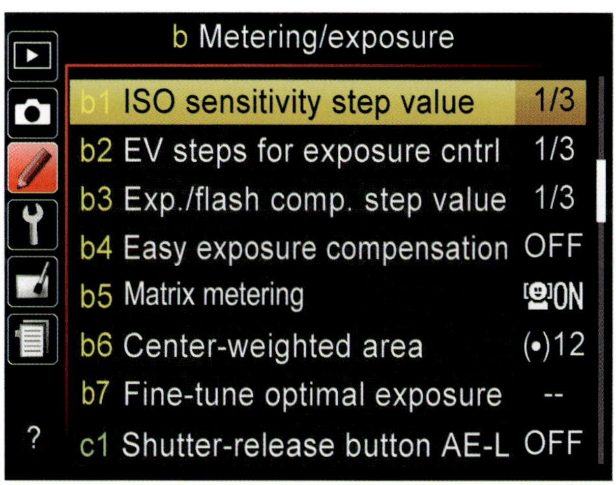

Figure 12.5
There are seven metering/exposure options.

increment can help you leap from one ISO setting to one that's much larger with one click in environments where you don't care to fine-tune sensitivity. As you've surmised, your choices include 1/3 step (the default); 1/2 step; and 1 step.

b2 EV Steps for Exposure Cntrl.

This setting tells the Nikon D810 the size of the "jumps" it should use when making exposure adjustments—either one-third, one-half, or one full stop. The increment you specify here applies to f/stops, shutter speeds, EV changes, and autoexposure bracketing. As with ISO sensitivity step value, you can select from 1/3 step (the default); 1/2 step; and 1 step increments.

Choose the 1/3 stop setting when you want the finest increments between shutter speeds and/or f/stops. For example, the D810 will use shutter speeds such as 1/60th, 1/80th, 1/100th, 1/125th, and 1/160th second, and f/stops such as f/5.6, f/6.3, f/7.1, and f/8, giving you (and the autoexposure system) maximum flexibility.

With 1/2 stop increments, you will have larger and more noticeable changes between settings. The D810 will apply shutter speeds such as 1/60th, 1/125th, 1/250th, and 1/500th second, and f/stops including f/5.6, f/6.7, f/8, f/9.5, and f/11. These coarser adjustments are useful when you want more dramatic changes between different exposures.

b3 Exp./Flash Comp. Step Value

This third "increment" setting functions identically to the other two but applies to exposure compensation and flash exposure compensation adjustments you make by holding down the relevant EV adjustment buttons on the camera. (The Exposure Compensation button is on the top panel, just southeast of the shutter release button, as introduced in Chapter 2.) The flash compensation button can be found on the left side of the pentaprism, just below the flash pop-up button. Both add or subtract from the exposure when held down while the main command dial is rotated. This setting tells the Nikon D810 the size of the "jumps" it should use when making these exposure adjustments. As with ISO sensitivity and exposure control step values, you can select from 1/3 step (the default); 1/2 step; and 1 step increments.

b4 Easy Exposure Compensation

This setting potentially simplifies dialing in EV (exposure value compensation) adjustments by specifying whether the Exposure Compensation button must be pressed while adding or extracting EV compensation. Because of the possibility of confusion or error, I tend to leave this setting turned off.

Your choices are as follows:

- **On (Auto reset).** This setting allows you to add or subtract exposure by rotating the sub-command dial when in Programmed (P) or Shutter-priority (S) exposure modes, or by rotating the main command dial when using Aperture-priority (A) mode. Rotating either dial has no effect in Manual (M) exposure mode. (If you've reversed the behavior of the command dials using Custom Setting f7, the "opposite" command dial must be used to make the changes.) Any adjustments you've made are canceled when the camera is shut off, or the meter-off time expires and the D810's exposure meters go back to sleep. That's a useful mode, because most of us have made an EV adjustment and then forgotten about it, only to expose a whole series of improperly exposed photos. You can still have "sticky" EV settings when Easy Exposure Compensation is turned on: just hold down the Exposure Compensation button when you make your changes.
- **On.** This setting brings the Easy Compensation mode into conformance with the D810's behavior when the Exposure Compensation button is pressed: in either case, any EV modifications you make will remain until you countermand them. As I have mentioned several times, forgetting to "turn off" EV changes after you've moved on to a different shooting environment is a primary cause of over and underexposure among those of us who are forgetful or who ignore the D810's flashing EV warnings.
- **Off.** With this default setting, you must always press the Exposure Compensation button while rotating the main command dial to add or subtract exposure. Use this choice when you don't want any EV changes unless you deliberately make them by pressing the button.

b5 Matrix Metering

Use this entry (On or Off) to enable/disable face detection when you're using matrix metering while using the viewfinder to frame your image.

b6 Center-Weighted Area

This setting changes the size of the center-weighted exposure spot when the D810 is used with a non-CPU (generally older AI and AI-S and earlier lenses that haven't been updated with a "computer" chip). Your choices include 8mm, 12mm, 15mm, 20mm, or full-frame average (which turns the metering mode from a center-weighted system to an old-fashioned averaging system). If you're using a non-CPU lens, the center-weighted area is fixed at 12mm, and the camera ignores whatever choice you may have entered here. Because the D810 shows the default 12mm area in the viewfinder, you have a visual indication of what area is being emphasized by the metering system. Figure 12.6 shows the relative size of the center-weight zones.

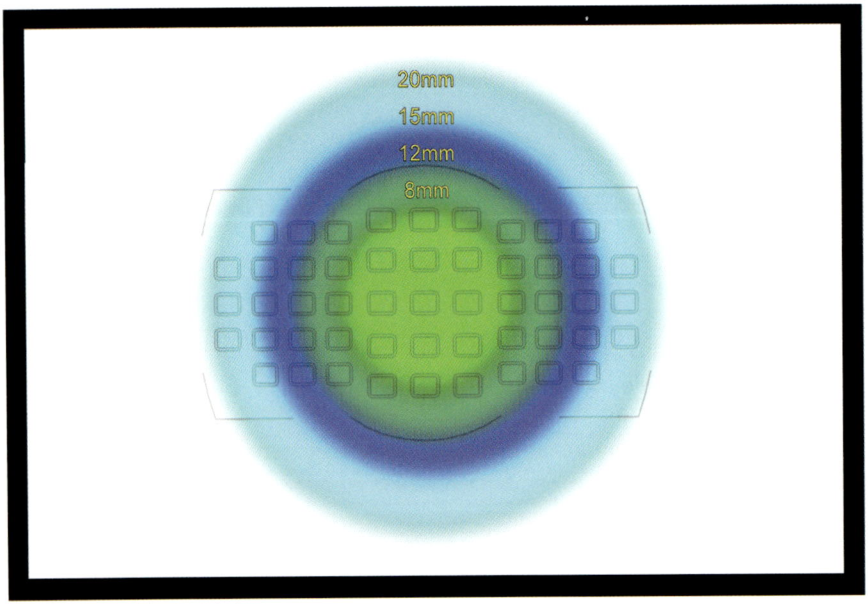

Figure 12.6
Center-weighting can use zones measuring 8, 12, 15, and 20mm.

b7 Fine-Tune Optimal Exposure

This setting is a powerful adjustment that allows you to dial in a specific amount of exposure compensation that will be applied, invisibly, to every photo you take using each of the three metering modes. No more can you complain, "My D810 always underexposes by 1/3 stop!" If that is actually the case, and the phenomenon is consistent, you can use this custom menu adjustment to compensate.

Exposure compensation is usually a better idea (does your camera *really* underexpose that consistently?), but this setting does allow you to "recalibrate" your D810 yourself. You can fine-tune exposure separately in each of the four A, B, C, D Custom Settings banks, and your dialed in modifications will survive a two-button reset. However, you have no indication that fine-tuning has been made, so you'll need to remember what you've done. After all, you someday might discover that your camera is consistently *over*exposing images by 1/3 stop, not realizing that your Custom Setting b6 adjustment is the culprit.

In practice, it's rare that the Nikon D810 will *consistently* provide the wrong exposure in any of the three metering modes, especially Matrix metering, which can alter exposure dramatically based on the D810's internal database of typical scenes. This feature may be most useful for Spot metering, if you always take a reading off the same type of subject, such as a human face or 18-percent gray card. Should you find that the gray card readings, for example, always differ from what you would prefer, go ahead and fine-tune optimal exposure for Spot metering, and use that to read your gray cards.

To use this feature:

1. **Select fine-tuning.** Choose Custom Setting b6, Fine-tune optimal exposure from the Custom Settings menu.
2. **Consider yourself warned.** In the screen that appears, choose Yes after carefully reading the warning that Nikon insists on showing you each and every time this option is activated.
3. **Select metering mode to correct.** Choose Matrix metering, Center-weighted, Spot, or Highlight-weighted metering in the screen that follows by highlighting your choice and pressing the multi selector right button.
4. **Specify amount of correction.** Press the up/down buttons to dial in the exposure compensation you want to apply. You can specify compensation in increments of 1/6 stop, half as large a change as conventional exposure compensation. This is truly *fine-tuning.*
5. **Confirm your change.** Press OK when finished. You can repeat the action to fine-tune the other two exposure modes if you wish.

c. Timers/AE Lock

This category (see Figure 12.7) is a mixed bag of settings, covering both entries that adjust delay times (c2 through c4) and how the shutter release and AE-L buttons interact (c1). I think the latter setting, changed slightly for the D810, should have been placed in the purple f-coded Controls section, especially since with the original D300, Nikon moved the assignment of the AE-L/AF-L button setting (which used to reside here with some earlier cameras) to that location. They moved one of the settings, but not the other. Go figure.

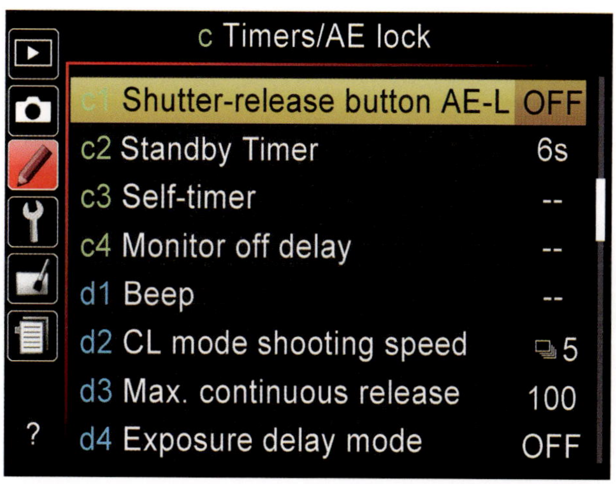

Figure 12.7
The Timers/AE Lock settings.

c1 Shutter-Release Button AE-L

This is another of Nikon's easily confusing options for controlling how and when autofocus and exposure are activated and locked. The intent is to allow you to separate autofocus and autoexposure activation and locking.

- **Off.** Exposure is locked *only* when the AE-L/AF-L button is pressed. This is the default.
- **On.** Exposure locks when either the shutter release button is depressed halfway or the AE-L/AF-L button is held down.

c2 Standby Timer

Use this setting to determine how long the D810's exposure meter continues to operate after the last operation, such as autofocusing, focus point selection, and so forth, was performed. The default value is 6 seconds, but you can also select 4, 6, 10, and 30 seconds, as well as 1, 5, 10, and 30 minutes, or No limit, which keeps the meter active until the camera is switched off.

To save power, you should select an intermediate value, such as 8, 16, or 30 seconds if the default 6 seconds is not long enough. When the Nikon EH-6 AC adapter is connected to the D810, the exposure meter will remain on indefinitely, just as if you'd specified No limit. Absent an external power source, any setting longer than 8 seconds will definitely eat up power.

Even so, sports shooters and some others prefer a longer delay, because they are able to keep their camera always "at the ready" with no delay to interfere with taking an action shot that unexpectedly presents itself. Extra battery consumption is just part of the price paid. For example, when I am shooting football, a meter-off delay of 16 seconds is plenty, because the players lining up for the snap is my signal to get ready to shoot. But for basketball or soccer, I typically set the meter-off delay for No Limit, because action is virtually continuous. My D810 has plenty of power, and I carry two sets of spares. I rarely shoot much more than 1,000-1,200 shots at any sports event, so that's often sufficient juice even with meter-off delay set for No Limit.

Of course, if the meters have shut off, and the power switch remains in the On position, you can bring the camera back to life by tapping the shutter button.

c3 Self-Timer

This setting lets you choose the length of the self-timer shutter release delay. The default value is 10 seconds. You can also choose 2, 5, or 20 seconds.

Your options include:

- **Self-timer delay.** The default value is 10 seconds. You can also choose 2, 5, 10, or 20 seconds. If I have the camera mounted on a tripod or other support and am too lazy to dig around for my wired or IR remote, I can set a two-second delay that is sufficient to let the camera stop vibrating after I've pressed the shutter release. I use a longer delay time if I am racing to get into the picture myself and am not sure I can make it in 10 seconds.
- **Number of shots.** After the timer finishes counting down, the D810 can take from 1 to 9 different shots. This is a godsend when shooting photos of groups, especially if you want to appear in the photo itself. You'll always want to shoot several pictures to ensure that everyone's eyes are open and there are smiling expressions on each face. Instead of racing back and forth between the camera to trigger the self-timer multiple times, you can select the number of shots taken after a single countdown. For small groups, I always take at least as many shots as there are people in the group—plus one. That gives everybody a chance to close their eyes. Of course, the ML-L3 IR remote is often your best choice, but this facility works well if you don't have one handy.
- **Interval between shots.** If you've selected 2 to 9 as your number of shots to be snapped off, you can use this option to space out the different exposures. Your choices are 0.5 seconds, 1, 2, or 3 seconds. Use a short interval when you want to capture everyone saying "Cheese!" The 3-second option is helpful if you're using flash, as 3 seconds is generally long enough to allow the flash to recycle and have enough juice for the next photo.

Tip

If you want a longer delay and are *really* lazy, just turn the D810's release mode dial to the Mup position. No menu changes required! When you press the shutter release all the way down, the mirror will raise (reducing vibration so you can take a picture immediately), but if you do nothing else, the picture will be taken anyway 30 seconds later. (To take a picture immediately after the mirror is raised, press the shutter release a second time.) Return the release mode dial to the single frame or continuous shooting modes to cancel this temporary self-timer option.

c4 Monitor Off Delay

You can adjust the amount of time the monitor remains on when no other operations are being performed. As with the meter-off delay, if the EH-6 AC adapter is attached, the monitor will remain on for the maximum amount, about 10 minutes. With the D810, you can specify separate values for Playback (the default is 10 seconds); Menus (the default is 1 minute); Information display (default is 10 seconds); Image review (4 seconds); and live view (10 minute default). Choosing a brief duration for all or each of these can help preserve battery power. However, the D810 will always override the review display when the shutter button is partially or fully depressed, so you'll never miss a shot because a previous image was on the screen.

SAVING POWER WITH THE Nikon D810

There are several settings and techniques you can use to help stretch the longevity of your D810's battery. To get the most from each charge, consider these steps:

- **Playback menu.** Image review: Turn off image review after each shot. You can still review your images by pressing the Playback button.
- **Auto meter-off delay.** Set to 4 seconds if you can tolerate such a brief active time.
- **Monitor off delay.** Set values for the minimum length, 10 seconds. That big 3.2-inch monitor uses a lot of juice, so reducing the amount of time it is used when you don't turn it off manually (either for automatic review or for playing back your images) can boost the effectiveness of your battery.
- **Reduce LCD illumination.** Set Custom Setting d8 to Off, so the control panel will be backlit only when you manually use the switch around the shutter release.
- **Reduce LCD brightness.** In the Setup menu, select the lowest of the seven brightness settings that work for you under most conditions. If you're willing to shade the monitor with your hand, you can often get away with lower brightness settings outdoors, which will further increase the useful life of your battery.
- **Cancel VR.** Turn off vibration reduction if your lens has that feature and you feel you don't need it.
- **Use a card reader.** When transferring pictures from your D810 to your computer, use a card reader instead of the USB cable. Linking your camera to your computer and transferring images using the cable takes longer and uses a lot more power.

d. Shooting/Display

This menu section (see Figure 12.8) offers a variety of mostly unrelated shooting and display options not found elsewhere, but which are not frequently changed, making them suitable for a Custom Settings entry. The figure shows only the first eight entries; you must scroll down to see the last three.

d1 Beep

The Nikon D810's internal beeper provides a (usually) superfluous chirp to signify various functions, such as the countdown of your camera's self-timer or autofocus confirmation in AF-S mode (unless you've selected release priority in Custom Setting a2). You can (and probably should) switch it off if you want to avoid the beep because it's annoying, impolite, distracting (at a concert or museum), or undesired for any other reason. It's one of the few ways to make the D810 a bit quieter. (I've actually had new dSLR owners ask me how to turn off the "shutter sound" the camera makes; such an option was available in the point-and-shoot camera they'd used previously.)

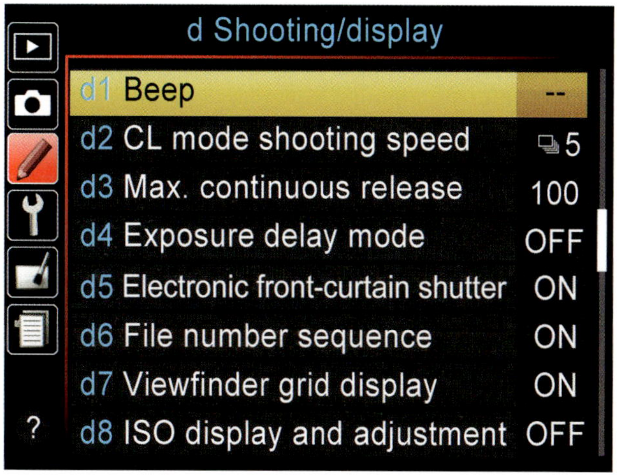

Figure 12.8
A mixed bag of entries is found in the Shooting/Display submenu.

Select d1 Beep from the Custom Setting menu, and select one of the following:

- **Volume.** Select Off to disable the beeper, or values of 1 (soft) through 3 (loud). A quarter-note icon appears in the monochrome control panel and the shooting information display.
- **Pitch.** Select High for a high-pitched beep, or Low for a deeper tone.

d2 CL Mode Shooting Speed

You can specify the frames per second shooting rate for continuous low speed mode (C_L), from 1 frame per second to 6 frames per second. Faster rates are better for sports action, such as the image shown in Figure 12.9.

Choose one of these firing speed ranges for C_L from among those available that is suitable for the kind of shooting environment you're in:

- **Normal continuous shooting.** I set my D810 to the 1 fps rate most of the time, so that I can take multiple shots quickly without needing to press the shutter release repeatedly. A one-second rate isn't so fast that I end up taking a bunch of shots that I don't want, but it is fast enough that I can shoot a series.
- **Bracketing.** When I'm using bracketing, I generally have the D810 set to shoot a bracketed set of three pictures: normal, over, and underexposure. With the camera set to 3 fps, I can press the shutter once and take all three bracketed shots, with basically the same framing, within about one second.
- **Slower action sequences.** The 6 fps rate available for sports photography often produces an embarrassing plethora of pictures that are a pain to wade through after the event is over. For some types of action, such as long distance running, golf, swimming, or routine baseball plays, a rate of 3 to 5 fps might be sufficient. You can make this more reasonable speed available by defining it here as the continuous low speed frame rate.

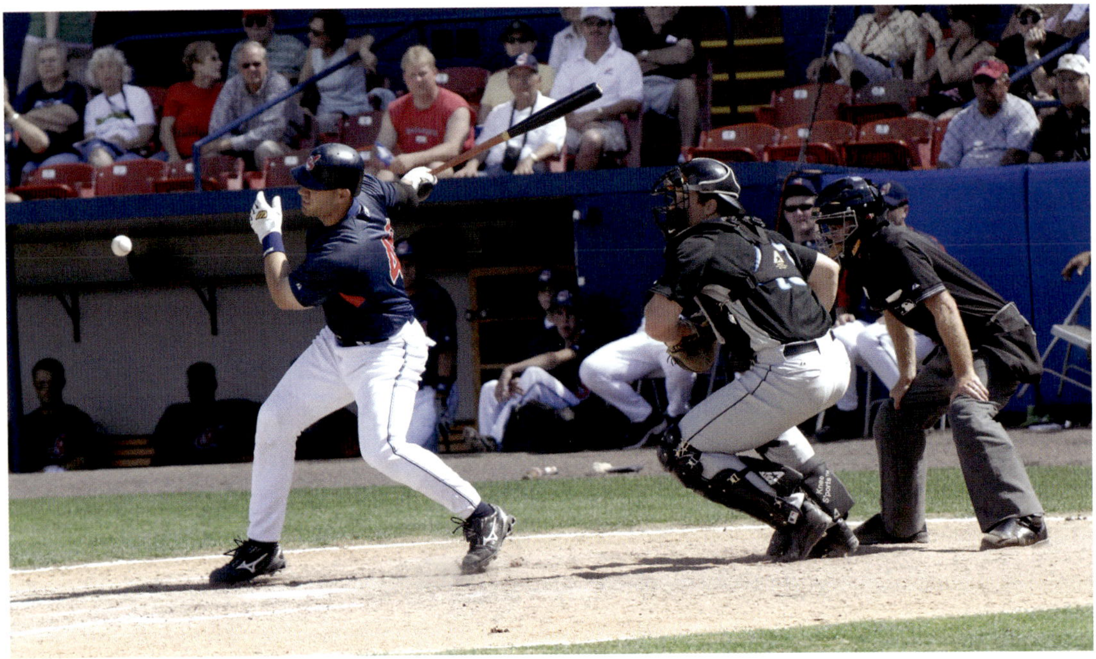

Figure 12.9 High frame rates can capture a critical moment when shooting sports action.

d3 Max. Continuous Release

Use this setting to limit the number of consecutive shots that can be taken in one burst when using continuous shooting modes. Your choices are any value between 1 and 100. Choosing a particular setting does not mean that the D810 will actually *take* that many shots if you hold down the shutter button long enough. As your buffer fills, continuous shooting will slow down and eventually pause while the D810 dumps pictures to the memory card. However, the D810's file sizes at 36 megapixels are quite large, so you can easily find yourself waiting for the memory card to store images, especially if you're shooting RAW+JPEG at a 6 fps rate. I have my D810 set to 30 shots maximum, but almost never reach that point when shooting.

d4 Exposure Delay Mode

This is a marginally useful feature (and mildly annoying if you forget to turn it off) that you can use to force the Nikon D810 to snap a picture about 1, 2, or 3 seconds (your choice) after you've pressed the shutter release button all the way. It's useful when you are using shutter speeds of about 1/8th to 1/60th second hand-held and want to minimize the effects of the vibration that results when you depress the shutter button. It can also be used when the camera is mounted on a tripod, although the self-timer function, set to a two-second delay, is more useful in that scenario. When switched On, the camera will pause while you steady your steely grip on the camera, taking the picture about one second later. When turned Off, the picture is taken when the shutter release is pressed, as normal. One interesting side-effect of this mode is that it separates the normally invisible pre-flash produced by any D810's external flash that's connected with the delay, so, if you're shooting living subjects (human or animal), they may be startled by the initial flash and close their eyes just before the main flash fires 1,000 milliseconds later.

d5 Electronic Front-Curtain Shutter

You can Enable or Disable this feature using this menu entry. The electronic front-curtain shutter operates *only* when the D810 is operated in Mup mode, and is used to elminate blur caused by shutter motion. To get the most from this feature, you'll need to have the camera mounted on a tripod. When enabled, the picture taking sequence is as follows:

1. **Shutter release pressed.** With the camera in Mup mode, pressing the shutter release down all the way initiates the exposure process.
2. **Mirror flips up.** The quick return mirror flips up, exposing the physical shutter that's covering the sensor plane. Any vibration caused by the mirror movement damps in a fraction of a second.
3. **Physical first curtain opens.** The first curtain opens, exposing the sensor to light—but the actual exposure does not begin yet. Instead, there is a slight pause to allow the motion of the shutter opening to be damped.
4. **Image on sensor is discarded.** Any current photons captured by the sensor are electronically dumped, effectively producing an electronic "first curtain" shutter opening.
5. **Picture captured.** The sensor remains uncovered for the length of time specified for the exposure—from 30 seconds to 1/2000th second (or longer if Bulb is selected). Note that shutter speeds shorter than 1/2000th second are not possible.
6. **Rear physical curtain closes.** Any vibrations from the rear curtain closing don't affect the exposure.

d6 File Number Sequence

The Nikon D810 will automatically apply a file number to each picture you take, using consecutive numbering for all your photos over a long period of time, spanning many different memory cards, starting over from scratch when you insert a new card, or when you manually reset the numbers. Numbers are applied from 0001 to 9999, at which time the D810 "rolls over" to 0001 again.

The camera keeps track of the last number used in its internal memory and, if File Number Sequence is turned On, will apply a number that's one higher, or a number that's one higher than the largest number in the current folder on the memory card inserted in the camera. You can also start over each time a new folder has been created on the memory card, or reset the current counter back to 0001 at any time.

Here's how it works:

- **On.** At this default setting, the D810 will use the number stored in its internal memory any time a new folder is created, a new memory card inserted, or an existing memory card formatted. If the card is not blank and contains images, then the next number will be one greater than the highest number on the card *or* in internal memory (whichever is higher). Here are some examples.
  - You've taken 1,235 shots with the camera, and you insert a blank/reformatted memory card. The next number assigned will be 1,236, based on the value stored in internal memory.
  - You've taken 1,235 shots with the camera, and you insert an old memory card you previously used with the D810, but which has a picture numbered 0728. The next picture will be numbered 1,236.
  - You've taken more than 9,999 shots with the camera and the counter has rolled over to 0001 again, and your new total is 1,235 shots. You insert an old memory card with a picture from before the rollover that's numbered 8,281. The next picture will be numbered 8,282, and that value will be stored in the camera's menu as the "high" shot number (and will be applied when you next insert a blank card). This misnumbering makes it a good idea to always reformat your memory cards before taking a photo, if at all possible.
- **Off.** If you're using a blank/reformatted memory card, or a new folder is created, the next photo taken will be numbered 0001. File number sequences will be reset every time you use or format a card, or a new folder is created (which happens when an existing folder on the card contains 999 shots).
- **Reset.** The D810 assigns a file number that's one larger than the largest file number in the current folder, unless the folder is empty, in which case numbering is reset to 0001. At this setting, new or reformatted memory cards will always have 0001 as the first file number.

HOW MANY SHOTS, REALLY?

The file numbers produced by the D810 don't provide information about the actual number of times the camera's shutter has been tripped—called actuations. For that data, you'll need a third-party software solution, such as the free Opanda iExif (www.opanda.com) for Windows or the non-free ($34.95) GraphicConverter for Macintosh (www.lemkesoft.com). These utilities can be used to extract the true number of actuations from the Exif information embedded in a JPEG file.

d7 Viewfinder Grid Display

The D810 can display a grid of lines overlaid on the viewfinder (see Figure 12.10), offering some help when you want to align vertical or horizontal lines. Note that the intersections of these lines do *not* follow the Rule of Thirds convention, and so are less useful for composition, assuming you want to follow the Rule of Thirds guideline in the first place. If you happen to subscribe to the Rule of Quarters, you're all set. Note that for critical applications, it's possible that your D810's viewfinder isn't absolutely accurate. I sometimes have to rotate images slightly in Photoshop because the grid is not perfectly aligned. Your options for this grid display are On and Off (the default).

d8 ISO Display and Adjustment

This entry controls whether ISO or frame count is displayed in the viewfinder and control panel. You have three options.

- **Show ISO sensitivity.** The viewfinder and control panel will display the current ISO sensitivity in the position where the frame count is normally shown.
- **Show ISO/Easy ISO.** This option also replaces the frame count with the ISO display, but when active you can change the ISO quickly by rotating the sub-command dial (when using P or S exposure modes) or by rotating the main command dial (when using A mode).
- **Show Frame Count.** In this default mode, the number of exposures remaining is shown in the viewfinder and control panel. To see the ISO setting on the monitor, press the INFO button.

d9 Screen Tips

Items highlighted in the *i*-button display are accompanied by a pop-up tool tip when this option is set to On. Turn Screen Tips off once you've learned the features of your camera, or find them annoying.

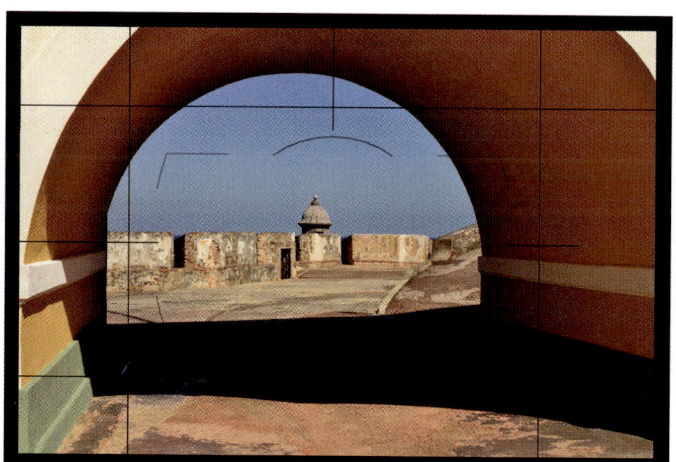

Figure 12.10
The D810's optional grid display can help with composing and aligning images in the viewfinder.

d10 Information Display

This menu entry (see Figure 12.11) refers to the shooting information display that appears when you press the Info button. You can set this display to change automatically from dark lettering on a light background to light lettering on a dark background, or you can select one or the other to be used all the time. The monitor will automatically change its brightness to provide the best contrast for the selected text display. Your choices are as follows:

- **Auto.** If the scene as viewed through the lens indicates a bright environment, the shooting info display will appear as black letters on a white background, producing an improved view in full daylight. If the scene appears dark, the display will have lighter letters on a dark background. Note that it's easy to "fool" the camera. Until you take the lens cap off, you'll see the dark background display regardless of your shooting environment. If you're standing in a darkened location, but point the camera at a bright scene, the D810 will show you the "daylight" display.
- **Manual.** Select this option and you can choose B (Dark on light) or W (Light on dark) to be used as the display at all times.

d11 LCD Illumination

When set to Off (the default), the control panel (and the status LCDs on any attached compatible Nikon Speedlight, such as the Nikon SB-910) will illuminate for as long as the exposure meters are active, but only when the switch around the shutter release is pressed toward the maximum clockwise direction, just past the On indicator. Choose On, and the panel will be illuminated any time the exposure meters are active (and thus using more power), without the need to press the switch.

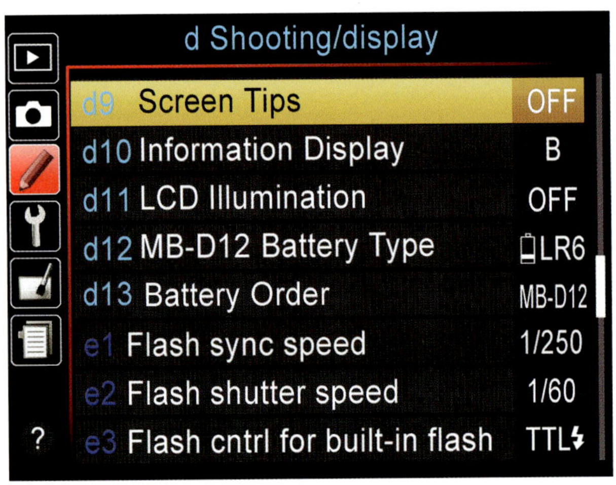

Figure 12.11
The second screen of Shooting/display options.

d12 MB-D12 Battery Type

This option is needed to communicate to the D810 what type of AA batteries are being used in the MB-D12 battery pack/grip, because the different varieties of AA batteries provide slightly different voltages, and change voltages at different rates as they are used up. The setting you select here has no effect when you're using an EN-EL15. Your choices include:

- **LR6 (AA alkaline).** For ordinary alkaline batteries
- **HR6 (AA NiMH).** For Nickel-Metal Hydride rechargeable batteries
- **FR6 (AA lithium).** For non-rechargeable lithium batteries

Because of their limited capacity, you'll want to use conventional AA alkaline batteries only as a last resort, and then only when the weather is warmer than 68 degrees Fahrenheit, because the chemical reactions that provide power decline at lower temperatures. Alkalines retain their power longer when not used, so they may be a reasonable choice if you rarely use your MB-D12 and want to keep it ready to go. But I expect few readers will have this useful accessory sitting on a shelf gathering dust.

d13 Battery Order

When using the MB-D12 battery pack/grip, the batteries in the pack and in your D810 are used consecutively. That is, one of them powers the camera until it is exhausted, and then the D810 switches to the other. You can choose the order in which this switch-off takes place.

The default setting is Use MB-D12 Batteries First. You can also specify Use Camera Battery First. If you were using AA alkaline batteries in the MB-D12 as an emergency reserve, you'd probably want to use the D810's internal battery first, so the alkalines wouldn't be prematurely exhausted and could live to shoot as backup another day. If you're using an EN-EL15 in the MB-D12, and shooting a lot, you might want to use the MB-D12 battery first, and use the camera's battery as a backup, because the MB-D12 battery can be changed more quickly, and without removing the grip from the D810.

e. Bracketing/Flash

There are lots of useful settings in this submenu (see Figure 12.12) that deal with bracketing and electronic flash (hence the cleverly concocted name). I provided a thorough description of using bracketing in Chapter 4, and a complete rundown of flash options in Chapters 9 and 10. Here, I'll offer a recap of the settings at your disposal.

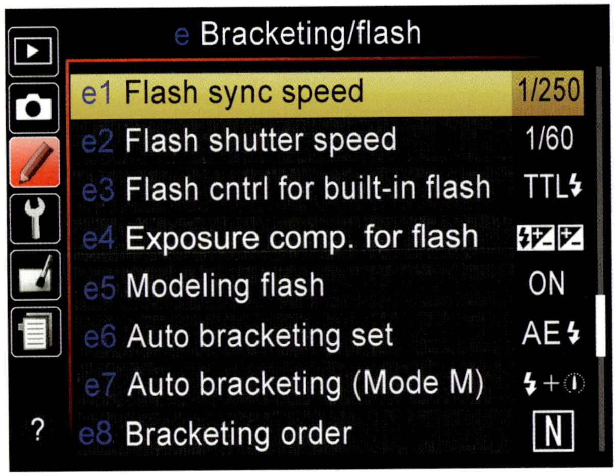

Figure 12.12
Bracketing and flash options are available in this menu.

e1 Flash Sync Speed

As you may already know (or will learn in Chapter 9), the focal plane shutter in the Nikon D810 must be fully open when the flash fires; otherwise, you'll image one edge or the other of the vertically traveling shutter curtain in your photo. Ordinarily, the fastest shutter speed during which the shutter is completely open for an instant is 1/250th second. However, there are exceptions when you can use faster shutter speeds with certain flash units (such as the Nikon SB-910, SB-700, and SB-R200) for automatic FP (focal plane) synchronization. There are also situations in which you might want to set flash sync speed to *less* than 1/250th second, say, because you *want* ambient light to produce secondary ghost images in your frame. (I'll address all these sync issues in Chapter 9.) You can choose the following settings:

- **1/320 s (Auto FP).** This setting allows using compatible external flash units with high-speed synchronization at 1/320th second or faster, and activates auto FP sync when the camera selects a shutter speed of 1/320th second or faster in Programmed and Aperture-priority modes. Other flash units, including the built-in flash, will be used at speeds no faster than 1/250th second.
- **1/250 s (Auto FP).** This similar setting allows using the named external flash units with high-speed synchronization at 1/250th second or faster, and activates auto FP sync when the camera selects a shutter speed of 1/250th second or faster in Programmed and Aperture-priority modes. Other flash units, including the flip-up internal flash, will be used at speeds no faster than 1/250th second.
- **1/250 s.** At this default setting, only shutter speeds up to 1/250th second can be used with flash, both internal and external. Note: To lock in shutter speed at 1/250th second, rotate the main control dial in M or S modes to choose the x250 setting located after the 30s and bulb speeds.
- **1/200 s-1/60 s.** You can specify a shutter speed from 1/200th second to 1/60th second to be used as the synchronization speed for flash units.

e2 Flash Shutter Speed

This setting determines the *slowest* shutter speed that is available for electronic flash synchronization when you're not using a "slow sync" mode (described in Chapter 9). As you may know, when you're using flash, the flash itself provides virtually all of the illumination that makes the main exposure, and the shutter speed determines how much, if any, of the ambient light contributes to that second, non-flash exposure. Indeed, if the camera or subject is moving, you can end up with two distinct exposures in the same frame: the sharply defined flash exposure, and a second, blurry "ghost" picture created by the ambient light.

If you *don't* want that second exposure, you should use the highest shutter speed that will synchronize with your flash. This setting prevents Programmed or Aperture-priority modes (which both select the shutter speed for you) from inadvertently selecting a "too slow" shutter speed. You can select a value from 30 s to 1/60 s, and the D810 will avoid using speeds slower than the one you specify with electronic flash (unless you've selected slow sync, slow rear-curtain sync, or red-eye reduction with slow sync, as described in Chapter 10). The "slow sync" modes do permit the ambient light to contribute to the exposure (say, to allow the background to register in night shots, or to use the ghost image as a special effect). For brighter backgrounds, you'll need to put the camera on a tripod or other support to avoid the blurry ghosts that can occur from camera shake, even if the subject is stationary.

If you are able to hold the D810 steady, a value of 1/30 s is a good compromise; if you have shaky hands, use 1/60 s or higher. Those with extraordinarily solid grips or a lens with vibration reduction can try the 1/15 s setting. Remember that this setting only determines the slowest shutter speed that will be used, not the default shutter speed.

e3 Flash Cntrl for Built-in Flash

The Nikon D810's built-in flash has four modes, which I described in a lot more detail in Chapter 9. Your four options are as follows:

- **TTL.** When the built-in flash is triggered, the D810 first fires a pre-flash and measures the light reflected back and through the lens to calculate the proper exposure when the full flash is emitted a fraction of a second later.
- **Manual.** You can set the level of the built-in flash from full power to 1/128 power.
- **Repeating flash.** The flash fires multiple bursts, producing a stroboscopic lighting effect. As I described in Chapter 9, when you choose repeating flash you'll be asked to select Output (flash power level), Times (the number of times the flash is fired at the output level you specify), and Frequency (how often the flash fires per second). Note that these factors are interdependent. For example, if you tell the flash to fire at 1/8 output power, you can select from 2 to 5 flashes, at a rate of 1 to 50 flashes per second. That's because the flash has only enough power for a maximum of 5 flashes at the 1/8 output setting. At 1/128 power, there's enough juice for 2 to 35 individual flashes, at a rate of no more than 50 flashes per second.

- **Commander mode.** If you never use external flash, you can safely ignore this setting. If you do, you'll want to set up the D810 for your most frequently used options, to avoid having to fiddle with the camera if you decide to pull your SB-910 out of your bag for some impromptu multi-flash shooting. In Commander mode, the built-in flash emits pre-flashes that can be used to wirelessly control one or more remote external flash units.

> **Tip**
>
> If the Nikon SB-400 flash unit is attached and turned on, this menu choice is not available, because the SB-400 unit, unlike the D810's built-in flash and other external flash units, cannot function in Commander mode. You'll be able to set flash compensation and flash mode for the built-in flash as well as individual "groups" of flashes (Groups A and B) and the triggering channels. As you'll see, using electronic flash with the Nikon D810 is worth a book of its own, but I'll do my best to explain the vagaries in Chapter 9.

e4 Exposure Compensation for Flash

Use this to specify how the camera modifies the flash level when you apply exposure compensation.

- **Entire frame.** Flash exposure compensation *and* ambient light exposure compensation are adjusted over the entire frame.
- **Background only.** Exposure compensation is applied only to the background areas of your image. Use this option when you want to adjust the brightness/darkness of the background.

e5 Modeling Flash

The Nikon D810, and certain compatible external flash units (like the SB-700 and SB-910/SB-900) have the capability of simulating a modeling lamp, which gives you the limited capability of previewing how your flash illumination is going to look in the finished photo. The modeling flash is not a perfect substitute for a real incandescent or fluorescent modeling lamp, but it does help you see how your subject is illuminated, and spot any potential problems with shadows.

When this feature is activated, pressing the depth-of-field button on the D810 briefly triggers the modeling flash for your preview. Selecting Off disables the feature. You'll generally want to leave it On, except when you anticipate using the depth-of-field preview button for depth-of-field purposes (imagine that) and do *not* want the modeling flash to fire when the flash unit is charged and ready. Some external flash units, such as the SB-910, have their own modeling flash buttons.

e6 Auto Bracketing Set

The Nikon D810 can automatically take several pictures using slightly different settings within a range that you specify, and apply the changes to automatic exposure, electronic flash, white balance, or (with the D810) Active D-Lighting. This setting allows you to specify whether bracketing is used for both automatic exposure *and* flash (AE & flash), automatic exposure only (AE), flash bracketing only (Flash only), white balance color bracketing alone (WB bracketing), or (with the D810) Active D-Lighting bracketing alone. No autoexposure or flash bracketing will be performed when white balance bracketing or ADL bracketing is activated. Because you can specify white balance manually when importing a RAW file, WB bracketing is not available when Quality has been set to NEF (RAW) or NEF (RAW)+JPEG. The results you get with flash bracketing can vary quite a bit, depending on the amount of ambient illumination and flash mode you've chosen, but exposure bracketing is fairly consistent. I tend to leave this option set to AE most of the time. White balance bracketing is useful when you're not quite sure of the color balance of your illumination. ADL bracketing with the D810 can come in handy when you're not sure which Active D-Lighting setting will work for a particular situation. You'll find more about bracketing in Chapter 4.

e7 Auto Bracketing Mode (Mode M)

If you're using Manual exposure mode to set the shutter speed and f/stop yourself, you can still take advantage of exposure bracketing. The Nikon D810 will take the basic settings you specified and adjust the exposure to provide over, under, and as-set variations. This setting determines whether shutter speed, aperture, or both are used to create the bracketing exposures. Remember, *you* set the basic exposure using shutter speed and aperture, and the D810 brackets around those values. If your flash is used and has been activated for bracketing using Custom Setting e5, the flash will be factored in, as well. The menu entries can be tricky to understand, so I'm going to spell them out:

- **Flash/Speed.** With this default value, the D810 will vary the shutter speed to produce bracketed exposures and, if flash bracketing is available, will vary flash output as well. Use this option to keep your aperture set at the f/stop you select, say, to provide a certain desired amount (or lack) of depth-of-field. This setting works best when bracketing a moderate number of shots—say, 2 to 5 exposures—because the shutter speed changes among the bracketed set won't be dramatic.
- **Flash/Speed/Aperture.** This option tells the D810 to vary both shutter speed and aperture from your manual settings, and to vary flash output if flash bracketing is available. This setting is useful when creating a large bracket set, up to nine different exposures, because you'll rarely want to vary shutter speed or aperture alone over such a large range of shots. The Flash/Speed/Aperture option spreads the variation over a combination of shutter speeds and apertures.

- **Flash/Aperture.** The D810 will use the aperture to bracket your photos taken by ambient light, and if flash bracketing is available, will use flash output as well. This option is best if you're shooting sports with manual exposure and want to lock in a specific shutter speed. As with Flash/Speed, this setting works best when the number of exposures in your bracket set is limited to 2 to 5 exposures; otherwise, the f/stop selected can vary wildly.
- **Flash Only.** The D810 will bracket only flash exposure.

e8 Bracketing Order

Use this setting to define the sequence in which bracketing is carried out. Your choices are the default: MTR > Under > Over (metered exposure, followed by the version receiving less exposure, and finishing with the picture receiving the most exposure) and Under > MTR > Over, which orders the exposures from least exposed to most exposed (for both ambient and flash exposures). The same order is applied to white balance bracketing, too, but the values are Normal > More Yellow > More Blue and More Yellow > Normal > More Blue. (Nikon actually calls "yellow" by the term "amber," but I've found "yellow" easier to understand.) You'll find lots more about bracketing in Chapter 4. When doing ADL bracketing with the D810, this setting has no effect.

f. Controls

You can modify the way various control buttons and dials perform by using the options in this submenu, shown in Figure 12.13.

f1 Illuminator Switch

When you rotate the power switch, located concentrically with the shutter release, all the way to the clockwise position, the control panel is backlit for approximately six seconds. Choose the monitor Backlight option, the default, and that's exactly what happens. The Switch and Information Display also turns on the shooting information display on the color monitor.

f2 Multi Selector Center Button

There are three groups of options available here, one for use when the camera is in shooting mode, and another when you're reviewing images in playback mode. The third is applied during live view mode. So the multi selector center button can have three different functions. In shooting mode:

- **RESET/Select center focus point.** This default setting lets you quickly select the center focus point in the viewfinder simply by pressing the multi selector center button.
- **Preset.** Preset the focus point to a saved location.
- **Highlight active focus point.** The active point is illuminated when you press the button.
- **Not used.** Nothing happens when the multi selector center button is pressed. If you find yourself sloppily pressing the center button in the heat of the moment while shooting, use this setting to deactivate it and avoid unwanted actions.

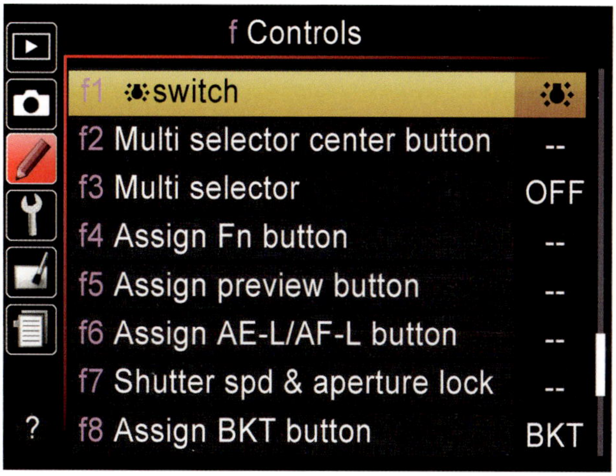

Figure 12.13
Modify the behavior of the D810's controls with these menu options.

In playback mode:

- **Thumbnail on/off.** This default setting alternates between full-frame and thumbnail playback.
- **View histograms.** When selected, a larger histogram is displayed while the multi selector center button is pressed.
- **Zoom on/off.** Use the multi selector center button to toggle between full-frame or thumbnail playback (whichever is active) and playback zoom. You can choose Low Magnification, Medium Magnification, and High Magnification.
- **Choose slot and folder.** This mode pops up the slot and folder selection screen.

In live view mode:

- **RESET/Select center focus point.** This setting selects the center focus point in the viewfinder by pressing the center button.
- **Zoom on/off.** Use the multi selector center button to toggle between full-frame or thumbnail playback (whichever is active) and playback zoom. You can choose Low Magnification, Medium Magnification, and High Magnification.
- **Not used.** Nothing happens when you press the multi selector center button.

f3 Multi Selector

By default, pressing the left/right or up/down buttons on the multi selector when the exposure meters are off does nothing. If you would rather have the meters activated instead, switch from the Do Nothing default to Reset Meter-Off Delay. The meters will spring to life when one of the directional buttons is pressed, and remain active until the delay you've set previously in Custom Setting c2 has elapsed.

f4 Assign Fn (Function) Button

You can define the action that the Fn button performs when pressed alone, or when pressed while the command dials are rotated. There are nearly two dozen 16 different actions you can define for the button alone (including None), and five for the Fn button + a command dial. For the Fn button alone you can choose from:

- **Preview.** Depth-of-field preview. Perhaps you'd like to use the DOF preview button for something else, and substitute the Fn button for DOF preview.
- **FV lock.** Press the Fn button to lock the value of the built-in or external flash, and press again to unlock it. This is the default value for the button.
- **AE/AF lock.** Lock both focus and exposure while the Fn button is pressed. Use this setting or one of the next three when you want to have a specific mode of operation normally available from the AE-L/AF-L button, but would prefer to trigger the behavior with the Fn button pressed instead.
- **AE lock only.** Lock only the exposure while the Fn button is pressed.
- **AE lock (Reset on Release).** Lock exposure when Fn button is pressed; unlock when the button is pressed a second time, or the shutter button is pressed down all the way, or the exposure meters time out and turn off.
- **AE lock (Hold).** Exposure is locked when the Fn button is pressed, and remains locked until the button is pressed again, or the exposure meter-off delay expires.
- **AF lock only.** Focus is locked in while the Fn button is held down.
- **AF-ON.** The AE-L/AF-L button is used to initiate autofocus.
- **Flash off.** The built-in flash (if elevated) and any external flash attached and powered up will not fire while the Fn button is held down. Handy if you want to temporarily disable the flash, say, to take a picture or two by available light, and then return to normal flash operation.
- **Bracketing burst.** If the Fn button is pressed while exposure or flash bracketing have been activated in Single frame mode, all the shots will be taken, one after another, each time the shutter release is pressed. If Continuous high speed or Continuous low speed shooting modes (C_H or C_L) are active (or if white balance bracketing is active), the D810 will repeat the bracketing bursts for as long as the shutter release button is pressed down.
- **+NEF (RAW).** If your D810 is currently set to shoot JPEG only, use this setting so that when you press the Fn button, the next shot will be recorded as a RAW+JPEG set. I use this option when shooting sports or other fast-moving events, then decide to shoot an image, say, along the sidelines, that could benefit from RAW manipulation later. If you change your mind before shooting, press the Fn button again to cancel.
- **Matrix metering.** Switch from the current metering mode to Matrix metering while the Fn button is held down. You can use this to switch rapidly, say, from Spot metering to Matrix metering in a single session.

- **Center-weighted metering.** Switch from the current metering mode to Center-weighted metering while the Fn button is held down.
- **Spot metering.** Switch from the current metering mode to Spot metering while the Fn button is held down. This is my favorite setting, because I like to switch from Matrix to Spot metering from time to time.
- **Highlight-weighted metering.** Switch from the current metering mode to Highlight-weighted metering while the Fn button is held down. If you find yourself using this new metering option frequently, you can use the Fn button to switch to it temporarily.
- **Viewfinder grid display.** Press Fn to turn the viewfinder grid display on or off.
- **Viewfinder virtual horizon.** Press the Fn button to view or hide the Virtual Horizon indicators at the bottom and sides of the viewfinder. The display shows the degree of tilt of the camera, with the bars to the left and right of center disappearing as the D810 is leveled in the roll orientation, and the bars at the right side of the viewfinder centering as pitch is corrected. (See Figure 12.14.)
- **Disable synchronized release.** When you're syncing several cameras with a wireless remote control, hold down the Fn button to disable activating the other cameras, and images will be captured only using this master camera.

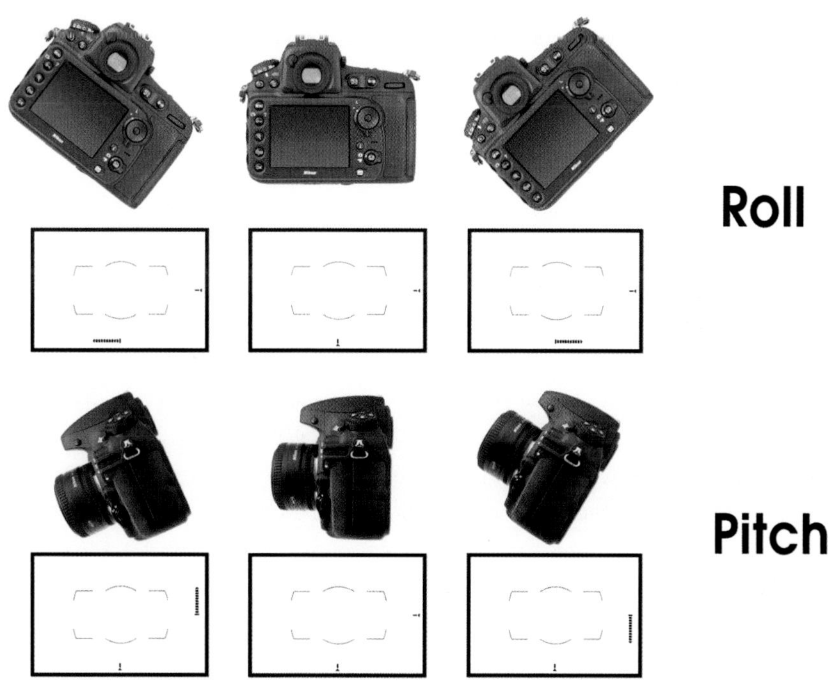

Figure 12.14
The scales at the bottom and right side of the viewfinder show the amount of horizontal and forward/back tilt of the camera.

- **Remote release only.** This is the opposite command; holding down the Fn button will cause only the remote cameras to capture images when you press the shutter release on the master camera.
- **My Menu.** Access the My Menu screen of favorite entries.
- **Access top item in My Menu.** Another new option, this summons the first entry in your My Menu roster. Effectively, you can select *any* menu item that you access frequently, place it at the top of My Menu (as described in Chapter 13), and jump to that item by pressing the Fn button.
- **Playback.** This option redefines the Fn button to provide the same function as the Playback button. You'll find this useful when a long, heavy lens is mounted on your camera and it's difficult to press the Playback button with the left hand.
- **None.** Deactivates the Fn button.

To define the Fn button + command dials options, choose one of the following. Note that setting any of these while Preview, FV lock, AE lock (Reset on release), or AE lock (Hold) are active will reset the Fn button (alone) to None:

- **Choose image area.** Select from DX, FX formats, 5:4, 1.2x, or Auto (the D810 will detect Nikon DX lenses, and some from third-party manufacturers).
- **Shutter Speed & Aperture Lock.** Hold down the Fn button and rotate the main command dial to lock shutter speed when using Shutter-priority and Manual exposure modes; rotate the sub-command dial to lock the aperture when using Aperture-priority and Manual exposure modes.
- **1 step spd/aperture.** If you sometimes prefer coarser exposure settings of 1 whole step (instead of the 1/3 or 1/2 step increments that are normally set), use this option. When holding down the Fn button and rotating a command dial, shutter speed and aperture changes are made in whole step increments instead.
- **Choose non-CPU lens number.** If you swap out older non-CPU manual lenses frequently, this option provides a quicker way of telling the D810 which lens number (1 to 9) to use. I often mount an old manual focus 85mm f/1.8 lens or 55mm f/3.5 Micro Nikkor on my D810, and can use this facility to switch back and forth between the lens settings I've manually entered for these lenses. (Chapter 13 will show you how to do that in the Setup menu.)
- **Active D-Lighting.** Press the Fn button and rotate the command dials to adjust Active D-Lighting, as discussed in Chapter 4.
- **Exposure delay mode.** Hold down the Fn button and rotate either command dial to choose an exposure delay mode.
- **None.** No action is performed when the Fn button is held down while the command dials are rotated.

USING BOTH FN PLUS FN + COMMAND DIALS

The settings that preclude the use of the Fn button + command dials combinations can be confusing. To make things simpler, you can define the Fn button to use AE/AF lock, AE lock only, AF lock only, Flash Off, bracketing burst, Matrix, Center-weighted, or Spot metering options with any of the Fn button + command dial options. If you define the Fn button to provide Preview, FV lock, AE lock (Reset on release), AE lock (Hold), Playback, or +NEF (RAW) functions, you cannot use *any* of the Fn button + command dial options at all. If you elect to use any Fn button + command dial settings, then the antagonistic Fn button functions are disabled. It's as simple (or complicated) as that.

f5 Assign Preview Button

The depth-of-field button can also be defined as you wish, with the same options and limitations as for the Fn button, except that AF-ON is not available, and the default action for the preview button is DOF Preview. The default setting is None.

f6 Assign AE-L/AF-L Button

As if the Nikon D810 didn't have enough buttons that are user-definable, you can change the behavior of the AE-L/AF-L button, too, both when it is used alone and when held down while command dials are rotated. The options and limitations are basically the same as for the Fn button described earlier, except that 1 Stp Spd./Aperture and Active D-Lighting are not available. The default value for the AE-L/AF-L button is AE/AF Lock; there is no default action for AE-L/AF-L button + command dials.

f7 Shutter Speed & Aperture Lock

Hold down the Fn button and rotate the main command dial to lock shutter speed when using Shutter-priority and Manual exposure modes; rotate the sub-command dial to lock the aperture when using Aperture-priority and Manual exposure modes. Shutter speed and aperture lock are not available when using the P exposure mode.

f8 Assign BKT Button

You can redefine the BKT button, located on the right side of the release mode dial. The options are as follows:

- **Auto Bracketing.** Press the BKT button and rotate the command dials to select the bracketing increment and number of shots in the sequence, as described in Chapter 4.
- **Multiple exposure.** Press and rotate the command dials to choose the multiple exposure mode and number of shots, as described in Chapter 11. If you shoot a lot of multiple exposures, or

shoot multiple exposures more than you bracket, this behavior can come in quite handy, as it's faster than accessing the Multiple Exposure menu entry in the Shooting menu.

- **HDR.** Press the button and rotate the command dials to choose the HDR mode and exposure differential, as described in Chapter 4.

f9 Customize Command Dials

This menu entry, the first in the next page of the Controls submenu (see Figure 12.15), can change the behavior of the command dials. Use the available tweaks to change the behavior of the dials to better suit your preferences, or if you're coming to the Nikon world from another vendor's product that uses a different operational scheme. Keep in mind that redefining basic controls in this way can prove confusing if someone other than yourself uses your camera, or if you find yourself working with other Nikon cameras that have retained the normal command dial behavior. The reason that the dials are set for their default directions is to match the direction of rotation of the aperture ring/sub-command dial (when changing the aperture). Turning any of the three to the left decreases exposure, while rotating to the right increases exposure. Your options include:

- **Reverse rotation.** Rotating the main command dial (both the regular camera dial and the one on the vertical grip) counterclockwise causes shutter speeds to become shorter in Manual and Shutter-priority modes; rotating the sub-command dial counterclockwise selects larger f/stops. If you want to reverse the directional orientation of the dials (so you'll need to rotate the main command dial clockwise to specify shorter shutter speeds, etc.), set this option to Yes. Set to No to return to the original D810 scheme of things.
- **Change main/sub.** Select On to exchange the functions of the main and sub-command dials. When activated, the main dial will set the aperture in Manual and Aperture-priority modes, and the sub-command dial will adjust the shutter speed in Manual and Shutter-priority modes. All other normal functions are swapped, as well. Select Off to return to the Nikon D810's default arrangement.

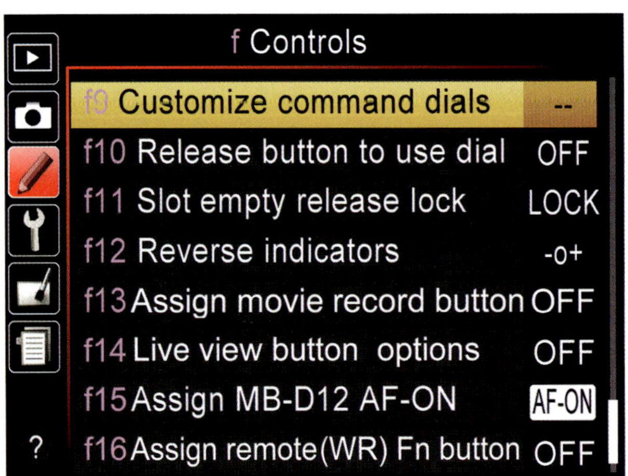

Figure 12.15
The second page of the Controls submenu.

- **Aperture setting.** Ordinarily, autofocus lenses having an aperture ring are locked at their smallest aperture when mounted on the Nikon D810 (and other Nikon models) and f/stops are set using the sub-command dial (unless you've used the Change Main/Sub option above). The default setting of sub-command dial retains this behavior. If you'd rather unlock the aperture ring on the lens and use that instead, choose Aperture Ring. Type G lenses, which lack an aperture ring, will still be adjusted using the sub-command dial, regardless of how this setting is made. Non-CPU lenses, which lack an electronic connection to the camera, are always set using the aperture ring.
- **Menus and playback.** You can change the orientation of the command dials when navigating menus and playback options, too. By default, the main command dial is used to select an image during full-frame playback; move the cursor left or right during thumbnail viewing, and move the menu highlighting up or down. The sub-command dial is used to display additional photo information in full-frame playback, to move the cursor up and down, and to move back and forth between menus and submenus. (Note that you can also use the multi selector directional buttons for these functions.) When set to On, the functions assigned to the dials are reversed.
- **Sub-dial frame advance.** If you've turned the Menus and Playback option to On, you can set the sub-command dial so that while reviewing images in full frame mode, the D810 skips ahead either 10 or 50 frames, or allows you to select a folder. This feature is new to the D810.

f10 Release Button to Use Dial

Normally, any button used in conjunction with a command dial must be held down while the command dial or sub-command dial is rotated. Choose Yes for this option if you want to be able to press the button and release it, and then rotate the command dial. You can continue to make adjustments until the button is pressed again, the shutter release button is pressed halfway, or the standby timer elapses. This option can be applied to the Mode, Exposure Compensation, Flash, BKT, ISO, Qual, WB, Metering Mode, AF mode, Fn, Pv, AE-L/AF-L, or movie record buttons. Chose No to return to the D810's default behavior, which requires that the button be held down while the adjustment is made.

f11 Slot Empty Release Lock

This option gives you the ability to snap off "pictures" without a memory card installed—or to lock the camera shutter release if that is the case. It is sometimes called play mode, because you can experiment with your camera's features or even hand your D810 to a friend to let them fool around, without any danger of pictures actually being taken.

Back in our film days, we'd sometimes finish a roll, rewind the film back into its cassette surreptitiously, and then hand the camera to a child to take a few pictures—without actually wasting any film. It's hard to waste digital film, but "shoot without card" mode is still appreciated by some, especially camera vendors who want to be able to demo a camera at a store or trade show, but don't want to have to equip each and every demonstrator model with a memory card. Choose Enable Release to activate "play" mode or Release Locked to disable it.

The pictures you actually "take" are displayed on the LCD monitor with the legend "Demo" superimposed on the screen, and they are, of course, not saved. Note that if you are using the optional Camera Control Pro 2 software to record photos from a USB-tethered D810 directly to a computer, no memory card is required to unlock the shutter even if Release Locked has been selected.

f12 Reverse Indicators

You can change the exposure indicators on the top control panel and information display so that the negative values are shown at the left (-0+) and positive values to the right, or the reverse (+0-). You might want to reverse indicators to match a "foreign" camera system you're coming to the Nikon world from, or, if you use the aperture ring on lenses that have them, to match what happens when the ring is rotated. (Older Nikon lenses have the smallest aperture on the ring to the left, and the largest to the right, so rotating the aperture ring to the right increases exposure; to the left decreases exposure.)

f13 Assign Movie Record Button

Define the action performed when you press the Movie Record button when the Lv selector switch is *not* set to the Movie position. When shooting stills, the button is, in effect, wasted, so you can use this entry to assign a useful behavior to it. Your choices are: White Balance, ISO Sensitivity, Choose Image Area, Shutter Spd & Aperture Lock, or None.

f14 Live View Button Options

If you find yourself accidentally pressing the Lv button, this entry lets you disable it. You'd use this only if you rarely shoot movies or use live view, as you must re-enable the button's function here to activate either feature. Choose Enable (Standby Timer Active), and the Lv button activates live view while the standby (meters) timer is active. If inactive, just tap the shutter release and press the Lv button to enter live view.

f15 Assign MB-D12 AF-ON Button

You can use the AF-ON button included in the MB-D12 grip for its intended purpose when firing the camera in vertical orientation, or you can redefine the button to a related function, depending on your working preferences. While the options for this button are similar to those for the main AF-ON button, this setting changes *only* the behavior of the AF-ON button on the vertical grip; the AF-ON button on the D810 camera body next to the viewfinder may be set up to do something different (which can be *very* confusing).

Your choices let you define the AF-ON button for three different functions: normal AF-ON behavior; AE-L/AF-L exposure lock/focus lock functions; and whatever action you've defined for the Fn button. Your choices are as follows:

- **AF-ON.** This default setting defines the AF-ON button as an AF-ON button, natch. Autofocus is initiated when the button is pressed.
- **FV lock.** The AF-ON button will lock the flash value for the D810's built-in flash and compatible dedicated flash units like the SB-910. Press again to cancel FV lock.
- **AE/AF lock.** With this setting, both focus and exposure are locked when the AF-ON button is held down.
- **AE lock only.** Exposure is locked while this button is held down.
- **AE lock (Reset on release).** Exposure locks when the button is held down, and remains locked even when the button is released. You can cancel the AE lock by pressing the button a second time, by taking a picture, or allowing the exposure meters to turn off at the end of their normal meter-off delay.
- **AE lock (Hold).** This exposure locks when the AF-ON button is pressed, and remains locked at that exposure until the button is pressed again, or the meters turn off.
- **Flash Value Lock.** This setting locks current flash value.
- **Same as Fn button.** The Fn button is a little hard to reach when using the vertical grip's controls, this setting sets the AF-ON button to perform the same setting that you've specified for Custom Setting f4.

f16 Assign Remote (WR) Fn Button

Your Nikon WR remote control has an Fn button, and you can use this setting to define the action taken when that remote button is pressed. Available behaviors include:

- **Preview.** Depth-of-field preview. Perhaps you'd like to use the DOF preview button for something else, and substitute the Fn button for DOF preview.
- **FV lock.** Press the Fn button to lock the value of the built-in or external flash, and press again to unlock it. This is the default value for the button.
- **AE/AF lock.** Lock both focus and exposure while the Fn button is pressed.
- **AE lock only.** Lock only the exposure while the Fn button is pressed.
- **AE lock (Reset on Release).** Lock exposure when Fn button is pressed; unlock when the button is pressed a second time, or the shutter button is pressed down all the way, or the exposure meters time out and turn off.
- **AF lock only.** Focus is locked in while the Fn button is held down.
- **AF-ON.** The AE-L/AF-L button is used to initiate autofocus.

- **Flash off.** Any external flash attached and powered up will not fire while the Fn button is held down. Handy if you want to temporarily disable the flash, say, to take a picture or two by available light, and then return to normal flash operation. If the flash is off, front-curtain sync will be selected.
- **+NEF (RAW).** If your D810 is currently set to shoot JPEG only, use this setting so that when you press the Fn button, the next shot will be recorded as a RAW+JPEG set. I use this option when shooting sports or other fast-moving events, then decide to shoot an image, say, along the sidelines, that could benefit from RAW manipulation later.
- **Live view.** Start and end live view.
- **None.** Deactivates the remote Fn button.

f17 Lens Focus Function Buttons

This option is not shown in Figure 12.15. Some Nikon lenses have a focus function button on the barrel. When the lens's focus function button selector switch is set to the AF-L position, you can activate one of the following functions using the focus function button.

- **AF lock only.** Focus is locked in while the button is held down.
- **AE/AF lock.** Lock both focus and exposure while Fn button is pressed.
- **AE lock only.** Lock only the exposure while the button is pressed.
- **Preset focus point.** Choose the preset focus point, as described earlier.
- **AF-area mode.** Press the button and use the right directional button to select an AF-area mode other than 3D-tracking. Release the button and the camera will return to the previously set AF-area mode.
- **Flash off.** Any external flash attached and powered up will not fire while the button is held down. Handy if you want to temporarily disable the flash, say, to take a picture or two by available light, and then return to normal flash operation. If the flash is off, front-curtain sync will be used.
- **Disable synchronized release.** When you're syncing several cameras wirelessly, hold down the button to disable activating the other cameras, and images will be captured only using this master camera.
- **Remote release only.** This is the opposite command; holding down the button will cause only the remote cameras to capture images when you press the shutter release on the master camera.

g. Movie

You can set separately for movie shooting some of the button assignments available for still shooting (Fn button, Preview button, AE-L/AF-L button), plus a new option, Shutter button. These entries include some options that aren't appropriate/useful for still photography, but which can come in handy for video capture. You'll find more about movie shooting in Chapters 14 to 16.

g1 Assign Fn (Function) Button

You can define the action that the Fn button performs when pressed in live view movie mode. For the Fn button alone you can choose from:

- **Power Aperture (Open).** When used in conjunction with the preview button defined as Power Aperture (Close), you can use the Fn and Pv buttons to close down the aperture to the f/stop that is used to capture video, allowing you to preview depth-of-field. The power aperture feature is available before you start shooting and not if photo information is being displayed, and only when the D810 is set for Aperture-priority or Manual exposure modes.
- **Index marking.** Press while capturing video to add an index marker at the current point. You can use the markers when editing and reviewing your movies.
- **View photo shooting info.** Normally, movie recording information appears on the monitor during capture. If you'd rather see shutter speed, aperture, and other settings, press this button to turn the photo shooting information display on or off.
- **None.** Deactivates the Fn button during movie shooting.

g2 Assign Preview Button

You can define the action that the Pv button performs when pressed in live view movie mode. For the Pv button alone you can choose from:

- **Power Aperture (Close).** When used in conjunction with the Fn button defined as Power Aperture (Open), you can use the Fn and Pv buttons to close down the aperture to the f/stop that is used to capture video, allowing you to preview depth-of-field. The power aperture feature is available before you start shooting and not if photo information is being displayed, and only when the D810 is set for Aperture-priority or Manual exposure modes.
- **Index marking.** Press while capturing video to add an index marker at the current point. You can use the markers when editing and reviewing your movies.
- **View photo shooting info.** Normally, movie recording information appears on the monitor during capture. If you'd rather see shutter speed, aperture, and other settings, press this button to turn the photo shooting information display on or off.
- **None.** Deactivates the Fn button during movie shooting.

g3 Assign AE-L/AF-L Button

The behavior of the AE-L/AF-L button can also be defined for movie mode. Your choices are as follows:

- **Index marking.** Press while capturing video to add an index marker at the current point. You can use the markers when editing and reviewing your movies.
- **View photo shooting info.** Normally, movie recording information appears on the monitor during capture. If you'd rather see shutter speed, aperture, and other settings, press this button to turn the photo shooting information display on or off.
- **AE/AF lock.** This is the default definition for the AE-L/AF-L button. When active, it locks both focus and exposure while the AE-L/AF-L button is pressed. Use this setting or one of the next four when you want to have a specific mode of operation normally available from the AE-L/AF-L button, but would prefer to trigger the behavior with the AE-L/AF-L button pressed instead.
- **AE lock only.** Lock only the exposure while the AE-L/AF-L button is pressed.
- **AE lock (Hold).** Exposure is locked when the AE-L/AF-L button is pressed, and remains locked until the button is pressed again, or the exposure meter-off delay expires. This is the fourth of the settings mutually exclusive with using an AE-L/AF-L button + command dial setting.
- **AF lock only.** Focus is locked in while the AE-L/AF-L button is held down.
- **None.** Deactivates the AE-L/AF-L button during movie capture.

g4 Assign Shutter Button

The behavior of the shutter release button can also be defined for live view and movie mode. Your choices are as follows:

- **Take Photos.** If you select this option, pressing the shutter release down all the way ends movie recording and captures a still photograph using the 16:9, 1920 × 1080 HD aspect ratio. This is a good option if you think you might want to take still pictures during a video session.
- **Record movies.** Although the D810 has a Movie button (located southwest of the shutter release) to activate video capture, you can also redefine the shutter release to start capture when the D810 is set to live view movie mode (the Lv switch must be rotated to the Movie position, and the Lv button pressed to initiate live view for this function to work). When activated, press the shutter release halfway to focus, and all the way down to initiate or end movie capture. With this mode set, you can also use remote controls attached to the 10-pin connector or MC-D10 wired remote linked to the D810 through the remote socket on the GP-1 GPS device to begin recording movies. I like this mode as a vibration-free way to focus and start capture when grabbing movies with the D810 mounted on a tripod. There's less vibration than when you manually press the D810's Movie button.

13

The Setup Menu, Retouch Menu, and My Menu

We're not done covering the Nikon D810's setup options yet. There are three more menus to deal with. These include the Setup menu (which deals with adjustments that are generally outside the actual shooting experience, such as formatting a memory card, adjusting the time, or checking your battery); the Retouch menu (which enables you to fine-tune the appearance of images by trimming, adding filter effects, or removing red-eye); and the My Menu/Recent Menu system, which can help you set up a customized menu that contains only the entries you want, or your most recently accessed entries.

Setup Menu Options

There is a long list of the 22 entries in the orange-coded Setup menu. The first page of entries is shown in Figure 13.1. All the Setup menu options let you make additional adjustments on how your camera *behaves* before or during your shooting session, as differentiated from the Shooting menu, which adjusts how the pictures are actually taken.

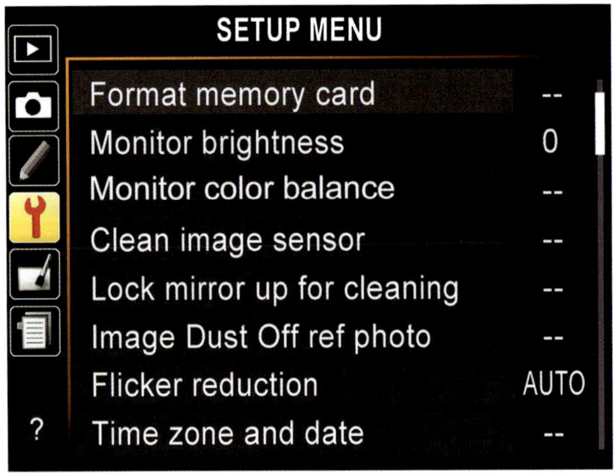

Figure 13.1
The Setup menu allows you to adjust how the D810 behaves.

Your choices include:

- Format Memory Card
- Monitor Brightness
- Monitor Color Balance
- Clean Image Sensor
- Lock Mirror Up for Cleaning
- Image Dust Off Ref Photo
- Flicker Reduction
- Time Zone and Date
- Language
- Auto Image Rotation
- Battery Info
- Image Comment
- Copyright Information
- Save/Load Settings
- Virtual Horizon
- Non-CPU Lens Data
- AF Fine-Tune
- HDMI
- Location Data
- Network
- Eye-Fi Upload
- Firmware version

Format Memory Card

I recommend using this menu entry to reformat your memory card after each shoot. Although you can move files from the memory card to your computer, creating a blank card, or delete files using the Playback menu's Delete feature, both of those options can leave behind stray files (such as those that have been marked as Hidden or Protected). Format removes those files completely and beyond retrieval (unless you use a special utility program as described in Appendix D) and establishes a spanking new fresh file system on the card. All the file allocation table (FAT) pointers (which tell the camera and your computer's operating system where all the images reside) are reset, efficiently pointing where they are supposed to on a blank card.

If you're an efficiency nut, you can reformat a memory card without a visit to the Setup menu by holding down the Mode and Trash buttons (both marked with red Format labels) for about two seconds, until "For" flashes on the control panel and a slot number appears below. Press the buttons a second time to format the card in the slot indicated. Or, select the Format Memory Card menu entry, and select Yes from the screen that appears. Press OK to begin the format process. Wait until the "For" indicator has finished flashing on the monochrome control panel.

Monitor Brightness

Choose this menu option and a grayscale strip appears on the monitor, with two options, Auto and Manual underneath. Choose Auto and the D810 will adjust brightness based on the ambient light levels using the sensor located just to the left of the speaker openings on the right side of the camera (see Figure 2.10 in the roadmap chapter to pinpoint its location). Choose Manual and the screen shown in Figure 13.2 appears. Use the multi selector up/down keys to adjust the brightness to a comfortable viewing level. Under the lighting conditions that exist when you make this adjustment, you should be able to see all 10 swatches from black to white. If the two left end swatches blend together, the brightness has been set too low. If the two whitest swatches on the right end of the strip blend together, the brightness is too high. Brighter settings use more battery power, but can allow you to view an image on the monitor outdoors in bright sunlight. When you have the brightness you want, press OK to lock it in and return to the menu.

Monitor Color Balance

Nikon users have been very vocal about what they saw as a green tinge in the monitors of some models when using live view and movie shooting, as well as when reviewing images during playback, or (less critically) when navigating menus. Nikon was quick to offer a firmware fix for this condition. The company went a step further and added a monitor color balance feature. You can adjust the monitor hue in live view or tweak it using this menu entry.

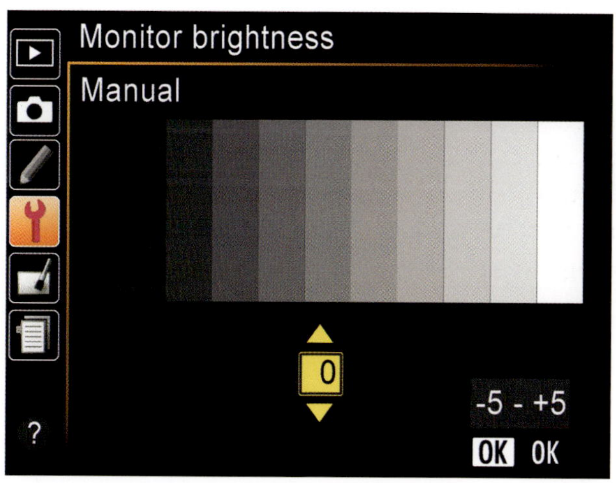

Figure 13.2
Adjust the monitor brightness so that all the grayscale strips are visible.

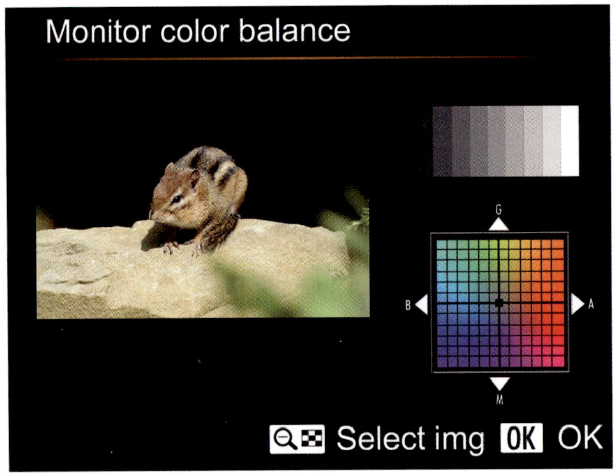

Figure 13.3
Fine-tune monitor color balance.

An adjustment screen, like the one shown in Figure 13.3, appears. The large thumbnail image at upper left will be the last photograph taken, or, if you are using Playback mode, the last photograph viewed. You can also press the Zoom Out/Index button to select an image on your memory card from a thumbnail list.

Use the multi selector directional buttons to bias the monitor hue along the blue/amber and/or green/magenta axes. The grayscale tone strip above helps you judge the neutrality of your selected balance settings. Press OK to confirm your adjustment. Note that changing the monitor color balance has *no* effect on the color balance of the photos you take.

Clean Image Sensor

This entry gives you some control over the Nikon D810's automatic sensor cleaning feature, which removes dust through a vibration cycle that shakes the sensor until dust, presumably, falls off and is captured by a sticky surface at the bottom of the sensor area. If you happen to take a picture and notice an artifact in an area that contains little detail (such as the sky or a blank wall), you can access this menu choice, place the camera with its base downward, and choose Clean Now. A Cleaning Sensor message now appears, and the dust you noticed has probably been shaken off.

You can also tell the D810 when you'd like it to perform automatic cleaning without specific instructions from you. Select from:

- **ON. Clean at startup.** This allows you to start off a particular shooting session with a clean sensor.
- **OFF. Clean at shutdown.** This removes any dust that may have accumulated since the camera has been turned on, say, from dust infiltration while changing lenses. Note that this choice does not turn off automatic cleaning; it simply moves the operation to the camera power-down sequence.

- **ON/OFF.** Clean at both startup and shutdown. Use this setting if you're paranoid about dust and don't mind the extra battery power consumed each time the camera is turned on or off. If you only turn off the D810 when you're finished shooting, the power penalty is not large, but if you're the sort who turns off the camera every time you pause in shooting, the extra power consumed by the dust removal may exceed any savings you get from leaving the camera off.
- **Cleaning Off.** No automatic dust removal will be performed. Use this to preserve battery power, or if you prefer to use automatic dust removal only when you explicitly want to apply it.

Lock Mirror Up for Cleaning

You can also clean the sensor manually. Use this menu entry to raise the mirror and open the shutter so you'll have access to the sensor for cleaning with a blower, brush, or swab, as described in Appendix D. You don't want power to fail while you're poking around inside the camera, so this option is available only when sufficient battery power (at least 60 percent) is available. Using a fully charged battery or connecting the D810 to an EH-5b/EP-5b AC adapter is an even better idea.

Image Dust Off Ref Photo

This menu choice lets you "take a picture" of any dust or other particles that may be adhering to your sensor. The D810 will then append information about the location of this dust to your photos, so that the Image Dust Off option in Capture NX 2 can be used to mask the dust in the NEF image.

To use this feature, select Image Dust Off Ref Photo, choose either Start or Clean Sensor and Then Start, and then press OK. If directed to do so, the camera will first perform a self-cleaning operation by applying ultrasonic vibration to the low-pass filter that resides on top of the sensor. Then, a screen will appear asking you to take a photo of a bright featureless white object 10 cm (about four inches) from the lens. Nikon recommends using a lens with a focal length of at least 50mm. Point the D810 at a solid white card and press the shutter release. An image with the extension .ndf will be created, and can be used by Nikon Capture NX as a reference photo if the "dust off" picture is placed in the same folder as an image to be processed for dust removal.

Flicker Reduction

This menu entry helps eliminate the banding and flickering effects that can result from unsynchronized video display when using live view or movie recording modes. All you need to do is match the AC power frequency in your area by selecting 50Hz (used in Europe and many other countries) or 60Hz (used in North America and other places). Some locations, such as Japan, use a mixture of 50Hz and 60Hz current. You can select Auto if you're not sure which is correct, and the D810 will choose a setting consistent with the location indicated by your current time setting. Or, you can try both settings to see which works best for you.

Another way to reduce flicker is to use Manual exposure and choose a shutter speed that is an approximate multiple of the local power frequency. For example, in countries using 60Hz current, 1/125th, 1/60th, and 1/30th second will produce the best results. If the local current is 50Hz, you're better off with 1/100th, 1/50th, or 1/25th second. You can adjust the D810's increments to produce appropriate speeds by visiting Custom Setting b2 and changing the EV Steps for Exposure Control to 1/3 EV (for 60Hz countries) or 1/2 EV (for 50Hz locations).

Time Zone and Date

Use this menu entry to adjust the D810's internal clock. Your options include:

- **Time zone.** A small map will pop up on the setting screen and you can choose your local time zone. I sometimes forget to change the time zone when I travel (especially when going to Europe), so my pictures are all time-stamped incorrectly. I like to use the time stamp to recall exactly when a photo was taken, so keeping this setting correct is important.
- **Date and time.** Use this setting to enter the exact year, month, day, hour, minute, and second.
- **Date format.** Choose from Y/M/D (year/month/day), M/D/Y (month/day/year), or D/M/Y (day/month/year) formats.
- **Daylight saving time.** Use this to turn daylight saving time On or Off. Because the date on which DST goes into effect each year has been changed from time to time, if you turn this feature on you may need to monitor your camera to make sure DST has been implemented correctly.

Language

Choose from 24 languages for menu display, choosing from Czech, Danish, German, English, Spanish, French, Indonesian, Italian, Dutch, Norwegian, Polish, Portuguese, Russian, Romanian, Finnish, Swedish, Turkish, Ukrainian, Arabic, Traditional Chinese, Simplified Chinese, Japanese, Korean, or Thai. This is the first entry on the second "page" of Setup menu entries (see Figure 13.4).

Auto Image Rotation

Turning this setting On tells the Nikon D810 to include camera orientation information in the image file. The orientation can be read by many software applications, including Adobe Photoshop, Nikon ViewNX, and Capture NX, as well as the Rotate Tall setting in the Playback menu. Turn this feature Off, and none of the software applications or Playback's Rotate Tall will be able to determine the correct orientation for the image. Nikon notes that only the first image's orientation is used when shooting continuous bursts; subsequent photos will be assigned the same orientation, even if you rotate the camera during the sequence (which is something I have been known to do myself when shooting sports like basketball).

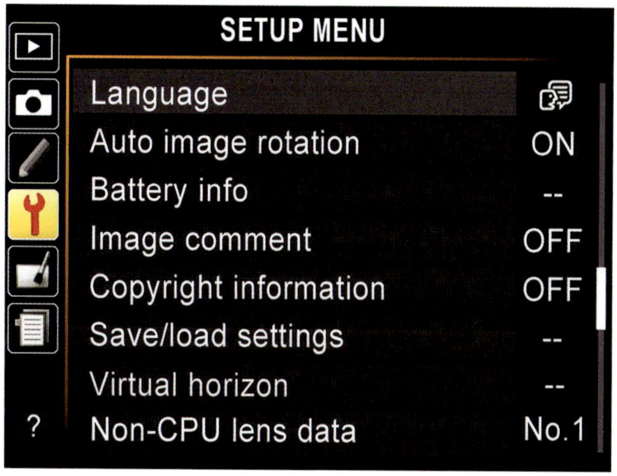

Figure 13.4
The second page of Setup menu options starts with the Language option.

Battery Info

This screen is purely informational; there are no settings to be made. When invoked, you can see the following information:

- **Charge.** The current battery level, shown as a percentage from 100 to 0 percent.
- **No. of shots.** This shows the number of actuations with the current battery since it was last recharged. This number can be larger than the number of photos taken, because other functions, such as white balance presetting, can cause the shutter to be tripped.
- **Battery Age.** Eventually, a battery will no longer accept a charge as well as it did when it was new, and must be replaced. This indicator shows when a battery is considered new (0); has begun to degrade slightly (1,2,3); or has reached the end of its charging life and is ready for replacement (4). Batteries charged at temperatures lower than 41 degrees F may display an impaired charging life temporarily, but return to their true "health" when recharged above 68 degrees F.

Note that when the MB-D12 pack is used, the Battery Info display will provide information about both the D810's internal battery and the EN-EL15 or EN-EL18 battery in the MB-D12. When AA batteries are used in the MB-D12, only the battery level is shown; number of shots and battery age will not be displayed.

Image Comment

The Image Comment is your opportunity to add a copyright notice, personal information about yourself (including contact info), or even a description of where the image was taken (e.g., Browns Super Bowl 2013), although text entry with the Nikon D810 is a bit too clumsy for doing a lot of individual annotation of your photos. (But you still might want to change the comment each time, say, you change cities during your travels.) The embedded comments can be read by many software programs, including Nikon ViewNX 2 or Capture NX 2/NX-D.

The standard text entry screen described in Chapter 2 can be used to enter your comment, with up to 36 characters available. For the copyright symbol, embed a lowercase "c" within opening and closing parentheses: (c). You can input the comment, turn attachment of the comment On or Off using the Attach Comment entry, and select Done when you're finished working with comments. If you find typing with a cursor too tedious, you can enter your comment in Nikon Capture NX 2 and upload it to the camera through a USB cable.

Copyright Information

This is an expansion of the Image Comment capability, allowing you to specify the name of the "artist" (photographer), and enter copyright information. Use the standard Nikon text entry screen described earlier. Highlight the Attach Copyright Information option and press the right multi selector button to mark/unmark it to control whether your copyright data is embedded in each photo as taken.

Save/Load Settings

You can store many camera settings to your memory card in a file named NCSETUP8, and then reload them later using this menu item. This is a good way to archive your favorite camera settings for the Playback menu, all four Shooting menu and Custom Setting menu banks, the Setup menu settings, and all My Menu items. You can restore your settings if you've messed them up, or save multiple sets of settings to multiple memory cards. You can save only one group of settings at a time to a particular card (always in the Primary slot); the default NCSETUP8 cannot be changed. Well, it *can* be changed in your computer, but if you do, the D810 will not be able to find it on the memory card. If you want to save multiple settings, simply use multiple memory cards. This might be a good use for all those 256MB SD cards you have left over from your point-and-shoot snap-shooting days.

Note that storing/restoration is an all-or-nothing proposition. When you select Save Settings, all your current settings are stored on the memory card; choose Load Settings, and the camera's current settings are replaced with the values stored on the memory card. The following settings are saved:

- **Playback.** Playback display options, Image review, After delete, Rotate tall.
- **Shooting menu.** Shooting menu bank, Extended menu banks, File naming, Primary slot selection, Secondary slot function, Image quality, Image size, Image area, JPEG compression, NEF (RAW) recording, White balance, Set Picture Control, Color space, Active D-Lighting, Vignette control, Long exp. NR, High ISO NR, ISO sensitivity settings, and Movie settings. The settings for all four banks (A, B, C, D) are stored.

- **Custom Settings menu.** All settings for all four banks (A, B, C, D) are stored.
- **Setup menu.** Clean image sensor, HDMI, Flicker reduction, Time zone and date, Language, Auto image rotation, Image comment, Copyright information, GPS, Non-CPU lens data, Eye-Fi upload.
- **My Menu/Recent Settings.** All My Menu entries, All recent settings, active tab.

Virtual Horizon

Your viewfinder has a leveling indicator displayed as a series of bars that show how far the D810 is tilted forward and back, or rotated along the lens axis. I showed you how to activate this feature using Custom Setting f4 in Chapter 12. Some people prefer to use the monitor's virtual horizon feature, visible when using live view, instead. It provides a virtual bubble level display on the monitor that acts like the horizon indicator in an airplane, ostensibly to help you keep your image level as you shoot.

When activated, a circular indicator like the one shown in Figure 13.5 appears on the monitor. When the camera is level, the reference lines will be displayed in green and a green dot will be shown in the center of the screen. It measures both pitch and roll, or side-to-side tilt (along the axis of the lens) and forward/back tilt (raising the lens up or down). Of course, you can't frame a picture through the viewfinder very easily while monitoring this display, and it's difficult to keep the camera on a level plane, so you'll find that the virtual horizon works best when the D810 is mounted on a tripod and/or when you're using live view, which has its own virtual horizon feature (discussed in Chapter 14).

I'm not crazy about the feature because, in my case, all my tripods and tripod heads already *have* bubble levels built in. So, when I'm using the D810 on a tripod, I don't need the virtual horizon feature as much. The bubble levels on my tripods and tripod heads can do that, with no problems.

Figure 13.5
The virtual horizon serves as a kind of bubble level for your camera.

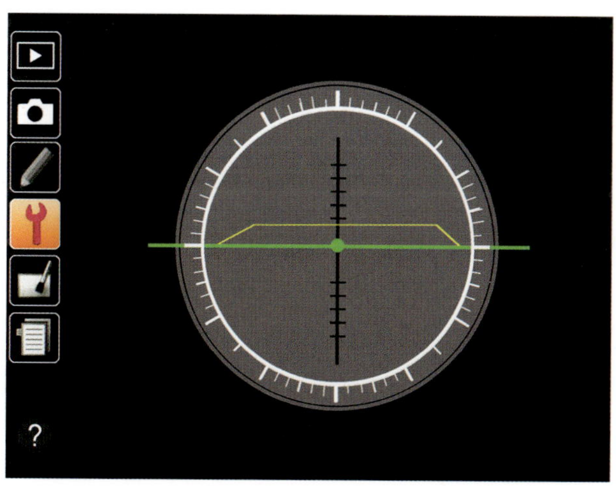

I know folks who like and use the virtual horizon; it's an extra way to use the sensor built into your camera which sends vertical/horizontal orientation information to the various rotation features. (Incidentally, if you listen carefully when you rotate the camera from horizontal to vertical, you can hear the pendulum-like sensor clanking around inside the D810.)

Non-CPU Lens Data

You can specify lens focal length data and maximum aperture for up to nine older manual focus, non-CPU chipped lenses, using this entry. When both values are entered, the D810 can use older lenses (including AI manual focus lenses) that are not equipped with a CPU chip for color matrix metering to calculate exposure in Aperture-priority and Manual exposure modes. The data also enables automatic power zoom when using the Nikon SB-910, SB-700, and some other Nikon electronic flash units; as well as improved flash exposures and balanced iTTL fill-flash. In addition, the current aperture can be listed in the monochrome control panel and camera viewfinder, as well as embedded in the photo playback display.

The Nikon D810 allows defining up to nine different lenses, and I can choose any of them with a quick trip to this menu entry (or to the equivalent menu item in My Menu, described later in this chapter), or using a control (such as the Fn, Pv, or AE-L/AF-L button plus command dial) as described for Custom Settings menu option f4, f5, or f6 in Chapter 12.

To enter this information, follow these steps using the screen shown in Figure 13.6:

1. Choose Non-CPU lens data from the Setup menu.
2. Highlight Lens Number and press the multi selector left/right buttons to choose a number between 1 and 9.

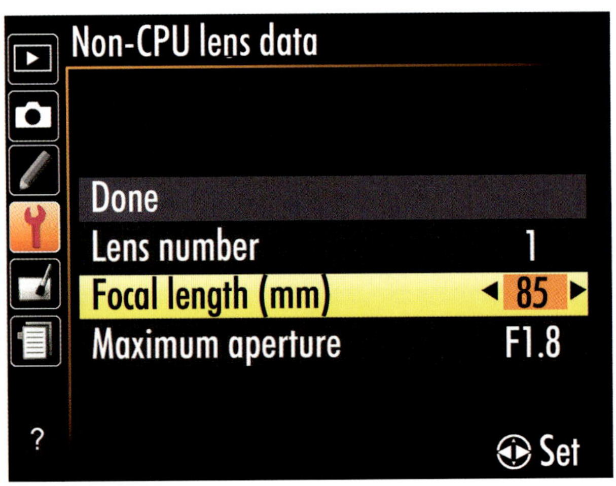

Figure 13.6
You can enter focal length and maximum aperture of up to nine manual focus lenses.

3. Scroll down to Focal Length (mm) and use the multi selector left/right buttons to choose a focal length between 6mm and 4000mm.
4. Scroll down to Maximum Aperture and use the multi selector left/right buttons to choose a maximum f/stop between f/1.2 and f/22.
5. Choose Done. You can now select the lens number using any of several controls you can define for the Fn button, depth-of-field preview button, AE-L/AF-L, or BKT buttons as described in Chapter 12 under Custom Setting f4, Custom Setting f5, or Custom Setting f6.

AF Fine Tune

This is the first entry in the last page of the Setup Menu (see Figure 13.7.) Troubled by lenses that don't focus exactly where they should, producing back focus or front focus problems? No need to send your lens and/or camera into Nikon for servicing. The Nikon D810 allows you to fine-tune focus for up to 12 different lenses. You'll probably never need to use this feature, but if you do, it's priceless. To fine-tune your lenses, first perform some tests to see just how much fine-tuning is required. The only problem I've run into is that with some lenses, particularly short focal length lenses, using large negative values (0 to -20) to move the focal point closer to the camera sometimes results in being unable to focus to infinity. If you run into that, you may be better off sending the lens to Nikon so they can recalibrate the focus for you.

This menu option has four choices, shown in Figure 13.8:

- **AF fine tune (On/Off).** Enable/disable application of your AF fine-tuning changes.
- **Saved value.** View or enter an adjustment for the lens currently mounted on your camera.

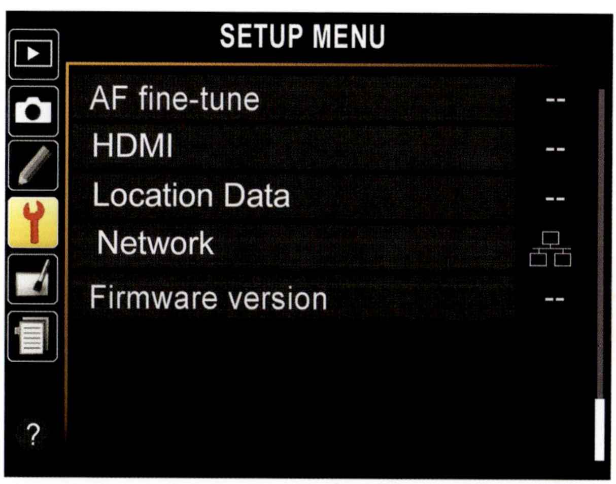

Figure 13.7
The last page of the Setup menu.

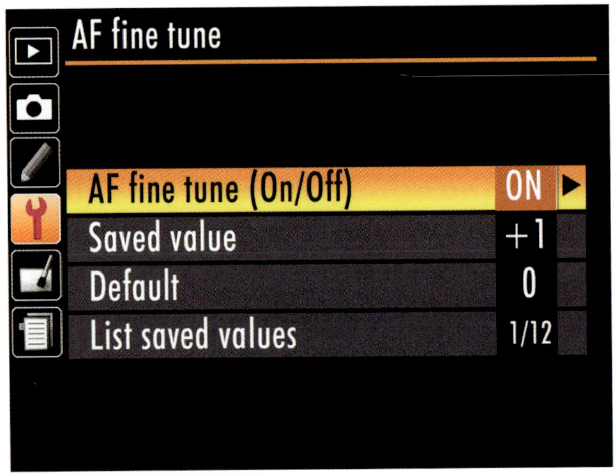

Figure 13.8
The autofocus of lenses can be adjusted here.

- **Default.** Set the default value to be applied to lenses that haven't been recalibrated. You'd use this if your D810 has a certain amount of front or back focus problems with all lenses. Use with caution, as it affects every CPU lens that you use.
- **List saved values.** View and delete tuning values you've saved for up to 12 different lenses.

Because the adjustments made with the AF Fine Tune setting are potentially so dangerous to your focusing health, I'm not even going to provide an overview in this chapter. (Knowing just enough to hurt yourself can be a real possibility.) Instead, you'll find a complete discussion of using this feature at the end of Chapter 7, which deals with lens issues.

HDMI

The Nikon D810 has a High-Definition Multimedia Interface (HDMI) video connection, so you can play back your camera's images on HDTV or HD monitors using a type A cable, which Nikon does not provide to you, but which is readily available from third parties. Before you link up you'll want to choose from the following options:

- **Output Resolution.** Select Auto and the camera will sense the correct output resolution to use. Auto will be applied (even if you select another resolution) when the HDMI port is used to display the camera's image during movie live view, movie capture, and movie playback. If you want to use a different resolution under other circumstances (say, when you're viewing still images), you can choose 480p (640 × 480 progressive scan); 576p (720 × 576 progressive scan); 720p (1280 × 720 progressive scan); 1080p (1920 × 1080 progressive scan); or 1080i (1920 × 1080 interlaced scan).

- **Advanced.** This cryptic entry leads you to a screen where you can select three more parameters:
  - **Output range.** Choose Auto (the default, and the best choice under most circumstances); Limited Range; or Full Range. In most cases, the camera will be able to determine the output range of your HDMI device. If not, Limited Range uses settings of 16 to 235, clipping off the darkest (0-16) and brightest (235-255) portions of the image. Use Limited Range if you're plagued with reduced detail in the shadows of your image. Full Range may be your choice if shadows are washed out or excessively bright. It accepts video signals with the full range from 0 to 255.
  - **Output Display Size.** Sometimes the image output needs to be adjusted to allow filling the frame on your HDMI device. You can select 95 percent to 100 percent coverage.
  - **Live View On-Screen Display.** If you're shooting the camera tethered, you may want to view a live view image exclusively on the connected HDMI monitor. Choose Off and the display of shooting information on your monitor will be suppressed.
  - **Dual Monitor.** Choose On to display on both the camera monitor *and* HDMI display. Off disables the camera monitor to save battery power. If you've set Live View On-Screen Display to Off, Dual Monitor is enabled automatically.

Location Data

This menu entry has options for using the Nikon GP-1a Global Positioning System (GPS) device. It has three options, none of which turn GPS features on or off, despite the misleading "Enable" and "Disable" nomenclature (what you're enabling and disabling is the automatic exposure meter turn-off):

- **Standby Timer.** Setting to Enable reduces battery drain by enabling turning off exposure meters while using the GP-1 after the time specified in Custom Setting c2 (Standby Timer, discussed in Chapter 12) has elapsed. When the meters turn off, the GP-1a becomes inactive and must reacquire at least three satellite signals before it can begin recording GPS data once more. Setting to Disable causes exposure meters to remain on while using the GP-1a, so that GPS data can be recorded at any time, despite increased battery drain.
- **Position.** This is an information display, rather than a selectable option. It appears when the GP-1 is connected and receiving satellite positioning data. It shows the latitude, longitude, altitude, and Coordinated Universal Time (UTC) values.
- **Set Clock From Satellite.** Choose Yes to allow the camera to update its internal clock from information provided by the GPS device when attached. No disables this updating feature. You might want to avoid updating the clock if you're traveling and want all the basic date/time information embedded in your image files to reflect the settings back home, rather than the date and time where your pictures are taken. Note that if the GPS device is active when shooting, the local date and time will be embedded in the GPS portion of the EXIF data.

Network

I'll bet you thought when you became a photographer you'd never be forced to become a wireless or local area networking guru, right? It's a topic worth a book of its own, and only a quick overview can be provided in a book like this size. I'm not going to discuss routers and firewalls or the installation and use of the Nikon Wireless Transmitter Utility here. Fortunately, Nikon provides a Networking Guide, 88 dense pages of information and step-by-step instructions that will bring you up to speed. In it, you'll find detailed directions for using the options found in this menu entry. Your choices include:

- **Choose Hardware.** Here you can select how you'd like to connect your camera to your network. If you're working in a studio, you might want to select Wired Lan, and plug in a standard Cat5 cable into the Ethernet port on the side of the camera. You can also choose Nikon WT-5 or WT-4 wireless connections if you have one of those devices attached to your camera. When linked through one of these, you can perform cool functions like:
  - **Tethered shooting.** Use FTP upload and image transfer to forward existing images or new captures to your computer or FTP file server.
  - **Control your camera remotely.** Your optional Camera Control Pro 2 software can adjust your camera settings and take pictures remotely, which means that you can sit at your computer and your camera can be in another location entirely as long as it's on the LAN.
  - **View and shoot using a browser.** A computer browser or your iPhone app can be used to review images and control your camera remotely.
  - **Synchronized release.** You can take pictures remotely using multiple cameras that are synchronized with a master camera.
- **Network Connection.** Use this to enable or disable your network connection. I didn't remember to disable my connection when unlinking from my LAN, which led to the mirror lockup bug I described earlier.
- **Network Settings.** Here you can create or choose a Network Profile from up to nine different profiles, or copy an existing profile from a memory card. A helpful Connection Wizard will allow you to choose from FTP/Image Transfer, Camera Control, or HTTP server. You can also name your profile, and choose an IP address (either obtained automatically or manually entered. These settings are where networking familiarity comes in handy.) If you selected Image Transfer or Camera Control earlier, you'll need to link your camera to the computer temporarily to pair the two using the Wireless Transmitter Utility. You can use the Wireless Transmitter Utility to create network profiles on your computer, rather than going through the tedious process entirely using camera controls.
- **Options.** This section allows you to edit some options, such as Auto Send; Delete After Send; whether to transfer both NEF and JPEG versions of an image, or just the JPEG copy; whether to overwrite files having the same name; protection status; which folder to use when sending; remove all markings; HTTP User Settings; Mac Address; and Power Saving Options. Whew.
- **Choose a profile.** Here you can choose which profile to activate.

Eye-Fi Upload

This option is displayed in the menu only when a compatible Eye-Fi memory card is being used in the D810. The Eye-Fi card looks like an ordinary SDHC memory card, but has built-in Wi-Fi capabilities, so it can be used to transmit your photos as they are taken directly to a computer over a Wi-Fi network. When an Eye-Fi card is inserted, and you've enabled the card by choosing Enable in this menu entry, one of four informational icons will appear in its shooting information screen.

Firmware Version

You can see the current firmware release in use in the menu listing. You can learn how to update firmware in Appendix D.

Retouch Menu

The Retouch menu contains the post-processing options you can apply to your images after you've taken a photo. When reviewing an image, press OK to jump directly to this menu and begin processing that image.

- D-Lighting
- Red-Eye Correction
- Trim
- Monochrome
- Filter Effects
- Color Balance
- Image Overlay
- NEF (RAW) Processing
- Resize
- Quick Retouch
- Straighten
- Distortion Control
- Fisheye
- Color Outline
- Color Sketch
- Perspective Control
- Miniature Effect
- Selective Color
- Edit Movie
- Side-by-Side Comparison

The Retouch menu (see Figure 13.9) is most useful when you want to create a modified copy of an image on the spot, for immediate printing or e-mailing without first importing into your computer for more extensive editing. You can also use it to create a JPEG version of an image in the camera when you are shooting RAW-only photos. You can retouch images that have already been processed by the Retouch menu, except for copies created with the Trim, Resize, or Save Selected Frame (in movie mode) options. Nor can you apply D-Lighting, red-eye correction, filter effects, and color balance to monochrome image copies. You may notice some quality loss when applying more than one retouch option. To create a retouched copy of an image:

1. **Choose image retouching option.** From the Retouch menu, select the option you want and press the multi selector right button. The Nikon D810's standard image selection screen appears. Scroll among the images as usual with the left/right multi selector buttons, press the Zoom In button to examine a highlighted image more closely, and press OK to choose that image.

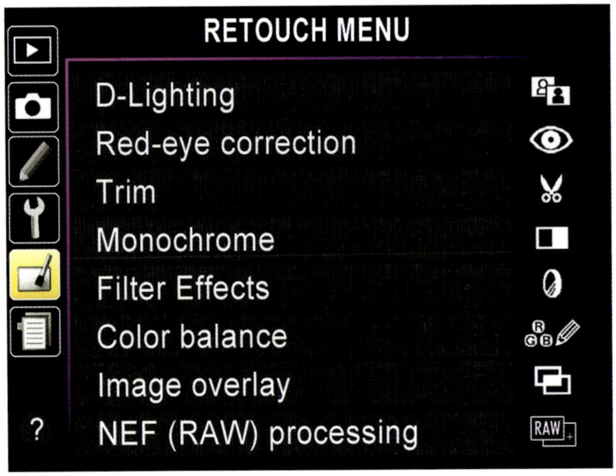

Figure 13.9
The Retouch menu allows simple in-camera editing.

2. **Manipulate image.** Work with the options available from that particular Retouch menu feature and press OK to create the modified copy, or Playback to cancel your changes.
3. **View copy.** A retouched JPEG image will be the same size and quality as the original, except for copies created from NEF and TIFF images (which are always saved as JPEG Fine images). During review, retouched copies are overlaid with a paint brush icon in their upper-left corner.

D-Lighting

This option brightens the shadows of pictures that have already been taken. Once you've selected your photo for modification, you'll be shown side-by-side images with the unaltered version on the left, and your adjusted version on the right. Press the multi selector's up/down buttons to choose from High, Normal, or Low corrections. (See Figure 13.10.) Press the Zoom In button to magnify the image. When you're happy with the corrected image on the right, compared to the original on the left, press OK to save the copy to your memory card. Typical results are shown in Figure 13.11.

Red-Eye Correction

This Retouch menu tool can be used to remove the residual red-eye look that remains after applying the Nikon D810's other remedies, such as the red-eye reduction lamp. (You can use the red-eye tools found in most image editors, as well.)

Your Nikon D810 has a fairly effective red-eye reduction flash mode. Unfortunately, your camera is unable, on its own, to totally *eliminate* the red-eye effects that occur when an electronic flash (or, rarely, illumination from other sources) bounces off the retinas of the eye and into the camera lens. Animals seem to suffer from yellow or green glowing pupils, instead; the effect is equally undesirable. The effect is worst under low-light conditions (exactly when you might be using a flash) as the

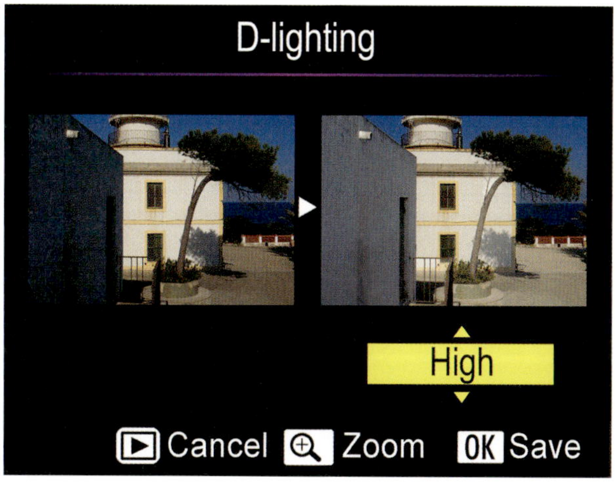

Figure 13.10 An image with dark shadows can be improved with post-shot D-Lighting.

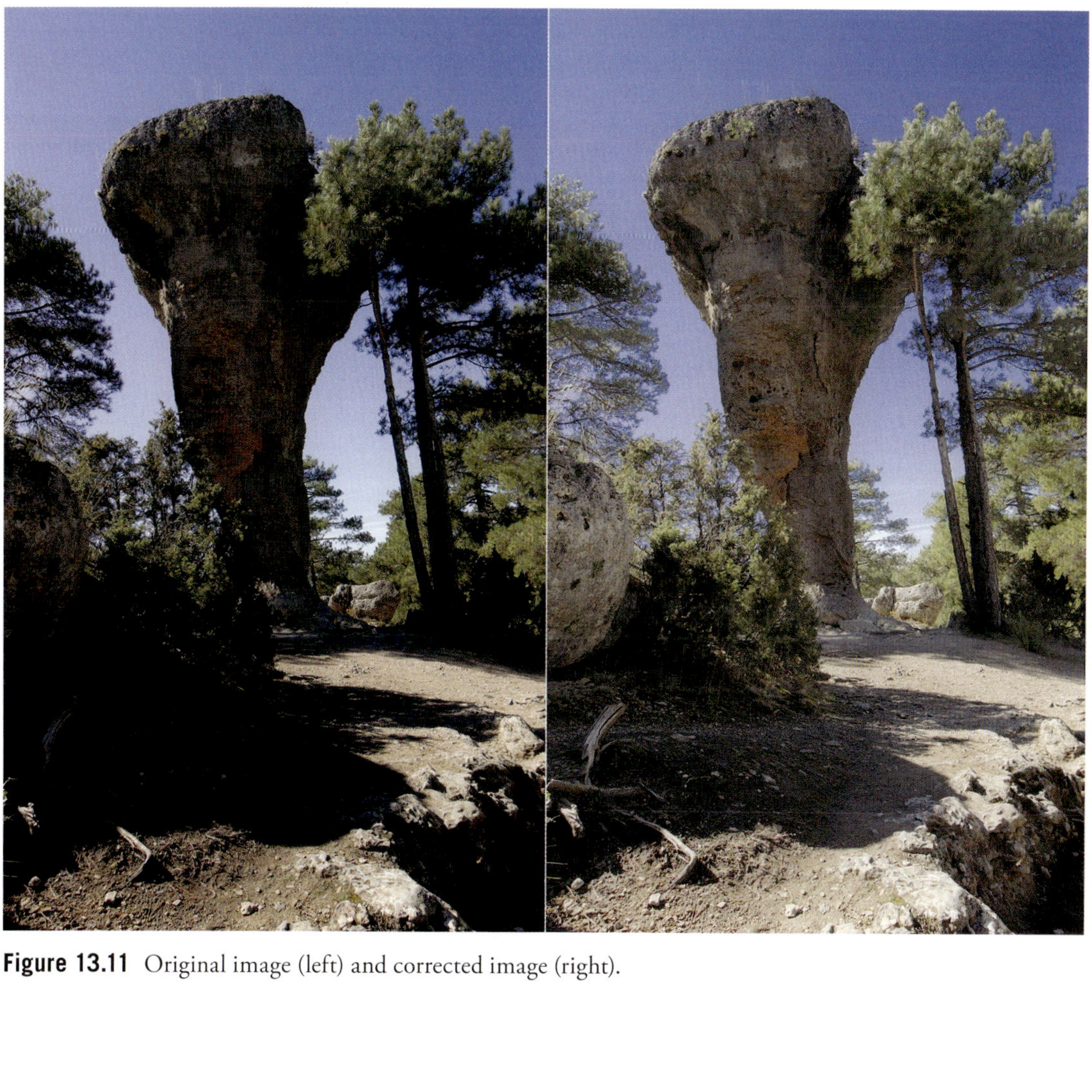

Figure 13.11 Original image (left) and corrected image (right).

pupils expand to allow more light to reach the retinas. The best you can hope for is to *reduce* or minimize the red-eye effect.

The best way to truly eliminate red-eye is to raise the flash up off the camera so its illumination approaches the eye from an angle that won't reflect directly back to the retina and into the lens. The extra height of the built-in flash may not be sufficient, however. That alone is a good reason for using an external flash. If you're working with your D810's built-in flash, your only recourse may be to switch on the red-eye reduction flash mode. That causes a lamp on the front of the camera to illuminate with a half-press of the shutter release button, which may result in your subjects' pupils contracting, decreasing the amount of the red-eye effect. (You may have to ask your subject to look at the lamp to gain maximum effect.)

If your image still displays red-eye effects, you can use the Retouch menu to make a copy with red-eye reduced further. First, select a picture that was taken with flash (non-flash pictures won't be available for selection). After you've selected the picture to process, press OK. The image will be displayed on the monitor. You can magnify the image with the Zoom In button, scroll around the zoomed image with the multi selector buttons, and zoom out with the Zoom Out button. While zoomed, you can cancel the zoom by pressing the OK button.

When you are finished examining the image, press OK again. The D810 will look for red-eye, and, if detected, create a copy that has been processed to reduce the effect. If no red-eye is found, a copy is not created. Figure 13.12 shows an original image (left) and its processed copy (right).

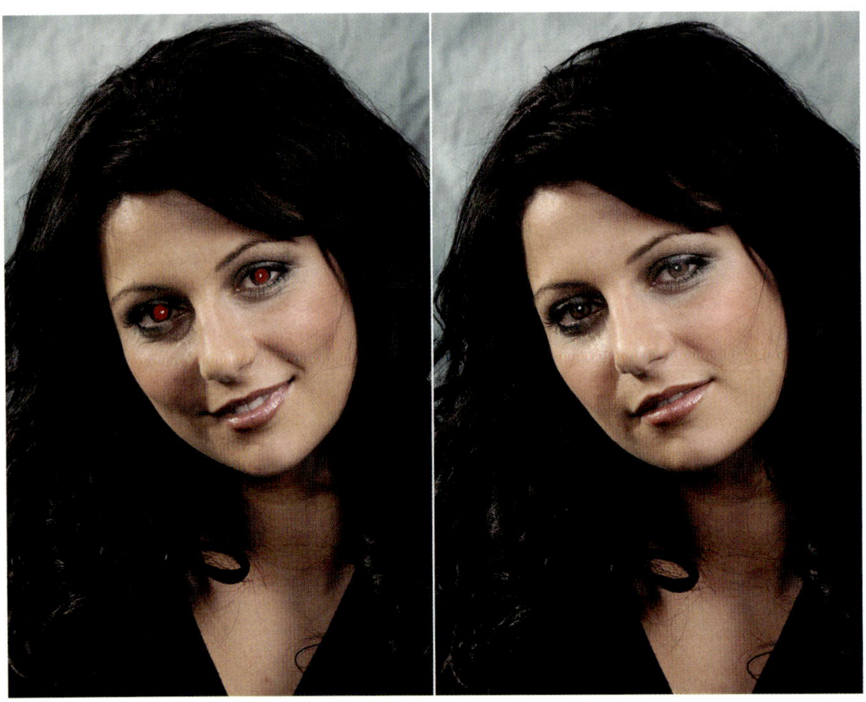

Figure 13.12
Wider pupils (left) can lead to red-eye effects; the Nikon D810's red-eye reduction lamp can cause pupils to contract (right).

Trim

This option creates copies in specific sizes based on the final size you select, chosen from among 3:2, 4:3, and 5:4 aspect ratios (proportions). You can use this feature to create smaller versions of a picture for e-mailing without the need to first transfer the image to your own computer. If you're traveling, create your smaller copy here, insert the memory card in a card reader at an Internet café, your library's public computers, or some other computer, and e-mail the reduced-size version. Just follow these steps:

1. **Select your photo.** Choose Trim from the Retouch menu. You'll be shown the standard Nikon D810 image selection screen. Scroll among the photos using the multi selector left/right buttons, and press OK when the image you want to trim is highlighted. While selecting, you can temporarily enlarge the highlighted image by pressing the Zoom In button.
2. **Choose your aspect ratio.** Rotate the main command dial to change from 3:2, 4:3, 5:4, 1:1, and 16:9 aspect ratios. These proportions happen to correspond to the proportions of common print sizes, including the two most popular sizes: 4 × 6 inches (3:2) and 8 × 10 inches (5:4).
3. **Crop in on your photo.** Press the Zoom In button to crop in on your picture. The pixel dimensions of the cropped image at the selected proportions will be displayed in the upper-left corner (see Figure 13.13) as you zoom. The sizes available are shown in Table 13.1. The current framed size is outlined in yellow within an inset image in the lower-right corner.
4. **Move cropped area within the image.** Use the multi selector left/right and up/down buttons to relocate the yellow cropping border within the frame.
5. **Save the cropped image.** Press OK to save a copy of the image using the current crop and size, or press the Playback button to exit without creating a copy. Copies created from JPEG Fine, Normal, or Standard have the same Image Quality setting as the original; copies made from RAW files or any RAW+JPEG setting will use JPEG Fine compression.

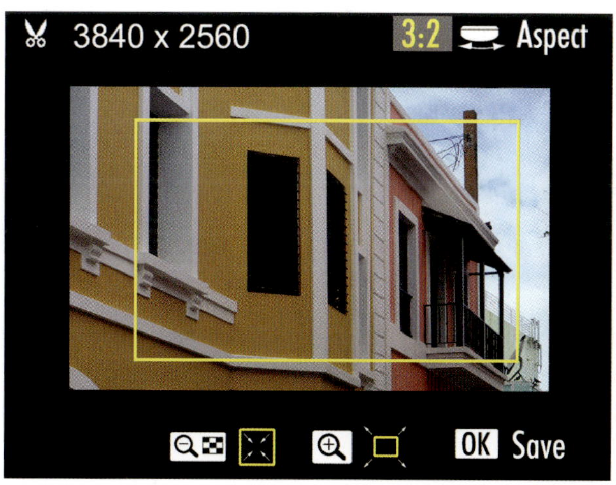

Figure 13.13 The Trim feature of the Retouch menu allows in-camera cropping.

Table 13.1 Trim Sizes

Aspect Ratio	Sizes Available in FX mode
3:2	7040 × 4688, 6400 × 4264, 5760 × 3840, 5120 × 3416, 4480 × 2984, 3840 × 2560, 3200 × 2128, 2560 × 1704, 1920 × 1280, 1280 × 856, 960 × 640, 640 × 424
4:3	6544 × 4912, 6400 × 4800, 5760 × 4320, 5120 × 3840, 4480 × 3360, 3840 × 2880, 3200 × 2400, 2560 × 1920, 1920 × 1440, 1280 × 960, 960 × 720, 640 × 480
5:4	6144 × 4912, 6000 × 4800, 5408 × 4320, 4800 × 3840, 4208 × 3360, 3600 × 2880, 3008 × 2400, 2400 × 1920, 1808 × 1440, 1200 × 960, 986 × 720, 608 × 480
1:1	4912 × 4912, 4800 × 4800, 4320 × 4320, 3840 × 3840, 3360 × 3360, 2880 × 2880, 2400 × 2400, 1920 × 1920, 1440 × 1440, 960 × 960, 720 × 720, 480 × 480
16:9	7360 × 4144, 7040 × 3960, 6400 × 3600, 5760 × 3240, 5120 × 2880, 4480 × 2520, 3840 × 2160, 3200 × 1800, 2560 × 1440, 1920 × 1080, 1280 × 720, 960 × 536, 640 × 480

Monochrome

This Retouch choice allows you to produce a copy of the selected photo as a black-and-white image, sepia-toned image, or cyanotype (blue-and-white). You can fine-tune the color saturation of the previewed Sepia or Cyanotype version by pressing the multi selector up button to increase color richness, and the down button to decrease saturation. When satisfied, press OK to create the monochrome duplicate. Cancel by pressing the Playback button.

Filter Effects

Add a warmer tone to your images using this Retouch option. You have two choices: Skylight, which makes the picture slightly less blue, and Warm filter, which adds a rich warm cast to the duplicate. Preview either effect in the color monitor before pressing OK to create the modified copy.

Color Balance

This Retouch effect allows you to create a copy with modified color balance. When you press the OK button while viewing a selected image, a screen like the one shown in Figure 13.14 appears with the photo shown in thumbnail size at the upper-left corner, and red/green/blue histograms at the right. You can bias the image along the magenta/green axis or blue/yellow (amber) axis based on

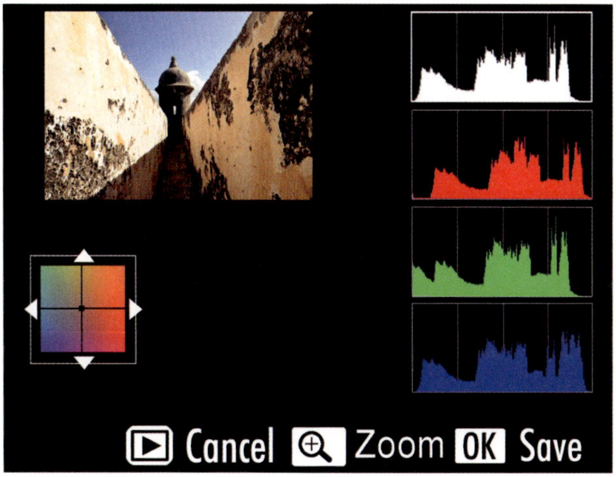

Figure 13.14 Fine-tune color balance in the camera using this Retouch menu screen.

your perception of the thumbnail or, as you gain experience, from your estimation of the distribution of tones as shown by the histograms.

Press the multi selector up button to increase the amount of green, the down button to increase the amount of magenta, the right button to increase the bias toward yellow/amber, and the left button to increase the amount of blue. As you make these modifications, the changes will be reflected in the histograms. Press OK to save the image, and MENU to back out of the feature.

Image Overlay

This feature allows you to combine two RAW photos (only NEF files can be used) in a composite image that Nikon claims is better than a "double exposure" created in an image-editing application, because the overlays are made using RAW data. To produce this composite image, follow these steps:

1. Choose Image Overlay. The screen shown in Figure 13.15 will be displayed, with the Image 1 box highlighted.
2. Press OK and the Nikon D810's image selection screen appears. Choose the first image for the overlay and press OK.
3. Press the multi selector right button to highlight the Image 2 box, and press OK to produce the image selection screen. Choose the second image for the overlay.
4. By highlighting either the Image 1 or Image 2 boxes and pressing the multi selector up/down buttons, you can adjust the "gain," or how much of the final image will be "exposed" from the selected picture. You can choose from X0.5 (half-exposure) to X2.0 (twice the exposure) for each image. The default value is 1.0 for each, so that each image will contribute equally to the final exposure.

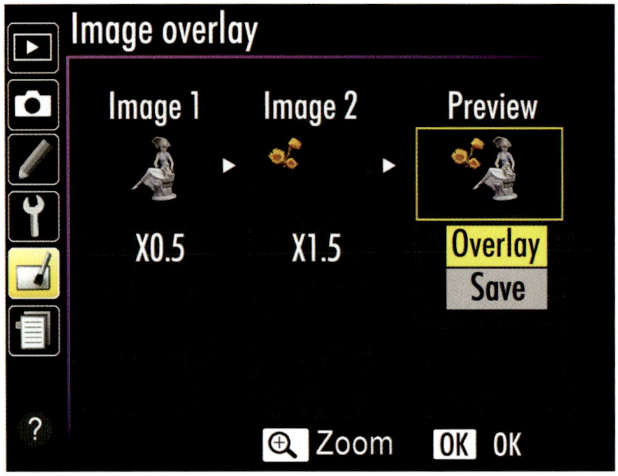

Figure 13.15
Overlay two RAW images to produce a "double exposure."

5. Use the multi selector right button to highlight the Preview box and view the combined picture. Press the Zoom In button to enlarge the view.
6. When you're ready to store your composite copy, press the multi selector down button when the Preview box is highlighted to select Save, and press OK. The combined image is stored on the memory card.

NEF (RAW) Processing

Use this tool to create a JPEG version of any image saved in either straight RAW (with no JPEG version) or RAW+Basic (with a Basic JPEG version). You can select from among several parameters to "process" your new JPEG copy right in the camera.

1. Choose a RAW image. Select NEF (RAW) processing from the Retouch menu. You'll be shown the standard Nikon D810 image selection screen. Use the left/right buttons to navigate among the RAW images displayed. Press OK to select the highlighted image.
2. In the NEF (RAW) processing screen, shown in Figure 13.16, you can use the multi selector up/down keys to select from five different attributes of the RAW image information to apply to your JPEG copy. Choose Image Quality (Fine, Normal, or Basic), Image Size (Large, Medium, or Small), White Balance, Exposure Compensation, Set Picture Control, and High ISO Noise Reduction.
3. Press the Zoom In button to magnify the image temporarily while the button is held down.
4. Press the Playback button if you change your mind, to exit from the processing screen.
5. When all parameters are set, highlight EXE (for Execute) and press OK. The D810 will create a JPEG file with the settings you've specified, and show an Image Saved message on the monitor when finished.

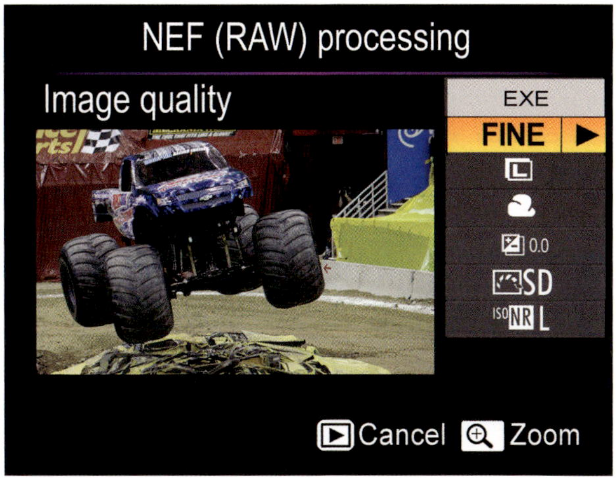

Figure 13.16
Adjust six parameters and then save your JPEG copy from a RAW original file.

Resize

This option, the first in the second page of the Retouch menu (see Figure 13.17), creates smaller copies of the selected images. It can be applied while viewing a single image in full-size mode (just press the OK button while viewing a photo), or accessed from the Retouch menu (especially useful if you'd like to select and resize multiple images).

1. **Select images.** If accessing from the Retouch menu, you can choose to select multiple images, or jump directly to the following two steps.
2. **Choose destination.** If two memory cards are inserted, you can choose either slot as the destination.
3. **Choose size.** Next, select the size for the finished copy, from 2.5, 1.1, 0.6, or 0.3 megabytes.
4. **Confirm.** Press OK to create your copy.

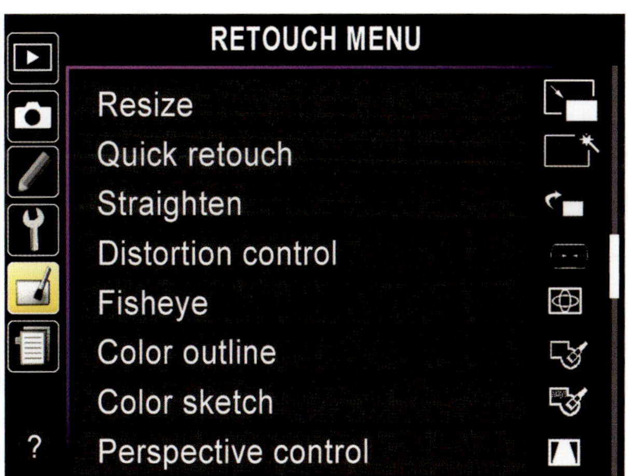

Figure 13.17
The second page of the Retouch menu.

Quick Retouch

This option brightens the shadows of pictures that have already been taken. Once you've selected your photo for processing, use the multi-selector up/down keys in the screen that pops up (see Figure 13.18). The amount of correction that you select (High, Normal, or Low) will be applied to the version of the image shown at right. The left-hand version of the image shows the uncorrected version. While working on your image, you can press the Zoom In button to temporarily magnify the original photo.

Quick Retouch brightens shadows, enhances contrast, and adds color richness (saturation) to the image. Press OK to create a copy on your memory card with the retouching applied.

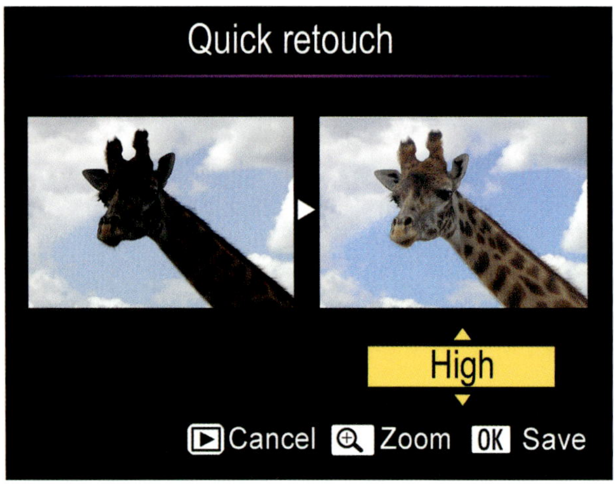

Figure 13.18
Quick Retouch applies D-Lighting, enhanced contrast, and added saturation to an image.

Straighten

Use this to create a corrected copy of a crooked image, rotated by up to five degrees, in increments of one-quarter of a degree. Use the right directional button to rotate clockwise, and the left directional button to rotate counterclockwise. Press OK to make a corrected copy, or the Playback button to exit without saving a copy.

Distortion Control

This option produces a copy with reduced barrel distortion (a bowing out effect) or pincushion distortion (an inward-bending effect), both most noticeable at the edges of a photo. You can select Auto to let the D810 make this correction, or use Manual to make the fix yourself visually. Use the right directional button to reduce barrel distortion and the left directional button to reduce pincushion distortion. In both cases, some of the edges of the photo will be cropped out of your image. Press OK to make a corrected copy, or the Playback button to exit without saving a copy. Note that

Auto cannot be used with images exposed using the Auto Distortion Control feature described earlier in this chapter. Auto works only with type G and type D lenses (see Chapter 7 for a description of what these lenses are), and does not work well with certain lenses, such as fisheye lenses and perspective control lenses.

Fisheye

This feature emulates the extreme curving effect of a fisheye lens. Use the right directional button to increase the effect, and the left directional button to decrease it. Press OK to make a processed copy, or the Playback button to exit without saving a copy. Figure 13.19 shows an example image.

Color Outline

This option creates a copy of your image in outline form (see Figure 13.20), which Nikon says you can use for "painting." You might like the effect on its own. It's a little like the Find Edges command in Photoshop and Photoshop Elements, but you can perform this magic in your camera!

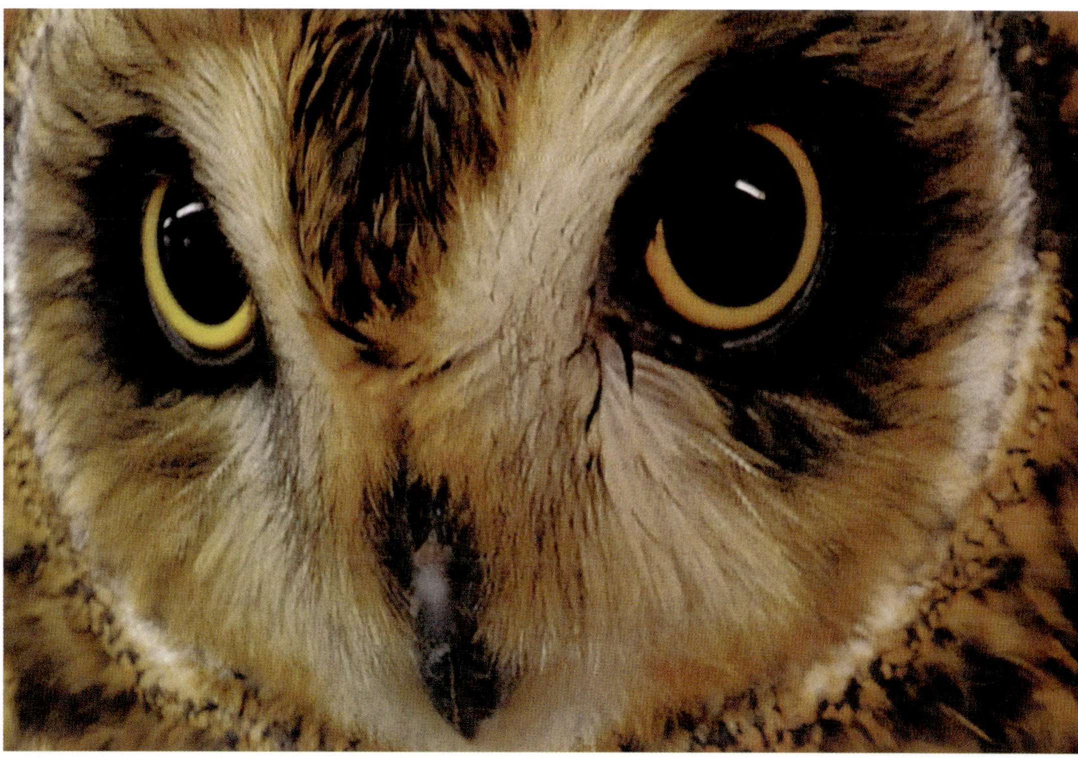

Figure 13.19 You can apply a fisheye effect to an image.

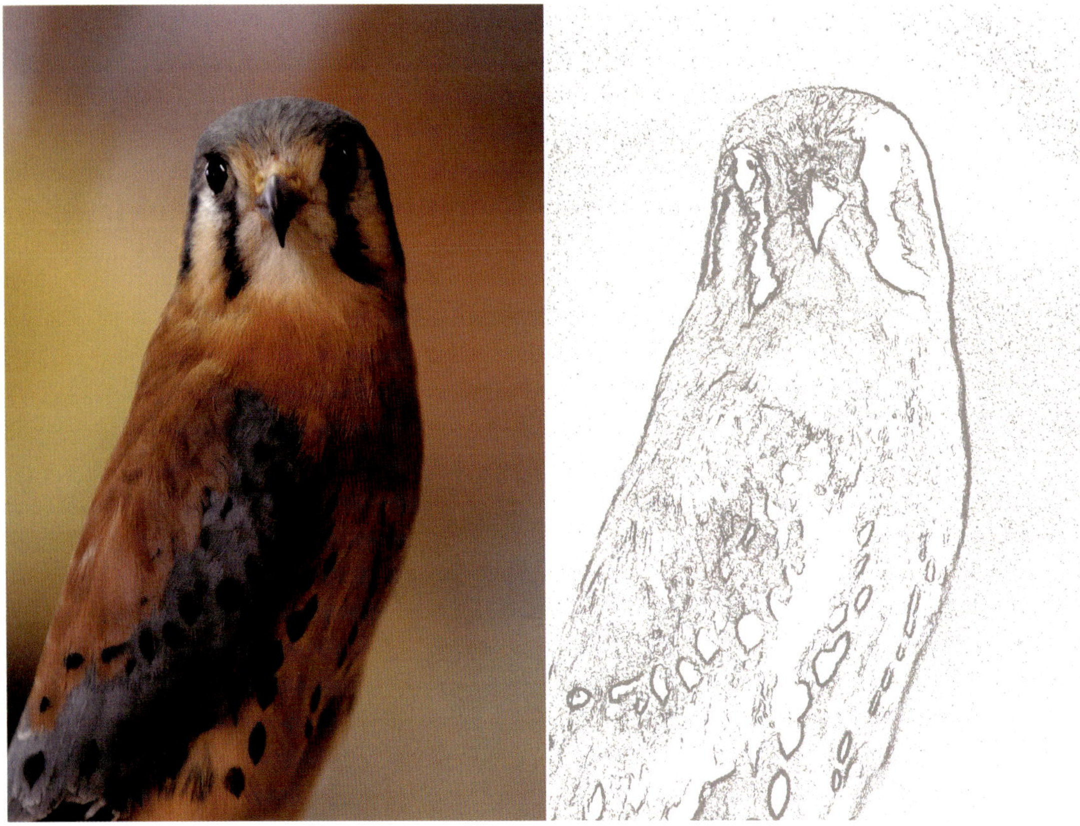

Figure 13.20 The Color Outline retouching feature creates an outline image (right), but it's not in color (like the original, left).

Color Sketch

This option transforms your photo into a colored pencil sketch. Press the up/down buttons to select Vividness or Outlines attributes, and the left/right buttons to increase/decrease saturation, or make the outlines thinner/thicker (respectively).

Perspective Control

This option lets you adjust the perspective of an image, reducing the falling back effect produced when the camera is tilted to take in the top of a tall subject, such as a building (see Figure 13.21). Use the multi selector buttons to "tilt" the image in various directions and visually correct the distortion.

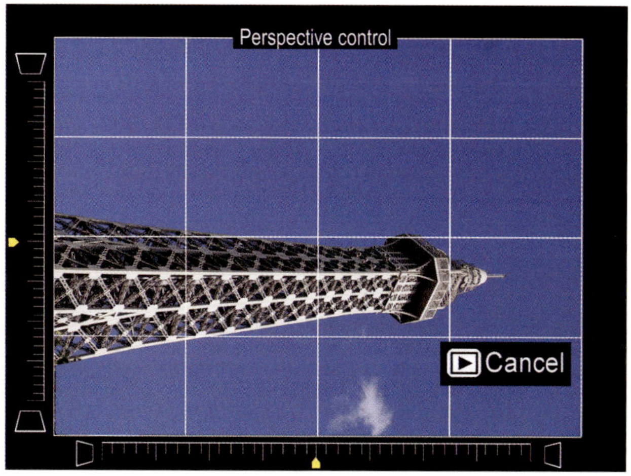

Figure 13.21
Perspective Control lets you fix "falling back" distortion when photographing tall subjects.

Miniature Effect

This is a clever effect, and it's hampered by a misleading name and the fact that its properties are hard to visualize (which is not a great attribute for a visual effect). This tool doesn't create a "miniature" picture, as you might expect. What it does is mimic tilt/shift lens effects that angle the lens off the axis of the sensor plane to drastically change the plane of focus, producing the sort of look you get when viewing some photographs of a diorama, or miniature scene. Confused yet?

Perhaps the best way to understand this capability is to actually modify a picture using it. Just follow these steps:

1. **Take your best shot.** Capture an image of a distant landscape or other scene, preferably from a slightly elevated viewpoint.
2. **Access Miniature Effect.** When viewing the image during playback, press the multi selector center button to access the Retouch menu, and select Miniature Effect. A screen like the one shown in Figure 13.22 appears.
3. **Adjust selected area.** A wide yellow box (or a tall yellow box if the image is rotated to vertical perspective on playback) highlights a small section of the image. (No, we're not going to create a panorama from that slice; this Nikon super-tricky feature has fooled you yet again.) Use the up/down buttons (or left/right buttons if the image is displayed vertically) to move the yellow box, which represents the area of your image that will be rendered in (fairly) sharp focus. The rest of the image will be blurred.
4. **Preview area to be in sharp focus.** Press the Zoom In button to preview the area that will be rendered in sharp focus. Nikon labels this control Confirm, but that's just to mislead you. It's actually just a preview that lets you "confirm" that this is the area you want to emphasize.
5. **Apply the effect.** Press the OK button to apply the effect (or the Playback button to cancel). Your finished image will be rendered in a weird altered-focus way, as shown in Figure 13.23.

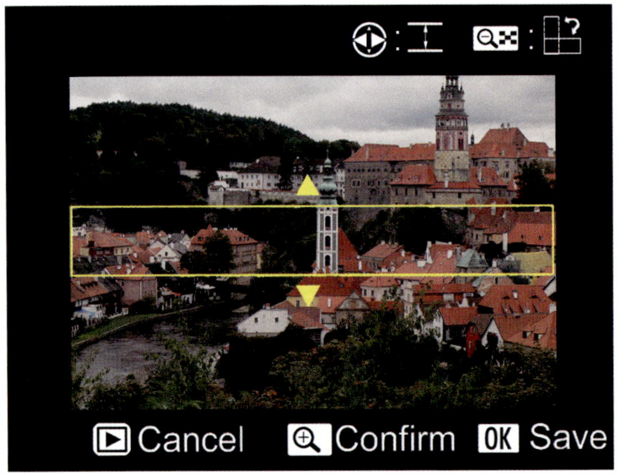

Figure 13.22 Choose the area for sharp focus by moving the yellow box within the frame.

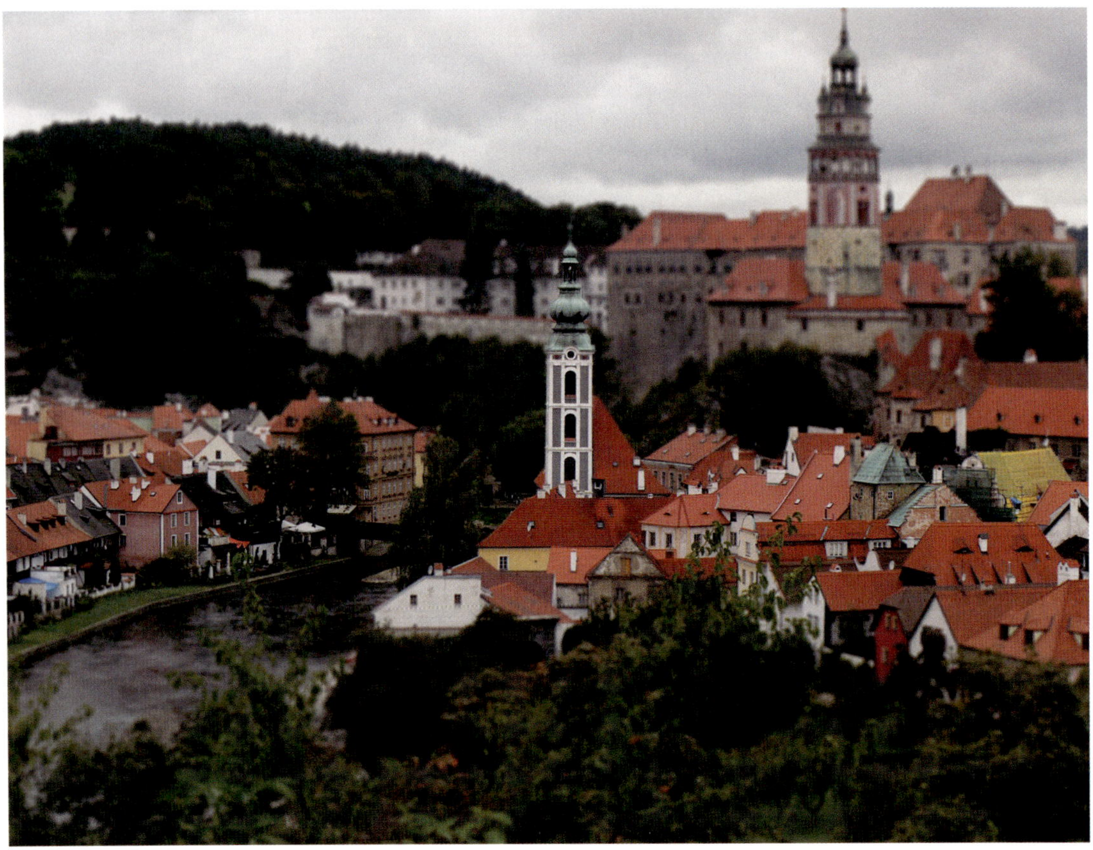

Figure 13.23 The same photo with the diorama/miniature effect applied.

Selective Color

This is a retouching effect that allows you to choose which colors appear in a finished image, with the other colors rendered in black-and-white, resembling the effects seen in movies like *Sin City*, and every single wedding picture of a monochrome bride holding a vivid red rose. Your D810 gives you access to this effect, to use creatively, or to reproduce some of the most popular clichés. To use it:

1. **Access Selective Color feature.** Choose Selective Color from the Retouch menu.
2. **Choose image.** When the Select Photo screen appears, highlight the one you want to process. You can preview the image in full frame by pressing the Zoom In button. When you've decided on the image, press the OK button. A screen like the one shown in Figure 13.24 appears.
3. **Specify a color.** Next, use the multi selector buttons to move the on-screen cursor over an area of the object with the color you want to specify and press the Protect/AE-L/AF-L button. The effect works best if you choose a rich, highly saturated color. You can enlarge a portion of the image by pressing the Zoom In button.
4. **Add the selected color to a color range.** Rotate the command dial to choose a color range specified by one of the three color range boxes.
5. **Increase/decrease "tolerance."** Press the up/down multi selector buttons to increase or decrease the range of similar colors that will be included, with values from 1 to 7. A very broad range may extend the color selection into adjoining colors, say, embracing dark blues as well as lighter blues or even cyans.
6. **Choose a different color range box to add more colors.** Rotate the command dial again to highlight one of the other three color range boxes and repeat Steps 3 to 5 to add more colors.
7. **Save image.** Press OK to create a modified copy of your original photograph. (See Figure 13.25.)

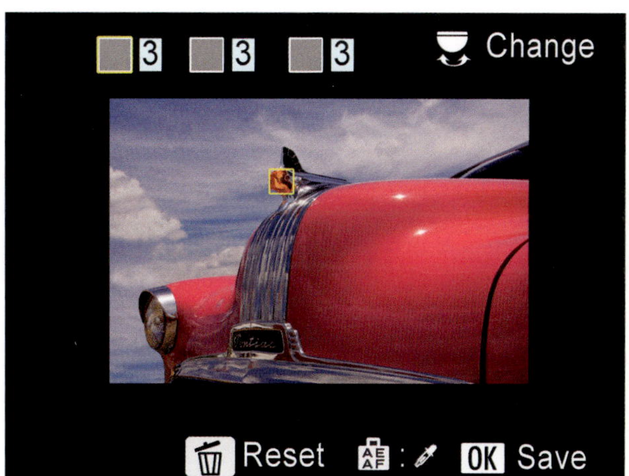

Figure 13.24
Select your colors and color ranges here.

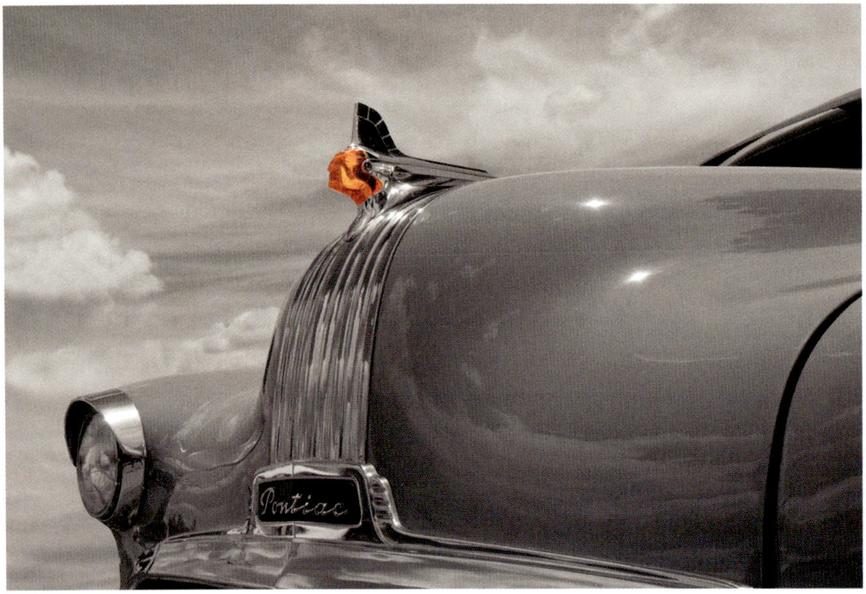

Figure 13.25
The finished effect looks like this.

Edit Movie

You can do limited editing of movies in the camera (actually, just modest trimming), choosing a start point, end point, and also storing a selected frame as a still image. I'll show you how to edit movies using this capability in Chapter 15.

Side-by-Side Comparison

Use this option to compare a retouched photo side-by-side with the original from which it was derived. Don't look for Side-by-Side Comparison in the Retouch menu. It doesn't appear there. Instead, this option is shown at the bottom of the pop-up menu that appears when you are viewing an image (or copy) full screen and press the OK button.

To use Side-by-Side Comparison:

1. Press the Playback button and review images in full-frame mode until you encounter a source image or retouched copy you want to compare. The retouched copy will have the retouching icon displayed in the upper-left corner. Press OK.
2. The original and retouched image will appear next to each other, with the retouching options you've used shown as a label above the images, as you can see in Figure 13.26.
3. Highlight the original or the copy with the multi selector left/right buttons, and press the Zoom In button to magnify the image to examine it more closely.

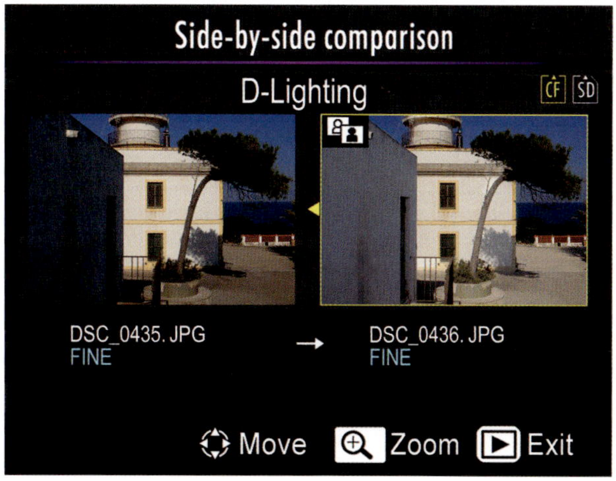

Figure 13.26
You can easily compare an original image and the retouched version side-by-side.

4. If you have created more than one copy of an original image, select the retouched version shown, and press the multi selector up/down buttons to view the other retouched copies. The up/down buttons will also let you view the other image used to create an Image Overlay copy.
5. When done comparing, press the Playback button to exit.

Using My Menu

The last menu in the D810's main menu screen has two versions: Recent Settings and My Menu. The default mode is Recent Settings, which simply shows an ever-changing roster of the 20 menu items you used most recently. You'll probably find it more useful to activate the My Menu option instead, which contains only those menu items that you deposit there extracted from the Playback, Shooting, Custom Settings, Setup, and Retouch menus, based on your own decisions on which you use most. Remember that the D810 always returns to the last menu and menu entry accessed when you press the MENU button. So you can set up My Menu (see Figure 13.27) to include just the items accessed most frequently, and (as long as you haven't used another menu) jump to those items instantly by pressing the MENU button.

Switching back and forth is easy. The My Menu and Recent Settings menus each has a menu choice called Choose Tab. Highlight that entry and press the right multi selector button to view a screen that allows you to activate either the My Menu or Recent Settings menu. Press OK to confirm.

I tend to include frequently used functions that aren't available using direct access buttons in My Menu. For example, I include High ISO NR and Long Exp. NR and Battery Info there, because I may want to turn noise reduction on or off, or check the status of my battery during shooting. I *don't* include ISO, Qual, or WB changes in My Menu, even though they are available in the menu system, because I can quickly change those values by pressing their dedicated buttons and rotating the main and sub-command dials.

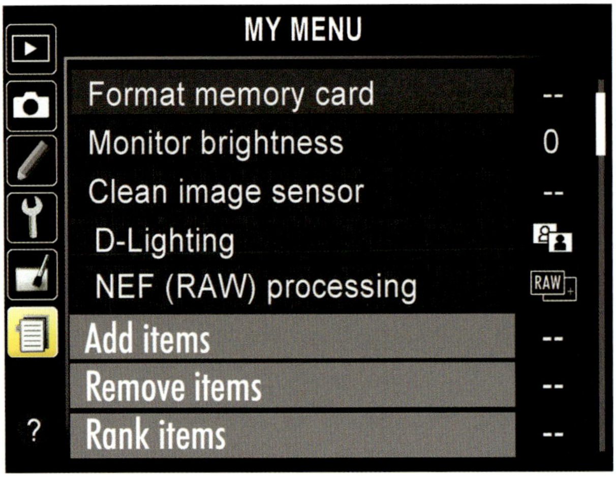

Figure 13.27
You can include your favorite menu items in the fast-access My Menu.

You can add or subtract entries on My Menu at any time, and reorder (or rank) the entries so the ones you access most often are shown at the top of the list. Here's all you need to know to work with My Menu. To add entries to My Menu:

1. Select My Menu and choose Add Items.
2. A list of the available menus will appear (Playback, Shooting, Custom Settings, Setup, and Retouch menus). Highlight one and press the multi selector's right button.
3. Within the selected menu, choose the menu item you want to add and press OK.
4. The label Choose Position appears at the top of the My Menu screen. Use the up/down buttons to select a rank among the entries, and press OK to confirm and add the new item.
5. Repeat steps 1-4 if you want to add more entries to My Menu.

To reorder the menu listings:

1. Within the My Menu screen, choose Rank Items.
2. Use the up/down buttons to select the item to be moved, and press OK.
3. Use the up/down buttons to relocate the selected item and press OK.
4. Repeat steps 2-3 to move additional entries.

To remove entries from the list, you can simply press the Trash button while an item is highlighted in the My Menu screen. To remove multiple items, follow these steps:

1. Within the My Menu screen, choose Remove Items.
2. A list with check boxes next to the menu items appears. Scroll down to an item you want to remove and press the multi selector right button to mark its box. If you change your mind, highlight the item and press the right button again to unmark the box.
3. When finished, highlight Done and press the OK button.
4. Press OK to confirm the deletion.

Part V

Introduction to Movie Making

In the next three chapters you'll find enough about movie making with the D810 to get you started shooting your own video. As you probably know, Nikon was the first camera manufacturer to offer HD movie capabilities in a digital SLR, specifically the Nikon D90, introduced in August, 2008. Every subsequent Nikon dSLR (other than the retro Df model) also had movie-making capabilities, but Nikon found itself in the odd position of having to play catch up as vendors like Canon offered highly improved video features (for example, full HD 1920 × 1080 video vs. the standard HD 1280 × 720 video Nikon pioneered).

With the Nikon D810 and its upscale stablemate the D4s, Nikon's video features take a backseat to no one. These cameras are equipped with a headphone jack that serious videographers need to monitor audio as it's recorded (usually with an external microphone or two), an HDMI port that can output raw video files to external storage or a monitor, and both full and standard HD formats with industry-standard H.264 encoding. Your D810 rivals the quality of some professional video capture gear—and goes them one better because its sensor is much larger, allowing exquisite control over selective focus and depth-of-field.

In this part, you'll find the following chapters:

- **Chapter 14:** The D810's live view feature is an important component of its movie-making capabilities. Video capture is, after all, continuous live view, stored on your memory card at a frame rate of 24, 25, 30, 50, or 60 frames per second (depending on mode). In this chapter I'll show you all the controls and capabilities of the D810's live view and movie modes.
- **Chapter 15:** Once you learn the basics of live view, you'll have much of what you need to know to begin shooting movies. This chapter shows you all the controls and settings you need to begin, and will have you shooting your first video in minutes.
- **Chapter 16:** If you want to take your products up a step from camcorder mode, you'll need to learn the basics of movie production. There's not enough room to give you the 200 or 300 page short course you really need, but this chapter will introduce you to the terminology and techniques so you can begin using them right away, while picking up on-the-job training.

14

Basics of Live View

You don't care about video, and never shoot movies? Get with the program! It's true that shooting video is quite a bit different from capturing stills, and requires a somewhat different skill set. Great still photographers aren't necessarily comfortable with visualizing a subject not as a moment, or series of moments, but as a story told using the dimension of time. However, photographers motivated enough to choose a Nikon D810 as their tool of choice are *at the very least* halfway up the learning curve that must be surmounted to make the transition to video.

And there's plenty of incentive to do so. Many professional photographers can easily gain an edge over their rivals by adding video shooting to their repertoire. Wedding photographers will find a ready market for video that they—or their second shooters—capture during the ceremony and reception. Photojournalists can supplement their picture stories with interviews and video coverage. Those who really enjoy shooting video can branch out and produce short films with their D810. The camera includes every capability you need for professional-quality movie magic.

Amateur photographers who don't intend to sell their work can appreciate not needing to tote along a camcorder on their outings, and the opportunity to express their creative side with video. This chapter and the next two can serve as your introduction to the basics of Nikon movie making, *and* capturing stills in live view mode (or while shooting video). Because live view forms the foundation of the D810's video capabilities, we'll start there.

The New Perspective of Live View

Live view, like movie making, is one of those features that experienced SLR users sometimes think they don't need—until they try it. It's also one of those features (like truly "silent" shooting, without any shutter click) that point-and-shoot refugees are surprised that digital SLRs (until recently) have lacked. Of course, all single lens reflex cameras have actual, mechanical shutters that can't be completely silenced, as can be done with point-and-shoot cameras. I've fielded almost as many queries from those who don't know about live view and want to preview their images on the LCD—just as they did with their point-and-shoot cameras. Indeed, these days many P & S models don't even *have* optical viewfinders, engendering a whole generation of amateur photographers who think the only way to frame and compose an image is to hold the camera out at arm's length so the back-panel LCD can be viewed more easily.

The Nikon D810 has a gorgeous 3.2-inch LCD monitor that can be viewed under a variety of lighting conditions and from wide-ranging angles (up to 170 degrees horizontally), so you don't have to be exactly behind the display to see it clearly. It offers a 100-percent view of the sensor's capture area, the same as the camera's optical viewfinder. It's large enough to allow manual focusing—but there is an automatic focus option, too. The D810 has a Monitor Color Balance option that allows you to neutralize any tint that may appear on the LCD during live view. The resulting colors aren't guaranteed to be 100 percent accurate, but they can allow you to better evaluate how your captured image or video will appear.

You still have to avoid pointing your camera at bright light sources (especially the Sun) when using live view, but the real-time preview can be used for fairly long periods without frying the sensor. Nikon's system works just like you'd want it to: the mirror flips up, the shutter opens, and what the sensor sees is displayed in full color on the monitor on the back of the camera.

What You Can Do with Live View

You may not have considered just what you can do with live view. Once you've played with it, you'll discover dozens of applications for this capability.

- **Preview your images on the monitor or a TV.** You can see a preview of your image on the LCD monitor. Or, connect your camera to a standard definition or high-definition television using an (optional) HDMI cable, and you can preview your image on a large screen. Because you're viewing the actual image that will be captured, you can check things like focus or white balance in real time, on a larger display. You can preview exposure with live view (just press the OK button), because the camera will adjust the monitor display to approximate the metered exposure. However, if you make EV changes that exceed +3/–3 EV (you can set up to +/–5EV), the monitor will not reflect the actual exposure. If you're using Bulb or x250 for a shutter speed, Active D-Lighting, HDR, or flash (for stills only, of course), or if the image is very bright or dark, the preview may not accurately reflect your final image.

- **Preview remotely.** Extend the cable between the camera and TV screen, and you can preview your images some distance away from the camera.
- **Improve your point of view.** If looking through the viewfinder to frame your subject is awkward (say, you have to hold the D810 over your head to clear obstructions such as a crowd of people), live view may allow you to see what you're going to shoot before you snap the shutter. (A remote release is a good idea in this mode.)
- **Shoot from your computer.** With Camera Control Pro 2 (an extra cost option) or Lightroom 4, you can control your camera from your computer in "tethered" mode, so you can preview images and take pictures without physically touching the D810.
- **Continuous shooting.** You can shoot bursts of images using live view.
- **Shoot from tripod or hand-held.** Of course, holding the camera out at arm's length to preview an image is poor technique, and will introduce a lot of camera shake. If you want to use live view for hand-held images, use an image-stabilized lens and/or a high shutter speed. A tripod is a better choice if you can use one.
- **Watch your power.** Live view uses a lot of juice and will deplete your battery rapidly. The optional AC adapter is a useful accessory.
- **Watch your usage times.** Nikon says live view can be used continuously for as long as one hour, but notes that after periods of more than a few minutes, the sensor warms up and increases image noise and color artifacts. Your D810 will shut down before your camera seriously overheats, and will give you a warning on the monitor 30 seconds before shut off. (If you've chosen an automatic monitor off delay for live view using Custom Settings menu option c4—other than No Limit—you'll be warned five seconds before the live view monitor shuts off automatically.)

Beginning Live View

Activate live view by rotating the Lv switch on the back of the camera (just to the lower right of the monitor) to the still position (represented by a camera icon). Then, press the Lv button (in the center of the Lv switch) to activate live view. The first thing to do when entering live view is to double-check three settings that affect how your image or movie is taken. These settings, which are basically set exactly as in non-live view mode, include:

Metering Mode

While using live view, you can press the Metering mode button and rotate the main command dial to select Matrix, Center-weighted, Spot, or Highlight-Weighted metering.

Focus Mode

Focus mode is also chosen using the same controls as when using the optical viewfinder. Set the focus mode selector switch on the side of the camera under the lens release button to AF (and set the lens focus mode switch to AF, as well). Then press the AF mode button and rotate the main command dial until either AF-S or AF-F is displayed on the back-panel LCD. The available modes differ slightly from those possible when not shooting in live view. To use manual focus, set the focus mode selector switch to M.

- **AF-S.** This single autofocus mode, which Nikon calls Single-servo AF, locks focus when the shutter release is pressed halfway. This mode uses focus-priority; the shutter can be fully released to take a picture only if the D810 is able to achieve sharp focus.
- **AF-F.** This mode is roughly the equivalent of AF-C. Nikon calls it Full-time servo AF. The D810 focuses and refocuses continually as you shoot stills in live view mode or record movies. Unlike AF-C, this mode also uses focus-priority. You can't release the shutter unless the camera has achieved sharp focus.
- **MF.** Manual focus. You focus the image by rotating the focus ring on the camera.

Focus Area

With the focus mode selector button pressed, rotate the sub-command dial to choose one of the following focus area modes. Your choices, which I also explained in Chapter 5, are as follows:

- **Face-priority AF.** The camera automatically detects faces, and focuses on subjects facing the camera, as when you're shooting a portrait. You can't select the focus zone yourself. Instead, a double yellow border will be displayed on the monitor when the camera detects a face. You don't need to press the shutter release to activate this behavior. Up to 35 faces may be detected; the D810 focuses on the face that is closest to the camera. To change to a different face, use the multi selector to shift the double-bordered box to the one you want. When you press down the shutter release halfway, the camera attempts to focus the face. As sharp focus is achieved, the border turns green. (See Figure 14.1.) If the camera is unable to focus, the border blinks red. Focus may also be lost if the subject turns away from the camera and is no longer detectable by Face-priority.
- **Wide-area AF.** This is the mode to use for non-portrait subjects, such as landscapes, as you can select the focus zone to be used manually. It's good for shooting hand-held, because the subjects may change as you reframe the image with a hand-held camera, and the wide-area zones are forgiving of these changes. The focus zone will be outlined in red. You can move the focus zone around the screen with the multi selector buttons. When sharp focus is achieved, the focus zone box will turn green. (See Figure 14.2.)
- **Normal-area AF.** This mode uses smaller focus zones for precise placement of the focus spot, and so is best suited for tripod-mounted images where the camera is held fairly steady. As with Wide-area AF, the focus zone will be outlined in red. You can move the focus zone around the

screen with the multi selector buttons. When sharp focus is achieved, the focus zone box will turn green. (See Figure 14.3.)

- **Subject-tracking AF.** This mode allows the camera to "grab" a subject, focus, and then follow the subject as it moves within the frame. You can use this mode for subjects that don't remain stationary, such as small children. When using Subject-tracking AF, a white border appears in the center of the frame, and turns yellow when focus is locked in. To select the subject to track, frame the image until the object you want to follow is within the box on the screen, then press the multi selector center button to lock it in. (See Figure 14.4.)
- **Manual focus.** In this non-automatic focus mode, you can move the focus area around the frame with the multi selector buttons, press the shutter release halfway, and then adjust focus manually by rotating the focus ring on the lens. When sharp focus is achieved, the red focus zone box will turn green, and the camera's beeper, if enabled, will sound.

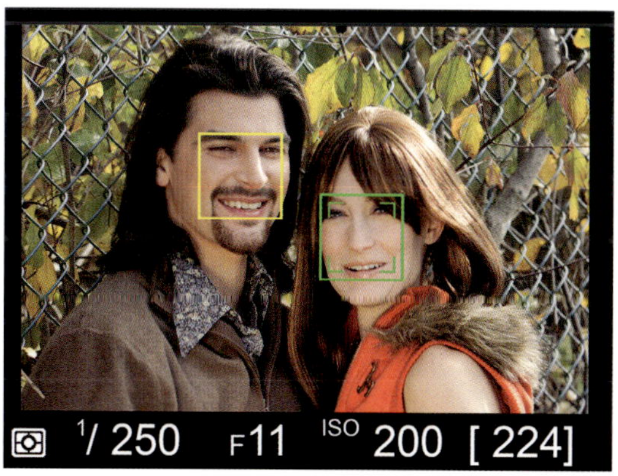

Figure 14.1 Face-priority AF attempts to focus on the face that's closest to the camera.

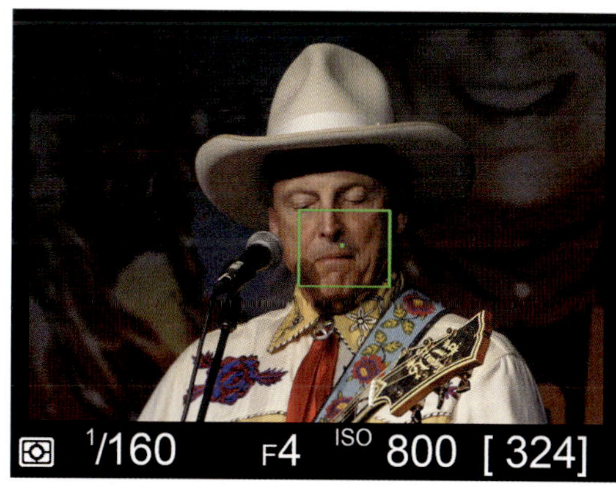

Figure 14.2 Wide-area AF is best for landscapes and other subjects with large elements.

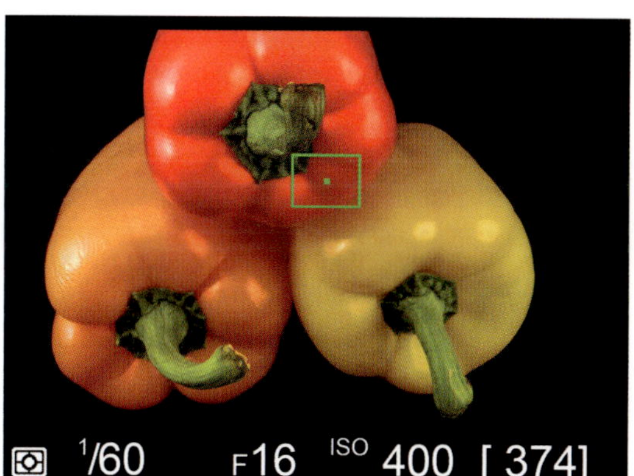

Figure 14.3 Normal-area AF allows you to zero in on a specific point of focus.

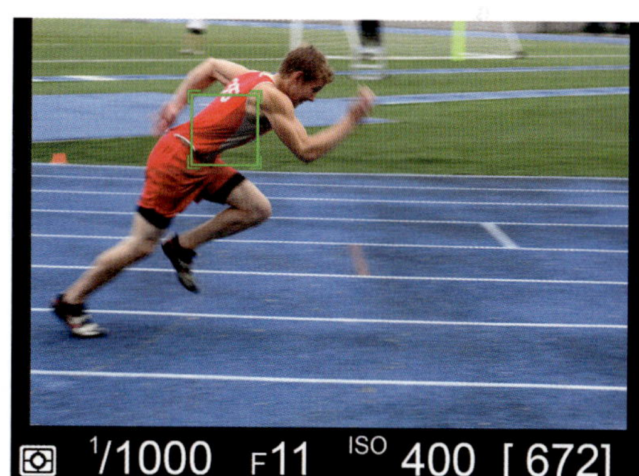

Figure 14.4 Subject-tracking AF allows you to follow moving subjects.

Viewing Live View Information

Once you've activated live view, a display like the one shown in Figure 14.5 appears. Not all of the information appears all the time. For example, the Time Remaining indicator shows only when there are 30 seconds or less remaining for live view shooting. The indicators overlaid on the image can be displayed or suppressed by pressing the Info button (that's to the lower right of the LCD).

As you press the button, the LCD cycles among these screen variations:

- Live view screen overlaid with shooting information, as shown in Figure 14.5.
- Live view screen overlaid with only minimal information. (Figures 14.1–14.4 are examples of this kind of display.)
- Live view screen overlaid with a 16-segment alignment grid. (See Figure 14.6.)
- Live view screen overlaid with a virtual horizon leveling aid. (See Figure 14.7.)
- Live view shooting information screen with a 16:9 aspect ratio of HD movie format indicated.

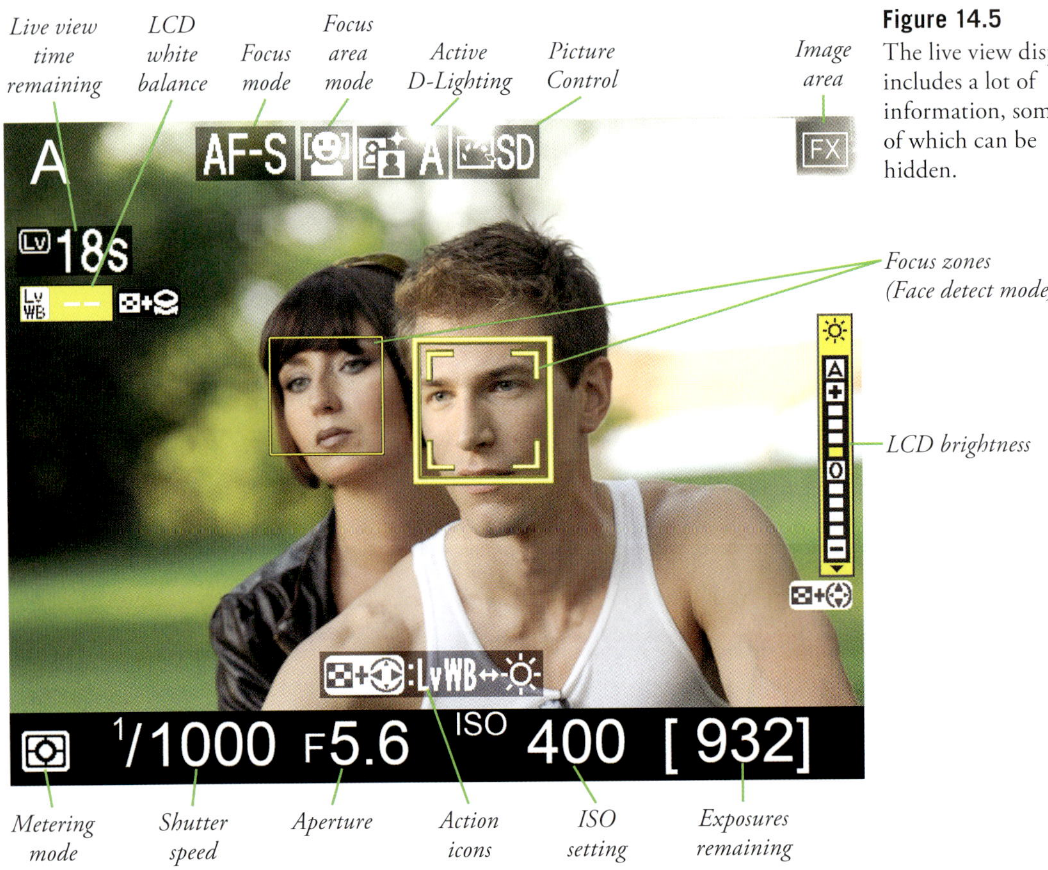

Figure 14.5
The live view display includes a lot of information, some of which can be hidden.

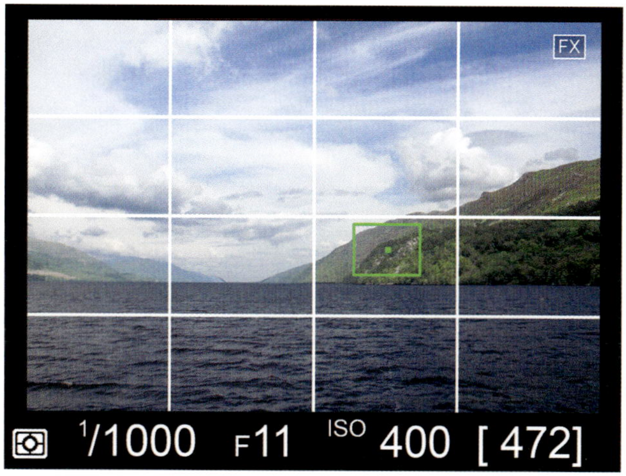

Figure 14.6
The live view display with alignment grid.

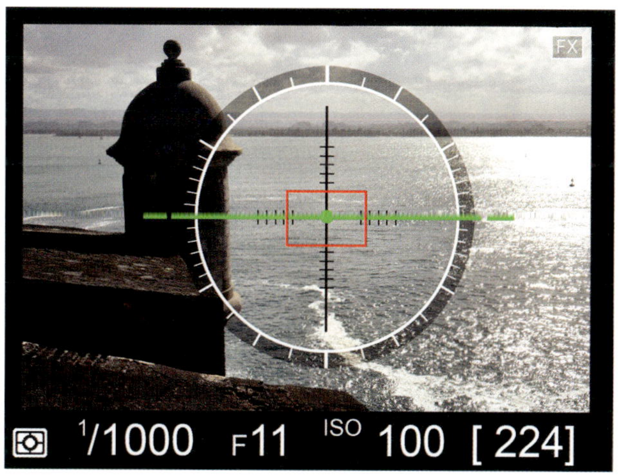

Figure 14.7
The live view display with virtual horizon.

If the Lv switch is set to the Movie position instead, the information screens that can be summoned by pressing the Info button are slightly different:

- Additional shooting data related to movie making, such as audio levels and movie format, appear on the shooting information screen.
- The minimal information screen (and all other live view screens) are masked to show the 16:9 aspect ratio of the HD movie format.
- The 16-segment grid screen and the virtual horizon leveling screen are both basically the same, except for the masking.
- An additional screen showing a live histogram is available.

The overlaid indicators include:

- **Focus mode.** Shows AF-S or AF-F when active. If you switch to Manual focus mode, this indicator disappears.
- **Focus Area mode.** Shows whether Face-priority, Wide-area, Normal-area, or Subject-tracking autofocus will be used.
- **Active D-Lighting status.** Shows the D-Lighting that will be applied.
- **Picture Control.** Shows the current active Picture Control.
- **White balance.** Displays the current white balance preset or WB Auto status.
- **Image Size.** Displays the current resolution, L (Large), M (Medium), or S (Small).
- **Image Quality.** Shows JPEG Image Quality: Fine, Norm, or Basic.
- **Image Area.** Shows current image area setting, such as FX, DX, 1.2X, or 5:4.
- **Live view time remaining.** This is displayed when the amount of shooting time in live view mode is 30 seconds or less. Although live view is possible for 60 minutes, if the D810 overheats, this countdown display appears and the camera exits live view before damage is done.
- **Focus zones.** Shows the appropriate focus indicator for the AF-area mode in use.
- **Monitor brightness.** This indicator shows the relative brightness of the back-panel monitor during live view as you make adjustments. Press the Zoom Out button, then use the left/right directional buttons to highlight either the LCD Brightness icon (at the right side of the screen) or LCD White Balance icon (on the left). To change monitor brightness, hold the Zoom Out button and press the up/down directional buttons while this icon is highlighted.
- **LCD White Balance/Monitor Hue.** The monitor will generally match the colors found in the final image. (Many early users of the D810 complained that the screen had a "green" cast, but Nikon insisted this was a more accurate rendition.) The exception is when you are using flash, or you have manually set a special color balance preset. You can adjust the monitor hue. Choose this icon with the Zoom Out button and left/right directional buttons, then rotate the main command dial to modify. Nikon has issued a firmware update that eliminates most of the green cast for you, but you may still want to fine-tune the balance of the monitor here.
- **Action icons.** These icons are a reminder that you can adjust the screen brightness and screen white balance by pressing Zoom Out and directional buttons to choose the mode.

Additional information is arrayed along the bottom of the monitor image, more or less duplicating much of the data in the LED display that is seen through the viewfinder when not using live view. These indicators include:

- **Metering method.** Shows whether Matrix, Center-weighted, or Spot metering is selected. Choose before entering live view.
- **Shutter speed.** The currently selected shutter speed.
- **F/stop.** The current f/stop.
- **ISO value.** Shows the ISO sensitivity setting, or ISO Auto.
- **Shots remaining.** Indicates the number of images remaining on your memory card at the current Image Size and Image Quality settings.
- **Flash ready.** Shows the electronic flash is fully charged and ready to shoot.

More icons not shown in the figure include the alignment grid, and indicators for movie modes:

- **Alignment grid.** (Shown in Figure 14.6.) This set of guides can be used to help line up horizontal or vertical lines.
- **Audio recording indicator.** Shows when a microphone is being used.
- **No Movies Possible.** This shows that it is not possible to shoot movies, because there is not enough space remaining on your memory card.
- **Movie time remaining.** Indicates the number of minutes and seconds remaining for movie shooting.
- **Movie frame size.** Displays the resolution of the movie frame and frames per second rate, from 1920 × 1080 pixels to 1280 × 720, down to 640 x 424, at your selected frame rate.

Shooting Stills (and Movies, Too!) in Live View

Shooting stills and movies in live view is easy. I'll show you more about movie making in Chapters 15 and 16, but you can begin shooting stills *or* movies right now with no further instruction. Just follow these steps:

1. **Rotate Lv switch.** Specify live view mode by rotating the switch to either the Still or Movie icons. Then press the Lv button. The D810 can be hand-held or mounted on a tripod. (Using tripod mode makes it easier to obtain and keep sharp focus.) You can exit live view at any time by pressing the Lv button again.
2. **Zoom in/out.** Check your view by pressing the Zoom In and Zoom Out buttons (located to the left of the color monitor). Five levels of magnification are available, up to 6.7X zoom. A navigation box appears in the lower right of the monitor with a yellow box representing the portion of the image zoomed, just as when you're reviewing photos you've already taken using Playback mode. Use the multi selector keys to change the zoomed area within the full frame. Press the Zoom Out button to zoom out again.

3. **Make exposure adjustments.** While using an automatic exposure mode, you can add or subtract exposure using the EV settings, as described in Chapter 4. Hold down the EV button (just southeast of the shutter release) and rotate the main command dial to add or subtract exposure when using P, S, and A modes. The back-panel color monitor will brighten or darken to represent the exposure change you make.
4. **Choose a focus mode.** Select from autofocus or manual focus with the AF/MF switch on the camera body. Choose AF-S or AF-F by pressing the focus mode button in the center of the AF/MF switch and rotating the main command dial.
5. **Choose an AF-area mode.** Select autofocus area by pressing the focus mode button in the center of the AF/MF switch and rotating the sub-command dial. Choices include Face-priority AF, Wide-area AF, Normal-area AF, or Subject-tracking AF. You'll find complete descriptions of focus and AF-area modes in Chapter 5.
6. **Shoot.** Lock focus and begin capture by pressing the shutter release all the way down to take a still picture, or the movie button to begin capturing video. Press the movie button a second time to stop.

i Button Options

In live view mode, pressing the *i* button produces a screen of settings and options that are especially useful for live shooting, including one—split-screen display zoom—that is sensational for comparing opposite sides of the frame under high magnification. The screen that appears is shown in Figure 14.8. The available options include:

- **Image area.** Select the image area used for live view photography, as described in Chapter 11.
- **Active D-Lighting.** Adjust the Active D-Lighting setting, described in detail under the Shooting menu in Chapter 11.
- **Electronic front-curtain shutter.** Enable or disable the electronic front-curtain shutter, as described under Custom Setting d5 in Chapter 12.
- **Monitor brightness.** Select this option and then press the up/down buttons to adjust the monitor brightness applied *only* during live view. A scale appears on the right side of the live view screen with +5 to –5 settings. The adjustment has *no* effect on the photographs or movies that you capture, nor on the brightness of the monitor during playback or menu access. To change the brightness for those other modes, use the Monitor Brightness entry in the Setup menu, as described in Chapter 13.

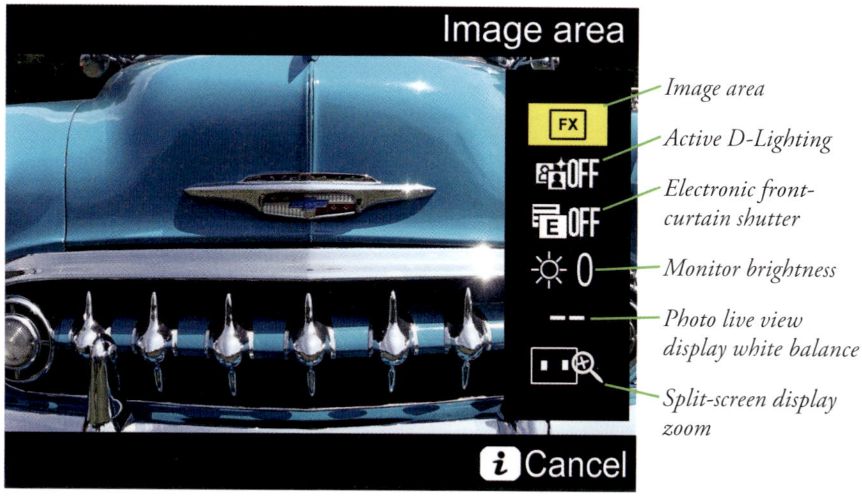

Figure 14.8
Press the *i* button while in live view to access these options.

- **Photo Live View Display White Balance.** This changes the hue (white balance) of the monitor (only) during live view, and is useful to help make what you see (on the screen) resemble what you get (in the finished photograph), if the lighting used to make the exposure is different from the lighting used to view the scene.

  For example, if you're using flash when working with live view, you'll have the D810 white balance set for Flash, in almost all cases. However, you might be framing the picture under lighting that is very different, perhaps much warmer incandescent lighting. Although our eyes adapt well visually to changes in white balance, your live view image won't be similar to the final image in terms of color. This control allows you to adjust the live view display white balance setting to more closely match the final image. If you want to use the same white balance for live view and the photograph, select None. This setting has no effect on the white balance of the captured image.
- **Split-screen Display Zoom.** This feature divides the live view display into two boxes, each of which shows a magnified view of a different area of the frame, as described next.

Split-Screen Display Zoom

When you activate this feature, the D810 divides the live view LCD display into two boxes, each showing a separate area of the frame side-by-side. To use this capability, just follow these steps.

1. **Split the screen.** While in live view, press the *i* button and scroll down to the bottom icon that appears on the right side of the screen. Press OK to activate.
2. **Areas are indicated by a navigation window.** The screen will split into two areas, shown next to each other. The relative positions of the two areas are shown in a magnification window, seen at lower right in Figure 14.9.

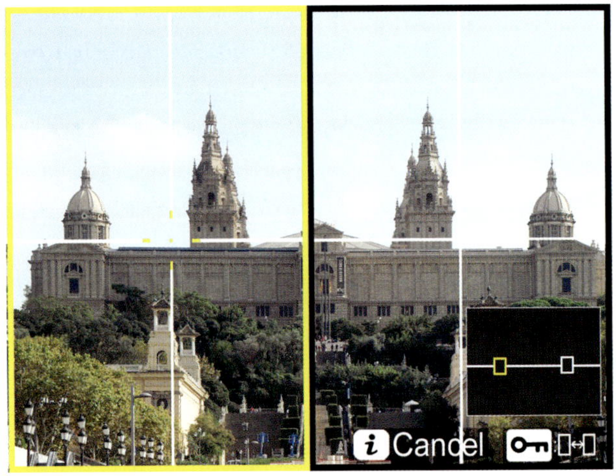

Figure 14.9
Split screen display in live view.

3. **Zoom in or out of the split display.** Use the Zoom In and Zoom Out buttons to magnify or reduce magnification of both portions of the image.
4. **Choose one of the two sides of the frame.** Press the Help (?) button to select one of the two sides of the frame.
5. **Move selected area horizontally.** You can use the left/right buttons to scroll that box's selected area from side to side.
6. **Move both areas vertically.** Press the up or down buttons to scroll *both* areas up or down simultaneously. In other words, the split screen images will always match horizontally, but you can adjust either of their positions left or right. Landscape photographers have already noted that they'd like the ability to change the locations in both horizontal and vertical directions.
7. **Focus on selected area.** When either box is selected, you can focus the image on *that* area by pressing the shutter release button halfway.
8. **Exit.** Press the *i* button again to exit the split-screen display.

You're probably wondering what this feature is useful for—unless you're way ahead of me. Here are some typical applications. These are all fairly technical in nature, and likely to be needed only for specialized types of photography, particularly in the architectural and landscape fields. But if you do need the split screen feature, you'll really need it.

- **Check horizontal alignment.** Some subjects lend themselves to symmetrical compositions (or, *demand* such treatment, in the case of buildings or other bi-laterally symmetrical scenes that look weird if the camera has been placed slightly to one side or the other). Use the split screen to view comparable parts of the same image simultaneously to see if the camera is aligned appropriately.

- **Check front/back tilt.** Sometimes you unintentionally lean the camera forward or back slightly, which can produce fall-back or fall-forward effects when shooting very tall or very deep subjects (*pitch*), or rotate the camera around its base (imagine a line running vertically through, say, the tripod socket; that's *yaw*). You might also *roll* the camera by rotating it along the axis that runs through the center of the lens.

  When these rotations are severe, you'll probably notice it visually; lean way back to take in the top of a building, and you'll see the effect on the screen. However, less drastic tilting may escape your attention. You can use the split screen feature in conjunction with the live view virtual horizon (discussed earlier in this chapter) to ensure the camera is completely level. The virtual horizon's indicators will show you when the camera is rolled around the lens axis running, or pitched forward or back. The split screen capability can help you counter yaw by comparing the two magnified sides of the image.
- **Control perspective and focus.** The split screen allows you to check the focus of different parts of a scene, which landscape photographers will like. Those using shift-tilt lenses will like the feature even more. These specialized lenses can be tilted without changing the position of the camera, providing control over which part of subjects photographed at an angle are in focus. The split screen can be used to select either side of the image, and focus on the side that you want to be rendered most sharply. These lenses can also be shifted side to side, say to allow photographing the top of a building while keeping the focal plane of the camera parallel to the structure. In such cases, you can use the D810 in portrait orientation (in which case the screen will be split top and bottom, rather than side to side) and then view both parts of the image before making additional shift adjustments for the best perspective control.

15

Shooting Movies with the D810

As you've probably gathered, movie making is an extension of the live view concept. Once you've directed the output of the sensor to the LCD, capturing it as a video file—with audio—is relatively easy. All the focus modes and AF-area modes described for plain old live view mode can be applied to movie making.

If you've absorbed all the basics of live view from Chapter 14, you need only a little more information to begin capturing video. First, here are some considerations to think about:

- **Stills, too.** If you've defined the shutter button to Take Photos using Custom Settings menu choice g4, as described in Chapter 12, you can take a cropped high resolution still photograph even while you're shooting a movie clip by pressing the shutter release all the way down. You won't miss a still shot because you're shooting video. However, movie shooting will cease after you take the still, and must be reactivated by pressing the red movie button again. The still image is saved using the current movie size aspect ratio (for example 16:9) image setting. In FX Large mode, the image will measure 4920 × 2768 pixels, or 13.6 MP.

  If you want to capture a frame without interrupting the movie, choose Live Frame Grab in Custom Settings g4 instead; you'll get JPEG Fine image at the current movie size (for example, 1920 × 1080 pixels).
- **Exposure compensation.** When shooting movies, exposure compensation is available in plus/minus 3EV steps in 1/3 EV increments.

- **Size matters.** Individual movie files can be up to 4GB in size (this will vary according to the resolution you select), and no more than 29 minutes, 59 seconds in length (20 minutes when shooting in high quality mode). The speed and capacity of your memory card may provide additional restrictions on size/length.
- **Use the right card.** You'll want to use a UDMA-compatible Compact Flash card with a read/write speed of 40/60 MB/second, or an SDHC/SDXC card with Class 6 or higher speed; if you use a slower card, like a Class 4 or especially Class 2, the recording may stop after a minute or two. In either case, choose a memory card with at least 4GB capacity; 8GB or 16GB are even better. If you're going to be recording a lot of HD video that could be a good reason to take advantage of the ability to use SDXC cards of 64GB capacity. Just make sure your memory card reader is compatible and your computer can read the files from that type of card.

  I've standardized on fast 32GB 600X Compact Flash cards and Class 10 32GB SDHC cards when I'm shooting movies; one of these cards will hold at least three to six hours of video. However, the camera cannot shoot a continuous movie scene for more than 29 minutes. You can start shooting the next clip right away, though, missing only about 30 seconds of the action. Of course that assumes there's enough space on your memory card and adequate battery power.

WHY THE 29-MINUTE LIMITATION?

Vendors are really cagey about revealing the reason for the seemingly arbitrary/non-arbitrary 29 minute, 59 second limitation on the length of a single video clip—not only with Nikon still cameras, but with other brands as well. So, various theories have emerged, none of which have proven to be definitive. That's especially true since Nikon puts a shorter, 20-minute limit on its so-called "high quality" movie files.

- The sensor will overheat when you shoot continuously. In a mirrorless camera, the sensor is active virtually all the time the camera is turned on, so that idea doesn't hold water. Plus, you can shoot one 29-minute clip, then immediately begin another one. Thermal protection doesn't seem to be a problem, or the reason for the limitation.
- Some countries, particularly in the European Union, classify cameras that can capture clips of 30 minutes or more as camcorders, at a higher duty rate.
- The FAT32 file format limits the size of video clips to 2GB, or about 30 minutes. Actually, it's the FAT16 file format (used in pre-SDHC memory cards) that has the 2GB limitation. All memory cards larger than 2GB will let you create a file that's 4GB in size. Further, my 64GB SDXC card allows files up to 2 terabytes in size, but when I insert one into my D810, I still can't exceed 29 minutes, 59 seconds.
- Theories aside, the only people who want to shoot clips longer than 30 minutes are the proud parents who plop the D810 down on a tripod and capture an entire Spring Pageant or high school musical. Those who want to go beyond camcorder ennui will shoot segments of only a few seconds each and, perhaps, piece them together into an effective production using easy-to-master editing software.

- **Carry extra cards.** You're probably used to shooting still photographs. It's easy to estimate how much of your memory card's capacity you've already consumed, and how much is left, based on the shots remaining indicator on the D810's LCD monitor and viewfinder displays. Video usage is a bit of a different animal. While the camera does show how much space you have remaining for a clip as you shoot, it's often difficult to make the connection to the remaining capacity of your memory card. It's necessary to make a trip to the Movie Settings entry in the Shooting menu to see exactly how much space you have left. So, the best practice is to carry along many more cards than you think you need. I stuff a pair of 64GB CF and SDXC cards in my D810—enough for 5 hours of video each—but always carry along five 32GB cards as backup.
- **Add an external mic.** For the best sound quality, and to avoid picking up the sound of the autofocus or zoom motor, get an external stereo mic. I'll have more advice about capturing sound in Chapter 16.
- **Minimize zooming.** While it's great to be able to use the zoom for filling the frame with a distant subject, think twice before zooming. Unless you are using an external mic, the sound of the zoom ring rotating will be picked up and it will be audible when you play a movie. Any more than the occasional minor zoom will be very distracting to friends who watch your videos. And digital zoom will definitely degrade image quality. Don't use the digital zoom if quality is more important than recording a specific subject such as a famous movie star far from a distance.

WHAT FRAME RATE: 24 fps or 30/60 fps?

Even intermediate movie shooters can be confused by the choice between 24 fps and 30/60 fps, especially since those are only nominal figures (with the D810, the 24 fps setting actually yields 23.976 frames per second; 30 fps gives you 29.97 actual "frames" per second; while 60 fps yields 59.94). The difference lies in the two "worlds" of motion images, film and video. The standard frame rate for motion picture film is 24 fps, while the video rate, at least in the United States, Japan, and other places using the NTSC standard, is 30 fps (actually 60 interlaced *fields* per second). Most computer video-editing software can handle either type, and convert between them. The choice between 24 fps and 30 fps is determined by what you plan to do with your video. Your camera can also shoot at 25/50 fps for use with PAL systems, which don't use NTSC standards.

The short explanation is that, for technical reasons I won't go into here, shooting at 24 fps gives your movie a "film" look, excellent for showing fine detail. (I'll have more to say about that later in this chapter.)

However, if your clip has moving subjects, or you pan the camera, 24 fps can produce a jerky effect called "judder." A 30/60 fps rate produces a home-video look that some feel is less desirable, but which is smoother and less jittery when displayed on an electronic monitor. I suggest you try both and use the frame rate that best suits your tastes and video-editing software.

- **Use a fully charged battery.** A fresh battery will allow about one hour of filming at normal (non-Winter) temperatures, but that can be shorter if there are many focus adjustments. Individual clips can be no longer than 29 minutes, however.
- **Keep it cool.** Video quality can suffer terribly when the imaging sensor gets hot so keep the camera in a cool place. When shooting on hot days especially, the sensor can get hot quicker than usual; when there's a risk of overheating, the camera will stop recording and it will shut down about five seconds later. Give it time to cool down before using it again.
- **Press the Movie button.** You don't have to hold it down. Press it again when you're done to stop recording.

Capturing Video

In the Movie Settings entry of the Shooting menu, you can make the following choices:

- **Frame size/Frame rate.** Choose from 1920 × 1080 at 60, 50, 30, 25, or 24 fps; 1280 × 720 at 60, 50, 30, or 25 fps. You can also select *cropped* capture using a 2.7X crop to achieve a telephoto effect for 1920 × 1080 pixels at 30, 25, and 24 fps.
- **Movie Quality.** Choose High Quality or Normal Quality.
- **Microphone Sensitivity.** Select from Auto Sensitivity and Manual Sensitivity settings with levels from 1–20. (See Figure 15.1.)
- **Frequency Response.** This entry lets you specify a Wide Range or Vocal Range response.
- **Wind noise reduction.** This setting allows you to turn your microphone's wind noise canceling circuitry on or off.

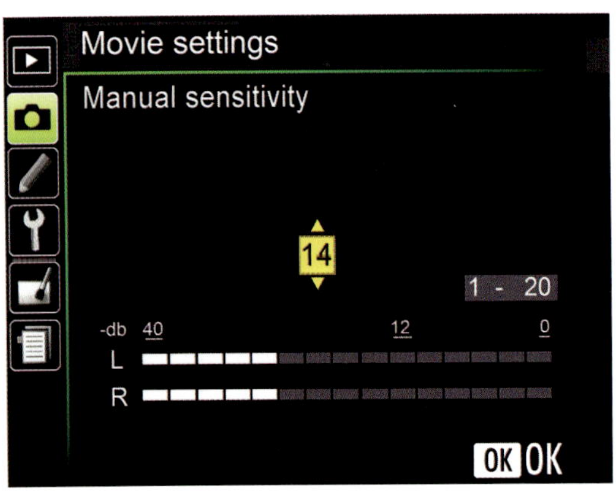

Figure 15.1 Microphone sensitivity can be set manually, using an audio meter (bottom) as a reference.

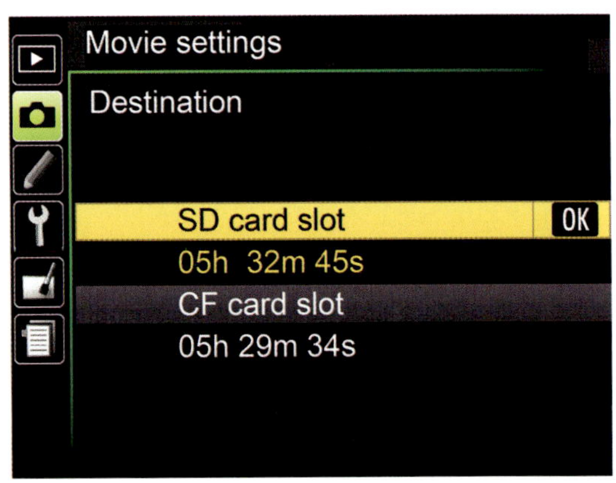

Figure 15.2 Choose the destination for your video clips; usually you'll want to select the fastest card or the card with the highest capacity.

NOT MUCH OF A LIMITATION

Unless you are shooting an entire performance from a fixed position, such as a stage play, the near-30-minute limitation on HDTV movie duration won't put much of a crimp in your style. Good motion picture practice calls for each production to consist of a series of relatively *short* clips, with 10 to 20 seconds a good average. You can assemble and edit your D810 movies into one long, finished production using one of the many movie-editing software packages available. Andy Warhol might have been successful with his 1963 five-hour epic *Sleep*, but the rest of us will do better with short sequences of the type produced by the Nikon D810.

- **Destination.** Choose the slot containing the memory card you want to store your movies on (Figure 15.2); generally, use the slot containing the fastest memory card.
- **Movie ISO sensitivity settings.** These settings allow you to choose ISO sensitivity in Manual exposure mode from ISO 200 to Hi 2, and turn Auto ISO On or Off while shooting movies in Manual exposure mode. Maximum sensitivity can be set from ISO 400 through Hi 2.

To shoot your movies, follow these steps, which are similar to those for using live view:

1. **Plug in microphone.** If you want to use an external monaural or stereo microphone with a 3.5mm stereo mini plug, attach it to the microphone jack on the left side of the camera.
2. **Choose an exposure mode.** Select Program, Shutter-priority, Aperture-priority, or Manual exposure. The D810 uses Matrix metering based on readings from the sensor itself to determine exposure.
3. **Adjust exposure.** The adjustments you can make depend on the exposure mode you select. You'll find more about exposure in the section that follows this one.
   - **Program/Shutter-priority.** Adjust only exposure compensation by pressing the EV button on top of the camera and rotating the main command dial. The screen image will brighten and darken as you make adjustments. Shutter speed and ISO sensitivity are selected for you by the D810.
   - **Aperture-priority.** You can change the f/stop by rotating the sub-command dial, and adjust exposure compensation with the EV button and the main command dial. Shutter speed and ISO sensitivity are selected for you by the D810.
   - **Manual exposure.** The main command dial changes the shutter speed (from 1/25th to 1/8000th second), and the sub-command dial adjusts the aperture. Press the ISO button and rotate the main command dial to change the ISO sensitivity.
4. **Start live view.** Activate live view by rotating the Lv switch to the movie position. Then press the Lv button.

5. **Choose a focus mode.** Select from autofocus or manual focus with the AF/MF switch on the camera body. Choose AF-S or AF-F by pressing the focus mode button in the center of the AF/MF switch and rotating the main command dial. Note that you can refocus by pressing the AF-ON button.
6. **Choose an AF-area mode.** Select autofocus area by pressing the focus mode button in the center of the AF/MF switch and rotating the sub-command dial. Choices include Face-priority AF, Wide-area AF, Normal-area AF, or Subject-tracking AF. You'll find complete descriptions of focus and AF-area modes in Chapter 5.
7. **Start/Stop recording.** Press the red movie recording button to lock in focus and begin capture. Press again to stop recording. The live view display as you're capturing video looks like Figure 15.3. You can press the Info button to increase or decrease the amount of information overlaid on the screen during movie recording. The displays in movie live view mode are similar to still mode and include: Information on, information off, grid framing guides, virtual horizon, and a live histogram.

- **Mark indices.** While you are shooting you can add an index to a specific spot that will enable you to locate a specific frame during editing. As many as 20 indices can be added for any given clip by pressing the Preview button during capture. A cyan balloon icon appears on the live view screen at the upper-right side to indicate that an index has been stored. The icon turns red when you exceed the 20-indice limit. To enable this capability, you must choose Index Marking as the function for the Preview button using Custom Settings menu choice g2, described in Chapter 12.

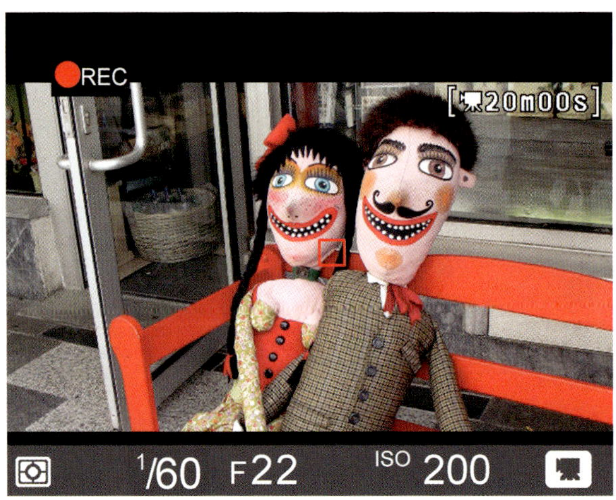

Figure 15.3
The live view display during movie capture.

Stop That!

You might think that setting your D810 to a faster shutter speed will help give you sharper video frames. But the choice of a shutter speed for movie making is a bit more complicated than that. First, you can't select the shutter speed at all for your movies when you're using P, S, or A exposure modes. You can select a shutter speed only if you switch to Manual exposure. Here's how it works:

- **Program and Shutter-priority modes.** The D810 selects the shutter speed (such as 1/30th second) and ISO sensitivity appropriate for your lighting conditions. Your only exposure adjustment option is to press the EV button and add/subtract exposure compensation. As you might guess, P and S modes are not the best choices for those who want to shoot creatively.
- **Aperture-priority mode.** This is the mode to use when you want to put selective focus to work by choosing an aperture that will provide more, or less, depth-of-field. In A mode, you can select any f/stop available with your lens, and the D810 will choose a shutter speed and ISO setting to suit. Generally, if you choose a large aperture, the camera will lower the ISO sensitivity as much as it can, to allow sticking with a shutter speed of 1/30th second. It will then select shorter shutter speeds, if necessary, under very bright illumination. My D810 has jumped up to 1/250th second outdoors under bright daylight when I try to shoot at f/1.8 or f/1.4. In A mode, you can still add or subtract exposure compensation.
- **Manual exposure mode.** In this mode, you have control of aperture, shutter speed (from 1/30th second all the way up to 1/8000th second), and ISO—even if your settings result in video that is completely washed out, or entirely black. Because video capture is in the range of 24 to 60 frames per second, you can't select a shutter speed that is longer than the frame interval. That is, if your video mode is 1920 × 1080 at 30 fps, you can't choose a shutter speed longer than 1/30th second. What you can't do in M mode is add or subtract exposure compensation, but with full control over all three legs of the exposure triangle, you shouldn't have to.

So, how do you select an appropriate shutter speed? As you might guess, it's almost always best to leave the shutter speed at 1/30th second, and allow the overall exposure to be adjusted by varying the aperture and/or ISO sensitivity. We don't normally stare at a video frame for longer than 1/30th or 1/24th second, so while the shakiness of the *camera* can be disruptive (and often corrected by VR), if there is a bit of blur in our *subjects* from movement, we tend not to notice. Each frame flashes by in the blink of an eye, so to speak, so a shutter speed of 1/30th second works a lot better in video than it does when shooting stills.

Higher shutter speeds actually introduce problems of their own. If you shoot a video frame using a shutter speed of 1/250th second, the actual moment in time that's captured represents only about 12 percent of the 1/30th second of elapsed time in that frame. Yet, when played back, that frame occupies the full 1/30th of a second, with 88 percent of that time filled by stretching the original image to fill it. The result is often a choppy/jumpy image, and one that may appear to be *too* sharp.

The reason for that is more social imprinting than scientific: we've all grown up accustomed to seeing the look of Hollywood productions that, by convention, were shot using a shutter speed that's half the reciprocal of the frame rate (that is, 1/48th second for a 24 fps movie). Movie cameras use a rotary shutter (achieving that 1/48th second exposure by using a 180 degree shutter "angle"), but the effect on our visual expectations is the same. For the most "film-like" appearance, use 24 fps and 1/60th second shutter speed.

Faster shutter speeds do have some specialized uses for motion analysis, especially where individual frames are studied. The rest of the time, 1/30th or 1/60th of a second will suffice. If the reason you needed a higher shutter speed was to obtain the correct exposure, use a slower ISO setting, or a neutral-density filter to cut down on the amount of light passing through the lens.

A good rule of thumb when shooting progressive video (as opposed to interlaced video, which is not offered by the D810) is to use 1/60th second or slower when shooting at 24 fps; 1/60th second or slower at 30 fps; and 1/125th second or slower at 60 fps.

Viewing Your Movies

Once you've finished recording your movies, they are available for review. Film clips show up during picture review, the same as still photos, but they are differentiated by a movie camera icon overlay. Press the center of the multi selector to start playback.

During playback, you can perform the following functions:

- **Pause.** Press the multi selector down button to pause the clip during playback. Press the multi selector center button to resume playback.
- **Rewind/Advance.** Press the left/right multi selector buttons to rewind or advance (respectively). Press once for 2X speed, twice for 8X speed, or three times for 16X speed. Hold down the left/right buttons to move to the end or beginning of the clip.
- **Skip to index.** Rotate the main command dial to skip to the next or previous index marker. If there are no indices saved, the command dial moves to the last or first frame of the clip.
- **Change volume.** Press the Zoom In and Zoom Out buttons to increase/decrease volume.
- **Trim movie.** Press the OK button and follow the steps in the next section.
- **Exit Playback.** Press the multi selector up button to exit playback.
- **Return to shooting mode.** Press the shutter release button to return to shooting mode.
- **View menus.** Press the MENU button to interrupt playback to access menus.

Trimming Your Movies

In-camera editing is limited to trimming the beginning or end from a clip, and the clip must be at least two seconds long. For more advanced editing, you'll need an application capable of editing AVI movie clips. Google "AVI Editor" to locate any of the hundreds of free video editors available, or use a commercial product like Corel Video Studio, Adobe Premiere Elements, or Pinnacle Studio. These will let you combine several clips into one movie, add titles, special effects, and transitions between scenes.

In-camera editing/trimming can be done from the Retouch menu, or during Playback. The procedure is the same. To do in-camera editing/trimming, follow these steps:

1. **Start movie clip.** Use the Playback button to start image review, and press the multi selector center button to start playback when you see a clip you want to edit. It will begin playing. Then follow the instructions beginning with Step 2. Or, when you see the clip on the screen that you want to edit, press the OK button to produce the Edit Movie screen shown in Figure 15.4. Highlight Choose Start/End Point, and press OK to continue.
2. **Activate edit.** To remove video from the beginning of a clip, view the movie until you reach the first frame you want to keep, and then press the down button to pause. The movie progress bar at the bottom left of the screen will show the current position in the movie, as shown in Figure 15.5. To trim video from the end of a clip, watch the movie until you reach the last frame you want to keep and then press the down button to pause. You can jump to the next saved index point in the clip by rotating the main command dial.
3. **Select start/end point.** When the video is paused, press the OK button to show the movie edit options, and select Choose Start/End Point. You'll be asked whether the current frame should be the start or end point. Highlight your choice and press OK again.

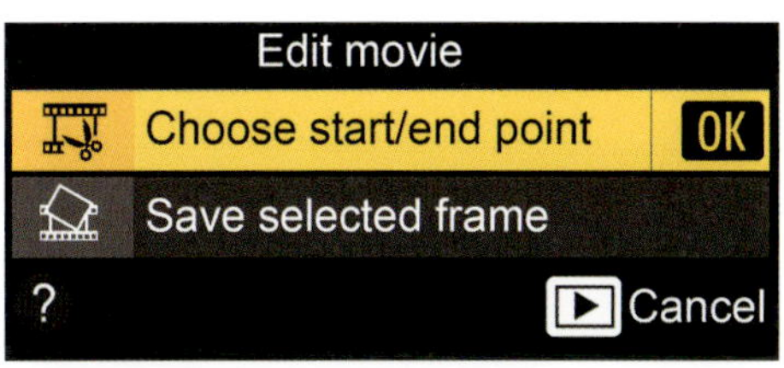

Figure 15.4 Choose editing options from this menu.

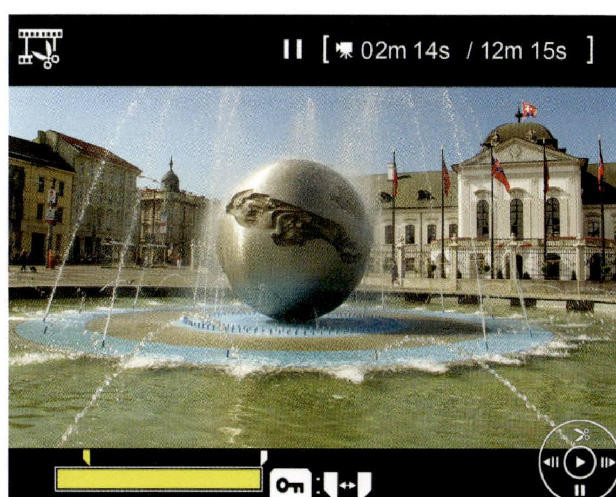

Figure 15.5 Edit your movie.

4. **Resume playback.** Press the center button of the multi selector to start or resume playback. You can use the Pause, Rewind, Advance, and Single frame controls plus the main control dial (to jump to the next saved index point) as described previously to move around within your clip.
5. **Confirm trim.** A Proceed? prompt appears. Choose Yes or No, and press OK.
6. **Save movie.** You have four choices when saving the trimmed movie:
   - **Save As New File.** The trimmed clip will be stored as a new file, and the original movie preserved.
   - **Overwrite Existing File.** The trimmed clip replaces the original movie on your memory card. Use this option with caution, as you'll be unable to restore your unedited clip.
   - **Cancel.** Return to the editing mode.
   - **Preview.** View the trimmed version. You can then save as a new file, overwrite, or cancel.

   You'll see a Saving Movie message and a green progress bar as the D810 stores the trimmed clip to your memory card. Storage takes some time, and you don't want to interrupt it to avoid losing your saved clip. So, make sure your camera has a fully charged battery before you start to edit a clip.

Saving a Frame

You can store any frame from one of your movies as a JPEG still, using the resolution of the current video format. Just follow these steps:

1. Pause your movie at the frame you want to save by pressing the down button.
2. Press the *i* button and choose Save Selected Frame.
3. Press the up button to save a still copy of the selected frame.
4. Choose Proceed and press OK to confirm.
5. Your frame will be stored on the memory card, and will be marked with a scissors icon.

The actual resolution of your video "stills" is shown in Table 15.1.

Table 15.1 Video Still Sizes

Image Area	Large Image Size	Medium Image Size	Small Image Size
FX	6720 × 3776 pixels (25MP)	5040 × 2832 pixels (14MP)	3360 × 1888 pixels (6.3MP)
DX	4800 × 2704 pixels (13MP)	3600 × 2024 pixels (7.3MP)	2400 × 1352 pixels (3.2MP)

16

Advanced Movie-Making Techniques

Once upon a time, the ability to shoot video with a digital still camera was one of those "Gee whiz" gimmicks camera makers seemed to include just to have a reason to get you to buy a new camera. That hasn't been true for a couple of years now, as the video quality of many digital still cameras has gotten quite good. The D810 is a stellar example. It's capable of HD-quality video and is actually capable of outperforming typical modestly priced digital video camcorders, especially when you consider the range of lenses and other helpful accessories available for it.

Tips for Shooting Better Video

Producing good-quality video is more complicated than just buying good equipment. There are techniques that make for gripping storytelling and a visual language the average person is very used to, but also pretty unaware of.

After all, by comparison we're used to watching the best productions that television, video, and motion pictures can offer. Whether it's fair or not, our efforts are compared to what we're used to seeing produced by experts. While this book can't make you a professional videographer, there is some advice I can give you that will help you improve your results with the camera.

There are a number of different things to consider when planning a video shoot, and when possible, a shooting script and storyboard can help you produce a higher-quality video.

VIDEO FORMATS

Your Nikon D810 captures its video in the standard MPEG-4/H.264 format, which compresses that stream of 1920 × 1080-pixel (or 1280 × 720-pixel) images as much as 50X. That's the *capture format.* The video is then saved as a MOV *file.*

Lens Craft

I covered the use of lenses with the D810 in more detail in Chapter 7, but a discussion of lens selection when shooting movies may be useful at this point. In the video world, not all lenses are created equal. The two most important considerations are depth-of-field, or the beneficial lack thereof, and zooming. I'll address each of these separately.

Depth-of-Field and Video

Have you wondered why professional videographers have gone nuts over still cameras that can also shoot video? The producers of *Saturday Night Live* could afford to have Alex Buono, their director of photography, use the niftiest, most expensive high-resolution video cameras to shoot the opening sequences of the program. Instead, Buono opted for a pair of digital SLR cameras. One thing that makes digital still cameras so attractive for video is that they have relatively large sensors, which provides improved low-light performance and results in the oddly attractive reduced depth-of-field, compared with most professional video cameras.

But wait! you say. No matter what size sensor is used to capture a full HD video frame, isn't the number of pixels in that frame exactly the same—1920 × 1080 pixels? That's true—the final resolution of the video image is exactly 1920 × 1080 pixels, whether you're capturing that frame with a point-and-shoot camera, a professional video camera, or a full-frame digital SLR like the Nikon D810. But that's only the *final* resolution. The number of pixels used to capture each video frame varies by sensor size.

For example, your D810 does *not* use only its central 1920 × 1080 pixels to capture a full HD video frame. If it did that, you'd have to contend with a 3.8X "crop" factor, and the field of view of, say, a 24mm wide angle would be the equivalent of a 90mm telephoto. That doesn't happen! (See Chapter 7 for a longer discussion of the effects of the so-called "crop" factor.)

Instead, the D810 captures a video frame using the proportions of a 16:9 area of its sensor. The capture area is only a little smaller than the full frame, as shown in Figure 16.1, producing a negligible 1.1X crop factor. Your wide-angle and telephoto lenses retain roughly their same fields of view, and you can frame and compose your video through the viewfinder normally, with only the top and bottom of the frame and a little off each side cropped off to account for the wider video aspect ratio. The image in that area is interpolated down to the final 1920 × 1080 rectangle shown in the center of the figure.

The pixels used to capture the image are processed to create the 2,073,600 pixels of the final video frame. That's why the D810 gives you such great video quality, and why your video images retain roughly the same field of view and exact same depth-of-field you get with full-frame still images.

Figure 16.2 provides a comparison of the relative size of sensors. The typical size of a professional video camera sensor is shown at lower left. The sensor of the typical point-and-shoot camera is shown just northeast of it, and an APS-C-sized sensor to the right of that. In comparison, the D810's FX image-grabber is *much* larger when compared with the sensors used in many pro video cameras and the even smaller sensors found in the typical computer camcorder.

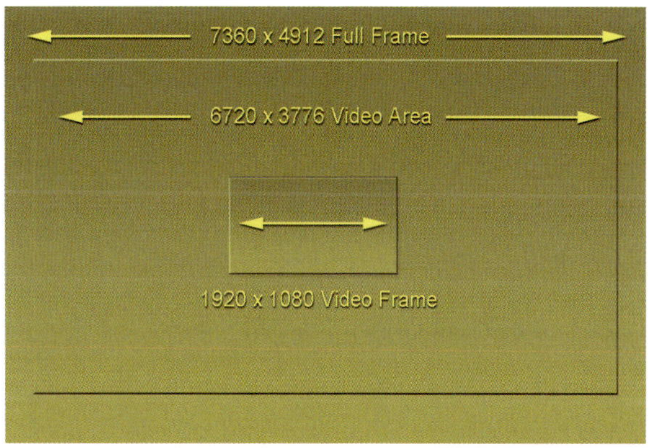

Figure 16.1 The D810's video capture area and final video frame size.

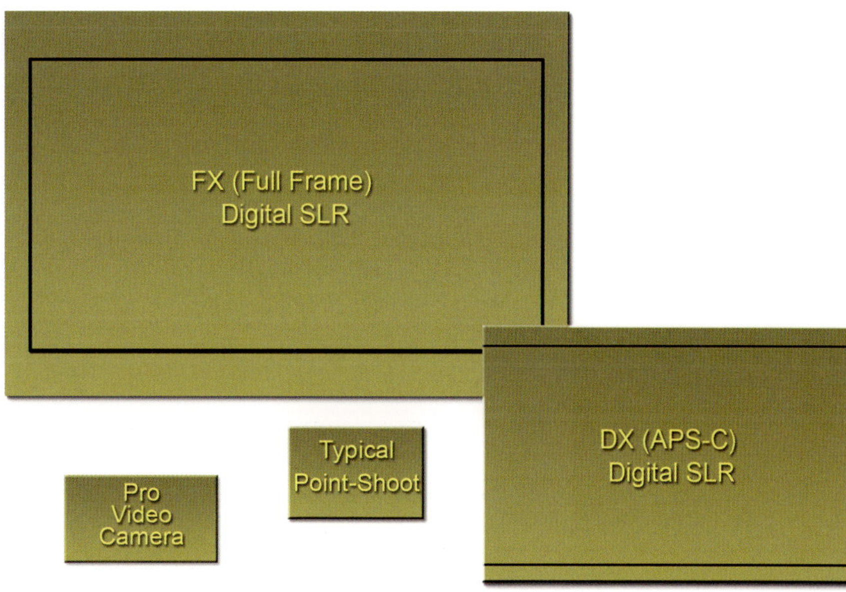

Figure 16.2 Sensor size comparison.

As you learned in Chapter 7, a larger sensor calls for the use of longer focal lengths to produce the same field of view, so, in effect, a larger sensor has reduced depth-of-field. And *that's* what makes cameras like the D810 attractive from a creative standpoint. Less depth-of-field means greater control over the range of what's in focus. Your D810, with its larger sensor, has a distinct advantage over consumer camcorders in this regard, and even does a better job than many professional video cameras.

Zooming and Video

When shooting still photos, a zoom is a zoom is a zoom. The key considerations for a zoom lens used only for still photography are the maximum aperture available at each focal length ("How *fast* is this lens?), the zoom range ("How far can I zoom in or out?"), and its sharpness at any given f/stop ("Do I lose sharpness when I shoot wide open?").

When shooting video, the priorities may change, and there are two additional parameters to consider. The first two I listed, lens speed and zoom range, have roughly the same importance in both still and video photography. Zoom range gains a bit of importance in videography, because you can always/usually move closer to shoot a still photograph, but when you're zooming during a shot most of us don't have that option (or the funds to buy/rent a dolly to smoothly move the camera during capture). But, oddly enough, overall sharpness may have slightly less importance under certain conditions when shooting video. That's because the image changes in some way many times per second (24/60 times per second with the D810), so any given frame doesn't hang around long enough for our eyes to pick out every single detail. You want a sharp image, of course, but your standards don't need to be quite as high when shooting video.

Here are the remaining considerations:

- **Zoom lens maximum aperture.** The speed of the lens matters in several ways. A zoom with a relatively large maximum aperture lets you shoot in lower light levels, and a big f/stop allows you to minimize depth-of-field for selective focus. Keep in mind that the maximum aperture may change during zooming. A lens that offers an f/3.5 maximum aperture at its widest focal length may provide only f/5.6 worth of light at the telephoto position.
- **Zoom range.** Use of zoom during actual capture should not be an everyday thing, unless you're shooting a kung-fu movie. However, there are effective uses for a zoom shot, particularly if it's a "long" one from extreme wide angle to extreme close-up (or vice versa). Most of the time, you'll use the zoom range to adjust the perspective of the camera *between* shots, and a longer zoom range can mean less trotting back and forth to adjust the field of view. Zoom range also comes into play when you're working with selective focus (longer focal lengths have less depth-of-field), or want to expand or compress the apparent distance between foreground and background subjects. A longer range gives you more flexibility.

- **Linearity.** Interchangeable lenses may have some drawbacks, as many photographers who have been using the video features of their digital SLRs have discovered. That's because, unless a lens is optimized for video shooting, zooming with a particular lens may not necessarily be linear. Rotating the zoom collar manually at a constant speed doesn't always produce a smooth zoom. There may be "jumps" as the elements of the lens shift around during the zoom. Keep that in mind if you plan to zoom during a shot, and are using a lens that has proved, from experience, to provide a non-linear zoom. (Unfortunately, there's no easy way to tell ahead of time whether you own a lens that is well suited for zooming during a shot.)

Keep Things Stable and on the Level

Camera shake's enough of a problem with still photography, but it becomes even more of a nuisance when you're shooting video. The image-stabilization feature found in many Nikon lenses (and some third-party optics) can help minimize this. That's why Nikon's 24-120mm f/4, 16-35mm f/4, and the 24-85mm VR FX lenses (described in Chapter 7) make an excellent choice for video shooting if you're planning on going for the hand-held cinema verité look.

Just realize that while hand-held camera shots—even image stabilized—may be perfect if you're shooting a documentary or video that intentionally mimics traditional home movie making, in other contexts it can be disconcerting or annoying. And even VR can't work miracles. As I'll point out in the next section, it's the camera movement itself that is distracting—not necessarily any blur in our subject matter.

If you want your video to look professional, putting the D810 on a tripod will give you smoother, steadier video clips to work with. It will be easier to intercut shots taken from different angles (or even at different times) if everything was shot on a tripod. Cutting from a tripod shot to a hand-held shot, or even from one hand-held shot to another one that has noticeably more (or less) camera movement can call attention to what otherwise might have been a smooth cut or transition.

Remember that telephoto lenses and telephoto zoom focal lengths magnify any camera shake, even with VR, so when you're using a longer focal length, that tripod becomes an even better idea. Tripods are essential if you want to pan from side to side during a shot, dolly in and out, or track from side to side (say, you want to shoot with the camera in your kid's coaster wagon). A tripod and (for panning) a fluid head built especially for smooth video movements can add a lot of production value to your movies.

Shooting Script

A shooting script is nothing more than a coordinated plan that covers both audio and video and provides order and structure for your video when you're in planned, storytelling mode. A detailed script will cover what types of shots you're going after, what dialogue you're going to use, audio effects, transitions, and graphics. A good script needn't constrain you: as the director you are free to make changes on the spot during actual capture. But, before you change the route to your final destination, it's good to know where you were headed, and how you originally planned to get there.

When putting together your shooting script, plan for lots and lots of different shots, even if you don't think you'll need them. Only amateurish videos consist of a bunch of long, tedious shots. You'll want to vary the pace of your production by cutting among lots of different views, angles, and perspectives, so jot down your ideas for these variations when you put together your script.

If you're shooting a documentary rather than telling a story that's already been completely mapped out, the idea of using a shooting script needs to be applied more flexibly. Documentary filmmakers often have no shooting script at all. They go out, do their interviews, capture video of people, places, and events as they find them, and allow the structure of the story to take shape as they learn more about the subject of their documentary. In such cases, the movie is typically "created" during editing, as bits and pieces are assembled into the finished piece.

Storyboards

A storyboard makes a great adjunct to a detailed shooting script. It is a series of panels providing visuals of what each scene should look like. While the ones produced by Hollywood are generally of very high quality, there's nothing that says drawing skills are important for this step. Stick figures work just fine if that's the best you can do. The storyboard just helps you visualize locations, placement of actors/actresses, props and furniture, and also helps everyone involved get an idea of what you're trying to show. It also helps show how you want to frame or compose a shot. You can even shoot a series of still photos and transform them into a "storyboard" if you want, such as in Figure 16.3.

Storytelling in Video

Today's audience is used to fast-paced, short-scene storytelling. In order to produce interesting video for such viewers, it's important to view video storytelling as a kind of shorthand code for the more leisurely efforts print media offers. Audio and video should always be advancing the story. While it's okay to let the camera linger from time to time, it should only be for a compelling reason and only briefly.

Above all, look for movement in your scene as you shoot. You're not taking still photographs! Perhaps your ideal still picture of an old castle in Segovia, Spain might be to show the edifice in its modern-day surroundings, but a movie needs to show something *moving,* like the hang glider who soared overhead when I captured the image shown in Figure 16.4.

It only takes a second or two for an establishing shot to impart the necessary information. For example, many of the scenes for a video documenting a model being photographed in a Rock and Roll music setting might be close-ups and talking heads, but an establishing shot showing the studio where the video was captured helps set the scene.

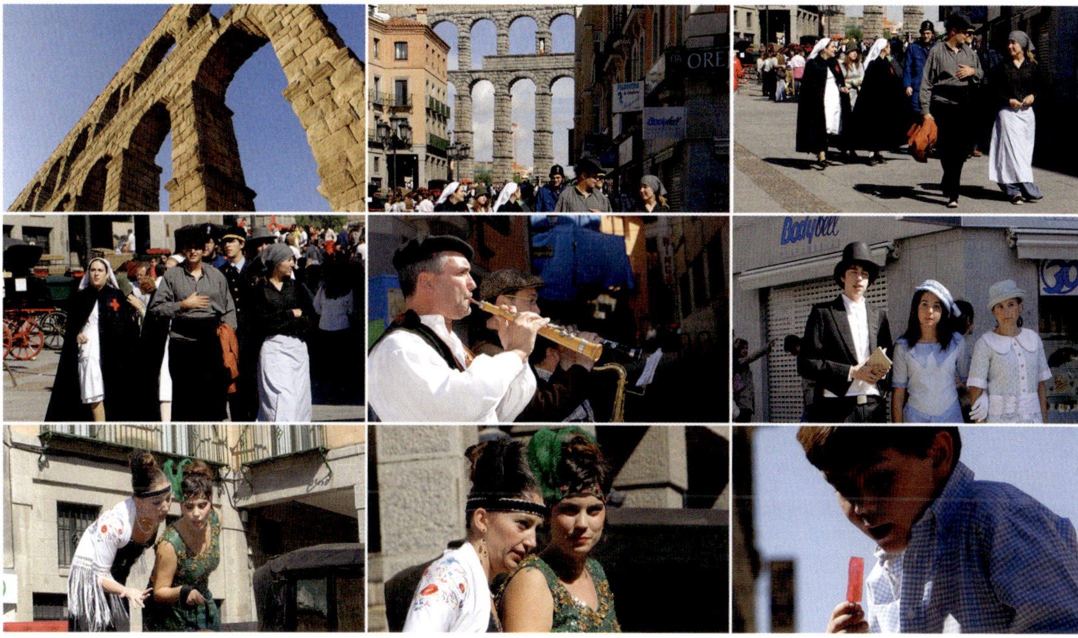

Figure 16.3 A storyboard is a series of simple sketches or photos to help visualize a segment of video

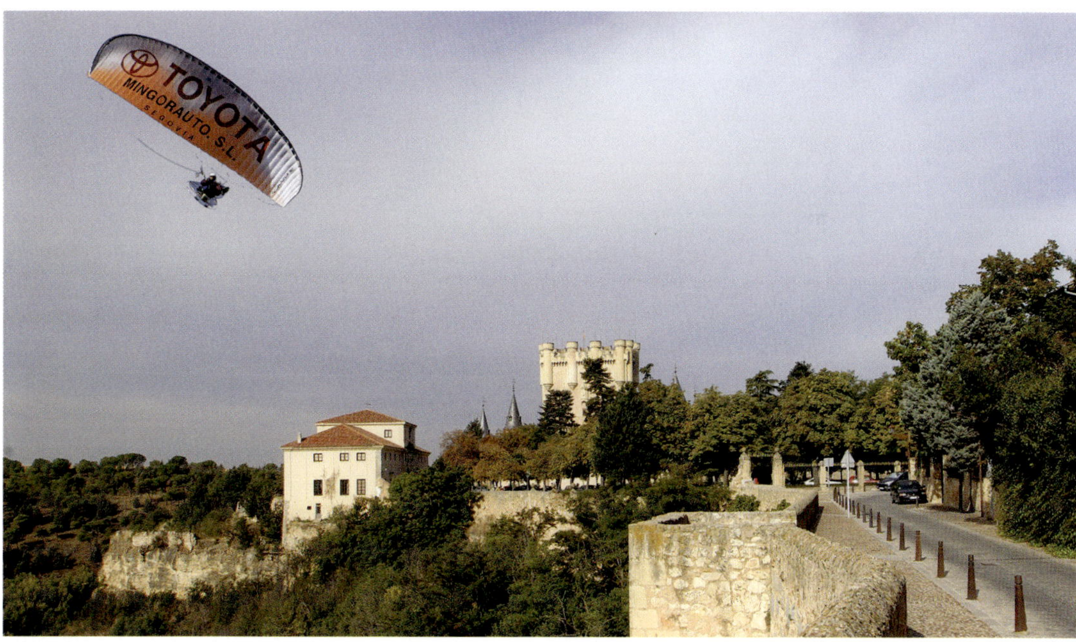

Figure 16.4 Movies need motion to come alive.

Provide variety too. If you put your shooting script together correctly, you'll be changing camera angles and perspectives often and never leave a static scene on the screen for a long period of time. (You can record a static scene for a reasonably long period and then edit in other shots that cut away and back to the longer scene with close-ups that show each person talking.)

When editing, keep transitions basic! I can't stress this one enough. Watch a television program or movie. The action "jumps" from one scene or person to the next. Fancy transitions that involve exotic "wipes," dissolves, or cross fades take too long for the average viewer and make your video ponderous.

Composition

In movie shooting, several factors restrict your composition, and impose requirements you just don't always have in still photography (although other rules of good composition do apply). Here are some of the key differences to keep in mind when composing movie frames:

- **Horizontal compositions only.** Some subjects, such as basketball players and tall buildings, just lend themselves to vertical compositions. But movies are shown in horizontal format only. So if you're interviewing a local basketball star, you can end up with a worst-case situation like the one shown in Figure 16.5. If you want to show how tall your subject is, it's often impractical to move back far enough to show him full-length. You really can't capture a vertical composition. Tricks like getting down on the floor and shooting up at your subject can exaggerate the perspective, but aren't a perfect solution.

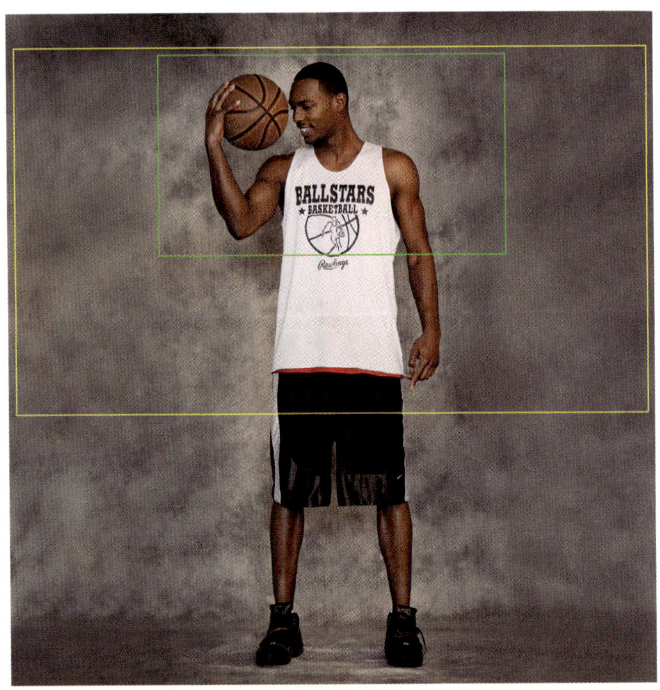

Figure 16.5
Movie shooting requires you to fit all your subjects into a horizontally oriented frame.

- **Wasted space at the sides.** Moving in to frame the basketball player as outlined by the yellow box in Figure 16.5 means that you're still forced to leave a lot of empty space on either side. (Of course, you can fill that space with other people and/or interesting stuff, but that defeats your intent of concentrating on your main subject.) So when faced with some types of subjects in a horizontal frame, you can be creative, or move in *really* tight. For example, if I was willing to give up the "height" aspect of my composition, I could have framed the shot as shown by the green box in the figure, and wasted less of the image area at either side.
- **Seamless (or seamed) transitions.** Unless you're telling a picture story with a photo essay, still pictures often stand alone. But with movies, each of your compositions must relate to the shot that preceded it, and the one that follows. It can be jarring to jump from a long shot to a tight close-up unless the director—you—is very creative. Another common error is the "jump cut" in which successive shots vary only slightly in camera angle, making it appear that the main subject has "jumped" from one place to another. (Although everyone from French New Wave director Jean-Luc Goddard to Guy Ritchie—Madonna's ex—have used jump cuts effectively in their films.) The rule of thumb is to vary the camera angle by at least 30 degrees between shots to make it appear to be seamless. Unless you prefer that your images flaunt convention and appear to be "seamy."
- **The time dimension.** Unlike still photography, with motion pictures there's a lot more emphasis on using a series of images to build on each other to tell a story. Static shots where the camera is mounted on a tripod and everything is shot from the same distance are a recipe for dull videos. Watch a television program sometime and notice how often camera shots change distances and directions. Viewers are used to this variety and have come to expect it. Professional video productions are often done with multiple cameras shooting from different angles and positions. But many professional productions are shot with just one camera and careful planning, and you can do just fine with your D810.

Here's a look at the different types of commonly used compositional tools:

- **Establishing shot.** Much like it sounds, this type of composition, as shown in Figure 16.6, establishes the scene and tells the viewer where the action is taking place. Let's say you're shooting a video of your offspring's move to college; the establishing shot could be a wide shot of the campus with a sign welcoming you to the school in the foreground. Another example would be for a child's birthday party; the establishing shot could be the front of the house decorated with birthday signs and streamers or a shot of the dining room table decked out with party favors and a candle-covered birthday cake. Or, in Figure 16.6, I wanted to show the studio where the video was shot.
- **Medium shot.** This shot is composed from about waist to head room (some space above the subject's head). It's useful for providing variety from a series of close-ups and also makes for a useful first look at a speaker. (See Figure 16.7.)

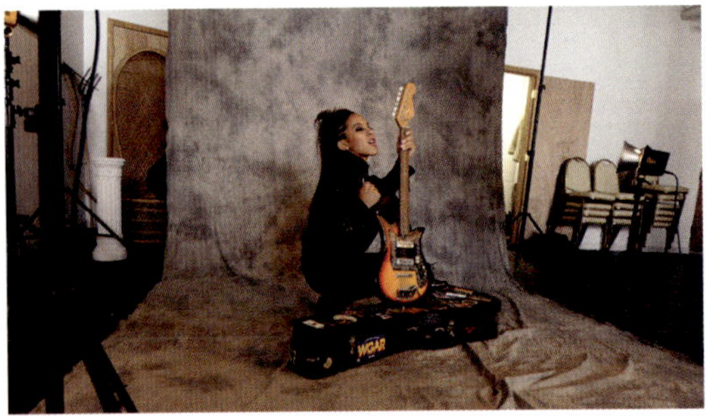

Figure 16.6 An establishing shot sets the stage for your video scene.

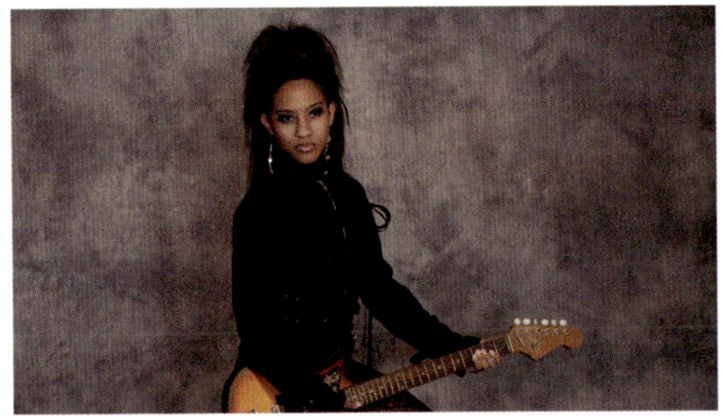

Figure 16.7 A medium shot is used to bring the viewer into a scene without shocking them. It can be used to introduce a character and provide context via their surroundings.

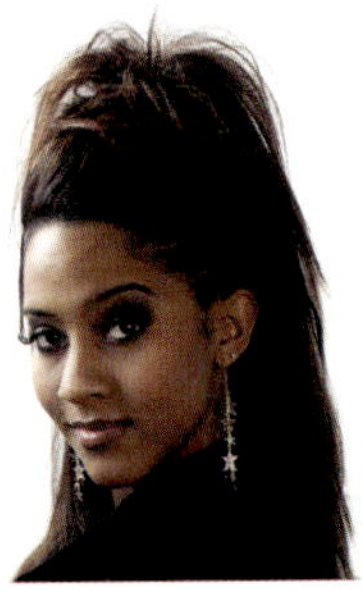

Figure 16.8 A close-up generally shows the full face with a little head room at the top and down to the shoulders at the bottom of the frame.

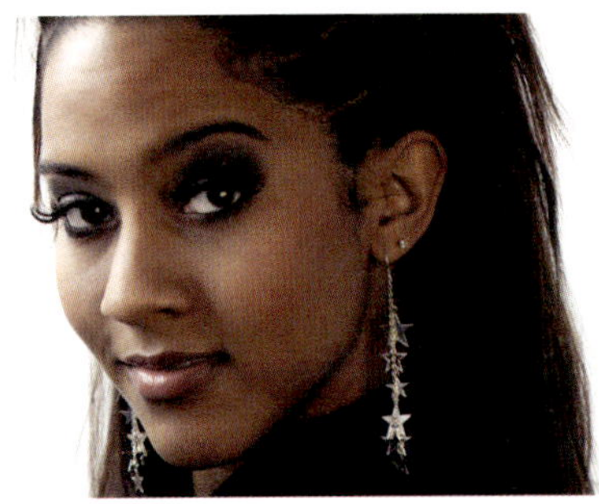

Figure 16.9 An extreme close-up is a very tight shot that cuts off everything above the top of the head and below the chin (or even closer!). Be careful using this shot since many of us look better from a distance!

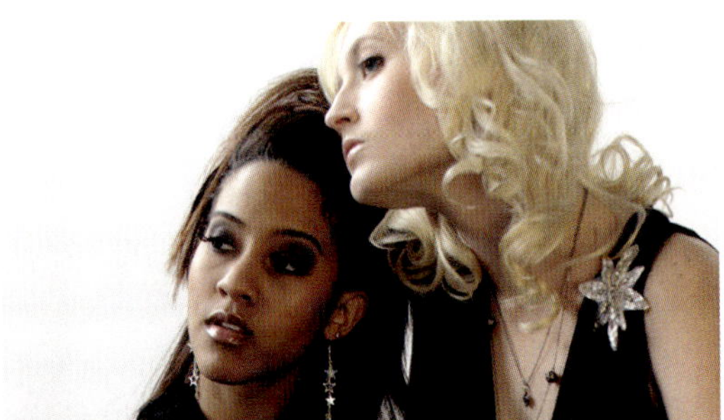

Figure 16.10 A "two shot" features two people in the frame. This version can be framed at various distances such as medium or close-up.

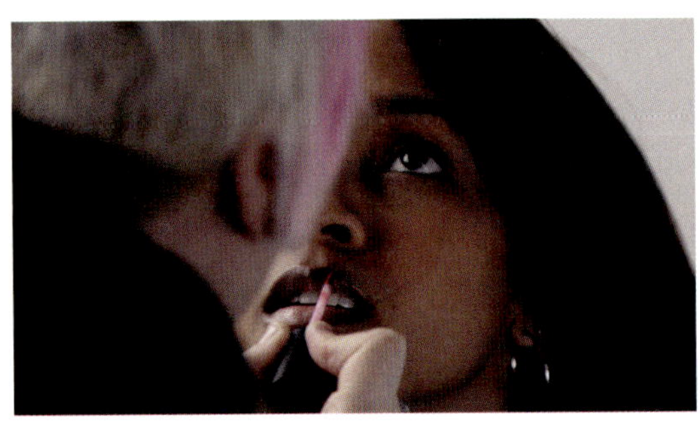

Figure 16.11 An "over-the-shoulder" shot is a popular shot for interview programs. It helps make the viewers feel like they're the one asking the questions.

- **Close-up.** The close-up, usually described as "from shirt pocket to head room," provides a good composition for someone talking directly to the camera. Although it's common to have your talking head centered in the shot, that's not a requirement. In Figure 16.8 the subject was offset to the right. This would allow other images, especially graphics or titles, to be superimposed in the frame in a "real" (professional) production. But the compositional technique can be used with D810 videos, too, even if special effects are not going to be added.
- **Extreme close-up.** When I went through broadcast training, this shot was described as the "big talking face" shot and we were actively discouraged from employing it. Styles and tastes change over the years and now the big talking face is much more commonly used (maybe people are better looking these days?) and so this view may be appropriate. Just remember, the D810 is capable of shooting in high-definition video and you may be playing the video on a high-def TV; be careful that you use this composition on a face that can stand up to high definition. (See Figure 16.9.)
- **"Two" shot.** A two shot shows a pair of subjects in one frame. They can be side by side or one in the foreground and one in the background. (See Figure 16.10.) This does not have to be a head to ground composition. Subjects can be standing or seated. A "three shot" is the same principle except that three people are in the frame.
- **Over-the-shoulder shot.** Long a composition of interview programs, the "over-the-shoulder shot" uses the rear of one person's head and shoulder to serve as a frame for the other person. This puts the viewer's perspective as that of the person facing away from the camera. (See Figure 16.11.)

Lighting for Video

Much like in still photography, how you handle light pretty much can make or break your videography. Lighting for video can be more complicated than lighting for still photography, since both subject and camera movement are often part of the process.

Lighting for video presents several concerns. First off, you want enough illumination to create a useable video. Beyond that, you want to use light to help tell your story or increase drama. Let's take a better look at both.

Illumination

You can significantly improve the quality of your video by increasing the light falling in the scene. This is true indoors or out, by the way. While it may seem like sunlight is more than enough, it depends on how much contrast you're dealing with. If your subject is in shadow (which can help them from squinting) or wearing a ball cap, a video light can help make them look a lot better.

Lighting choices for amateur videographers are a lot better these days than they were a decade or two ago. An inexpensive incandescent video light, which will easily fit in a camera bag, can be found for $15 or $20. You can even get a good-quality LED video light for less than $100. Work lights sold at many home improvement stores can also serve as video lights since you can set the camera's white balance to correct for any color casts. You'll need to mount these lights on a tripod or other support, or, perhaps, to a bracket that fastens to the tripod socket on the bottom of the camera.

Much of the challenge depends upon whether you're just trying to add some fill-light on your subject versus trying to boost the light on an entire scene. A small video light will do just fine for the former. It won't handle the latter. Fortunately, the versatility of the D810 comes in quite handy here. Since the camera shoots video in Auto ISO mode, it can compensate for lower lighting levels and still produce a decent image. For best results though, better lighting is necessary.

Creative Lighting

While ramping up the light intensity will produce better technical quality in your video, it won't necessarily improve the artistic quality of it. Whether we're outdoors or indoors, we're used to seeing light come from above. Videographers need to consider how they position their lights to provide even illumination while up high enough to angle shadows down low and out of sight of the camera.

When considering lighting for video, there are several factors. One is the quality of the light. It can either be hard (direct) light or soft (diffused). Hard light is good for showing detail, but can also be very harsh and unforgiving. "Softening" the light, but diffusing it somehow, can reduce the intensity of the light but make for a kinder, gentler light as well.

While mixing light sources isn't always a good idea, one approach is to combine window light with supplemental lighting. Position your subject with the window to one side and bring in either a supplemental light or a reflector to the other side for reasonably even lighting.

Lighting Styles

Some lighting styles are more heavily used than others. Some forms are used for special effects, while others are designed to be invisible. At its most basic, lighting just illuminates the scene, but when used properly it can also create drama. Let's look at some types of lighting styles:

- **Three-point lighting.** This is a basic lighting setup for one person. A main light illuminates the strong side of a person's face, while a fill light lights up the other side. A third light is then positioned above and behind the subject to light the back of the head and shoulders. (See Figure 16.12.)

- **Flat lighting.** Use this type of lighting to provide illumination and nothing more. It calls for a variety of lights and diffusers set to raise the light level in a space enough for good video reproduction, but not to create a particular mood or emphasize a particular scene or individual. With flat lighting, you're trying to create even lighting levels throughout the video space and minimize any shadows. Generally, the lights are placed up high and angled downward (or possibly pointed straight up to bounce off of a white ceiling). (See Figure 16.13.)
- **"Ghoul lighting."** This is the style of lighting used for old horror movies. The idea is to position the light down low, pointed upward. It's such an unnatural style of lighting that it makes its targets seem weird and "ghoulish."

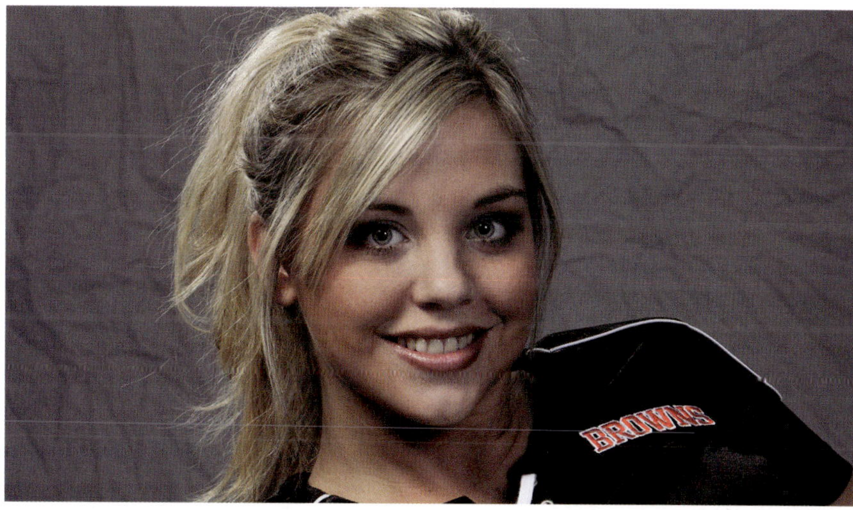

Figure 16.12
With three-point lighting, two lights are placed in front and to the side of the subject (45-degree angles are ideal) and positioned about a foot higher than the subject's head. Another light is directed on the background in order to separate the subject and the background.

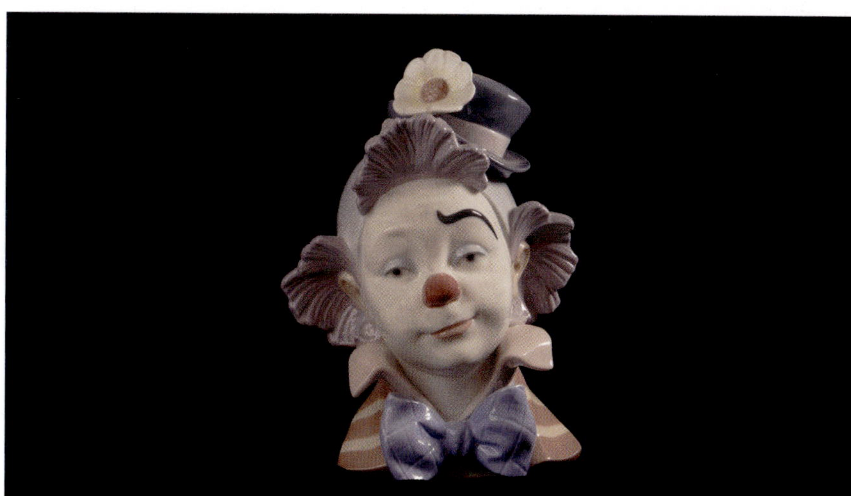

Figure 16.13
Flat lighting is another approach for creating even illumination. Here the lights can be bounced off of a white ceiling and walls to fill in shadows as much as possible. It is a flexible lighting approach since the subject can change positions without needing a change in light direction.

- **Outdoor lighting.** While shooting outdoors may seem easier because the sun provides more light, it also presents its own problems. As a general rule of thumb, keep the sun behind you when you're shooting video outdoors, except when shooting faces (anything from a medium shot and closer) since the viewer won't want to see a squinting subject. When shooting another human this way, put the sun behind her and use a video light to balance light levels between the foreground and background. If the sun is simply too bright, position the subject in the shade and use the video light for your main illumination. Using reflectors (white board panels or aluminum foil covered cardboard panels are cheap options) can also help balance light effectively.

Audio

When it comes to making a successful video, audio quality is one of those things that separates the professionals from the amateurs. We're used to watching top-quality productions on television and in the movies, yet the average person has no idea how much effort goes in to producing what seems to be "natural" sound. Much of the sound you hear in such productions is actually recorded on carefully controlled sound stages and "sweetened" with a variety of sound effects and other recordings of "natural" sound.

Tips for Better Audio

Since recording high-quality audio is such a challenge, it's a good idea to do everything possible to maximize recording quality. Here are some ideas for improving the quality of the audio your camera records:

- **Get the camera and its microphone close to the speaker.** The farther the microphone is from the audio source, the less effective it will be in picking up that sound. While having to position the camera and its built-in microphone closer to the subject affects your lens choices and lens perspective options, it will make the most of your audio source. Of course, if you're using a very wide-angle lens, getting too close to your subject can have unflattering results, so don't take this advice too far. It's important to think carefully about what sounds you want to capture. If you're shooting video of an acoustic combo that's not using a PA system, you'll want the microphone close to them, but not so close that, say, only the lead singer or instrumentalist is picked up, while the players at either side fade off into the background.
- **Use an external microphone.** You'll recall the description of the camera's external microphone port in Chapter 2. As noted, this port accepts a stereo mini-plug from a standard external microphone, allowing you to achieve considerably higher audio quality for your movies than is possible with the camera's built-in microphones (which are disabled when an external mic is plugged in). An external microphone reduces the amount of camera-induced noise that is picked up and recorded on your audio track. (The action of the lens as it focuses can be audible when the built-in microphones are active.)

The external microphone port can provide plug-in power for microphones that can take their power from this sort of outlet rather than from a battery in the microphone. Nikon provides optional compatible microphones such as the ME-1; you also may find suitable microphones from companies such as Shure and Audio-Technica. If you are on a quest for really superior audio quality, you can even obtain a portable mixer that can plug into this jack, such as the affordable Rolls MX124 (around $150) (www.rolls.com), letting you use multiple high-quality microphones (up to four) to record your soundtrack.

An exciting new option designed specifically for still cameras like the Nikon D810 is the Beachtek DXA-SLR PRO HDSLR Audio Adapter. It's more expensive, at around $450, but has even more professional sound options and clips right onto the bottom of your camera using the tripod mounting socket.

One advantage that a sound mixing device like the DXA-SLR PRO or the Beachtek-SLR Ultra offers over the stock D810 is that it adds a headphone output jack to your camera, so you can monitor the sound being recorded (you can also listen to your soundtrack through the headphones during playback, which is *way* better than using the D810's built-in speaker). The adapter has two balanced XLR microphone inputs and can also accept line input (from another audio source), and provides cool features like AGC (automatic gain control), built-in limiting, and VU meters you can use to monitor sound input.

- **Hide the microphone.** Combine the first few tips by using an external mic, and getting it as close to your subject as possible. If you're capturing a single person, you can always use a lapel microphone (described in the next section). But if you want a single mic to capture sound from multiple sources, your best bet may be to hide it somewhere in the shot. Put it behind a vase, using duct tape to fasten the microphone, and fix the mic cable out of sight (if you're not using a wireless microphone).
- **Turn off any sound makers you can.** Little things like fans and air handling units aren't obvious to the human ear, but will be picked up by the microphone. Turn off any machinery or devices that you can plus make sure cell phones are set to silent mode. Also, do what you can to minimize sounds such as wind, radio, television, or people talking in the background.
- **Make sure to record some "natural" sound.** If you're shooting video at an event of some kind, make sure you get some background sound that you can add to your audio as desired in postproduction.
- **Consider recording audio separately.** Lip-syncing is probably beyond most of the people you're going to be shooting, but there's nothing that says you can't record narration separately and add it later. It's relatively easy if you learn how to use simple software video-editing programs like iMovie (for the Macintosh) or Windows Movie Maker (for Windows PCs). Any time the speaker is off-camera, you can work with separately recorded narration rather than recording the speaker on-camera. This can produce much cleaner sound.

External Microphones

The single most important thing you can do to improve your audio quality is to use an external microphone. The D810's internal stereo microphones mounted on the front of the camera will do a decent job, but have some significant drawbacks, partially spelled out in the previous section:

- **Camera noise.** There are plenty of noise sources emanating from the camera, including your own breathing and rustling around as the camera shifts in your hand. Manual zooming is bound to affect your sound, and your fingers will fall directly in front of the built-in mics as you change focal lengths. An external microphone isolates the sound recording from camera noise.
- **Distance.** Anytime your D810 is located more than 6–8 feet from your subjects or sound source, the audio will suffer. An external unit allows you to place the mic right next to your subject.
- **Improved quality.** Obviously, Nikon wasn't able to install a super-expensive, super high quality microphone, even on a $6,000-plus dSLR. Not all owners of the D810 would be willing to pay the premium, especially if they didn't plan to shoot much video themselves. An external microphone will almost always be of better quality.
- **Directionality.** The D810's internal microphone generally records only sounds directly in front of it. An external microphone can be either of the directional type or omnidirectional, depending on whether you want to "shotgun" your sound or record more ambient sound.

You can choose from several different types of microphones, each of which has its own advantages and disadvantages. If you're serious about movie making with your D810, you might want to own more than one. Common configurations include:

- **Shotgun microphones.** These can be mounted directly on your D810, although, if the mic uses an accessory shoe mount, you'll need the optional adapter to convert the camera's shoe to a standard hot shoe. I prefer to use a bracket, which further isolates the microphone from any camera noise. One thing to keep in mind is that while the shotgun mic will generally ignore any sound coming from *behind* it, it will pick up any sound it is pointed at, even *behind* your subject. You may be capturing video and audio of someone you're interviewing in a restaurant, and not realize you're picking up the lunchtime conversation of the diners seated in the table behind your subject. Outdoors, you may record your speaker, as well as the traffic on a busy street or freeway in the background.
- **Lapel microphones.** Also called *lavalieres*, these microphones attach to the subject's clothing and pick up their voice with the best quality. You'll need a long enough cord or a wireless mic (described later). These are especially good for video interviews, so whether you're producing a documentary or grilling relatives for a family history, you'll want one of these.

- **Hand-held microphones.** If you're capturing a singer crooning a tune, or want your subject to mimic famed faux newscaster Wally Ballou, a hand-held mic may be your best choice. They serve much the same purpose as a lapel microphone, and they're more intrusive—but that may be the point. A hand-held microphone can make a great prop for your fake newscast! The speaker can talk right into the microphone, point it at another person, or use it to record ambient sound. If your narrator is not going to appear on-camera, one of these can be an inexpensive way to improve sound.
- **Wired and wireless external microphones.** This option is the most expensive, but you get a receiver and a transmitter (both battery-powered, so you'll need to make sure you have enough batteries). The transmitter is connected to the microphone, and the receiver is connected to your D810. In addition to being less klutzy and enabling you to avoid having wires on view in your scene, wireless mics let you record sounds that are physically located some distance from your camera. Of course, you need to keep in mind the range of your device, and be aware of possible signal interference from other electronic components in the vicinity.

WIND NOISE REDUCTION

Always use the wind screen provided with an external microphone to reduce the effect of noise produced by even light breezes blowing over the microphone. Many mics, such as the Nikon ME-1 (about $180), include a low-cut filter to further reduce wind noise. However, these can also affect other sounds. You can disable the low-cut filters for the ME-1 by changing a switch on the back from L-cut (low cutoff) to Flat. Other external mics also have their own low-cut filter switch.

Special Features

The D810 has some special features that lend themselves to professional video production. It has the ability to save raw, uncompressed ("clean") video to an external storage device using the built-in HDMI port, and, if you prefer, simultaneously to an internal memory card. The camera also enables Auto ISO during manual exposure while shooting video, which can help improve your captures under changing lighting conditions, because the shutter speed and aperture setting won't shift (causing depth-of-field and other modifications).

The D810 also has two audio frequency ranges (Wide and Vocal Range) so you can tailor your microphone capture to your subject matter (for ambient sound or voice recording). Audio levels can be adjusted while recording, and the camera's internal microphones have improved wind noise reduction.

Part VI

Bonus Material

When I seek to explain the mysteries of Nikon's more advanced cameras, I seem to get an equal number of comments from experienced shooters and beginners. The veterans urge me to confine my explanations solely to more advanced topics and techniques, because explanations of basic f/stops and shutter speeds are old hat to them. Yet, I also hear from less experienced owners of these cameras, courageous folk who have invested in an advanced camera that they don't expect to grow out of, and who want to know all the details, with plenty of background material to help them get up to speed. They want me to blend explanations of camera operation with basic photography in a book that is, after all, titled *David Busch's Nikon D810 Guide to Digital SLR Photography.*

Although I do combine basics and advanced material throughout the book, this Part VI is a recognition of the needs of both groups. Here, you'll find "bonus" material of a more basic sort, accessible to those who need it (as well as to those who just need a refresher), while removing it from the main body of the book. Even the most advanced photographers will concede that there was a time when they, too, wished they had explanations of this sort available. In this part you'll find:

- **Appendix A:** This appendix has everything the new Nikon D810 owner needs to unpack and set up the camera prior to beginning shooting. And if, as I expect, you've already started shooting, it's not too late to glean some useful information from this checklist.
- **Appendix B:** Here is a simple explanation of what different types of lenses do, and how to choose among the available focal lengths and ranges Nikon offers. You'll discover that this is a supplement to Chapter 7, where I describe specific lenses and their applications.
- **Appendix C:** Learn about Nikon Capture NX 2, NX-D, Nikon Camera Control Pro 2, and other offerings, as well as alternative tools like Adobe Photoshop and Lightroom.
- **Appendix D:** This is a simple explanation of updating firmware, protecting your image files, cleaning your sensor, and other maintenance chores.

A

Nikon D810: Pre-Flight Checklist

The Nikon D810 appeals to more advanced users, including those who have previously owned full-frame Nikon cameras (especially the Nikon D700). However, I recognize that a significant number of serious photographers were inspired by the features and capabilities of the Nikon D810 to make the jump from a "cropped" sensor model to the full-frame (FX) world. Others are switching to Nikon from another brand of camera, and still others are brave souls who have decided to make the Nikon D810 their first digital SLR or even first digital camera.

The D810 has such broad appeal that I didn't want to leave those of you who need some extra information behind in the lurch when it comes to initial setup of the camera. So, I'm providing the most basic setup information here, and tucking it away for easy access, yet out of the way of more experienced shooters who want to skip over this kind of information. You can absorb this Appendix easily, as each section has a brief summary that will help you decide if you want to skim over it, read it quickly, or study it.

> This section helps get you oriented with all the things that come in the box with your Nikon D810, including what they do. I'll also describe some optional equipment you might want to have. If you want to get started immediately, skim through this section and jump ahead to "Initial Setup" later in the appendix.

The Nikon D810 comes in an impressive gold box filled with stuff, including connecting cords, booklets, a CD, and lots of paperwork. The most important components are the camera and lens (if you purchased your D810 with a lens), battery, battery charger, and, if you're the nervous type, the neck strap. You'll also need a memory card as one is not included. If you purchased your D810 from a camera shop, as I did, the store personnel probably attached the neck strap for you, ran through some basic operational advice that you've already forgotten, tried to sell you a memory card, and then, after they'd given you all the help you could absorb, sent you on your way with a handshake.

Perhaps you purchased your D810 from one of those mass merchandisers that also sell washing machines and vacuum cleaners. In that case, you might have been sent on your way with only the handshake, or, maybe, not even that if you resisted the efforts to sell you an extended warranty. You save a few bucks at the big box stores, but you don't get the personal service a professional photo retailer provides. It's your choice. There's a third alternative, of course. You might have purchased your camera from a mail order or Internet source, and your D810 arrived in a big brown (or purple/red) truck. Your only interaction when you took possession of your camera was to scrawl your signature on an electronic clipboard.

In all three cases, the first thing to do is to carefully unpack the camera and double-check the contents with the checklist on one end of the box, helpfully designated under a "This package includes" listing. While this level of setup detail may seem as superfluous as the instructions on a bottle of shampoo, checking the contents *first* is always a good idea. No matter who sells a camera, it's common to open boxes, use a particular camera for a demonstration, and then repack the box without replacing all the pieces and parts afterwards. Someone might actually have helpfully checked out your camera on your behalf—and then mispacked the box. It's better to know *now* that something is missing so you can seek redress immediately, rather than discover two months from now that the video cable you thought you'd never use (but now *must* have) was never in the box. I once purchased a brand-new Nikon dSLR kit that was supposed to include a second focusing screen; it wasn't in the box, but because I discovered the deficiency right away, the dealer ordered a replacement for me post haste.

At a minimum, the box should have the following:

- **Nikon D810 digital camera.** It almost goes without saying that you should check out the camera immediately, making sure the back- and top-panel LCDs aren't scratched or cracked, the memory and battery doors open properly, and, when a charged battery is inserted and lens mounted, the camera powers up and reports for duty. Out-of-the-box defects like these are rare, but they can happen. It's probably more common that your dealer played with the camera or, perhaps, it was a customer return. That's why it's best to buy your D810 from a retailer you trust to supply a factory-fresh camera.

- **Rechargeable Li-ion battery EN-EL15.** You'll need to charge this 7.0V, 1900mAh (milliampere hour) battery before use, and then navigate immediately to the Setup menu's Battery Info entry to make sure the battery accepted the juice and is showing a 100% charge. (You'll find more on accessing this menu item in Chapter 13.) You'll want a second EN-EL15 battery as a spare (trust me), so buy one as soon as possible.
- **Quick charger MH-25a.** This charger comes with both a power cable and a power adapter that can be used instead of the cable to plug the charger directly into a wall outlet.
- **USB cable UC-E22.** You can use this cable to transfer photos from the camera to your computer (I don't recommend that because direct transfer uses a lot of battery power), to upload and download settings between the camera and your computer (highly recommended), and to operate your camera remotely using Nikon Camera Control Pro software (not included in the box).

Note

This cable has a special connector at the camera end, as it is a USB 3.0-compatible cable with a Micro-B connector. The computer end of the cable is compatible with USB 1.0, USB 2.0, and the latest USB 3.0 connections. Also in the box is a USB cable clip, which you can attach to prevent the cable from being disconnected.

- **AN-DC12 neck strap.** Nikon provides you with a neck strap emblazoned with your camera model. It's not very adjustable, and, while useful for showing off to your friends exactly which nifty new camera you bought, the Nikon strap also can serve to alert observant unsavory types that you're sporting a higher-end model that's worthy of their attention. I never attach the Nikon strap to my cameras, and instead opt for a more serviceable strap from UPstrap (www.upstrap-pro.com). An UPstrap is shown in Figure A.1, with its patented non-slip pad that keeps your D810 on your shoulder, and not crashing to the ground. If you order one of these, tell inventor-photographer Al Stegmeyer that I sent you.
- **BF-1B body cap.** The body cap keeps dust from infiltrating your camera when a lens is not mounted. Always carry a body cap (and rear lens cap) in your camera bag for those times when you need to have the camera bare of optics for more than a minute or two. (That usually happens when repacking a bag efficiently for transport, or when you are carrying an extra body or two for backup.) The body cap/lens cap nest together for compact storage.

Note

If you happen to have one of the earlier BF-1 body caps for older film cameras, do not use it, as they don't accommodate the electronic contacts in newer lenses.

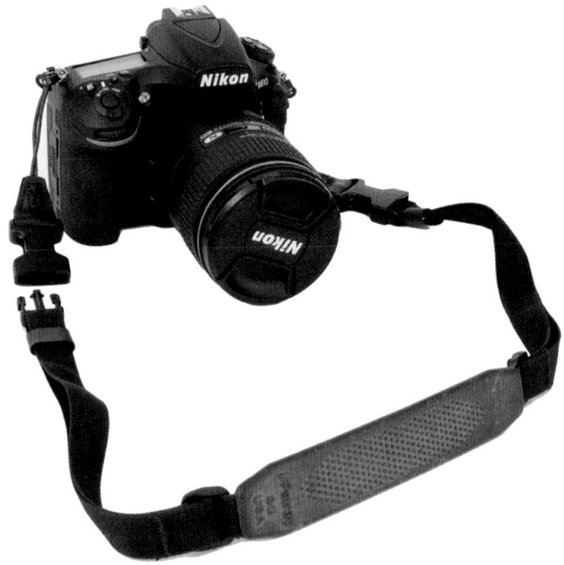

Figure A.1
Third-party neck straps like this UPstrap model are often preferable to the Nikon-supplied strap.

- **BS-1 accessory shoe cover.** This little piece of plastic protects the electrical contacts of the "hot" shoe on top of the D810. You can remove it when mounting an electronic flash, Nikon GP-1 GPS device, or other accessory, and then safely leave it off for the rest of your life. I've never had an accessory shoe receive damage in normal use, even when not protected. The paranoid among you who use accessories frequently can keep removing/mounting the shoe cover as required. Find a safe place to keep it between uses, or purchase replacements for this easily mislaid item. (Visit www.bocaphoto.com for many Nikon-related items.)
- **LCD monitor cover BM-12.** The glass covering the D810's big 3.2-inch LCD monitor is tough, but this plastic cover adds another layer of protection, and it can be replaced for a few dollars if scratched. If I were going to worry about shielding the LCD from damage, I'd use a less obtrusive acrylic cover from various vendors who sell GGS or Giottos glass protectors.
- **User's manuals.** Even if you have this book, you'll probably want to check the user's guide that Nikon provides, if only to check the actual nomenclature for some obscure accessory, or to double-check an error code. Copy a PDF version to store on your laptop, a CD-ROM, or other media in case you want to access this reference when the paper version isn't handy. If you have an old memory card that's too small to be usable on a modern dSLR (I still have some 128MB and 256MB cards), you can store the PDF on that. But an even better choice is to put the manual on a low-capacity USB "thumb" drive, which you can buy for less than $10. You'll then be able to access the reference anywhere you are, because you can always find someone with a computer that has a USB port and Adobe Acrobat Reader available. You might not be lucky enough to locate a computer with a memory reader. Nikon offers a Manual Reader app for iOS and Android devices that you can use to peruse the PDF manual, so you can carry a manual on your phone or tablet. An e-book version of this book is available in Kindle, iBook, and Nook formats, as well.

- **Quick Start guide.** This little booklet tucked away in the camera's paperwork offers a reasonable summary of the Nikon D810's basic commands and settings, and can be stowed in your camera bag.
- **Software CD-ROM.** Here you'll find the Nikon ViewNX 2 software, a useful image management program. I'll cover a variety of other software offerings later in Appendix C.
- **Warranty and registration card.** Don't lose these! You can register your Nikon D810 by mail or online (in the USA, the URL is www.nikonusa.com/register), and you may need the information in this paperwork (plus the purchase receipt/invoice from your retailer) should you require Nikon service support.

Don't bother rooting around in the box for anything beyond what I've listed previously. There are a few things Nikon classifies as optional accessories, even though you (and I) might consider some of them essential. Here's a list of what you *don't* get in the box, but might want to think about as an impending purchase. I'll list them roughly in the order of importance:

- **Compact Flash and Secure Digital card.** First-time digital camera buyers are sometimes shocked that their new tool doesn't come with a memory card. Why should it? The manufacturer doesn't have the slightest idea of what capacity or speed card you prefer, so why should they pack one (or even two) in the box and charge you for it? That's especially true for the Nikon D810, which is likely to be purchased by photographers who have quite definite ideas about their ideal memory card. Perhaps you want to use tiny 4GB cards—and lots of them, as the D810 will store only 172 JPEG Fine images on a 4GB card, or just 38 RAW+JPEG Fine pairs. I've met many paranoid wedding photographers who like to work with a horde of smaller cards (and then watch over them *very* protectively), on the theory that they are reducing their chances of losing a significant chunk of the event or reception at one time (of course, that's why you hire a second shooter as backup). Others, especially sports photographers, instead prefer 16GB or 32GB cards with room to spare. If you are shooting fast action at continuous frame rates, or transfer lots of photos to your computer with a speedy card reader, you might opt for the speediest possible memory card. I personally use 64GB 400X Compact Flash cards with my D810 (although 600X and 1000X are also available), paired with an SDXC with similar speed and capacity. Buy one (or two, or three) of your own and have your flash memory ready when you unpack your D810.
- **Extra EN-EL15 battery.** I mentioned the need for an extra battery earlier, and I'll mention it here, again. Even though you might get 1,000 or more shots from a single battery, it's easy to exceed that figure in a few hours of shooting sports. Batteries can unexpectedly fail, too, or simply lose their charge from sitting around unused for a week or two. If you're using the MB-D12 battery/vertical grip offered for the D810, you'll definitely want an additional EN-EL15 battery. Buy an extra (I own four, in total), keep it charged, and free your mind from worry. Just don't buy the one of the defective "exploding" batteries that are involved in the recall!

- **Nikon Capture NX 2 software.** You can download a free try-out copy of this software from Nikon's website, but if you want to use it after the free period expires, you'll need to buy it. Nikon has said it will continue supporting this utility, but is pushing its free NX-D software that has many of the same features.
- **Camera Control Pro 2 software.** This is the utility you'll use to operate your camera remotely from your computer. Nikon charges extra for this software, but you'll find it invaluable if you're hiding near a tethered, tripod-mounted camera while shooting, say, close-ups of hummingbirds. There are lots of applications for remote shooting, and you'll need Camera Control Pro to operate your camera. Buy a suitably longer USB cable, too, unless you plan to use the Nikon WT4a wireless transmitter (described below).
- **Add-on Speedlight.** One of the best uses for your Nikon D810's built-in electronic flash is as a remote trigger for an off-camera Speedlight such as the Nikon SB-910. Your built-in flash can function as the main light, diffused and used for fill, or dialed down in power so it has virtually no effect on the finished photo at all (other than triggering your remote flash units). But, you'll have to own one or two (or more) external flash units to gain that flexibility. If you do much flash photography at all, consider an add-on Speedlight as an important accessory.
- **Nikon GP-1a global positioning system (GPS) device.** This accessory attaches to the accessory shoe on top of the Nikon D810 and captures latitude, longitude, and altitude information, which is imprinted in a special data area of your image files. The "geotagging" data can be plotted on a map in Nikon ViewNX or other software programs.
- **Power connector EP-5b/AC adapter EH-5b.** There are several typical situations where this AC adapter for your D810 can come in handy: when you're cleaning the sensor manually and want to totally eliminate the possibility that a lack of juice will cause the fragile shutter and mirror to spring to life during the process; when in the studio shooting product photos, portraits, class pictures, and so forth for hours on end; when using your D810 for remote shooting as well as time-lapse photography; for extensive review of images on your standard-definition or high-definition television; or for file transfer to your computer. These all use prodigious amounts of power, which can be provided by this AC adapter. (Beware of power outages and blackouts when cleaning your sensor, however!)

  The EP-5b is the connector that fits in the battery compartment of *either* the D810 or the MB-D12 multi-power battery pack. It's then connected to the EH-5b AC adapter. **Note:** The Nikon EH-5 and EH-5a AC adapters can also be used.
- **Multi-power battery pack MB-D12.** Lots of photographers consider this battery pack/vertical grip to be an essential item, but you must buy it as an extra. Unfortunately, it is delivered "bare," with no extra power sources at all. You'll need to purchase AA batteries (alkalines or rechargeables) for the supplied AA battery tray, or have an extra EN-EL15 battery to use this accessory. (I *told* you that you'd need that extra battery.)

- **DR-4/DR-5 right-angle viewers.** Fasten in place of the standard rubber eyecup and it provides a 90-degree view for framing and composing your image at right angles to the original viewfinder, useful for low-level (or high-level) shooting. (Or, maybe, shooting around corners!)
- **DK-17M magnifying eyepiece.** Provides a 1.17X magnification factor of the entire viewing area (unlike the 2X DG-2 eyepiece, which enlarges the center of the image), making it easier to check focus. You might have to move your eye around a little to see all the indicators outside the image frame, but this magnifier is still suitable for everyday use.
- **Eyepiece Magnifier DG-2.** This magnifies the center of the scene only, helping you to focus more accurately.
- **Eyepiece Adapter DK-18.** This adapter is required to attach the DG-2 magnifier or DR-4 right-angle viewer to the D810's eyepiece.
- **SC-28 TTL flash cord.** Allows using Nikon Speedlights off-camera, while retaining all the automated features.
- **SC-29 TTL flash cord.** Similar to the SC-28, this unit has its own AF-assist lamp, which can provide extra illumination for the D810's autofocus system in dim light (which, not coincidentally, is when you'll probably be using an electronic flash).

Initial Setup

This section helps you become familiar with the three important controls most used to make adjustments: the multi selector and the main and sub-command dials. You'll also find information on charging the battery, setting the clock, mounting a lens, and making diopter vision adjustments. If you're comfortable with all these things, you're ready for my Quick Start in Chapter 1 of this book.

Once you've unpacked and inspected your camera, the initial setup of your Nikon D810 is fast and easy. Basically, you just need to charge the battery, attach a lens, and insert a memory card. I'll address each of these steps separately, but if you already are confident you can manage these setup tasks without further instructions, feel free to skip this section entirely. While most buyers of a D810 tend to be experienced photographers, I realize that some readers are ambitious, if inexperienced, and should, at the minimum, skim the contents of the next section, because I'm going to list a few options that you might not be aware of.

Mastering the Multi Selector and Command Dials

You'll find descriptions of most of the controls used with the Nikon D810 in Chapter 2, which provides a complete "roadmap" of the camera's buttons and dials and switches. However, you may need to perform a few tasks during this initial setup process, and most of them will require the MENU button and the multi selector pad. The MENU button is easy to find: it's located to the left of the LCD monitor, the first button in the series of four located to the left of the LCD.

It requires almost no explanation; when you want to access a menu, press it. To exit most menus, press it again.

The multi selector pad may remind you of the similar control found on many point-and-shoot cameras, and other digital SLRs. It consists of a thumbpad-sized button with projections at the north, south, east, and west positions, plus a button in the center. It can also be pushed in diagonal directions to give you northeast, southeast, southwest, and northwest orientations. (See Figure A.2.)

The multi selector on the D810 functions slightly differently than its counterpart on some other cameras. For example, some point-and-shoot models assign a function, such as white balance or ISO setting, to one of the directional buttons (usually in conjunction with a function key of some sort). The use of the multi selector varies, even within the Nikon dSLR line up. For example, some early Nikon digital SLRs (such as the Nikon D50/D70/D80) had no center button in the multi selector at all. Advanced Nikon cameras (including the D810) allow assigning a function of your choice to the multi selector center button.

With the D810, the multi selector is used extensively for navigation—for example, to navigate among menus on the LCD monitor or to choose one of the 51 focus points, to advance or reverse display of a series of images during picture review, or to change the kind of photo information displayed on the screen. The center button is used to select a highlighted item from a menu.

So, from time to time in this chapter (and throughout this book) I'll be referring to the multi selector and its left/right/up/down buttons, and center button.

The main command dial and sub-command dial are located on the rear and front of the D810, respectively. The main command dial is used to change settings such as shutter speed, while the sub-command dial adjusts an alternate or secondary setting. For example, in Manual exposure mode, you'd use the sub-command dial to change the aperture, while the main command dial is used to change the shutter speed. (In both cases, the dial is "active" for these adjustments only when the D810's exposure meter is On.) The meter will automatically go to sleep after an interval (you'll learn how to specify the length of time in Chapter 12), and you must waken the camera (just tap the shutter release button) to switch the meter back on and activate the main and sub-command dials.

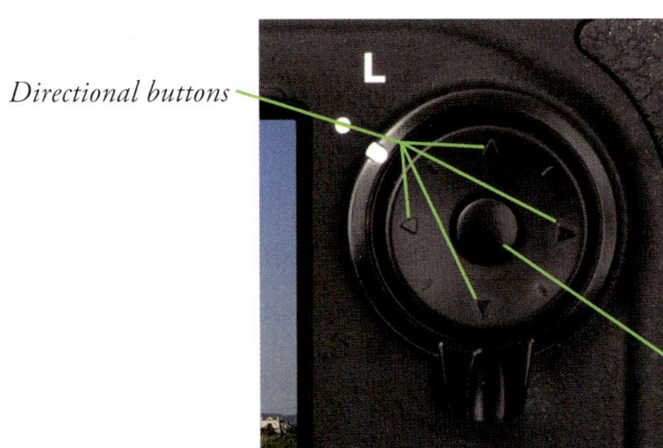

Figure A.2
The multi selector pad has four directional positions for navigating up/down/left/right, and a center button to confirm your selection.

Setting the Clock

It's likely that your Nikon D810's internal clock hasn't been set to your local time, so you may need to do that first. If so, the flashing CLOCK indicator on the top control panel LCD will be the giveaway. You'll find complete instructions for setting the four options for the date/time (time zone, actual date and time, the date format, and whether you want the D810 to conform to Daylight Savings Time) in Chapter 13. However, if you think you can handle this step without instruction, press the MENU button, use the multi selector (that thumb-friendly button I just described, located to the immediate right of the back-panel color LCD monitor) to scroll down to the Setup menu, press the multi selector button to the right, and scroll down to Time Zone and Date choice, and press right again. The options will appear on the screen that appears next. Keep in mind that you'll need to reset your camera's internal clock from time to time, as it is not 100-percent accurate, unless you're using the GP-1 GPS device and have specified Use GPS to Set Camera Clock to On in the Setup menu's GPS entry.

Battery Included

Your Nikon D810 is a sophisticated hunk of machinery and electronics, but it needs a charged battery to function, so rejuvenating the EN-EL15 lithium-ion battery pack furnished with the camera should be your first step. A fully charged power source should be good for approximately 1200 shots, based on standard tests defined by the Camera & Imaging Products Association (CIPA) document DC-002. Nikon's own standards are quite a bit more optimistic (it predicts as many as 3,860 shots from a single charge). In the real world, of course, the life of the battery will depend on how much image review you do, how many shots you take with the built-in flash, and many other factors. You'll want to keep track of how many pictures *you* are able to take in your own typical circumstances, and use that figure as a guideline, instead.

A BATTERY AND A SPARE

I always recommend purchasing Nikon brand batteries (for about $75) over less-expensive third-party packs, even though the $30 substitute batteries may offer more capacity at a lower price (some may even top the 1,900 mAh offered by the Nikon battery). My reasoning is that it doesn't make sense to save $20 on a component for a $3,000-$3,300 camera, especially since batteries have been known to fail in potentially harmful ways. You need only look as far as Nikon's own recall of these very batteries, which forced the company to ship out thousands of free replacement cells. You're unlikely to get the same support from a third-party battery supplier that sells under a half-dozen or more different product labels and brands, and may not even have an easy way to get the word out that a recall has been issued.

If your pictures are important to you, always have at least one spare battery available, and make sure it is an authentic Nikon product.

All rechargeable batteries undergo some degree of self-discharge just sitting idle in the camera or in the original packaging. Lithium-ion power packs of this type typically lose a few percent of their charge every few days, even when the camera isn't turned on. The small amount of juice used to provide the "shots remaining" figure on the top control panel when the D810 is turned off isn't the culprit; Li-ion cells lose their power through a chemical reaction that continues when the camera is switched off. It's very likely that the battery purchased with your camera is at least partially pooped out, so you'll want to revive it before going out for some serious shooting.

Charging the Battery

When the battery is inserted into the MH-25a charger properly (it's impossible to insert it incorrectly), a Charge light begins flashing, and remains flashing until the status lamp glows steadily indicating that charging is finished, in about 2.5 hours. You can use the supplied connector cable (at left in Figure A.3) or attach a handy plug adapter that allows connecting the charger directly to a wall outlet (as shown at right in Figure A.3). When the battery is charged, flip the lever on the bottom of the camera and slide the battery in, as shown in Figure A.4. Check the Setup menu's Battery Info entry as I recommended earlier to make sure the battery is fully charged. If not, try putting it in the charger again. One of three things may be the culprit: a.) the actual charging cycle sometimes takes longer than you (or the charger) expected; b.) the battery is new and needs to be "seasoned" for a few charging cycles, after which it will accept a full charge and deliver more shots; c.) you've got a defective battery. The last is fairly rare, but before you start counting on getting a particular number of exposures from a battery, it's best to make sure it's fully charged, seasoned, and ready to deliver.

Final Steps

Your Nikon D810 is almost ready to fire up and shoot. You'll need to select and mount a lens, adjust the viewfinder for your vision, and insert a memory card. Each of these steps is easy, and if you've used any Nikon before, you already know exactly what to do. I'm going to provide a little extra detail for those of you who are new to the Nikon or SLR worlds.

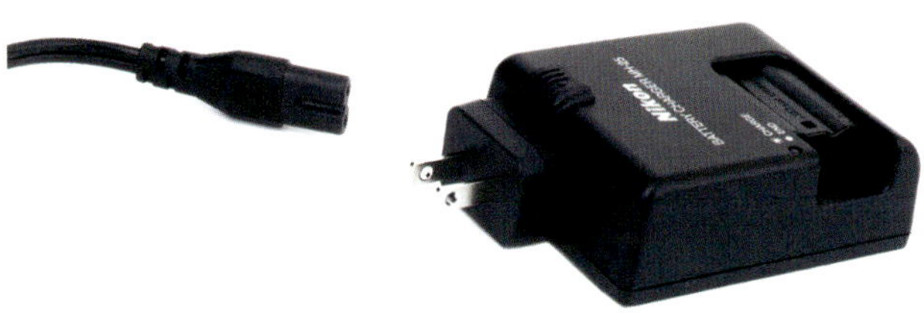

Figure A.3 Charge the battery before use.

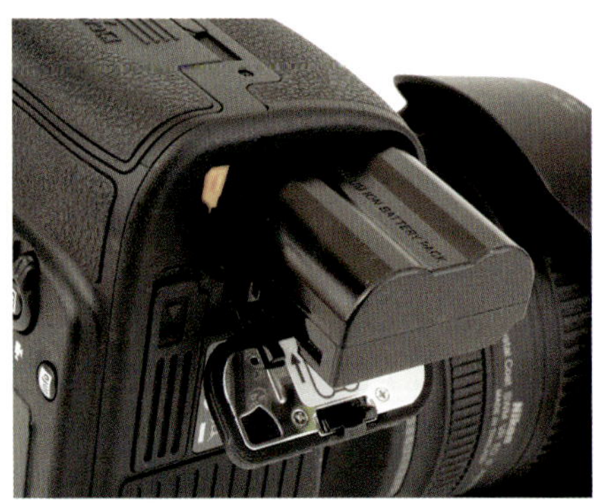

Figure A.4 Insert the battery in the camera; it only fits one way.

Mounting the Lens

As you'll see, my recommended lens mounting procedure emphasizes protecting your equipment from accidental damage and minimizing the intrusion of dust. If your D810 has no lens attached, select the lens you want to use and loosen (but do not remove) the rear lens cap. I generally place the lens I am planning to mount vertically in a slot in my camera bag, where it's protected from mishaps, but ready to pick up quickly. By loosening the rear lens cap, you'll be able to lift it off the back of the lens at the last instant, so the rear element of the lens is covered until then.

After that, remove the body cap by rotating the cap away from the release button. You should always mount the body cap when there is no lens on the camera, because it helps keep dust out of the interior of the camera, where it can settle on the mirror, focusing screen, interior mirror box, and potentially find its way past the shutter onto the sensor. (While the D810's sensor cleaning mechanism works fine; the less dust it has to contend with, the better.) The body cap also protects the vulnerable mirror from damage caused by intruding objects (including your fingers, if you're not cautious).

Once the body cap has been removed, remove the rear lens cap from the lens, set it aside, and then mount the lens on the camera by matching the alignment indicator on the lens barrel with the raised white bump on the camera's lens mount. (See Figure A.5.) Rotate the lens toward the shutter release until it seats securely. Some lenses are trickier to mount than others, particularly telephotos and telephoto zooms with swiveling collars that allow the lens to be fastened to a tripod. You might need to rotate the collar so the tripod foot doesn't bump into the front overhang of the D810's prism.

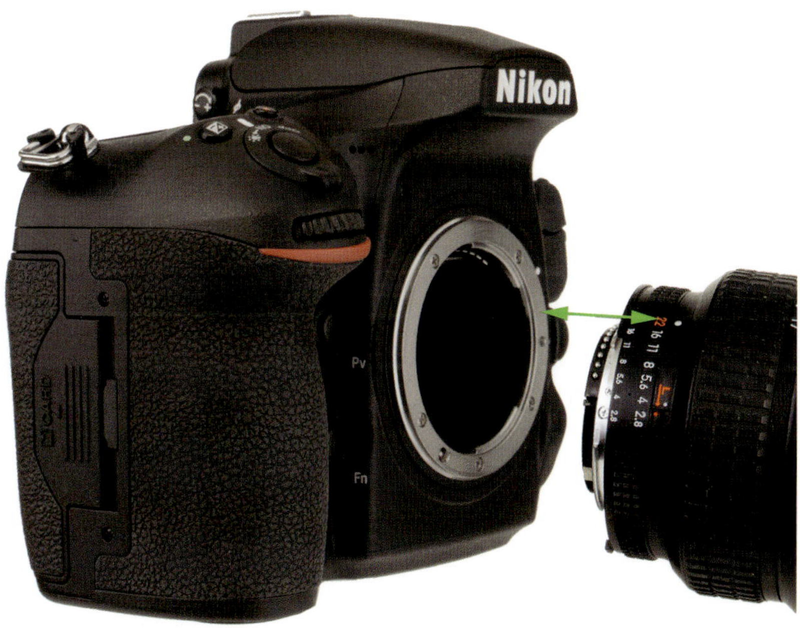

Figure A.5
Match the indicator on the lens with the white dot on the camera mount to properly align the lens with the bayonet mount.

DEALING WITH ERRORS

After you've mounted your lens properly (or *think* you have), you might find various error codes appearing on the control panel LCD, viewfinder, and back-panel color monitor. Here are the most common error codes, and what you should do next:

- **FE E.** This error code, with a smaller uppercase F followed by two Es, indicates that you've mounted a lens that has an aperture ring, but haven't set the lens to its smallest f/stop (usually f/22 or f/32). Nikon autofocus lenses with an aperture ring have a lock lever that allows you to set the minimum aperture and lock it there so that this problem doesn't occur. However, you may have unlocked the aperture ring when you needed to set the aperture manually with the lens mounted on an older camera that didn't allow setting the aperture electronically. Or, you might have mounted the lens on a non-autoaperture extension tube, bellows, or other accessory.
- **E r r.** Some other error has taken place. Release the shutter, turn off the camera, remove the lens, and remount it. Try another lens. If the message persists, then there is a problem unrelated to your lens, and your D810 may need service.

Set the focus mode switch on the lens to AF or M-AF (autofocus). If the lens hood is bayoneted on the lens in the reversed position (which makes the lens/hood combination more compact for transport), twist it off and remount with the "petals" (found on virtually all Nikon lens hoods) facing outward. (See Figure A.6.) A lens hood protects the front of the lens from accidental bumps, and reduces flare caused by extraneous light arriving at the front element of the lens from outside the picture area.

Adjusting Diopter Correction

Those of us with less than perfect eyesight can often benefit from a little optical correction in the viewfinder. Your contact lenses or glasses may provide all the correction you need, but if you are a glasses wearer and want to use the D810 without your glasses, you can take advantage of the camera's built-in diopter adjustment, which can be varied from –3 to +1 correction. Press the shutter release halfway to illuminate the indicators in the viewfinder, then pull out and rotate the diopter adjustment dial next to the viewfinder (see Figure A.7) while looking through the viewfinder until the indicators appear sharp. Push the dial back in to lock the setting.

If more than one person uses your D810, and each requires a different diopter setting on the camera itself, you can save a little time by noting the number of clicks and direction (clockwise to increase the diopter power; counterclockwise to decrease the diopter value) required to change from one user to the other. Should the available correction be insufficient, Nikon offers Diopter-Adjustment Viewfinder Lens DK-17C for the viewfinder window, ranging from –3 to +2, at a cost of $15-$20 each.

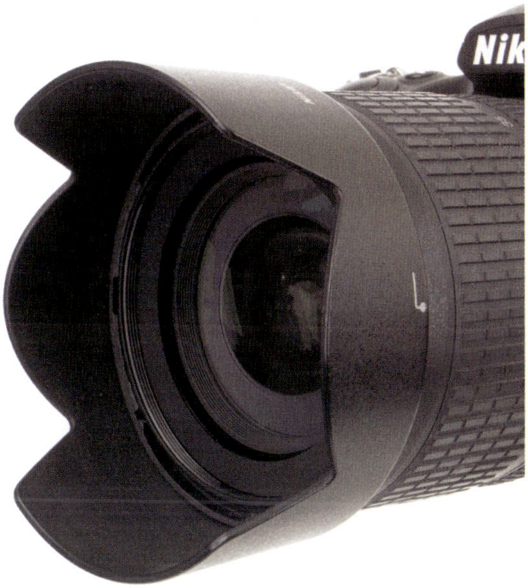

Figure A.6 A lens hood protects the lens from extraneous light and accidental bumps.

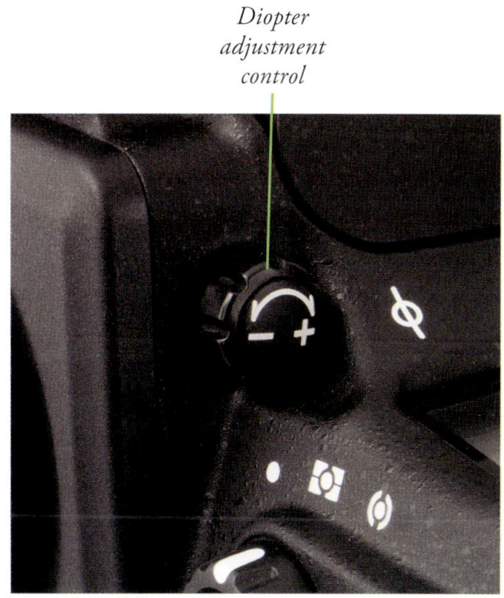

Figure A.7 Viewfinder diopter correction from –3 to +1 can be dialed in.

Inserting a Memory Card

You've probably set up your D810 so you can't take photos without a memory card inserted. (There is a Slot Empty Release Lock entry, Custom Setting f11 that enables/disables shutter release functions when a memory card is absent—learn about that in Chapter 12.) So, your final step will be to insert a memory card. Slide the door on the back right edge of the body toward the back of the camera to release the cover, and then open it. (You should only remove a memory card when the camera is switched off, or, at the very least, the yellow-green memory access light that indicates the camera is writing to the card is not illuminated.)

Inside, you'll find a Compact Flash slot and an SD card slot. (See Figure A.8.) You can specify one of them as the Primary slot, and the other becomes the Secondary slot, with functions designated for each, as I'll show you in Chapter 11. Insert either memory card with the label facing the back of the camera oriented so the edge with the contacts goes into the slot first. Close the door, and, if necessary, format the card. A Secure Digital card can be removed just by pressing it inward; it will pop out far enough that you can extract it. To remove the Compact Flash card, press the gray button at the bottom of the card chamber.

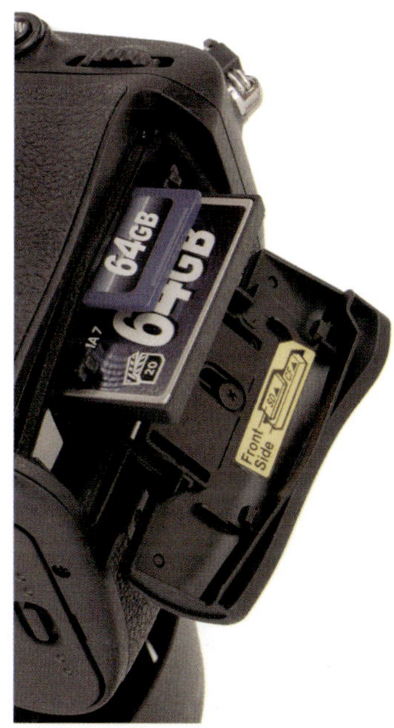

Figure A.8 The memory card in either slot is always inserted with the label facing the back of the camera.

MORE ABOUT CSM OPTIONS IN CHAPTER 3

Chapter 3 suggests other "default" settings you might want to adjust before you get started. You'll find a complete list of Custom Setting menu options and parameters in Chapter 12.

Formatting a Memory Card

There are four ways to create a blank memory card for your D810, and two of them are wrong. Here are your options, both correct and incorrect:

- **Transfer (move) files to your computer.** When you transfer (rather than copy) all the image files to your computer from the memory card (either using a direct cable transfer or with a card reader, as described later in this chapter), the old image files are erased from the card, leaving the card blank. Theoretically. Unfortunately, this method does *not* remove files that you've labeled as Protected (by pressing the Protect button to the left of the LCD while viewing the image on the monitor), nor does it identify and lock out parts of your memory card that have become corrupted or unusable since the last time you formatted the card. Therefore, I recommend always formatting the card, rather than simply moving the image files, each time you want to make a blank card. The only exception is when you *want* to leave the protected/unerased images on the card for awhile longer, say, to share with friends, family, and colleagues.
- **(Don't) Format in your computer.** With the memory card inserted in a card reader or card slot in your computer, you can use Windows or Mac OS to reformat the memory card. Don't! The operating system won't necessarily install the correct file system. The only way to ensure that the card has been properly formatted for your camera is to perform the format in the camera itself. The only exception to this rule is when you have a seriously munged memory card that your camera refuses to format. Sometimes it is possible to revive such a corrupted card by allowing the operating system to reformat it first, then trying again in the camera.
- **Setup menu format.** To use one of the recommended methods to format a memory card, press the MENU button, use the up/down buttons of the multi selector (that thumb-pad-sized control to the right of the monitor) to choose the Setup menu (which is represented by a wrench icon), navigate to the Format Memory Card entry with the right button of the multi selector, choose which memory card to format (CF or SD), and select Yes from the screen that appears. Press OK to begin the format process.

- **Two-button format.** The second recommended method requires no menus. Hold down the mode button (on top of the camera, just southwest of the shutter release button) and the trash can button (on the upper-left corner of the back) simultaneously for about two seconds. (A Format label [color-coded red] appears next to each button, as shown in the yellow boxes in Figure A.9.) The characters "For" and the exposures remaining displays will blink in the viewfinder and top control panel LCD. If you have memory cards inserted in both the Secure Digital card slots, Slot 1 will be selected. If you'd rather format the other card, rotate the main command dial to select that slot. Then press the pair of buttons again, and the D810 will format your card. To cancel the format, press any other button.

Table A.1 shows the typical number of shots you can expect using 14-bit color depth and an 8GB memory card. (Hold down the QUAL button [the front button on the dial at the top-left edge of the camera] and rotate the main command dial to change the file/formats in column 1, and rotate the sub-command dial to change the image sizes in columns 2, 3, and, 4.) The current file format appears in the control panel along with the number of exposures possible with the current memory card.

At this point, your camera is set up and ready to shoot. You can move on to Chapter 1, where I show you how to make basic settings.

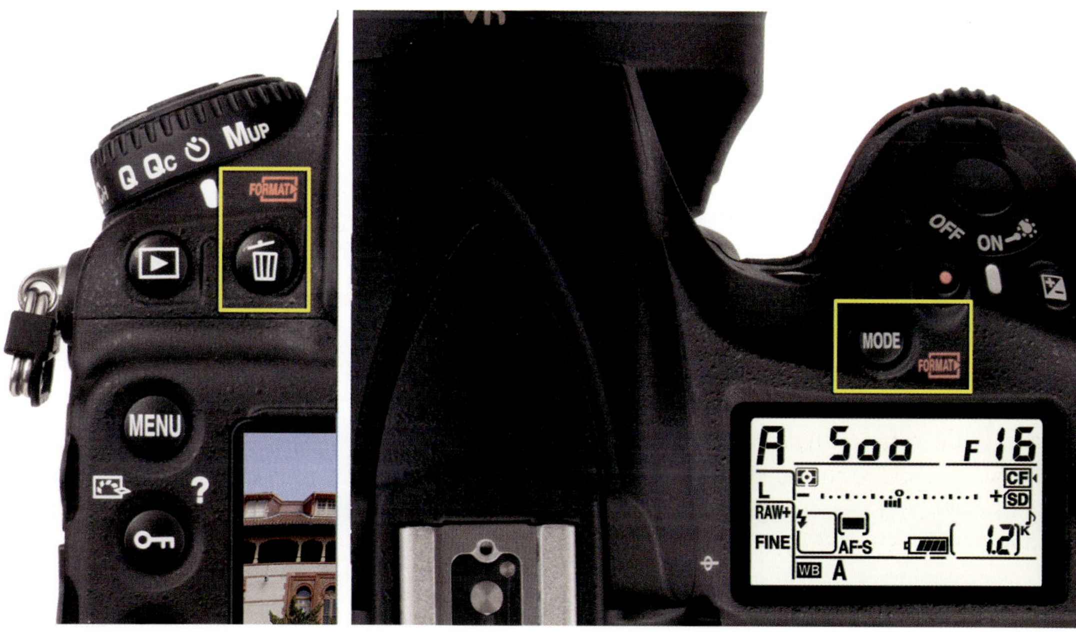

Figure A.9 Hold down the buttons marked Format to initiate reformatting of a memory card.

Table A.1 File Capacity of 8GB Card

	Large	Medium	Small
JPEG Fine	349	598	1,200
JPEG Normal	697	1,100	2,300
JPEG Basic	1,300	2,300	4,600
TIFF	69	122	268
RAW	100	N/A	N/A
RAW+JPEG Fine	77	85	92
RAW+JPEG Normal	87	92	96
RAW+JPEG Basic	93	96	98

HOW MANY SHOTS?

The D810 provides a fairly accurate estimate of the number of shots remaining on the control panel at all times (even when the camera is turned off), as well as at the lower-right edge of the viewfinder display when the display is active. (Tap the shutter release button to activate it.)

It is only an estimate, because the actual number will vary, depending on the capacity of your memory card, the file format(s) you've selected, and the content of the image itself. (Some photos may contain large areas that can be more efficiently compressed to a smaller size.)

For example, an 8GB card can hold about 349 JPEG Fine shots in full resolution (Large) format; 697 shots using Normal JPEG compression; or 1,300 shots with Basic JPEG compression. When numbers exceed 1,000, the D810 displays a figure and decimal point, followed by a K superscript, so that 1,300 shots (or thereabouts) is represented by $[1.3]^{K}$ in the LCD and viewfinder. The D810 offers three different resolution settings that provide different numbers of exposures: Large (7360 × 4912; 24 megapixels), Medium (5520 × 3680; 20.3 megapixels), and Small (3680 × 2456; 9 megapixels). For example, JPEG Basic using the Small resolution setting yields 4.6K exposures on a single 8GB memory card!

Using RAW/NEF format (more on that later) reduces the number of shots. An 8GB card has enough room for about 100 RAW photos in Nikon's NEF format (depending on the type of compression you choose, as described later) or just 77 pictures if you're shooting RAW+JPEG Fine pairs. Table A.1 shows some typical capacities for an 8GB memory card. You should know that the D810 has various compression options for JPEG and RAW files, as well as 12-bit and 14-bit dynamic range settings for the RAW format; we looked into those options in more detail in Chapter 11.

B

What Lenses Can Do for You

This appendix is intended for those who need a little updating on the capabilities of wide-angle, normal, or telephoto lenses and special-purpose optics. This is fairly basic stuff, but I've received more than a few requests from readers who want me to spell out these distinctions for them. Those of you who have a solid understanding of the most common lens types can return to Chapter 7, where I provide my recommendations about specific lenses.

I'm something of a lens nut. Because my work requires me to evaluate many different lenses and provide recommendations for specific lenses that may have overlapping focal lengths and features, I'm able to justify owning many more optics than the average person wants or needs. It probably wouldn't make sense for you to own 14-24mm, 17-35mm, 24-70mm, 24-85mm, 24-120mm, and 28-200mm zooms as I do. Indeed, a much saner approach to expanding your lens collection is to consider what each of your options can do for you and then choosing the type of lens and specific model that will really boost your creative opportunities.

So, in the sections that follow, I'm going to provide a general guide to the sort of capabilities you can gain for your D810 by adding a lens to your repertoire. In Chapter 7, I provided a more detailed discussion of some specific lenses and how they might fit into your camera bag toolkit.

- **Wider perspective.** Your mid-range zoom lens has served you well for moderate wide-angle shots. Now you find your back is up against a wall and you *can't* take a step backwards to take in more subject matter. Perhaps you're standing on the rim of the Grand Canyon, and you want to take in as much of the breathtaking view as you can. You might find yourself just behind the baseline at a high school basketball game and want an interesting shot with a little perspective distortion tossed in the mix. There's a lens out there that will provide you with what you need, such as the 14-24mm zoom I described in Chapter 7.

- **Bring objects closer.** A long lens brings distant subjects closer to you, offers better control over depth-of-field, and avoids the perspective distortion that wide-angle lenses provide. They compress the apparent distance between objects in your frame. The image shown in Figure B.1 was taken using a wide 16mm lens, while Figures B.2 and B.3 were taken from the same position as Figure B.1, but with focal lengths of 70mm and 200mm, respectively.
- **Bring your camera closer.** Macro lenses allow you to focus to within an inch or two of your subject. Nikon's best close-up lenses are all fixed focal length optics in the 60mm to 200mm range. But you'll find good macro zooms available from Sigma and others. They don't tend to focus quite as close, but they provide a bit of flexibility when you want to vary your subject distance (say, to avoid spooking a skittish creature).
- **Look sharp.** Many lenses are prized for their sharpness and overall image quality. While your run-of-the-mill lens is likely to be plenty sharp for most applications, the very best optics are even better over their entire field of view (which means no fuzzy corners), are sharper at a wider range of focal lengths (in the case of zooms), and have better correction for various types of distortion. You can read lens evaluations to help locate the sharpest lenses in online forums like www.popphoto.com and www.dpreview.com.
- **More speed.** Your Nikon 70-300mm f/4.5-5.6 telephoto zoom lens might have the perfect focal length and sharpness for sports photography, but the maximum aperture won't cut it for night baseball or football games, or, even, any sports shooting in daylight if the weather is cloudy or you need to use some ungodly fast shutter speed, such as 1/4,000th second. You might be happier to gain a full f/stop with an AF-S Nikkor 300mm f/4D IF-ED or even the Nikon AF-S VR II Zoom-Nikkor 70-200mm f/2.8G IF-E mated to a 1.4x teleconverter (giving you a 98-280mm f/4 lens). If money is no object, you can spring for Nikon's superfast 400mm f/2.8 and 600mm f/4 (both with vibration reduction and priced in the $10,000-and-up stratosphere). Or, maybe you just need the speed and can benefit from an f/1.8 or f/1.4 prime lens. They're all available in Nikon mounts (there's even an 85mm f/1.4 and 50mm f/1.4 for the real speed demons). With any of these lenses you can continue photographing under the dimmest of lighting conditions without the need for a tripod or flash.
- **Special features.** Accessory lenses give you special features, such as tilt/shift capabilities to correct for perspective distortion in architectural shots. You'll also find macro lenses, including the AF-S Micro-Nikkor 60mm f/2.8G ED, and all VR (vibration reduction) lenses also count as special-feature optics.

Zoom or Prime?

Zoom lenses have changed the way serious photographers take pictures. One of the reasons that I own 12 SLR film bodies dating back to the pre-zoom days is that in ancient times it was common to mount a different fixed focal length prime lens on various cameras and take pictures with two or three cameras around your neck (or tucked in a camera case) so you'd be ready to take a long shot or an intimate close-up or wide-angle view on a moment's notice, without the need to switch

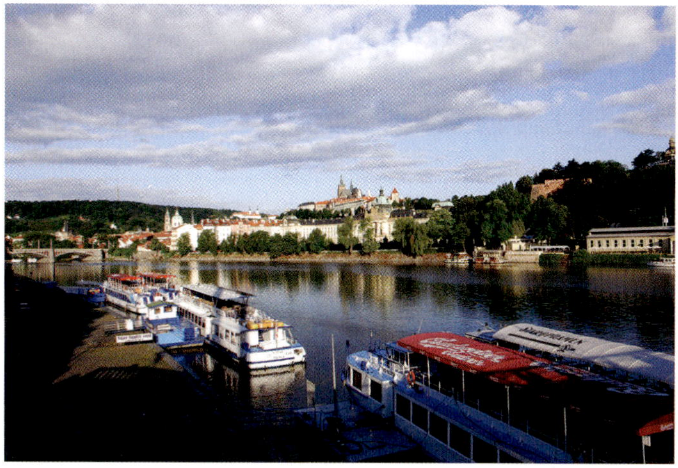

Figure B.1
An ultra-wide-angle lens provided this view of Prague Castle.

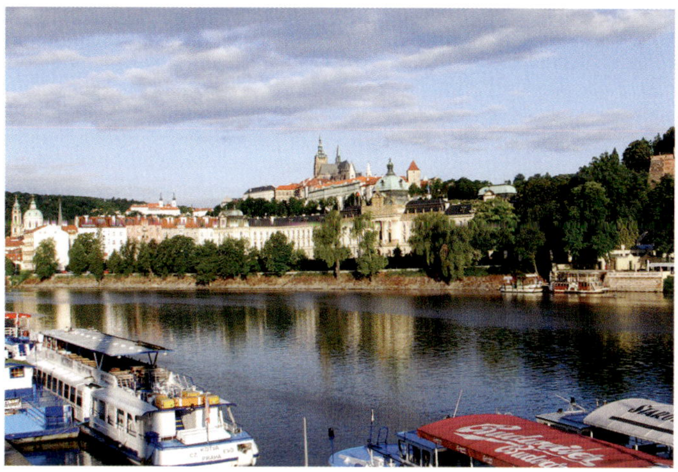

Figure B.2
This photo, taken from roughly the same distance, shows the view using a short telephoto lens.

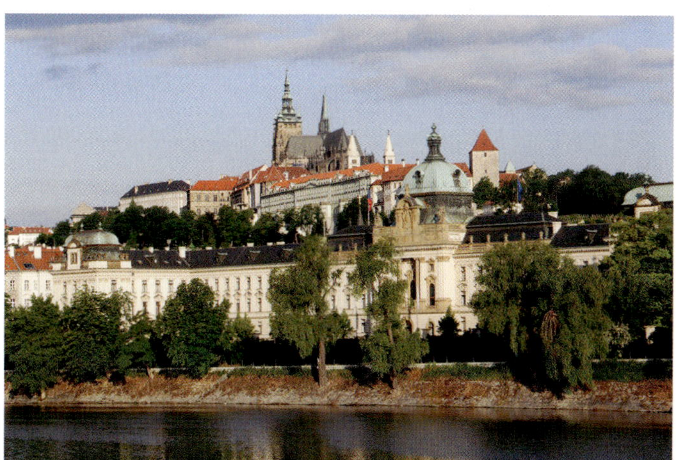

Figure B.3
A long telephoto lens captured this close-up view of Prague Castle from approximately the same shooting position.

lenses. It made sense (at the time) to have a half-dozen or so bodies (two to use, one in the shop, one in transit, and a couple backups). Zoom lenses of the time had a limited zoom range, were heavy, and not very sharp (especially when you tried to wield one of those monsters hand-held).

That's all changed today. Lenses like the razor-sharp AF-S Nikkor 70-200 f/2.8G ED VR II boast longer zoom ranges, in a package that's about 8.5-inches long, and while not petite at 3.2 pounds, quite usable hand-held (especially with VR switched on). Although such a lens might seem expensive at around $2,400-plus, it's actually much less costly than the six or so lenses it replaces. I'll explain more about this particular lens in Chapter 7.

When selecting between zoom and prime lenses, there are several considerations to ponder. Here's a checklist of the most important factors. I already mentioned image quality and maximum aperture earlier, but those aspects take on additional meaning when comparing zooms and primes.

- **Logistics.** As prime lenses offer just a single focal length, you'll need more of them to encompass the full range offered by a single zoom. More lenses mean additional slots in your camera bag, and extra weight to carry. Just within Nikon's line alone you can choose from a good selection of general-purpose prime lenses in 28mm, 35mm, 50mm, 85mm, 100mm, 135mm, and 200mm focal lengths, all of which are overlapped by the 28-200mm zoom I mentioned earlier. Even so, you might be willing to carry an extra prime lens or two in order to gain the speed or image quality.
- **Image quality.** Prime lenses usually produce better image quality at their focal length than even the most sophisticated zoom lenses at the same magnification. Zoom lenses, with their shifting elements and f/stops that can vary from zoom position to zoom position, are in general more complex to design than fixed focal length lenses. That's not to say that the very best prime lenses can't be complicated as well. However, the exotic designs, aspheric elements, and low-dispersion glass can be applied to improving the quality of the lens, rather than wasting a lot of it on compensating for problems caused by the zoom process itself.
- **Maximum aperture.** Because of the same design constraints, zoom lenses usually have smaller maximum apertures than prime lenses, and the most affordable zooms have a lens opening that grows effectively smaller as you zoom in. The difference in lens speed verges on the ridiculous at some focal lengths. For example, an 18mm-55mm basic zoom gives you a 55mm f/5.6 lens when zoomed all the way out, while prime lenses in that focal length commonly have f/1.8 or faster maximum apertures. Indeed, the fastest f/2, f/1.8, f/1.4, and f/1.2 lenses are all primes, and if you require speed, a fixed focal length lens, is what you should rely on. Figure B.4 shows an image taken with a Nikon 85mm f /1.4 lens.
- **Speed.** Using prime lenses takes time and slows you down. It takes a few seconds to remove your current lens and mount a new one, and the more often you need to do that, the more time is wasted. If you choose not to swap lenses, when using a fixed focal length lens you'll still have to move closer or farther away from your subject to get the field of view you want. A zoom lens allows you to change magnifications and focal lengths with the twist of a ring and generally saves a great deal of time.

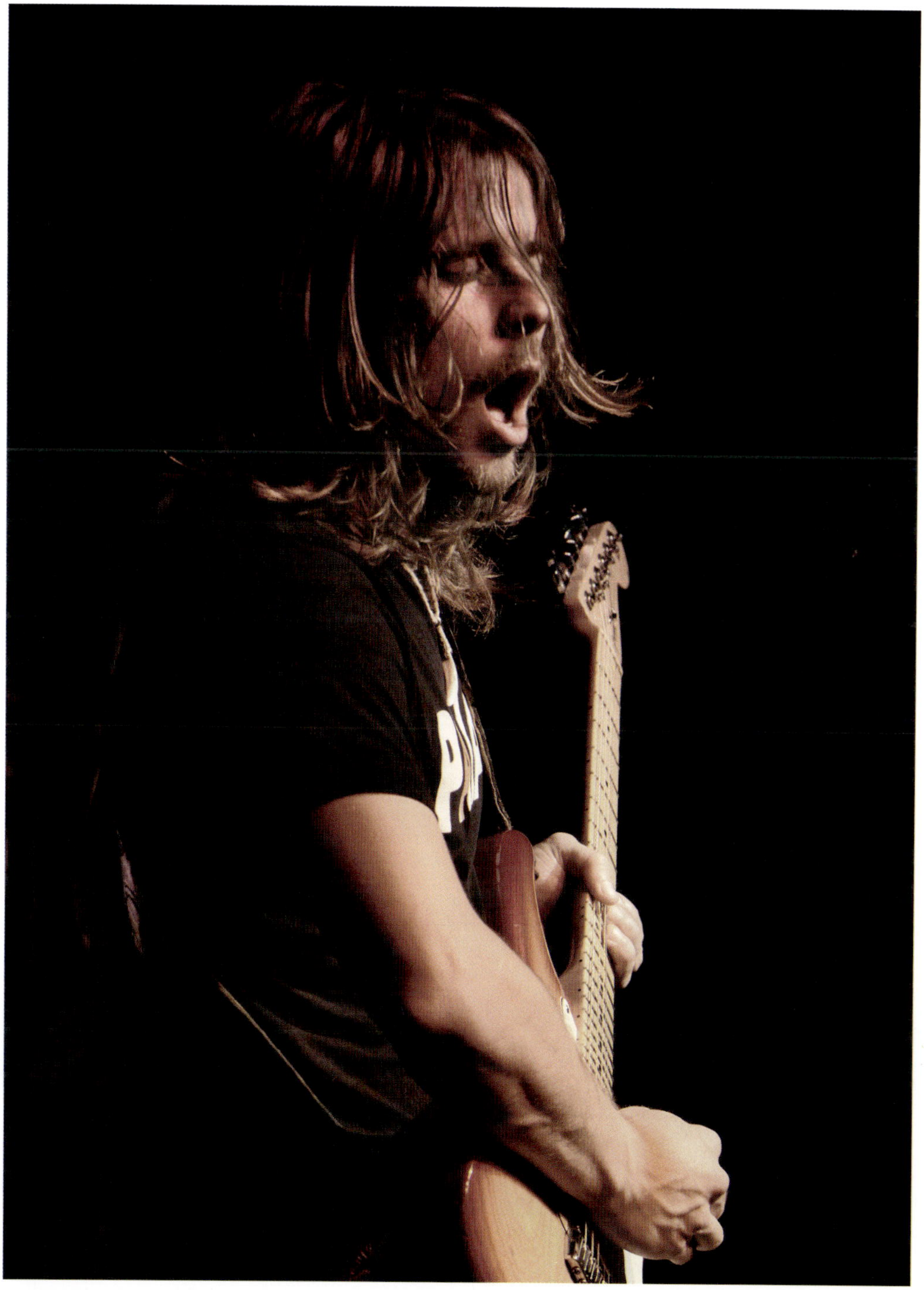

Figure B.4 The 85mm f/1.4 lens was perfect for this hand-held photo of Willie Nelson's guitar-slinger son Lukas.

Categories of Lenses

Lenses can be categorized by their intended purpose—general photography, macro photography, and so forth—or by their focal length. The range of available focal lengths is usually divided into three main groups: wide-angle, normal, and telephoto. Prime lenses fall neatly into one of these classifications. Zooms can overlap designations, with a significant number falling into the catch-all wide-to-telephoto zoom range. This section provides more information about focal length ranges, and how they are used.

Any lens with a focal length of 10mm to 16mm is said to be an *ultra-wide-angle lens*; from about 16mm to 30mm is said to be a *wide-angle lens. Normal lenses* have a focal length roughly equivalent to the diagonal of the film or sensor, in millimeters, and so fall into the range of about 40mm to 55mm on a D810. *Short telephoto lenses* start at about 70mm to 85mm, with anything from 105mm to 300mm qualifying as a conventional *telephoto.* For the Nikon D810, anything from about 300mm-400mm or longer can be considered a *super-telephoto.*

Using Wide-Angle and Wide-Zoom Lenses

To use wide-angle prime lenses and wide zooms, you need to understand how they affect your photography. Here's a quick summary of the things you need to know.

- **More depth-of-field.** Practically speaking, wide-angle lenses offer more depth-of-field at a particular subject distance and aperture. (But see the sidebar below for an important note.) You'll find that helpful when you want to maximize sharpness of a large zone, but not very useful when you'd rather isolate your subject using selective focus (telephoto lenses are better for that).
- **Stepping back.** Wide-angle lenses have the effect of making it seem that you are standing farther from your subject than you really are. They're helpful when you don't want to back up, or can't because there are impediments in your way.
- **Wider field of view.** While making your subject seem farther away, as implied above, a wide-angle lens also provides a larger field of view, including more of the subject in your photos.
- **More foreground.** As background objects retreat, more of the foreground is brought into view by a wide-angle lens. That gives you extra emphasis on the area that's closest to the camera. Photograph your home with a normal lens/normal zoom setting, and the front yard probably looks fairly conventional in your photo (that's why they're called "normal" lenses). Switch to a wider lens and you'll discover that your lawn now makes up much more of the photo. So, wide-angle lenses are great when you want to emphasize that lake in the foreground, but problematic when your intended subject is located farther in the distance.
- **Super-sized subjects.** The tendency of a wide-angle lens to emphasize objects in the foreground, while de-emphasizing objects in the background, can lead to a kind of size distortion that may be more objectionable for some types of subjects than others. Shoot a bed of flowers

up close with a wide angle, and you might like the distorted effect of the larger blossoms nearer the lens. Take a photo of a family member with the same lens from the same distance, and you're likely to get some complaints about that gigantic nose in the foreground.

- **Perspective distortion.** When you tilt the camera so the plane of the sensor is no longer perpendicular to the vertical plane of your subject, some parts of the subject are now closer to the sensor than they were before, while other parts are farther away. So, buildings, flagpoles, or NBA players appear to be falling backwards, as you can see in Figure B.5. While this kind of apparent distortion (it's not caused by a defect in the lens) can happen with any lens, it's most apparent when a wide angle is used.

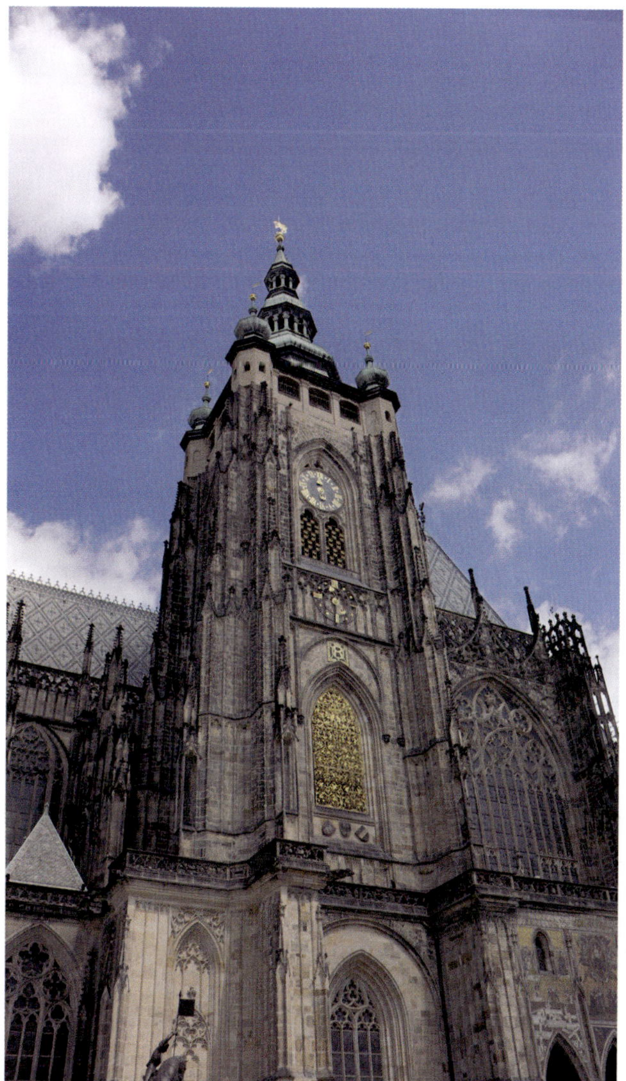

Figure B.5
Tilting the camera back produces this "falling back" look in architectural photos.

- **Steady cam.** You'll find that you can hand-hold a wide-angle lens at slower shutter speeds, without need for vibration reduction, than you can with a telephoto lens. The reduced magnification of the wide-lens or wide-zoom setting doesn't emphasize camera shake like a telephoto lens does.
- **Interesting angles.** Many of the factors already listed combine to produce more interesting angles when shooting with wide-angle lenses. Raising or lowering a telephoto lens a few feet probably will have little effect on the appearance of the distant subjects you're shooting. The same change in elevation can produce a dramatic effect for the much closer subjects typically captured with a wide-angle lens or wide-zoom setting.

DOF IN DEPTH

The DOF advantage of wide-angle lenses is diminished when you enlarge your picture; believe it or not, a wide-angle image enlarged and cropped to provide the same subject size as a telephoto shot would have the *same* depth-of-field. Try it: take a wide-angle photo of a friend from a fair distance, and then zoom in to duplicate the picture in a telephoto image. Then, enlarge the wide shot so your friend is the same size in both. The wide photo will have the same depth-of-field (and will have much less detail, too).

Avoiding Potential Wide-Angle Problems

Wide-angle lenses have a few quirks that you'll want to keep in mind when shooting so you can avoid falling into some common traps. Here's a checklist of tips for avoiding common problems:

- **Symptom: converging lines.** Unless you want to use wildly diverging lines as a creative effect, it's a good idea to keep horizontal and vertical lines in landscapes, architecture, and other subjects carefully aligned with the sides, top, and bottom of the frame. That will help you avoid undesired perspective distortion. Sometimes it helps to shoot from a slightly elevated position so you don't have to tilt the camera up or down.
- **Symptom: color fringes around objects.** Lenses are often plagued with fringes of color around backlit objects, produced by *chromatic aberration*, which comes in two forms: *longitudinal/axial*, in which all the colors of light don't focus in the same plane; and *lateral/transverse*, in which the colors are shifted to one side. Axial chromatic aberration can be reduced by stopping down the lens, but transverse CA cannot. Both can be reduced by using lenses with low diffraction index glass (or ED elements, in Nikon nomenclature) and by incorporating elements that cancel the chromatic aberration of other glass in the lens. For example, a strong positive lens made of low-dispersion crown glass (made of a soda-lime-silica composite) may be mated with a weaker negative lens made of high-dispersion flint glass, which contains lead.

- **Symptom: lines that bow outward.** Some wide-angle lenses cause straight lines to bow outward, with the strongest effect at the edges. In fisheye (or *curvilinear*) lenses, this defect is a feature, as you can see in Figure B.6. When distortion is not desired, you'll need to use a lens that has corrected barrel distortion. Manufacturers like Nikon do their best to minimize or eliminate it (producing a *rectilinear* lens), often using *aspherical* lens elements (which are not cross-sections of a sphere). You can also minimize barrel distortion simply by framing your photo with some extra space all around, so the edges where the defect is most obvious can be cropped out of the picture. Some image editors, such as Photoshop and Photoshop Elements have a lens distortion correction feature.
- **Symptom: light and dark areas when using polarizing filter.** If you know that polarizers work best when the camera is pointed 90 degrees away from the sun and have the least effect when the camera is oriented 180 degrees from the sun, you know only half the story. With lenses having a focal length of 14mm-28mm, the angle of view is extensive enough to cause problems. Think about it: when a 14mm lens is pointed at the proper 90-degree angle from the sun, objects at the edges of the frame will be oriented at 135 to 41 degrees, with only the center at exactly 90 degrees. Either edge will have much less of a polarized effect. The solution is to avoid using a polarizing filter with lenses having an actual focal length of less than 28mm.

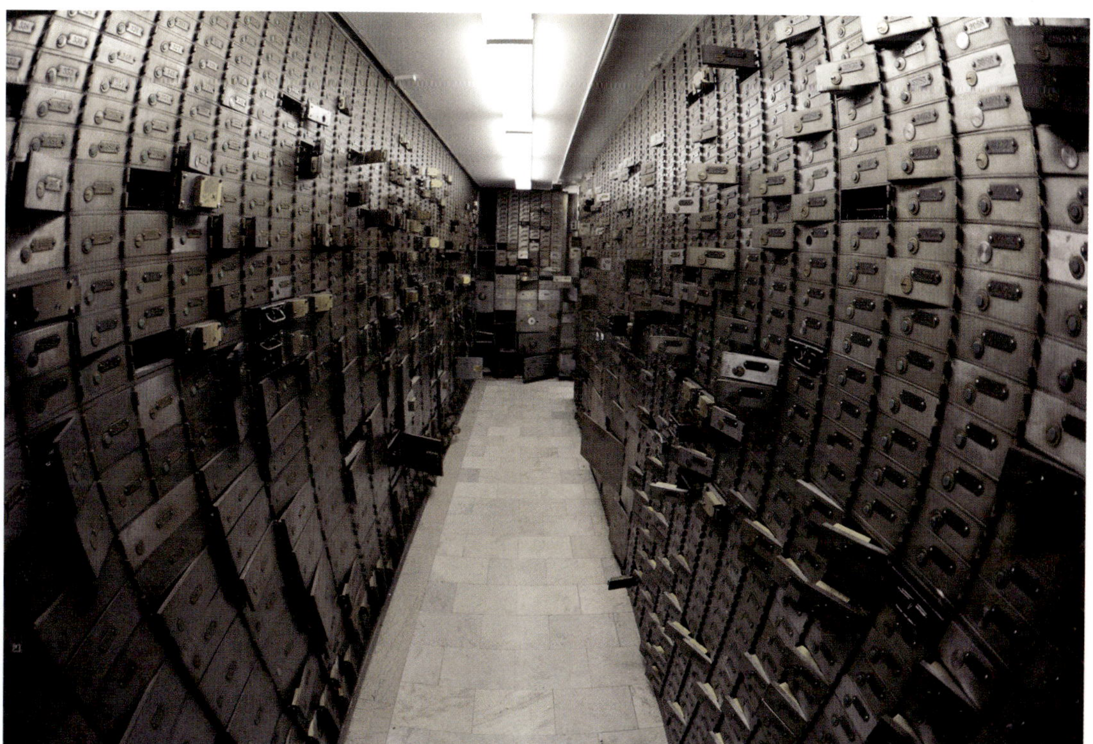

Figure B.6 Many wide-angle lenses cause lines to bow outward toward the edges of the image; with a fisheye lens, this tendency is considered an interesting feature.

Using Telephoto and Tele-Zoom Lenses

Telephoto lenses also can have a dramatic effect on your photography, and Nikon is especially strong in the long-lens arena, with lots of choices in many focal lengths and zoom ranges. You should be able to find an affordable telephoto or tele-zoom to enhance your photography in several different ways. Here are the most important things you need to know. In the next section, I'll concentrate on telephoto considerations that can be problematic—and how to avoid those problems.

- **Selective focus.** Long lenses have reduced depth-of-field within the frame, allowing you to use selective focus to isolate your subject. You can open the lens up wide to create shallow depth-of-field, or close it down a bit to allow more to be in focus. The flip side of the coin is that when you *want* to make a range of objects sharp, you'll need to use a smaller f/stop to get the depth-of-field you need. Like fire, the depth-of-field of a telephoto lens can be friend or foe. Figure B.7 shows a photo of a François' langur monkey, photographed using a telephoto lens and wider f/stop to de-emphasize a distracting background.
- **Getting closer.** Telephoto lenses bring you closer to wildlife, sports action, and candid subjects. No one wants to get a reputation as a surreptitious or "sneaky" photographer (except for paparazzi), but when applied to candids in an open and honest way, a long lens can help you capture memorable moments while retaining enough distance to stay out of the way of events as they transpire.
- **Reduced foreground/increased compression.** Telephoto lenses have the opposite effect of wide angles: they reduce the importance of things in the foreground by squeezing everything together. This compression even makes distant objects appear to be closer to subjects in the foreground and middle ranges. You can use this effect as a creative tool to squeeze subjects together.
- **Accentuates camera shakiness.** Telephoto focal lengths hit you with a double whammy in terms of camera/photographer shake. The lenses themselves are bulkier, more difficult to hold steady, and may even produce a barely perceptible see-saw rocking effect when you support them with one hand halfway down the lens barrel. Telephotos also magnify any camera shake. It's no wonder that vibration reduction is popular in longer lenses.
- **Interesting angles require creativity.** Telephoto lenses require more imagination in selecting interesting angles, because the "angle" you do get on your subjects is so narrow. Moving from side to side or a bit higher or lower can make a dramatic difference in a wide-angle shot, but raising or lowering a telephoto lens a few feet probably will have little effect on the appearance of the distant subjects you're shooting.

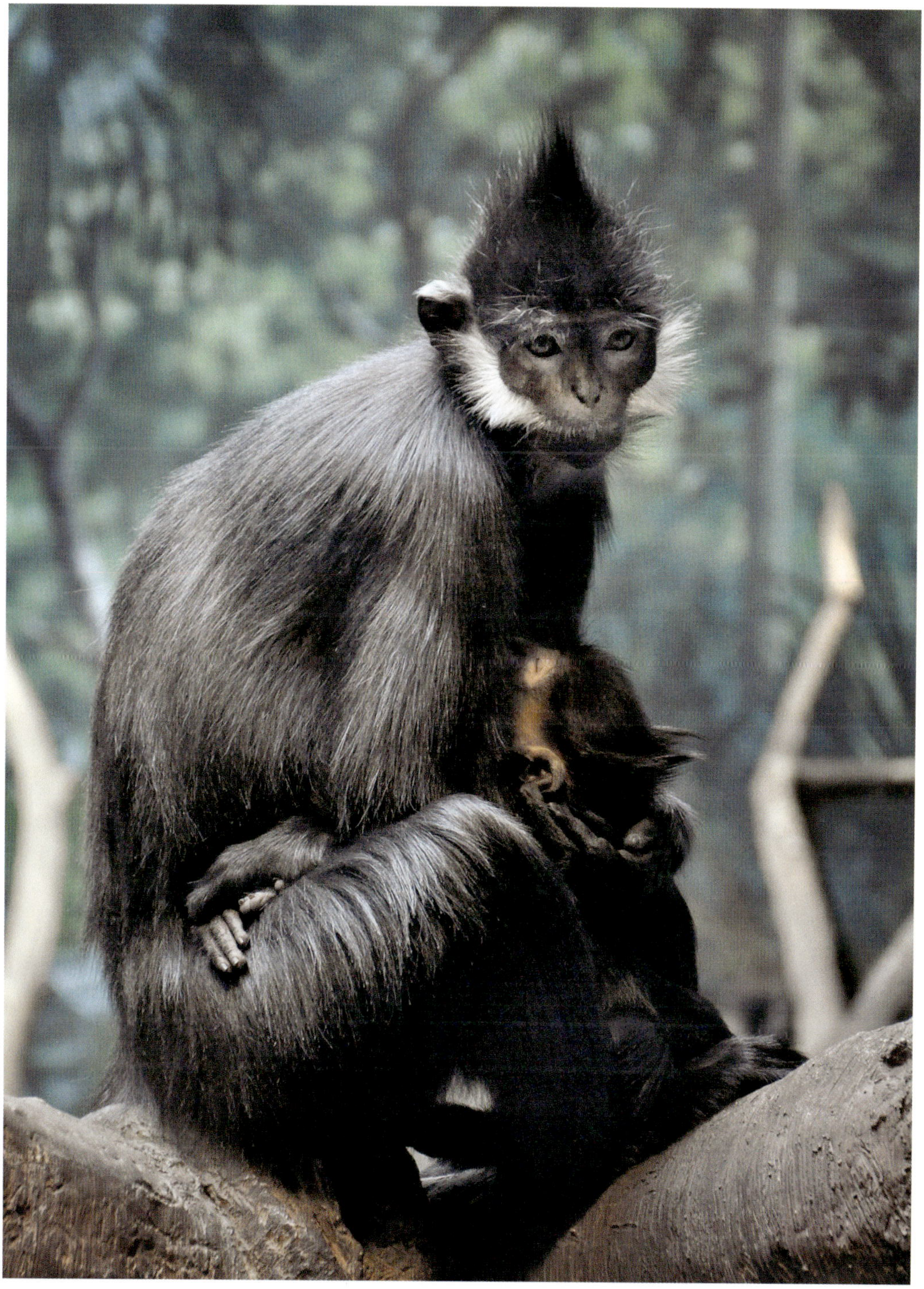

Figure B.7 A wide f/stop and lighting helped isolate this leaf monkey and her child from its background.

Avoiding Telephoto Lens Problems

Many of the "problems" that telephoto lenses pose are really just challenges and not that difficult to overcome. Here is a list of the seven most common picture maladies and suggested solutions.

- **Symptom: flat faces in portraits.** Head-and-shoulders portraits of humans tend to be more flattering when a focal length of 50mm to 85mm is used. Longer focal lengths compress the distance between features like noses and ears, making the face look wider and flat. A wide angle might make noses look huge and ears tiny when you fill the frame with a face. So stick with 50mm to 105mm focal lengths, going longer only when you're forced to shoot from a greater distance, and wider only when shooting three-quarters/full-length portraits, or group shots.
- **Symptom: blur due to camera shake.** Use a higher shutter speed (boosting ISO if necessary); consider an image-stabilized lens; or mount your camera on a tripod, monopod, or brace it with some other support. Of those three solutions, only the first will reduce blur caused by *subject* motion; a VR lens or tripod won't help you freeze a race car in mid-lap.
- **Symptom: color fringes.** Chromatic aberration is the most pernicious optical problem found in telephoto lenses. There are others, including spherical aberration, astigmatism, coma, curvature of field, and similarly scary-sounding phenomena. The best solution for any of these is to use a better lens that offers the proper degree of correction, or stop down the lens to minimize the problem. But that's not always possible. Your second best choice may be to correct the fringing in your favorite RAW conversion tool or image editor. Photoshop's Lens Correction filter offers sliders that minimize both red/cyan and blue/yellow fringing.
- **Symptom: lines that curve inward.** Pincushion distortion is found in many telephoto lenses. You might find after a bit of testing that it is worse at certain focal lengths with your particular zoom lens. Like chromatic aberration, it can be partially corrected using tools like the correction tools built into Photoshop and Photoshop Elements. You can see an example in Figure B.8; pincushion distortion isn't always this obvious.
- **Symptom: low contrast from haze or fog.** When you're photographing distant objects, a long lens shoots through a lot more atmosphere, which generally is muddied up with extra haze and fog. That dirt or moisture in the atmosphere can reduce contrast and mute colors. Some feel that a skylight or UV filter can help, but this practice is mostly a holdover from the film days. Digital sensors are not sensitive enough to UV light for a UV filter to have much effect. So you should be prepared to boost contrast and color saturation in your Picture Controls menu or image editor if necessary.
- **Symptom: low contrast from flare.** Lenses are furnished with lens hoods for a good reason: to reduce flare from bright light sources at the periphery of the picture area, or completely outside it. Because telephoto lenses often create images that are lower in contrast in the first place, you'll want to be especially careful to use a lens hood to prevent further effects on your image (or shade the front of the lens with your hand).

- **Symptom: dark flash photos.** Edge-to-edge flash coverage isn't a problem with telephoto lenses as it is with wide angles. The shooting distance is. A long lens might make a subject that's 50 feet away look as if it's right next to you, but your camera's flash isn't fooled. You'll need extra power for distant flash shots. The Nikon SB-910 Speedlight, for example, can automatically zoom its coverage down to that of a 105mm medium telephoto lens, providing a theoretical full-power shooting aperture of about f/11 at 30 feet and ISO 400.

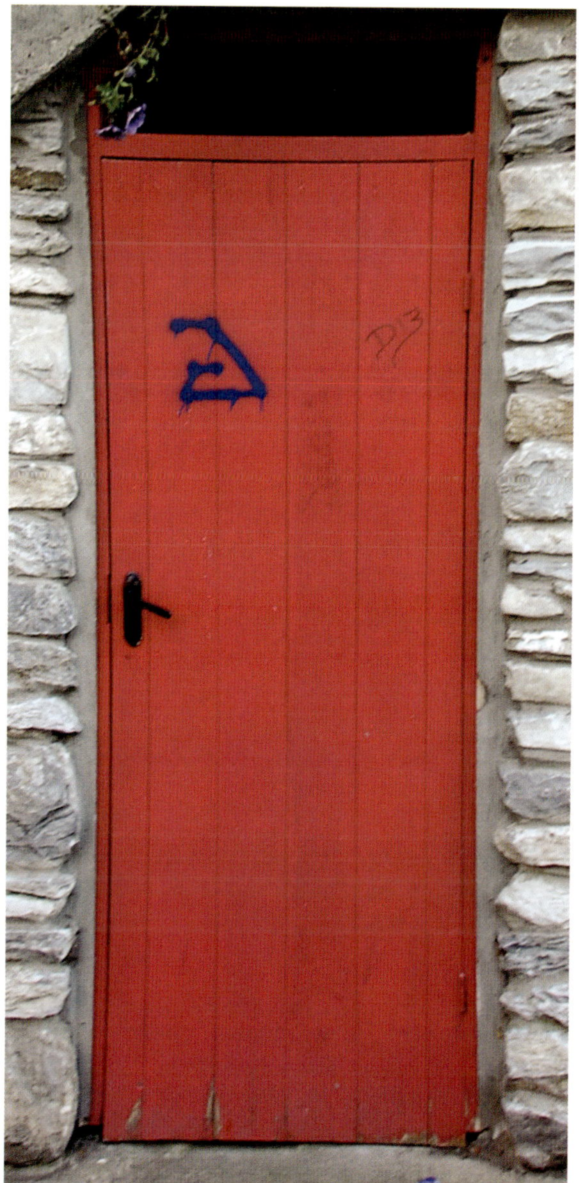

Figure B.8
Pincushion distortion in telephoto lenses causes lines to bow inward from the edges.

Telephotos and Bokeh

Bokeh describes the aesthetic qualities of the out-of-focus parts of an image and whether out-of-focus points of light—circles of confusion—are rendered as distracting fuzzy discs or smoothly fade into the background. *Boke* is a Japanese word for "blur," and the h was added to keep English speakers from rendering it monosyllabically to rhyme with *broke.* Although bokeh is visible in blurry portions of any image, it's of particular concern with telephoto lenses, which, thanks to the magic of reduced depth-of-field, produce more obviously out-of-focus areas.

Bokeh can vary from lens to lens, or even within a given lens depending on the f/stop in use. Bokeh becomes objectionable when the circles of confusion are evenly illuminated, making them stand out as distinct discs, or, worse, when these circles are darker in the center, producing an ugly "doughnut" effect. A lens defect called spherical aberration may produce out-of-focus discs that are brighter on the edges and darker in the center, because the lens doesn't focus light passing through the edges of the lens exactly as it does light going through the center. (Mirror or *catadioptric* lenses also produce this effect.)

Other kinds of spherical aberration generate circles of confusion that are brightest in the center and fade out at the edges, producing a smooth blending effect, as you can see at right in Figure B.9. Ironically, when no spherical aberration is present at all, the discs are a uniform shade, which, while better than the doughnut effect, is not as pleasing as the bright center/dark edge rendition. The shape of the disc also comes into play, with round smooth circles considered the best, and nonagonal or some other polygon (determined by the shape of the lens diaphragm) considered less desirable.

If you plan to use selective focus a lot, you should investigate the bokeh characteristics of a particular lens before you buy. Nikon user groups and forums will usually be full of comments and questions about bokeh of particular lenses, so the research is fairly easy.

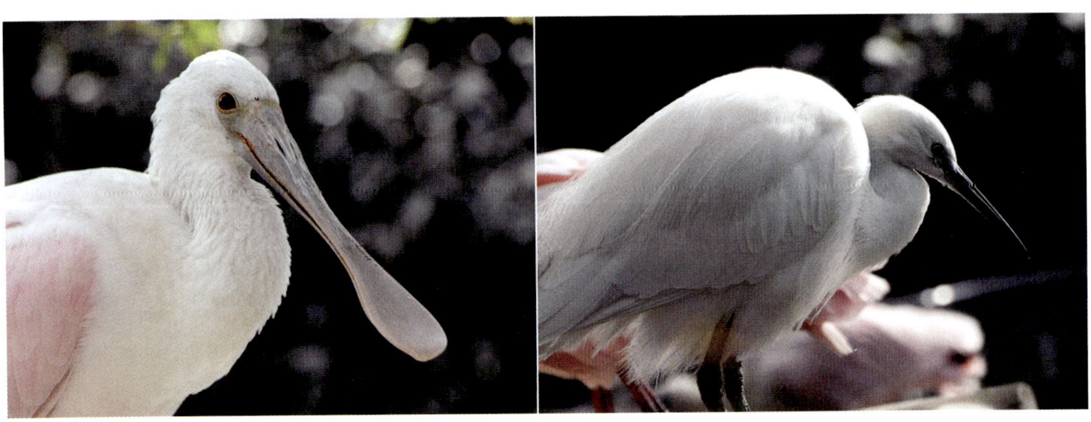

Figure B.9 Bokeh is less pleasing when the discs are prominent (left), and less obtrusive when they blend into the background (right).

Add-ons and Special Features

Once you've purchased your telephoto lens, you'll want to think about some appropriate accessories for it. There are some handy add-ons available that can be valuable. Here are a couple of them to think about.

Lens Hoods

Lens hoods are an important accessory for all lenses, but they're especially valuable with telephotos. As I mentioned earlier, lens hoods do a good job of preserving image contrast by keeping bright light sources outside the field of view from striking the lens and, potentially, bouncing around inside that long tube to generate flare that, when coupled with atmospheric haze, can rob your image of detail and snap. In addition, lens hoods serve as valuable protection for that large, vulnerable, front lens element. It's easy to forget that you've got that long tube sticking out in front of your camera and accidentally whack the front of your lens into something. It's cheaper to replace a lens hood than it is to have a lens repaired, so you might find that a good hood is valuable protection for your prized optics.

When choosing a lens hood, it's important to have the right hood for the lens, usually the one offered for that lens by Nikon or the third-party manufacturer. You want a hood that blocks precisely the right amount of light: neither too much light nor too little. A hood with a front diameter that is too small can show up in your pictures as vignetting. A hood that has a front diameter that's too large isn't stopping all the light it should. Generic lens hoods may not do the job.

When your telephoto is a zoom lens, it's even more important to get the right hood, because you need one that does what it is supposed to at both the wide-angle and telephoto ends of the zoom range. Lens hoods may be cylindrical, rectangular (shaped like the image frame), or petal shaped (that is, cylindrical, but with cut-out areas at the corners which correspond to the actual image area). Lens hoods should be mounted in the correct orientation (a bayonet mount for the hood usually takes care of this).

Telephoto Converters

Teleconverters (often called telephoto extenders outside the Nikon world) multiply the actual focal length of your lens, giving you a longer telephoto for much less than the price of a lens with that actual focal length. These converters fit between the lens and your camera and contain optical elements that magnify the image produced by the lens. Available in 1.4X, 1.7X, and 2.0X configurations from Nikon, a teleconverter transforms, say, a 200mm lens into a 280mm, 340mm, or 400mm optic, respectively. In effect, converters restore the "lens multiplier" factor you lost when you adopted the FX format. At around $500, converters are quite a bargain, aren't they?

There are other downsides. While extenders retain the closest focusing distance of your original lens, autofocus is maintained only if the lens's original maximum aperture is fairly large (f/2.8 or f/4 in most cases). The components reduce the effective aperture of any lens they are used with, by one f/stop with the 1.4X converter, 1.5 f/stops with the 1.7X converter, and 2 f/stops with the 2X extender. So, your 200mm f/2.8 lens becomes a 280mm f/4 or 400mm f/5.6 lens. Although Nikon converters are precision optical devices, they do cost you a little sharpness, but that improves when you reduce the aperture by a stop or two. Each of the converters is compatible only with a particular set of lenses greater, so you'll want to check Nikon's compatibility chart to see if the converter can be used with the lens you want to attach to it.

If your lenses are compatible and you're shooting under bright lighting conditions, the Nikon extenders make handy accessories. I recommend the 1.4X version because it robs you of very little sharpness and only one f/stop. The 1.7X version also works well, but I've found the original 2X teleconverter to exact too much of a sharpness and speed penalty to be of much use. The new version III is much better.

Macro Focusing

Some telephotos and telephoto zooms available for the Nikon D810 have particularly close focusing capabilities, making them *macro* lenses. Of course, the object is not necessarily to get close (get too close and you'll find it difficult to light your subject). What you're really looking for in a macro lens is to magnify the apparent size of the subject in the final image. Camera-to-subject distance is most important when you want to back up farther from your subject (say, to avoid spooking skittish insects or small animals). In that case, you'll want a macro lens with a longer focal length to allow that distance while retaining the desired magnification.

I discussed Nikon's array of macro lenses in Chapter 7. In addition to Nikon's close-up lenses, you'll also find macro lenses, macro zooms, and other close-focusing lenses available from Sigma, Tamron, and Tokina. Macro lenses let you shoot images like the one shown in Figure B.10. If you want to focus closer with a macro lens, or any other lens, you can add an accessory called an *extension tube*, or a *bellows extension*. These add-ons move the lens farther from the focal plane, allowing it to focus more closely. Nikon also sells add-on close-up lenses, which look like filters, and allow lenses to focus more closely.

Vibration Reduction

Nikon has a burgeoning line of about a dozen and a half lenses with built-in vibration reduction (VR) capabilities. I expect another half dozen or so new VR lenses to be introduced rather early in the life of this book.

The VR feature uses lens elements that are shifted internally in response to vertical or horizontal motion of the lens, which compensates for any camera shake in those directions. Vibration reduction is particularly effective when used with telephoto lenses, which magnify the effects of camera

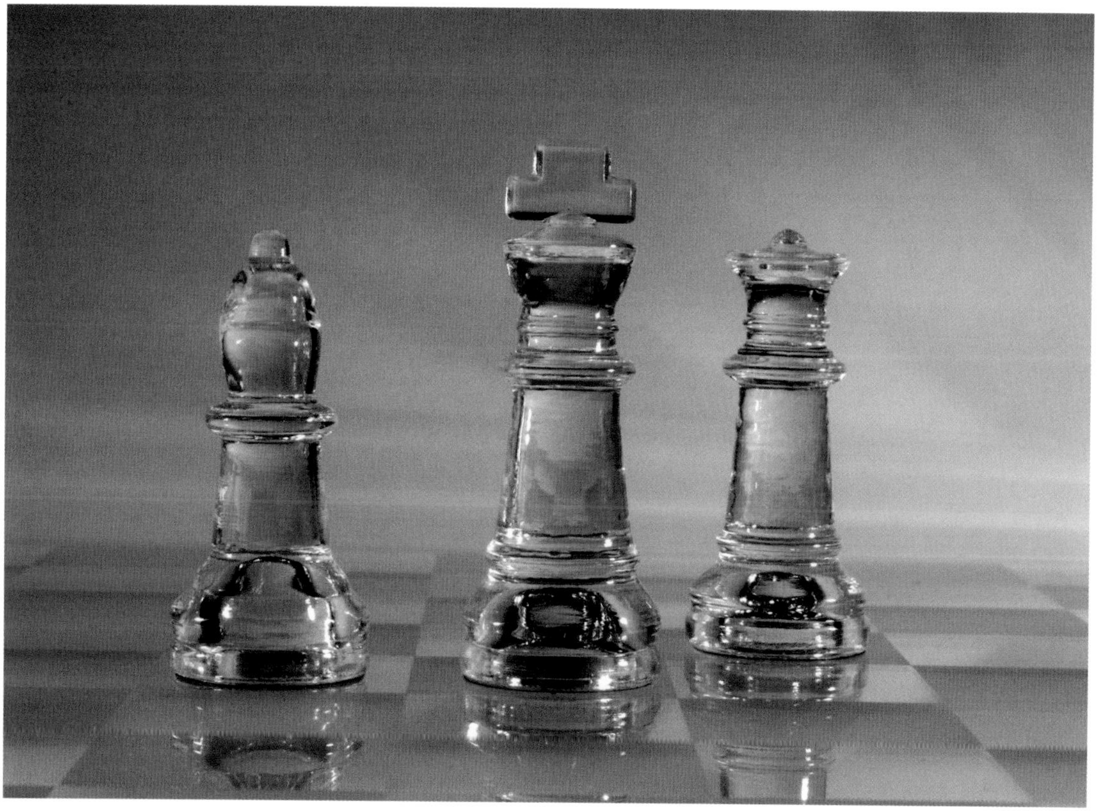

Figure B.10 Macro lenses aren't limited to shooting wildlife or flowers. You can create some interesting still life images out of everyday objects.

and photographer motion. However, VR can be useful for lenses of shorter focal lengths, such as Nikon's 24-120mm full-frame zoom or the new 24-85mm VR zoom.

Vibration reduction offers two to three shutter speed increments' worth of shake reduction. (Nikon claims a four-stop gain, which I feel may be optimistic.) This extra margin can be invaluable when you're shooting under dim lighting conditions or hand-holding a lens for, say, wildlife photography. Perhaps that shot of a foraging deer would require a shutter speed of 1/2,000th second at f/5.6 with your AF-S VR Zoom-Nikkor 200-400mm f/4G IF-ED lens. Relax. You can shoot at 1/250th second at f/11 and get a photo that is just as sharp, as long as the deer doesn't decide to bound off. Or, perhaps you're shooting indoors and would prefer to shoot at 1/15th second at f/4. However, consider these facts:

- **VR doesn't freeze subject motion.** Vibration reduction won't freeze moving subjects in their tracks, because it is effective only at compensating for *camera* motion. It's best used in reduced illumination, to steady the up-down swaying of telephoto lenses, and to improve close-up photography. If your subject is in motion, you'll still need a shutter speed that's fast enough to stop the action.

- **VR adds to shutter lag.** The process of adjusting the lens elements, like autofocus, takes time, so vibration reduction may contribute to a slight increase in shutter lag. If you're shooting sports, that delay may be annoying, but I still use my VR lenses for sports all the time!
- **Use when appropriate.** You may find that your results are worse when using VR while panning, although newer Nikon VR lenses work fine when the camera is deliberately moved from side to side during exposure. Older lenses can confuse the panning motion with camera wobble and provide too much compensation. You might want to switch off VR when panning or when your camera is mounted on a tripod.
- **Do you need VR at all?** Remember that an inexpensive monopod might be able to provide the same additional steadiness as a VR lens, at a much lower cost. If you're out in the field shooting wild animals or flowers and think a tripod isn't practical, try a monopod first. Or, you might be able to shift to a much higher ISO setting and use faster shutter speeds.

C

Software Tools

Unless you only take pictures, and then immediately print them directly to a PictBridge-compatible printer, somewhere along the line you're going to need to make use of the broad array of software available for the Nikon D810. The picture-fixing options in the Retouch menu let you make only modest modifications to your carefully crafted photos. If your needs involve more than fixing red-eye, cropping and trimming, and maybe adjusting tonal values with D-Lighting, you're definitely going to want to use a utility or editor of some sort to perfect your images. After you've captured some great images and have them safely stored on your Nikon D810's memory card, you'll need to transfer them from your camera and memory card to your computer, where they can be organized, fine-tuned in an image editor, and prepared for web display, printing, or some other final destination.

Fortunately, there are lots of software utilities and applications to help you do all these things. This chapter will introduce you to a few of them. Please note that this is *not* a "how-to-do-it" software chapter. There's no space, even in this massive volume, to explain how to use all the features of Nikon Capture NX 2 or NX-D, nor how to tweak RAW file settings in Adobe Camera Raw. Entire books have been written about both products. This chapter is intended solely to help you get your bearings among the large number of utilities and applications available, to help you better understand what each does, and how you might want to use them.

Nikon's Applications and Utilities

If nothing else, Nikon has made sorting through the software for its digital cameras an interesting pursuit. Through the years, we've had various incarnations of programs with names like PictureProject, Nikon View, and Nikon Capture. Some have been compatible with both the Nikon dSLR and amateur Coolpix product lines. Many of them have been furnished on disk with the cameras. Others, most notoriously Nikon Capture NX 2, have been an extra-cost option, which particularly infuriated those of us who had paid several thousand dollars for a Nikon dSLR, and found that we'd need to pay more to get the software needed for the camera. Note that while Nikon updates its software offerings periodically, adding new features is fairly rare. Most updates simply add support for the latest camera introductions, such as the Nikon D4s or Nikon Df. So, if your current Nikon utilities support your camera, there is no rush to install the very latest version unless the notification mentions bug fixes. The next few sections provide some descriptions of the Nikon software you'll want to use with your camera.

Nikon ViewNX 2

This latest incarnation of Nikon's basic file viewer is better than ever, making it easy to browse through images, convert RAW files to JPEG or TIFF, and make corrections to white balance and exposure, either on individual files or on batches of files. It works in tandem with Nikon Transfer and Nikon Capture NX, as you can open files inspected in ViewNX in one of the other programs—or within a third-party application you "register."

First and foremost, Nikon ViewNX is a great file viewer. There are five modes for looking at images: a Thumbnail Grid mode for checking out an array of small previews of your images; a Thumbnail List that presents the tiny previews in a single column you can scroll through rapidly; an Image Viewer mode that shows a group of thumbnails along with an enlarged version of a selected image; a Geotag View that can place images with embedded GPS information (say, from the Nikon GP-1a device) on a Google map; and Full Screen mode, which allows you to examine an image in maximum detail. The program senses whether you have a secondary display (as I do), and when you press F will show the selected image full screen on that other monitor.

If you like to shoot RAW+JPEG, you can review image pairs as if they were a single image (rather than view the RAW and JPEG versions separately), and work with whichever version you need. The active focus area can be displayed in the image, and there are histogram, highlight, and shadow displays to help you evaluate an image. You can crop and straighten images, fix red-eye automatically, boost color, and make simple adjustments for exposure compensation, white balance, Picture Controls, Sharpness, Contrast, Brightness, and other parameters. That's a lot of control for a simple file viewer.

Should you want to organize your images, there are 10 color-coded labels available to classify images by criteria such as images printed, images copied, or images sent as e-mail, and you can mark your best shots for easier retrieval with a rating system of one to five stars. ViewNX also allows you to edit embedded XMP/IPTC Information in fields such as Creator, Origin, Image Title, and suitable keywords. The utility can be downloaded from the support/download pages of the Nikon website at www.nikonusa.com.

Nikon Transfer

It seems like everyone offers some sort of image transfer system that automatically recognizes when a memory card is inserted in a reader, or a digital camera like the Nikon D810 is attached to a computer using a USB cable. The most popular operating systems, from Mac OS X to Windows XP, Vista, and Windows 7 have their own built-in transfer programs, and Adobe includes one in its utilities for Bridge, and Photoshop Elements includes one in its suite of utilities.

Nikon Transfer is particularly well suited for Nikon D810 owners, because it integrates easily with other Nikon software products, including ViewNX, Nikon Capture NX 2, and Capture NX-D. You can download photos to your computer, and then continue to work on them in the Nikon application (or third-party utility) of your choice.

When a memory card is inserted into a card reader, or when the Nikon D810 is connected to your computer through a USB cable, Nikon Transfer recognizes the device, searches it for thumbnails, and provides a display where you can preview the images and mark the ones you want to transfer with checks to create a Transfer Queue.

Then, click on the Primary Destination tab and choose a location for the photos that will be transferred. Nikon Transfer can create a new folder for each transfer based on a naming convention you set up (click the Edit button next to the box at top center in the figure), or copy to a folder named after the current folder in the Nikon D810's memory card. You can keep the current filename as the files are transferred, or assign a new name with a prefix you designate, such as Prague12_. The program will add a number from 001 to 999 to the filename prefix you specify.

One neat feature is the ability to name a Backup Destination location, so that all transferred pictures can also be copied to a second folder, which can be located on a different hard disk drive or other media. You can embed information such as copyright data, star ratings, and labels in the images as they are transferred. When the file transfer is complete, Nikon Transfer can launch an application of your choice, set with a few clicks in the Preferences tab.

Nikon Capture NX 2 "Becomes" NX-D

Capture NX is a pretty hefty chunk of software for the typical entry-level Nikon owner, but you, as a Nikon D810 buyer, should be up to it. However, this program is challenging to master (and was somewhat expensive at about $180, but available for about $130 from various sources). Because Capture NX 2 was developed by Nik Software, which has been acquired by Google, Nikon intends to replace it with an in-house product, NX-D, which was introduced as a free application while I was finishing this book. The company has said it will continue to support NX 2 but has said that NX-D will remain free of charge in the future.

NX-D works with Nikon's RAW image formats, both NEF used by Nikon dSLRs, and NRW used by its non SLR cameras, and can process/adjust JPEG and TIFF files as well. The D stands for development (as in what some of us did in film darkrooms).

Its features include:

- **RAW conversion.** You can use NX-D to convert NEF/NRW files for editing in Photoshop, Elements, or another image editor, making adjustments to many in-camera settings that are locked in with JPEG and TIFF files, such as white balance.
- **Broad adjustments.** The program can also make *limited* adjustments to JPEG and TIFF files, including tone curves, brightness, and contrast, and correcting lateral color aberration caused by lenses.
- **Flexibility.** NX-D has floating palettes that can be moved around the screen and onto multiple monitors, as well as before-and-after comparison images (with automatic enlargement of both when you zoom in). Thumbnail, filmstrip, single-image, and full-screen displays are available.
- **Non-destructive.** Like Adobe Camera Raw and Lightroom, NX-D is able to preserve your original RAW files untouched, storing all the modifications in separate "sidecar" files that can be applied to the original at any time, modified, or discarded.
- **Image management.** NX-D has filtering functions that let you locate particular images using criteria such as focal length or camera name. Batch processing can be used to apply changes to multiple images.

Photographers tended to love the old Capture NX 2 or hate it, and it's easy to separate the fans from the furious. Those who are enamored of the program have invested a great deal of time in learning its quirky paradigm and now appreciate just how powerful Capture NX 2 is. The detractors are usually those who are comfortable with another program, such as Photoshop or Lightroom and are upset that even the simplest functions can be confoundingly difficult for a new user to figure out. Capture NX 2's murky Help system isn't a lot of help; there's room for a huge book (or two) to explain how to use this program. I think most are going to love NX-D—especially its price.

Nikon Camera Control Pro

Nikon's Camera Control Pro ($180) is a versatile utility that allows you to communicate directly with your camera from your computer through a USB cable. Once the two are linked, you can perform a variety of functions:

- **Shoot stills and movies remotely.** Just about any shooting function you can adjust on the camera can be performed remotely, as you can see from the cluster of tabbed dialog boxes. Set exposure mode, adjust the aperture, add or subtract exposure compensation, choose a focus area, change ISO sensitivity or white balance—all are at your command through the software. You can even change Quality and Size settings, turn on auto bracketing, and change image optimization settings. You can optionally disable the controls on the camera, to prevent having settings you made at the computer changed accidentally.

- **Preview your shots remotely.** Of course, shooting remotely is most useful only when you can *see* what you're capturing from your computer. Camera Control Pro has a full tethered shooting mode for the camera that shows the live view image on your computer display. If you're capturing video, you can even see the current audio levels at the bottom of the screen.
- **Download directly to your computer.** When shooting, especially when doing time-lapse photography, it's convenient to use Camera Control Pro to transfer the images you take directly to the computer in tethered mode.
- **Upload comments.** Frustrated by the Nikon D810's text entry screen? Edit your Image Comment and upload it directly to the camera from your computer keyboard.
- **Create and save custom curves.** You can load a sample image and create a special tone compensation custom curve for that image using tools similar to those found in Photoshop.
- **View and change Custom Settings.** This is one of my favorite features. While changing the Custom Settings for any of the Custom Settings options using the camera's menus isn't difficult (particularly after you've absorbed the information in Chapter 12), Camera Control Pro makes playing with these options a joy.

The amount of control you have over the camera's shooting functions is amazing:

- **Make exposure adjustments.** Choose exposure mode, shutter speed (in Shutter-priority mode), aperture (in Aperture-priority mode), or both (in Manual mode), and exposure compensation. You can preview the effects of your exposure adjustments on the screen of your remote computer using live view.
- **Set focus point, ISO, white balance, etc.** Select the exact focus point when using an AF-area mode where the point is user selectable, plus parameters like metering mode, flash sync mode, ISO, and white balance.
- **Choose file format.** Set all your image size and quality parameters, including bit depth and compression, plus destination for your captured images—PC, memory card slot (your choice), or both.
- **Fine-tune focus and other settings.** You can choose AF-area mode, select an AF mode, activate bracketing, and monitor battery level.
- **Use Picture Controls, HDR, or A-DL.** Select a Picture Control or Active D-Lighting setting on the fly, launch into automatic HDR mode, and adjust things like noise reduction.
- **Select movie settings.** Every setting you can make from the camera for movie shooting is available, including your choice of destination memory card and whether to store your clip in the camera, on your PC, or both.

The Creative Cloud Surrounding Photoshop and Lightroom

I've been using Photoshop since Version 2.0, and as far back as the 1980s struggled with a variety of other programs with names like Digital Darkroom, Image Studio, Picture Publisher, SuperPaint, UltraPaint, Dr. Halo, and Gray F/X (believe it or not, many early image editors could not handle *color* photos). Over the years, Photoshop has grown from being a simple image-editing program that was difficult to learn to a complete suite with basic and "extended" versions, and the capability to satisfy everyone from photographers to graphic designers to 3D artists working on motion picture production. It's gone from being difficult to learn to something akin to quantum mechanics: nobody seems to know everything about it, and most of us could spend a lifetime adding little pieces of expertise in it to our repertoires.

Today Photoshop—whether you're using the "frozen" CS6 standalone version or the constantly morphing Creative Cloud subscription version—folds the capabilities of many other applications into its bulk. It does a decent job of assembling multiple RAW images into an HDR photograph. It retouches, it color corrects, it does an amazing job of compositing, and it can tame noise and create animations. My biggest relief when I upgraded to Photoshop CS6 was that, unlike some previous versions, the new edition was enough like the old one that I was able to use it comfortably from Day One. Drastic paradigm shifts are not as bad as they appear to be—but not when I'm trying to get work done. Until Creative Cloud adds new features that I actually *need,* I'll probably stick with the "old" CS6 for a few more years.

Lightroom, on the other hand, is a newer tool that has some limited image-editing features similar to some of the pixel manipulation tools in Photoshop. However, the intent of Lightroom is to function as a workflow management application. Photoshop can do just about anything, except help you manage 100,000 different images effectively (even using its Bridge and Mini-Bridge organizing tools). Lightroom *can't* do everything, but it excels at giving you a way to manage tens or hundreds of thousands of images easily. In these days of inexpensive, huge hard drives, bracketing, and ridiculously fast continuous shooting rates, it's easy to amass that many photos. Two 3TB internal hard drives in my computer are dedicated to storing the images I shoot. (Don't worry, all those photos are safely backed up to a pair of 6TB RAID-like arrays, plus multiple duplicate hard drives stored offsite.) It would be impossible to manage all those images without something like Lightroom.

The secret behind Lightroom's image management prowess is a database it builds automatically from the EXIF data embedded in each image, with information that includes the camera model, date and time the image was captured, shutter speed, aperture, ISO, white balance, and other information. You can add more information to its catalog, including keywords that will help you retrieve a specific image later and star ratings.

Lightroom's Develop module includes correction using histograms, cropping/straightening, the ability to remove spots and correct red-eye problems, along with white balance. The exposure tools include recovery, fill light, blacks, brightness/contrast, clarity, vibrance, and saturation modules, similar to those found in Adobe Camera Raw. You can also adjust curves, perform sharpening and noise reduction, correct lens distortion, chromatic aberration, and vignetting from profiles specific for each lens. When you're done with your images, you can assemble them into slide shows or web galleries quickly.

Photoshop CS6/CC has all those image manipulation tools—many of them embedded in Adobe Camera Raw. Indeed, when a new release of ACR becomes available, the update fine-tunes both Lightroom and Camera Raw to offer the same functionality. But while Photoshop has more extensive image-editing features, including sophisticated selection (including Skin-Tone Selection), layering, and masking tools, its changes to your files are usually "destructive." You'll need to save snapshots as you work, or use a limited history of Undo steps to reverse your changes. Lightroom, in contrast, never applies permanent changes to the original file.

Which to choose? If you have large numbers of images to catalog and don't need the most advanced Photoshop editing tools, Lightroom may be your best bet for organizing your workflow. While Photoshop includes image management in its Bridge module, there is no database catalog system comparable to Lightroom available in Photoshop. Lightroom is also best for batch processing many files quickly. You'll probably find it easier to learn.

If you need to manipulate your images in complex ways, including compositing to combine objects from one image to another (or to move objects around within the same image), or to creatively *remove* unwanted image areas, dig in and learn Photoshop in more depth. My favorite capabilities are probably Photoshop's Content Aware editing tools, including the Content Aware Move tool in CS6 that lets you seamlessly replace part of an image with a pattern that resembles the surrounding area. Should you be shooting a lot of movies with your Nikon camera, Photoshop CS6 is a great deal more video-friendly than the last edition of the program.

Now, should you need *both* the most sophisticated editing tools available *and* comprehensive workflow/image management capabilities, you probably will want both Photoshop and Lightroom. Buying both—even if you qualify for upgrades for one or the other—isn't cheap, especially since Adobe has essentially discontinued the standalone licensed version of Photoshop, freezing its feature set at Photoshop CS6. At this writing, all future upgrades will be in the form of Adobe Creative Cloud (CC) subscriptions, for which you will pay a monthly or annual fee to use Photoshop or any of the other applications in the Creative Cloud Suite (such as Adobe InDesign or Adobe Illustrator). The software still physically resides on your computer, but periodically "phones home" to Adobe over the internet, and if your subscription has expired, so does your access to Photoshop CC and your other tools.

Adobe has said that Lightroom will retain both standalone and CC versions, and remains an option for those who don't like subscribing to software. Photoshop Elements also remains on the standalone track, but lacks some of the tools that owners of an advanced camera like your Nikon D810 require.

D

Nikon D810: Troubleshooting and Prevention

One of the nice things about modern electronic cameras like the Nikon D810 is that they have fewer mechanical moving parts to fail, so they are less likely to "wear out." No film transport mechanism, no wind lever or motor drive. If you use AF-S lenses instead of the older AF models, you don't even have to worry about complicated mechanical linkages from camera to lens to physically stop down the lens aperture. Instead, tiny, reliable motors are built into each AF-S lens (and you lose the use of only *that* lens should something fail), and one of the few major moving parts in the camera itself is a lightweight mirror that flips up and down with each shot when you're not using live view mode.

Of course, the camera also has a moving shutter that can fail, but the shutter is built rugged enough that you can expect it to last several hundred thousand shutter cycles or more. Unless you're shooting sports in continuous mode day in and day out, the shutter on your D810 is likely to last as long as you expect to use the camera.

The only other things on the camera that move are switches, dials, buttons, the flip-up electronic flash, and the door that slides open to allow you to remove and insert the memory card. Unless you're extraordinarily clumsy or unlucky and manage to bend the internal pins in the memory card slot, or give your built-in flash a good whack while it is in use, there's not a lot that can go wrong mechanically with your Nikon D810.

On the other hand, one of the chief drawbacks of modern electronic cameras is that they are modern *electronic* cameras. Your D810 is fully dependent on two different batteries. Without them, the camera can't be used. There are numerous other electrical and electronic connections in the camera (many connected to those mechanical switches and dials), and components like the color LCD and top-panel status LCD that can potentially fail or suffer damage. The camera also relies on its "operating system," or *firmware*, which can be plagued by bugs that cause unexpected behavior. Luckily, electronic components are generally more reliable and trouble-free, especially when compared to their mechanical counterparts from the pre-electronic film camera days.

Of course, film cameras of the last 10 to 20 years had almost as many electronic features as digital cameras, but, believe it or not, there were whole generations of film cameras that had *no* electronics or batteries. I still own a dozen Nikon F/F2 cameras that don't even have a built-in light meter!

Digital cameras have problems unique to their breed, too; the most troublesome being the need to clean the sensor of dust and grime periodically. This chapter will show you how to diagnose problems, fix some common ills, and, importantly, learn how to avoid them in the future.

Moiré and the Nikon D810

Back when the original D800 was introduced, there was a lot of indecision among potential buyers as to whether they should purchase the D800E, which offered 36 megapixels of resolution untainted by the dreaded "anti-aliasing" filter (technically known as an *optical low-pass filter,* or OLPF); or whether they could settle for the ordinary D800, priced $300 less, which also had a mere 36 megapixels of resolution. A lot of the tempest was generated by those who had no idea whether the D800 would be best for them, but all they could hear was "No AA filter! Sharper!" The majority, however, selected either the D800 or D800E, based on their actual needs. The difference between the two wasn't all that great, and Nikon has since solved the dilemma by introducing the D810, which is available only in an untainted, OLPF-less version.

The tempest might have been in a teapot, as Nikon also introduced D3300, D5300, and D7100 DX-format models that also lack an OLPF, and the world has not come to an end. The difference between the D800E and D810 is that, with the D800E, Nikon didn't actually *remove* the OLPF from the D810, it simply replaced it with an optically-neutral module that doesn't provide any anti-aliasing properties. Does that mean Nikon has eliminated moiré from the D810—or does it indicate that the company feels that problems caused by sensor without anti-aliasing will be minimal, or easily fixed? To understand the question, you might want to delve into exactly what moiré is, and what it does. You can skip ahead to the next section if moiré doesn't concern you.

Moiré is a visual phenomenon that occurs when two regular patterns that are very close in spacing between elements overlap. You might see it on your television when a guest wears a checked shirt with a pattern that's very close to the interval, or frequency, of the lines that produce the video

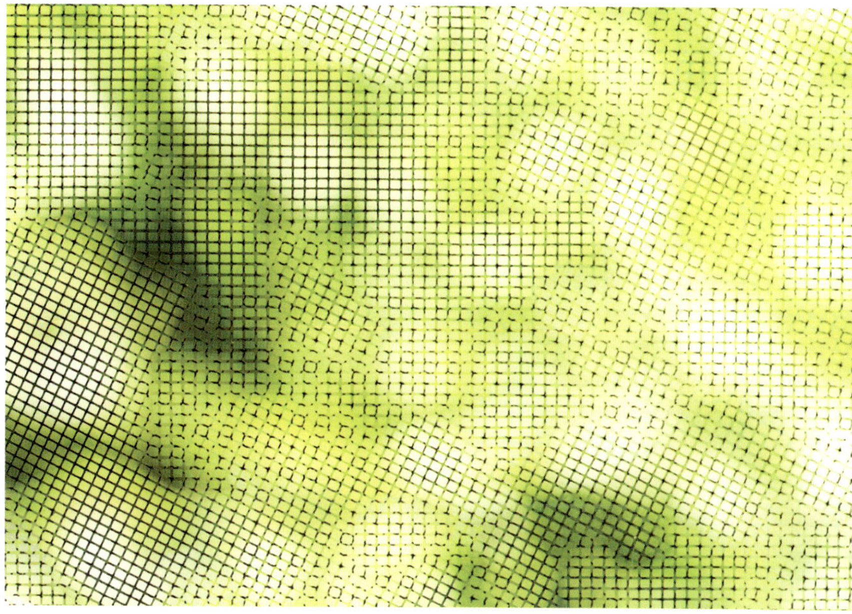

Figure D.1
Photographing a window screen is the easiest way to intentionally produce moiré effects.

image. You probably see moiré effects when you zoom in and out of a patterned image in your image editor, as the frequency coincides with the dot pattern of your display. Moiré rears its ugly head when you photograph a window screen from two angles (rotating the camera between shots) and then overlay the images, as I did to produce Figure D.1.

The interference is caused by the conflict of the patterns you photograph, and the regular pattern that makes up your D810's sensor mosaic. With 36 million pixels stuffed onto a sensor measuring just 24 × 36mm, the tight pattern is that much more likely to create unwanted effects, including false colors (the "rainbow" look). The ravages of moiré are distracting, undesirable, and to be avoided whereever possible. Fixing moiré in an image editor is sometimes easy, but more often time-consuming, and software like Nikon Capture NX 2 has moiré-mending features built in.

No matter which D800-series model you own, you're likely to get *some* moiré in shots that you shoot of fabrics, buildings with strong vertical lines, or anything with grids (including window screens). Indeed, most digital SLRs can exhibit the phenomenon to one extent or another. With the D810, moiré happens to be slightly more likely, and stronger. It's unlikely that you'll see moiré in subjects that are not human-made, as nature's patterns tend to be more variable and random, enough to thwart the intrusion of moiré. In short, you may not get moiré, nor notice it; and, if it's there, you can usually fix it in your image editor.

Diffraction

Diffraction is another phenomenon that can cause a reduction in the apparent sharpness of your image due to scattering and interference of photons as they pass through smaller lens openings. In effect, the edges of your lens aperture affects proportionately more photons as the f/stop grows smaller. The relative amount of space available to pass freely decreases, and the amount of edge surface that can collide with incoming light increases.

So, an f/stop of f/11 may produce a slight loss of overall sharpness compared to an opening of f/8 (although depth-of-field will increase); and f/16 will be less sharp than f/11. With the D810, images are softened by an almost undetectable amount at every aperture—including wide open—but diffraction becomes more noticeable only at f/stops smaller than f/8. With the D810, you shouldn't see any diffraction effects until you stop down smaller than f/8. Again, as with moiré, the difference is very slight. I regularly shoot product shots on a seamless background (such as the camera images in this book) with a macro lens (at f/32), and, because the final printed images are so small, the gains in depth-of-field far outweigh any loss of sharpness from diffraction.

Theoretically, the limit on sharpness caused by diffraction should be independent of the resolution of the sensor, or the size of the sensor. The effects of diffraction *should* be the same at, say, f/11, regardless of what type of sensor is being used. However, in practice, smaller pixels do show the effects of diffraction more readily. The diffraction produces a multi-ringed pattern called an *airy disk* (it has nothing to do with air; the phenomenon was named after scientist George Airy), and when the peak area of this disk is large enough, compared to the pixel size of the sensor, or if two disks overlap, an effect may be visible in the image.

Typically, this happens at a particular f/stop with a particular pixel size, and that f/stop is said to be the diffraction limit for that camera/sensor. Point-and-shoot cameras, with their tiny sensors, may begin to show diffraction effects at f/5.6; a cropped-sensor camera at f/11; a lower-resolution full-frame camera (like the Nikon D4s) at f/16; and a camera with *extremely* small pixels, like the Nikon D810 at f/11.

The photons striking the edges of the diaphragm are disrupted from their paths, and begin to interfere with those passing through the center of the lens. While this phenomenon takes place at all apertures, it is most pronounced at smaller f/stops, when the edges of the iris are proportionately larger compared to the entire lens opening.

The best analogy I can think of is a pond with two floating docks sticking out into the water, as shown in Figure D.2. Throw a big rock in the pond, and the ripples pass between the docks relatively smoothly if the structures are relatively far apart (top). Move them closer together (bottom), and some ripples rebound off each dock to interfere with the incoming wavelets. In a lens, smaller apertures produce the same effect.

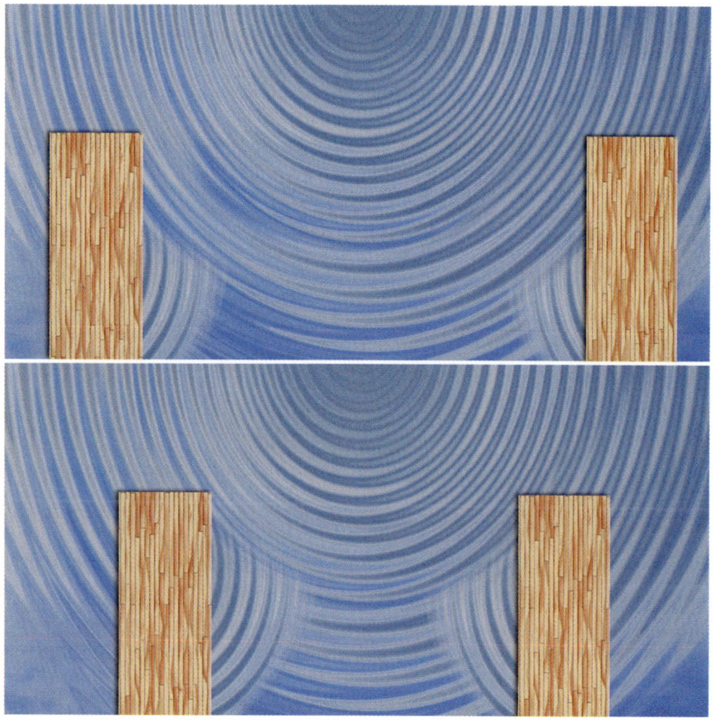

Figure D.2 Diffraction interference can be visualized as ripples on a lake.

There's no "cure" for diffraction-limited images, other than to use larger f/stops, or to apply some sharpening of the image in your editor (which is likely to be a losing cause). It is important, then, to be aware of the effects of diffraction on images captured with the D810, and take them into account before choosing a small aperture.

Battery Powered

I've grown to live with the need for batteries even though I shot for years using all-mechanical Nikon cameras that had no batteries (or even a built-in light meter!). The need for electrical power is the price we pay for modern conveniences like autofocus, autoexposure, LCD image display, backlit menus, and, of course, digital images.

One of the batteries you rely on is the EN-EL15 battery installed in the grip. It's rechargeable, can last for as long as 1,000 shots, and is user-replaceable if you have a spare. The second power cell in your camera is a so-called *clock battery,* which is also rechargeable, but is tucked away within the innards of the camera and can't be replaced by the user. The clock battery retains the settings of the camera when it's powered down, and, even, when the main battery is removed for charging. If you remove the EN-EL15 for long periods, the clock battery may discharge, but it will be quickly rejuvenated when you replace the main battery. (It's recharged by juice supplied by the EN-EL15.)

Although you can't replace this battery yourself, you can expect it to last for the useful life of the camera.

So, your main concern will be to provide a continuous, reliable source of power for your D810. As I noted in Appendix A, you should always have a spare battery or two so you won't need to stop shooting when your internal battery dies. I recommend buying Nikon-brand batteries: saving $20 or so for an after-market battery may save you a few dollars, but can cost you much more than that if the battery malfunctions and damages your camera. We all saw how quickly Nikon replaced the initial "bad" EN-EL15 batteries that were discovered shortly after the original D800 was introduced.

A good use for those extra batteries is in the Nikon MB-D12 Multi-Power Battery Pack, which holds an EN-EL15 battery, effectively doubling your total shooting time. The MB-D12 can also be used with the included AA Battery Holder, allowing you to use six AA batteries in a pinch so users can have AA batteries as a power backup.

The MB-D12 power pack is sometimes called a *vertical grip*, because it includes a supplemental AE-L/AF-L button, vertically oriented shutter release button with lock, and front and rear command dials. The control combo makes it more convenient to shoot vertically oriented photos with the camera rotated 90 degrees.

KEEPING TRACK OF YOUR BATTERIES AND MEMORY CARDS

Here's a trick I use to keep track of which memory cards are blank/exposed, and which batteries are fresh/discharged. I cut up some small slips of paper and fold them in half, forming a tiny "booklet." Then I write EXPOSED in red on the "inside" pages of the booklet and UNEXPOSED in green on the outside pages. Folded one way, the slips read EXPOSED; folded the other way, the slips read UNEXPOSED. I slip them inside the plastic battery cover, which you should *always* use when memory cards or batteries are not in the camera, folded so the appropriate "state" of the batteries is visible. For my purposes, EXPOSED means the same as DISCHARGED, and UNEXPOSED is the equivalent of CHARGED, so I can use the same slips for both batteries and memory cards. The red/green color coding is an additional clue as to which batteries/memory cards are good to go, or not ready for use. (See Figure D.3.)

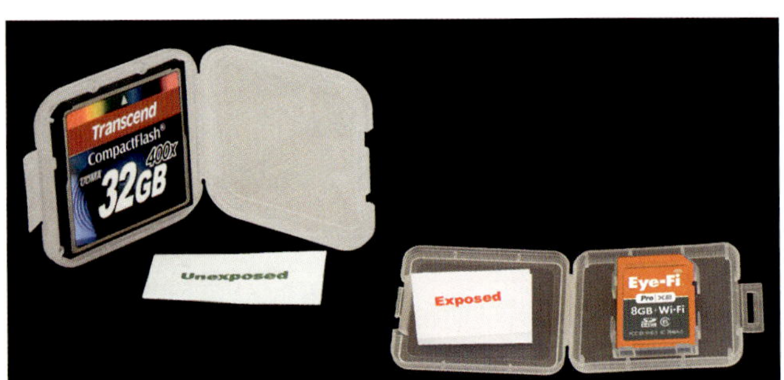

Figure D.3
Mark your memory cards—or batteries—so you'll know which are ready for use.

Upgrading Your Firmware

The camera relies on its "operating system," or *firmware*, which should be updated in a reasonable fashion as new releases become available. The firmware in your Nikon D810 handles everything from menu display (including fonts, colors, and the actual entries themselves), what languages are available, and even support for specific devices and features. Upgrading the firmware to a new version makes it possible to add or fine-tune features while fixing some of the bugs that sneak in.

The exact changes made to the firmware are generally spelled out in the firmware release announcement. You can examine the remedies provided and decide if a given firmware patch is important to you. If not, you can usually safely wait a while before going through the bother of upgrading your firmware—at least long enough for the early adopters (such as those who haunt the Digital Photography Review forums at www.dpreview.com) to report whether the bug fixes have introduced new bugs of their own. Each new firmware release incorporates the changes from previous releases, so if you skip a minor upgrade you should have no problems.

WHEN TO UPGRADE YOUR FIRMWARE

I *always* recommend waiting at least two weeks after a firmware upgrade is announced before changing the software in your camera. This is often in direct contradiction to the online Nikon "gurus" who breathlessly announce each new firmware release on their web pages, usually with links to where you can download the latest software. *Don't do it!* Yet. Nikon has, in the past, introduced firmware upgrades that were buggy and added problems of their own. If you own a camera affected by a new round of firmware upgrades, I urge you to wait and let a few million over-eager fellow users "beta test" this upgrade for you. Within a few weeks, any problems (although I don't expect there will be any) will surface and you'll know whether the update is safe. Your camera is working fine right now, so why take the chance?

How It Works

If you're computer savvy, you might wonder how your Nikon D810 is able to overwrite its own operating system—that is, how can the existing firmware be used to load the new version on top of itself? It's a little like lifting yourself by reaching down and pulling up on your bootstraps.

Not ironically, that's almost exactly what happens: At your command (when you start the upgrade process), the D810 shifts into a special mode in which it is no longer operating from its firmware but, rather, from a small piece of software called a *bootstrap loader*, a separate, protected software program that functions only at startup or when upgrading firmware. The loader's function is to look for firmware to launch or, when directed, to copy new firmware from a memory card to the internal memory space where the old firmware is located. Once the new firmware has replaced the old, you can "reboot" the camera using the new operating system.

Why Three Firmware Modules?

Your Nikon D810's firmware is divided into three parts. The main firmware model is labeled C (for camera). So, what are Firmware L and Firmware S, found in current Nikon models, like the D810? The L firmware is a database of lens information that helps the camera integrate new lenses with its features, such as distance information and barrel and pincushion distortion, while the S firmware provides a similar database for strobes (or Speedlights, take your pick). Nikon regularly updates the C firmware to correct for mistakes or add features/support for new accessories, and the L and S modules to account for new lens and electronic flash introductions. Note that the S firmware will be shown in the Firmware Version menu *only* if you have an external dedicated flash unit installed and powered up. (See Figure D.4.)

WARNING

Use a fully charged EN-EL15 charged battery or a Nikon EH-5/EH-5a AC adapter to ensure that you'll have enough power to operate the camera for the entire upgrade. Moreover, you should not turn off the camera while your old firmware is being overwritten. Don't open the memory card door or do anything else that might disrupt operation of the D810 while the firmware is being installed.

Getting Ready

Before you get started, I have to emphasize that at the time this book was written, only one firmware release has been made available, Version 1.01, which fixed some problems with movie shooting. So, the procedure I am going to describe is the recommended process used for that update. But when it comes time to do an actual firmware upgrade for your D810, you should double check the instructions below against the recommended procedure that Nikon implements at that time. It should be very close to the steps I outline, but there may be some small differences.

The first thing to do is determine whether you need the current firmware update. First, confirm the version number of your Nikon D810's current firmware:

1. Turn on the D810.
2. Press the MENU button and select *Firmware Version* from the Setup menu. The camera's firmware version will be displayed. (See Figure D.4.) If you have an external dedicated flash unit available, attach it and turn on the power.
3. Write down the Version number for Parts C, L, and S (if needed).
4. Turn off the D810.

Next, go to the Nikon support site, locate, and download the firmware update. In the USA, the place to go is http://support.nikonusa.com/, which will offer a list of choices, including one that says Current Firmware Downloads available for Nikon Products. Click that link, then click the DSLR link on the page displayed next. Scroll down to the D810 row in the table, and review the version number for the current update.

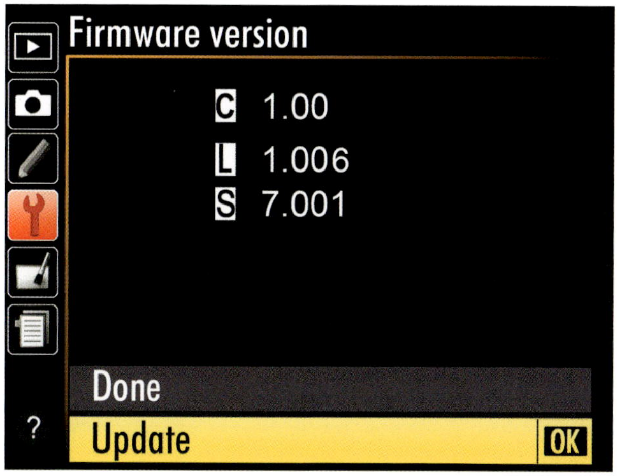

Figure D.4
View your current firmware versions before upgrading.

If the version is later than the one you noted in your camera, click the firmware link in either the Windows or Macintosh columns (depending on your computer) to download the file. It will have a name like D810-V101W.exe (Windows) or F-D810-V101M.dmg (Macintosh). Extract the file to a folder on your computer using the unzipping or unstuffing software of your choice.

The D810's firmware may come in several parts. The actual update files will be named something like:

D810_0101.bin

The final preparation you need to make is to decide whether you'd like to upgrade your firmware using a memory card reader, or by transferring the software to the D810 using the USB cable. In either case, you'll need to format a memory card in the D810. Then, perform one of the sets of steps in the sections that follow.

Updating from a Card Reader

To update from a card reader, use a reader connected to your computer with a USB cable. Then, follow these steps:

1. Insert a formatted memory card into the card reader. If you have been using Nikon Transfer or the "autoplay" features of your operating system to transfer images from your memory card to the computer, the automated transfer dialog box may appear. Close it.
2. The memory card will appear on your Macintosh desktop, or in the Computer/My Computer folders under Windows 7/Windows Vista/Windows XP.
3. Drag one of the firmware files to the memory card. You can install any of them in any order. If your particular upgrade consists of only one of the files, drag that to the memory card. Remember to copy the firmware to the *root* (top) directory of the memory card. The D810 will be unable to find it if you place it in a folder.

Updating with a USB Connection

You can also copy the firmware to the D810's memory card using a USB connection. Just follow these steps:

1. With the camera turned off, insert the formatted memory card. Then, turn the camera on.
2. Press the MENU button and navigate to the Setup menu.
3. Turn the D810 off and connect it to your computer using the USB cable.
4. Turn the camera back on. If you have been using Nikon Transfer or the "autoplay" features of your operating system to transfer images from your memory card to the computer, the automated transfer dialog box may appear. Close it.
5. The camera will appear on the Macintosh desktop, or in the Computer/My Computer folders under Windows 8/Windows 7/Windows Vista/Windows XP.
6. Drag one of the firmware files to the memory card. It doesn't matter which you install first. If your particular upgrade consists of only one .bin file, drag that to the memory card. Remember to copy the firmware to the *root* (top) directory of the memory card. The D810 will be unable to find it if you place it in a folder.
7. Disconnect the camera from the computer.

Starting the Update

To perform the actual update, follow these steps:

1. With the memory card containing the firmware update software in the camera, turn the camera on.
2. Press the **MENU** button and select **Firmware Version** in the Setup menu.
3. Select Update and press the multi selector button to the right.
4. When the firmware update screen appears, highlight **Yes** and press **OK** to begin the update.
5. The actual process may take a few minutes (from two to five). Be sure not to turn off the camera or perform any other operations while it is underway. (See Figure D.5.)
6. When the update is completed, the warning message will no longer be displayed on the screen. You can turn off the camera when the message disappears.
7. Remove the memory card.
8. Turn the D810 back on to load the updated firmware.
9. Press the **MENU** button and select **Firmware Version** in the Setup menu to view the current firmware number. If it matches the update, you've successfully upgraded that portion of the firmware.
10. If there is a second part to your firmware upgrade, then repeat all the steps for the additional firmware software.
11. Reformat the memory card to return it to a "clean" condition.

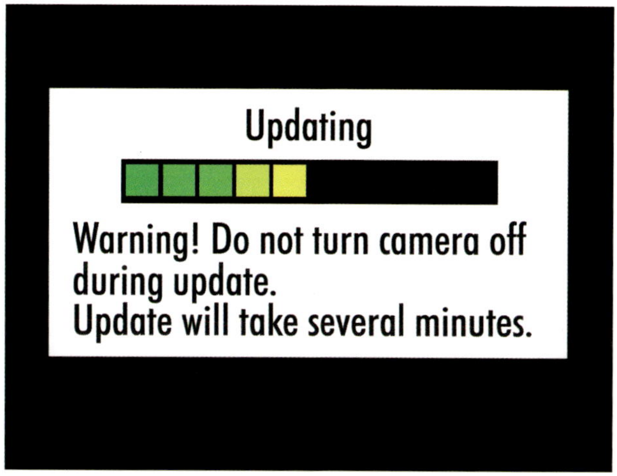

Figure D.5
Don't turn the camera off while updating is underway.

Troubleshooting Memory Cards

Sometimes good memory cards go bad. Sometimes good photographers can treat their memory cards badly. It's possible that a memory card that works fine in one camera won't be recognized when inserted into another. In the worst case, you can have a card full of important photos and find that the card seems to be corrupted and you can't access any of them. Don't panic! If these scenarios sound horrific to you, there are lots of things you can do to prevent them from happening, and a variety of remedies available if they do occur. You'll want to take some time—before disaster strikes—to consider your options.

All Your Eggs in One Basket?

The debate about whether it's better to use one large memory card or several smaller ones has been going on since even before there were memory cards. I can remember when computer users wondered whether it was smarter to install a pair of 200MB (not *gigabyte*) hard drives in their computer, or if they should go for one of those new-fangled 500MB models. By the same token, a few years ago the user groups were full of proponents who insisted that you ought to use 128MB memory cards rather than the huge 512MB versions. Today, with the huge file size of D810 images, most of the arguments involve 16GB cards versus 32GB cards, or even 64GB (and larger) cards.

Why all the fuss? Are 8GB memory cards more likely to fail than 16GB cards? Are you risking all your photos if you trust your images to a larger card? Isn't it better to use several smaller cards, so that if one fails you lose only half as many photos? Or, isn't it wiser to put all your photos onto one larger card, because the more cards you use, the better your odds of misplacing or damaging one and losing at least some pictures?

In the end, the "eggs in one basket" argument boils down to statistics, and how you happen to use your D810. The rationales can go both ways. If you have multiple smaller cards, you do increase your chances of something happening to one of them, so, arguably, you might be boosting the odds of losing some pictures. If all your images are important, the fact that you've lost 100 rather than 200 pictures isn't very comforting.

After all, the myth assumes that a damaged card will always be full before it becomes corrupted. Fortunately, memory cards don't magically wait until they are full before they fail. In a typical shooting session, it doesn't matter whether you've shot 7GB worth of pictures on an 8GB card or 7GB worth of pictures on a 16GB card. If either card fails, you've lost exactly the same number of images. Your risk increases *only* when you start shooting additional photos on the larger card. In the real world, most of us who use larger memory cards don't fill them up very often. We just like having the extra capacity there when we need it. I've standardized on a pair of 64GB cards for my D810, one SDXC card and one CF card.

The myth also says that by using several smaller cards, you're spreading the risk around so that only some pictures will be lost in case of a failure. What is more important to you, your photographs or the members of your family? When going on vacation, do you insist on splitting your kin up and driving several smaller cars? Of course not.

If you shoot photojournalist-type pictures, you probably change memory cards when they're less than completely full in order to avoid the need to do so at a crucial moment. (When I shoot sports, my cards rarely reach 80 to 90 percent of capacity before I change them.) Using multiple smaller cards means you have to change them that more often, which can be a real pain when you're taking a lot of photos. As an example, if you use 4GB memory cards with a Nikon D810 and shoot RAW+JPEG FINE, you may get only a few dozen pictures on the card. That's not even twice the capacity of a 36-exposure roll of film (remember those?). In my book, I prefer keeping all my eggs in one basket, and then making very sure that nothing happens to that basket.

Preventive Measures

Here are some options for preventing the loss of valuable images:

- **Interleaving.** One option is to *interleave* your shots. Say you don't shoot weddings, but you do go on vacation from time to time. Take 100 or so pictures on one card, or whatever number of images might fill about 25 percent of its capacity. Then, replace it with a different card and shoot about 25 percent of that card's available space. Repeat these steps with diligence (you'd have to be determined to go through this inconvenience), and, if you use four or more memory cards you'll find your pictures from each location scattered among the different memory cards. If you lose or damage one, you'll still have *some* pictures from all the various stops on your trip on the other cards. That's more work than I like to do (I usually tote around a portable hard disk and copy the files to the drive as I go), but it's an option.

- **In-camera backup.** Fortunately, if you own a Nikon D810, you don't need to restrict yourself to a single basket. Load your camera with two memory cards, then go to the Shooting menu and set Role Played by Secondary Card to Backup, so that each shot you take is copied to both cards simultaneously. This will slow down your maximum shooting speed significantly (don't try this backup method when shooting sports), but for ordinary photography, this provides the peace of mind of knowing you're making a spare copy of each image right on the spot.
- **Transmit your images.** Another option is to transmit your images, as they are shot, over a network to your laptop, assuming a network and a laptop are available. You can use Nikon's Wireless Transmitter WT-4a, and beam the images over to a computer as you shoot them using the gadget's Image Transfer mode. A company called Eye-Fi (www.eye.fi) markets a clever memory card with wireless capabilities built-in.
- **External backup.** You can purchase external hard disk gadgets called Personal Storage Devices, which can copy files from your memory cards automatically. More expensive models have color LCD screens so you can review your images. I tend to prefer my 11-inch MacBook Air, which fits in a pocket of my ScotteVest. I can store images on the computer's internal storage, and make an extra backup copy to an external drive as well. Plus, I can access the Internet from Wi-Fi hotspots (including the one built into my iPhone), all using a very compact device. Lately, I've been backing up many images on my iPad, which has 64GB of storage—enough for short trips.

EXTREME BACKUP

I probably took the dual-card technique to the extreme recently while on a trip. I had my camera stocked with a pair of 64GB cards, and was shooting in RAW+JPEG mode. I happened to be shooting three-exposure brackets, which I was going to process as HDR (high dynamic range) photos. With the camera set to copy to both cards at the same time, and using Continuous high, every time I pressed the shutter release, the camera took a three-shot set in both RAW+JPEG Fine (six pictures) and copied them to both cards (12 files in all). I managed the dubious feat of filling up 128GB of memory cards while pressing the shutter release fewer than 300 times.

What Can Go Wrong?

There are lots of things that can go wrong with your memory card, but the ones that aren't caused by human stupidity are statistically very rare. Yes, a memory card's internal bit bin or controller can suddenly fail due to a manufacturing error or some inexplicable event caused by old age. However, if your card works for the first week or two that you own it, it should work forever. There's really not a lot that can wear out.

The typical memory card is rated for a Mean Time Between Failures of 1,000,000 hours of use. That's constant use 24/7 for more than 100 years! According to the manufacturers, they are good for 10,000 insertions in your camera, and should be able to retain their data (and that's without an external power source) for something on the order of 11 years. Of course, with the millions of cards in use, there are bound to be a few lemons here or there.

Given the reliability of solid-state memory compared to magnetic memory, though, it's more likely that your problems will stem from something that you do. Secure Digital and memory cards are small and easy to misplace if you're not careful. For that reason, it's a good idea to keep them in their original cases or a "card safe" offered by Gepe (www.gepe.com), Pelican (www.pelican.com), and others. Always placing your memory card in a case can provide protection from the second-most common mishap that befalls memory cards: the common household laundry. If you slip a card in a pocket, rather than a case or your camera bag often enough, sooner or later it's going to end up in the washing machine and probably the clothes dryer, too. There are plenty of reports of relieved digital camera owners who've laundered their memory cards and found they still worked fine, but it's not uncommon for such mistreatment to do some damage.

Memory cards can also be stomped on, accidentally bent, dropped into the ocean, chewed by pets, and otherwise rendered unusable in myriad ways. It's also possible to force a Compact Flash card into your D810's memory card slot incorrectly if you're diligent enough, doing little damage to the card itself, but bending the connector pins in the camera, eliminating its ability to read or write to any memory card. Fortunately, the SD card slot isn't susceptible to this kind of damage.

Or, if the card is formatted in your computer with a memory card reader, your D810 may fail to recognize it. Occasionally, I've found that a memory card used in one camera would fail if used in a different camera (until I reformatted it in Windows, and then again in the camera). (Don't do this with SDXC cards, which use the exFAT format, and have a special protected data area that can be destroyed by that type of formatting.) Every once in a while, a card goes completely bad and—seemingly—can't be salvaged.

Another way to lose images is to do commonplace things with your card at an inopportune time. If you remove the card from the D810 while the camera is writing images to the card, you'll lose any photos in the buffer and may damage the file structure of the card, making it difficult or impossible to retrieve the other pictures you've taken. The same thing can happen if you remove the memory card from your computer's card reader while the computer is writing to the card (say, to erase files you've already moved to your computer). You can avoid this by *not* using your computer to erase files on a memory card but, instead, always reformatting the card in your D810 before you use it again.

What Can You Do?

Pay attention: If you're having problems, the *first* thing you should do is *stop* using that memory card. Don't take any more pictures. Don't do anything with the card until you've figured out what's wrong. Your second line of defense (your first line is to be sufficiently careful with your cards that you avoid problems in the first place) is to *do no harm* that hasn't already been done. Read the rest of this section and then, if necessary, decide on a course of action (such as using a data recovery service or software described later) before you risk damaging the data on your card further.

Now that you've calmed down, the first thing to check is whether you've actually inserted a card in the camera. If you've set the camera so that shooting without a card has been turned on, it's entirely possible (although not particularly plausible) that you've been snapping away with no memory card to store the pictures to, which can lead to massive disappointment later on. Of course, the –E- warning appears on the LCD when the camera is powered up, and the Demo message is superimposed on the review image after every shot (assuming you've enabled the D810 to take photos when a card is not inserted), but maybe you're inattentive or aren't using picture review. You can avoid all this by setting the Slot Empty Release Lock in Custom Setting f11 to Release Locked, and leaving it there.

Things get more exciting when the card itself is put in jeopardy. If you lose a card, there's not a lot you can do other than take a picture of a similar card and print up some Have You Seen This Lost Flash Memory? flyers to post on utility poles all around town.

If all you care about is reusing the card, and have resigned yourself to losing the pictures, try reformatting the card in your camera. You may find that reformatting removes the corrupted data and restores your card to health. Sometimes I've had success reformatting a card in my computer using a memory card reader (this is normally a no-no because your operating system doesn't understand the needs of your D810), and *then* reformatting again in the camera.

If your memory card is not behaving properly, and you *do* want to recover your images, things get a little more complicated. If your pictures are very valuable, either to you or to others (for example, a wedding), you can always turn to professional data recovery firms. Be prepared to pay hundreds of dollars to get your pictures back, but these pros often do an amazing job. You wouldn't want them working on your memory card on behalf of the police if you'd tried to erase some incriminating pictures. There are many firms of this type, and I've never used them myself, so I can't offer a recommendation. Use a Google search to turn up a ton of them.

A more reasonable approach is to try special data recovery software you can install on your computer and use to attempt to resurrect your "lost" images yourself. They may not actually be gone completely. Perhaps your card's "table of contents" is jumbled, or only a few pictures are damaged in such a way that your camera and computer can't read some or any of the pictures on the card. Some of the available software was written specifically to reconstruct lost pictures, while other utilities are more general-purpose applications that can be used with any media, including floppy disks and hard disk drives. They have names like OnTrack, Photo Rescue 2, Digital Image

Recovery, MediaRecover, Image Recall, and the aptly named Recover My Photos. You'll find a comprehensive list and links, as well as some picture recovery tips at www.ultimateslr.com/memory-card-recovery.php. I like the RescuePRO software that SanDisk supplies, especially since it originally came on a mini-CD that I was totally unable to erase by mistake, and more recently became downloadable from a URL SanDisk supplies with the memory card.

Cleaning Your Sensor

Yes, the Nikon D810 has a two-pronged sensor dust prevention scheme: an innovative air control system that keeps dust away from the sensor in the first place, and a sensor-shaking cleaning mechanism. But no dust-busting technology is 100-percent effective.

Indeed, there's no avoiding dust. No matter how careful you are, some of it is going to settle on your camera and on the mounts of your lenses, eventually making its way inside your camera to settle in the mirror chamber. As you take photos, the mirror flipping up and down causes the dust to become airborne and eventually make its way past the shutter curtain to come to rest on the anti-aliasing filter atop your sensor. There, dust and particles can show up in every single picture you take at a small enough aperture to bring the foreign matter into sharp focus. No matter how careful you are and how cleanly you work, eventually you will get some of this dust on your camera's sensor. Some say that CMOS sensors, like the one found in the Nikon D810, "attract" less dust than CCD sensors found in cameras from other vendors. But even the cleanest-working photographers using the Nikon D810 are far from immune.

Fortunately, one of the Nikon D810's most useful features is the automatic sensor cleaning system that reduces or eliminates the need to clean your camera's sensor manually. The sensor vibrates ultrasonically each time the D810 is powered either on or off (or both, at your option), shaking loose any dust.

Although the automatic sensor cleaning feature operates when you power the camera up or turn it off (depending on the behavior you specify in the Setup menu), you can activate it manually at any time. Choose Clean Image Sensor from the Setup menu, and select Clean Now. If you'd rather specify when automatic cleaning occurs, choose On (clean at power up), Off (clean when the camera is switched off), On/Off (clean at both power up and power down), or Cleaning Off (no automatic sensor cleaning will take place).

If some dust does collect on your sensor, you can often map it out of your images (making it invisible) using software techniques with the Image Dust Off Ref Photo feature in the Setup menu. Operation of this feature is described in Chapter 13.

Of course, even with the Nikon D810's automatic sensor cleaning/dust resistance features, you may still be required to manually clean your sensor from time to time. This section explains the phenomenon and provides some tips on minimizing dust and eliminating it when it begins to affect your shots.

Dust the FAQs, Ma'am

Here are some of the most frequently asked questions about sensor dust issues.

Q. I see tiny specks in my viewfinder. Do I have dust on my sensor?

A. If you see sharp, well-defined specks, they are clinging to the underside of your focus screen and not on your sensor. They have absolutely no effect on your photographs, and are merely annoying or distracting.

Q. I can see dust on my mirror. How can I remove it?

A. Like focus-screen dust, any artifacts that have settled on your mirror won't affect your photos. You can often remove dust on the mirror or focus screen with a bulb air blower, which will loosen it and whisk it away. Stubborn dust on the focus screen can sometimes be gently flicked away with a soft brush designed for cleaning lenses. I don't recommend brushing the mirror or touching it in any way. The mirror is a special front-surface-silvered optical device (unlike conventional mirrors, which are silvered on the back side of a piece of glass or plastic) and can be easily scratched. If you can't blow mirror dust off, it's best to just forget about it. You can't see it in the viewfinder, anyway.

Q. I see a bright or dark spot in the same place in all of my photos. Is that sensor dust?

A. You've probably got a "hot" pixel, a "dead" pixel, or one that is permanently "stuck" due to a defect in the sensor. A hot pixel is one that shows up as a bright spot only during long exposures as the sensor warms. These are often removed automatically if you use Long Exposure Noise Reduction, or can disappear if you work with shorter exposures. A dead pixel is always dark and represents a defect in the sensor. A pixel stuck in the "on" position always appears in the image. Hot and stuck pixels show up as bright red, green, or blue pixels, usually surrounded by a small cluster of other improperly illuminated pixels, caused by the camera's interpolating the hot or stuck pixel into its surroundings, as shown in Figure D.6. Hot, dead, and stuck pixels are likely to show up when they contrast with plain, evenly colored areas of your image.

Figure D.6 A stuck pixel is surrounded by improperly interpolated pixels created by the D810's demosaicing algorithm.

Finding one or two hot or stuck pixels in your sensor is unfortunately fairly common. They can be "removed" by telling the D810 to ignore them through a simple process called *pixel mapping*. If the bad pixels become bothersome, Nikon can remap your sensor's pixels with a quick trip to a service center.

Bad pixels can also show up on your camera's color LCD panel, but, unless they are abundant, the wisest course is to just ignore them.

Q. I see an irregular out-of-focus blob in the same place in my photos. Is that sensor dust?

A. Yes. Sensor contaminants can take the form of tiny spots, larger blobs, or even curvy lines if they are caused by minuscule fibers that have settled on the sensor. They'll appear out of focus because they aren't actually on the sensor surface but, rather, a fraction of a millimeter above it on the filter that covers the sensor. The smaller the f/stop used, the more in-focus the dust becomes. At large apertures, it may not be visible at all.

Q. I never see any dust on my sensor. What's all the fuss about?

A. Those who never have dust problems with their Nikon D810 fall into one of four categories: those for whom the camera's automatic dust removal features are working well; those who seldom change their lenses and have clean working habits that minimize the amount of dust that invades their cameras in the first place; those who simply don't notice the dust (often because they don't shoot many macro photos or other pictures using the small f/stops that makes dust evident in their images); and those who are very, very lucky.

Identifying and Dealing with Dust

Sensor dust is less of a problem than it might be because it shows up only under certain circumstances. Indeed, you might have dust on your sensor right now and not be aware of it. The dust doesn't actually settle on the sensor itself, but, rather, on a protective filter a very tiny distance above the sensor, subjecting it to the phenomenon of *depth-of-focus*. Depth-of-focus is the distance the focal plane can be moved and still render an object in sharp focus. At f/2.8 to f/5.6 or even smaller, sensor dust, particularly if small, is likely to be outside the range of depth-of-focus and blur into an unnoticeable dot.

However, if you're shooting at f/16 to f/22 or smaller, those dust motes suddenly pop into focus. Forget about trying to spot them by peering directly at your sensor with the shutter open and the lens removed. The period at the end of this sentence, about .33mm in diameter, could block a group of pixels measuring 40 × 40 pixels (160 pixels in all!). Dust spots that are even smaller than that can easily show up in your images if you're shooting large, empty areas that are light colored. Dust motes are most likely to show up in the sky, as in Figure D.7, or in white backgrounds of your seamless product shots and are less likely to be a problem in images that contain lots of dark areas and detail.

To see if you have dust on your sensor, take a few test shots of a plain, blank surface (such as a piece of paper or a cloudless sky) at small f/stops, such as f/22, and a few wide open. Open Photoshop or another image editor, copy several shots into a single document in separate layers, then flip back and forth between layers to see if any spots you see are present in all layers. You may have to boost contrast and sharpness to make the dust easier to spot.

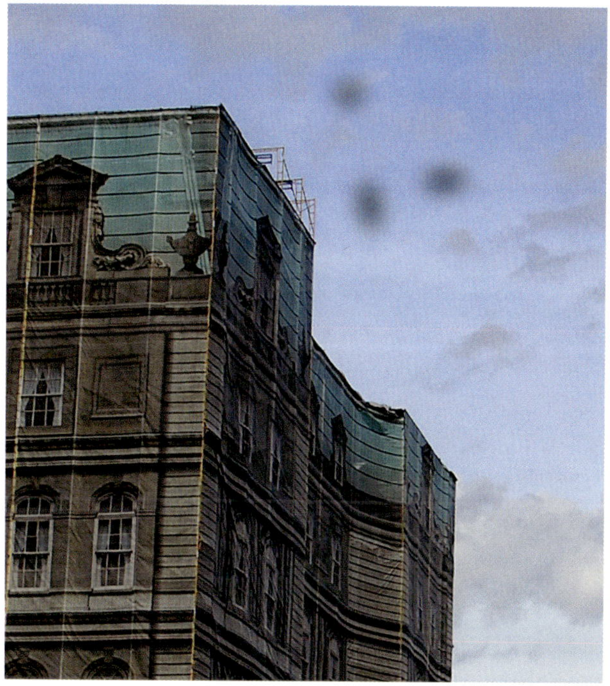

Figure D.7
Only the dust spots in the sky are apparent in this shot.

Avoiding Dust

Of course, the easiest way to protect your sensor from dust is to prevent it from settling on the sensor in the first place. Here are my stock tips for eliminating the problem before it begins.

- **Clean environment.** Avoid working in dusty areas if you can do so. Hah! Serious photographers will take this one with a grain of salt, because it usually makes sense to go where the pictures are. Only a few of us are so paranoid about sensor dust (considering that it is so easily removed) that we'll avoid moderately grimy locations just to protect something that is, when you get down to it, just a tool. If you find a great picture opportunity at a raging fire, during a sandstorm, or while surrounded by dust clouds, you might hesitate to take the picture, but, with a little caution (don't remove your lens in these situations, and clean the camera afterwards!) you can still shoot. However, it still makes sense to store your camera in a clean environment. One place cameras and lenses pick up a lot of dust is inside a camera bag. Clean your bag from time to time, and you can avoid problems.
- **Clean lenses.** There are a few paranoid types that avoid swapping lenses in order to minimize the chance of dust getting inside their cameras. It makes more sense just to use a blower or brush to dust off the rear lens mount of the replacement lens first, so you won't be introducing dust into your camera simply by attaching a new, dusty lens. Do this before you remove the current lens from your camera, and then avoid stirring up dust before making the exchange.

- **Work fast.** Minimize the time your camera is lens-less and exposed to dust. That means having your replacement lens ready and dusted off, and a place to set down the old lens as soon as it is removed, so you can quickly attach the new lens.
- **Let gravity help you.** Face the camera downward when the lens is detached so any dust in the mirror box will tend to fall away from the sensor. Turn your back to any breezes, indoor forced air vents, fans, or other sources of dust to minimize infiltration.
- **Protect the lens you just removed.** Once you've attached the new lens, quickly put the end cap on the one you just removed to reduce the dust that might fall on it.
- **Clean out the vestibule.** From time to time, remove the lens while in a relatively dust-free environment and use a blower bulb like the one shown in Figure D.8 (*not* compressed air or a vacuum hose) to clean out the mirror box area. A blower bulb is generally safer than a can of compressed air, or a strong positive/negative airflow, which can tend to drive dust further into nooks and crannies.
- **Be prepared.** If you're embarking on an important shooting session, it's a good idea to clean your sensor *now*, rather than come home with hundreds or thousands of images with dust spots caused by flecks that were sitting on your sensor before you even started.
- **Clone out existing spots in your image editor.** Photoshop and other editors have a clone tool or healing brush you can use to copy pixels from surrounding areas over the dust spot or dead pixel. This process can be tedious, especially if you have lots of dust spots and/or lots of images to be corrected. The advantage is that this sort of manual fix-it probably will do the least damage to the rest of your photo. Only the damaged pixels will be affected.
- **Use filtration in your image editor.** A semi-smart filter like Photoshop's Dust & Scratches filter can remove dust and other artifacts by selectively blurring areas that the plug-in decides represent dust spots. This method can work well if you have many dust spots, because you won't need to patch them manually. However, any automated method like this has the possibility of blurring areas of your image that you didn't intend to soften.

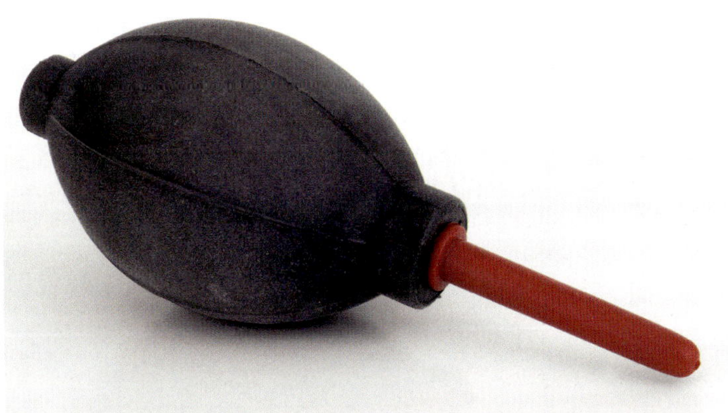

Figure D.8
Use a robust air bulb for cleaning your sensor.

Sensor Cleaning

Those new to the concept of sensor dust actually hesitate before deciding to clean their camera themselves. Isn't it a better idea to pack up your D810 and send it to a Nikon service center so their crack technical staff can do the job for you? Or, at the very least, shouldn't you let the friendly folks at your local camera store do it?

Of course, if you choose to let someone else clean your sensor, they will be using methods that are more or less identical to the techniques you would use yourself. None of these techniques are difficult, and the only difference between their cleaning and your cleaning is that they might have done it dozens or hundreds of times. If you're careful, you can do just as good a job.

Of course vendors like Nikon won't tell you this, but it's not because they don't trust you. It's not that difficult for a real goofball to mess up a camera by hurrying or taking a shortcut. Perhaps the person uses the "Bulb" method of holding the shutter open and a finger slips, allowing the shutter curtain to close on top of a sensor cleaning brush. Or, someone tries to clean the sensor using masking tape, and ends up with goo all over its surface. If Nikon recommended *any* method that's mildly risky, someone would do it wrong, and then the company would face lawsuits from those who'd contend they did it exactly in the way the vendor suggested, so the ruined camera is not their fault.

You can see that vendors like Nikon tend to be conservative in their recommendations, and, in doing so, make it seem as if sensor cleaning is more daunting and dangerous than it really is. Some vendors recommend only dust-off cleaning, through the use of reasonably gentle blasts of air, while condemning more serious scrubbing with swabs and cleaning fluids. However, these cleaning kits for the exact types of cleaning they recommended against are for sale in Japan only, where, apparently, your average photographer is more dexterous than those of us in the rest of the world. These kits are similar to those used by official repair staff to clean your sensor if you decide to send your camera in for a dust-up.

As I noted, sensors can be affected by dust particles that are much smaller than you might be able to spot visually on the surface of your lens. The filters that cover sensors tend to be fairly hard compared to optical glass. Cleaning the 24mm × 36mm sensor in your Nikon D810 within the tight confines of the mirror box can call for a steady hand and careful touch. If your sensor's filter becomes scratched through inept cleaning, you can't simply remove it yourself and replace it with a new one.

There are three basic kinds of cleaning processes that can be used to remove dusty and sticky stuff that settles on your dSLR's sensor. All of these must be performed with the shutter locked open. I'll describe these methods and provide instructions for locking the shutter later in this section.

- **Air cleaning.** This process involves squirting blasts of air inside your camera with the shutter locked open. This works well for dust that's not clinging stubbornly to your sensor.
- **Brushing.** A soft, very fine brush is passed across the surface of the sensor's filter, dislodging mildly persistent dust particles and sweeping them off the imager.
- **Liquid cleaning.** A soft swab dipped in a cleaning solution such as ethanol is used to wipe the sensor filter, removing more obstinate particles.

Placing the Mirror/Shutter in the Locked and Fully Upright Position for Landing

Make sure you're using a fully charged battery or an AC adapter. Fortunately, the Nikon D810 is smart enough that it won't let you try to clean the sensor manually unless the battery has a sufficient charge.

1. Remove the lens from the camera and then turn on the camera.
2. You'll find the Lock Mirror Up for Cleaning menu choice in the Setup menu. Select it.
3. Choose Start. The mirror will flip up and the shutter will open.
4. Use one of the methods described below to remove dust and grime from your sensor. Be careful not to accidentally switch the power off or open the memory card or battery compartment doors as you work. If that happens, the shutter may be damaged if it closes onto your cleaning tool.
5. When you're finished, turn off the power, replace your lens, and switch your camera back on.

Air Cleaning

Your first attempts at cleaning your sensor should always involve gentle blasts of air. Many times, you'll be able to dislodge dust spots, which will fall off the sensor and, with luck, out of the mirror box. Attempt one of the other methods only when you've already tried air cleaning and it didn't remove all the dust.

Here are some tips for doing air cleaning:

- **Use a clean, powerful air bulb.** Your best bet is bulb cleaners designed for the job, like the Giottos Rocket or the one shown in Figure D.9. Smaller bulbs, like those air bulbs with a brush attached sometimes sold for lens cleaning or weak nasal aspirators may not provide sufficient air or a strong enough blast to do much good.

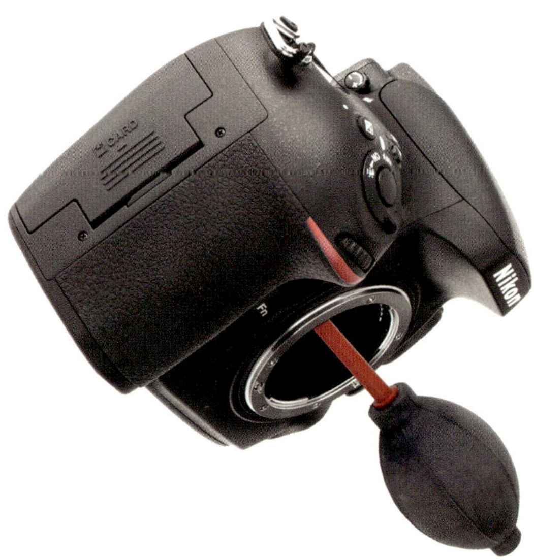

Figure D.9
Hold the camera upside down and blow the dust off the sensor.

- **Hold the camera upside down.** Then look up into the mirror box as you squirt your air blasts, increasing the odds that gravity will help pull the expelled dust downward, away from the sensor. You may have to use some imagination in positioning yourself. (See Figure D.9, which illustrates how I clean my Nikon D810.)
- **Never use air canisters.** The propellant inside these cans can permanently coat your sensor if you tilt the can while spraying. It's not worth taking a chance.
- **Avoid air compressors.** Super-strong blasts of air are likely to force dust under the sensor filter.

Brush Cleaning

If your dust is a little more stubborn and can't be dislodged by air alone, you may want to try a brush, charged with static electricity, which can pick off dust spots by electrical attraction. One good, but expensive, option is the Sensor Brush sold at www.visibledust.com. A cheaper version can be purchased at www.copperhillimages.com. You need a 24mm version, like the one in Figure D.10. It can be stroked across the short dimension of your D810's sensor.

Ordinary artists' brushes are much too coarse and stiff and have fibers that are tangled or can come loose and settle on your sensor. A good sensor brush's fibers are resilient and described as "thinner than a human hair." Moreover, the brush has a wooden handle that reduces the risk of static sparks.

Brush cleaning is done with a dry brush by gently swiping the surface of the sensor filter with the tip. The dust particles are attracted to the brush particles and cling to them. You should clean the brush with compressed air before and after each use, and store it in an appropriate air-tight container between applications to keep it clean and dust-free. Although these special brushes are expensive, one should last you a long time.

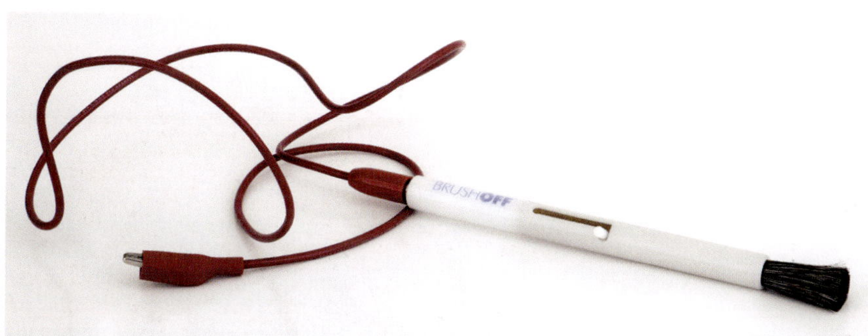

Figure D.10
A proper brush is required for dusting off your sensor.

Liquid Cleaning

Unfortunately, you'll often encounter really stubborn dust spots that can't be removed with a blast of air or flick of a brush. These spots may be combined with some grease or a liquid that causes them to stick to the sensor filter's surface. In such cases, liquid cleaning with a swab may be necessary. During my first clumsy attempts to clean my own sensor, I accidentally got my blower bulb tip too close to the sensor, and some sort of deposit from the tip of the bulb ended up on the sensor. I panicked until I discovered that liquid cleaning did a good job of removing whatever it was that took up residence on my sensor.

You want a sturdy swab that won't bend or break so you can apply gentle pressure to the swab as you wipe the sensor surface. Use the swab with methanol (as pure as you can get it, particularly medical grade; other ingredients can leave a residue), or the Eclipse solution also sold by Photographic Solutions. Eclipse is actually quite a bit purer than even medical-grade methanol. A couple drops of solution should be enough, unless you have a spot that's extremely difficult to remove. In that case, you may need to use extra solution on the swab to help "soak" the dirt off.

You can make your own swabs out of pieces of plastic (some use fast food restaurant knives, with the tip cut at an angle to the proper size) covered with a soft cloth or Pec-Pad, as shown in Figure D.11. However, if you've got the bucks to spend, you can't go wrong with good-quality commercial sensor cleaning swabs, such as those sold by Photographic Solutions, Inc. (www.photosol.com/swabproduct.htm).

Once you overcome your nervousness at touching your D810's sensor, the process is easy. You'll wipe continuously with the swab in one direction, then flip it over and wipe in the other direction. You need to completely wipe the entire surface; otherwise, you may end up depositing the dust you collect at the far end of your stroke. Wipe; don't rub.

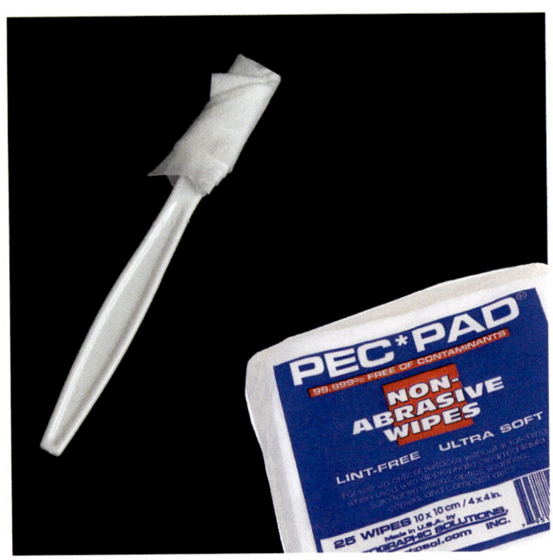

Figure D.11
Carefully wrap a Pec-Pad around a plastic knife that you've truncated.

Magnifier Assisted Cleaning

Using a magnifier to view your sensor as you clean it is a good idea. I rely on two types. I have four Carson MiniBrite PO-55 magnifiers (see Figure D.12), and keep one in each camera bag. So, no matter where I am shooting, I have one of these $8.95 gadgets with me. You can read more about this great tool at my blog (http://dslrguides.com/carson). When I'm not traveling, I use a SensorKlear loupe. It's a magnifier with a built-in LED illuminator. There's an opening on one side that allows you to insert a SensorKlear cleaning wand, a lens pen-like stylus with a surface treated to capture dust particles. (See Figure D.13.) Both the SensorKlear loupe and the SensorKlear wand are available from www.lenspen.com.

When I'm using the MiniBrite, I locate the dust on the sensor with the magnifier, remembering that the position of the dust will be *reversed* from what I might have seen on an image on the camera's LCD (because the camera lens flips the image when making the exposure). Then, I use the SensorKlear wand, a carbon-tip tool similar to a LensPen, or the blower brush to remove the artifact.

The SensorKlear loupe actually allows you to keep your eye on the prize as you do the cleaning. You can peer through the viewer, rotate the opening to the side opposite the position of the dust, then insert the hinged wand to tap the dust while you're watching. This method allows removing a bunch of dust particles quickly, so it's my preferred procedure when I have the loupe with me.

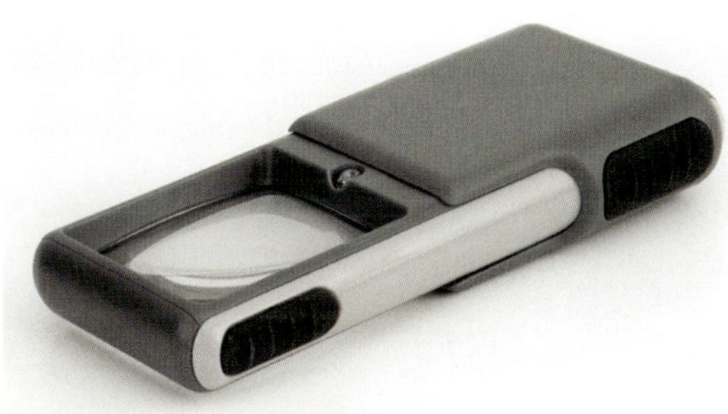

Figure D.12 The Carson MiniBrite is a good value sensor magnifier.

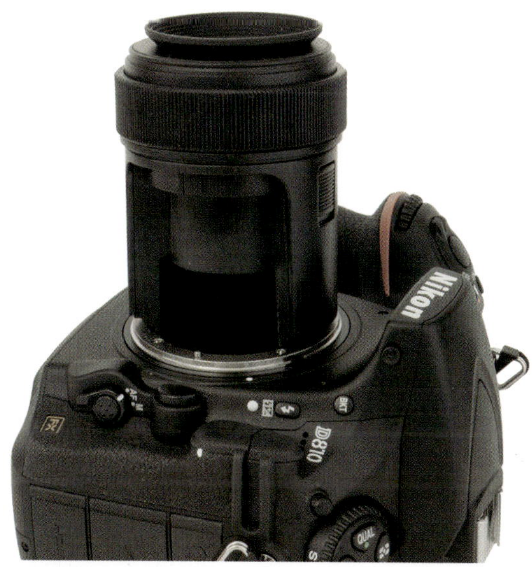

Figure D.13 The SensorKlear Loupe and wand allow quickly removing multiple dust particles.

Index

A

B

C

D

F

J

K

L

M

N

O

P

S

V

W

Z

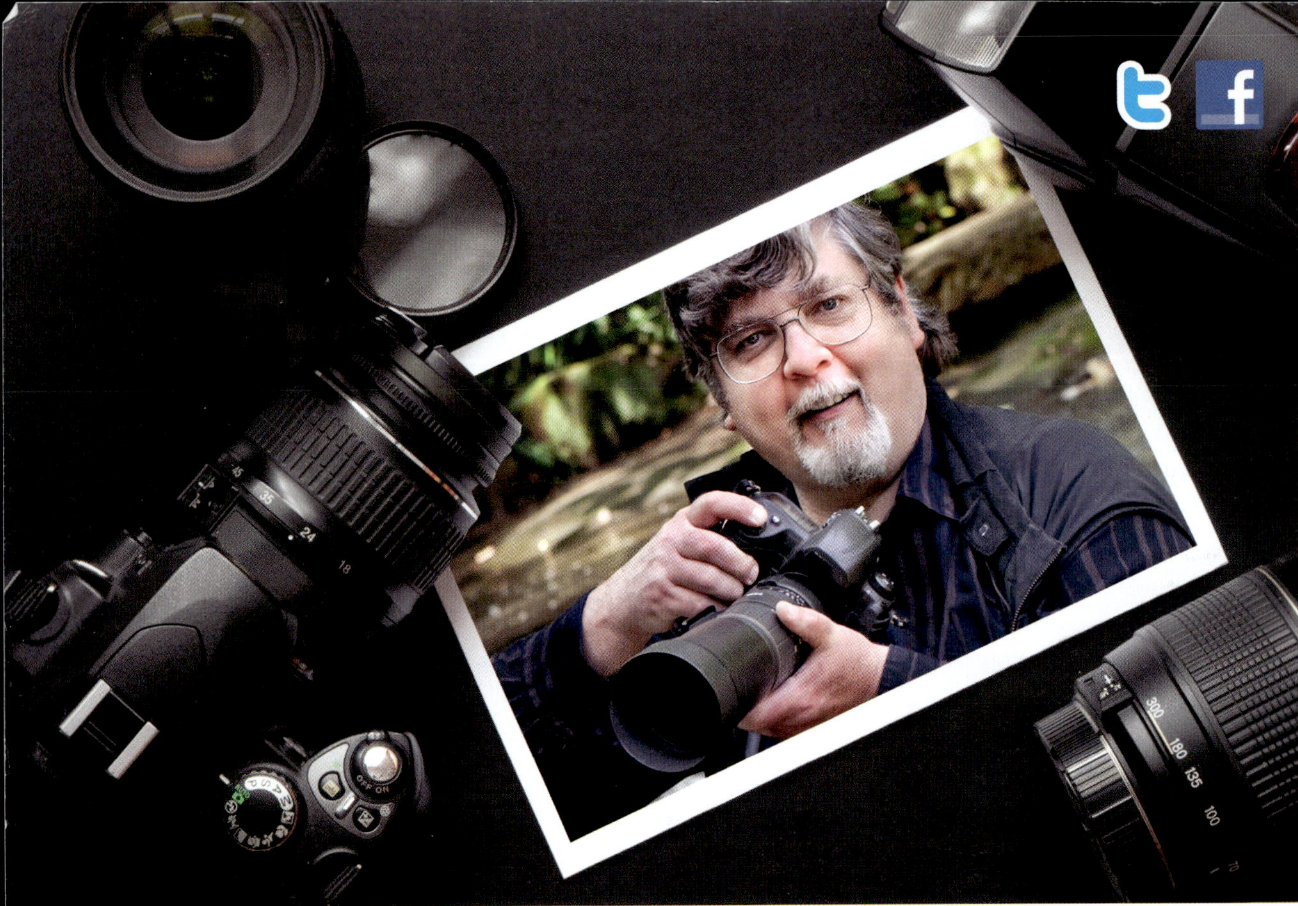

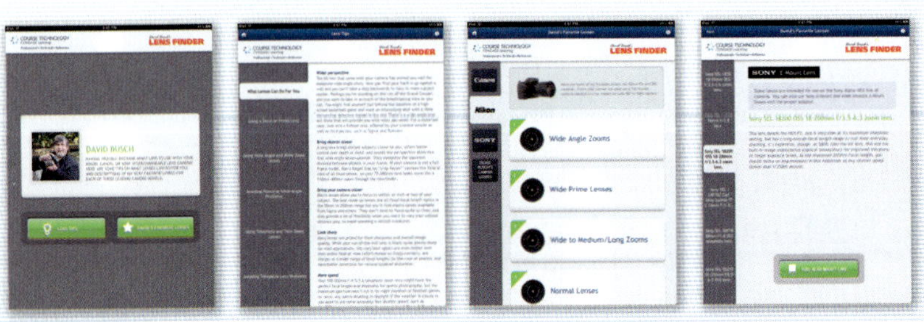